Creating Web Sites

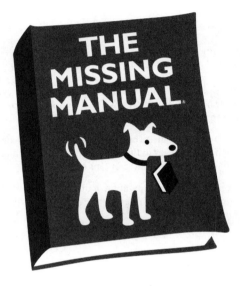

Matthew MacDonald

POGUE PRESS™
O'REILLY®

Beijing · Cambridge · Farnham · Köln · Paris · Sebastopol · Taipei · Tokyo

Creating Web Sites: The Missing Manual
by Matthew MacDonald

Copyright © 2006 O'Reilly Media, Inc. All rights reserved.
Printed in the United States of America.

Published by O'Reilly Media, Inc., 1005 Gravenstein Highway North, Sebastopol, CA 95472.

O'Reilly books may be purchased for educational, business, or sales promotional use. Online editions are also available for most titles (*safari.oreilly.com*). For more information, contact our corporate/institutional sales department: (800) 998-9938 or *corporate@oreilly.com*.

Printing History:

   October 2005:   First Edition.

 This book uses RepKover,™ a durable and flexible lay-flat binding.

ISBN-13: 978-0-596-00842-0

[M]

Table of Contents

Part Three: Connecting with Your Audience

Part Four: Web Site Frills

Part Five: Blogs

Part Six: Appendixes

The Missing Credits

About the Author

 **Matthew MacDonald** is an author, educator, and programmer extraordinaire. He is the author of over a dozen books about .NET programming, and the author of *Excel: The Missing Manual*. In a dimly remembered past life, he studied English literature and theoretical physics.

About the Creative Team

Peter Meyers (editor) works as an editor at O'Reilly Media on the Missing Manual series. He lives with his wife and cat in New York City. Email: *peter.meyers@gmail.com*.

Michele Filshie (editor) is O'Reilly's assistant editor for Missing Manuals and editor of four Personal Trainers (another O'Reilly series). Before coming to O'Reilly, Michele spent many happy years at Black Sparrow Press. She lives in Sebastopol and loves to get involved in local politics. Email: *mfilshie@oreilly.com*.

Jamie Barnett (copy editor) is a freelance copy editor and technical editor based in San Francisco and has copy edited over a thousand articles for O'Reilly's Web sites. He wrote a couple of books a while back, but likes the editing side better. He's also a painter and printmaker, under the nom de brush El Rey. His Web site is at *www.elreyart.com*.

Jim Goodenough (tech reviewer) was born and raised in California and he currently lives in Sebastopol with his wife Kati and his son Graham and daughter Anna. Jim is a Stanford graduate with a BS and MS in Mechanical Engineering. Jim owns and operates his Web site design and maintenance business named "Goodenough Web Site Services." Jim and Kati are avid SCUBA divers. Email: *jim@goodenoughwebsiteservices.com.*

Rhea Howard (tech reviewer) is excited to have finally taken the plunge into Web site creation. When she is not exploring the newly discovered intricacies of HTML and CSS, she is working in the O'Reilly operations department and inching ever closer to finishing her BA. Rhea lives and works in beautiful Sebastopol, CA. Email: *rheah@oreilly.com.*

Mark Levitt (tech reviewer) is a Senior Web Producer for O'Reilly Media's Online Publishing Group. His background includes Computer Science, Interactive & Educational Media, and Web Development. He has been known to eat cereal at all hours of the day. Email: *markl@oreilly.com.*

Rose Cassano (cover illustration) has worked as an independent designer and illustrator for 20 years. Assignments have ranged from the nonprofit sector to corporate clientele. She lives in beautiful Southern Oregon, grateful for the miracles of modern technology that make working there a reality. Email: *cassano@highstream. net.* Web: *www.rosecassano.com.*

Acknowledgements

No author could complete a book without a small army of helpful individuals. I'm deeply indebted to the whole Missing Manual team, especially Sarah Milstein and Peter Meyers, who kept me on track with relentless questions, solid feedback, and late night emails. I also owe a hearty thanks to Jim Goodenough, Rhea Howard, and Mark Levitt, who performed the technical review, and numerous others who've toiled behind the scenes indexing pages, drawing figures, and proofreading the final copy.

Finally, I'd never write *any* book without the support of my wife Faria and these special individuals: Nora, Razia, Paul, and Hamid. Thanks everyone!

The Missing Manual Series

Missing Manuals are witty, superbly written guides to computer products that don't come with printed manuals (which is just about all of them). Each book features a handcrafted index; cross-references to specific page numbers (not just "see Chapter 14"); and RepKover, a detached-spine binding that lets the book lie perfectly flat without the assistance of weights or cinder blocks.

Recent and upcoming titles include:

Introduction

These days, it's almost impossible to find someone who *hasn't* heard of the Internet. Companies create Web sites before they make business plans. Ordinary people build obsessively detailed pages that describe their lives and swizzle-stick-collecting hobbies. Even the language has changed: *blog* is a verb (see Chapter 17 for that story), and *surfing* doesn't necessarily involve California coastlines.

Everyone wants their own piece of Web real estate. Unfortunately, building a Web site isn't as easy as it should be. Even though people have been building Web sites for years, Web site design has only become more complicated. That's because tech gurus have been busy creating new standards to solve problems, add features, and just fill in the gaps. If you want to create a modern Web site (one that doesn't look as hokey as a 1960s yearbook portrait), you need to understand all these different ingredients, and how they fit together.

That's where this book comes in. The bookstore shelves are chock full of Web design books that were created years ago, but they leave out most of the contemporary innovations you need to make a Web site look truly grand. In this book, you'll learn how to:

- **Create Web pages.** HTML (HyperText Markup Language) is the pretty-easy-to-use but maddeningly inflexible language that powers almost all pages on the Web today. You'll quickly learn how to get the most out of HTML.

- **Make pages look beautiful using CSS (Cascading Style Sheets).** CSS picks up where HTML leaves off, adding formatting muscle that can transform the drabbest of sites into eye candy. Best of all, once you understand the *right* way to use

CSS, you'll be able to apply a new look to your entire Web site by tweaking a single file.

- **Put your Web site online.** The world's greatest Web site isn't much help if no one gets to see it. That's why you'll spend ample time learning how to choose the best Web hosting company, pick a *domain name* (like *www. HotToTrotHorses.com*), and get your masterpiece online. Don't panic—there are plenty of cheap Web hosting companies ready to show off your site for pennies a day.

- **Attract visitors.** You'll learn how to make sure Web surfers can find your site using popular search engines. You'll also get some tips for creating a community with discussion boards.

- **Get rich (or earn some spare change).** The Web's a lynchpin of modern commerce. But even ordinary people can make money selling products (using PayPal) or showing other people's ads (with Google). You'll learn how to get in on the action.

- **Pile on the frills.** Every Web site worth its weight in salt has a few cool tricks. You'll learn how to dazzle visitors with cool buttons, slick menus, and other flashy things, courtesy of JavaScript and Dynamic HTML. You'll even learn how to (shudder) serenade visitors with background music

What You Need to Get Started

This book assumes you don't have anything more than a reasonably up-to-date computer and raw ambition. Although there are dozens of high-powered Web editing programs to help you build a Web site, you *don't* need one to use this book. In fact, if you use a Web editor before you understand how Web sites work, you're liable to create more problems than you solve. That's because, as helpful as these programs are, they shield you from learning all the Web design nitty-gritty that can sometimes be the difference between an okay-looking Web site and a fantastic-looking one.

Once you master the basics, you're welcome to use a fancy Web page editor like FrontPage or Dreamweaver. You'll learn how these two leading programs work—and you'll see a great free (!) alternative—in Chapter 4.

Note: Under no circumstances do you need to know anything about complex Web programming technologies like Java and ASP.NET. You also don't need to know anything about databases or XML. These topics are fascinating, but insanely difficult to implement without some solid computer coding experience. In this book, you'll learn how to create the best possible Web site without becoming a programmer. (However, you *will* learn just enough about JavaScript to use many of the free samples you can find online.)

About This Book

No one owns the Web. As a result, no one has the responsibility to teach people how to use it or how to build a home for themselves online. That's where this book comes in. If the Web did have an instruction manual—one that painstakingly details the basic ingredients, time-saving tricks, and fancy frills every Web site needs—this would be it.

Note: This book periodically recommends *other* books, covering topics that are too specialized or tangential for a manual about creating Web sites. Careful readers may notice that not every one of these titles is published by Missing Manual parent O'Reilly Media. While we're happy to mention other Missing Manuals and books in the O'Reilly family, if there's a great book out there that doesn't happen to be published by O'Reilly, we'll still let you know about it.

Macintosh and Windows

One of the best things about the Web is that it truly is World Wide: Wherever you live, from Aruba to Zambia, the Web eagerly awaits your company. The same goes for whatever kind of computer you're using to design your Web site. From an early model Windows PC to the latest and greatest Mac, the tactics, tools, and tricks described in this book can be implemented with pretty much whatever kind of computer you might have. (Of course, there are a few programs that favor one operating system over another, and you'll hear about those differences whenever they come up.) The good news is that this book is usable and suitable for owners of computers of all stripes.

On occasion, you'll see a keyboard shortcut mentioned to help you perform a quick maneuver like saving or printing a document. When these occur, you'll see the Windows keystroke listed first (with + symbols, as is customary in Windows documentation); the Macintosh keystroke follows in parentheses (with - symbols, in time-honored Mac fashion). In other words, you might read, "The keyboard shortcut for saving a file is Ctrl+S (⌘-S)."

About the Outline

This book is divided into five parts, each containing several chapters.

- **Part 1: Welcome to the Web.** In this part, you'll start planning the Web site you want (Chapter 1). You'll learn the basics behind HTML, the language of the Web (Chapter 2); and you'll put your page online with a reputable hosting company (Chapter 3). Finally, you'll look at how you can simplify your life by using Web page editing software (Chapter 4).

- **Part 2: Building Better Web Pages.** This part shows you how to use Web page essentials like pictures, links, and tables. You'll learn your way around the CSS standard, which lets you add fancy colors, fonts, and borders (Chapter 6). You'll master slick layouts (Chapter 9 and Chapter 10), and create an entire Web site with linked pages.

- **Part 3: Connecting with Your Audience.** The third part explains how to get your site noticed in popular Web search engines like Google (Chapter 11), and how to foster a community by making your site more interactive with features like discussion boards (Chapter 12). Finally, you'll consider how you can get on the path to Web riches by showing ads or selling your own products (Chapter 13).

- **Part 4: Web Site Frills.** Now that you can create a professional, working Web site, why not deck it out with fancy features like glowing buttons and pop-out menus? You won't learn the brain-bending details of how to become a JavaScript programmer, but you will learn enough to find great scripts online, and use them in your own creations.

- **Part 5: Blogs.** In this short part, you'll take a look at *blogs* (or Web logs) and the free software that helps you create them. (Blogs are a type of Web page that consists of regular, dated postings—like an online journal. In recent years, blogs have become a self-publishing phenomenon and a great place to rant, rave, and spill company gossip.)

At the end of this book, you'll find two appendixes. The first gives you a quick reference for HTML that explains its tags and points you to more detailed discussions in the various chapters of this book.

The second appendix lists a pile of useful Web links culled from the chapters in this book, which can help you learn more, get free stuff (like pictures, Web software, and handy examples), and sign up for services (like Google's ad program and PayPal's shopping cart tools). Don't worry—you don't need to type this information in by hand. It's all waiting for you on the "Missing CD" page at *www. missingmanuals.com.*

About → These → Arrows

Throughout this book, you'll find sentences like this one: "Open the My Computer → C: → Windows folder." That's shorthand for a much longer instruction that directs you to open three nested folders in sequence, like this: "On your hard drive, there's an icon called My Computer. Open that. Inside My Computer, there's a folder for your C: drive. Open that. Inside your C: drive is your Windows folder. Open that." Similarly, this kind of arrow shorthand helps to simplify the business of choosing commands in menus, such as File → New → Window, as shown in Figure I-1.

Downloadable Examples

As you read this book, you'll see a number of examples that demonstrate different Web page designs. Most of these examples are available for your downloading pleasure, and playing with them is a great way to learn more. Just surf to the site *www.missingmanuals.com* and click the "Missing CD" page link. There you'll find a list of files that includes the examples, organized by chapter.

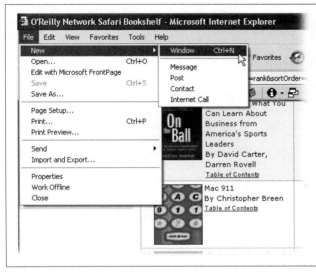

Figure I-1:
In this book, arrow notations help to simplify folder and menu instructions. For example, "Choose File → New → Window" is a more compact way of saying "From the File menu, choose New; from the submenu that appears, choose Window," as shown here.

About MissingManuals.com

At *www.missingmanuals.com*, you'll find news, articles, and updates to the books in the Missing Manual and Power Hound series.

But the Web site also offers corrections and updates to this book (to see them, click the book's title, and then click Errata). In fact, you're invited and encouraged to submit such corrections and updates yourself. In an effort to keep the book as up to date and accurate as possible, each time we print more copies of this book, we'll make any confirmed corrections you've suggested. We'll also note such changes on the Web site, so that you can mark important corrections into your own copy of the book, if you like.

In the meantime, we'd love to hear your own suggestions for new books in the Missing Manual and Power Hound lines. There's a place for that on the Web site, too, as well as a place to sign up for free email notification of new titles in the series.

Safari® Enabled

When you see a Safari® Enabled icon on the cover of your favorite technology book, that means it's available online through the O'Reilly Network Safari Bookshelf.

Safari offers a solution that's better than e-books: it's a virtual library that lets you easily search thousands of top technology books, cut and paste code samples, download chapters, and find quick answers when you need the most accurate, current information. Try it for free at *http://safari.oreilly.com*.

Part One: Welcome to the Web

1

Preparing for the Web

The Web's an exciting place. Every day, it chews through millions of financial transactions, serves up late-breaking news and scandalous rumors, and provides a thriving meeting place for every type of community, from political anarchists to Beanie Baby collectors.

Since you're reading this book, you've probably decided to move in and join the Web. Congratulations! Just as you need to prepare when it's time to find a home in the real world, you'll also need to undertake some basic planning before you can make the move to your new online neighborhood. In this chapter, you'll get a good look at the Web and what it takes to establish your own Web site. You'll also learn how the Web really works (behind the scenes), and what ingredients you need to build your site.

Introducing the World Wide Web

Although it doesn't show its age, the Internet is older than you might think. The computer visionaries who created the Internet began developing the idea in the early 1960s. In 1969, the first transmission over the Internet took place, between a computer at the University of California at Los Angeles and one at the Stanford Research Institute. As far as pioneering moments go, it wasn't much to brag about—the computer crashed when it reached the G in the word "LOGIN." Still, the revolution was underway.

The early Internet was mostly traveled by academic and government types. It flourished as a tool for research and collaboration, allowing scientists everywhere to share information. In 1993 the first Web browser hit the scene. In the following years, the Internet was colonized by new types of people, including book shoppers, news junkies, hobbyists, and a lot of lonely computer programmers.

Tip: History buffs can follow the saga of the early Internet in much more detail at *www.isoc.org/internet/history* and *www.walthowe.com/navnet/history.html*.

Of course, the early Internet doesn't have much in common with today's Internet. In 1969, the Internet community consisted of four computers, all of which were beastly, complex machines that no one but a government lab or academic institution could love (or afford). In 1981, there were still fewer than 200 mainframe computers on the Internet, and most of the people using them were computer experts or scientists going about their day-to-day work. Today, well over eight million Web sites—and many more Web surfers—are online. No wonder there's so much junk email flying around with shady sales pitches for anatomical self-improvement.

FREQUENTLY ASKED QUESTION

The Web vs. the Internet

Is there a difference between the Web and the Internet?

Newscasters, politicians, and regular people often use these terms interchangeably. However, technically, the concepts are different—and confusing them is likely to put computer techies and other self-respecting nerds on edge.

The *Internet* is a network of connected computers that spans the globe. These computers are connected together to share information, but there are a number of ways to get the job done, including emailing, instant messaging, transferring files through *FTP* (short for File Transfer Protocol), and downloading MP3 songs through peer-to-peer applications (which of course you don't do). The *World Wide Web* is one of the many ways to exchange information across the Internet. And how does this information get exchanged? You guessed it—people use special programs called *Web browsers* to visit Web sites and Web pages spread across the globe.

Browsers

As you no doubt already know, a Web browser is a piece of software that you use to navigate (or, in techy speak, *surf*) through Web pages. Without browsers, the Web would still exist, there just wouldn't be any way for you to turn on your computer and take a look at it.

A browser is surprisingly simple—in fact, the bulk of its work consists of two tasks. First of all, it can *request* a Web page, which happens when you type in a Web site address (like *www.google.com*) or click something on the current Web page. At this point, the browser sends a request for a Web page to another computer. This far-off computer, called a *Web server*, is typically much more powerful than a home computer, because it needs to handle multiple browsers that are all clamoring for its attention at the same time. The Web server deals with the request by firing the desired Web page back to the browser.

When the browser gets the Web page it wants, it puts its second skill into action and *renders,* or draws, the Web page. Technically, this means the browser converts the plain text it received from the Web server into a display document, based on formatting instructions that a Web site author has embedded into the page. The end result is a graphically rich page with different typefaces, colors, and links. Figure 1-1 shows the process.

You type
1 *http://www.CrazyCoolSite.com*
into the address bar of your browser

2 Your browser requests http://www.CrazyCoolSite.com
The web server returns an HTML document **3**

Your computer **4** Your browser renders the document, displaying it for you to see

Web server

Figure 1-1:
A Web browser is designed to do two things really well—contact remote computers to ask for Web pages, and then display them in a graphical window. Technically, browsers are called client-side programs, which means they run on your humble personal computer. The server-side is the part of the equation that takes place on the Web server, where the Web page content is actually stored (or, in a dynamic Web application, generated on the fly).

Choosing your Web browser

Depending on your personality type, choosing a Web browser is either a) a bore or b) an important expression of your personality, individuality, and overall computer savvy. If you fall into the latter camp, you've probably already settled on your favorite browser. But if you're searching for something a little different, or you're curious what else is out there, the following quick overview sums up your options.

Even if you're not interested in changing your browser, it's a good idea to be familiar with the most common options out there. That's because when you design your Web site, you'll need to prepare for a wide audience of people with different browsers. To make sure your nifty graphics don't turn funky when viewed in other browsers, it's a good idea to test your Web site on other computers, using other screen resolutions, and with other Web browsers. At a bare minimum, all Web authors need a copy of Internet Explorer, which is by far the most commonly used browser, so that you can see what your hard work will look like to 95 percent of the world.

• **Internet Explorer** is the world's most used (and sometimes most reviled) Web browser. For better or for worse, Internet Explorer sets the standard that other browsers need to follow. The clear advantage of using Internet Explorer (or IE, as it's known for short) is that you'll never run into a Web page you can't read—with a market share of over 90 percent, IE is simply too successful to ignore. The downside is that the developers at Microsoft have grown complacent, which means you might not see dramatic innovations in IE in future versions. Success can also attract a little too much interest—if you use IE, unethical marketers have a bull's eye on your computer with the latest spyware (see the sidebar "Spyware: When Good Browsers Go Bad" on page 13).

To download an updated version of Internet Explorer, visit *www.microsoft.com/ windows/ie.*

Note: Mac owners with OS X will probably give Internet Explorer a pass. Not only does the Macintosh include a built-in Web browser of its own (see Safari, later in this list), Microsoft has now halted development of IE on the Mac. However, many Mac-heads running earlier operating systems like OS 9 report that Internet Explorer is still one of the best choices. For a full roundup of Mac browsers, check out *http:// darrel.knutson.com/mac/www/browsers.html.*

- **Firefox** is the modern response to Internet Explorer—a Web browser that's lean, secure, and knows how to block those annoying pop-up ads. You can easily extend Firefox with eye-catching *themes* (customizations that let you revamp the way Firefox buttons and icons look) and *extensions* (handy tools that enhance Firefox with extra features). Firefox is currently enjoying wide popularity with computer geeks, and a growing number of disillusioned Internet Explorer veterans are also trying it out. Best of all, Firefox is completely free, and kept rigorously up-to-date by an army of volunteer programmers, including many who designed the original Netscape browser.

Give Firefox a go at *www.mozilla.org/products/firefox.*

- **Netscape Navigator** is one of the first Web pioneers, and was once a formidable challenger to Internet Explorer. These days, Netscape is well past its prime. Although it's still the choice of a few nostalgic Web surfers, most find its installation process, user interface, and far-from-blistering speed as clunky as a '57 Chevy with a broken rear axle. Netscape development has slowed dramatically, with Firefox becoming the new successor.

Download Netscape at *http://channels.netscape.com/ns/browsers/download.jsp.*

- **Opera** is a slimmed down, easy to install browser that has existed for several years as an antidote to the bloated size and pointless frills of Internet Explorer. Opera's chief disadvantage is that you need to pay for an ad-free version (the free version shows a small banner advertisement), unlike the other browsers in this list. You'll also need to adjust to its somewhat cluttered interface, which inspires either love or an intense headache. However, Opera has a small but loyal following, and it's clearly survived the browser wars.

Check out Opera at *www.opera.com.*

- **Safari** is the only browser in this list that's limited to Macs. Safari is an Apple-designed Web browser that's provided with the OS X operating system. It's quick, elegant, and sports a nifty Google toolbar for quick searches.

  Go on Safari at *www.apple.com/safari.*

Along with the browsers listed above, there are some specialty niche browsers. The most important of these is Lynx, one of the earliest Web browsers and one that's changed the least. Lynx is an entirely text-based browser that's perfectly suited for terminals that don't support graphics. (You can sometimes find these beasts lurking about computer labs in universities and colleges.) Lynx also supports the visually impaired, who can use Lynx in conjunction with a device that reads the text of a Web page aloud.

TROUBLESHOOTING MOMENT

Spyware: When Good Browsers Go Bad

Even though a Web browser is deceptively simple, many browsers are bloated up with plug-ins, extra frills (like the ability to send email), or even (shudder) spyware. *Spyware* is among the most hideous forms of computer software you'll encounter. Essentially, a spyware program is an unwanted plug-in that attaches itself, leech-like, to your browser or operating system without your permission. It then harasses you with advertisements, or just bogs down your computer with unnecessary operations (like recording your surfing habits and sending them to a Big-Brother-like marketing company). Spyware thrives like a weed, particularly on the Windows operating system.

Spyware is notoriously difficult to remove. If you see the telltale signs—a sudden slowdown in Web access, Web page requests that get redirected to the wrong place, or pop-up ads that materialize out of nowhere, even when you aren't using your Web browser—you should have your computer checked out. The best remedy is a spyware removal tool that scans for delinquent programs and removes them, much like a virus scanner. Good bets include Spybot Search & Destroy (*www.safer-networking. org*), Microsoft's AntiSpyware tool (*www.microsoft.com/ athome/security/spyware*), and Lavasoft's Ad-Aware (*www.lavasoftusa.com/software/adaware*).

Web Servers

On the other end of the line, the Web server receives browser requests and sends back the correct Web page. For a busy Web site, this basic task can require a lot of work. As a result, Web servers tend to be industrial-strength computers. Even though the average Windows PC with the right setup can host a Web site, it's rarely worth the effort (see the sidebar "Becoming a Web Host"). Instead, most normal people get another company to give them a little space on an existing Web server, usually for a monthly fee. In other words, you need to rent some space on the Web.

Often, you can rent this space from the same company you use for Internet access, or it may already be included with your Internet connection package for free. Alternatively, you can turn to a dedicated Web hosting company. Either way, you're going to take the Web sites you build and copy them to some far off computer that will make sure your talents can be enjoyed by a worldwide audience.

In Chapter 3, you'll learn more about how a Web browser navigates the Web to find a specific Web page. But for now, keep focusing on the big picture so you can start planning your first Web site.

FREQUENTLY ASKED QUESTION

Becoming a Web Host

Can I run a Web server?

In theory, you definitely can. The Web was designed to be an open community, and no one is out to stop you. But in practice, it's not at all easy—no matter how many computer-savvy relatives you may have.

Several monumental challenges prevent all but the most ambitious people from running their own Web servers. The first problem is that you need to have a reliable computer that runs 24 hours a day. That computer also needs to run special Web hosting software that's able to serve up Web pages when browsers request them.

The next problem is that your computer requires a special type of connection to the Internet, called a *fixed IP address*. The IP address (described on page 54) is a numeric address that identifies your computer on the Web.

In order to have your computer run a Web site and make sure others can find it, you need to make sure your IP address is fixed—in other words, you need to lock it down so it's not constantly changing. Most ISPs (Internet Service Providers) randomly assign new IP addresses as they're needed and change them at a whim, which means most people can't use their computers to host a permanent Web site.

If you're still interested, you can call your ISP to ask them if they provide a fixed IP address service. The typical cost is usually far above what you'd pay for ordinary Web access.

Planning a Web Site

The last thing you need is to be buried under an avalanche of theory before you've had the joy of performing your first few Web creation tricks. However, every new Web site author can save time and effort by doing a little bit of planning before diving in to create a complete Web site. In the following sections, you'll consider some quick guidelines to get you on the right path.

Types of Sites

You don't have much chance of creating a successful Web site if you haven't decided what it's *for*. Some people have a very specific goal in mind (like getting hired for a job or promoting a book) while others are just planning to unleash their self-expression. Either way, take a look at the following list to get a handle on the different types of Web sites you might want to create:

- **Personal** sites are all about you. As the world gets more Web-savvy, it seems everyone is building online homes. Whether it's to share pictures of Junior with the relatives, chronicle a trip to Kuala Lumpur, or just post your latest thoughts and obsessions, it's no longer unusual to have a personal Web site. In fact, everyone from tweens to grandmothers are jumping in.

If your plan is to create a personal Web site, think about what its format should be, and how you'll use it. Do you want to post regularly updated news tidbits in a chronological format (in which case, you might be interested in creating a blog, covered below)? Or perhaps you want to create something more ambitious, like an online picture album or a site featuring your family's history. Either way, you should decide what you want your Web site to focus on before you start slapping together Web pages.

• **Online diaries or blogs** (Figure 1-2) are personal Web sites that are rapidly gaining popularity. The typical diary Web site provides a list of entries in reverse chronological order, which means whenever you surf to the site, you see the latest news at the top of the page. These online diaries, also known as *blogs* (short for Web logs) are a great way to while away the hours and keep in touch with friends in far-off places. But before you choose this type of site, make sure you have plenty of free time. Nothing says "dead site" like a blog that hasn't been updated in eight months. By contrast, personal Web sites that aren't in a date-specific format can linger on quite happily without regular updates.

Figure 1-2:
Blogs are a great way to keep in touch, allowing you to share pictures and day-to-day reflections with an unlimited audience. If blogs satisfy your Web needs, you might not need to learn HTML or add anything else to your Web site. Instead, skip straight to Chapter 17 to learn about the blogging software that makes it easy.

If you just want to create a blog, you can sacrifice your independence and join the masses on a Web site like The Open Diary (a huge online diary community at *www.opendiary.com*) or MSN Spaces (a free blogging from Microsoft at *http://spaces.msn.com*). Alternatively, you can set out to create and host your own blog. However, if you plan on blogging regularly, you should at least consider a *blogging* tool, which makes it easy to post quick updates even when you aren't at your computer. Depending on the tool you use, you might not even need to know HTML (a standard for writing Web pages, as described in Chapter 2) or have your own Web space. If this sounds like your cup of tea, skip straight to Chapter 17.

Note: Blogs aren't just for your personal life. They've become tremendously popular with computer geeks and IT workers as a way to share information and chat about a variety of topics, computer-related or otherwise. Microsoft programmers are the latest audience to get in on the trend (see *www.microsoft.com/communities/blogs*).

- **Résumé** sites can be powerful career-building tools. Rather than photocopy a suitcase full of paper résumés, why not send emails and distribute business cards that point to your online résumé? Best of all, with a little planning you can add more details to your résumé Web site, like links to companies where you've worked, online portfolio samples, and even background music playing "YMCA" (which is definitely not recommended).

- **Topical** sites focus on a particular subject that interests you. If you're more interested in building a Web site about your favorite music, art, books, food, or Beanie Babies than you are in talking about your own life, then a topical Web site is for you.

  Before you set out to create a topical Web site, consider whether other people with a similar interest will be interested in visiting your site, and take a look at existing sites on the topic. The best topical Web sites invite others with the same interest to join in. (If your Web site is really successful, you might want to use the techniques in Chapter 12 to let visitors talk to you and each other.) The worst Web sites present the same dozen links you can find anywhere else. Remember, the Web is drowning in information. The last thing it needs is another *Pamela Anderson Fan Emporium*.

- **Event** sites aren't designed to weather the years—instead, they revolve around a specific event. A common example is a wedding Web site. The event hosts create it to provide directions, background information, links to gift registries, and a few romantic photos. When the wedding is over, the Web site disappears—or morphs into something different (like a personal Web site chronicling the honeymoon). Other events that might be treated in a similar way include family reunions, costume parties, or do-it-yourself protest marches.

- **Promotion** sites are ideal when you have a personally produced CD or a hot-off-the-presses book to boast about. They're geared to get the word out about a specific item, whether it's handmade pottery or your own shareware program. Sometimes, these Web sites evolve into small business Web sites, where you actually sell your wares (see the "Small business" item next).

- **Small business (or e-commerce)** sites show off the most successful use of the modern Web—selling everything from portable music players to prescription

---

drugs. E-commerce sites are so widespread that it's hard to believe that when the Web was first created, making a buck was far from anyone's mind.

Creating a full-blown e-commerce Web site like Amazon or eBay is far beyond the abilities of a single person. These Web sites need the support of complex applications and computer-genius-level programming languages. Fortunately, if you've come to the Web to make some money, you don't need to give up hope yet! Innovative companies like PayPal and Yahoo now provide subscription services that can help you build shopping-cart-style Web sites and accept credit card payments. You can also show Google AdSense ads to start raking in the cash. You'll learn about these great tricks in Chapter 13.

Understanding Your Audience

Once you've firmed up your Web site's *raison d'être,* you should start to have a better idea about who your visitors will be. Knowing and understanding your audience is crucial to making sure your Web site is effective. (And don't even try to suggest you're creating a Web site just for yourself—if you were, there's no reason to get your hard work onto the Internet at all!)

Not only do you need to understand your audience, but you also need to single out the lowest common denominator in that audience. Good Web designers avoid using fancy frills unless *everyone* can experience them. Nothing is more disappointing than creating a Web site using the latest graphical wizardry, only to find out that the site's illegible on a friend's less powerful computer. To avoid these letdowns and reach as many people as possible, you need to keep your visitors' PC capabilities in mind as you build and improve your Web pages.

Unfortunately, there's no single set of specifications you can use to build your Web pages—everyone has a slightly different setup. The best thing to do is try out your Web site on different computers, which can be time-consuming. Some paid services can do this for you (see, for example, *www.netmechanic.com*, which tests your Web site with different browsers and sends you pictures), but they aren't cheap. You can minimize your risk by keeping this point about visitor diversity in mind while you create your Web site. Look for the design tips throughout the book, and watch out for these common problem areas:

- **Computer monitors** aren't all created equal. Some computers use a smaller *screen resolution* (number of pixels), so they can't show as much content. If you create the perfect Web site for your wide-screen monitor, you might find that it's unbearably cramped (or even worse, partly amputated) on another monitor.

- **Colors** cause a similar problem. Graphics that look rich and nuanced on your monitor might turn ugly on computers that don't support as many colors.

- **Non-standard fonts** are another headache. Imagine you create a Web page for a rent-a-clown service using a font named FunnyKidzScript. When you check your page out on another computer that doesn't have the same font, your text will revert to a completely different typeface. At best, it's not what you intended; at worst, it's indecipherable.

- **Large graphics** are another trap that's easy to fall into if you're testing your Web site on a speedy computer with a fast Internet connection. When dial-up Web surfers try to see your work, they'll be stuck waiting for the goods, and might just give up. Fortunately, there's a lot you can do to slim down your graphics (which you'll learn in Chapter 7).

- **Plug-ins, movies, and browser-specific features** are temptations you need to treat with caution. In the world of the Web, anything that limits how many visitors can enjoy your work is a danger. Steer clear of cutting-edge features that aren't widely supported.

The creators of the most popular Web sites have carefully considered all these issues. For example, think about the number of people whose computers won't let them buy a book on Amazon, make a bid on eBay, or conduct a search on Google. (Are you thinking of a number that's close to 0?)

It's been widely remarked that the average Web designer goes through three stages of maturity: 1) "I'm just learning, so I'll keep it simple;" 2) "I'm a Web guru, and I'll prove it by piling on the features;" 3) "I've been burned by browser compatibility problems, so I'll keep it simple."

The Lifespan of Your Site

The Web is a constantly changing place. Today's Web isn't the same as last year's—or even the Web of 15 seconds ago.

Here are two valuable truths about Web site lifetimes:

- **The best Web sites are constantly improving.** Their creators add support for new browser features, tweak their looks to match new style trends, and—most importantly of all—constantly add new content.

- **When a Web site stops changing, it's on life support.** Many great Web sites have crumbled through neglect.

Think about your favorite Web sites. Odds are, they change daily. A good Web site isn't one you consult once and then move on. It's a site that you can bookmark and return to periodically. In a sense, a Web site is like a television channel. If you aren't putting up new information, your Web site's showing reruns.

This problem poses a significant challenge. Making a Web site is hard enough, and keeping it up to date is even more challenging. Here are a few tips that can help you out:

- **Think in stages.** When you put your first Web site online, it won't be complete. Instead, think of it as version 1, and start planning a few changes for the next version. Bit by bit, and stage by stage, you can add everything that you want to your Web site.

- **Select the parts you can modify regularly, and leave the rest alone.** There's no way you can review and revise an entire Web site weekly or even monthly. Instead, your best strategy is to identify the sections that change regularly. For example, on a personal Web site, you might put news on a separate page, and update just that page. On a small business Web site, you might concentrate your changes on the home page to advertise new products and upcoming specials.

- **Design a Web site that's easy to change.** This is the hardest principle to follow, because it requires not only planning, but a dash of experience. As you become a more experienced Web maven, you'll learn how to simplify your life by making it easier to update pages. One method is to start out by separating information into several pages, so you can add new content without needing to reorganize everything. Another technique is to use style sheets to separate the formatting from your content (see Chapter 6). That way, you can easily insert new material without having to re-format it from scratch to make sure it matches the rest of your page.

Practice Good Design

Every year, hundreds of Web sites win awards for being abjectly awful. Sometimes, they have spinning globes and hot pink text on a lime green background. Other times, they have clunky navigation systems and grotesque flashing backgrounds. But no matter what the design sins, Web sites that are bad—hideously bad—are strangely common.

Maybe it's because creating a Web site really isn't that hard. Or maybe it's because we all have an impulse to play with color, texture, and sound, and sometimes new-fangled Web tools encourage our ugliest instincts. For a glimpse at some of the all-too-familiar mistakes go to *www.angelfire.com/super/badwebs* (see Figure 1-3). You can also visit Web sites like *www.webpagesthatsuck.com* and *www.worstoftheweb.com*, which tally not only yearly winners in the worst-of-show category, but also pick out new offenders every month.

This book won't teach you to become a professional Web designer. However, it will guide you in the time-honored Art of Not Making Bad Web Sites. Throughout this book, you'll find helpful tips, suggestions, and warnings about usability and design. Look specifically for the "Design Time" boxes. In the meantime, here are a few general principles that can help make sure you never wind up on a worst-of-the-Web list (unless you absolutely want to).

- **Stay simple (and don't annoy your visitors).** You can cram a lot of frills and goodies into a Web page. But unless they serve a purpose, just say no. You'll find that exercising restraint can make a few fancy touches seem witty and sophisticated. (Whereas adding a *lot* of fancy touches can make your site seem heady and delusional.) If you pare down the graphical tricks and distractions, you'll also make sure that the content of your Web site isn't overshadowed, and your visitors aren't driven away in annoyance.

• **Be consistent.** No matter how logical you think your Web site is, the majority of visitors probably won't think the same way. To cut down on the confusion, from one page to another, use similar organization, similar headings, similar graphics and links, a single navigation bar, and so on. These touches help make visitors feel right at home.

• **Know your audience.** Every type of Web site has its own unwritten conventions. You don't need to follow the same design in an e-commerce Web store as you do in a promotional page for an experimental electric harmonic band. To help decide what is and isn't suitable, be sure to check out lots of other sites that deal with the same sort of material as yours.

Figure 1-3:
Here's a Web site that gets it all wrong—deliberately. With a combination of scrolling titles, a crazily blinking background, and unreadable text, www. angelfire.com/super/ badwebs does a good job at demonstrating everything you should try to avoid in your own Web pages. Check out this actual web site to see for yourself.

The Ingredients of a Web Site

The trickiest part about building a Web site is coordination. To get it right, you not only need the right tools to create Web pages, but you also need to coordinate with other companies to get your Web site onto the World Wide Web and (optionally) to give it a catchy address like *www.StylinViolins.com*. In this section, you'll create a quick Web shopping list that maps out what you need—and tells you where you'll learn about it in the rest of this book.

- **Web pages.** Every Web site is built with individual pages. In order to create a basic Web page, you need to understand HTML (HyperText Markup Language), the language of the Web. You'll create your first Web page next, in Chapter 2.

- **Web space.** Creating Web pages is fun, but in order to let other people take a look at them, you need to put them on a Web server. In Chapter 3, you'll consider your options for getting your first Web page online, either through a fee-based service or a free alternative.

- **A domain name.** There's a world of difference between the Web site address *www.inetConnections.com/Users/~jMallone012/web* and *www.JackieMallone.com*. You can get your own personalized *domain name,* if it's available. It's not free, but the cost is usually quite low. If you want to put your Web site address on a business card or a brochure for a small business, there's really no better choice. In Chapter 3, you'll learn how to buy your own domain name.

Note: The domain name is the first part of the Web address, which identifies the Web server that's storing and serving up your site. In the URL *www.ebay.com/help/index.html*, the domain name is *www.ebay.com*. You'll learn much more about domain names and URLs (short for Universal Resource Locator) and how they work in Chapter 3.

- **Web design tools.** Creating Web pages from scratch is a great way to learn, but it's far too slow and painful to create a complete Web site that way. To get to the next level, you'll need to step up to a professional Web design tool. If you have a commercial program like FrontPage or Dreamweaver, you're in good hands. Even if you don't, there are many good free and shareware products that can help you out. Chapter 4 explains your options and helps you get started.

- **Hyperlinks.** On its own, a Web page can do only so much. The real magic begins when you bind multiple Web pages together using links. Chapter 8 introduces the versatile hyperlink, which allows visitors to surf around your Web site.

- **Indispensable extras.** Once you've mastered the basics of Web pages and Web sites, there's still more ground to conquer. You can get your site listed in a search engine catalog (Chapter 11), establish your own forum (Chapter 12), and sell items (Chapter 13). Still hungry for more frills? Why not animate your page with a sprinkling of JavaScript (Chapter 14), create eye-catching buttons (Chapter 15), and add audio and video (Chapter 16)? All these features take you beyond ordinary HTML and well on the road to becoming a genuine Web guru.

Creating Your First Page

Every Web site is a collection of one or more Web pages. You jump from page to page by clicking various *elements* in your Web browser, like links, pictures, or buttons. It may not sound very high-tech, but putting an entire Web site together and polishing it up is a significant undertaking. However, the first step to Web mastery is just building a single Web page. That's the task you'll tackle in this chapter.

Web pages are the basic unit of Web design. The ideal Web page contains enough information to fill up a browser window, but not so much that the reader needs to scroll from morning until lunchtime to get to the end. In other words, the ideal Web page strikes a balance—it avoids the lonely feeling caused by too much white space, and the stress induced by an avalanche of information.

The best way to get a handle on what a Web page should hold is to look at your favorite Web sites. On a news site like *www.nytimes.com,* every news article is a separate page (and longer stories are subdivided into several pages). On an e-commerce shop like *www.amazon.com,* every product has its own page. Similarly, a personal Web site like *www.MyUndyingLoveForPigTrotters.com* may be divided into separate Web pages with titles like "About Me," "Vacation Photos," "Résumé," and "Top Secret Recipes for Pig Parts."

For now, don't worry too much about how to divide up your Web site—it's a task you'll revisit in Chapter 8 when you start linking Web pages together. Instead, your first goal is to understand how a basic Web page works, and how to create one of your own.

The Anatomy of a Web Page

Web pages are written in *HTML* (HyperText Markup Language), which is the language of the Web. It doesn't matter whether your Web page contains a series of plain text blog entries, a dozen pictures of your pet lemur, or a heavily formatted screenplay—odds are if you're looking at it in a browser, it's an HTML page.

HTML plays two key roles:

• **HTML tells a Web browser how to format a page.** Although there are plenty of computer programs that can format text (take Microsoft Word, for instance), it's almost impossible to find a single standard that's supported on every type of computer, operating system, and Web-enabled device. HTML fills the gap by supplying information that any browser can interpret. These formatting details include specifications about colors, headings, text alignment, and so on.

• **HTML links different documents together.** These links can take several forms. You can use hyperlinks (discussed in Chapter 8) to let people surf from one Web page to another. You can also use HTML instructions to call up pictures (Chapter 7) or even other Web pages (Chapter 10) and combine them into a single Web page.

HTML is such an important standard that you'll spend a good portion of this book digging through most of its features, frills, and shortcomings. Every Web page you'll build along the way is a bona fide HTML document.

Cracking Open an HTML Document

On the inside, an HTML page is actually nothing more than a plain-vanilla text file. That means every Web page consists entirely of letters, numbers, and just a few special characters (like spaces, punctuation, and everything else you can spot on your keyboard). This file is quite different than what you would find if you cracked open a typical *binary file* on your computer. (A binary file contains genuine computer language—a series of 1s and 0s. If another program is foolish enough to try and convert this binary information into text, you end up with gibberish.)

To understand the difference, take a look at Figure 2-1, which examines a Word document under the microscope. Compare that with what you see in Figure 2-2, which dissects an HTML document containing the same content.

To take a look at an HTML document, all you need is an ordinary text editor, like Notepad, which is included on all Windows computers. To run Notepad, click the Start button and select Programs → Accessories → Notepad. Then choose File → Open and begin hunting around for the HTML file you want. On the Mac, try TextEdit, which you can find at Applications → TextEdit. Choose File → Open and then find the HTML file. If you've downloaded the companion content for this book (all of which you'll find on the "Missing CD" page at *www.missingmanuals. com*), try opening the *popsicles.htm* file, shown in Figure 2-2.

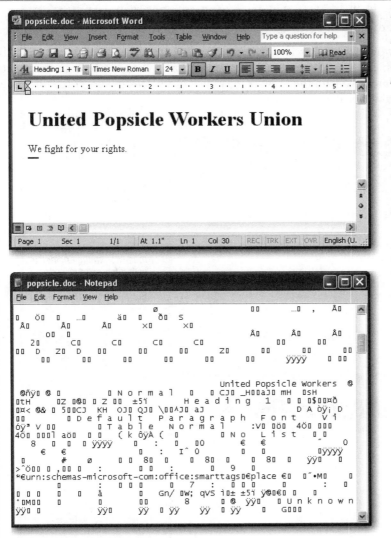

Figure 2-1:
Word documents are stored as binary information, as are documents in most file formats used by most computer programs.

Top: Even if your document looks relatively simple in the Word window, it doesn't look nearly as pretty when you bypass Word and open the file in an ordinary text editor like Notepad or TextEdit.

Bottom: Depending on the program you use, the string of ones and zeroes in the file is usually converted into a meaningless stream of intimidating gibberish. The actual text is there somewhere, but it's buried in computer gobbledygook.

Unfortunately, most text editors don't let you open a Web page directly from the Internet. In order to do that, they'd need to be able to send a request over the Internet to a Web server, which is a job that's best left to the Web browser. However, most browsers *do* give you the chance to look at the raw HTML for a Web page. Here's what you need to do:

1. **Open your preferred browser.**

2. Navigate to the Web page you want to examine.

3. In your browser, look for a menu command that allows you to view the source content of the Web page. In Internet Explorer (or Opera), select View → Source. In Firefox and Netscape, use View → Page Source. In Safari, View → View Source does the trick. Isn't diversity a wonderful thing?

Once you make your selection, a new window appears showing you the HTML used to create the Web page. This window may represent a built-in text viewer that's included with the browser, or it may just be Notepad or TextEdit. Either way, you'll see the raw HTML.

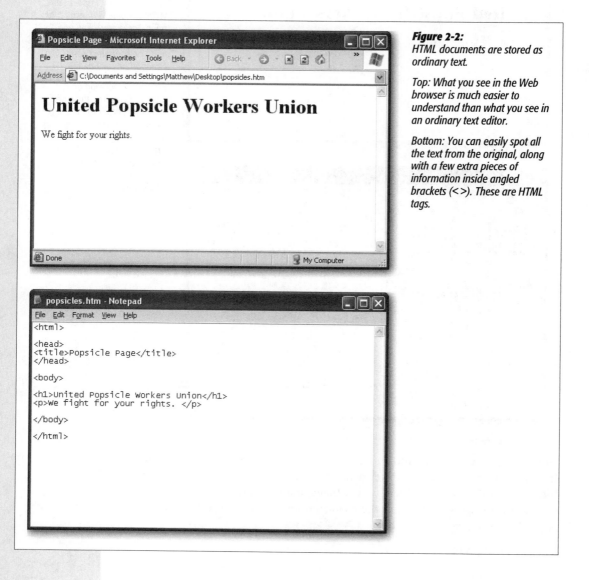

Figure 2-2:
HTML documents are stored as ordinary text.

Top: What you see in the Web browser is much easier to understand than what you see in an ordinary text editor.

Bottom: You can easily spot all the text from the original, along with a few extra pieces of information inside angled brackets (<>). These are HTML tags.

Tip: Firefox has a handy feature that lets you home in on part of the HTML in a complex page. Just select the text you're interested in on the page, right-click it, and then choose View Selection Source.

Most Web pages are considerably more complex than the *popsicles.htm* example shown in Figure 2-2, so you'll need to wade through many more HTML tags. But once you've acclimated yourself to the jumble of information, you'll have an extremely useful way to peer under the covers of any Web page. In fact, professional Web developers often use this trick to check out the snazziest work of their competitors.

POWER USERS' CLINIC

Going Beyond HTML

The creators of HTML designed it perfectly for putting research papers and other unchanging documents on the Web. They didn't envision a world of Internet auctions, e-commerce shops, and browser-based games. To add all these features to the modern Web browsing experience, crafty people have supplemented HTML with some tricky workarounds. And although it's more than a little confusing to consider all the ways you can extend HTML, doing so is the best way to really understand what's possible on your own Web site.

Here's an overview of the two most common ways to go beyond HTML:

- **Embedded applications.** Most modern browsers support *Java applets,* which are small programs than run inside your Web browser, and display information in a window inside a Web page. (To try one out and play some head-scratching Java Checkers against a computer opponent, surf to *http://thinks.com/java/checkers/checkers.htm.*) Internet Explorer can also host special tools called *ActiveX controls.* ActiveX is a Microsoft-backed technology for sharing useful widgets between different programs and Web pages. (To see an ActiveX control in use, check out TrendMicro's free virus scanner at *http://housecall.trendmicro.com.*) Both Java applets and ActiveX controls are miniature programs that can be used in a Web page (if the browser supports it), but neither are written in HTML.

- **Browser plug-ins.** Browsers are designed to deal with HTML, and they don't recognize other types of content. For example, browsers don't have the ability to interpret an Adobe PDF document, which is a specialized format used to preserve the formatting of documents. However, depending on how your browser is configured, you may find that when you click a hyperlink that points to a PDF file, a PDF reader launches. The automatic launch happens if you've installed a plug-in from Adobe that runs the Acrobat software (which displays PDF files). (To see for yourself, request the sample chapter *www.oreilly. com/catalog/exceltmm/chapter/ch04.pdf* from *Excel: The Missing Manual.*) Another example of a common plug-in is Macromedia Flash, which shows animations on a Web page. If you surf to a page that includes a Flash animation and you don't have the plug-in, you'll be asked if you want to download it. (Check out *www.orsinal.com* to play some of the best free Flash games around.)

Unfortunately, there's no surefire way to tell what extensions are at work on a particular page. In time, you'll learn to spot many of the telltale signs, because each type of content looks distinctly different.

Creating Your Own HTML Files

Here's one of the best-kept secrets of Web page writing: You don't need a live Web site to start creating your own Web pages. That's because you can easily build and test Web pages using only your own computer. In fact, you don't even need an Internet connection.

The basic approach is simple:

1. **Fire up your favorite text editor.**

2. **Start writing HTML content.**

   Of course, this part is a little tricky because you haven't explored the HTML standard yet. Hang on—help is on the way in the next section.

3. **When you've finished your Web page, save the document (a simple File → Save usually does it).**

   By convention, HTML documents typically have the file extension *.htm* or *.html*, as in *LimeGreenPyjamas.html*. Strictly speaking, these extensions aren't necessary, because browsers are perfectly happy displaying Web pages with any file extension. You're free to choose any file extension you want for your Web pages. The only rule is that the file has to contain valid HTML content. However, using the *.htm* or *.html* file extensions is still a good idea; not only does it save confusion, it also helps your computer recognize that the file contains HTML in other situations. For example, when you double-click a file with the *.htm* or *.html* extension, it opens in your Web browser automatically.

4. **To take a look at your work, open the file in a Web browser.**

   If you've used the extension *.htm* or *.html*, it's usually as easy as double-clicking the file. If not, you may need to type in the full file path in your Web browser's address bar, as shown in Figure 2-3.

   Remember, when you compose your HTML document in a text editor, you won't be able to see what the formatting actually looks like. All you'll see is the plain text and the HTML formatting instructions.

Tip: If you change and save the file *after* you open it in your Web browser, you can take a look at your recent changes by hitting the Refresh button.

The HTML Tag

Now that you know how to peer into existing HTML files and create your own, the next step is to understand what goes *inside* the average HTML file. It all revolves around a single concept—*tags*.

HTML tags are the formatting instructions that tell the browser how to transform ordinary text into something that's visually appealing. If you were to take all the tags out of an HTML document, you'd be left with nothing more than plain, unformatted text.

Note: Technically, HTTP (HyperText Transport Protocol) is the low-level communication system that allows two computers to exchange data over the Internet. If you were to apply the analogy of a phone conversation, the telephone line would use HTTP, and the juicy tidbits of gossip you're exchanging with your Aunt Martha would be the HTML documents.

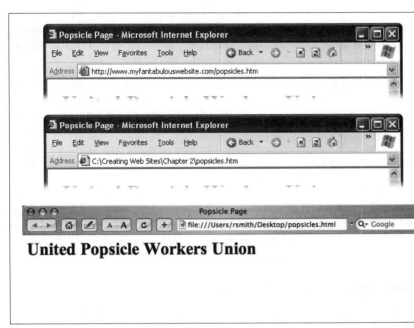

Figure 2-3:
The address bar indicates where the Web page you're viewing is really located (in geek-speak this is known as the file path). If you see "http://" your page is on a Web server somewhere out on the Internet (top). If you're looking at a Web page on your own computer, you'll just see an ordinary file path instead (middle, showing a Windows PC), or you'll see a URL that starts with the prefix "file:///" (bottom, showing a Mac). It all depends on the browser and operating system you're using.

What's in a Tag

You can recognize a tag by looking for the angle brackets, which are two special characters that look like this: < >. The angle brackets contain a code. This code is for the browser's eyes only, and it's never shown to Web surfers (unless they use the View → Source trick to peek at the HTML). Essentially, the code is an instruction that conveys some information to the browser about how it should format the text that follows the code.

For example, one simple tag is the <b> tag, which stands for bold. When the browser encounters this tag, it switches on boldface formatting, which affects all the text that appears after this tag. Here's an example:

```
This text isn't bold. <b>This text is bold.
```

In a browser, you don't see the <b>. You're just left with the end result, which looks something like this:

This text isn't bold. **This text is bold.**

As you can see, the browser has a fairly simple job. It scans through an HTML document, looking for tags and switching on and off various formatting settings. It sends everything else (everything that isn't a tag) straight to the Web browser window.

Note: Adding tags to ordinary text is known as *marking up* a document, and the tags themselves are known as HTML *markup*. When you look at raw HTML, you may be interested in looking at the content (the text that's nestled between the tags), or the markup (the HTML tags themselves).

Many tags come in pairs. That means there's a starting tag and an ending tag. The end tag marks the end of the instruction that was given by the start tag. In the bold text example, that means the end tag switches off the bold formatting, returning the text to normal.

End tags are easy to recognize. They always look the same as the start tag, except they start with the characters </ instead of <. So the end tag for bold formatting is </b>. Here's an example:

```
This isn't bold. <b>Pay attention!</b> Now we're back to normal.
```

Which the browser displays as:

This isn't bold. **Pay attention!** Now we're back to normal.

This example demonstrates another important principle in how a browser works. The browser always processes the tags in order, based on where they show up in your text. To get the bold formatting in the right place, you need to make sure you position the <b> and </b> tags appropriately.

Container Tags and Standalone Tags

It's considered good HTML style to always use tags in pairs. If you don't, it could conceivably confuse some browsers (and anyway, it's lazy). To get into the right habit, it helps to think of the start and end tags as a container into which you insert some text. In other words, when you use the <b> and </b> tags, you aren't exactly telling the browser to turn bold formatting on and off—more accurately, you're telling it to bold a specific piece of text.

Of course, life wouldn't be much fun (and computer books wouldn't be nearly as thick) without exceptions. When you get right down to it, there are really two types of tags:

- **Container tags**

  The container tag is, by far, the most common type of tag. With a container tag, you're usually applying some sort of formatting that affects only the content that's nestled in between the start and the end tags. The <b> tag is a container tag, and should always be accompanied by a </b>.

• **Standalone tags**

There are some tags that don't come in pairs. These standalone tags don't turn formatting on or off. Instead, they insert something on the page, like an image. One example is the <hr> tag, which inserts a horizontal line on the page. Standalone tags are often called *empty* tags because there's no way to put any text inside them.

Figure 2-4 puts it in perspective.

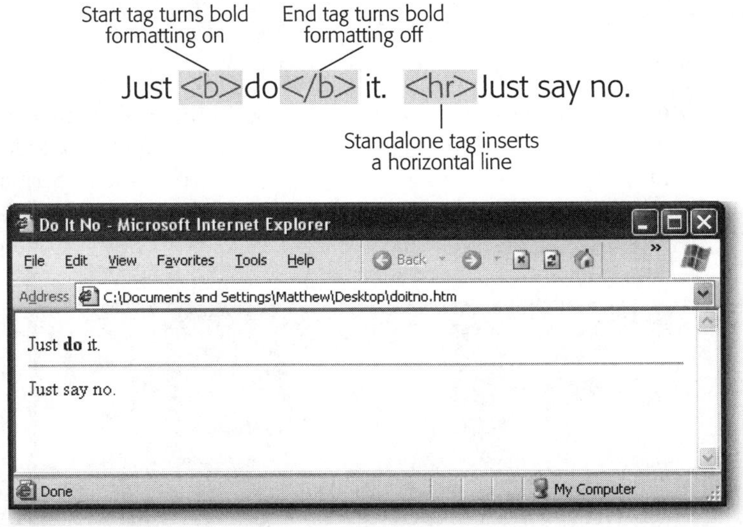

Figure 2-4:
Top: This snippet of HTML shows both a container tag and a standalone tag.

Bottom: The browser shows the resulting Web page.

Note: Standalone tags sometimes include a slash character, like this <hr /> (sort of like an opening and a closing tag rolled into one). This syntax is handy, because it clearly indicates that you have a standalone tag on your hands. It isn't official HTML, but it's used for a new standard called XHTML, which you'll learn about at the end of this chapter (page 47).

Nesting Tags

In the previous example, you saw how to apply a simple <b> tag for bold formatting. Between the <b> and </b> tags, you place the text that you want to make bold. However, text isn't the only thing that you can put between a start and an end tag. You can also nest one tag *inside* another. In fact, nesting tags is one of the basic building block techniques of Web pages. Nesting lets you apply more detailed formatting (for example, bold, underlined, italicized text), by piling in all the tags you need in the same place. Nesting is also required for more complicated structures (like bulleted lists).

To see nesting in action, you need another tag to work with. For the next example, consider both the familiar <b> tag and the <i> tag, which lets you italicize text.

The question is what happens if you want to make a piece of text bold and italicized? HTML doesn't include a tag for this purpose, so you need to combine the two. Here's an example:

```
This <b><i>word</i></b> has italic and bold formatting.
```

When the browser chews through this scrap of HTML, it produces text that looks like this:

This *word* has italic and bold formatting.

Incidentally, it doesn't matter if you reverse the order of the <i> and <b> tags. The following HTML produces exactly the same result.

```
This <i><b>word</b></i> has italic and bold formatting.
```

However, you should always make sure that you close tags in the *reverse* order that you opened them. In other words, if you apply italic formatting and then bold formatting, you should always switch off bold formatting first, and then italic formatting next. Here's an example that breaks this rule:

```
This <i><b>word</i></b> has italic and bold formatting.
```

FREQUENTLY ASKED QUESTION

Telling the Browser to Ignore a Tag

What if I really do want the text "<b>" to appear on my Web page?

The tag system works great until you actually want to use an angle bracket (< or >) in your text. Then you're in a tricky position.

For example, imagine you want to write the following bit of text as part of remarkable insight you've achieved:

```
The expression 5 < 2 is clearly false,
because 5 is bigger than 2.
```

When the browser reaches the less than (<) symbol, it becomes utterly bewildered. Its first instinct is to assume you're starting a tag, and the text following "2 is clearly false…" is part of a long tag name. Obviously, this isn't what you intended. The end result is unpredictable, but usually the text after the < character disappears into a nonexisting tag.

To solve this problem, you need to replace angle brackets with the corresponding HTML *character entity*. Character entities always begin with an ampersand (&) and end with a semicolon (;). The character entity for the less than symbol is *<* because the lt stands for "less than." Similarly, *>* is the character entity for the greater than symbol.

Here's the corrected example:

```
The expression 5 &lt; 2 is clearly false,
because 5 is bigger than 2.
```

In your text editor, this doesn't look like what you want. However, when the browser interprets this document, it automatically changes the < into a < character, without confusing it with a tag. You'll learn more about character entities on page 46 (at the end of this chapter).

Most Web browsers are savvy enough to figure out what you're trying to do and give you the right result. However, in some cases, violating this rule can cause different browsers to render the same document in different ways. To avoid these glitches, always close your tags in the reverse order that you open them.

Finally, it's worth noting that HTML gives you many more complex ways to nest tags. For example, you can nest one tag inside another, and then nest another tag inside that one, and so on, indefinitely. Just to give you some ideas, consider the following example, which uses a combination of italic, bold, and underline formatting with the <i>, <b>, and <u> tags.

```
<u>The <b>easiest</b> way to <b>confuse</b> a Web surfer is with <i>too much
<b>formatting</b></i>.</u>
```

If you follow through all the tags, you'll discover that this example produces the following dizzying line of text:

The **easiest** way to **confuse** a Web surfer is with *too much **formatting***.

To break down complex snippets of HTML like this, it's often handy to use a *tree model*. You'll use the tree model later in this chapter to analyze a complete HTML document.

Tip: If you're a graphic-design type, you're probably itching to get your hands on more powerful formatting tags to change alignment, spacing, and fonts. Unfortunately, in the Web world you can't always control everything you want. Chapter 5 has the lowdown, and Chapter 6 introduces the best solution (style sheets).

The HTML Document

So far, you've been considering HTML snippets—portions of a complete HTML document. In this section, you'll learn how to put it all together and create your first genuine Web page.

To create a true HTML document, you need a minimum of three container tags: <html>, <head>, and <body>. These three tags work together to describe the basic structure of your page.

- **<html>**

  This tag wraps everything else in your Web page. It tells the browser that you're using HTML.

- **<head>**

  This tag designates the *header* portion of your document. The header can include some optional information about your Web page, including the title (which is displayed in your browser's title bar), search keywords, and a style sheet (which you'll learn about in Chapter 6).

- **<body>**

  This tag holds the meat of your Web page, including the actual content you want to display to the world.

There's only one right way to combine these tags. Here's the correct arrangement:

```
<html>

<head>
...
</head>

<body>
...
</body>

</html>
```

Every Web page uses this basic framework. The ellipsis (…) shows where you'll want to insert additional information. The spaces in between the lines aren't required; they're just to help you see the tag structure more easily.

Note: Almost all browsers let you bend these rules, and create a document that lacks these three basic tags. Of course, if you wanted to learn the wrong way to write Web pages, you probably wouldn't be reading this book!

To transform this barebones template into a real document, you just need to start adding some content. For example, let's say you're starting a basic résumé page. Here's a very basic first go at it:

```
<html>

<head>
</head>

<body>
I am Lee Park. Hire me for your company, because my work is <b>off the
hizzle</b>.
</body>

</html>
```

The only change is the addition of text in the <body> section. A single <b> tag is also used, just to dress it up a little. Before you go any further, you may want to try creating this sample file in your own text editor, and opening it in your favorite Web browser (see Figure 2-5). You're then ready to try out all the upcoming HTML tricks.

Note: Even if you have high-powered HTML editing software (like FrontPage or Dreamweaver), don't use it yet. To get started learning HTML, it's best that you do it by hand so you understand every detail that's going into your Web page. Later on, when you've mastered the basics and are ready to create more sophisticated Web pages, you'll probably want to switch to other tools (see Chapter 4).

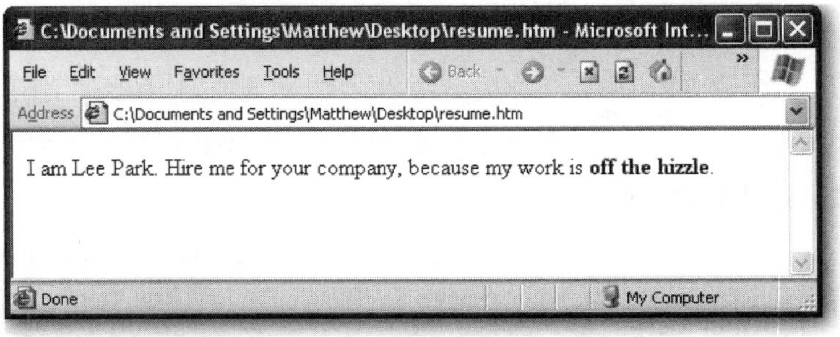

Figure 2-5:
Welcome to the Web. This page isn't much in the way of HTML goodies (and it probably won't get Lee hired), but it does represent one of the simplest possible HTML pages you can create.

Adding a Title

The first improvement you can make to the simple résumé page is to add a title. Without it, most browsers show the URL or file path (where the Web page is stored) in the title bar. Once you add a title that information disappears, and is replaced with your custom text (see Figure 2-6).

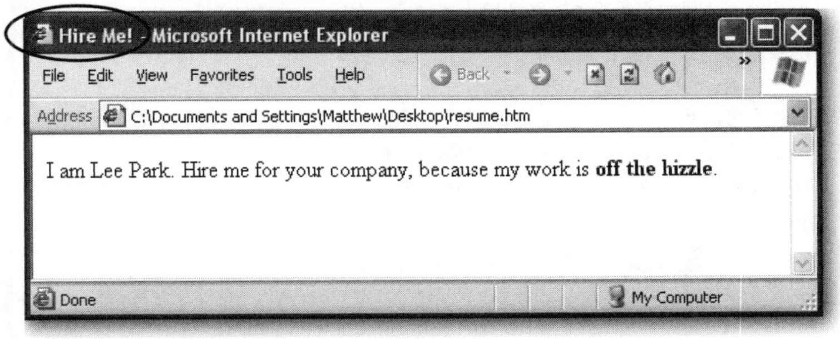

Figure 2-6:
When displaying a Web page that doesn't have a title, the Web browser title bar just tells you where the page is located (see Figure 2-5). When displaying a Web page with a title (shown here), you'll see the title and a bit of extra text that the Web browser tacks onto the end).

The title information isn't a part of the content of your Web page. Instead, it's added using a <title> tag in the <head> section. Here's the example shown in Figure 2-6:

```
<html>

<head>
<title>Hire Me!</title>
</head>
```

```
<body>
I am Lee Park. Hire me for your company, because my work is <b>off the
hizzle</b>.
</body>


</html>
```

Tip: Titles are important. When a Web surfer bookmarks your page, the title is what shows up in the browser's Bookmark (or Favorites) menu. Titles are also used by many search engines to identify your page.

Line Breaks and Text Flow

As you start to create more detailed Web pages, you'll quickly discover that building a Web page isn't as straightforward as, say, creating a page in Microsoft Word. For example, you may decide to enhance the résumé page by creating a list of skills. Here's a reasonable first try:

```
<html>

<head>
<title>Hire Me!</title>
</head>

<body>
I am Lee Park. Hire me for your company, because my work is <b>off the
hizzle</b>.

My skills include:
    * Fast typing (nearly 12 words/minute).
    * Extraordinary pencil sharpening.
    * Inventive excuse making.
    * Negotiating with officers of the peace.
</body>


</html>
```

The problem occurs when you open this seemingly innocent document in your Web browser (Figure 2-7).

The problem is that HTML ignores extra white space. That includes tabs, line breaks, and extra spaces (anything more than one consecutive space). The first time this happens to you, you'll probably stare dumbfounded at the computer screen and wonder why Web browsers are designed this way. But it actually makes a fair bit of sense when you consider the fact that HTML needs to work as a *universal standard*.

Say you were to customize your hypothetical Web page (like the one shown in Figure 2-7) with the perfect spacing, indenting, and line width for *your* computer monitor. The problem is it may not look as good on someone else's monitor. For example, some of the text may scroll off the right side of their page, making it difficult to read. And different monitors are only part of the problem—today's Web pages need to display on different types of *devices*. Lee Park's future boss might conceivably view his résumé on anything from the latest iBook laptop to a fixed-width terminal or a Web-enabled cell phone.

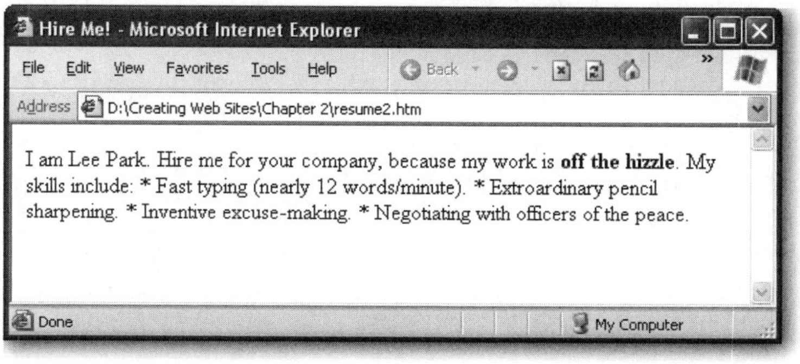

Figure 2-7:
HTML disregards line breaks and consecutive spaces, so neatly organized text files can easily turn into a jumble of text like this.

To deal with this wide range of display options, HTML lets you define the *structure* of your text with tags. Instead of telling the browser, "Here's where you go to the next line and here's where you add four extra spaces," HTML tells the browser, "Here are two complete paragraphs and here's a bulleted list." It's then up to the browser to display your Web page according to the instructions contained in your HTML.

To correct the résumé example, you need to use three new container tags:

• <p>

Indicates a paragraph. Web browsers don't indent paragraphs, but they do add a little space in between consecutive paragraphs.

• <ul>

Indicates the start of an unordered list (which is usually displayed with a bullet next to each item). This is the perfect way to detail Lee's skills.

• <li>

Indicates an individual item in a bulleted list. Each list item is indented, and has a bullet (•) preceding it. The <li> tag can only be used inside a <ul> tag. In other words, every list item needs to be a part of a bulleted list.

Here's the corrected Web page (shown in Figure 2-8), with the new tags high-lighted in bold:

```
<html>

<head>
<title>Hire Me!</title>
</head>

<body>
<p>I am Lee Park. Hire me for your company, because my work is <b>off the
hizzle</b>.</p>
<p>My skills include:</p>
<ul>
    <li>Fast typing (nearly 12 words/minute).</li>
    <li>Extraordinary pencil sharpening.</li>
    <li>Inventive excuse making.</li>
    <li>Negotiating with officers of the peace.</li>
</ul>
</body>

</html>
```

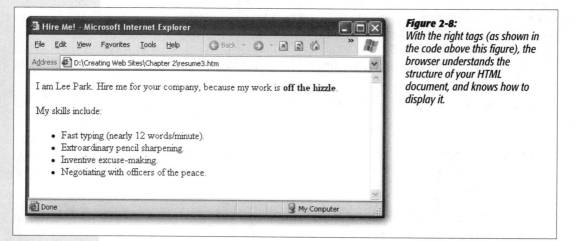

Figure 2-8:
With the right tags (as shown in the code above this figure), the browser understands the structure of your HTML document, and knows how to display it.

Figure 2-9 shows how you can analyze the HTML document so far using a tree model. The tree model is a handy way to get familiar with the anatomy of a Web page, because it shows the overall structure at a glance. However, as your Web pages get more complicated, they'll probably include too much information to comfortably see in a tree model diagram.

You can turn the browser's habit of ignoring line breaks to your advantage. To help make your Web documents more readable, add line breaks and spaces wherever you want. Web gurus often use indentation to make the structure of nested tags easier to understand. In the résumé example, you can already see this trick in action. Notice how the list items (the lines starting with the <li> tag) are indented. This has no effect on the browser, but it makes it easier to see the structure of the HTML document, and how it will be rendered in the browser.

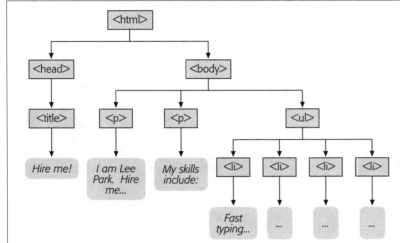

Figure 2-9:
Here's another way to look at the HTML you've created. The tree model is designed to show you, at a glance, how tags are nested. By following the arrows, you can see that the top-level <html> tag contains <head> and <body> tags. Inside the <head> tag is the title, and inside the <body> tag are two paragraphs and a bulleted list with four items. If you stare at the tree model long enough, you'll start to understand why all these tags are called container tags.

Of course, if you're a masochist, you don't need to use any spaces. The previous example is exactly equivalent to the following much-less-readable HTML document that omits white space entirely:

```
<html><head><title>Hire Me!</title></head><body><p>I am Lee Park. Hire me for
your company, because my work is <b>off the hizzle</b>.</p><p>My skills
include:</p><ul><li>Fast typing (nearly 12 words/minute).</li><li>
Extraordinary pencil sharpening.</li><li>Inventive excuse making.</li><li>
Negotiating with officers of the peace.</li></ul></body></html>
```

Of course, it's nearly impossible for a human to write HTML like this without making a mistake.

Where Are All the Pictures?

Whether it's a stock chart, a logo for your underground garage band, or doctored photos of your favorite celebrities, the Web would be a pretty drab place without pictures. But so far, you've only seen how to put text into an HTML document. What happens when you need an image?

Although it may surprise you, there's actually no way to store a picture inside an HTML file. There are plenty of good reasons why you wouldn't want to anyway—your Web page files would become really large, it would be hard to modify your pictures or do other things with them, and you'd have a fiendish time editing your pages in a text editor because the image data would make a mess. The solution is to store your pictures as separate files, and then *link* them to your HTML document. This way, the pictures will show up exactly where you want them in your Web page when it's displayed by a browser. The pictures just aren't stored in the HTML file.

Have Something to Hide?

When you're working with a complex Web page, you may want to temporarily remove a tag or a section of content. This is a handy trick when you have a page that doesn't quite work right, and you want to try and find out where the problem lies. One way to do this is with the good ol' fashioned cut-and-paste features in your text editor. However, HTML has a simpler solution—*comments*.

To create an HTML comment, you use the <!-- character sequence to mark the start of the comment, and the --> character sequence to mark the end. Everything in between these two markers, whether it's content or tags, is completely ignored by the browser. The comment markers can appear on the same line, or you can use them to hide an entire section of your HTML document.

Here's an example that hides two list items. When you open this document in your Web browser, the list will show only the last two items ("Inventive excuse making" and "Negotiating with officers of the peace").

```
<ul>
<!-- <li>Fast typing (nearly 12 words/minute).
</li>
    <li>Extraordinary pencil sharpening.</li>
  -->
    <li>Inventive excuse making.</li>
    <li>Negotiating with officers of the
    peace.</li>
</ul>
```

When you want to return the list to its original glory, just remove the comment markers.

The linking tool that performs this trick is the *<img>* tag (short for image). The image tag is a standalone tag that points to an image file, which the browser then retrieves and inserts into the Web page. The image file can be placed in the same folder as your Web page (which is the easiest option) or located on a completely different Web site.

Although you'll learn everything you ever wanted to know about Web graphics in Chapter 7, it's worth considering a simple example right now. To try this out, you need a Web-ready image handy. (The most common supported file types are JPEG, GIF, and PNG.) If you've downloaded this book's companion content (from the "Missing CD" page at *www.missingmanuals.com*), you can use the sample picture *leepark.jpg*. Assuming this file is in the same folder as your Web page file, you need the following image tag to display the picture:

```
<img src="leepark.jpg">
```

This example introduces something new. Although <img> is a standalone tag, it isn't self-sufficient. In order for the tag to mean anything, you also need to supply the file name. To incorporate this extra information into the image tag, HTML uses *attributes*. Attributes are extra pieces of information that appear *after* the tag name, but before the closing > character. In many cases, you can use multiple attributes, in which case you separate each attribute using a space.

The attribute itself has two parts—a name (this is the code that tells the browser what the attribute does) and a value (this is the piece of information you're supplying). In the <img> example, the attribute you're using is named *src*, which is shorthand for source. The value of the source attribute tells the browser where to find the image file you want to use.

Once you've unraveled the image tag, you're ready to use it in an HTML document. Just place it inside an existing paragraph, wherever it makes sense.

```
<html>

<head>
<title>Hire Me!</title>
</head>

<body>
<p>I am Lee Park. Hire me for your company, because my work is <b>off the
hizzle</b>.
<img src="leepark.jpg"></p>
<p>My skills include:</p>
<ul>
    <li>Fast typing (nearly 12 words/minute).</li>
    <li>Extraordinary pencil sharpening.</li>
    <li>Inventive excuse making.</li>
    <li>Negotiating with officers of the peace.</li>
</ul>
</body>

</html>
```

Figure 2-10 shows exactly where the picture is displayed.

Note: You'll learn many more tricks for Web graphics, including how to change their size and wrap text around them, in Chapter 7.

The 10 Most Important Tags (and a Few More)

You've now reached the point where you can create a basic HTML document, and you're well on your way to HTML mastery with several tags under your belt. You know the fundamentals—all that's left is to expand your knowledge by learning more tags.

HTML has a relatively small set of tags. In fact, there are just over 60 in all. You'll most likely use fewer than 25 tags on a regular basis.

Note: You can't define your own tags and use them in an HTML document because Web browsers won't know how to interpret them.

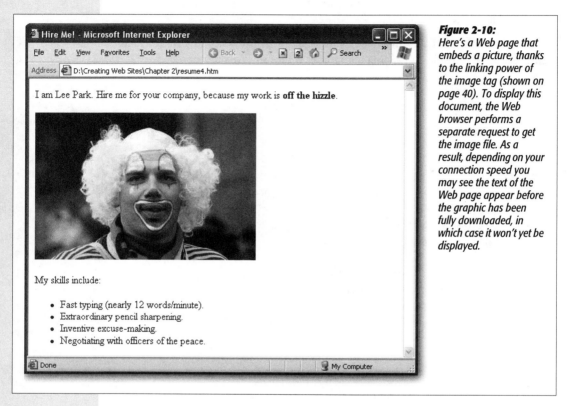

Figure 2-10:
Here's a Web page that embeds a picture, thanks to the linking power of the image tag (shown on page 40). To display this document, the Web browser performs a separate request to get the image file. As a result, depending on your connection speed you may see the text of the Web page appear before the graphic has been fully downloaded, in which case it won't yet be displayed.

Table 2-1 provides a quick overview of some the most fundamental building blocks in HTML, several of which you've already seen.

Table 2-1. *The Basic HTML Tags*

Tag	Name	Type	Description
<b>, <i>, <u>	Bold, Italic, Underline	Container	These three tags apply character styling—either bold, italic, or underline formatting.
<p>	Paragraph	Container	As your high school English teacher probably told you, the paragraph is the basic unit for organizing text. When you use more than one paragraph tag in a row, the browser inserts a certain amount of space in between the two paragraphs—just a bit more than a full blank line. Full details appear in Chapter 5.

Table 2-1. *The Basic HTML Tags (continued)*

Tag	Name	Type	Description
 	Line Break	Standalone	Sometimes, all you want is text separated by simple line breaks, not separate paragraphs. This keeps your text closer together than when you use paragraph tags. You'll learn more about text layout in Chapter 5.
<h1>, <h2>, <h3>, <h4>, <h5>, <h6>	Heading	Container	If you need a title to stand out, the heading tags are a good choice. They display text in large, bold letters. The lower the number, the larger the text, so <h1> is for the largest heading. By the time you get to <h5>, the heading size has dwindled down to the normal text size, and <h6>, although bold, is actually smaller than normal text.
<hr>	Horizontal Line	Standalone	A horizontal line can help you split one section from another. The line automatically matches the width of the browser window. (Or, if you put it inside another element like a cell in a table, it takes on the width of its container.)
<img>	Image	Standalone	To display an image inside a Web page, use this tag. Make sure you specify the *src* attribute to indicate the file name of the picture you want the browser to show.
<a>	Anchor	Container	The anchor tag is the starting point for creating hyperlinks that allow Web surfers to jump from one page to another. You'll learn about this indispensable tag in Chapter 8.
<ul>, <li>	Unordered List, List Item	Container	These tags let you build basic bulleted lists. The browser automatically puts individual list items on separate lines and indents each one. For a quick change of pace, you can substitute <ul> with <ol> to get an automatically numbered list instead of bullets (ol stands for ordered list).

In order to make the résumé really look respectable, you can use a few tricks from Table 2-1. Figure 2-11 shows this revised version of the Web page:

```
<html>

<head>
<title>Hire Me!</title>
</head>
```

```
<body>
<h1>Hire Me!</h1>
<p>I am Lee Park. Hire me for your company, because my work is <b>off the
hizzle</b>. As proof of my staggering computer skills and monumental work
ethic, please enjoy this electronic resume.</p>
<h2>Indispensable Skills</h2>
<p>My skills include:</p>
<ul>
    <li>Fast typing (nearly 12 words/minute).</li>
    <li>Extraordinary pencil sharpening.</li>
    <li>Inventive excuse making.</li>
    <li>Negotiating with officers of the peace.</li>
</ul>
<p>And I also know HTML!</p>
<h2>Previous Work Experience</h2>
I have had a long and illustrious career in a variety of trades. Here are
some highlights:
<ul>
    <li>2000-2003 - Worked as a typist at <i>Flying Fingers</i></li>
    <li>2003-2004 - Performed cutting-edge Web design at <i>Riverdale
    Farm</i></li>
    <li>2004-2005 - Starred in Chapter 2 of <i>Creating Web Pages: The
Missing Manual</i></li>
</ul>
<hr>
</body>

</html>
```

Common Mistakes

Now that you've seen some Web pages that get it right, it's worth considering a few common mistakes that can mangle the best of pages.

Missing a closing tag

You know the rule—container tags should always appear in pairs. That means if you use a tag like <h1> to switch on heading 1 style, make sure you use </h1> soon after to turn it off. The problem occurs if your closing tag isn't quite kosher. For example, maybe you left out the ever important slash character (/). Try to guess what the result of this mistake will be:

```
<h1>The Tile That Never Ends<h1>
```

The first tag turns on the heading style, and the second tag tries to turn it on *again*, which has no effect. The end result is that the heading 1 style is never switched off, and the entire Web page is rendered in gigantic bold letters. Ouch.

Here's what you really want:

```
<h1>The Tile That Never Ends</h1>
```

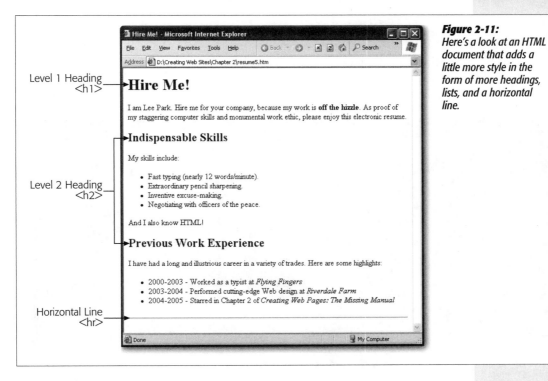

Figure 2-11:
Here's a look at an HTML document that adds a little more style in the form of more headings, lists, and a horizontal line.

Endless tags

As you can see, a minor typo can wreak a great deal of havoc. If you leave out the slash, you'll be faced with the unmistakable Entire Web Page In Giant Bold Letters syndrome. If you make another common mistake and leave out one of the angle brackets, you'll encounter the equally common Disappearing Page disorder.

Here's the mistake:

```
<pThe invisible paragraph.</p>
```

In this case, the starting <p> tag is missing the closing > character. As a result, the browser tries to interpret the entire line of text "<pThe invisible paragraph.</p>" as some sort of tag it's never seen before. And you know what browsers do with tags they don't recognize? They ignore them completely. As a result, the contents of that paragraph won't appear in your Web page at all. If you expected to see something that's mysteriously absent, an improperly closed tag is probably at the root of it.

Incidentally, a similar problem can occur with attributes if you include only one quotation mark instead of two. Here's an example that shows this mistake with the *src* attribute in the image tag, which is the only attribute you've seen so far.

```
<img src="leepark.jpg>
```

Because the closing quotation mark is missing, the rest of the HTML document (until the next quotation mark is found) is interpreted as an incredibly long file name. As a result, the browser won't display the picture, and a great deal of text will vanish.

FREQUENTLY ASKED QUESTION

The Difference Between <b> and <B>

Should I use uppercase or lowercase tags?

HTML isn't case-sensitive. That means that your tags can use any mix of lowercase letters or uppercase letters without disrupting the browser.

Of course, just because something's allowed doesn't mean it's necessarily a good idea. Although Web browsers won't make a distinction, most professional Web designers use only lowercase (as does this book) for a number of reasons:

- Newer Web standards like XHTML (see page 47) aren't as lenient. They'll force you to use lowercase tags.

- Following suit, Web authoring tools like FrontPage and Dreamweaver always use lowercase tags.

That said, a few Web fans still like uppercase tags because they sometimes stand out better in a sea of HTML. So feel free to go uppercase if you like, but just be warned that the rest of the world won't follow suit.

Handling special characters with caution

In HTML, certain characters have a special meaning—namely angle brackets (< >) and the ampersand (&). You can't enter these characters directly into a Web page, because the browser will assume you're trying to give it a super-special instruction. Instead, you need to replace these characters with the equivalent HTML *character entities,* as described in the box "Telling the Browser to Ignore a Tag" on page 32. Table 2-2 shows the basic HTML character entities.

Table 2-2. HTML Character Entities

To Get This:	Type This:
<	&lt;
>	&gt;
&	&amp;
"	&quot;

Strictly speaking, you don't need all of these entities. Quotation marks are always acceptable, except inside attribute names. Browsers are usually intelligent enough to handle the ampersand (&) character appropriately, but it's better style to use the entity & because that way there's no chance the browser will confuse the ampersand with another character entity. Finally, the character entities for the angle brackets are absolutely, utterly necessary.

Here's some flawed text that won't display correctly:

```
I love the greater than (>) and less than (<) symbols. Problem is, when I
type them my browser thinks I'm trying to use a tag.
```

And here's the correction with the HTML character entities. When the browser processes this text and displays it, it replaces the entities with the characters you really want.

```
I love the greater than (&gt;) and less than (&lt;) symbols. Problem is, when
I type them my browser thinks I'm trying to use a tag.
```

Tip: Character entities are also a handy way to insert symbols like non-English characters, the copyright mark, and the Euro currency symbol. You'll learn more in Chapter 5.

XHTML

The current version of HTML (as implemented by all modern browsers and taught in this book) is HTML 4.01. HTML 4.01 became an official standard at the end of 1999, so it's definitely not a new kid on the block. This raises an interesting question—in all the years since HTML 4.01 hit the Web, why haven't there been more changes?

The fact is, HTML 4.01 has essentially finished its evolution. There isn't much more that can be improved—at least not without radically changing the way the language is now. In the years since 1999, developers have largely concentrated on extending HTML with browser plug-ins for new types of content (like Flash movies) and building massive Web applications that can generate HTML on the fly.

That doesn't mean the world of Web standards has been quiet. The next big thing is *XHTML,* a revised version of HTML that incorporates some of the philosophy of another standard called *XML* (Extensible Markup Language). XHTML is a stricter form of HTML, so it doesn't allow sloppy mistakes (like improperly nested tags) that browsers tolerate happily. However, the real goal of XHTML isn't to hassle lazy Web developers. Instead, because XHTML is more consistent, it makes life easier for Web search engines and scaled-down Web browsers on specialized platforms (like telephones, pocket computers, and even kitchen appliances). And because XHTML has XML underpinnings, it's great for hardcore computer programmers that want to create and analyze Web pages using development tools.

So why aren't we all focusing on XHTML? Even though XHTML has been around for several years, HTML 4.01 is still the undisputed popularity champ. It's more compatible with older browsers and works well with piles of popular Web editors. Most Web page creators still pass on XHTML because it doesn't add any new features. At the time of this writing, top sites like Amazon, eBay, and Google are still

XHTML-free. In fact, XHTML is used only when companies have powerful Web application software that's smart enough to serve up different types of Web pages (HTML or XHTML) depending on how capable the requesting browser is.

Creating a Valid XHTML Page

In this book, you won't explore XHTML. However, if you're interested, it's just a short step up from HTML.

The basics

First of all, whereas a few HTML conventions are *guidelines* (that is, they're optional), in XHTML, they're unbreakable rules. These rules are recommended in this chapter and followed throughout this book, but they're not actually enforced by HTML:

- Always include the <html>, <head>, <title>, and <body> tags.

- Use proper nesting so that different start and end tags don't overlap (see page 32).

- Write all of your HTML tag names and attributes in lowercase letters.

- Understand the difference between block elements and inline elements (see page 116). Inline elements (like images and links) must always be placed inside a block element (like the paragraph).

Along with these rules are a few new wrinkles that you don't follow in ordinary HTML.

First of all, you need a *namespace* that indicates that you're using XHTML tags. Adding this ingredient is easy—just replace this <html> tag at the beginning of your document:

```
<html>
```

with this:

```
<html xmlns="http://www.w3.org/1999/xhtml">
```

Second, you need to add a space and a slash character to the end of every empty tag. That means instead of this:

```
<hr>
```

use this:

```
<hr />
```

And instead of this:

```
<img src="leepark.jpg">
```

use this:

```
<img src="leepark.jpg" />
```

Tip: The single space immediately before the /> characters ensures that the tag still works with browsers that don't understand XHTML.

To make life even more interesting, there are some rules for specific tags. For example, the <img> tag always needs to provide some alternate text, which is used in cases where the picture can't be downloaded (see page 183). Here's a valid <img> tag that's ready for XHTML:

```
<img src="leepark.jpg" alt="Lee Park Portrait" />
```

The document type definition

All XHTML documents must start with something called a *document type definition* (DTD). This is a cryptic code that's inserted at the very top of your document, just before the <html> tag. The DTD tells the world what type of XHTML you're using. The key difference between different flavors of XHTML is whether they support old-fashioned HTML features that XHTML gurus frown upon.

For example, if you have pure XHTML that's unadulterated by any old-fashioned HTML trickery, you can use the *strict* DTD. That means you'll insert this at the top of your page:

```
<!DOCTYPE html PUBLIC "-//W3C//DTD XHTML 1.0 Strict//EN"
 "http://www.w3.org/TR/xhtml1/DTD/xhtml1-strict.dtd">
```

In order to be considered strict XHTML, your page can't use the quirky formatting hacks that are present in HTML. Instead, it needs to use the more powerful and better organized style sheet standard (which is introduced in Chapter 6). Most of the examples in this book can be converted into strict XHTML, because they use style sheets. For the most part, you won't see any old-fashioned HTML tricks unless they're difficult to duplicate by other means.

If you decide you want the flexibility to use some of the unpopular parts of HTML, you can use the *transitional* DTD, which looks like this:

```
<!DOCTYPE html PUBLIC "-//W3C//DTD XHTML 1.0 Transitional//EN"
 "http://www.w3.org/TR/xhtml1/DTD/xhtml1-transitional.dtd">
```

The word transitional hints at the fact that this approach is only a temporary fix. Later versions of XHTML won't give you this option.

Finally, you can use the *frameset* DTD when you want to create a Web page that uses frames (see Chapter 10).

```
<!DOCTYPE html PUBLIC "-//W3C//DTD XHTML 1.0 Frameset//EN"
 "http://www.w3.org/TR/xhtml1/DTD/xhtml1-frameset.dtd">
```

Frames are a handy feature for splitting a browser window so it shows more than one page at a time. Many Web gurus refuse to deal with frames due to their quirks and limitations, preferring to build high-powered Web applications that custom-build each page instead. However, frames still play an important role for do-it-yourself designers.

A valid XHTML page

Here's a version of the résumé page reworked as a strict XHTML 1.0 document. The changes are highlighted in bold.

```
<!DOCTYPE html PUBLIC "-//W3C//DTD XHTML 1.0 Strict//EN"
 "http://www.w3.org/TR/xhtml1/DTD/xhtml1-strict.dtd">
<html xmlns="http://www.w3.org/1999/xhtml">

<head>
<title>Hire Me!</title>
</head>

<body>
<p>I am Lee Park. Hire me for your company, because my work is <b>off the
hizzle</b>.</p>
<img src="leepark.jpg" alt="Lee Park Portrait" />
<p>My skills include:</p>
<ul>
    <li>Fast typing (nearly 12 words/minute).</li>
    <li>Extraordinary pencil sharpening.</li>
    <li>Inventive excuse making.</li>
    <li>Negotiating with officers of the peace.</li>
</ul>
</body>

</html>
```

When you request this page in a browser, you won't notice any changes from the HTML version. However, you are now officially on the cutting edge (for a few minutes, anyway).

Note: XHTML pages still use the file extension .*htm* or .*html*.

You won't find much more about XHTML in this book. However, if the standard intrigues you, check out the quick tutorial at *www.w3schools.com/xhtml*. If you'd like to test your pages to see if they meet the rules of XHTML, you can use the handy online validator at *www.htmlhelp.com/cgi-bin/validate.cgi*.

Putting Your Page on the Web

In the previous chapter you learned the basics of HTML by considering a simple one-page résumé. There's still a lot more you can do to perfect that page, but before going any further it's worth taking a careful look at one of the most important pieces of the Web puzzle—getting your pages online.

In this chapter, you start by taking a closer look at how Web servers work. Once you're armed with these high-tech nerd credentials, you'll be ready to search for your own *Web host*—the company that's going to let you park your Web site on its Web server. All you need to do is figure out your requirements, assess the possibilities, and then start shopping!

How Web Hosting Works

As you learned in Chapter 1, the Web isn't stored on any single computer, and no company owns the Web. Instead, the individual pieces (Web sites) are scattered across millions of computers (Web servers). Only a subtle illusion makes all these Web sites seem to be part of a single environment. In reality, the Internet is just a set of standards that let independent computers talk to each other.

So how does your favorite browser navigate this tangled network of computers to find the Web page you want? It's all in the URL—the Web site address you type into your browser.

Understanding the URL

A *URL* (Uniform Resource Locator) consists of several pieces. Some of these pieces are optional, because they can be filled in by the browser or Web server automatically. Others are always required. Figure 3-1 dissects the URL *http://www. SellMyJunkForMillions.com/Buyers/listings.htm.*

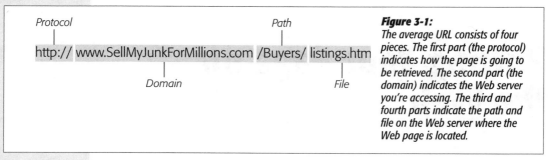

Figure 3-1:
The average URL consists of four pieces. The first part (the protocol) indicates how the page is going to be retrieved. The second part (the domain) indicates the Web server you're accessing. The third and fourth parts indicate the path and file on the Web server where the Web page is located.

Altogether, the URL packs a lot of information into one place, including:

- **The protocol** is the way you communicate over the Web. Technically, it's the way that request and response messages are transmitted across your Internet connection. Web pages always use HTTP (HyperText Transport Protocol), which means the protocol is always *http://* or *https://*. (The latter establishes a super-secure connection over HTTP that encrypts sensitive information you type in, like credit card numbers or passwords.) In most browsers, you can get away without typing this part of the URL. For example, when you type *www. google.com*, your browser will automatically convert it to the full URL *http:// www.google.com.*

Tip: Although http:// is the way to go when surfing the Web, depending on your browser you may also use other protocols for other tasks. Common examples include *ftp://* (File Transfer Protocol) for uploading and downloading files and *file:///* for retrieving a file directly from your own computer's hard drive.

- **The domain** identifies the Web server—the computer that hosts the Web site you want to see. As a convention, these computers usually have names that start with *www* to identify them as Web servers, although this isn't always the case. As you'll discover in this chapter, the friendly seeming domain name is really just a façade hiding a numeric address.

- **The path** identifies the location on the Web server where the Web page is stored. This part of the URL can have as many levels as is needed. For example, the path */MyFiles/Sales/2005/* refers to a MyFiles folder that contains a Sales folder that, in turn, contains a folder named 2005. Windows fans, take note— the slashes in the path portion of the URL are ordinary forward slashes, not the backward slashes used in Windows file paths (like *c:\MyFiles\Current*). This convention is designed to match the file paths used by Unix-based computers, which were the first machines to host Web sites. It's also the convention used in modern Macintosh operating systems (OS X and later).

Tip: Some browsers are smart enough to correct the common mistake of typing the wrong type of slash. However, you shouldn't rely on this happening, because similar laziness can break the Web pages you create. For example, if you use the <img> tag to link to an image (as demonstrated on page 40) and you use the wrong type of slash, your picture won't appear.

- **The file name** is the last part of the path. Often, you can recognize it by the file extension *.htm* or *.html*, both of which stand for HTML.

Tip: Web pages often end with *.htm* or *.html*, but they don't need to. Even if you look in the URL and see the extension *.blackpudding*, odds are you're still looking at an HTML document. In most cases, the browser ignores the extension as long as the file contains information that the browser can interpret. However, just to keep yourself sane, this is one convention that you shouldn't break.

- **The bookmark** is an optional part of a URL that identifies a specific position in a page. You can recognize a bookmark because it always starts with the hash character (#), and is placed after the file name. For example, the URL http:// www.LousyDeals.com/index.html#New includes the bookmark #New. When clicked, it takes the visitor to the section of the index.html page where the New bookmark is placed. You'll learn about bookmarks in Chapter 8.

- **The query string** is an optional part of the URL that some Web sites use to send extra instructions from one Web page to another. You can identify the query string because it starts with a question mark (?) character, and is placed after the file name. To see a query string in action, surf to *www.google.com* and perform a search for "pet platypus." When you click the Search button, you're directed to a URL like *http://www.google.ca/search?hl=en&q=pet+platypus&meta=*. This URL is a little tricky to analyze, but if you search for the question mark in the URL you'll discover that you're on a page named "search." The information to the right of the question mark indicates that you're performing an English language search for pages that match both the "pet" and "platypus" keywords. When you request this URL, a specialized Google Web application analyzes the query string to determine what type of search it needs to perform.

Note: You won't use the query string in your own Web pages, because it's designed for heavy-duty Web applications like the one that powers Google. However, by understanding the query string, you get a bit of insight into how other Web sites work.

How Browsers Analyze the URL

Clearly, the URL packs a lot of useful information into one place. But how does a browser actually use the URL to request the Web page you want? To understand how this works, it helps to take a peek behind the scenes (see Figure 3-2).

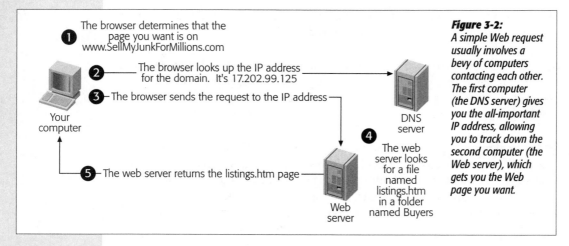

Figure 3-2:
A simple Web request usually involves a bevy of computers contacting each other. The first computer (the DNS server) gives you the all-important IP address, allowing you to track down the second computer (the Web server), which gets you the Web page you want.

The following list of steps shows a breakdown of what the browser needs to do when you type *http://www.SellMyJunkForMillions.com/Buyers/listings.htm* into the address bar and hit Enter:

1. **First, the browser needs to figure out what Web server to contact. It does this by extracting the domain from the URL.**

   In this example, the domain is *www.SellMyJunkForMillions.com*.

2. **In order to find the Web server named *www.SellMyJunkForMillions.com*, the browser needs to convert the domain name into a more computer-friendly number, which is called the *IP address*. Every computer on the Web—Web servers and regular PCs alike—has an IP address. To find the IP address for the Web server, the browser looks up the Web server's domain name in a giant catalog called the DNS (Domain Name Service).**

   An IP address looks like a set of four numbers separated by periods (or, in techy speak, dots). For example, the *www.SellMyJunkForMillions.com* Web site may have the IP address 17.202.99.125.

Note: The DNS catalog isn't stored on your computer, so your browser actually needs to grab this information from the Internet. You can see the advantage that this approach provides. In ordinary circumstances, a company's domain name will never change, because that's what customers use and remember. But an IP address may change, because the company may need to move their Web site from one Web server to another. As long as the company remembers to update the DNS, this won't cause any disruption. Fortunately, you won't need to worry about managing the DNS yourself, because that process is automatically handled for you by the company that hosts your Web site.

3. **Using the IP address, the browser sends the request to the Web server.**

   The actual route that the message takes is difficult to predict. It may cross through a number of other networking devices on the way.

4. **When the Web server receives the request, it looks at the path and file name in the URL.**

   In this case, the Web server sees that the request is for a file named *listings.htm* in a folder named *Buyers*. It looks up that file, and then sends it back to the Web browser. If the file doesn't exist, it sends back an error message instead.

5. **The browser gets the HTML page it's been waiting for (the *listings.htm* file), and renders it for your viewing pleasure.**

The URL *http://www.SellMyJunkForMillions.com/Buyers/listings.htm* is a typical example. However, in the wild, you'll sometimes come across URLs that seem a lot simpler. For instance, consider *http://www.amazon.com*. It clearly specifies the domain name (*www.amazon.com*), but it doesn't include any information about the path or file name. So what's a Web browser to do?

When your URL doesn't include a file name, the browser just sends the request as is, and lets the Web server decide what to do. The Web server sees that you aren't requesting a specific file, and so it sends you the site's default Web page, which is often named *index.htm* or *index.html*. However, the Web administrator can configure the Web server to use any Web page file name as the default.

Now that you understand how URLs work, you're ready to integrate your own pages into the fabric of the Web.

Domain Names

Shakespeare may have famously written "What's in a name? That which we call a rose / By any other name would smell as sweet." But he may not see things the same way if he has to type in *www.thesweetsmellingredflowerwiththorns.biz* into his browser instead of *www.rose.com*. Short, snappy domain addresses attract attention and are easier to remember. Today, cheap personalized domain addresses are within the reach of every Web site creator. If you decide to get one of your own, it's worth taking the time to get it right.

Searching for a Name

Your first step should be to start checking domain name availability. You can start this process even if you haven't chosen a Web hosting company. In fact, the Web abounds with tools that let you check if a domain name is available. These tools will also stop you if you try to use illegal characters (only letters, numbers, and dashes are allowed in a domain name).

POWER USERS' CLINIC

Internet vs. Intranet

As you already know, the Internet is a huge network of computers that spans the globe. An *intranet* is a lot smaller—it's a network inside a specific company, organization, or home that joins together a much smaller number of computers. In fact, an intranet could have as few as two computers.

An intranet makes sense anytime you need to have a Web site that's only available to a small number of people in one location. For example, a company can use an intranet Web site to share marketing bulletins (or the latest office gossip). In your own home, you could use an intranet to let your housemates browse your Web creations from multiple computers. The only limitation is that a Web site on an intranet is only accessible to the computers on that network. Other Web surfers won't be able to visit it.

Setting up a Web site for an intranet is easier than setting it up for the Internet, because you don't need to register the domain name. Instead, you can use the network computer name. For example, if your computer has the network name "SuperServer," you could access a Web page with a URL like *http://SuperServer/MySite/MyPage.htm*.

To set up your own intranet, you need to start by setting up a local network, and then you need to make sure you have some Web hosting software. These tasks are outside the scope of this book, but if you're eager to give this do-it-yourself project a try, you'll need to start by setting up a home network. Check out *Home Networking: The Missing Manual* for complete instructions.

Just about every Web hosting company provides its own version of a domain name search tool. Figure 3-3 shows an example from *www.domaindirect.com*.

After you've performed a search, the Web hosting company gives you an option to purchase one of the available domains. But don't register anything yet. Most people sign up for a Web hosting package and domain name all at once, for the easiest setup and best value.

Note: You may think you could check if a domain is free just by typing it into your Web browser. But this method of checking takes longer, and it doesn't give you a definitive result. Someone can buy a domain name without setting up a Web site, so even if you can't find a Web site using your browser, the domain may not be available.

Getting the Right Name

You'll find that most short, clever word combinations have long since disappeared from the Web. Even if they aren't in use, they've been purchased by domain squatters, who hope to sell them later to a desperate high bidder. Give up on *www.*

worldsbestchocolate.com—it's gone. However, you may find success with names that are a little longer or more specific (*www.worldsbestdarkchocolate.com*), use locations or the names of people (*www.bestvermontchocolate.com* or *www.anniesbestchocolate.com*), or introduce made-up words (*www.chocolatech.com*). All of these domain names are available at the time of this writing.

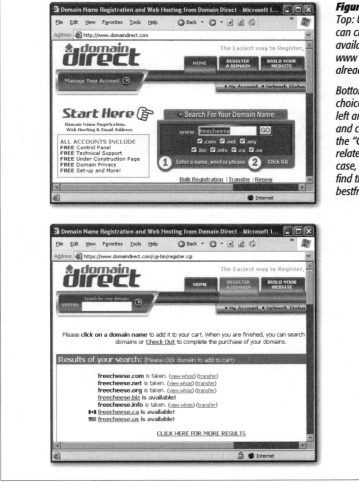

Figure 3-3:
Top: Using this free domain search tool, you can check if your preferred domain name is available. Notice that you don't type in the www at the start of the domain name (it's already indicated to the left of the box).

Bottom: The results aren't good. The first choice, www.freecheese.com is gone. All that's left are the less-catchy www.freecheese.biz and country-specific domains. You can click the "Click Here for More Results" link to see related domains that are available (in this case, if you asked to see more results, you'd find that www.allfreecheese.com and www.bestfreecheese.com are available).

Anyone who's chosen the wrong domain name knows that there are some clear-cut traps you want to avoid. Here are some mistakes to watch out for:

- **Dashes.** It may be tempting to get exactly the domain name you want by adding extra characters, like dashes, in between the words. For example, you have no chance at getting *www.reliablebusiness.com*, but *www.reliable-business.com* is still there for the taking. Don't do it. For some reason, dashes seem to confuse everyone. People are likely to leave them out, confuse them with underscores, or have trouble finding them on the keyboard.

- **Phrases that look confusing in lowercase.** Domain names aren't case-sensitive, and when you type a domain name into a browser, the browser converts it to all lowercase. The problem is that some phrases can blend together in lowercase, particularly if you have words that start with vowels. Take a look at what happens when the documentation company Prose Xact puts their business name into a lowercase domain name: *www.prosexact.com*. You get the picture.

Note: Even though domain names don't distinguish case, that doesn't stop business from using capital letters in business cards, promotions, and marketing material to make the domain name more readable. Whether customers type *www.google.com* or *wWw.gOOgLE.cOm* into their browsers, they'll get to the same site.

- **Names that don't match the business.** It's a classic business mistake. You set up a flower shop in New York called Roses are Red. Unfortunately, the domain *www.rosesarered.com* is already taken so you go for the next best choice, *www. newyorkflorist.com*. Huh? What you've actually done is created two separate names, and a somewhat schizophrenic identity for your business. To avoid these problems, if you're starting a new business, try to choose your business name and your domain name at the same time so they match. If you already have a business name, settle on an URL that has an extra word or two, like *www.rosesaredflorist.com*. This name may not be as snappy as *www. newyorkflorist.com*, but it avoids the inevitable confusion of creating a whole new identity.

- **Settling for .org.** The last few letters of the domain (the part after the last period) is called the *top-level domain*. Everyone wants a .com for their business, and as a result they're the hardest domain name to get. Of course, there are other top-level domains like .net, .org, .biz, and so on. The problem is, every Web surfer expects a .com. If you have the domain name *www.SuperShop.biz*, odds are someone will type *www.SuperShop.com* while trying to find your site. That mistake can easily lead your fans to a competitor (or to a vastly inferior Web site). In other words, it's sometimes worth taking a second-choice name to get your first choice of top-level domain (a .com).

Note: The top-level domain .org was originally intended for non-profit organizations. It's now free for anyone to use and abuse. However, if you're setting up a non-profit of your own, the .org domain may make more sense than .com and be almost as recognizable.

Domain name searches are an essential bit of prep work. Experiment—try to come up with as many variations and unusual name combinations as possible. Aim to record at least a dozen available name possibilities, so you can give yourself lots of choice. Once you've compiled the list, why not make a few late night phone calls to pester friends and relatives for their first reactions?

Registering Your Name

Once you've found an available name, you can register it, but you probably want to wait until you're ready to sign up for a Web hosting plan (which you'll read about in the next section), since most Web hosting companies offer free or discounted domain name registration when you rent space from them. That's also the easiest way to set up your domain name, because it's all taken care of automatically.

However, there are some cases where you may want to register a domain name separately from your Web hosting package. Here are some examples:

- You don't actually want to create a Web site. You just want to register a name so that no one else can grab it (a tactic known as *domain parking*). Sometime in the future, you may develop the Web site for that name.

- You already have Web space, possibly through your ISP (Internet Service Provider). All you need to make your Web site seem more professional is to get a custom domain name. This option can get a little tricky, and you may need to use a procedure called *domain forwarding* (which you'll read about in a moment).

- Your Web hosting company can't register the type of domain you want. This can occur if you need a domain name with a country-specific top-level domain.

If you don't fall into one of these special categories, skip ahead to the section "Getting Web Space" to start searching for the right Web host. Otherwise, keep reading for more details about registering and managing a domain name on its own.

Note: All Web hosting companies allow you to register more than one domain for the same Web site. That means you can register both *www.FancyPants.com* and *www.FancyPants.org*, and have them point to the same Web site. Of course, you'll need to pay an extra domain name registration fee.

FREQUENTLY ASKED QUESTION

International Domain Names

Some domain names end with a country code. Should I get one?

A .com address is a Web site creator's best friend. Other top-level domains (.net, .org, .biz, and so on), generally aren't worth the trouble. However, there is one exception: regional domain names. If you can't get the .com you need, it just might make sense to go with a country-specific top-level domain like .us (USA) or .ca (Canada).

For example, if you're offering piano lessons in England, *www.pianolessons.co.uk* isn't a bad choice. However, if you're planning to sell products to an international audience,

www.HotRetroRecords.co.uk is likely to frighten away otherwise interested buyers, who may assume it's too much trouble to deal with a British seller.

There are special rules about who can registrar country-specific names. Due to these restrictions, many Web hosting companies can't sell certain country-specific domains. To search for domain names with a specific country code, use Google to find the right registrar. For example, to find a registrar for Australian domains, search for "Australia domain names."

Domain parking

Domain parking (Figure 3-4) is just another name for domain registration. Essentially, domain parking means you've registered a domain name but haven't yet purchased any other services, like renting Web storage space.

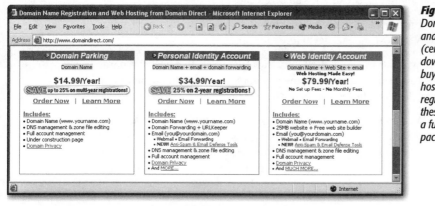

Figure 3-4:
Domain parking (left) and domain forwarding (center) are two scaled-down alternatives to buying a complete Web hosting package. This registrar offers both these options, along with a full Web hosting package (right).

Most people use domain parking to put a domain name away on reserve. In the increasingly crowded world of the Web, many people use domain parking to protect their names (for example, *www.matthewmalone.com*). Domain parking is also useful if you want to secure several potential business names that you may use in the future.

Tip: If you do reserve a domain name, it's a good idea to do your research, and pick a company that you'd like to use to host your Web site. Switching domain names from one Web hosting firm to another is possible, but it's a bit of a pain. Contact the Web host you're working with for specific instructions about how to pull this off.

The real appeal of domain parking is that it's cheap. You pay a nominal registration fee (as little as $10/year) and you get to keep the domain name for as long as you're willing to pay for it.

Domain forwarding

Domain forwarding is a budget option. It makes sense if you already have complimentary Web space that you want to use. For example, you may have free Web space through your ISP, your school, your job, from a (shudder) free Web hosting service (discussed on page 73), or from a crazy uncle with a Web server in the basement. In these situations, you can save some money because you don't need to pay a Web hosting company. However, you may still want to use a snappy URL for your Web site. In this situation, you can buy the URL separately, and use domain forwarding to point your brand new URL to your site on your Web space.

For example, if you have Web space on an ISP, you might be stuck with a URL like *http://member.magicisp.com/members/personalwebspace/~henryj420/home*, which clearly isn't as catchy as *www.HenryTheFriendly.com*. However, you can buy the domain name *www.HenryTheFriendly.com* and use domain forwarding to point it to your Web space.

FREQUENTLY ASKED QUESTION

A Host Here, a Domain There

Can I buy my domain name and Web space from different companies, and still make them work together?

The best approach is to get both from the same company, but that's not always possible. Maybe you bought your domain name before you set up your Web site, and you don't want to pay the cost of transferring the domain. Or maybe you have a country-specific domain name (like *www.CunningPets.co.uk*) that your Web hosting company can't register.

To make this multiple-company tango work, you'll need some technical support from your Web hosting company. Contact their help desk and let them know what you plan to do. They'll give you specific instructions about what steps to take, and they'll configure their name servers (more on what those are in a moment) to have the right information for your domain.

The next step is to change the registration information for your domain. Here are the steps that you'll need to follow:

1. Find out the name of the *domain name servers (DNS servers)* at your Web hosting company. These are the computers that convert domain names into the numeric IP addresses (see page 54 for full details on how DNS servers work). The technical support staff can give you this information.

2. Go to the company where you've registered the domain name, and update your domain registration settings. Change the name server setting to match the name servers you found out about in step 1. The figure in this sidebar shows an example with the name servers named *ns1.brinkster.com* and *ns2.brinkster.com*.

Due to the way that DNS servers work, the change can take 24 hours to take effect.

When you make this change, you're essentially saying that your Web host company is now responsible for giving out the IP address of your Web site. When someone types your domain name into a browser, the browser will contact the name server at your Web hosting company to get the IP address. From that point on, it's smooth sailing.

Once you've modified your domain name registration, you'll still have the same two bills to pay. You'll pay your hosting fees to the Web hosting company and the yearly domain name registration fee to the company where you registered your domain name.

Tip: Even if the URL from your ISP isn't that bad, it's still a good idea to buy a custom domain. Otherwise, if the ISP changes its configuration or if you switch from one ISP to another, your Web visitors won't be able to find your Web site anymore. But if you use domain forwarding, you simply need to update the domain settings with the new URL, and your custom domain keeps working. No one will even notice the change.

First you need to register a domain name that comes with forwarding as an included service (see Figure 3-4). Then, you can log in and set the forwarding settings (see Figure 3-5).

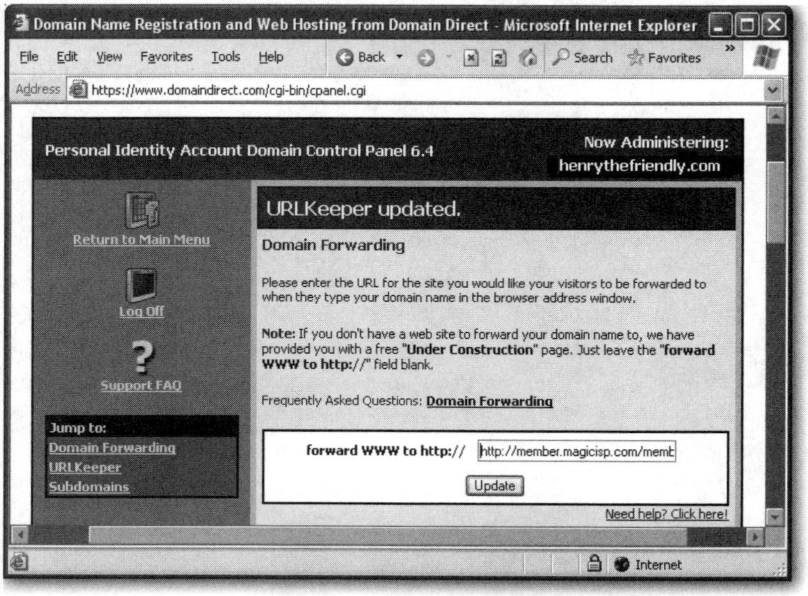

Figure 3-5:
Here, the catchy domain www.HenryTheFriendly. com seamlessly forwards all visitors to a much more awkward URL where the Web site is actually located. Usually, domain forwarding is implemented in such a way that the address bar keeps showing the original domain name (in this case, www. HenryTheFriendly.com) even when the visitor is directed to the second site.

With domain forwarding, most Web hosting firms give you the added ability to forward *subdomains*. Subdomains look like your domain name, but instead of starting with www they start with another word or phrase you choose. For example, if you get a forwarding account for *www.PremiumPencils.com*, you could choose to create a subdomain named *help.PremiumPencils.com* for customer support or *resume.PremiumPencils.com* for quick access to your electronic résumé (see Figure 3-6).

Domain forwarding can come in handy in other scenarios. For example, say you have an account with a Web hosting company and you want to use it to create several separate Web sites (like a personal site, a business site, a site for someone else in your family, and so on). Conceptually, it's easy—you just need to place each Web site in a separate folder. However, this tactic can muck up your URLs. If you have the business domain name *www.PremiumPencils.com* and you want to create a personal site for your upcoming marriage, you're stuck with something like *www.PremiumPencils.com/WeddingForDebbie*. A low-cost alternative is to buy one Web hosting account, and buy several domain names (like *www.PremiumPencils. com* and *www.DebbiesWedding.com*) with domain forwarding. Then, just direct each domain name to the appropriate subfolder. Presto—the wedding guests will never be asked to stock up on office stationery.

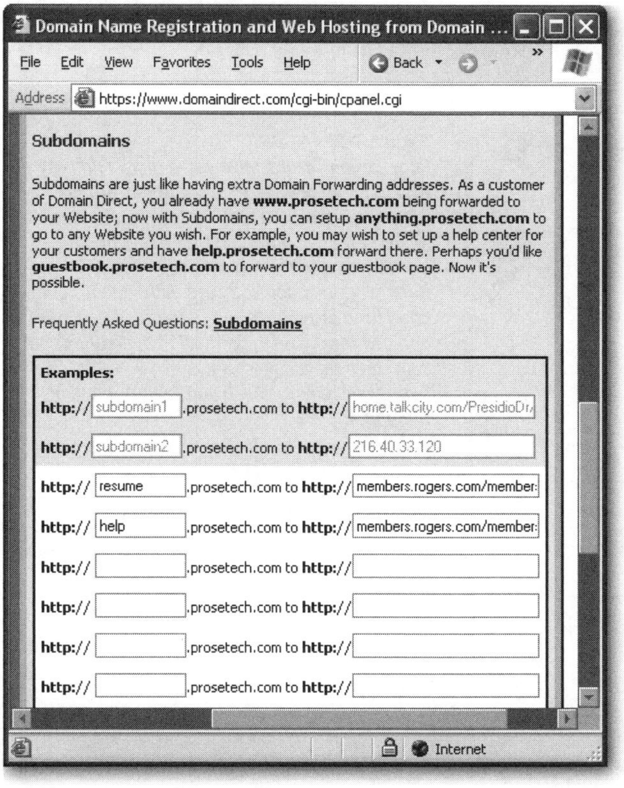

Figure 3-6:
Thanks to subdomains, you can provide easy access to several different pages in your Web site, or even several different Web sites. All you need to do is forward each domain to a different URL, as shown here with the subdomains resume.prosetech.com and help.prosetech.com.

Getting Web Space

All you need to achieve Web superstardom is a domain name and a small amount of space on a Web server. There's no one-size-fits-all solution when it comes to finding a Web host. Instead, you'll choose the right Web hosting company based on your budget, what you want your Web site to be able to do, and your own capricious whims (let's face it—some Web hosts just have way cooler names than others).

Finding the right Web host can take a bit of searching, and it may require making a few phone calls or just surfing around the Web. Before you start tapping away, it helps to take a look at the big picture.

The Big Picture

Nowadays, Web hosting packages come in three main flavors:

- **Simplified Web site creation.** In this case, the Web hosting company offers special software that promises to help you create a Web site in two or three easy steps. These tools range from terrible to awful (see Figure 3-7). After all, if you're content to create the same cookie-cutter Web site as everyone else, you probably aren't interested in HTML, and you wouldn't have picked up this book in the first place. Instead, go for standard Web site hosting and unleash your inner Web *artiste*.

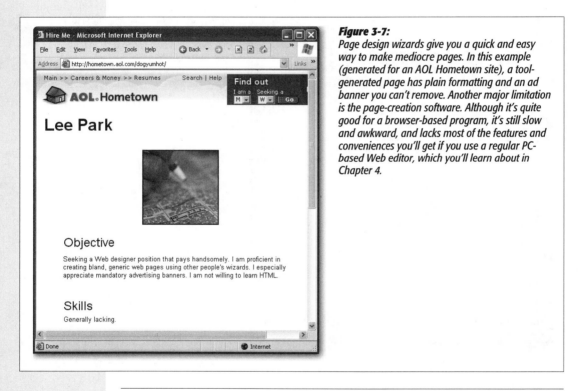

Figure 3-7:
Page design wizards give you a quick and easy way to make mediocre pages. In this example (generated for an AOL Hometown site), a tool-generated page has plain formatting and an ad banner you can't remove. Another major limitation is the page-creation software. Although it's quite good for a browser-based program, it's still slow and awkward, and lacks most of the features and conveniences you'll get if you use a regular PC-based Web editor, which you'll learn about in Chapter 4.

Note: There's one case where simplified Web site creation makes sense—if all you want to do is create a *blog* (a personal site that consists of short, chronological postings about anything that interests you). Chapter 17 shows how you can create a blog on your own Web site, or how you can set one up at a free blogging host so you don't need to buy a domain name or pay for Web space.

- **Standard Web site hosting.** Here, you're given a slot of space on a Web server to manage as you see fit. You create the Web page files you want using your own computer, and then copy these files to the Web server so that others can see them. This type of Web hosting is all you need to use this book.

- **Web application hosting.** This option makes sense if you're a programmer at heart, and you need a Web server that can run your Web applications. A Web application can be quite neat—it can perform complex calculations, read vast amounts of information from a database, and spit out made-to-measure HTML on the fly. However, programming a Web application is far from easy. In this book, you'll focus on creating ordinary Web sites, and using third-party services when you need more complex features like an e-commerce shopping cart. That means Web application hosting is overkill.

Web hosting packages usually charge a monthly fee. For basic Web hosting, this fee starts at the reasonable sum of $5–$10 per month. Of course, it can escalate quickly, depending on what features you want.

Assessing Your Needs

You need to ask yourself one important question—what features do you need? Web hosts are quick to swamp their ads and Web sites with techie jargon, but they don't tell you which services are truly useful. Here's a quick overview that describes what Web hosts sell (and what you need to know about each offering). If you'd like to keep track of which features you need, there's a checklist you can fill out on page 67, or you can download it from the "Missing CD" page at *www.missingmanuals.com*.

- **Web space** is how much space you're renting to store your Web site. Although HTML pages are extremely small, you may need more space to fit in images or files you want others to download. A modest Web site can easily survive with 20 MB (megabytes) of space, unless you're stuffing it full of pictures or videos. Many Web hosts throw in much more, often as much as 500 MB or 1 GB (gigabyte), knowing you'll probably never use it.

Note: For the numerically challenged, a Gigabyte (GB) is the same as 1024 Megabytes (MB). To put it in perspective, modern hard drives can offer 200 GB of space or more, which gives you room for thousands of Web sites.

- **Bandwidth** (or Web traffic, as it's sometimes called) is the maximum amount of information you can deliver to everybody who surfs to your Web site in a month. Usually, you can make do with the lowest bandwidth numbers offered by your Web hosting company (with 1 GB being more than enough). For more information, see "The Riddle of Bandwidth" on page 66.

- **A domain name** is a custom Web site address, as in *www.HenryTheFriendly.com*. If you decide to get a custom domain name, you don't necessarily need to get it from the same company that hosts your Web site. However, it does make life easier, and a custom domain name is often thrown in for a discounted price when you sign up for a Web hosting plan.

POWER USERS' CLINIC

The Riddle of Bandwidth

Most Web hosting companies set their pricing, at least in part, based on your Web space and bandwidth needs. This can be a problem, because the average Web site creator has no idea how to calculate these numbers. It's even harder to come up with realistic estimates.

Fortunately, you can save a lot of time and effort by understanding one dirty little secret: for the average personal or small business Web site, you don't need much disk space *or* bandwidth. You can probably take the smallest amounts on offer from any Web hosting company and live quite happily. The only real exception is if your Web site is ridiculously popular, if you're showcasing a huge catalog of digital photos, or if you want to store extremely large files and let visitors download them.

If you still insist on calculating bandwidth, here's how it works. Let's say you've got a Web site with 100 relatively modest pages that are each about 50 KB (kilobytes), including graphics. Right away, you can calculate your Web space requirement—it's 50 KB * 100, or 5 MB.

To calculate the bandwidth, you need to make estimates about how many visitors will surf through your site, and how much content they'll request over each visit. Suppose your Web site is doing well, and receives about 10 visitors in a day. Say an average visitor browses through 20 pages before leaving. In a day, your bandwidth usage is 10 visitors

* 20 pages * 50 KB, or 10 MB. Over a 30-day month, that's 300 MB, still less than a third of the 1 GB bare minimum that most Web hosting companies offer.

So why do Web hosting companies focus on Web space and bandwidth numbers? It's partly to satisfy large customers who really do have greater requirements, but it's also to confuse everyone else into buying more than they need.

Here's another scenario: you create a Web site and add links that allow visitors to download MP3 files of your underground all-percussion garage band. You offer up three songs, each of which is a 4 MB MP3 file. Now the equation changes. Assuming a steady stream of 10 visitors a day, and assuming each visitor downloads all three songs, you've hit a bandwidth of 10 visitors * 3 songs * 4 MB, or 120 MB. Now your monthly bandwidth usage tops 3 GB. You're probably still in the clear, because many Web hosting companies offer 7 or 10 GB in their starter packages. However, you'll want to pay more attention to the bandwidth number.

If bandwidth *is* important for you, you need to know what will happen if you surpass your bandwidth limit in a month. Some Web hosting companies cut your Web site off entirely at this point (or just show your visitors an explanatory page saying the site is temporarily inactive). Other Web hosting companies tack on extra fees. So ask.

- **Email addresses.** Odds are, you already have some of these. But you may want an email address that matches your Web site address, especially if you're paying for a customized domain name. For example, if you own *www. HenryTheFriendly.com*, you'd probably like to use an email address like *Hank@HenryTheFriendly.com*. Web hosting companies give you different options here—some may just forward the email to another email address (which you'd need to supply them with), while better packages will give you a dedicated email inbox with plenty of space for receiving and storing messages.

- **Upload-ability**—how easy it is to transfer files to the Web server—is another important detail. As you saw in the previous chapter, you can perfect your Web pages on your own computer before you upload them. But once your Web site's ready for prime time, you need a convenient way to copy all the files to your Web server. For greatest convenience, look for FTP (File Transfer Protocol) support, which lets you easily copy a number of files at once. Some Web hosts may also provide integration with popular Web design tools like FrontPage and Dreamweaver, allowing you to upload pages without leaving your Web editing program.

- **Frills.** In an effort to woo you to their side, Web hosting companies often pack in a slew of frills. For example, sometimes they'll boast about their amazing, quick-and-easy, Web site creation tools. Translation: they'll let you use a clumsy piece of software on their Web site to build yours. You'll end up with a cookie-cutter result and not much opportunity to express yourself. Steer clear of these pointless features. More usefully, a Web hosting company can provide Web site *statistics*—detailed information about how many visitors are flocking to your site on a daily or monthly basis. Some Web hosting companies also offer support for *server-side scripts* (essentially, miniature programs that can run in your Web site) with catchy acronyms like CGI, JSP, PHP, and ASP.NET. Although these features are powerful, they require programmer credentials. They're all beyond the scope of this book.

Note: Although server-side applications aren't covered in this book, you will learn about *client-side scripts* in Chapter 14. Client-side scripts run right inside your Web site visitor's browser, and are much more limited in ability than server-side scripts. They're commonly used for special effects like animated buttons. The nice thing about client-side scripts is that even programming novices can drop a simple script into their Web pages and enjoy the benefits. But you don't need to worry about any of this right now, because unlike server-side scripts, client-side scripts don't require any special support from your Web hosting company.

A Web host checklist

✓ _____ **Web space.** 20 MB is acceptable if you're getting free Web space from your ISP, but insist on at least 50 MB if you're paying for it with a monthly fee. If you want to offer photos, audio, or other large files, go for 250 MB to be safe.

✓ _____ **Bandwidth.** You don't need much. 1 GB works for normal Web sites, but look for 5 GB or more if you want to provide large files or are expecting to create a popular Web destination.

✓ **Domain name.** This is your identity—*www.You.com*. Ideally, the domain name should be thrown in for free.

✓ **Email addresses.** These go with the domain name. Look for at least one POP mailbox. It's better to have five or more, because it allows you to give separate email addresses to family members, or use them for different purposes. Also look for Web-based access to your email.

✓ **FTP access.** This ensures easy uploading of your files.

✓ **Tech support.** The best companies provide 24-hour tech support, ideally through a toll-free number or a live chat feature that lets you ask a tech support person questions through your browser.

✓ **Statistics.** These are useful if you want to check out how popular your Web site really is. If you want to analyze traffic patterns and more detailed statistics, look for a Web host that provides access to *raw server logs*. You can download these and use them with a high-powered analysis tool.

✓ **FrontPage extensions.** Useful if you're using FrontPage to create your Web site, and want to take advantage of a few extra frills.

Choosing Your Host

Now that you have your requirements in mind, it's time to start shopping for a Web host. The following sections take you through your options.

Your ISP (Internet Service Provider)

As you may have already realized, your ISP—the company that provides your access to the Internet—may have its own Web hosting services. In fact, these services are sometimes included in the basic subscription price, meaning you may already have a dedicated amount of Web space that you don't even know about. If you're in this situation, congratulations—you don't need to take any extra steps. If you're unsure, a quick call to your ISP will fill you in. Make sure you ask for "personal Web space." Many ISPs also provide large-scale Web hosting packages for a monthly fee.

Note: In some cases, your ISP may provide Web hosting that you decide not to use. For example, they may not give you enough space, or they may force you to use their limited Web site creation software (which is a definite drag). In these cases, you'll want to use one of the other Web hosting solutions described below.

Obviously, ISPs differ in whether or not they provide Web space. You're more likely to get a small amount of Web space if you have a high-speed broadband connection (cable or DSL) rather than a dial-up account. Often, the space is as little as 5 or 10 MB, which is much smaller than what you receive from a Web hosting company. And no matter what ISP you have, you won't get a customized domain name as part of your package (although you can purchase one separately).

Before continuing any further, it might be worth it to make a quick call to your ISP or visit their Web site to see if they provide Web hosting services. In the meantime, Table 3-1 lists some popular ISPs and their support for Web hosting (at the time of this writing).

Table 3-1. *ISPs and Personal Web Space*

ISP	Personal Web Space	Verdict
America Online (AOL)	Provides a wizard-based hosting service that anyone can use for free, called AOL Hometown (*http:// hometown.aol.com*). Existing AOL customers have added features, like FTP. Web space is limited, and ugly advertisement banners are mandatory.	Not worth the trouble.
United Online (NetZero, Juno, and BlueLight)	No.	No.
Comcast	Yes.	Suitable for small sites.
Earthlink	Yes. Also offers a premium Web hosting service for a monthly fee.	Suitable for small sites.
Verizon	Yes. Also offers a premium Web hosting service for a monthly fee.	Suitable for small sites.
SBC Yahoo!	The only free service is through GeoCities, which has no FTP access and forces you to use advertisements. Better Web hosting is available for an additional fee.	No.
AT&T	Yes (depending on your plan).	Suitable for small sites.
BellSouth	Yes (depending on your plan).	Suitable for small sites.
Road Runner	Yes.	Suitable for small sites.
MSN	Provides a free service called MSN Spaces (*http:// spaces.msn.com*) that lets you build a blog (Chapter 17) or a personal site with pictures. The service doesn't let you upload your own Web pages. Microsoft also offers real Web hosting, but it's a little pricey.	Too limited.

Web Hosting Companies

Technically, anyone that provides Web space is a Web host, but there's a class of companies that specialize in Web hosting and don't do anything else. You can find these companies all over the Internet, or in computer magazines. The disadvantage is that Web hosting companies always charge by the month. You won't get anything for free.

The sad truth is that it's almost impossible to research Web hosting companies online, because the Web is swamped with more Web hosting advertisements than those for cut-rate pharmaceuticals. Fortunately, there are many good choices.

Table 3-2 lists just a few good ones to get you started. If you're curious, be sure to check out these Web sites and start comparison shopping.

Table 3-2. *A Few of the Internet's Many Web Hosting Firms*

Name	URL
Brinkster	*www.brinkster.com*
Insider Hosting	*www.insiderhosting.com*
Pair Networks	*www.pair.com*
Sonic.net	*www.sonic.net*

Tip: For a recent *PC World* article that's packed full of Web host advice (and based on 6,000 reader reviews), surf to *www.pcworld.com/reviews/article/0,aid,120341,00.asp*.

As you consider different Web hosting companies, you'll need to sort through a dizzying array of options on different Web sites. In the following sections, you'll learn how to dig through the marketing haze and find the important information on the Web sites of two Web hosting companies.

A Web host walkthrough (#1)

Figure 3-8 shows how you can assess the home page for the popular Web hosting company Aplus.Net. The company offers Web hosting, dedicated servers, and Web design services. All three options are designed to help you get online, but the Web hosting option is what you're really looking for. The dedicated server option is a premium form of Web hosting. It means that your Web site will run on a separate computer that doesn't host anyone else's Web site. This is primarily of interest to large business customers with high-powered Web sites that chew up computer hardware resources. Most personal and small business Web sites run on shared servers without any noticeable slowdown. The Web design option is mainly of interest to HTML-phobes. It allows you to pay a Web design team to craft all the HTML pages and graphics for your Web site. But where's the fun in that?

The choices don't end there. Figure 3-9 invites you to narrow down your choice based on the type of operating system you want for your Web server. Unless you're a programmer planning to create special software to run on the server, there's no reason to care what type of operating system runs on the Web server. Assuming the Web hosting company does its job and distributes the Web sites they host over multiple computers, your Web site will be just as fast and reliable on any system. When was the last time you asked yourself what operating system runs eBay (Windows) or Amazon (Linux)?

At the end of your search, you've discovered that the cheapest option is currently $6/month for a 50 MB Web site with 1 GB of bandwidth. A free domain and five email addresses are thrown in for good measure. The virus and spam protection is much less interesting—it simply indicates that your email will have automatic filtering to catch dubious messages. The Web Control Panel refers to the page where you can configure your Web site settings—but every Web hosting company offers that. For the final assessment, click "more info" and you'll see mostly the same list with a few more details, including FTP support (page 76).

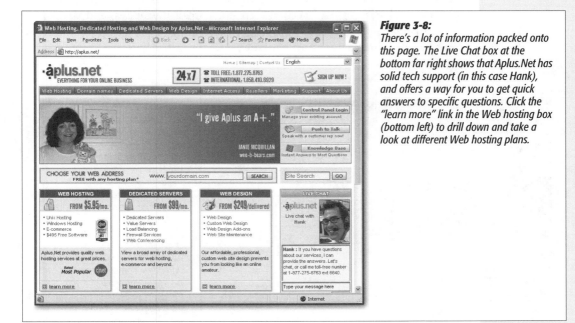

Figure 3-8:
There's a lot of information packed onto this page. The Live Chat box at the bottom far right shows that Aplus.Net has solid tech support (in this case Hank), and offers a way for you to get quick answers to specific questions. Click the "learn more" link in the Web hosting box (bottom left) to drill down and take a look at different Web hosting plans.

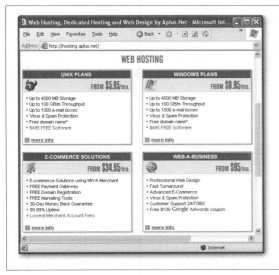

Figure 3-9:
Choices, choices. Unix hosting is the cheapest option on Aplus.net. (Unix refers to the type of computer that powers your Web site; on your own PC, you can stick with whatever operating system you normally use.) The cheapest plan offered (Solo) is $6/month for a 50 MB Web site.

A Web host walkthrough (#2)

Overall, the Aplus.Net search turned up a solid offer at a fair price. Discerning Web shoppers may be hoping to save a few dollars or get a little bit more space.

Figure 3-10 shows another Web hosting company—Brinkster. Brinkster's target audience includes personal Web site creators, small businesses, and developers, rather than large institutional customers. As a result, you won't find premium features like dedicated server hosting. However, you just may find a better deal for your Web site.

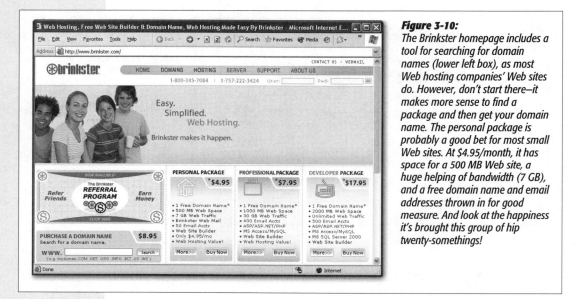

Figure 3-10:
The Brinkster homepage includes a tool for searching for domain names (lower left box), as most Web hosting companies' Web sites do. However, don't start there—it makes more sense to find a package and then get your domain name. The personal package is probably a good bet for most small Web sites. At $4.95/month, it has space for a 500 MB Web site, a huge helping of bandwidth (7 GB), and a free domain name and email addresses thrown in for good measure. And look at the happiness it's brought this group of hip twenty-somethings!

To get the full details, click the More button in the Personal Package box. You'll see the details in Figure 3-11.

Now that you've taken a tour of two Web hosting company Web sites, you're ready to evaluate some more. Or, if you're really impatient, you can set up your Web site using one of the hosting companies you've seen. It doesn't take anything more than a couple of mouse clicks, and you'll be completely online in only a few hours.

Tip: If your Web host is letting you down, don't panic. It's not too hard to switch hosts. The key thing to remember is when you change hosts, you're essentially abandoning one Web server and setting up shop on another one. It's up to you to copy your Web pages to the new Web server—no one will do it for you. As long as you have a copy of your Web site on your personal computer (which you always should), this part is easy. If you're still a little skeptical of the company you choose, look for a 30-day, money-back guarantee.

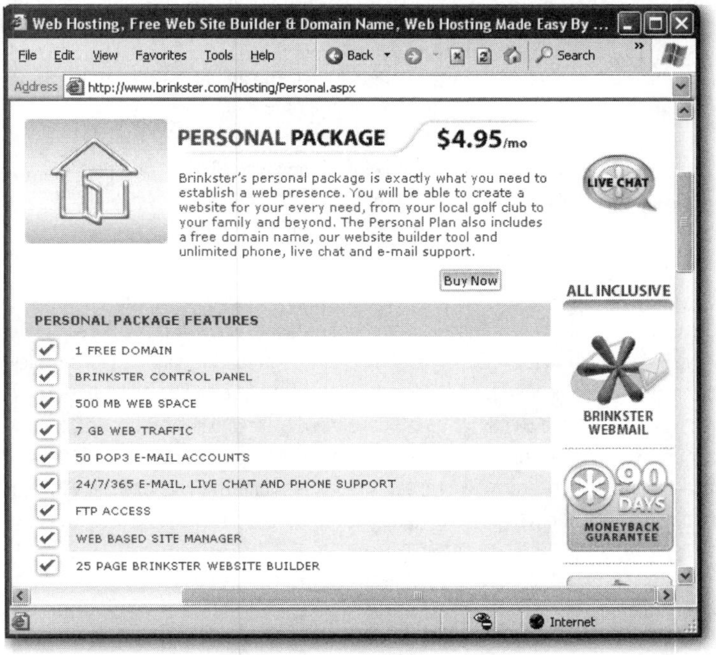

Figure 3-11:
Everything checks out in the listing here, including FTP access. You'll also notice features that every Web hosting company provides (like virus scanning and a control panel for managing your site) and some that aren't that useful at all (like the Website Builder).

Free Web Hosts

Not yet swayed by any of the hundreds of Web hosting companies on the Web? Not tempted by the offer of a little Web space from your ISP? If you're hoping to save a monthly fee at all cost, there is a solution, but it may not be worth the aggravation. The Web has a significant number of free Web hosts. These free hosts are companies that give you a small parcel of Web space without charging anything. Sometimes it's because they hope to get you to upgrade to a cost-based service in the future when you outgrow the strict limitations of the free package. Other times, they may just be interested in the advertisement revenue. That's because free Web sites universally force you to include an obnoxious ad banner at the top your Web pages.

If you're still interested in joining The Dark Side of the Web, Table 3-3 lists some well-known free Web hosts.

Table 3-3. *Free Web Hosts*

Web Host	Service	Verdict
Yahoo GeoCities *http://geocities.yahoo.com*	Fair space and bandwidth, but you're stuck with an ad bar and forced to use limited page-creation software. You can upgrade to FTP access (which gives you the ability to upload your own HTML creations) for a monthly fee.	Not worth the trouble.
Angelfire *http://angelfire.lycos.com*	Fair space and bandwidth, along with FTP support (allowing you to avoid those dodgy Web site creation tools). The ad bar is mandatory, unless you upgrade to a monthly fee plan.	Acceptable, if you can stand the ad bar.
Tripod *www.tripod.lycos.com*	Fair space and bandwidth, along with FTP support and a mandatory ad bar. Similar to Angelfire, along with the option to upgrade to a fee-based plan.	Acceptable, if you can stand the ad bar.

Tip: Looking to save some money but craving a custom domain name? You could use a free hosting service in conjunction with domain forwarding. But if you shop around, you may be surprised to find a few better deals. If you use the hosting company *www.catalog.com*, you can get a year of free Web hosting for a flat $35 fee. That price gives a respectable 50 MB with 3 GB of bandwidth, five email accounts, and, best of all, a custom domain name. A subsidiary company, *www.onesite.com*, offers more or less the same deal, but the first year is free, and students get an impressive five years of free hosting. The only catch? If you decide to transfer your domain name to another Web hosting company, you will pay an onerous cancellation fee.

Transferring Files

Once you've signed up for Web hosting, you're ready to transfer some files to your Web space. To perform this test, you can use Lee Park's résumé from the previous chapter (which you can download from the "Missing CD" page at *www.missingmanuals.com*). The final version has the filename *resume5.htm*.

Browser-Based Uploading

Browser-based uploading is fairly easy, but it's not always convenient. The idea is you go to a special Web page on your host's site, where you can specify the files you want to transfer. Many Web hosting companies provide both browser-based uploading and FTP-based uploading. If you're using a budget plan or a free Web host, you may not have the FTP option at all. To perform browser-based uploading, follow these steps:

1. **Surf to the Web site of your Web hosting company.**

2. **Log in to your account with the user name and password you created when you signed up.**

    Usually you'll find a login box somewhere on the first page.

3. **Browse through the icons until you find the right page for managing files.**

Each Web hosting provider has its own slightly different site layout. Figure 3-12 shows what things look like at Brinkster.

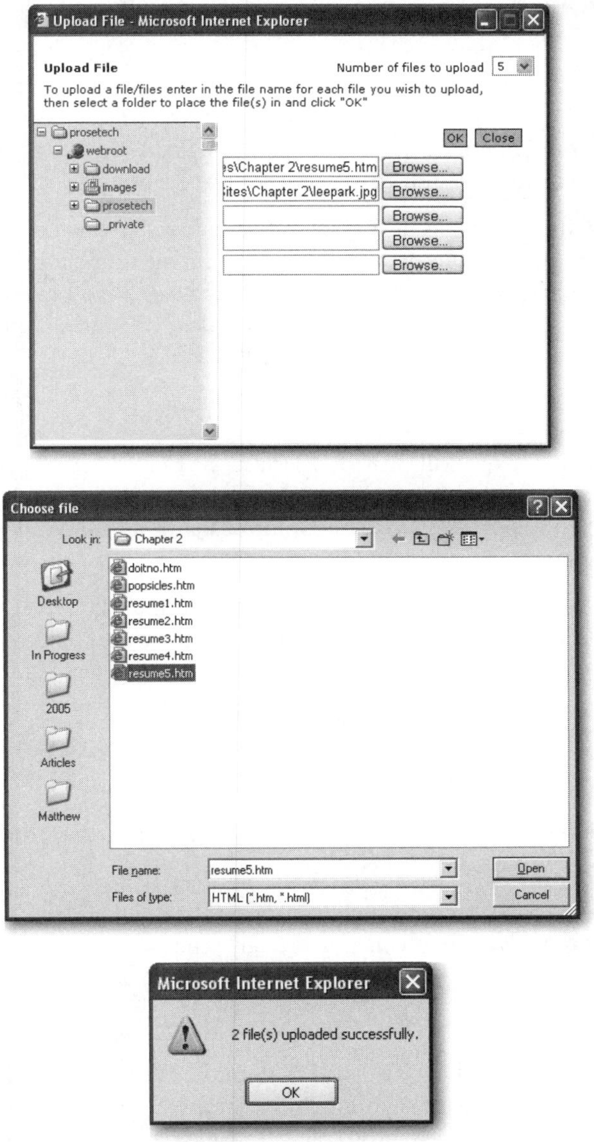

Figure 3-12:
Every Web hosting provider's site looks a little different, but you'll eventually find a set of text boxes that allows you to upload pages. These text boxes always work in the same way. First you click the Browse button (top image), which shows an Open File dialog box (middle). Then you browse to the file you want, select it and click Open. If you have several files to upload at once, repeat this process using different text boxes. When you've chosen all the files you want (or just run out of text boxes), click OK, and wait until the files are copied and you get a confirmation message (bottom).

4. **Specify the files you want to upload. You need to specify each file individually, by clicking the Browse button next to the text box.**

   In order for the résumé example to work properly, make sure you upload both the *resume5.htm* file and the linked picture, *leepark.jpg,* to the same place.

5. **Log out when you're finished.**

   Now you can test your work by entering your domain name followed by the Web page name. For example, if you uploaded the résumé example to your Web site *www.supersavvyworker.com,* try requesting *www.supersavvyworker.com/resume5. htm* in your browser. You don't need to wait—once you upload the file to your Web server, it's available almost instantly to any browser that requests it.

Unfortunately, the possibilities for mistakes with browser-based uploading are endless. The most common problem occurs when you have a large number of files to copy at once. Not only is it time consuming to pick out each one, it's all too easy to forget something. Other headaches include trying to upload files to different folders, and having to use another window to rename or delete files.

FTP

Ideally, your Web hosting company will provide FTP access. FTP access lets you transfer groups of files from your computer to the Web server (or vice versa), in much the same way that you copy files from one folder to another in Windows Explorer or the Mac's Finder.

Before you can upload files using FTP, you need the address for the FTP server, as well as a user name and password. These are usually the same as the user name and password of your Web hosting account, but not always.

To upload files using FTP, you can use a standalone FTP program. However, in these modern times you probably don't need to. Internet Explorer includes its own built-in FTP browser that handles the task comfortably. Here's how it works:

1. **Start by typing the FTP address into the Internet Explorer address bar. Make sure the URL starts with *ftp://*.**

   In other words, if you're trying to visit *ftp.myhost.com*, enter the URL *ftp://ftp. myhost.com*, not *http://ftp.myhost.com*, which incorrectly sends your browser off looking for Web pages.

2. **The next step is to log in by choosing File → Login (see Figure 3-13).**

   Once you've logged in, you'll see the folders and files on the Web server, which you can copy, delete, rename, and move in much the same way you work with your local folders and files. Seeing as you haven't uploaded anything yet, the folder may be empty, or it may contain a generic *index.htm* file that shows an "under construction" message.

Tip: As in Windows Explorer, you can choose to view files and folders using the traditional large icon view, or a more compact list (just make your selection from the View menu).

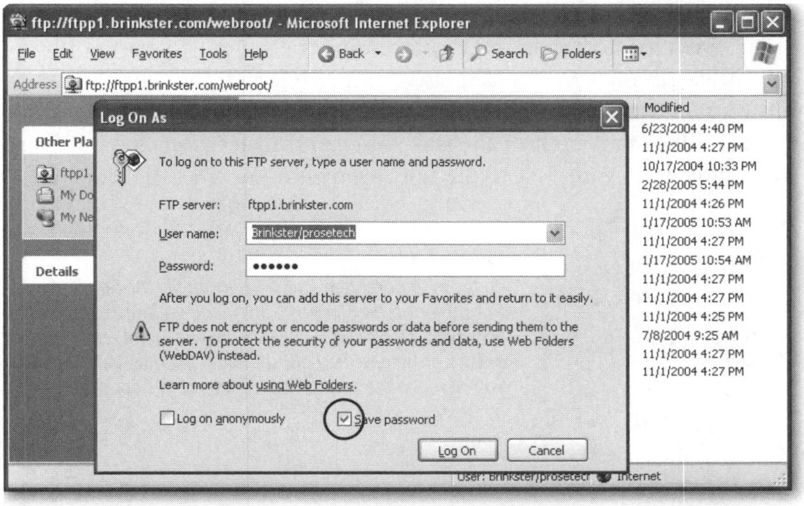

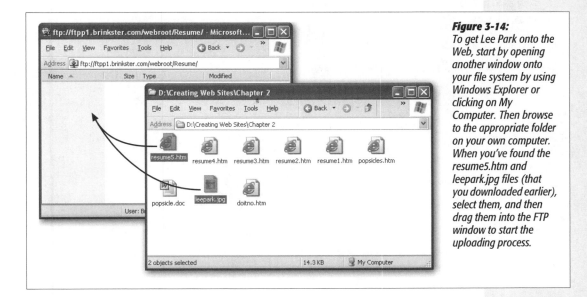

Figure 3-13:
When you first enter the FTP site address, Internet Explorer will probably try to log you in anonymously, and fail, at which point it will show an error message. Click OK, and then select File → Login As from Internet Explorer's menu to enter your user name and password. If you turn on the "Save password" checkbox, (circled), you don't need to repeat this process on subsequent visits.

3. **The next step is to copy your files to the Web server. The easiest way to do this is to drag the files from another open window, and drop them on the FTP window.**

Figure 3-14 shows the steps you need to upload the résumé example.

Figure 3-14:
To get Lee Park onto the Web, start by opening another window onto your file system by using Windows Explorer or clicking on My Computer. Then browse to the appropriate folder on your own computer. When you've found the resume5.htm and leepark.jpg files (that you downloaded earlier), select them, and then drag them into the FTP window to start the uploading process.

Tip: Drag-and-drop isn't the only way to transfer files. You can use all the familiar Windows shortcuts, including the Cut, Copy, and Paste commands in the Edit menu, and the Ctrl+C (copy) and Ctrl+V (paste) keyboard shortcuts.

If you're working on a Mac, you'll need to use a separate FTP program. Fortunately, you've got loads of free options, including the super-easy-to-use Rbrowser (available at *www.rbrowser.com*). Things work pretty much the same way they do for your Windows brethren. First, fire up Rbrowser. You'll be asked to log in (Figure 3-15). Once that's out of the way, you can transfer your files by dragging them from a folder on your Mac to the Rbrowser window.

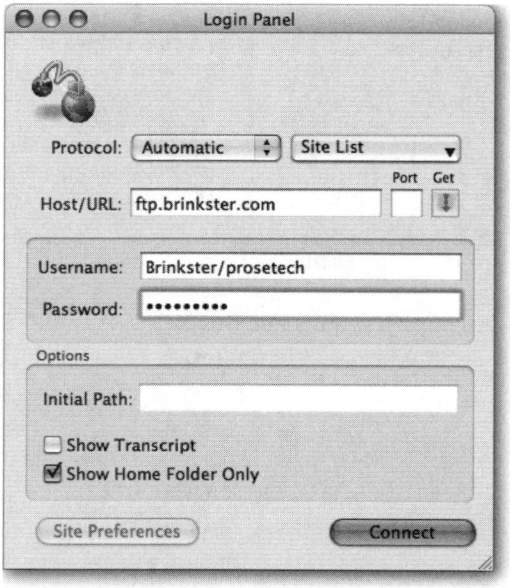

Figure 3-15:
To log in to Rbrowser, you need to supply the name of the FTP server (in the Host/URL box), and your user name and password. Don't worry about setting an initial path—you can always browse to the right subfolder in your Web site once you've made the connection. Finally, click Connect to seal the deal.

Power Tools

In Chapter 2, you built your first HTML page with nothing but a plain text editor and a lot of nerve. This is how all Web page gurus begin their careers. In order to really understand HTML (and establish your HTML street cred), you need to start from scratch.

However, very few Web authors stick with plain text editors or use them to create anything other than simple test pages. That's because the average HTML page is filled with tedious details. If you're forced to write every paragraph, line break, and formatting tag by hand, you'll probably make a mistake somewhere along the way. Even if you don't, it's hard to visualize what the end result will look like when you spend all day staring at angle brackets. This is especially true when you start to tackle more complex pages, such as those that introduce a slew of graphics or organize the layout of a page with tables.

There's a definite downside to outgrowing Notepad or TextEdit—namely, it can get expensive. Professional Web design tools can cost hundreds of dollars. At one point, software companies planned to include basic Web editors in common operating systems like Windows and Mac OS. In fact, some older versions of Windows shipped with a scaled-down version of FrontPage called FrontPage Express. That's not the case today, so if you want an HTML editor, you'll have to find one on your own. Fortunately, there are free alternatives for even the most cash-strapped Web designer.

In this chapter, you'll learn how HTML editors work, and how to evaluate them to find the one that's right for you. You'll also tour some of the better free and shareware offerings that are currently out there. When it comes to the basics, most Web page editors are surprisingly similar. That means you'll learn how to get started with your tool of choice, whether it's FrontPage, Dreamweaver, or a nice piece of freeware called Nvu.

Choosing Your Tools

Tools like Notepad and TextEdit aren't all that bad for starting out. They keep it simple, and they don't mess with your HTML (unlike a word processing program). Seeing the result of your work is just a browser refresh away. So why are you destined to outgrow your favorite text editor?

- **Nobody's perfect.** With a text editor, it's just a matter of time before you make a mistake, like typing <b> instead of </b>. Unfortunately, you might not realize your mistake even when you view your page in your browser. (Remember, some browsers compensate for some types of mistakes; other browsers don't.) A good HTML editor can highlight problems and help you get rid of faulty HTML.

- **Edit-Save-Refresh. Repeat 1,000 times.** Text editors are convenient for small pages. But what if you're trying to size a graphic perfectly, or line up a table column? You need to jump back and forth between your text editor and your Web browser (saving and refreshing each time). This process can literally take hours. With a good HTML editor, you get conveniences like drag-and-drop editing to fine tune your Web page. You make a few adjustments, and your editor tweaks your HTML appropriately.

- **Help, I'm drowning in HTML!** One of the nicest little frills in an HTML editor is color coding. Color coding helps make sure those pesky HTML tags stand out against a sea of text. Without this feature, you'll be cross-eyed in hours.

- **Just type <ul><li></li></ul>.** To create a bulleted list, of course. You haven't forgotten already, have you? The truth is, most Web authors don't memorize every tag there is. With a Web editor, you don't need to. If you forget something, there's usually a help link or a menu command to fill it in. Without a tool to guide you, you're on your own.

Of course, there are also risks to using a graphical HTML editor. That's why you started out with a simple text editor, and why you'll spend a good portion of this book learning more about HTML. If you don't understand HTML properly, there are a number of traps waiting for you.

For example, you might use a slick HTML editor to apply fancy fonts to your text. Imagine your surprise when you take a look at your page on another computer (where the same fonts aren't installed) and your page reverts to an ugly or illegible typeface. (Chapter 6 has more about this problem.) Similarly, your editor can unwittingly lead you to insert HTML that's not supported by all browsers, or graphics that won't display properly on other computers. Finally, even with the best HTML editor you'll spend a significant amount of time looking at raw HTML to see exactly what's going on, clean up a mess, or copy and paste useful bits to other pages.

Types of HTML Editors

There's a wide range of different HTML editors, but they all tend to fall into one of three categories.

- **Text-based** editors require you to work with the text and tags of raw HTML. The difference between an ordinary text editor and a text-based HTML editor is convenience. Unlike Notepad or TextEdit, text-based HTML editors usually include buttons to quickly insert common tags or tag combinations, and a one-click way to save your file and open it in a separate browser window. Essentially, text-based HTML editors are text editors with some useful Web features stapled on.

- **Split window** editors also make you write HTML by hand. The difference is that a separate window shows the results of your work *as you type*. In other words, you get a live preview, which means you don't need to keep stopping to see what you've accomplished.

- **WYSIWYG** (What You See Is What You Get) editors work more like word processors. That means you don't need to write the HTML tags. Instead, you type in some text, format it, and insert pictures just like you would in a word-processing program. Behind the scenes, the editor generates the HTML markup you need.

Any of these types of HTML editors makes a good replacement to a simple text editor. The type you choose depends mainly on how many features you want, how you prefer to work, and how much money you're willing to shell out. The best HTML editors blur the lines between these different types, and give you the freedom to switch back and forth between different views.

It's important to understand that no matter what type of HTML editor you use, you still need to know a fair bit about HTML to get the result you want. Even if you have a WYSIWYG editor, you'll almost always want to fine-tune the HTML by hand. Also, understanding the quirks of HTML will help you determine what you can and can't do—and what strategies you need to get the most sophisticated results. Even in a WYSIWYG editor, you'll inevitably use a code view to look at the HTML underbelly of your Web pages.

Finding a Free HTML Editor

Unless you're one of the lucky few who already has a copy of a cutting-edge Web editor like FrontPage or Dreamweaver, you're probably wondering how you can find a good HTML editor for as little money as possible. After all, the Web's all about getting goodies for free. And while you can't find an industrial strength FrontPage-killer for free, you can get a good basic editor without opening your wallet.

Note: *Shareware*, as you no doubt already know, is software that's free to try, play with, and pass along to friends. If you like it, you're politely asked to pay for it (or not-so-politely locked out when the trial period expires). *Freeware* is software that has no cost at all—if you like it, it's yours! Usually, you won't get niceties like technical support. Some freeware is supported by donations.

FREQUENTLY ASKED QUESTION

Save As HTML

My word processing/page layout/spreadsheet program has a feature for saving Web pages. Should I use it?

Over the last decade, the Internet has become the hottest marketing buzzword around. Every computer program imaginable is desperate to boast about new Web features. For example, virtually every modern word processor has a feature for exporting your documents to HTML. Don't use it.

Unfortunately, HTML export features don't work very well. Often, the problem is that these features take a document that's designed for one medium (usually print) and try to wedge it into another (the Web). But word processor documents just don't look like Web pages—they tend to have larger margins, fancier fonts, more text, more generous spacing around that text, no links, and a radically different layout.

Another problem is the fact that HTML export features often create wildly complex markup. At the end of this process, you end up with an ungainly Web page that's nearly impossible to edit because it's choked with custom HTML. And unless you take a close look at the underlying HTML, you won't know whether your exported Web page will be displayed properly on other computers and browsers.

The lesson? If you can, steer clear of these features. You're better off copying and pasting your document content into an HTML file as plain text, and then formatting it with standard HTML tags on your own.

If you'd like to do your own research (always a good idea), and don't mind installing several dozen programs onto your computer until you find what you like, head to one of the following shareware Web sites to look for HTML editors (Figure 4-1):

- *http://downloads-zdnet.com*. This leading computer publisher has provided a vast catalog of shareware since before the Internet existed. You can search, browse through thoughtfully organized category listings, or read editor reviews. It's highly recommended.

- *www.download.com*. Another high-tech media company—CNET—provides this top-tier Web site for shareware.

- *www.tucows.com*. This fan favorite is cluttered with ads, but still boasts a solid shareware collection

You'll quickly find out that there's a sea of free HTML editors out there. Many have awkward and clunky button and menu arrangements. Some have outright errors. Finding one that's right for you might take a little time.

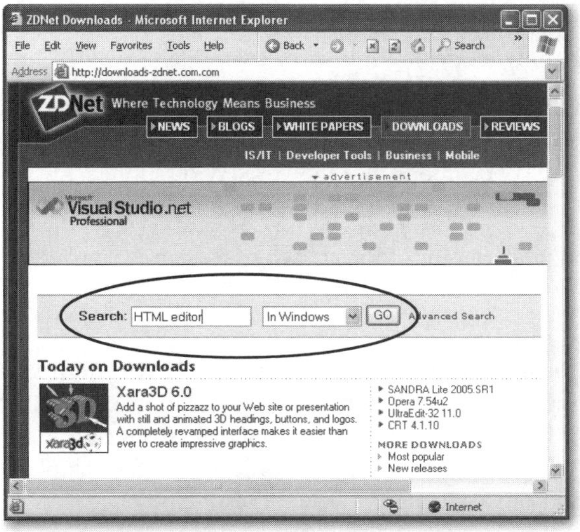

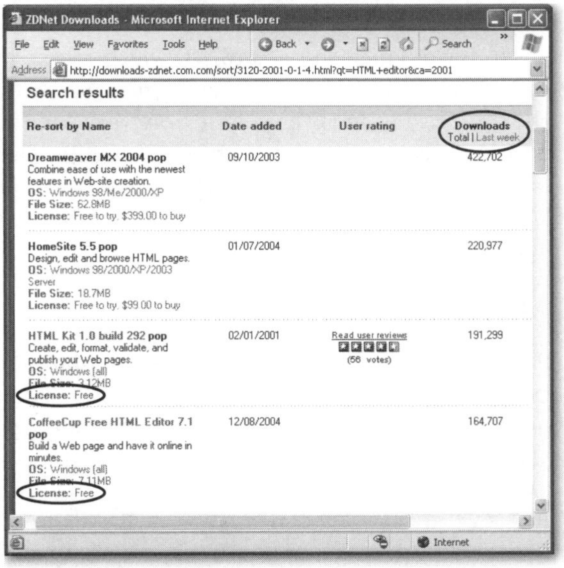

Figure 4-1:
Top: ZDNet has a rich catalog of shareware. Start by typing "HTML editor" in the search box and click GO. (If you're looking for Mac software, you should also change the list selection from "In Windows" to "In Downloads" and add the word "Mac" to your search.)

Bottom: In the table of lists, click the heading "Downloads." This sorts the results so the most popular show up first, which is a good shortcut. Make sure you read the license details next to each item to find out whether its trialware (like Dreamweaver and HomeSite) or completely free (like HTML-Kit and CoffeeCup). Then, select the item and follow the instructions to download and install it on your computer.

Here are three worthwhile candidates:

- **Nvu** is a newcomer that's already shaping up as the best free HTML editor around, and the only one with versions for Windows, Mac, and Linux. It lets you edit HTML documents using a WYSIWYG mode or a text-only mode.

- **HTML-Kit** is a popular—but slightly eccentric—free HTML editor for Windows. It lets you use a text-only mode or a split-preview mode.

- **CoffeeCup Free HTML Editor** is a scaled-down version of the full-blown Windows product CoffeeCup HTML Editor 2005. The full-blown version offers both a text-only mode and a WYSIWYG mode, but the WYSIWYG mode is switched off in the free version.

In the following sections, you'll take a quick look at each of these free editors.

Nvu

Nvu (pronounced "n-view," as in "new view") is the only free HTML editor in this roundup that works on Windows, Mac, and Linux. It's also the most current (providing regular releases), and it boasts an easy-to-understand layout and a set of nifty features. Nvu is a new kid on the block—its first official release took place in June 2005 (before then, it had been available as a beta, or test, release).

Nvu was created using some of the pieces from the Mozilla browser (godfather to the increasingly popular Firefox browser), with features that were copied from FrontPage shamelessly grafted on. It's an open source project, which means that not only is it free to download and copy, but if you're a programmer type, you're welcome to browse through the source code and even submit your own improvements. As a Web-head, you're most likely to fall in love with Nvu's multiple views, which give you several useful ways to look at your HTML, including a color-coded HTML tag view and a WYSIWYG preview (see Figure 4-2). Nvu's biggest limitation is that it doesn't give you any way to see more than one view at once, which means that if you want to edit in Source view, you won't see the results of your work until you switch to one of the other views.

Nvu is packed full of common-sense features that you get in most professional programs, like last-action undo (select Edit → Undo), a spell checker (Edit → Check), an option for inserting special characters (Insert → Characters and Symbols), and a helpful tip of the day. To download Nvu, surf to *www.nvu.com*.

Note: Since Nvu works so well, and is growing ever more popular, you'll find occasional tips on how to use it throughout this book.

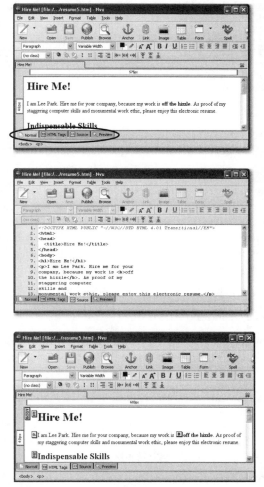

Figure 4-2:
Top: Nvu's normal view lets you edit formatted text instead of the raw HTML, just like in a word processor. You begin in normal view when you start Nvu and open a file. To switch from one view to another, use the tabs at the bottom of the window.

Middle: If you need to fine-tune your HTML markup, just switch to the Source view. You'll get handy line numbers and color-coded tags.

Bottom: Need something in between? The HTML Tags view lets you edit formatted text, but shows you what the tags are with floating yellow boxes. That way, if you find something amiss, you can switch to the Source view to clean it up.

HTML-Kit

HTML-Kit has an interface only a programmer could love. It's unusual, cluttered, and more than a little confusing. But on the good side, HTML-Kit is 100 percent free, relatively reliable, and ridiculously customizable.

HTML-Kit (*www.html-kit.com*) is a split-preview editor, which means you can see a live preview of your HTML document as you code it. However, HTML-Kit doesn't make this behavior immediately obvious. Instead, you need to coax HTML-Kit into showing both at the same time. Here's how to do it:

1. **Start HTML-Kit. (Choose Programs → HTML-Kit → HTML-Kit from the Start menu.)**

   The Open File dialog box appears, giving you a choice to create a new document or open an existing file.

2. **Select the "Open an existing file" option and click OK.**

   A typical Open dialog box appears.

3. **Browse to one of the résumé files that you used in Chapter 2 (also available for download from the "Missing CD" page at *www.missingmanuals.com*), select it, and click OK.**

   The HTML for the document appears in a tabbed window. You can click the Preview tab to see a graphical representation of your document, and the Editor tab to jump back to the HTML tag view. You can also use the Split View tab to take a look at both at the same time. However, for most people this feature is mysteriously broken, providing a blank page instead of an HTML preview. If that's what you encounter, continue on to the next step.

4. **Select View → Preview → Active Preview Window (or just press Ctrl+F8).**

   A separate preview window appears above the tabbed HTML view.

5. **Select Window → Tile Horizontally (if you want to stack the two windows one above the other) or Window → Tile Vertically (if you'd prefer to see them side by side).**

   The windows are rearranged so you can comfortably view both the HTML document and the preview window at the same time (see Figure 4-3).

   Periodically, HTML-Kit refreshes the preview window to show your latest edits. To trigger an immediate refresh, just press Ctrl+F8 at any time.

The most significant drawback to HTML-Kit (other than its charmingly baroque program layout) is the lack of handy buttons to quickly insert common HTML tags. If you love shortcut keys, you can browse the menu to find ways to insert angle brackets and jump from one tag to another. However, they're only useful if you think it's easy to remember odd keystrokes like Ctrl+, (the shortcut for jumping to the previous tag) and Ctrl+period (the shortcut for jumping to the next tag).

For more HTML-Kit fun, check out the wide array of HTML-Kit plug-ins at *www. html-kit.com*, as long as you're not scared off by perplexing names like avwEncodeEmail and hkMakeOptionsList. (Slightly more helpful descriptions are provided at the Web site.) One interesting plug-in is the HTML reference found at *www.chami.com/html-kit/plugins/info/hkh_w3c_offline*. Once you install this plug-in, you can get technical help about any HTML element in HTML-Kit. Just move your cursor over the tag in your document (using the arrow keys) and press F1.

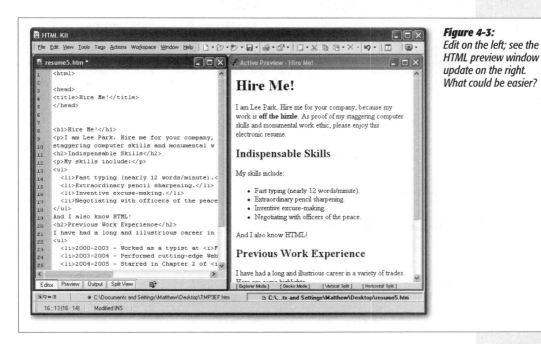

Figure 4-3:
Edit on the left; see the HTML preview window update on the right. What could be easier?

CoffeeCup

CoffeeCup Free HTML Editor is a scaled-down version of the full-blown Coffee-Cup HTML Editor 2005. It boasts a streamlined arrangement of buttons and menu options (see Figure 4-4), complete with an integrated file list (which shows you a list of all the HTML files you have in the current folder), and quick buttons for inserting common HTML tags.

CoffeeCup Free HTML Editor does come with a few drawbacks. In order to see an HTML preview, you need to constantly switch from the Code Editor tab to the Preview tab—there's no way to see both at once. Even more annoying is the Visual Editor tab, which offers to give you WYSIWYG editing abilities, but is disabled in the free version. If you accidentally click it, you'll receive a message asking you to upgrade. As a result, this product works best as a text-based HTML editor. It's effective, but not fantastic.

To download CoffeeCup Free HTML Editor, surf to this web page: *http://coffeecup.com.*

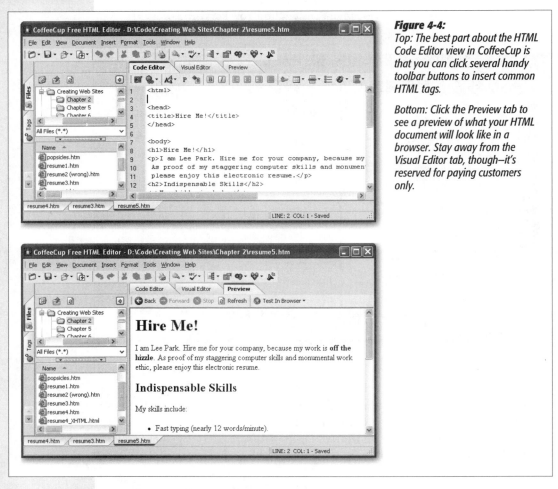

Figure 4-4:
Top: The best part about the HTML Code Editor view in CoffeeCup is that you can click several handy toolbar buttons to insert common HTML tags.

Bottom: Click the Preview tab to see a preview of what your HTML document will look like in a browser. Stay away from the Visual Editor tab, though—it's reserved for paying customers only.

Professional HTML Editors

Fed up with settling for a low-powered HTML editor and an editing environment that seems like it was designed by M. C. Escher? If you're ready to move on to a professional Web design package, take heart—your choice is surprisingly simple. That's because there are really only two top-tier HTML editors on the market today.

- **Macromedia Dreamweaver** is the favorite of graphic designers and hard-core HTML gurus. It's packed with features and gives you fine-grained control of every HTML ingredient.

- **Microsoft FrontPage** is a Microsoft powerhouse. Start typing, and you'll immediately see why FrontPage is popular with HTML novices. Its WYSIWYG mode is so seamless that it's hard to tell you aren't using a word processor. The menus, toolbars, and automatic spell check carefully duplicate what you find in Word.

One of the reasons that these products are so much better than their competitors is that they include a lot of other tools that you're sure to need when you start designing Web pages. For example, both let you create style sheets (an advanced feature you'll learn about in Chapter 6), resize images and drag them around your Web pages, and manage an entire Web site. FrontPage even includes a tool for generating fancy buttons. Another reason is that they're just so darned easy to use. Even though both are packed with sophisticated features, editing a simple HTML file couldn't be easier.

In the past, Dreamweaver had a reputation for being complicated enough to scare away HTML novices. On the other hand, FrontPage was known for being easy to use but having a few bad habits—like inserting unnecessary tags or relying on frills that only work when your Web site is hosted on a Web server that supports the FrontPage server extensions (see "FrontPage Folders" for more information). However, recent versions of both programs have tackled their weaknesses. Now, Dreamweaver is virtually as easy to use as FrontPage, and FrontPage 2003 is almost as mature and well-rounded as Dreamweaver. In fact, common tasks in these two programs are surprisingly similar. The bottom line? You can't go wrong with either tool.

If you're still itching to be convinced, you can try a free 30-day trial of either product. Surf to *www.microsoft.com/office/frontpage/prodinfo/trial.mspx* to order a free trial version of FrontPage, or *www.macromedia.com/go/trydreamweaver* to download a working Dreamweaver demo.

Note: For an in-depth exploration of every Dreamweaver feature, check out *Dreamweaver MX 2004: The Missing Manual*. For the low-down on FrontPage, pick up a copy of *FrontPage 2003: The Missing Manual*.

Working with Your HTML Editor

Once you've chosen an HTML editor, the next step is to take it for a spin. In this section, you'll learn how to create a sample HTML document and get it online, all without leaving the comfort of your editor.

Software companies have spent the last decade copying features from their competitors and as a result, common tasks in FrontPage, Dreamweaver, and Nvu are startlingly similar. That means that no matter which program you use, the following sections will teach you the basics. Once you're comfortable with your editor, you can move on to the rest of the book and learn more about how HTML works.

Tip: Although future chapters won't lead you step by step through any of these HTML editors, look for sidebars and tips to point out occasional shortcuts, tricks, and techniques for your favorite editor.

UP TO SPEED

Mid-Level HTML Editors

A few years ago, there were a number of mid-level HTML editors in hot competition. Today, most have died out. The mid-level HTML editors that remain often aren't worth the expense. Instead, your best bet is to save up for one of the two leading edge HTML editors—Macromedia Dreamweaver or Microsoft FrontPage. Of the two, FrontPage is the more affordable, while Dreamweaver is more often used by professional Web developers. You may be able to find academic (or "student and teacher") editions of both programs. These editions are scaled down but still powerful, and they have a much lower price tag. You'll need to prove you're a student or starving academic to get in on the action.

One mid-level option that's actually worth considering is Macromedia HomeSite, a less powerful Web design tool that Macromedia purchased from another company to complement its line of professional Web development software. HomeSite is priced at about $100, which makes it more affordable than FrontPage or the lofty Dreamweaver. However, there's a good case to be made for sticking with the nifty (and free) Nvu editor until you're ready to move up to a more full-featured program.

Starting Out

Here's what you need to get started with your editor of choice:

1. **The first step is to launch your program by double-clicking the appropriate icon or making a quick trip to the Start menu.**

   Your HTML editor appears.

2. **Some HTML editors start you off with a tip of the day (Nvu) or a start page (Dreamweaver). Close these windows to get to the main program window.**

   You may also need to remove a few more distractions. In FrontPage, you'll see a pesky Getting Started panel on the right-hand side—close this by clicking the X in the top-right corner. In Dreamweaver, you may want to shunt the panels out of the way (see Figure 4-5).

3. **Now, choose File → Open and select one of the HTML file samples you worked on in Chapter 2 (also available on the "Missing CD" page at *www. missingmanuals.com*).**

This step is easy—opening a document in an HTML editor is exactly the same as opening a document in any other self-respecting program.

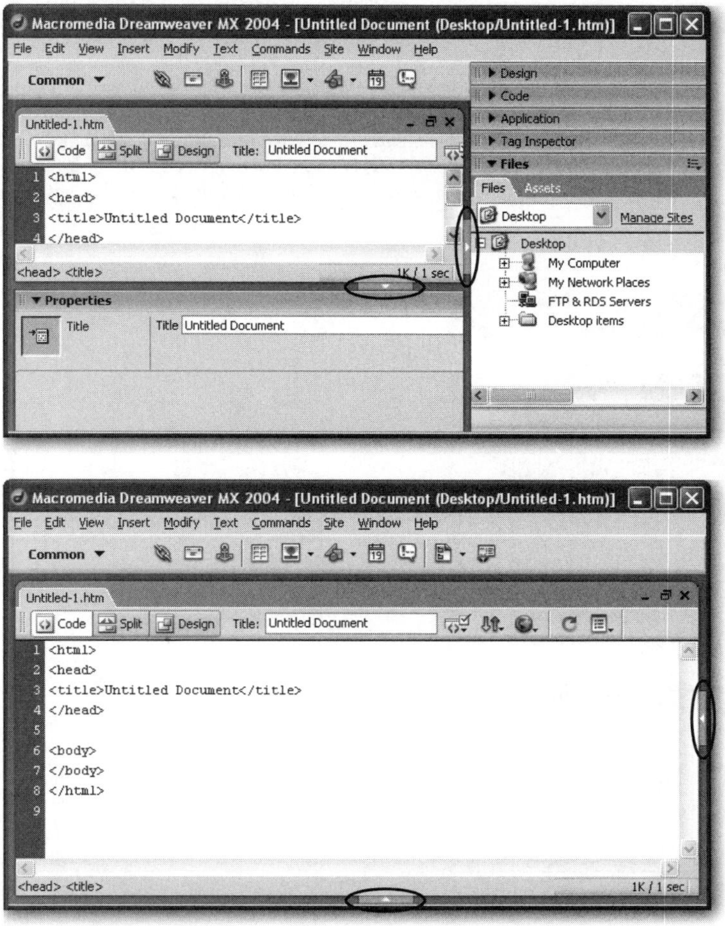

Figure 4-5:
Top: Dreamweaver is packed with features, many of which sit at your fingertips in specialized panels, which latch on to the right side and bottom of the main window. In this figure, you see the view that appears automatically when you open Dreamweaver. But until you've learned the basics, it's easiest to push the clutter out of the way by clicking the arrows circled here.

Bottom: You can also hide all panels at once by choosing View → Hide Panels. (Just choose View → Show Panels when you're psychologically ready for them to return.) In this figure, the special features are hidden, enlarging your main window view.

Multiple Views

As you've already learned, there are several different ways to look at an HTML document, depending on whether you want the convenience of a word processor or the complete control of working directly with HTML code. Most HTML editors give you a choice of how you want to work, and let you switch rapidly from one view to another. To switch views, you need to find a small series of buttons, which are usually displayed just above or just below the document you're working on. Figure 4-6 helps you spot these buttons.

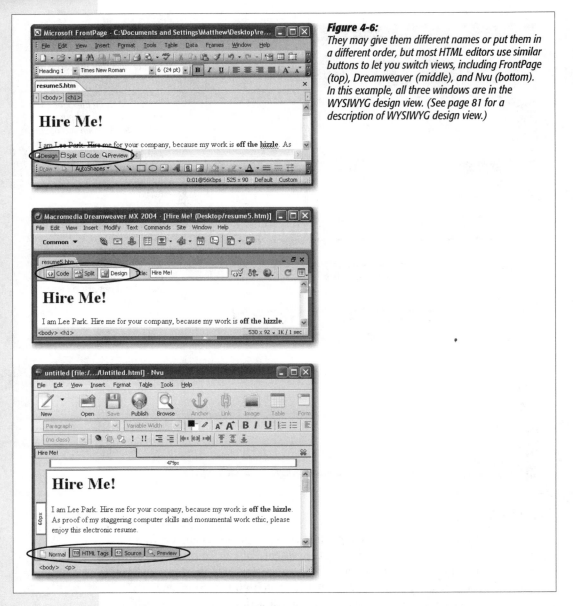

Figure 4-6:
They may give them different names or put them in a different order, but most HTML editors use similar buttons to let you switch views, including FrontPage (top), Dreamweaver (middle), and Nvu (bottom). In this example, all three windows are in the WYSIWYG design view. (See page 81 for a description of WYSIWYG design view.)

Most HTML editors start you out in a WYSIWYG view that shows the formatted HTML—in other words, an approximation of what the page will look like in a Web browser. When you switch to the HTML code view, you'll see the real story—the familiar text-only display of color-coded tags and text. These views are the two staples of HTML editing. However, the most useful choice just might be split view, which shows both views at once (see Figure 4-7).

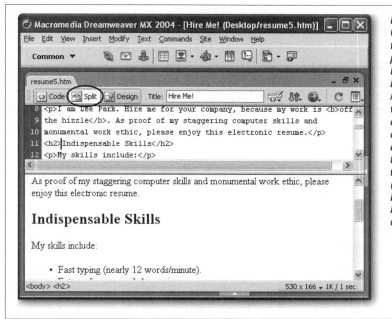

Figure 4-7:
One handy option is the split view, which splits the window into two panes. This figure shows a Dreamweaver screen after the Split button (circled) has been clicked. Most commonly, you'll use this view so you can edit the HTML tags and see a preview that's updated as you type. However, you could also work the other way, by editing the WYSIWYG preview, and seeing what HTML tags are inserted (which is a great way to learn HTML). Both Dreamweaver and FrontPage provide a split view option, but Nvu doesn't.

Some HTML editors also give you an interesting hybrid view that shows a WYSI-WYG preview with extra tag information. In Nvu, this is the HTML Tags view, which shows a formatted preview window with the corresponding tags shown in floating yellow boxes (see Figure 4-2, bottom). You can achieve a similar look in FrontPage by choosing View → Reveal Tags.

Creating a Web Page

The best way to understand how your HTML editor works is to create a new HTML document.

Use HTML view, as described above, so that you can have complete control over the HTML markup. Just enter all the tags and text content from beginning to end, just as though you were using Notepad or TextEdit (pop back to Chapter 2 for a refresher on HTML code writing basics). Along the way, you'll notice a few short-cuts. For example, when you start to type a tag in FrontPage or Dreamweaver, a drop-down menu appears with suggestions. You can choose a valid HTML tag from the list, or just keep typing. Also, when you add the start tag for a container element (like <h1> for a heading), FrontPage (or Dreamweaver) automatically inserts the end tag (like </h1>) so you won't forget it.

Creating and formatting a page in WYSIWYG view is a more interesting challenge, because you need to a know where to find the various formatting options in your editor.

FrontPage, Dreamweaver, and Nvu help you out by packing a fair bit of HTML smarts right into their toolbars. To add a tag in the WYSYWIG view, you first select a piece of text you want to format, and then click the appropriate toolbar button. You can then switch to the HTML tag view to verify that you got the result you expected. For example, to make text bold, select it and look for a toolbar button with the letter B. Clicking this button inserts the <b> tag just before your selection and the </b> tag just after it. Figure 4-8 shows you the most useful toolbar buttons in Nvu.

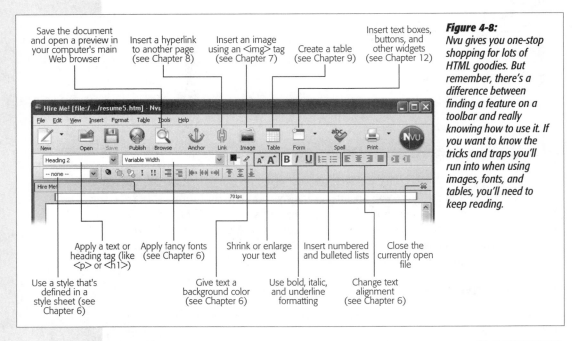

Save the document and open a preview in your computer's main Web browser

Insert a hyperlink to another page (see Chapter 8)

Insert an image using an <img> tag (see Chapter 7)

Create a table (see Chapter 9)

Insert text boxes, buttons, and other widgets (see Chapter 12)

Apply a text or heading tag (like <p> or <h1>)

Apply fancy fonts (see Chapter 6)

Shrink or enlarge your text

Insert numbered and bulleted lists

Close the currently open file

Use a style that's defined in a style sheet (see Chapter 6)

Give text a background color (see Chapter 6)

Use bold, italic, and underline formatting

Change text alignment (see Chapter 6)

Figure 4-8:
Nvu gives you one-stop shopping for lots of HTML goodies. But remember, there's a difference between finding a feature on a toolbar and really knowing how to use it. If you want to know the tricks and traps you'll run into when using images, fonts, and tables, you'll need to keep reading.

Tip: It's up to you whether you want to write your Web pages in HTML view or using the WYSIWYG preview mode. The WYSIWYG view is always quicker and more convenient at first, but it can leave you with a lot of HTML to check and review, adding to future complications.

To practice your WYSIWYG editing, you can re-create one of the examples from Chapter 2 (the mini-résumé you see on page 41 works well). But instead of entering the tags by hand, just enter the text and format it using the toolbar and menu options in your editor. Here are a few steps to get you started on this challenge:

1. **Start by choosing File → New to create the Web page.**

   Your editor asks you what type of file you want to create.

2. **In FrontPage, just click the "Blank page" link to start from scratch. In Dreamweaver, choose Basic page as your category, and HTML as the subcategory. In Nvu, choose the option "A blank document," and then click Create.**

A blank document appears, showing the bare HTML skeleton. If you take a look at your new document in the HTML code view, you'll see the basic <html>, <head>, and <body> tags.

Tip: Some HTML editors, like FrontPage, include all sorts of templates for quickly creating various site designs. The options in Dreamweaver aren't bad, but they're quite complex, and require styles, which are introduced in Chapter 6. The options in FrontPage are fairly limiting—although they look nice, there isn't much room for diversity. You're best off to avoid them until you've learned enough to create your own unique designs.

---

3. **Switch to WYSIWYG design view, and type the title "Hire Me!"**

The text appears at regular size.

4. **Select the text, and find a toolbar or menu option that can convert your text to a heading by adding the <h1> and </h1> tags.**

In FrontPage, the quickest approach is to select Heading 1 from the drop-down Style list. In Dreamweaver, there are several worthwhile choices. You can choose Text → Paragraph Format → Heading 1 for a fairly labor-intensive approach, or use the shortcut key Ctrl+1 for instant gratification. You can also use the toolbar, as explained in Figure 4-9, or the Properties window (choose Window → Properties if it isn't visible). In Nvu, your only option is to choose Format → Paragraph → Heading 1. This tag didn't make it into the toolbar.

5. **Hit the Enter key to move to the next paragraph.**

Your typeface reverts to normal, and you can begin typing the rest of the document. The next challenge is creating the bulleted list. FrontPage, Dreamweaver, and Nvu all let you do so by using buttons on their toolbars.

It's easy to lose yourself in a thicket of tags. To make it easier to orient yourself, FrontPage, Dreamweaver, and Nvu all include a quick tag selector bar at the top or bottom of your document (Figure 4-10).

6. **For a change of pace, try inserting a picture.**

Nvu provides easy access with an Image button on the toolbar. FrontPage and Dreamweaver have similar buttons, but it's easier to head straight to the menu (choose Insert → Picture → From File in Front Page or Insert → Image in Dreamweaver).

Note: For this test, the picture should be in the same directory as your Web page. Otherwise, some editors may add an <img> tag that's linked to a specific location on your hard drive. This is a problem, because Web surfers can't access your hard drive, and so they won't see the picture. To double-check that everything's in order, look at the <img> tag in HTML view, and make sure the src attribute doesn't start with *file:///*. If it does, edit it by hand so it looks like the <img> tag you used in Chapter 2 (page 40).

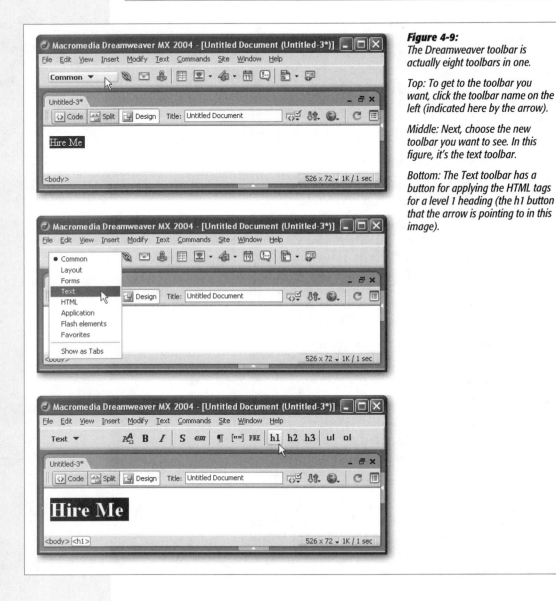

Figure 4-9:
The Dreamweaver toolbar is actually eight toolbars in one.

Top: To get to the toolbar you want, click the toolbar name on the left (indicated here by the arrow).

Middle: Next, choose the new toolbar you want to see. In this figure, it's the text toolbar.

Bottom: The Text toolbar has a button for applying the HTML tags for a level 1 heading (the h1 button that the arrow is pointing to in this image).

7. When you're prompted to pick an image file, browse to the *leepark.jpg* sample, and select it. (You can download this image from the "Missing CD" page at *www.missingmanuals.com.*)

The program inserts the appropriate <img> tag. Once the picture is inserted into your document, you'll really start to appreciate the benefits of the WYSI-WYG view. In all of the HTML editors covered here, you can drag the edges of the picture to move or resize it.

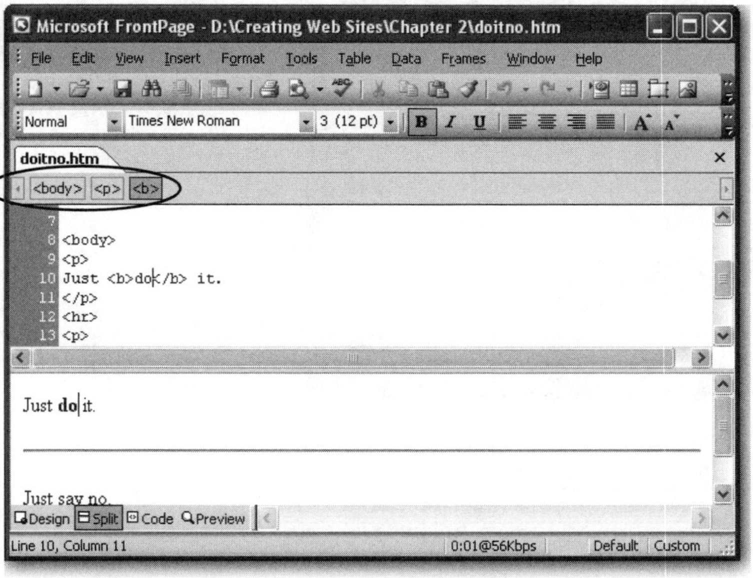

Figure 4-10:
The tag selector (circled) is handy if you're looking for a specific section of a Web page you need to edit. Once you've scrolled to the right place, double-check the tag selector to see if you're where you think you are. The tag selector lists all the tags that are in action at your current location. In this example, the cursor is positioned inside the <b> tag (for bold formatting), which itself is placed inside a <p> (paragraph) tag, which is nested inside the <body> tag that wraps the complete HTML document. You can quickly select any one of these tags by clicking it in the bar.

Managing a Web Site

HTML editors aren't limited to viewing a single Web page at a time. They almost always give you the ability to look at more than one document at once. In FrontPage, Dreamweaver, and Nvu, multiple open files are represented in the same way—the program adds tabs at the top of the document window. Figure 4-11 shows an example with FrontPage.

Along with the ability to edit more than one Web page at once, many HTML editors also let you manage an entire Web site.

Note: A Web site is simply a collection of one or more Web pages, along with any related files (like pictures). It's often useful to manage all these files together in an HTML editor. This way, it's easier to add links from one page to another (see Chapter 8) and keep things consistent. You also get the ability to upload all your Web pages with just a couple of clicks.

Another open document   The current document

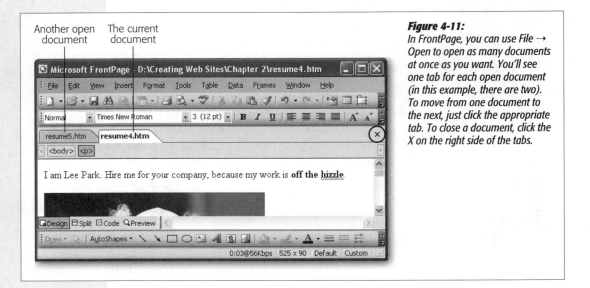

Figure 4-11:
In FrontPage, you can use File → Open to open as many documents at once as you want. You'll see one tab for each open document (in this example, there are two). To move from one document to the next, just click the appropriate tab. To close a document, click the X on the right side of the tabs.

Defining a site in FrontPage

To create a Web site in FrontPage, follow these steps:

1. **Select File → Open Site.**

   The Open Site dialog box appears. It looks like an ordinary Open File dialog box, except that for one difference—it doesn't show any files. Instead, you can only see folders.

2. **Browse to the folder you want to open, select it, and then click Open. For example, you could use the Chapter 2 folder that's included with the downloadable samples to see all the different résumé files.**

A dialog box appears asking if you want to add FrontPage information to your Web site (see Figure 4-12).

Figure 4-12:
In order to use FrontPage's Web site management features, you need to let it add specialized subfolders to your Web site folder. You can see these subfolders in Windows Explorer—they have names like _private, _vti_cnf, and _vti_pvt. FrontPage also adds a subfolder named images that you can use to store pictures you want to use in your Web site. This figure shows the dialog box that appears when you first open a new folder in FrontPage as a Web site.

3. **Click Yes to add FrontPage information.**

Once FrontPage adds the subfolders, a Folder List panel appears on the right site of the window with a list of all the files in your Web site (see Figure 4-13).

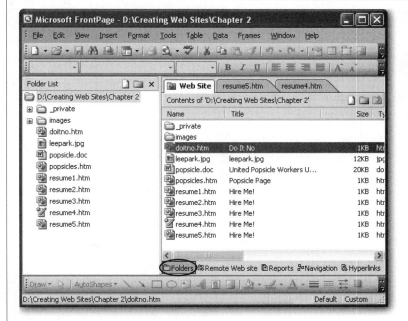

Figure 4-13:
The Folder List (the left column of this figure) makes it easy to see the contents of your Web site at a glance. To open a document, just double-click it. You can also select a file and right-click it to see additional options for renaming or deleting files.

Uploading a site in FrontPage

One of FrontPage's most popular features is its support for updating a Web site without needing to use a separate FTP program (see page 76 for the rundown on what FTP programs do). To take advantage of this support, you need to follow the steps described above to make sure FrontPage understands your folder is part of a complete Web site. Then, you can upload your Web site by following these steps:

1. **Choose File → Publish Site.**

   The first time you publish your site, a Remote Web Site Properties dialog box appears. You use this window to set your connection options, like the name of your FTP server (see Figure 4-14).

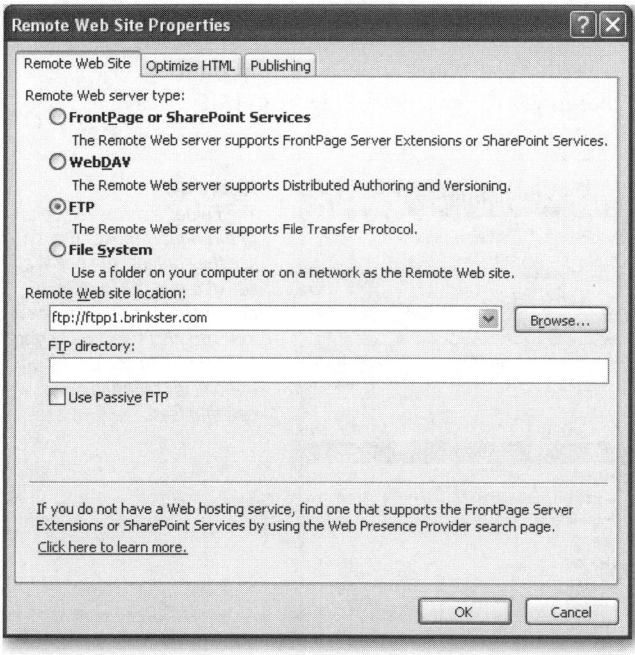

Figure 4-14:
Your Web hosting company should tell you the exact choices to make in the Remote Web Site Properties dialog box. Typically, you'll need the name of your FTP server, the directory (folder) on the server used for your Web site, and your FTP account and password. You only need to complete this step once. If you're successful, FrontPage will use this information the next time you choose to publish your Web site.

2. **Fill in the information about how you want to connect to your Web server, and then click OK.**

   You can also set some advanced options using the Publishing tab of this dialog box. Most usefully, you can set whether FrontPage uploads only changed or new pages (which is the standard setting), or always uploads everything in the copy of the Web site stored on your PC.

3. **At this point, FrontPage may prompt you for a user name and password to connect to your FTP server. Enter the correct information and then click OK.**

FrontPage stores the user name you enter for future use, but it's up to you to remember the password and supply it each time you connect.

Once you're connected, FrontPage shows a side-by-side file list that compares the contents of your Web site as stored on your PC with the contents that's located on the Web server.

FREQUENTLY ASKED QUESTION

FrontPage Folders

How can I get rid of the subfolders FrontPage adds to my Web site?

Few Web authors like it when an HTML editor adds unexpected and unwanted stuff to a Web site. Unfortunately, FrontPage doesn't give you a choice. If you use its Open Site feature, FrontPage adds several extra subfolders inside the folder where your site is stored. These folders have names like _private, _vti_cnf, and _vti_pvt. (Web trivia: The VTI acronym stands for Vermeer Technologies—the company that originally created FrontPage and sold it to Microsoft.)

These FrontPage folders have several purposes. First, they keep track of what files you've uploaded to your Web server. That makes it incredible easy to update a Web site, because FrontPage simply needs to transfer the changed files to the Web server, not the entire site. The FrontPage folders also track information about the pages and resources of your Web site, which helps with features like link checking (a nifty trick you'll learn about on page 227).

If you want to use these features, there's no way to get rid of the FrontPage subfolders. Just learn to accept them— honestly, they won't interfere with the rest of your Web site.

If you're not planning to use the Web site uploading feature in FrontPage, you may not need to copy the FrontPage subfolders to your Web server. It all depends if you're using one of a small set of FrontPage-specific features that need these folders. (If you're using these features, you had better know about it already, because you'll need a Web hosting company that supports the FrontPage *server extensions*.) For more information, surf to Microsoft's support site at *http://support.microsoft.com* and search for *281532*, which is the number of the knowledge base article that describes what features require the FrontPage server extensions. If you aren't using any of these, you don't need to upload these subfolders.

Finally, if you don't want to have the FrontPage folders on your Web server *or* on your personal computer, you can't use the Open Site feature. Instead, you can open your HTML files in FrontPage individually. This probably isn't worth the trouble, because you'll sacrifice some handy features that can help you manage a large Web site.

---

4. **To bring your Web server up to date, select the "Local to remote" option and click the Publish Web Site button. This starts the publishing process (see Figure 4-15).**

The "Remote to local" option is handy if a file on the Web server is more recent than the copy on your own computer. This might happen if you're editing the same Web site on more than one computer. The Synchronize option is like the

"Remote to local" and "Local to remote" operations rolled into one. It examines each file, and makes sure any old versions on your computer or the Web server are updated.

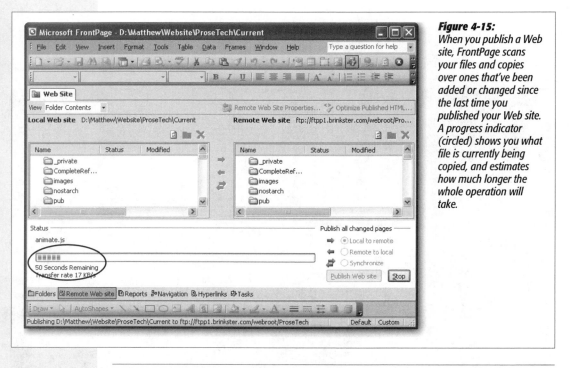

Figure 4-15:
When you publish a Web site, FrontPage scans your files and copies over ones that've been added or changed since the last time you published your Web site. A progress indicator (circled) shows you what file is currently being copied, and estimates how much longer the whole operation will take.

Tip: You may have trouble uploading a Web site using FrontPage if you've already copied some of the files manually using an FTP program. To fix this problem, delete the files from your Web server, and use FrontPage to transfer the whole Web site. FrontPage will then copy every file from your local Web site folder to your Web server.

Defining a site in Dreamweaver

Dreamweaver gives you two different ways to work with a Web site. The simplest approach is to use the integrated file browser to look at the files in any folder on your computer (see Figure 4-16).

Although using the Files panel is convenient, it's also limiting. The problem is that Dreamweaver doesn't have any way to tell what file and folders make up your Web site. In order to support Web site uploading and a few other tools, you may want to define your folder as a Web site. To do this, follow these steps:

1. **Click the Manage Sites link in the Files panel, or just select Site → Manage Sites.**

The Manage Sites dialog box appears, with a list of all the Web sites you've configured so far. Initially, this list is empty.

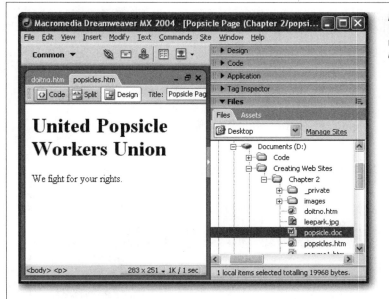

Figure 4-16:
*You can browse your file system
without leaving Dreamweaver by
using the Files panel.*

2. **To define a new Web site, click the New button and choose Site.**

   Dreamweaver walks you through a Site Definition wizard that asks you several
   questions.

3. **Enter a descriptive Web site name and click Next.**

   The site name is just the name you use to keep track of your Web site. It also
   appears in the Files panel.

4. **Choose "No, I do not want to use a server technology" and then click Next.**

   A *server technology* is the framework on a Web server that runs complex Web
   applications like database searches. Because you aren't creating a full-blown
   application (just ordinary HTML files), you don't need this support.

5. **Choose "Edit local copies directly on my machine."**

   Some Web servers give you the ability to modify files stored on the server. However, even if you have this specialized support, it's probably better to edit your
   files on your local computer, and only update them on the live Web server
   when you're ready. This gives you several advantages. First, you won't derail
   your Web site if you make a minor mistake. Second, you have a valuable
   backup if anything happens to your Web server. And third, you have the ability
   to experiment with changes and different designs that may take days to finish,
   without affecting the live version of your Web site.

6. In the "Where on your computer do you want to store your files" text box, type in the full file path for your Web site folder (usually something like *C:\ Creating Web Sites*\Chapter 2), and then click Next.

   If you aren't sure where your Web site folder is, you can click the folder icon next to the text box to browse for it.

7. **The next step asks how you want to connect to your Web server. Fill in your connection information, and then click Next.**

   The option you choose depends on the support offered by your Web hosting company, but FTP is a common choice (see Figure 4-17). Depending on what option you choose, there are a number of extra settings you have to supply.

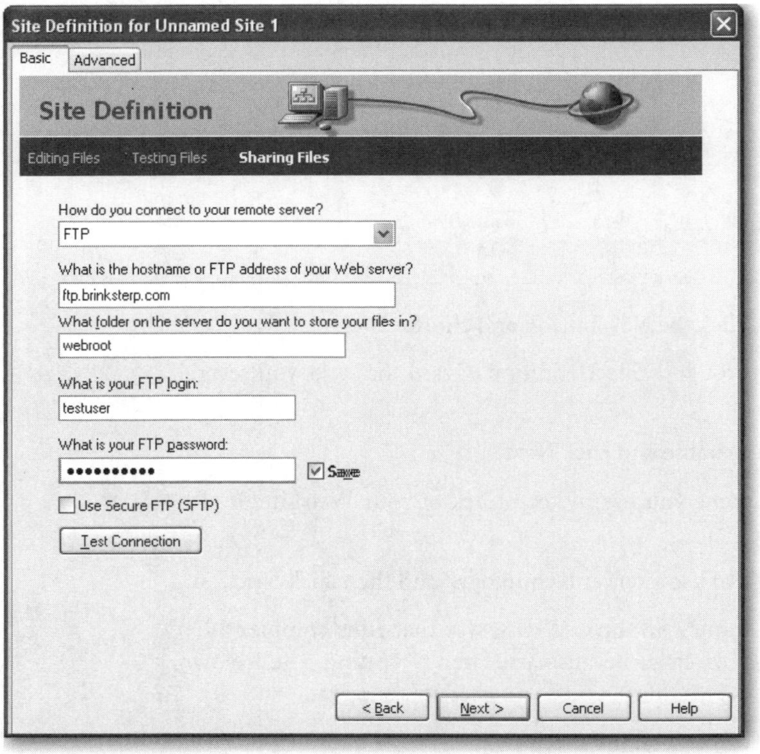

Figure 4-17:
In the "Sharing files" step of the Wizard, you choose how you want to transfer your files to the remote Web Server. Your remote server is the location where you plan to publish your Web site. Typically, this is a Web site that you'll communicate with using a communication method like FTP, but it could also be an ordinary directory on a local network.

8. **Choose "Do not allow check in and check out" and then click Next.**

   Check in and *check out* features allow you to collaborate with a group of coworkers to edit different parts of a Web site simultaneously. For information about this and other advanced Dreamweaver features, check out *Dreamweaver MX 2004: The Missing Manual.*

9. **The last step summarizes the information you've entered. Click Done.**

You return to the Manage Sites dialog box.

10. **Click Done.**

You return to the Dreamweaver main window.

Uploading a site in Dreamweaver

Once you've defined your Web site, you'll see it in the Files panel. You can then browse your remote Web server, or transfer files back and forth. Dreamweaver doesn't make things quite as intuitive as FrontPage, but it's still pretty convenient.

To transfer files from your local computer to the Web server, you use an operation that Dreamweaver jargon calls a *put*. It works like this:

1. **In the Files panel, choose your Web site from the drop-down menu at the top left.**

2. **Now, choose "Local view" from the drop-down menu at the top right.**

The Files panel shows a list of the files on your computer (see Figure 4-18).

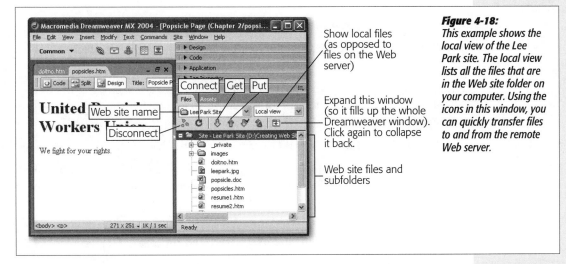

Figure 4-18:
This example shows the local view of the Lee Park site. The local view lists all the files that are in the Web site folder on your computer. Using the icons in this window, you can quickly transfer files to and from the remote Web server.

3. **Select the files you want to transfer to the Web server.**

You can select multiple files by holding down Ctrl while you click each file's icon.

4. **Once you've selected the files, click the Put arrow (a blue arrow icon pointing up), or right-click the files and then choose Put from the shortcut drop-down menu.**

Dreamweaver asks if you want to copy dependent files.

5. **Choose Yes if you want to copy linked files. For example, if you're copying a Web page that uses the <img> tag to show graphics, you should click Yes to make sure the graphics are also uploaded. If there aren't any dependent files, your choice has no effect.**

   Dreamweaver connects to your Web server and transfers the files.

To perform the reverse trick, and transfer files from your Web server *to* your computer, you need to use a *get* operation. Follow these steps:

1. **In the Files panel, choose your Web site from the drop-down menu at the top left.**

2. **Next, choose "Remote view" from the drop-down menu at the top right.**

   Dreamweaver doesn't automatically show a list of files on the Web server, because getting that list could take a little time. So you need to specifically ask Dreamweaver for an updated view of the files on your Web server, which you'll learn how to do in the next step.

3. **Click the refresh button, which looks like a circular arrow icon.**

   Dreamweaver connects to the Web server, retrieves the list of files in your Web site, and displays it.

4. **Select the files you want to transfer to your computer.**

   You can select multiple files by holding down Ctrl while you click each file's name.

5. **Once you've selected the files, click the Get arrow (a green arrow icon pointing down), or right-click the files and choose Get from the shortcut drop-down menu.**

   Dreamweaver asks if you want to copy dependent files.

6. **Choose Yes if you want to copy linked files. For example, if you're copying a Web page that uses the <img> tag to show graphics, you should click Yes to make sure the graphics are also downloaded. If there aren't any dependent files, your choice has no effect.**

   Dreamweaver connects to your Web server and copies the files to the folder on your computer that contains your Web site.

Part Two: Building Better Web Pages

2

HTML Text Tags

Getting text into a Web page is easy. All you need to do is open an HTML file, drop in your content, and add the occasional formatting tag. Unfortunately, getting text to look *exactly* the way you want is a completely different story.

One of the first things you'll notice when you start working on a site is how little control HTML gives you. When you create a Web page, you're at the mercy of your viewers' Web browsers, their bizarre preference settings, and a dozen other details beyond your control. Under these conditions, writing a perfect page feels like trying to compose a 90-minute symphony with a triangle and a pair of castanets.

Faced with these limitations, what's an enterprising Web developer to do? The first step is to learn the basic tags you can use to structure your text by marking up paragraphs, sections, and lists. That's the task you'll tackle in this chapter. The second step—which you won't dive into until the next chapter—is to apply *style sheets,* a powerful page formatting technology that lets you unleash your markup skills across multiple pages or even your entire site.

Understanding Text and the Web

Sooner or later, every Web site creator discovers that designing for the Web is pretty different than designing something that's going to be printed out. Before you can unleash your inner graphic designer, there are a few conceptual hurdles to clear.

To understand the problem you're facing, it helps to consider the difference between an HTML page and a document you might create in a program like Microsoft Word. Word processing programs help you prepare your content so that you can print it out. In that environment, you know all the details about your *output medium* (things like the paper size, whether or not the printer supports color, what fonts are available, and so on). As a result, your word processor gives you absolute control over every detail.

HTML is a more freewheeling standard. When you create an HTML document, you have no idea who's going to look at it or what kind of monitor, screen settings, Web browser, and so on they'll be using to view it. The way your document appears could change dramatically, depending on whether the person viewing your page turns on large text, shrinks the browser window to microscopic proportions, or switches off pictures. And if people surf to your site using a trendy pocket-sized PC, they'll get a completely different view compared to those who have the latest widescreen computer monitor.

Tip: HTML was designed to avoid compatibility problems by giving you *less* control. Instead of allowing you to place everything in an exact spot, HTML forces you to use tags to shape the basic structure of your work (for example, to indicate paragraphs, headings, and lists). However, it's up to the Web browser to decide *how* to display these details on a given computer. In other words, HTML was designed as a compromise that sacrifices control for the sake of simplicity, flexibility, and compatibility.

UP TO SPEED

Understanding Resolution

A resolution of 800 x 600 means that the entire monitor shows a grid that's 800 pixels wide and 600 pixels high. A pixel is the smallest unit of measurement on a computer monitor, and is otherwise known as a "dot." In other words, a resolution of 800 x 600 gives programs 480,000 pixels to play with, while a mediocre 640 x 480 resolution offers only 307,200. Clearly, higher resolutions can fit in a lot more content.

It's important to realize screen resolution isn't directly tied to the size of your monitor. In other words, a 17" monitor can have a higher resolution (and show more information) than a 19" monitor. However, it makes sense for larger monitors to use higher resolutions. That's because on a small monitor, high resolutions look cramped. Monitors support a wide range of resolutions, and you can choose the best compromise between showing lots of content (a higher resolution) and making sure that content isn't too small (a lower resolution).

The Problem of Layout

One of the most important considerations in print design is the physical size of the document. For example, you need to use much larger text on a poster than a business card. In the world of the Web, you don't have the luxury of worrying about size. Web surfers can shrink your window at will, changing it drastically (see

Figure 5-1). You need to accept this reality, and make sure your Web page looks good regardless of who's viewing it or what kind of browser they're using.

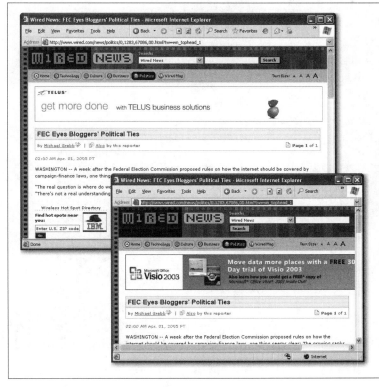

Figure 5-1:
Size matters. A paragraph that occupies just a couple of lines in a full-size window requires many more lines in a narrow window.

Left: At 800 x 600 pixels (a common monitor resolution), you get a great view of this article.

Right: At the smaller, but still supported resolution of 640 x 480, the Web page is still readable, albeit much more cramped. Designing for variable window sizes is one of the endless headaches that confronts every Web artist.

In some rare cases, you might know how big a browser window your visitors will use. For example, if you're designing a private Web site for an internal company network, where computers are all configured the same way, you can depend on everyone having the same view. But in most cases, you'll need to aim for a design that satisfies a broad range of viewers.

The first step in your quest for design equilibrium is to determine the smallest window size you want to support. See the box "How Big Is Your Window?" below for some good tips on choosing the right size for your pages.

Once you know the window sizes you're aiming for, the next step is to resize your Web browser window to match these dimensions. That way, as you're creating your pages, you can preview each page in a browser and make sure it looks okay. Fortunately, many HTML editors have a feature that opens your page in a browser window set to a fixed size. For example, in FrontPage you can choose File → Preview in Browser, which has options for common window sizes.

DESIGN TIME

How Big Is Your Window?

Here are three good guidelines that the Web's most successful sites follow:

- Your page should be usable in a window that's 640 x 480 pixels. In other words, maybe folks whose monitors are set to this resolution will have to scroll a bit (up or down, or left or right) to see your initial screen, but for the most part everything you want them to see will be viewable. Most ancient Windows-95–era computers came with monitors whose screens could display a maximum of 640 x 480 pixels; designing with these people in mind means you won't be alienating any of these antique PC owners.

- Your page should look its *best* at 800 x 600 pixels. This is the most common full-screen size for today's generation of computers, although higher resolutions (like 1024 x 768) are becoming increasingly common.

- Your page should still look respectable at sizes above 800 x 600 pixels.

For an example, surf over to read an article on the New York Times Web site (*www.nytimes.com*). If you adjust the size of your browser window so that it measures 640 x 480, you'll be able to see the full width of an article along with the links for moving from one page to the next. (Any narrower, and some text is cut off.) At 800 x 600, you see the outskirts of the page, which includes related links and advertising banners. At 1024 x 768, life doesn't change very much—you just wind up with an extra margin of blank space on the right-hand side.

To achieve this kind of good-for-all-viewers result, you'll need to use the layout features described in Chapter 9. However, you can start following good design principles right away, by testing your pages at all these sizes.

Logical Structure vs. Physical Formatting

Before you start tagging up your Web pages, there's one other concept you should understand—the difference between *structuring* a document (arranging it into sections like headings, paragraphs, and lists) and *formatting* a document (making the sections look different). Novice Web masters who don't understand this difference always end up formatting when they should be structuring, which leads to messy HTML that's difficult to edit.

In keeping with this distinction, HTML has two types of tags:

- **Logical tags** (sometimes called *idiomatic tags*) describe the type of content. For example, logical tags identify headings, paragraphs, quotations, code snippets, and emphasized text. However, logical tags don't determine the specific formatting details about how your content is displayed in the browser.

- **Physical tags** (sometimes called *typographic tags*) are all about formatting. Examples include tags that apply italics, boldface, underlining, and different fonts. Physical tags don't tell you anything about the content of the text within them.

These two types of tags represent two different ways of thinking about HTML. When you use logical tags, you define the structure of your document. For example, you use logical tags to organize the résumé document in Chapter 2 into separate sections, including a heading, several paragraphs, and a bulleted list.

POWER USERS' CLINIC

Using JavaScript to Resize a Window

If you can't (or don't want) to use your HTML editor's preview tool, there is a devious workaround. You can add a block of JavaScript code into your Web page that takes charge and automatically resizes your browser window. (JavaScript is a simple scripting language that allows you to give browsers additional instructions. You'll learn more about it in Chapter 14.)

Assuming your browser supports JavaScript (and almost all do), you can embed JavaScript code using a <script> tag. Here's an example, with the JavaScript code highlighted:

```
<html>

<head>
    <title>Resizable Page</title>
    <script type="text/javascript">
      self.resizeTo(640, 480);
    </script>
</head>
```

```
<body>
    <p>Put your normal Web page here...</p>
</body>

</html>
```

In this example, the self.resizeTo( ) command changes the size of the window while the page is loading. The first number in parentheses is the width, and the second number is the height. Replace these numbers with your own numbers to test different window sizes. Just remember to remove the <script> block when you're finished testing.

You could use the same devious trick in your finished page to resize a window without your visitors' permission. But don't. This tactic is guaranteed to drive visitors away from your site in record time.

When you use logical tags, it's up to the browser to decide what formatting to use. The perfect example of a logical tag is <address>, which is occasionally used to identify contact information (like a Web or postal address):

```
<address>IHateSpam@webremailers.com</address>
```

Most browsers format addresses in italics, just as though you used the <i> tag. But the important point is that a browser doesn't *need* to format address tagged-content in italics. Instead, you're using the <address> tag to identify the type of content.

On the other hand, when you use a physical tag, you specify the exact formatting you want to appear—in other words, you're micromanaging your Web page. It's like telling the browser: "Listen up. Put *this* word in italics; and put **that phrase** in bold face." In fact, two of the most popular physical tags are the <b> and <i> tags (for bold and italics) that you learned about in Chapter 2.

Tip: This book focuses on the HTML tags that are most widespread today. That means you'll learn about the most popular logical and physical tags, which makes it easier to carry on a conversation with other Web-heads.

Logical tags have ruled the roost ever since HTML was invented. The creators of HTML imagined a world where document writers didn't want the hassle of formatting, particularly because different types of browsers would present the same document in different ways, depending on the capabilities of the Web surfer's computer. Even better, logical tags let programs other than Web browsers analyze HTML documents. For example, someone could create an automated search program that scans Web pages, and extracts just the top-level headings to give you a barebones outline. Or browses Amazon to find book reviews. Or creates a junk-mail list by reading <address> tags. A comparable program that came across a Web page filled with nothing but physical tags wouldn't be nearly as interesting. For example, who cares how much text is in bold on eBay?

Tip: The vision of a Web where tags indicate what a page contains (prices, size information, email addresses, and so on) rather than how a page looks, is called the *semantic Web*. According to the visionaries who first built the Internet, the semantic Web could usher in a golden age of information access and super-smart searching. Many of the same gurus are still at work planning the semantic Web with new XML-based standards. For a preview of the possible future, surf to *http://logicerror.com/semanticWeb*.

CSS (Cascading Style Sheets)

All of this discussion raises a good question—if Web page writers are supposed to describe the content and structure of their pages, what's left to make sure the page looks good? The HTML powers-that-be could create more tags just for formatting, but that would force page creators to do more work, make HTML more complicated, and choke the average Web page in a swamp of ugly details about fonts, colors, and alignment. Even worse, because the content and the formatting information would be glued together, it would be hard to change. Imagine a page in which you not only had to tag every paragraph, but you also had to indicate which font you wanted to use. What a headache. To avoid problems like these, HTML only has a few, idiosyncratic formatting tags like the aforementioned <i> and <b> tags. Web purists hate them.

The solution that HTML gurus finally hit on was to separate the formatting information from the document's content, and place these two pieces into separate files. Here's how it works. First of all, the HTML documents you create in this scenario continue to look more or less the same—just like the ones you learned how to create in Chapter 2. They keep the same tags for paragraphs, headings, and lists, but not much more. This is good news already—it means you don't need to change your approach or throw out the basic tags once you've mastered them.

Next, you create a separate document using a standard called CSS (Cascading Style Sheets). The style sheet defines how every type of element in your HTML document should be formatted. For example, it contains instructions like "make every heading bright red" and "give all paragraphs a 15-pixel margin."

Once you've perfected your Web site's look and feel, you link your Web page to the style sheet and the transformation takes place (see Figure 5-2).

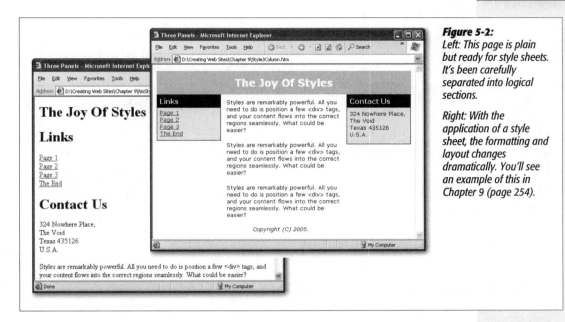

Figure 5-2:
Left: This page is plain but ready for style sheets. It's been carefully separated into logical sections.

Right: With the application of a style sheet, the formatting and layout changes dramatically. You'll see an example of this in Chapter 9 (page 254).

There are many benefits to the style sheet system. First of all, you can reuse the same style sheet for many Web pages. Because getting your formatting right can be a long and tedious chore, this is a major timesaver. Even better, when you're ready for a new look, you don't need to mess with your HTML documents—instead, just tweak the style sheet and every linked page gets an instant facelift.

Tip: Now that you've understood the role of style sheets, you'll understand why this chapter concentrates on *structuring* your text, rather than *formatting* it. There are some formatting features built into HTML, but they aren't as powerful as style sheets, and they're a lot messier. Now that you're thinking with style sheets in mind, you're ready to steer clear of those headaches, and concentrate on becoming comfortable with the staples of the HTML diet—the tags for structuring text.

Basic Text Tags

Some text tags are so important they'll crop up in virtually every HTML document. Many of these tags are used to create *block elements*—chunks of content that are separated (by a line break and a little bit of extra space) on a Web page. Headings and paragraphs are two examples of block elements. When you end a block element, the browser automatically adds a line break and a little extra space before the next bit of content.

For example, consider this fragment of HTML:

```
<h1>Bread and Water</h1>This economical snack is really
all you need to sustain life.
```

This snippet has a title in large, bold letters followed immediately by some ordinary text. You might expect to see both parts (the heading and the ordinary text) appear on the same line. However, the <h1> tag is a block element. When you close it, the browser does a little housecleaning, and adds a line break and some extra space. The text starts on a new line, as you can see in Figure 5-3.

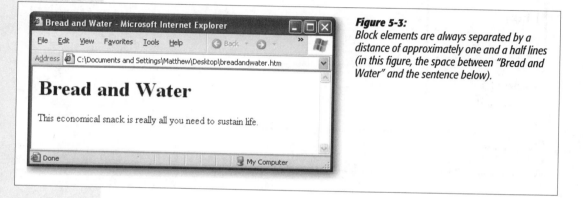

Figure 5-3:
Block elements are always separated by a distance of approximately one and a half lines (in this figure, the space between "Bread and Water" and the sentence below).

Tip: Block elements are nice because they make it easy to format a document. For example, the spaces that exist between block elements helps insure that one section of text doesn't run into another section. However, there's also a clear downside. In some cases, you won't be happy with the automatic spacing between block elements. For example, in dense, information-laden pages, the standard spacing looks far too generous. To tighten up your text and shrink the spaces in between block elements, you need style sheets (see Chapter 6).

Interestingly, the previous example is equivalent to this more explicit HTML:

```
<h1>Bread and Water</h1><p>This economical snack is really
all you need to sustain life.</p>
```

Although it's basically the same, the second version is the one that's technically correct, and it's the approach you'll see in this book. The reason that it's better is because it's clearer that the text after the heading actually occupies a separate paragraph. In the first example, the text after the heading is floating free without any container. The second example makes it clear that the document really contains a heading followed by a paragraph. Conceptually, this makes more sense.

Tip: Remember, sticking to good style has other benefits. For example, it will help you if you decide to upgrade to XHTML someday (see page 47), and it will make it easier for search engines and other computer programs to scan and analyze your pages.

Not all HTML elements are block elements. There are also *inline elements*, which are tags that should be placed inside other block elements. Examples of inline elements include the <img> tag for inserting images and the <br> tag for inserting line breaks. You can insert inline elements in other paragraphs, headings, or lists.

Now that you've learned how block elements work, it's time to take a closer look at your basic toolkit of tags.

Paragraphs

You've already seen the basic <p> paragraph tag. It's a container tag that defines a paragraph of text.

```
<p>It was the best of times, it was the worst of times...</p>
```

As you've no doubt noticed by now in your travels across the Internet, HTML paragraphs don't get indented like they do in print media. That's just the way of the Web, although you can change this with style sheets (page 165). Figure 5-4 shows an example of paragraph tags in action.

These extra paragraph tags don't create any extra line breaks

Figure 5-4:
When you put several paragraphs in a row, each paragraph is separated with a space of about one and a half lines. However, browsers ignore empty paragraph tags completely, and don't add any extra space for them.

You should get into the habit of thinking of the text in your Web pages as a series of paragraphs. In other words, before you type some text, add the <p></p> tags to serve as a container. It's the first level of structure your page gets.

Usually, when you type a long paragraph in an HTML file, you'll split it up over multiple lines so that you can read what you've written without having to scroll from one side of your window to the other. But remember, even if you split your text into separate lines in the HTML file, it doesn't mean the text gets displayed that way in the browser. Browsers treat a line break (like the one you see at the end of this line) as a single space, and they stubbornly ignore multiple spaces that you enter by hitting the Space bar. As a result, when a browser displays a paragraph, it wraps the text to fit the width of the current browser window. If you want to insert a real break between your lines, check out the next section.

Getting More Space

The way that browsers ignore spaces can be exasperating. What if you really do want to add several spaces in a row? The trick is the non-breaking space– –which is a special HTML character entity (see page 46) that forces browsers to insert a space.

When the browser sees this entity, it interprets it as a space that can't be ignored. So if you create a paragraph like this:

```
<p>Hello   Bye</p>
```

You end up with this text:

```
Hello   Bye
```

Most WYSIWYG HTML editors automatically add non-breaking spaces when you press the space key in design view, which is why those spaces don't disappear. But try not to use non-breaking spaces more than you need to. (If you really want indented paragraphs, you'll get a better solution with style sheets, which you'll learn about in Chapter 6.) And never, ever use spaces to try and align columns of text–that always ends badly, with the browser scrambling your attempts. Instead, you'll need to use the layout features described in Chapter 9.

Line Breaks

Sometimes you want to start a new line but not a whole new paragraph. The most common reason is when you want to avoid the extra spacing the browser puts between paragraphs. In this situation, the line break tag <br> comes in handy.

Tip: Remember, if you're following the XHTML standard (page 47), all empty tags need to include a slash character. That means instead of <br>, you write the equivalent code <br />.

Line breaks are exceedingly simple—they simply tell the browser to move to the start of the following line. They aren't container tags or block elements, so you can use them on their own, anywhere (see Figure 5-5).

Line breaks aren't block elements, so they should always be placed inside of a block element, like a paragraph:

```
<p>This paragraph appears<br>
on two lines</p>
```

Don't overuse line breaks. Remember, when you resize the browser window, your text is reformatted to fit. If you try to perfect your paragraphs with line breaks, you'll just end up with pages that look bizarre at different sizes. A good rule of thumb is to avoid line breaks in ordinary paragraphs. Instead, use them the to force breaks in addresses, outlines, poems, and other types of text whose spacing

you want to tightly control. Don't use them for bulleted and numbered lists—
you'll learn about tags for those on page 126.

Figure 5-5:
The <br> line break tag is great for separating addresses. If you want to skip down several lines, you can use a series of <br> tags in a row (but it's a better idea to use empty paragraphs, as described in the box "The Mystery of Empty Paragraphs").

In some cases, you might want to *prevent* a line break. This is a fairly specialized
trick, but it can come in handy if you're afraid of the browser mangling product
names, or other phrases that contain a space, that you want to appear on a single
line. The trick is to use a non-breaking space character (which looks like * *)

instead of just hitting the Space bar. The browser still displays the space in the Web page, but won't wrap the words on either side of it (see Figure 5-6).

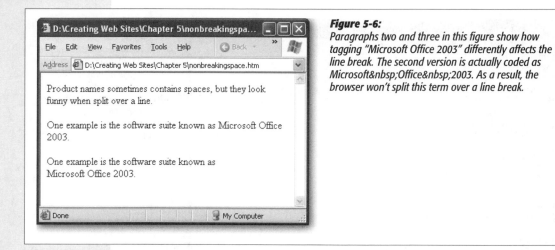

Figure 5-6:
Paragraphs two and three in this figure show how tagging "Microsoft Office 2003" differently affects the line break. The second version is actually coded as Microsoft Office 2003. As a result, the browser won't split this term over a line break.

HOW'D THEY DO THAT?

The Mystery of Empty Paragraphs

In authoring tools like Dreamweaver and FrontPage, every time you press Enter, when you're in design view, a new paragraph is created. This seems a little counterintuitive, as you've seen how empty paragraph tags normally get ignored by the browser (see Figure 5-4).

The trick is that both these programs add what's called a *non-breaking space.* This character is entered using the HTML entity   (see page 46 for an introduction to HTML entities). Unlike regular spaces, a non-breaking space is never ignored by the browser. That means if you put three non-breaking spaces in a row, you wind up with three spaces when you view the page in a browser. (If you use regular spaces, you'll only see one, because extra spaces are summarily dismissed.)

The trick is that you can also put a non-breaking space into a <p> tag. When you do, the paragraph tag becomes an empty paragraph, which is sometimes useful for spacing out your work. Here's an example of a paragraph with the non-breaking space:

```
<p> </p>
```

Incidentally, Dreamweaver and FrontPage do allow you to use more ordinary <br> line break tags instead of empty paragraphs. To do this, press Shift+Enter instead of Enter. Nvu doesn't use the empty paragraph trick, so pressing Enter always inserts a line break.

Headings

Headings are section titles—for example, the word "Headings just above this paragraph. They display in bold lettering, at various sizes. The size of the heading depends on the *heading level.* There are six heading levels, starting at <h1> (the biggest) and dwindling down to <h6> (the smallest). Both <h5> and <h6> are actually smaller than regularly sized text, and aren't used too often. Figure 5-7 shows all the heading levels you can use.

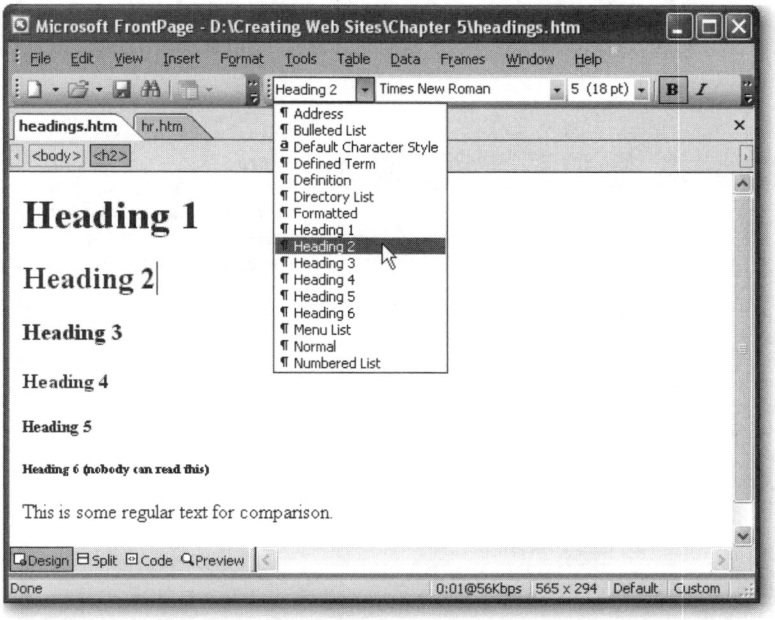

Figure 5-7:
Most HTML editors give you a single-click way to apply headings. In FrontPage and Nvu, you can find a drop-down menu that lets you choose whether the current section of text is a paragraph or one of the various headings. This figure shows a FrontPage example, but in Dreamweaver you can find a similar drop-down menu in the Properties panel.

Headings aren't just useful for formatting—they also delineate the structure of your document. To make sure your document makes sense, it's a good idea to start with the largest headings (level one) and work your way down. For instance, don't jump straight to a level three heading just because you like the way it looks.

Tip: It's probably occurred to you that if everyone uses the same heading levels in the same order, the Web will become as bland as a bagel in a chain supermarket. Don't panic—it's not as bad as it seems. When you add style sheets into the mix (Chapter 6), you'll see that you can completely change the look of any and every heading you use. So for now, stick to using the right levels in the correct order.

Horizontal Lines

Paragraphs and line breaks aren't the only way to separate sections of text. Another neat trick is the <hr> tag, which translates to "horizontal rule." A horizontal rule is a horizontal line that stretches from one side of its container to the other, separating everything above and below it.

Tip: Usually, you'll put a horizontal break in between paragraphs, which means it stretches from one side of the page to the other. However, you can also put a rule in a smaller container, like a table cell, in which case it won't turn out nearly as big.

Rules are block elements, so you can stick them in between paragraphs (see Figure 5-8).

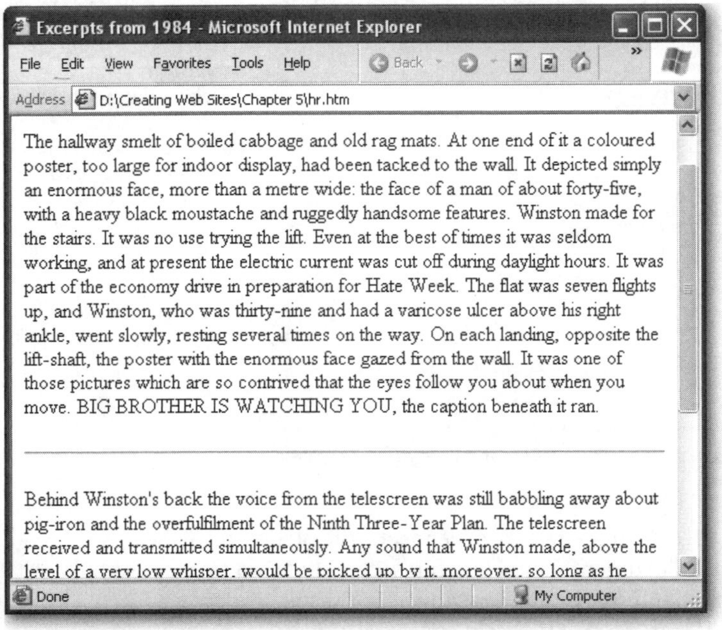

Figure 5-8:
In this example, there are two paragraphs, with an <hr> tag in between, which is the tag that inserts the solid line you see here.

Preformatted

Preformatted text is a unique concept in HTML that breaks the rules you've read about so far. As you've seen, Web browsers ignore multiple spaces and flow your text to fit the width of the page. Although you can change this to a certain extent by using line breaks and non-breaking spaces, some types of documents are still hard to deal with.

For example, imagine you want to display a bit of poetry or a snippet of code from a programming language. Using non-breaking spaces to try and line everything up is time-consuming and difficult to read. The <pre> tag gives you a different option. Inside the <pre> tag, the browser pays close attention to every space and line break you use, and it duplicates that precisely on the Web page it displays. Additionally, the Web browser puts all your text into a monospaced font (typically Courier). Figure 5-9 shows an example.

Tip: In a *monospaced* font, every letter occupies the same amount of space. HTML documents and books like this one use proportional fonts, where letters like W and M are much wider than l and i. Monospaced fonts are useful in preformatted text, because it allows you to line up rows of text exactly. However, it doesn't look as polished.

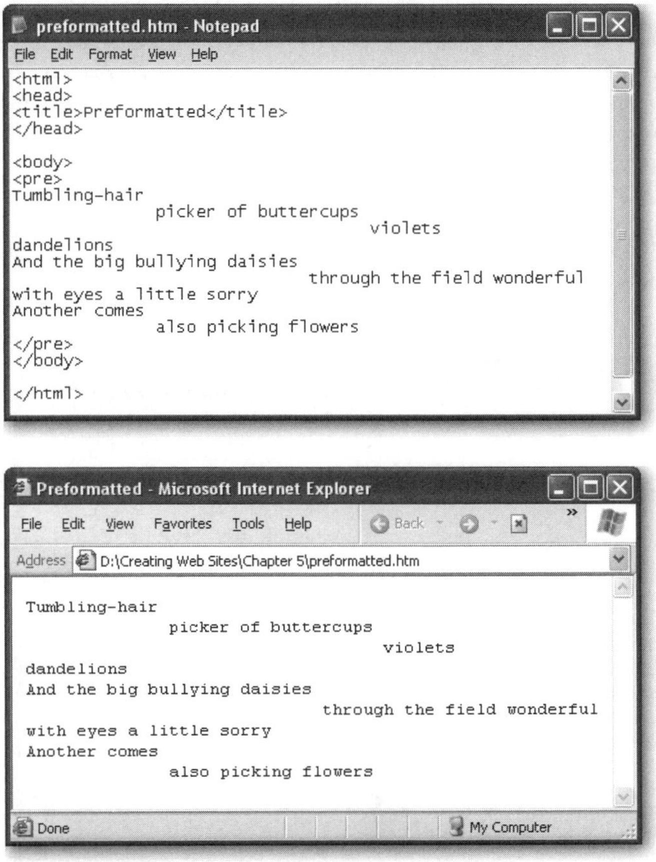

Figure 5-9:
There's no mystery in how this e. e. cummings poem will turn out. Because it's in a <pre> block, you get the exact spacing and line breaks that appear in your HTML file. The <pre> tag also works well for blocks of programming code.

Quotes

It may be a rare Web page that spouts poetry, but the architects of the HTML standard created a block element named <blockquote>, which is designed especially for long quotations. When you use this element, your text is indented on the left and right edges.

Here's an example:

```
<p>Some words of wisdom from "A Tale of Two Cities":</p>

<blockquote>It was the best of times, it was the worst of times, it was the
age of wisdom, it was the age of foolishness, it was the epoch of belief, it
was the epoch of incredulity, it was the season of Light, it was the season
of Darkness, it was the spring of hope, it was the winter of despair, we had
everything before us, we had nothing before us, we were all going direct to
Heaven, we were all going direct the other way—in short, the period was so
far like the present period, that some of its noisiest authorities insisted
on its being received, for good or for evil, in the superlative degree of
comparison only.</blockquote>

<p>It's amazing what you can fit into one sentence.</p>
```

Figure 5-10 shows how this appears in the browser.

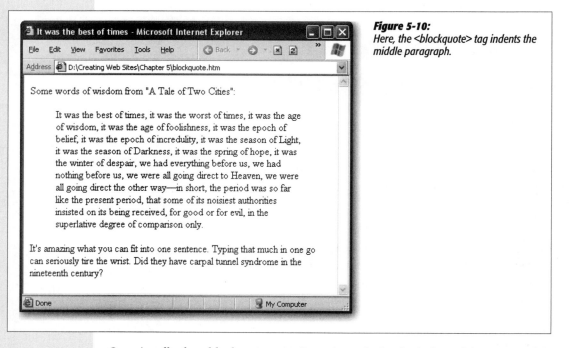

Figure 5-10:
Here, the <blockquote> tag indents the middle paragraph.

Occasionally the <blockquote> tag is used purely for the indented formatting that it gives you. Of course, this compromises the spirit of the tag, and you'd be better off to use style sheets to achieve a similar effect. However, it's a fairly common technique, so it's more or less accepted.

The <blockquote> tag is a block element, which means it always appears separately from other block elements like paragraphs and headings. HTML also defines an element for shorter quotations that are nested inside another block—the <q> element, which stands for quotation:

```
<p>As Charles Dickens once wrote, <q>It was the best of times, it was the
worst of times</q>.</p>
```

Most browsers won't format the <q> element, so you might want to add some italics of your own. You can do this by applying a style sheet rule that formats the <q> element (see Chapter 6).

And if you're dreaming of the semantic Web (page 114), you can add a URL that points to the source of your quote (assuming it's on the Web) using the *cite* attribute:

```
<p>As Charles Dickens once wrote, <q
 cite="http://www.literature.org/authors/dickens-charles/two-cities">It
 was the best of times, it was the worst of times</q>.</p>
```

The information in the *cite* attribute isn't shown in the page, but other applications that analyze your Web page can retrieve this information.

Divisions

The last block element you'll learn about—<div>—is one of the least interesting, at least at first glance. That's because on its own, it doesn't actually do anything. <div> is used to group together one or more block elements. That means you could group together several paragraphs, a paragraph and heading, and so on. Here's an example:

```
<div>
    <h1>...</h1>
    <p>...</p>
    <p>...</p>
</div>
<p>...</p>
```

Given the fact that <div> doesn't do anything, you're probably wondering why it exists. In turns out that the lowly <div> becomes a lot more interesting when it's combined with style sheets (Chapter 6). That's because you can apply formatting directly to a <div> tag. For example, if a <div> tag contains three paragraphs, that means you can format three paragraphs for the price of one.

The <div> tag also has an important relative—the <span> tag. The difference is that <div> groups together block elements. The <span> tag is placed *inside* a block element, around some section of text. Here's an example:

```
<p>In this paragraph, some of the text is wrapped in a span tag.
That <span>gives you the ability</span> to format it in some fancy
way later on.</p>
```

Once again, the <span> tag doesn't accomplish anything on its own. However, with style sheets, you can use it to format just a portion of a paragraph, which is very handy.

HTML Tags for Lists

Once you've mastered paragraphs and headings, it's time to move to HTML's other set of tags for organizing text—the list tags. HTML gives you three types of lists you can create:

- **Ordered lists** give each item in a list a number or a letter (as in 1, 2, 3 or A, B, C). They're handy when sequence is important, like when you're listing off a series of steps that tell your relatives how to drive to your house.

- **Unordered lists** are also known as bulleted lists, because next to each item is a bullet. You can control what the bullet looks like, to some degree. You're reading a bulleted list right now.

- **Definition lists** are handy for displaying terms followed by definitions or descriptions. For example, the dictionary is one huge definition list. In a Web page, the terms are left-aligned, and the definition is indented underneath.

In the following sections you'll learn how to create all three types.

Ordered Lists

In an ordered list, each item is numbered consecutively, starting at some value (usually 1). The neat part about ordered lists in HTML is that you don't need to supply the numbers. Instead, the browser automatically adds one to the left of each list item (sort of like the autonumber feature in Microsoft Word). This is handy for two reasons. First, it allows you to wildly insert and remove list items without screwing up your numbering. Second, the numbers and list items are carefully lined up, which isn't as easy if you're doing it on your own.

To create an ordered list, you use the <ol> tag, which is a block element. (<ol> stands for ordered list.) Then, inside the <ol> tag, you place an <li> tag for each list item you want, in order.

For example, here's an ordered lists with three items:

```
<p>To wake up in the morning:</p>
<ol>
    <li>Rub eyes.</li>
    <li>Assume erect position.</li>
    <li>Turn on light.</li>
</ol>
```

In a browser, you'd see this:

To wake up in the morning:

1. Rub eyes.
2. Assume erect position.
3. Turn on light.

In other words, a space is inserted between the preceding paragraph and the list, as with all block elements. Next, each list item is given a number.

Ordered lists get more interesting when you mix in the *start* and *type* attributes. The start attribute allows you to start the list at a value other than 1. Here's an example that starts the counting at 5:

```
<p>To wake up in the morning:</p>
<ol start="5">
...
</ol>
```

The next numbers will be 5, 6, and 7. Unfortunately, there's no way to count backward (or to automatically continue counting from a previous list elsewhere on the page).

You aren't limited to numbers in your ordered list. The *type* attribute lets you choose the style of numbering. You can use letters and roman numerals, as described in Table 5-1. Figure 5-11 shows a few examples.

Table 5-1. *Types of ordered lists*

type Attribute	Description	Example
1	Numbers	1, 2, 3, 4…
a	Lowercase letters	a, b, c, d…
A	Uppercase letters	A, B, C, D…
i	Lowercase roman numerals	i, ii, iii, iv…
I	Uppercase roman numerals	I, II, III, IV…

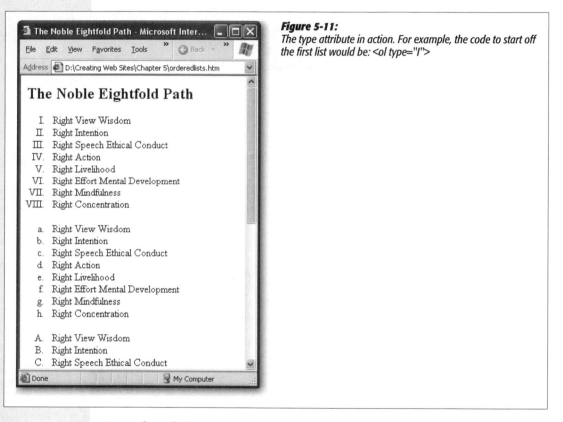

Figure 5-11:
The type attribute in action. For example, the code to start off the first list would be: <ol type="I">

Unordered Lists

Unordered lists are quite similar to ordered lists. The outer tag is <ul>, and each item inside is wrapped in a <li> tag. The browser indents each item in the list, and automatically draws the bullets.

The most interesting frill that comes with unordered lists is the *type* attribute, which lets you change the style of bullet. You can use *disc* (a black dot, which is the default), *circle* (an empty circle), or *square* (an empty square). Figure 5-12 shows the difference.

Tip: Most HTML editors have handy links for quickly creating the different types of lists. In Dreamweaver, look for the "ul" and "ol" icons in the Text toolbar, or select Text → List. In FrontPage, choose Format → Bullets and Numbering to get started.

Figure 5-12:
Three flavors of the same list.

Definition Lists

Definition lists are perfect for creating your own online glossary. Each list item actually has two parts—a term (which isn't indented) and a definition (which is indented underneath the term.

Definition lists use a slightly different tagging system than ordered and unordered lists. First, the whole list is wrapped in a <dl> tag. Inside the <dl> tag (which stands for dictionary list), you place pairs of terms and definitions. The term is wrapped in the <dt> tag (dictionary term), and the definition is placed in a <dd> tag (dictionary definition).

Here's an example:

```
<dl>
<dt>eat</dt>
<dd>To perform successively (and successfully) the functions of mastication,
humectation, and deglutition.</dd>
<dt>eavesdrop</dt>
<dd>Secretly to overhear a catalogue of the crimes and vices of another or
yourself.</dd>
<dt>economy</dt>
<dd>Purchasing the barrel of whiskey that you do not need for the price of
the cow that you cannot afford.</dd>
</dl>
```

In a browser you'd see this:

eat
To perform successively (and successfully) the functions of mastication, humectation, and deglutition.

eavesdrop
Secretly to overhear a catalogue of the crimes and vices of another or yourself.

economy
Purchasing the barrel of whiskey that you do not need for the price of the cow that you cannot afford.

Nesting Lists

Lists work well on their own, but you can also get fancier by placing one complete list inside another. This technique is called *nesting* lists, and it allows you to build multilayered outlines and detailed sequences of instructions.

To nest a list, just declare the new list inside an <li> tag in the previous list. For example, the following daily to-do list has three levels:

```
<ul>
  <li>Monday
    <ol>
      <li>Plan schedule for week</li>
      <li>Complete Project X
        <ul style="square">
      <li>Preliminary Interview</li>
          <li>Wild Hypothesis</li>
          <li>Final Report</li>
      </ul>
      </li>
      <li>Abuse underlings</li>
    </ol>
  </li>
  <li>Tuesday
    <ol>
      <li>Revise schedule</li>
      <li>Procrastinate (time permitting). If necessary, put off
        procrastination until another day.</li>
    </ol>
  </li>
  <li>Wednesday
  ...
</ul>
```

Tip: When using nested lists, it's a good idea to use indents in your HTML document so you can see the different levels at a glance. Otherwise, you'll find it difficult to determine where each list item belongs.

In a nested list, the different list styles really start to become useful for distinguishing each level. Figure 5-13 shows the result of this example.

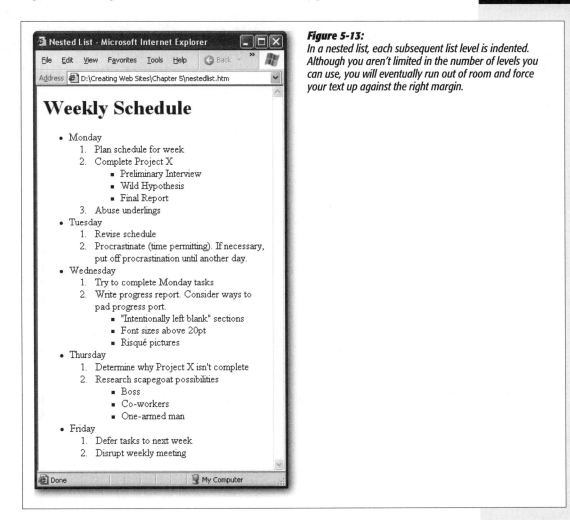

Figure 5-13:
In a nested list, each subsequent list level is indented. Although you aren't limited in the number of levels you can use, you will eventually run out of room and force your text up against the right margin.

Inline Formatting

As you learned earlier in this chapter, it's best not to format HTML too heavily. Instead, to get the maximum control and make it easy to update your Web site's look later on, you should head straight to style sheets (as described in the next chapter). However, there are a few formatting tags in HTML that are so commonly used that you should know them. These are *inline character styles*—tags you can use inside another block element, like a paragraph, heading, or list.

Italics, Bold, and Underline

You've already seen these tags in Chapter 2. They're staples in HTML, allowing you to quickly format snippets of text in a few simple ways. Here's an example that uses all three—<i> for italics, <b> for bold, and <u> for underline:

```
<p>
<b>Stop!</b> The mattress label says <u>do not remove under penalty
of law</u> and you <i>don't</i> want to mess with mattress companies.
</p>
```

It's displayed like this in a browser:

> **Stop!** The mattress label says <u>do not remove under penalty of law</u> and you *don't* want to mess with mattress companies.

Emphasis and Strong

The <em> tag (for emphasized text) is the logical equivalent of the physical tag <i>. In just about every browser these two tags have the same effect—they italicize text. Philosophically, the <em> tag is a better choice, because it's more generic. When you use <em>, you're simply indicating that you want to emphasize a piece of text, but you aren't saying *how* to emphasize it. You can use a style sheet later on to change how emphasized text is displayed. Possibilities include making it a different color, a different font, or a different size.

Tip: Technically, you can use style sheets to redefine the <i> tag in the same way. However, it seems confusing to have the <i> tag do anything except apply italics. After all, that's its name.

The <strong> tag is the logical equivalent of the <b> tag. If you aren't using style sheets, this simply applies bold formatting to a piece of text. Overall, the <i> and <b> tags are more commonly used than <em> and <strong>, but the latter are preferred because they're more flexible.

Here's the previous example rewritten to use the <em> and <strong> tags:

```
<p>
<strong>Stop!</strong> The mattress label says <u>do not remove under penalty
of law</u> and you <em>don't</em> want to mess with mattress companies.
</p>
```

There's no logical equivalent for the <u> underline tag, although you can always use one of the generic tags discussed earlier, like <span> (see page 125).

Subscript, Superscript, and Strikethrough

You can use the <sub> tag for *subscript*—text that's smaller and placed at the bottom of the current line. The <sup> tag is for *superscript*—smaller text at the top of the current line. Finally, wrapping text in a <strike> tag tells the browser to cross it out. Figure 5-14 shows an example.

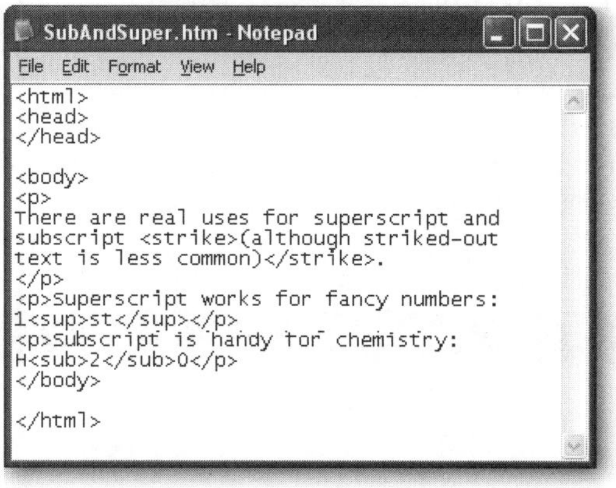

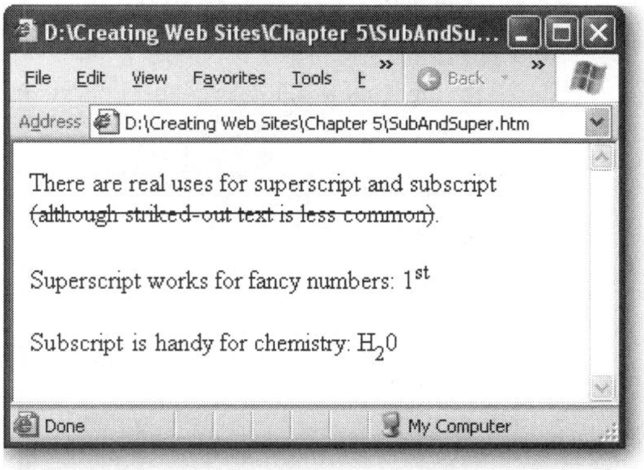

Figure 5-14:
Strikeout text, superscript, and subscript and in action.

Teletype

Text within a <tt> element displays using a fixed-width (monospaced) font, like Courier. Programmers sometimes use it for snippets of code in a paragraph.

```
<p>To solve your problem, use the <tt>Fizzle( )</tt> function.</p>
```

Which renders like this:

To solve your problem, use the Fizzle( ) function.

Teletype text (or typewriter text) looks exactly like the text in a <pre> block (see page 122), but <tt> text is meant to be placed inside another block element. Unlike preformatted text, spaces and line breaks in <tt> text are ignored, as they are in every other HTML tag.

Special Characters

Not all characters are available directly on your keyboard. For example, what if you want to add a copyright symbol (©), a paragraph mark (¶), or an accented e (é)? Good news: they're all supported by HTML, along with about 250 relatives, including mathematical symbols and Icelandic letters. However, to add them, you'll need to use some sleight of hand. The trick is to use *HTML character entities*—special codes that the browser recognizes as requests for unusual characters. Table 5-2 has some common options, with a sprinkling of accent characters. For the complete list, see *http://webmonkey.wired.com/webmonkey/reference/special_characters*.

Table 5-2. *Common Special Characters*

Character	Name of Character	What to Type
©	Copyright	&copy;
®	Registered trademark	&reg;
¢	Cent sign	&cent;
£	Pound sterling	&pound;
¥	Yen sign	&yen;
€	Euro sign	€ (but € is better supported)
°	Degree sign	&deg;
±	Plus or minus	&plusmn;
÷	Division sign	&divide;
×	Multiply sign	&times;
µ	Micro sign	&micro;
¼	Fraction one-fourth	&frac14;
½	Fraction one-half	&frac12;
¾	Fraction three-fourths	&frac34;
¶	Paragraph sign	&para;
§	Section sign	&sect;
«	Left angle quote, guillemot left	&laquo;
»	Right angle quote, guillemot right	&raquo;
¡	Inverted exclamation	&iexcl;
¿	Inverted question mark	&iquest;
æ	Small ae diphthong (ligature)	&aelig;
ç	Small c, cedilla	&ccedil;
è	Small e, grave accent	&egrave;
é	Small e, acute accent	&eacute;
ê	Small e, circumflex accent	&ecirc;
ë	Small e, dieresis or umlaut mark	&euml;
ö	Small o, dieresis or umlaut mark	&ouml;
É	Capital E, acute accent	&Eacute;

Tip: The euro symbol is a relative newcomer to HTML. Although you can use the character entity € you'll have the best support using the numeric code € because it works with older browsers like Internet Explorer 4 and Netscape Navigator 6.

Many HTML editors have features for easily inserting special characters, without forcing you to look up the character entity in a list (see Figure 5-15).

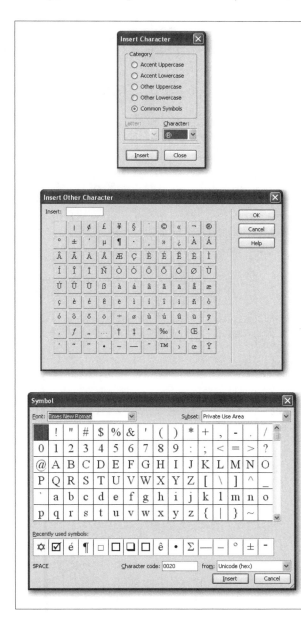

Figure 5-15:
Top: In Nvu, just choose Insert → Characters and Symbols.

Middle: Dreamweaver forces you to do more work and choose Insert → HTML → Special Characters → Other to see a relatively small set of special characters.

Bottom: Choose Insert → Symbol to see FrontPage's more comprehensive list. Note that FrontPage inserts Unicode characters (not just character entities). As a result, if you insert a special character in FrontPage, it might not appear correctly in older operating systems.

CHAPTER 6

Style Sheets

Last chapter, you learned HTML's dirty little secret—it doesn't have much formatting muscle. If you want your Web pages to look sharp, you need to add style sheets into the mix.

Style sheets are separate documents that are filled with formatting rules. The browser reads these rules and uses them to format your Web page. For example, a style sheet rule might say, "make all headings bold and fuchsia and draw a box around each one."

There's several reasons that you place formatting instructions in a style sheet instead of directly in a Web page. The most obvious one is *reuse*. For example, thanks to style sheets, you can create a single rule that you can use with every level three heading in every Web page on your Web site. The second reason is that style sheets help you make tidy, manageable HTML. Because they do all the formatting, your HTML code doesn't need to. All your HTML needs to do is organize the page into logical sections. (For a quick recap of the difference between structuring and formatting a Web page, refer back to page 112.)

The formatting choices in style sheets are much more extensive (and much more overwhelming) than those in HTML alone. Using style sheets, you can control colors, borders, margins, alignment, and (to a limited degree) fonts. You'll use style sheets in this chapter and throughout this book. As you'll see, style sheets give you options that can jazz up the dullest HTML.

Style Sheet Basics

Style sheets are officially known as the *cascading style sheet* (CSS) standard. CSS is a system for defining rules about how one or more Web pages should be formatted. When you use CSS in a Web page, the browser reads both the page's HTML and the style sheet rules. It then uses the style sheet rules to format the page. Figure 6-1 diagrams the process.

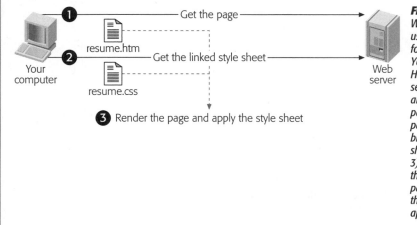

Figure 6-1:
When you surf to a page that uses a style sheet, the following things happen. 1) Your browser requests the HTML page from the Web server. 2) The browser finds an instruction in the HTML page that indicates that the page uses a style sheet. The browser then grabs that style sheet with a separate request. 3) The browser chews through the HTML in the Web page, and uses the rules in the style sheet to adjust its appearance.

This system gives Web weavers the best of both worlds—a rich way to format pages and a way to avoid mucking up your HTML beyond recognition. In an ideal world, the HTML document describes only the structure of a Web page (what's a header, what's a paragraph, what's a list, and so on), and the style sheet explains how to give that Web page a hot new look.

The Three Types of Styles

Before you even get started learning how to write CSS rules, you first have to think about *where* you're going to place those instructions. CSS gives you three different ways to apply style sheets to a Web page:

- An **external style sheet** is a style sheet that's stored in a separate file. This is the most powerful approach, because it completely separates the formatting rules from your HTML pages. It also gives you an easy way to apply the same rules to many pages.

- An **internal style sheet** is a style sheet that's embedded inside an HTML document (it goes right inside the <head> element). You still have the benefit of separating the style information from the HTML, and if you really want, you can copy the embedded style sheet from one page to another (although it gets difficult to keep all of those copies synchronized). Really, the only time you'll use an internal style sheet is if you want to give someone a Web page in a single file—for example, if you're emailing someone a Web page.

- An **inline style** is a method for inserting style sheet language directly inside an HTML tag. You've already learned that it's a bad idea to embed formatting inside a Web page document, because these details are ugly and long. However, you might occasionally use this approach to apply one-time formatting in a hurry. It's not all that clean or structured, but it does work.

UP TO SPEED

The "Other Way" to Format a Web Page

Style sheets aren't the only way to format a Web page—they're just the most capable tool. But you've also got a few formatting options built right into the HTML tags you learned about in Chapter 5. For example, you can change a page's background color or center text without touching a style sheet. For the most part, this book doesn't use these formatting options, for several good reasons:

- **They're patchy and incomplete.** Many features (like paragraph indenting and borders) are completely missing—no HTML tags exist to achieve these effects. Even worse, the model isn't consistent—for example, you might be able to line up text in one type of tag, but not the text that's contained in another type of tag. This makes the model difficult to learn and remember.

- **According to the HTML standard, these formatting options are deprecated.** That means that even though these formatting tweaks are still supported by most browsers, they're considered obsolete by the official rulemakers of the HTML standard—that'd be the good people who work at World Wide Web Consortium (W3C). Many people didn't like these fancy flourishes in the first place, but they were wedged in by over-eager software companies such as Microsoft and Netscape. Newer devices (for example, browsers on tiny mobile phones) are

more likely to ignore these instructions altogether. Even worse, if you use them, your hard-core Web designer friends won't sit with you at restaurants.

- **They don't allow you to easily reuse formatting changes.** So after you format one page, you need to start all over again to fix the next page. And so on, and so on, and so on.

- **They won't work in XHTML.** Right now you might not be concerned about creating XHTML pages (page 47), but by using style sheets, you'll simplify your life if you ever decide to switch your Web site over to this new Web standard.

- **Why learn something you don't need?** Seeing as style sheets offer so much more power and flexibility, and now that style sheets are supported (with certain limitations) on virtually every browser around (old and new), it doesn't make sense to waste time with something you'll outgrow anyway.

CSS does have one strike against it. If you plan to support Paleolithic browsers like Netscape 4, you'll run into quirks with many parts of the CSS standard. In that case, you'd be better off sticking with pure HTML.

These three levels give you the flexibility to either follow the CSS philosophy wholeheartedly (with external style sheets), or to use the occasional compromise (with internal style sheets or inline styles). Because the style sheet language is always the same, even if you use the "lazier" approach, like internal style sheets, you can always cut-and-paste your way to an external style sheet when you're ready to get more structured.

Browser Support for CSS

Before you embrace style sheets, you need to make sure that they work on all the browsers your visitors are using. But determining what browsers support cascading style sheets isn't as easy a question as it should be. The first problem is that there is actually more than one version of the CSS standard—there's both CSS1 and CSS2. This book concentrates exclusively on CSS1, because support for CSS2 is lacking in most browsers. (Internet Explorer is a notable laggard in this department.) But the real problem is that browsers don't necessarily support the entire CSS standard, and when they do, they don't always support it in exactly the same way. The discrepancies range from minor to troubling. As a result, in this book you'll focus on CSS properties that are known to be well supported among all the major browsers. (That said, don't forget to test your pages in a wide variety of browsers to be sure they're appearing correctly.)

As a basic rule of thumb, you can count on good all-around CSS support in Netscape Navigator 6, Internet Explorer 5 for Windows, Internet Explorer 4.5 for Macintosh, Opera 3.6, and any version of Firefox or Safari. In later browser versions, the support just gets stronger.

Many people who've used the Web for a few years still remember an earlier generation of browsers—namely, Netscape 4.x and Internet Explorer 4.x. Both of these browsers are unreliable when it comes to some of the fancier features in CSS. However, you're unlikely to run into these browsers anymore outside of a museum. If you're in doubt, just take a look at some recent browser statistics to see who's online.

Table 6-1 shows the log results—a record of which visitors are using which browsers over a period of several months—at a popular HTML teaching site, W3Schools. Given the fact that W3Schools doesn't cater to power users or computer professionals, this table's a pretty good yardstick for the kinds of browsers your visitors are likely to be using. Every browser in this table supports CSS.

Table 6-1. Current browser usage

2005	IE 6	IE 5	Opera 7/8	Firefox	Mozilla	Opera 8	Netscape 7
July	67.0%	6.7%	0.4%	19.7%	2.6%	0.8%	0.5%
June	65.0%	6.8%	0.5%	20.7%	2.9%	0.7%	0.6%
May	64.8%	6.8%	0.6%	21.0%	3.1%	0.7%	0.7%
April	63.5%	7.9%	1.0%	20.9%	3.1%	0.4%	0.9%
March	63.6%	8.9%	1.6%	18.9%	3.3%	0.3%	1.0%

Tip: For more up-to-date information, surf to *www.w3schools.com/browsers/browsers_stats.asp*.

Of course, statistics can be misleading. Web sites can attract wildly divergent groups of people, and you know your audience best. If you're still concerned about whether a specific CSS feature is supported in a specific browser version, see the sidebar "A Browser Compatibility Reference." Also, look for the Oldest Supported Browsers column in the property tables shown throughout this chapter. For example, if the Oldest Supported Browsers column indicates Internet Explorer 5, you can bet that the property won't work (or works erratically) in Internet Explorer 4.5.

FREQUENTLY ASKED QUESTION

A Browser Compatibility Reference

How can I tell if a CSS feature is supported in a particular browser?

If you're a hard-core Web maven, you may be interested in one of the Web browser compatibility charts for CSS that are on the Web. Two good resources are *www.corecss. com/properties/full-chart.php* and *www.quirksmode.org*. These charts specify which CSS features are supported in different browser versions.

But chart-reader beware: These tables also include many rarely used or new and poorly supported features (such as CSS2 features). For example, you probably don't care that virtually no browser supports the *pitch range* property, which is used in conjunction with text-reading devices. Unfortunately, the CSS charts can cause panic in those who don't know the standards. However, they can be handy if you need to check out support for a potentially risky feature.

The Anatomy of a Rule

Style sheets contain one thing: *rules*. Each rule is a formatting instruction that applies to a part of your Web page. A style sheet can contain a single rule, or it can hold dozens (or even hundreds) of them.

Here's a simple rule that tells the browser to display all <h1> headings in blue:

```
h1 { color: blue }
```

CSS rules don't look like anything you've seen in HTML. But you'll have no trouble with them once you realize all rules are built out of three ingredients: *selectors, properties,* and *values.* Here's the format that every rule follows:

```
selector { property: value }
```

And here's what each part means:

- The *selector* identifies what you want to format. The browser hunts down all the parts of the Web page that match the selector. For now, you'll concentrate on selectors that match every occurrence of a specific tag. But as you'll learn later in this chapter (page 173), you can create more sophisticated selectors that pick out just specific sections of your page.

- The *property* identifies the type of formatting you're applying. Here's where you choose whether you want to change colors, fonts, alignment, or something else.

- The *value* sets the property. This is where you bring it all home. For example, if your property is color, the value could be light blue or dead-salmon pink.

Of course, it's rarely enough to format just one property. Usually, you'll want to change several characteristics at the same time. You can do this with style sheets by creating a selector like this:

```
h1 { text-align: center;
     color: black; }
```

This example changes the color *and* centers the text inside an <h1> tag. That's why selectors use the funny curly braces ({ and })—so you can put as many formatting instructions inside them as you want. Each rule is separated from the next using a semicolon (;). It's up to you whether you want to include a semicolon at the end of the last rule. Although it's not necessary, Webheads often include one so that it's easy to add another formatting property onto the end of the selector when needed.

Tip: As in an HTML file, CSS files let you use spacing and line breaks pretty much wherever you want. However, people usually put each formatting instruction on a separate line (as in the example above) in order to make style sheets easy to read.

Conversely, you might want to create a formatting instruction that affects several different tags. For example, imagine you want to make sure the first three heading levels all use blue formatting. Rather than writing three separate rules, you can create a selector that includes all three tags, separated by commas. Here's an example:

```
h1, h2, h3 { color: blue }
```

Believe it or not, selectors, properties, and values are the essence of CSS. Once you understand these three ingredients, you're on your way to style sheet gurudom.

Here are a few side effects of the style sheet system that you might not have realized yet:

- A single rule can format a whole whack of HTML. With the selectors you're considering right now (called *type selectors*), every part of your page that uses the tag is affected.

- It's up to you how much you format. You can choose to fine-tune every HTML tag in your Web page, or you can write rules that affect only a single tag, using the techniques you'll see at the end of this chapter (page 173).

- You can create two different rules for the same element. For example, you could create a rule that changes the font of every heading level (<h1>, <h2>, <h3>, and so on), and then add another rule that changes the color of just <h1> elements. Just make sure you don't try to set the same property multiple times with conflicting values, or the results will be more difficult to predict.

- Some tags have built-in style rules. For example, text in a <b> tag is always displayed with bold text, and text in an <h1> heading is always displayed in a large font. But you can override any or all of these rules using style rules. For example, you could explicitly set the font size of an <h1> heading so that it appears *smaller* than the following text. Similarly, you can take the underline off of a link.

Don't worry about learning the specific properties and values yet. Later in this chapter, after you see how style sheets work, you'll get acquainted with all the different types of formatting instructions you can use.

Applying a Style Sheet

Now it's time to see style sheets in action. Before you go any further, dig up the *resume.htm* file you worked on in Chapter 2 (it's also available from the "Missing CD" page at *www.missingmanuals.com*). You'll use it to test out a new style sheet. Just follow these steps:

1. **First, create the style sheet. You can do this by creating a new file in any text editor like Notepad or TextEdit.**

   Creating a style sheet is no different than creating an HTML page—it's all text. Many HTML editors have built-in support for authoring style sheets (see the box "Creating Style Sheets with HTML Editors" on page 145 for more information).

Note: Remember, Word is *not* a candidate for Best HTML Editor of the Year. In fact, if you make the mistake of editing an HTML page in Word, you're likely to end up with problems (like invalid characters), so don't do it.

---

2. **Type the following rule into your style sheet:**

   ```
   h1 { color: fuchsia }
   ```

   This rule instructs the browser to display all <h1> tags in bright fuchsia lettering.

3. **Save the style sheet with the name *resume.css*.**

   Like an HTML document, a style sheet can have just about any file name. However, as a matter of convention, style sheets almost always use the extension .css. Make sure you save the style sheet in the same folder as the HTML page.

4. **Next, open the *resume.htm* file.**

   If you don't have the *resume.htm* file handy, you can test this style sheet with any HTML file that has at least one <h1> tag.

5. **In order to use the style sheet with your HTML file, you need to add a link to the HTML file. This link is a special <link> tag, which you must place in the <head> section of the Web page. Here's the revised <head> section with the <link> tag you need to add:**

   ```
   <head>
     <link rel="stylesheet" href="resume.css" type="text/css" >
     <title>Hire Me!</title>
   </head>
   ```

   The link tag includes three directions. The *rel* attribute indicates that the link points to a style sheet. The *type* attribute describes how the document is encoded. You should copy both of these attributes exactly as shown above, as they never change. The *href* attribute is the important bit—it indicates the location of the style sheet. ("href" stands for hypertext reference.) Assuming the style sheet is located in the same folder as the HTML file, all you need to supply is the file name. (If the files were located in different folders you'd need to specify the location of the .css file using a file path notation system that you'll learn about on page 215.)

6. **Save the HTML file, and open it in a browser.**

    Here's what happens. The browser begins processing the HTML document and finds the <link> attribute, which tells the browser to find the associated style sheet and apply all its rules. The browser than reads the first (and only) rule in the style sheet. In order to apply this rule, it starts by analyzing the selector, which targets all <h1> tags. The browser then finds all the <h1> tags, and applies the fuchsia formatting.

The style sheet in this example isn't terribly impressive. In fact, it probably seems like a lot of work to get a simple pink heading. However, once you've got this basic model in place, you can quickly take advantage of it. For example, you could edit the style sheet to change the color. Or, you could add new rules to format other parts of the document. Simply save the new style sheet and refresh the page to see the new rules come into effect.

To see this at work, try changing the style sheet so that it has these rules:

```
body {
  font-family: Verdana,Arial,sans-serif;
  font-size: 83%;
}

h1 {
  border-style: double;
  color: fuchsia;
  text-align: center;
}

h2 {
  color: fuchsia;
  margin-bottom: 0px;
  font-size: 100%;
}

li {
  font-style: italic;
}

p {
  margin-top: 2px;
}
```

These rules change the font style for the entire document (through the <body> tag), tweak the two heading levels, italicize the list items, and shave off some of the spacing between paragraphs. Although you won't recognize all these rules at first glance, the overall model hasn't changed. Figure 6-2 shows the result.

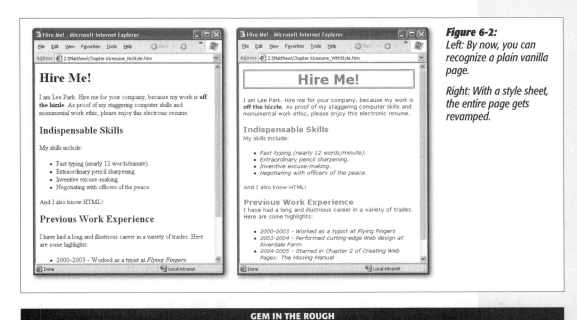

Figure 6-2:
Left: By now, you can recognize a plain vanilla page.

Right: With a style sheet, the entire page gets revamped.

GEM IN THE ROUGH

Creating Style Sheets with HTML Editors

Some HTML editors have handy features for creating style sheets. You won't find this frill in the free Nvu editor, but it does turn up in FrontPage and Dreamweaver.

To create a style sheet in FrontPage, choose File → New to show the "New page" task window on the right. Then, click the "More page templates" link to show the Page Templates dialog box. Choose the Templates tab (which is confusingly called the Style Sheets tab in some older versions of FrontPage). You'll see a list of predefined templates—choose one of these and you'll start off with a pile of color-coordinated rules you can apply to a Web page right away. (And of course, you're free to change or replace the rules as you see fit.)

Dreamweaver goes one better than FrontPage. It also includes a list of prebuilt style sheets—to see it, choose File → New and then select the Templates tab in the New Document dialog box (shown in this illustration). Not only will

you see a list of style sheets, but you'll also see a small preview window that shows you a sample of what the rules in the style sheet look like.

Internal style sheets

The previous example demonstrated an external style sheet. External style sheets are everybody's favorite way to use CSS, because they allow you to link a single lovingly crafted style sheet to as many Web pages as you want. However, sometimes you don't have an entire Web site in mind, and you'd be happy with a solution that's a little less ambitious.

An internal style sheet is a style sheet that's not linked, but instead is *embedded* in the <head> area of a Web page. Yes, it bulks up your Web pages and it forces you to give each Web page a separate style sheet. But occasionally, the convenience of having just one page with its own style rules makes it worthwhile.

To change the earlier example so that it uses an internal style sheet, remove the <link> element and add the style rules in a <style> element inside the <head> section of the Web page, as shown here:

```
<head>
  <style type="text/css">
    h1 { color: fuchsia }
  </style>
</head>
```

To ensure optimum compatibility with really old browsers, there's another trick Web gurus often use—they put the style information in between comment tags:

```
<head>
  <style type="text/css">
<!--
    h1 { color: fuchsia }
-->
  </style>
</head>
```

This way, ancient browsers that have no understanding of style sheets (like Netscape 3), won't inadvertently display the style information in the Web page because it's hidden in the page. (On the other hand, browsers that are CSS-conversant see the instructions just fine.) Of course, you're unlikely to run into this problem these days, but many Web authors still follow this best practice.

Inline styles

If you want to avoid writing a style sheet altogether, there's another approach you can use. Inline styles allow you to insert the property and value portion of a style sheet rule right into an HTML tag. (You don't need the selector because it's obvious that you want to format the current tag.) For example, here's how you format a single heading with an inline style:

```
<h1 style="color: fuchsia">Hire Me!</h1>
```

When you use this approach, it affects only the tag where the style rule is placed. If there are other <h1> headings in the Web page, they aren't affected.

WORD TO THE WISE

Boosting Style Sheet Speed

External style sheets are more efficient in Web sites because of the way that browsers use *caching*. (Caching is a performance-improving technique where browsers store a copy of some downloaded information on the Web surfer's computer, so they don't need to download it again.)

When you link to a style sheet, the browser makes a separate request to get that style sheet file, as shown back in Figure 6-1. However, if you have another Web page that requests the *same* style sheet, the browser is intelligent enough to realize it already has the right style sheet on hand. As a result, it doesn't make the request. Instead, it just

reuses the cached copy of the style sheet, which makes the page load a little bit faster. (Of course, browsers only cache things for so long. If you surf to the same site tomorrow, the browser will re-request the style sheet in case it's changed.)

If you put the style sheet into each Web page, the browser always downloads the full Web page with the duplicate copy of the style sheet. It has no way to realize that you're reusing the same rules. Although this probably won't make a huge difference, in a Web site with lots of pages it could start to add up. Speed is just one more reason Web veterans prefer external style sheets.

Inline styles may seem appealing at first glance, because they're clear and straightforward. You define the formatting information exactly where you want to use it. However, if you try to format a whole Web page this way, you'll realize why Web gurus universally shun them. Quite simply, the average CSS formatting rule is long. If you need to put it inside an HTML page alongside your content, and copy it each time you use the tag, you'll quickly end up with a Web page that's mangled beyond all recognition. For example, consider a more complex heading that needs several style rules:

```
<h1 style="border-style: double; color: fuchsia; text-align: center">Hire
Me!</h1>
```

Even if this occurs only once in the document, it's already becoming a loose and baggy monstrosity. Try to avoid inline styles if you can.

Note: Novice Web designers often get into trouble with inline styles when they use WYSIWYG editors like FrontPage to format their Web pages. Every time you change a formatting detail in FrontPage (like the color, alignment, and so on), it quietly adds a dollop of style information to your HTML. That makes these files quite difficult to edit (and gives FrontPage a bit of a bad reputation). Now that you know better, you'll be able to use a WYSIWIG editor *and* styles to make sure your HTML stays neat and tidy.

The Cascade

By now, you might be wondering what the "cascading" part of "cascading style sheets" means. It refers to the way the browser decides which rules take precedence in case you've got multiple sets of rules.

For example, if you indicate that <h1> headings should have blue letters using an external style sheet, and then apply bold formatting with an inline style, you'll end up with the sum of both changes: a bold blue-letter heading. However, it's not as clear what happens if the rules conflict—for example, if one rule specifies blue text while another mandates red. Which color setting wins?

To determine the answer, you need to consult the following list to find out which rule has highest priority. This list indicates the steps the browser follows when applying styles. The steps toward the bottom are the most powerful: they're performed after the steps at the top, and so they overwrite any earlier formatting.

1. Browser default

2. External style sheet

3. Internal style sheet (inside the <head> tag)

4. Inline style (inside an HTML element)

So, if an external style sheet property conflicts with an internal style sheet, the internal style sheet wins.

Based on this behavior, you might think that you can use this cascading behavior to your advantage by defining general rules in external style sheets, and overriding them with the occasional exception using inline styles. However, there's actually a much better option. Rather than formatting every matching tag, you can specifically format individual tags by using class selectors (see page 173 for details).

Note: The "cascading" in cascading style sheets is a little misleading, because in most cases you won't use more than one type of style sheet (for the simple reason that it can quickly get confusing). Most Web artistes favor external style sheets primarily and exclusively.

Inheritance

Along with the idea of cascading styles, there's another closely related concept—style *inheritance*. In order to understand style inheritance, you need to remember that in HTML documents, one tag can contain other tags. For example, the <ul> (unordered list) tag contains <li> (list item) tags. Similarly, a <p> paragraph tag can contain character formatting tags like <b> and <i>, and the <body> tag contains the whole document.

Thanks to inheritance, when you apply formatting to an element that contains *other* elements, the rule is applied to *everything*. For example, if you set the <body> element to use a specific font (as in the résumé style sheet shown earlier), the font applies to every element inside the <body> element, including all the headings, paragraphs, lists, and so on.

Note: There are some style properties that break the rules (for example, margin settings are never inherited) but most don't. Look for the Can Be Inherited column in each table in this chapter to figure out whether a property will be inherited.

However, there's a trick. Sometimes, formatting rules may overlap. In this case, the most specific rule—that is, the one closest to the tag—wins. For example, settings in an <h1> element override settings in a <body> element for all level 1 headings. Or consider this style sheet:

```
body {
  color: black;
  text-align: center;
}

ul {
  color: fuschia;
  font-style: italic;
}

li {
  color: red;
  font-weight: bold;
}
```

These rules can overlap. In a typical document (see Figure 6-3) a <li> (list item) is placed inside a list tag like <ul>, which in turn exists inside the <body> tag.

Crafty style sheet designers can use this behavior to their advantage. For example, you might apply a font to the <body> element so that everything in your Web page—headings, paragraph text, lists, and so on—has the same font. Then, you can judiciously override this font for a few specific tags by applying more formatting rules.

Although you probably won't see cascading styles in action very often, you'll almost certainly use style inheritance.

Note: Now that you've learned how style sheets work, you're ready to start with the hard part—learning about the dozens of different formatting properties you can change. In this chapter, you won't learn about every property. For example, there are some properties that apply primarily to pictures and tables. You'll learn about these properties in later chapters.

Colors

It isn't difficult to inject some color into a Web page. There are really just two color-related properties that you'll use, and they're listed in Table 6-2.

Table 6-2. *Color Properties*

Property	Description	Common Values	Oldest Supported Browsers	Can Be Inherited
color	The color of the text. This is a handy way to make headings or emphasized text stand out.	A color name, HTML color code, or RGB color value.	IE 3, Netscape 4	Yes
background-color	The color behind the text, for just that tag.	A color name, HTML color code, or RGB color value. You can also use transparent.	IE 4, Netscape 4	No [a]

[a] The background-color isn't inherited (page 148), which means a tag doesn't get the same background color as the tag that contains it. However, there's a trick. If you don't explicitly assign a background color to a tag, its color is transparent. That means the color of the containing tag will still show through, which has the same effect.

The *color* property is easy to understand—it's the color of your text. The *background-color* property is a little more unusual. If you apply a background color to the <body> tag, the whole Web page is affected, as you might expect. However, if you use the background color on an individual element, the results are a bit stranger. In CSS, what's inside of each tag is treated as though it exists in an invisible rectangle.

When you apply the background color to an element, the color applies just to this rectangle.

For example, the following style sheet applies different background colors to the page, headings, paragraphs, and any bold text:

```
body {
  background-color: yellow;
}

h1 {
  color: white;
  background-color: blue;
}
```

```
p {
   background-color: lime;
}

b {
   background-color: white;
}
```

Figure 6-4 shows the result.

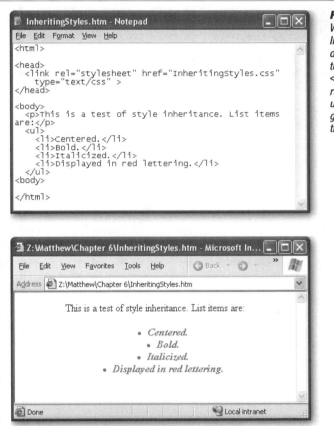

Figure 6-3:
When rules collide, the most specific tag wins. In this example, that means that list items are displayed in red, because the rule for the <li> tag overrides the inherited properties from the <ul> and <body> tags. However, any part of a rule that doesn't conflict with another rule is used. In this example, that means the <li> tag gets italics, bold, and center alignment, all through inheritance.

Specifying a Color

The trick to using colors is finding the appropriate code that indicates the exact shade of electric blue you love. You have several ways to go about this. First of all, you can indicate your color of choice with a plain English name, as you've seen in the examples so far. Unfortunately, this system only works with a small set of 16 color names (aqua, black, blue, fuchsia, gray, green, lime, maroon, navy, olive, purple, red, silver, teal, white, and yellow). Some browsers accept other names, but none are guaranteed to be widely supported, so it's best to use another approach. CSS gives you two more options: hexadecimal (or HTML) color values, and RGB (or red-green-blue) values.

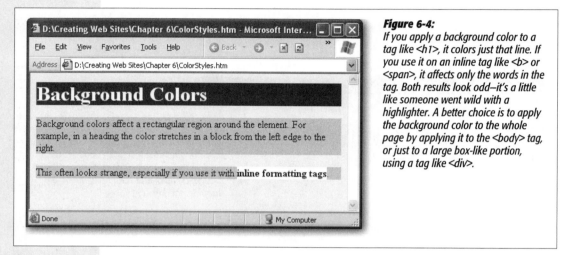

Figure 6-4:
If you apply a background color to a tag like <h1>, it colors just that line. If you use it on an inline tag like <b> or <span>, it affects only the words in the tag. Both results look odd—it's a little like someone went wild with a highlighter. A better choice is to apply the background color to the whole page by applying it to the <body> tag, or just to a large box-like portion, using a tag like <div>.

Hexadecimal color values

With *hexadecimal color values* you use a strange-looking code with a pound sign (#) at the beginning. Technically, hexadecimal colors are made up of three numbers representing the red, green, and blue component of the color (similar to the RGB colors you'll learn about in the next section). However, these colors have been combined in a manner that's perfectly understandable to computers, but utterly baroque to normal people. You'll find hexadecimal color notation kicking around the Web a lot, because it's the original format that was designed for HTML. However, it's about as intuitive as reading the ones and zeroes that power your computer.

Here's an example:

```
body {
   background-color: #E0E0E0
}
```

Even a computer nerd can't tell that this applies a light gray background. (See "Finding the Right Color" for some tips on how to pick out hexadecimal color values, if you're determined to use this system.)

RGB color values

The other approach to specifying color values is to use RGB (or *red-green-blue*) values. According to this more logical approach, you simply specify how much of each color you want to "mix in" to create your final color. Each component takes a number from 0 to 255. For example, a color that's composed of red, green, and blue, each set to 255, appears white; on the other hand, all those values set to 0 generates black.

Here's an example of a nice lime color:

```
body {
  background-color: rgb(177,255,20)
}
```

Web-Safe Colors

Will the colors I pick show up on other computers?

When colors began appearing as the latest fad in Web pages, the computing world was very different. The average computer couldn't handle a really wide variety of colors. Many computers were limited to a relatively small set of 256 colors, and had to deal with other colors by *dithering* (a dubious process that combines little dots of several colors to simulate a different color, leading to an unattractive speckled effect). To avoid dithering, Web designers came up with a standard called *Web-safe colors*, which identifies a set of 216 colors that can be reliably used on any computing platform. Even better, they always look almost exactly the same.

Today, the world is a little different, and you'd be hard pressed to find a computer that can't display at least 65,536 colors (a standard called 16-bit color, or *high color*). Most support a staggering 16.7 million (a standard called 32-bit color, or *true color*). In this environment, it's rarely worth worrying about the Web-safe colors anymore, and the standard is just another piece of computing history.

However, there is one exception. If you plan to create Web pages for very small devices (like cell phones or palmtop computers), which have much leaner hardware, you might change your mind and decide to pare down your Web pages and limit yourself to Web-safe colors only. To check out the list of safe colors, surf to *www.w3schools.com/css/css_colors.asp*.

Even if you aren't concerned about serving this still relatively small audience of tiny devices, it's still a good idea to look at your Web pages on a variety of computers. That's because different monitors don't always display the same colors—some tend to tint colors unexpectedly, and Windows computers tend to produce darker colors than their Macintosh counterparts (even when using the same monitor). Pick colors carefully, because a color combination that looks great on your computer can look nauseating (or worse, be illegible) on someone else's.

Finding the Right Color

Style sheets can handle absolutely any color you can imagine. But how do you find the color code for the perfect shade of sunset orange (or dead salmon) that you need?

Sadly, there's no way this black and white book can show you your choices. But there are a great number of excellent color-picking programs online. You have two options here—you can download a free color-picking program, or you can hunt around on the Web to find an online color-picking program, which is often more convenient.

For example, try *www.webtemplates.com/colors*, where all you need to do is click a picture to preview the color you want (and see its hexadecimal code). Other handy online color pickers include *http://mediagods.com/tools/rgb2hex.htm* and *www.colorschemer.com/online.html* (where you can see groups of colors that match).

Note: The RGB system lets you pick any of 16.7 million colors, which means that none of these Web sites will actually show you every single possible RGB color code (if they do, make sure you don't hit print; even with ten colors per line, you'd wind up with thousands of pages). Instead, most sites limit you to a representative sampling of colors. This works, because many colors are so similar that they're nearly impossible to distinguish by eye.

If you're using an HTML editor like FrontPage, Dreamweaver, or Nvu, life gets a little easier. These programs have built-in color picking tools (see Figure 6-5).

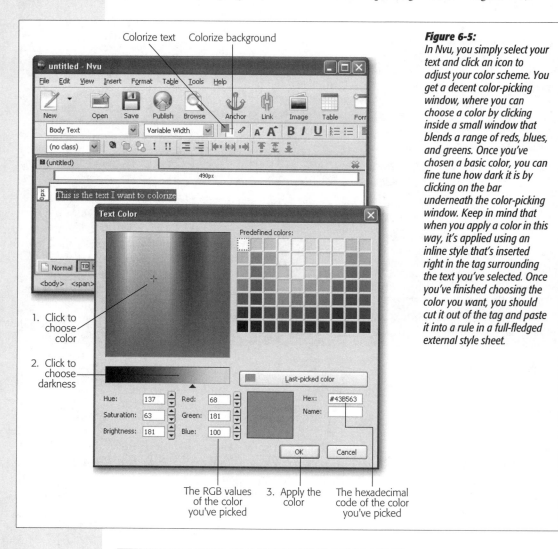

Figure 6-5:
In Nvu, you simply select your text and click an icon to adjust your color scheme. You get a decent color-picking window, where you can choose a color by clicking inside a small window that blends a range of reds, blues, and greens. Once you've chosen a basic color, you can fine tune how dark it is by clicking on the bar underneath the color-picking window. Keep in mind that when you apply a color in this way, it's applied using an inline style that's inserted right in the tag surrounding the text you've selected. Once you've finished choosing the color you want, you should cut it out of the tag and paste it into a rule in a full-fledged external style sheet.

Tip: The RGB color standard is alive and well in many computer programs. For example, if you see a color you love in a professional drawing program, odds are there's a way to get the red, green, and blue values for that color, which you can then use in a style sheet. This gives you a great way to match the text in your Web page with a color in a picture. Now that's a trick that pleases the strictest interior designer!

DESIGN TIME

Making Color Look Good

Nothing beats black on white for creating a crisp, clean, easy-to-read Web page with real presence. Black text and white backgrounds also work best in Web pages that have a lot of colorful pictures. It's no accident that almost every top Web site, from news sites (*www.cnn.com*) to search engines (*www.google.com*) to e-commerce shops (*www.amazon.com*) and auction houses (*www.ebay.com*) all use the winning combination of black on white.

But what if you're just too colorful a person to leave your Web page in plain black and white? The best advice is to follow the golden rule of color: *use restraint*. Unless you're creating a sixties revival site or a Led Zeppelin tribute page, you don't want color to run wild. Here are some ways that you can inject a splash of color without letting it take over your Web page:

- **Go monochrome.** That means use black, white, and one other dark color. For example, Time magazine's Web site (*www.time.com*) uses its familiar bold red color for headlines.

- **Use a lightly shaded background.** Sometimes, a faint wash of color in the background is all you need to perk up a site. For example, a gentle tan or gold

can suggest elegance or sophistication (see the Harvard library at *http://lib.harvard.edu*). Or, light pinks and yellows can get shoppers ready to buy sleepwear and other feminine accoutrements (see Victoria's Secret at *www.victoriassecret.com*).

- **Use color in a box.** Shaded boxes are a frequently used technique to highlight important areas of a Web page (see Wikipedia at *http://en.wikipedia.org*). You'll learn how to create boxes later in this chapter on page 169.

- **Be careful about using white text.** White text on a black or dark blue background can be striking—and strikingly hard to read. The rule of thumb is avoid it, unless you're trying to make your Web site seem futuristic, alternative, or gloomy. (And even if you do fall into one of these categories, you might still get a stronger effect with a white background and a few well-chosen graphics with splashy electric colors.)

Fonts

Using the CSS font properties, you can choose a font family, the font weight (its boldness setting), and font size (see Table 6-3). Be prepared, however, for a bit of Web-style uncertainty; this is one case where life isn't as easy as it seems.

The inescapable problem you face when using CSS font properties is that no two computers have the same set of fonts. A simple way to solve this would be to create Web browsers that could automatically download new fonts they don't have—but this would be a Web nightmare. First, it could swamp the average computer's hard drive with thousands of (potentially low-quality) fonts. Second, it would infuriate the software companies who sell fonts. (Fonts aren't free, and so copying them wantonly from one computer to another isn't kosher.)

Table 6-3. *Font Properties*

Property	Description	Common Values	Oldest Supported Browsers	Can Be Inherited
font-family	A list of font names. The browser scans through the list until it finds a font that's on the browser's PC. If no supported font is found, it uses the standard font it always uses.	A font name (like Verdana, Times, or Arial) or one of the generic family names: serif sans-serif monospace	IE 3, Netscape 4	Yes
font-size	Sets the size of the font.	A specific size, or one of these values: xx-small x-small small medium large x-large xx-large smaller larger	IE 3, Netscape 4	Yes
font-weight	Sets the weight of the font (how bold it appears).	normal bold bolder lighter	IE 4, Netscape 4	Yes
font-style	Lets you apply italic formatting.	normal italic	IE 4, Netscape 4	Yes
font-variant	Lets you apply small caps, which turns lowercase letters into smaller capitals (LIKE THIS).	normal small-caps	IE 4, Netscape 6	Yes
text-decoration	Applies a few miscellaneous text changes, like underlining and strikeout. Technically speaking, these aren't part of the font (they're added in by the browser).	none underline overline line-through	IE 4, Netscape 4	Yes
text-transform	Transforms text so that it's all capitals or all lowercase.	none uppercase lowercase	IE 4, Netscape 4	Yes

There may be practical solutions to these problems, but unfortunately, browser companies and the people who make Web standards have never agreed on any. As a result, any font settings you specify are just recommendations. If a browser doesn't have the font you request, it reverts to the standard font that the browser uses whenever it's on a site that doesn't have special font instructions.

Given that caveat, you're probably wondering why you should bother to configure font choices at all. Well, here's one bit of good news. Instead of requesting a font and blindly hoping that the browser has it, you can create a list of *font preferences*. That way, the browser will try to match your first choice and, if that fails, your second choice, and so on. At the end of this list, you should use one of the few standard fonts that almost all platforms are known to support in some variation. You'll see this technique at work in the next section.

DESIGN TIME

Graphical Text

The only guaranteed cure for font woes is *graphical text*. With graphical text, you don't type your content in an HTML file. Instead, you perfect it in a drawing program, and then save it as a picture. Finally, you display the picture of the text in your page using the <img> tag.

Graphical text is clearly unsuitable for large amounts of text. First of all, it bloats the size of your Web page horribly. It's also much less flexible. For example, graphical text can't adjust itself to fit the width of the browser window or take into account your visitors' browser preference settings. There's also no way for a Web surfer to search through your page hunting for specific words (or for a Web search engine to figure out what's on your Web site).

However, graphical text is commonly used for menus, buttons, and headings, where these issues aren't nearly as important. You'll find this technique used on countless Web sites. For just one example, look at the children's site in this illustration. There's only a little real text here—the distinctive navigation buttons and headings are all graphics.

Often, graphical text isn't as obvious. For example, you may have never noticed that the section headings on your favorite online newspaper are actually images. To figure out if a Web site is using graphical text or the real deal, try to select the text. If you can't, the text is really a picture.

You'll learn how to use graphics (including graphical text) in Chapter 7.

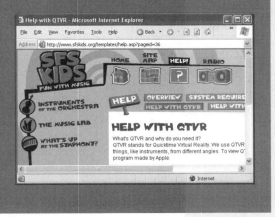

Specifying a Font

To select a font, you use the *font-family* attribute. Here's an example that changes the font for an entire page:

```
body {
  font-family: Arial;
}
```

Arial is a *sans-serif* font that's found on just about every modern computer, including those that run the Windows, Mac, Unix, and Linux operating systems. (See Figure 6-6 for more about the difference between serif and sans-serif.)

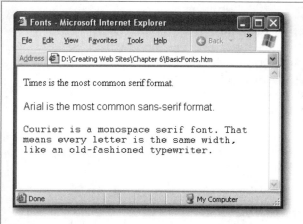

Figure 6-6:
Serif fonts use adornments, or serifs, that make them easier to read in print. This book is written using a serif font. If you look closely at the letter "S," you'll see tiny curlicues in the top-right and bottom-left corners. On the other hand, sans-serif fonts have a spare, streamlined look. Depending on the font, they can seem less bookish, less formal, more modern, and colder.

To be safe, when you specify a font, you should always use a font list that ends with a generic font family name. Every browser supports generic family names, which include serif, sans-serif, and monospace.

Here's the modified rule:

```
body {
   font-family: Arial, sans-serif;
}
```

Tip: If your font has a space in the name, make sure you enclose the whole font name in quotations.

At this point, you might be tempted to get a little creative with this rule by adding support for a less common sans-serif format. Here's an example:

```
body {
   font-family: Eras, Arial, sans-serif;
}
```

If Eras is relatively similar to Arial, this technique might not be a problem. But if it's significantly different, this is a bad idea.

The first problem is that by using on a non-standard font, you're creating a Web page whose appearance may vary dramatically depending on the fonts on the Web surfer's computer. Whenever pages vary, it becomes more difficult to really tweak them to perfection, because you don't know exactly how they'll be displayed. Different fonts take up different amounts of space, and if text grows or shrinks, the layout of other elements (like pictures) changes, too. Besides, is it really that pleasant to read KidzzFunScript or SnoopDawg font for long periods of time?

A more insidious problem occurs if another browser has a font with the same name that looks completely different. Even worse, browsers may access an online database of fonts to try and find a similar font that is installed on the Web surfer's computer. This approach can quickly get ugly. At worst, either of these problems can lead to illegible text.

Note: Most HTML editors won't warn you when you apply a non-standard font. So be on your guard. If your font isn't one of a small set of widely distributed Web fonts (more on which those are in a moment), you shouldn't try to use it.

Finding the Right Font

To make sure your Web page displays correctly, you should use a standard font that's widely available. But just what are these standard fonts? Unfortunately, Web gurus don't completely agree.

But if you want to be really conservative, you won't go wrong with any of these fonts:

- Times
- Arial and Helvetica
- Courier

Of course, all of these fonts are insanely boring. If you want to take on more risk, you can use one of the following fonts, which are found on almost all Windows and Mac computers (but not necessarily on other operating systems like Unix):

- Verdana
- Georgia
- Tahoma
- Comic Sans
- Arial Black
- Impact

To compare these different fonts, see Figure 6-7.

Verdana, Georgia, and Tahoma can all help give your Web pages a more modern look. However, Verdana and Tahoma usually need to be ratcheted down one notch in size (a technique described in the next section).

For good resources that discuss different fonts, what platforms reliably support them, and the pros and cons of each font family (for example, some fonts look nice on screen but generate lousy printouts) see *http://web.mit.edu/jmorzins/www/fonts.html* and *www.upsdell.com/BrowserNews/res_fontsamp.htm*.

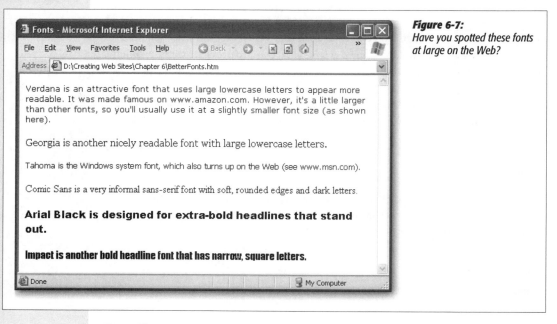

Figure 6-7:
Have you spotted these fonts at large on the Web?

Font Sizes

Once you've sorted out the thorny issue of choosing your font, you may also want to change the size. It's important that you select a text size that's readable and looks good. Resist the urge to shrink or enlarge text to suit your personal preferences. Instead, aim to match the standard text size that you see on other popular Web sites.

Despite what you might expect, you don't have complete control over the font size in your Web pages. Most Web surfers use browsers that let them scale font sizes up or down, either to fit more text on screen or (more commonly) to make text easy to read on a high-resolution monitor. In Internet Explorer and FireFox, you'll find these options in the View → Text Size menu.

The browser's font size settings don't completely override the size you've set in your Web page. Instead, they just tweak it up or down. For example, if you choose to use a large font size (which corresponds to a setting of about 15 points in a word processor) and an Internet Explorer surfer selects View → Text Size → Larger, the text size grows about 20 percent in size (to 18 points).

The fact that your visitors have this kind of control is another reason you shouldn't use particularly small or large font sizes in your Web pages. When they're combined with the browser preferences, a size that's a little on the large size could become gargantuan, and text that's slightly small could turn unreadable. The best defense for these problems is to test out your Web page with different browsers *and* different font size preferences.

As you'll discover in the following sections, you have three choices for setting font sizes.

Tip: Getting the right font size is trickier than you might think, because different browsers will interpret your font sizes differently. If you want to explore Web typography in even more detail, check out the incredibly in-depth information that's available at *http://usabletype.com/css*. It's somewhat technical, but remarkably thorough.

Absolute sizes (keywords and percentages)

The simplest approach for specifying the size of your text is to use one of the size values listed in Table 6-3. For example, to create a really big heading and ridiculously small text, you could use these two rules:

```
body {
  font-size: xx-small;
}
h1 {
  font-size: xx-large;
}
```

These size keywords are often called *absolute sizes*, because they apply an exact size. Exactly what size, you ask? Well, that's where it gets a bit complicated. These details actually aren't set in stone—different browsers are free to interpret them in different ways. The basic rule of thumb is that the font size *medium* corresponds to the standard text size that the browser uses. Every time you go up a size level, you add about 20 percent in size. (For math geeks, that means every time you go down a size you lose about 17 percent.)

A typical standard font size for most computers is 12 points (although text at this size typically appears smaller on Mac computers than on Windows computers). That means *large* text is approximately 15 points, *x-large* text is 18 points, and *xx-large* text is 27 points.

Figure 6-8 shows the basic sizes you can choose from.

There's one serious drawback to using the size keywords—they really aren't absolute. As described above, when you set a font to *medium* you're supposed to get a browser's standard text size. Unfortunately, that's not how Internet Explorer sees it. Instead, IE displays its standard text size when it sees font that's set to *small*. That means if you want to get a little smaller (which is useful for some large fonts, like Verdana), you actually need to choose *x-small*. Unfortunately, other, more standards-aware browsers (like Firefox) don't have this idiosyncrasy. As a result, pages that look perfect on Internet Explorer are likely to look smaller on Firefox when you use size keywords.

The best solution to correct this problem is to use percentage sizes instead of size keywords. For example, if you want to make sure text is normal size, use this rule:

```
body {
  font-size: 100%;
}
```

And if you want to make text smaller, use something like this:

```
body {
  font-family: Verdana,Arial,sans-serif;
  font-size: 83%;
}
```

This sets text to be 83 percent of the standard size. It doesn't matter whether the standard size is considered *small* (Internet Explorer) or *medium* (most other browsers). This particular example creates nicely readable text with the Verdana font.

It's just as easy to upsize text:

```
h1 {
  font-size: 120%;
}
```

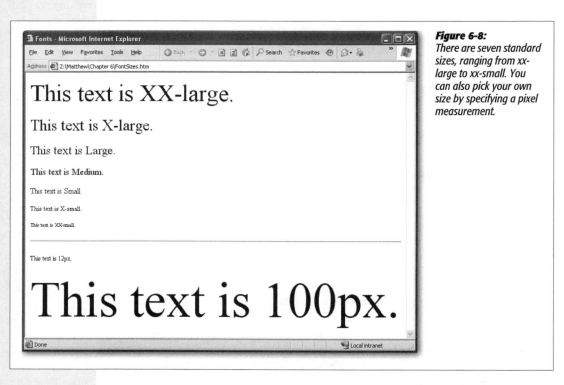

Figure 6-8:
There are seven standard sizes, ranging from xx-large to xx-small. You can also pick your own size by specifying a pixel measurement.

But keep in mind that 100 percent always refers to the standard size of normal *paragraph* text (not the standard size of the element you're styling). So if you create a heading with 120 percent sized text, your heading is going to be only a little bigger than normal paragraph text, which is actually quite a bit smaller than the normal size of an <h1> heading.

Using percentage sizes is the safest, most reliable way to size text. Not only does it provide consistent results across all browsers, it also works in conjunction with the browser size preferences described earlier.

Tip: When you use absolute sizes, you create flexible pages. If the visitor ratchets up the text size using his browser's preferences, all your other fonts are resized proportionately.

Relative sizes

Another approach for setting fonts is to use one of two *relative size* values—larger or smaller. This is a bit confusing, because as you just learned in the last section, absolute sizes are already relative—they're all based on the browser setting for standard text.

The difference is that relative sizes are influenced by the font of the element that contains them. The easiest way to understand how this works is to consider the following style sheet, which has two rules:

```
body {
   font-size: xx-small;
}
b {
   font-size: larger;
}
```

The first rule applies an absolute *xx-small* size to the whole page. The second rule (the relative one) *inherits* the *xx-small* size (see page 146 for a recap about inheritance). However, it then steps the font size up one notch to *x-small*.

Now consider what happens if you edit the body style to use a larger font, like this:

```
body {
   font-size: x-small;
}
```

Now all bold text will be shown one level up from *x-small,* which is *small.*

The only limit of the two relative sizes is that they can step up or down only one level. You can get around this limitation by using font numbers. For example, a size of +2 is a relative size that increments a font two levels. Here's an example:

```
body {
   font-size: x-small;
}
```

```
b {
  font-size: +2;
}
```

Now the bold text is shown in *medium* text, because *medium* is two levels up from *x-small*.

Relative sizes are a little trickier to get used to than absolute sizes. You're most likely to use them if you have a style sheet that has a lot of different sizes. For example, you might use a relative size for bold text if you want to make sure bold text is always a little bit bigger than the text around it. If you were to use an absolute size instead, the bold text would appear large in relation to a small-sized paragraph, but it wouldn't stand out in a large-sized heading.

Exact sizes (pixels)

Most of the time, you should rely on absolute and relative sizing. However, if you really must have more control, you can customize your font size precisely by specifying a *pixel size*. Pixel sizes can range wildly, with 12px and 14px being about normal for body text. To specify a pixel size, use the number immediately followed by the letters *px*, as shown here:

```
body {
  font-size: 11px;
}
h1 {
  font-size: 24px;
}
```

> **Tip:** Don't put a space between the number and the letters px. If you do, your rule may work in Internet Explorer but thoroughly confuse other browsers.

As always, you need to test, refine, and retest to get the right sizes. Some fonts look bigger than others, and require smaller sizes. Other fonts work well at larger sizes, but become less legible as you scale them down in size.

Web purists avoid using exact sizes because they are horribly inflexible on Internet Explorer. For example, if a near-sighted surfer has upped the text size settings in Internet Explorer, it won't have any effect on your page. (For some reason, other browsers don't suffer from this problem—they're able to resize pages even if you use pixel sizes.) As a result, when you use pixel sizes you could inadvertently lock out certain audiences or create pages that are difficult to read or navigate on certain types of browsers. It just goes to show that in the Web world there's a price to be paid for getting complete control over formatting.

Text Alignment and Spacing

CSS includes a great many properties for controlling how text appears on a Web page. If you've ever wondered how to indent paragraphs, space out lines, or center a title, these are the tools you need.

Table 6-4 has the details on all your alignment options.

Table 6-4. *Alignment and Spacing Properties*

Property	Description	Common Values	Oldest Supported Browsers	Can Be Inherited
text-align	Lines the text up on one or both edges of the page.	left right center justify	IE 4, Netscape 4	Yes
text-indent	Indents the first line of text (typically in a paragraph).	A pixel value (indicating the amount to indent) or percentage of the width of the containing tag.	IE 4, Netscape 4	Yes
margin	Sets the spacing that's added around the outside of a block element (page 116). You can also use the similar properties margin-bottom, margin-left, margin-right, and margin-top to change the margin on just one side.	A pixel value or percentage indicating the amount of space to add around the element.	IE 4, Netscape 4	No
padding	Sets the spacing that's added around the inside of a block element. Has the same effect as margin, unless you have an element with a border or background color (see page 151 for more).	A pixel value or percentage indicating the amount of space to add around the element.	IE 4, Netscape 4	No
word-spacing	Sets the space between words.	A pixel value or percentage.	IE 6, Netscape 6	Yes
letter-spacing	Sets the space between letters.	A pixel value or percentage.	IE 6, Netscape 6	Yes

Table 6-4. Alignment and Spacing Properties (continued)

Property	Description	Common Values	Oldest Supported Browsers	Can Be Inherited
line-height	Sets the space between lines.	A pixel value or percentage. You can also use a multiple (i.e., use 2 for double-spacing).	IE 4, Netscape 4	Yes

For example, if you want to create a page that has indented paragraphs (like a novel or newspaper), use this style sheet rule:

```
p {
    text-indent: 20px
}
```

In the following sections, you'll see examples that use the alignment and margin properties.

Alignment

Ordinarily, all text in a Web page is lined up on the left side of the browser window. Using the *text-align* property, you can center text, line it up on the right edge, or justify it. Figure 6-9 shows your options.

The most interesting choice is full justification, which tries to line text up so it lines up on both sides. Full justification, which you get by using the *justify* setting, is common in print (including books like this one). Originally, printers preferred full justification because it helps cram more words into each page (thereby reducing the number of pages and the printing cost). These days, it's a way of life. Many people feel text with full justification looks neater and cleaner than text with a ragged edge, even though tests show plain, unjustified text is easier to read.

Justification doesn't work as well in the Web world as in print. A key problem is the lack of word-splitting rules, which allow long words to be divided in a printed page. The method browsers use to justify text is relatively simplistic. Essentially, the browser adds words one at a time to a line, until no more words can fit, at which point spacing is added between the words to pad it to full length. By comparison, the best page layout systems for print can analyze an entire paragraph as a whole, and find the optimum justification strategy that best satisfies every line. In problematic cases, a skilled typesetter may need to step in and adjust the line breaking manually. Compared to this approach, Web browsers are irredeemably primitive, as you can see in Figure 6-10.

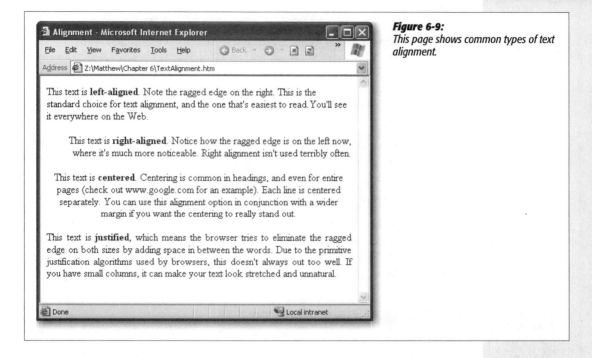

Figure 6-9:
This page shows common types of text alignment.

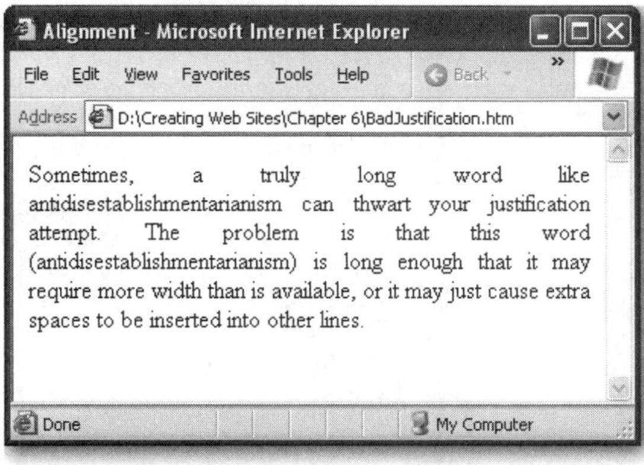

Figure 6-10:
If you decide to use full justification in a Web page, make sure your text lines are fairly long. Otherwise, you'll quickly wind up with gaps and rivers of white space. Few Web sites use justification.

Spacing

To adjust the spacing around any element, you use the *margin* property. For example, here's a rule that adds a fixed spacing of eight pixels to all sides of a paragraph:

```
p {
   margin: 8px;
}
```

Tip: You can supply margins as fixed pixel values (in which case you always get the exact same size) or as percentages (in which case the margin is a percentage of the width or height of the current document window).

This particular rule doesn't have much effect, because eight pixels is the standard margin that Web browsers apply around block elements (on all sides). The eight-pixel margin ensures a basic bit of breathing space. However, if you're looking to create dense pages of information, this space allowance can be a bit too generous. Therefore, many Web site developers look for ways to slim down the margins a little bit.

One common trick is to close the gap between headings and the text that follows them. Here's an example that puts this into action using inline styles:

```
<h2 style="margin-bottom: 0px">This heading has no bottom margin</h2>
<p style="margin-top: 0px">This paragraph has no top margin.</p>
```

You'll notice that this style rule uses the more targeted *margin-top* and *margin-bottom* properties to home in on just one margin. You can also use *margin-left* and *margin-right* to set different margins on all sides. Figure 6-11 compares some different margin choices.

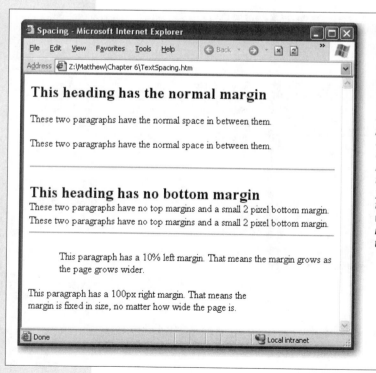

Figure 6-11:
When you want to change the spacing between page elements like headers and paragraphs, you need to consider both the top and bottom tags. For example, if you stack two paragraphs on top of each other, two factors come into play—the bottom margin of the top paragraph, and the top margin of the bottom paragraph. The browser uses the largest of these two values. That means there's no point in shrinking the top margin of the bottom tag unless you also shrink the bottom margin of the top tag. On the other hand, if you want more space, you only need to increase the margin of one of the two tags.

If you're daring, you can even use *negative* margins. Taken to its extreme, this can cause two tags to overlap.

Note: Unlike most other CSS properties, margin settings are never inherited. That means if you change the margins of an element, other elements inside that element aren't affected.

Borders

The last group of style sheet properties that you'll learn about in this chapter let you add borders to your Web pages (Figure 6-12). Borders are a great way to separate pieces of content. The only thing that's better than borders for organizing information are tables, which you'll learn about in Chapter 9.

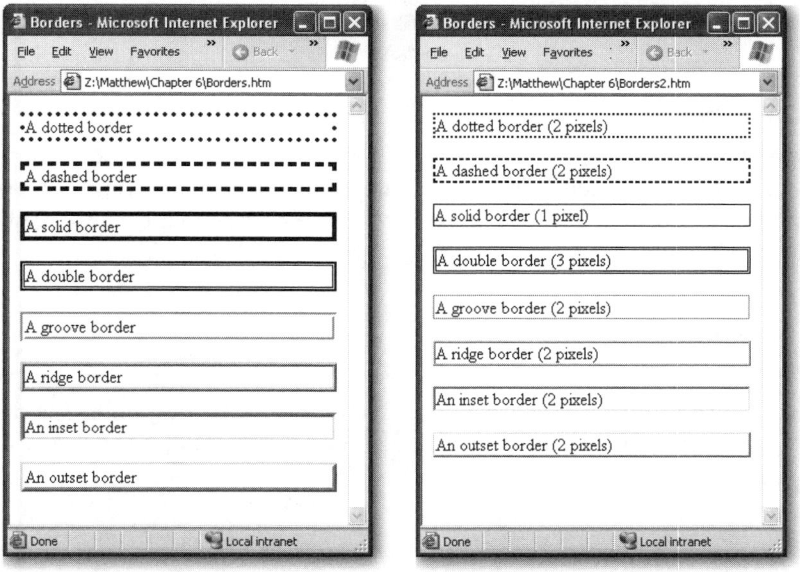

Figure 6-12:
Left: The basic border styles look a bit old-fashioned in today's sleek Web.

Right: Shrink these borders down to one or two pixels, and they blend in much better.

Table 6-5 lists the three key border properties.

Table 6-5. *Border Properties*

Property	Description	Common Values	Oldest Supported Browsers	Can Be Inherited
border-width	The border width sets the thickness of the border line. Usually, you'll want to pare this down.	A pixel width.	IE 4, Netscape 4	No

Table 6-5. *Border Properties (continued)*

Property	Description	Common Values	Oldest Supported Browsers	Can Be Inherited
border-style	Browsers have eight built-in border styles. The border style determines what the border line looks like.	none dotted dashed solid double groove ridge inset outset	IE 4, Netscape 4	No
border-color	The color of the border line.	A color name, hexadecimal color code, or RGB value (see page 152).	IE 4, Netscape 6	No

Basic Borders

The first choice you make when creating a border is the style. Depending on the style you pick, you can add a dashed or dotted line, a groove or a ridge, or just a normal thin hairline (which often looks best). Here's a rule that creates a dashed border:

```
p {
   border-style: dashed;
}
```

To make a border look respectable, you need to reduce the border width. The standard border width is almost always too clunky. You should reduce it to one or two pixels (depending on the style):

```
p {
   border-style: dashed;
   border-width: 2px;
}
```

Tip: You can also use properties like *border-top-style* and *border-left-width* to set different styles, width, and colors for every side of your element. Using many properties at once can occasionally create an unusual effect, but usually you don't need to get this detailed. Instead, check out the border optimization tips in the next section.

Making Better Borders

In Figure 6-12 the actual borders look fine, but they are squashed too close to the text inside the boxes formed by the borderlines, as well as by the edges of the page.

To make a border stand out, consider using the *border* property in conjunction with three other properties:

- **background-color** (page 151) applies a background color to your element. When used in conjunction with a border, it makes your element look like a floating box.

- **margin** (page 165) lets you set the spacing between your border box and the rest of the page. Increase the margin so that your boxes aren't crowded up against the rest of the content in your page or the sides of the browser window.

- **padding** works like the *margin* property, but it sets spacing *inside* your element, between the invisible edges and the actual content. Increase the padding so that there's a good amount of space between the border and your text. Figure 6-13 shows the difference between margin and padding.

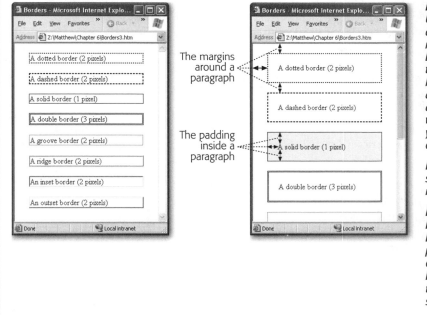

Figure 6-13:
Usually, you can't tell the difference between margins and padding, because you can't see the edges of the element. For example, a <p> tag displays a paragraph in an invisible box, but you won't see its sides. When you add a border, this changes.

Left: These boxes have some extra margin, but no more padding.

Right: The result is much better when you increase both the margin and padding. For added effect, throw in a light background color (like the solid border box shown here).

Here's an example of a paragraph that looks like a shaded box:

```
p {
    background-color: #FDF5E6;
    margin: 20px;
    padding: 20px;
    border-style: solid;
    border-width: 1px;
}
```

Figure 6-13 shows how the *margin, padding,* and *background-color* properties change an ordinary paragraph into a shaded box.

Using Borders to Separate Sections

In Chapter 5 (page 121), you learned about the unremarkable <hr> tag, which gives you a quick and easy way to separate one section of text from another with a horizontal line. With style sheets, you get several more ways to create attractive separators.

The first line of attack is to style the <hr> tag itself. You can use the *width* property to shrink the separator down. You supply length in terms of the percentage of a line's full length. For example, here's a half-length line that's centered on the page:

```
hr {
   width: 50%;
}
```

You can also thicken the line by using the *height* property and supplying a thickness in pixels. Here's a thick line:

```
hr {
   height: 5px;
}
```

For a variety of more interesting effects, you can bring borders into the mix. For example, here's a rule that heightens the horizontal line, applies the *double border* style, and adopts a modern light gray color:

```
hr {
  height: 3px;
  border-top-width: 3px;
  border-top-style: double;
  border-top-color: #D8D8D8;
}
```

This gives you a quick way to revitalize all your separators. However, if you aren't already using the <hr> tag, you don't need to start now. Another option is to bind the horizontal line to another tag, like a heading. For example, the following <h1> tag adds a grooved line at the top. The *margin* property sets the space between the line and previous tag, while the padding sets the space between the line and the heading text.

```
h1 {
  margin-top: 30px;
  margin-bottom: 20px;
  padding-top: 10px;
  border-top-width: 2px;
```

```
    border-top-style: groove;
  }
```

Figure 6-14 shows both these examples.

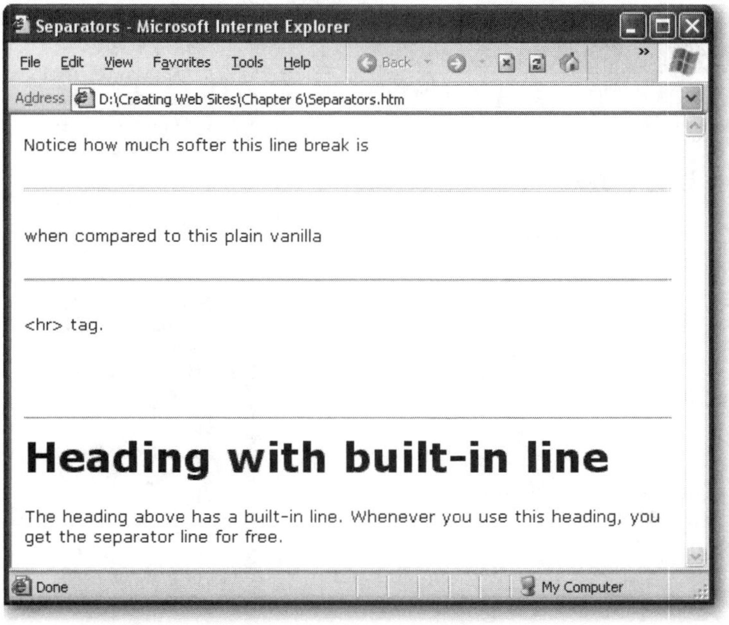

Figure 6-14:
This document includes (from top to bottom), a customized <hr> line, a normal <hr> separator, and a <h1> heading with a top border.

Class Selectors

So far, you've seen how to apply formatting rules on a tag-by-tag basis. These selectors are called *type selectors*. They apply formatting by matching every occurrence of an HTML tag. The only exception is inline styles (page 139), which act only on the tag where they're placed.

Type selectors are powerful, but not that flexible. Sometimes you need a little more flexibility to modify whole sections or small portions of an HTML document. Fortunately, style sheets have the perfect solution with *class selectors*.

Class selectors are one of the most practical style sheet tricks around. They allow you to separate your rules from your tags, and use them wherever you please. The basic idea is that you separate your Web page content into conceptual groups, or *classes*. Once you've taken this step, you can apply different formatting to each class. The trick is, you choose where you want to use each class in your Web page. For example, you might have two identical <h1> headings, but give them separate classes so the formatting is different for each heading.

For a more detailed example, consider the page shown in Figure 6-15. In the following sections, you'll work with this example to apply class-based style rules.

Creating Class Rules

To use classes, begin by mentally dividing your page into different kinds of content. In this case, it makes sense to create a specialized class for book reviews, and the author byline.

Figure 6-15:
In the average HTML document, you have a sea of similar tags—even a complex page often boils down to just headings and paragraph tags. This page has a general introduction followed by a series of book reviews. The general introduction, the author credits, and the book summaries are all marked up with <p> tags, but they shouldn't be formatted in the same way, because they represent different types of content. Instead, a better system would be one in which each different type of content (title, author, or description) gets formatted in a different way.

To create a class-specific rule, you use a two part name, like this:

```
p.review {
  ...
}
```

The first part of the name indicates the tag that the rule applies to—in this case, the paragraph tag. The second part (the part after the period) is the class name. You can choose whatever class name you want, as long as you stick to letters, digits, and dashes, and make sure the first character is always a letter.

The point of the class name is to provide a succinct description of the type of content you want to format. In this example, the class name is review, because it's going to be applied to all the paragraphs that contain the actual reviews.

So how does the browser know when to apply a rule that uses a class selector? It turns out that class rules are never applied automatically. Instead, it's up to you to add the class name to the appropriate tags using the class attribute in your HTML file. Here's an example that links a paragraph to the review class:

```
<p class="review">The actual review would go right here.</p>
```

As long as the class name in the tag matches the class name in the style sheet, the browser applies the formatting.

Note: Class rules work *in addition* to any other rules. For example, if you create a rule for the <p> tag, that rule applies to all paragraphs, including those that are part of a specialized class. However, if the class rule conflicts with any other rules, the class rule wins.

Here's the complete style sheet you might use to format the book review page:

```
/* Set the font for the whole page. */
body {
  font-family: Georgia,serif;
}

/* Set some standard margins for paragraphs. */
p
{
  margin-top: 2px;
  margin-bottom: 6px;
}

/* Format the heading with a background color. */
h1 {
  background-color: #FDF5E6;
  padding: 20px;
  text-align: center;
}

/* Make the bylines small and italicized. */
p.byline {
  font-size: 65%;
  font-style: italic;
  border-bottom-style: outset;
  border-bottom-width: 1px;
  margin-bottom: 5px;
```

```
    margin-top: 0px;
  }

  /* Make book reviews a little smaller, and justified. */
  p.review {
    font-size: 83%;
    text-align: justify;
  }

  /* Make the review headings blue. */
  h2.review {
    font-size: 100%;
    color: blue;
    margin-bottom: 0px;
  }
```

This style sheet includes three type selector rules. The first formats the <body> tag, thereby applying the same font to the whole Web page. The second gives every <p> tag the same margins, and the third changes the alignment and background color of <h1> headings. Next, two new paragraph classes are defined—one for the byline, and one for the review body. Lastly, a class is created for the review headings.

This example also introduces another feature—CSS comments. CSS comments don't look like HTML comments. They always start with the characters /* and end with the characters */. Comments allow you to document what each class represents. Without them, it's all too easy to forget what each style rule does in a complicated style sheet.

And here's how the page applies the classes in the style sheet. (To save space, most of the text is left out, but the essential structure is still here.)

```
<html>

<head>
<link rel="stylesheet" href="PessimistReviews1.css"
   type="text/css" >
  <title>The Pessimist</title>
</head>

<body>

  <h1>The Pessimist's Review Site</h1>
  <p>...</p>
  <p>...</p>
  <br>
```

```
<h2 class="review">How To Lose Friends and Fail in Life</h2>
<p class="byline">Chris Chu</p>
<p class="review">...</p>
<h2 class="review">Europe 2005: Great Places to Miss</h2>
<p class="byline">Antonio Cervantes</p>
<p class="review">...</p>

</body>
</html>
```

Figure 6-16 shows the result.

Figure 6-16:
Class rules allow you to format different parts of a document differently, even if they use the same tag (like the ever-common <p> tag).

Tip: Creating style sheets is an art and takes a fair bit of practice. To make the best use of them, you need to become comfortable with class rules. Not only do class rules give you complete flexibility, they also help you think in a more logical, structured way about your Web site.

Saving Work with the <div> Tag

It can get tedious to apply the class attribute to every tag in your Web page. Fortunately, there's a great shortcut, courtesy of the <div> tag.

You may remember the <div> tag from the last chapter (page 125). It lets you group together arbitrary sections of your Web page. You can put as many elements in the <div> tag as you want, including headings, paragraphs, lists, and more.

Thanks to style sheet inheritance, if you apply a class name to the <div> tag, it's automatically applied to all the nested elements. That means you can change this:

```
<p class="review">...</p>
<p class="review">...</p>
<p class="review">...</p>
```

into this:

```
<div class="review">
  <p>...</p>
  <p>...</p>
  <p>...</p>
</div>
```

This works because of style sheet inheritance (page 148). Essentially, when you format the <div> tag, all the <p> tags inside of it inherit the settings. And although there are some settings that can't be inherited in this way (like margin and padding), most can. Figure 6-17 shows this example.

The <div> tag is a great way to save loads of time. Web gurus use it all the time.

More Generic Class Rules

You can also create a rule that has a class name but doesn't specify a tag name. All you need to do is leave the first part of the selector (the portion before the period) blank. Here's an example:

```
.emphasize {
  color: red;
  font-weight: bolder;
}
```

The great thing about a rule like this is that you can use it with *any* tag, as long as you use the right class name. In other words, you can use it to format paragraphs, headings, lists, and more with bold, red lettering. The class name reflects this more general-purpose use. Instead of indicating the type of content, it indicates the type of formatting.

Figure 6-17:
In this example, each review is wrapped in a <div> tag. The <div> tag applies a background color and some borders, separating the reviews from the rest of the page. Techniques like these can help organize dense pages with lots of information.

Most Web designers use both tag-specific class rules, and more generic class rules. Although you could stick exclusively with generic rules, if you know that a certain set of formatting options will only be used with a specific tag, it's good to clearly indicate this fact with a tag-specific rule. That way, you won't forget the purpose of your rule when you edit your Web site later on.

Creating a Style Sheet for Your Entire Web Site

Class rules aren't just useful for separating different types of content. They also come in handy if you want to define the rules for your entire Web site in a single style sheet.

In a typical Web site, you'll have pages or groups of pages that need to be formatted differently. For example, you might have several pages that make up an online photo gallery, another group of pages chronicling your trip to Guadeloupe, and a separate page with your résumé. Rather than create three style sheets, you can create a single style sheet that handles everything. The trick is to use different class names for each section. In other words, you'll create a résumé class, a trip diary class, and a photo gallery class. Here's a basic outline of this approach:

```
/* Used for the resume pages. */
p.resume { ... }
h1.resume { ... }
h2.resume { ... }
...
/* Used for the trip diary pages. */
p.trip { ... }
h1.trip { ... }
h2.trip { ... }
...
/* Used for the online photo gallery. */
p.gallery { ... }
h1.gallery { ... }
h2.gallery { ... }
...
```

Obviously, each page will use only a few of these rules. However, it's often easier to maintain your site when you keep your styles together in one place.

Adding Graphics

It's safe to say that the creators of the Internet never imagined the way it looks today—thick with pictures, ads, and animated graphics. They expected a meeting place for leading academic minds; we ended up with something closer to a Sri Lankan bazaar. No one's complaining, but the Web would be an awfully drab place without its graphics.

In this chapter, you'll learn to master the art of images. You'll learn how to add images to ordinary Web pages and position them perfectly. You'll also consider what it takes to prepare a picture for the Web—or just find a good candidate online.

Understanding Images

In order to understand how images work on the Web, you need to know two things:

- Images aren't stored in your HTML files. Instead, you store each image in a separate file.

- In order to show a picture in your page, you use the <img> tag in your HTML file.

You'll use images throughout your site, even in spots where you might think ordinary text would work just fine (see Figure 7-1).

Tip: If you just can't tell if a piece of content on a page is a graphic or not, try right-clicking it. If it is, browsers like Internet Explorer and Firefox will give you a Save Picture option in a drop-down menu.

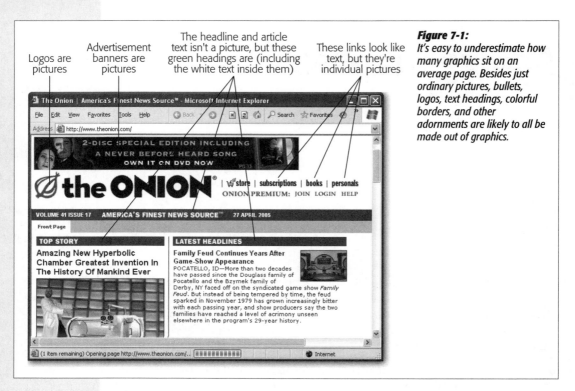

Logos are
pictures

Advertisement
banners are
pictures

The headline and article
text isn't a picture, but these
green headings are (including
the white text inside them)

These links look like
text, but they're
individual pictures

Figure 7-1:
*It's easy to underestimate how
many graphics sit on an
average page. Besides just
ordinary pictures, bullets,
logos, text headings, colorful
borders, and other
adornments are likely to all be
made out of graphics.*

The <img> Tag

Pictures appear on your page courtesy of the <img> tag, which points to the picture you want to show. For example, here's an <img> tag that shows the file named *photo01.jpg*:

```
<img src="photo01.jpg">
```

Note: XHTML fans (see page 47) add a slash character before the closing angle bracket, which indicates that <img> is a standalone tag:

```
<img src="photo01.jpg" />
```

Pictures are inline elements (page 116), which means you put them inside other block elements like paragraphs:

```
<p><img src="photo01.jpg"></p>
```

When the browser reads this <img> tag, it sends out a new request for the *photo01.jpg* file. Once the browser retrieves the file, it inserts it into the Web page wherever the <img> tag is located. If the image file is large or the Internet connection is slow, you might notice this two-stage process, because the rest of the Web page (for example, the text) may appear before the image.

Note: Often, you'll want to organize your site's many files by placing your images in a separate sub-folder inside the main folder that holds your Web pages. You'll learn how to do this in Chapter 8 (page 215).

Although it may seem surprising, the <img> tag is the only piece of HTML you need to show pictures. However, in order to get the result you want, you'll need to understand a few more issues, such as how to modify the size of your images, the many graphical file formats out there in Web-land, and how to align your images.

The alt Attribute

Technically, all <img> tags should have two attributes. You've already seen the *src* attribute (for source), which points to the image file. The other attribute is *alt*, which represents alternate text that should be displayed if the image can't be displayed. Here's an example:

```
<img src="photo01.jpg"
 alt="There's no picture, so all you get is this alternate text.">
```

The alternate text provides a short bit of text that's used instead of the graphic, when necessary. Here are some scenarios when the alt is used:

- The Web browser that requests the page doesn't support images. (This is understandably rare these days.)

- The Web surfer has switched off pictures to save time. (This isn't terribly common today, either.)

- The Web browser tries to request the picture, but can't find it. (Perhaps you forgot to copy it to the Web server?)

- The Web surfer is viewing-impaired and is using a *screen-reading* program (a program that "speaks" text on a Web page).

- A search engine (like Google) is analyzing your Web page, and is trying to determine the content of a picture so it can index it in a search catalog.

The last two reasons are the most important. Web gurus always use the alt attribute to help ensure their Web pages are accessible to screen readers and search engines. In XHTML, the alt attribute is a requirement.

These days, many Web browsers have resorted to using the alternate text for a completely different purpose—as a pop-up message that appears when you move the mouse over the picture (see Figure 7-2). This behavior is a little controversial, because it makes it difficult to use the alternate text the way it was designed (as replacement text for missing graphics).

If you want a bit of pop-up text like the one shown in Figure 7-2, there's a better solution. You should use the *title* attribute, which is designed exclusively for this purpose. Here's an example:

```
<img src="bullhero.jpg" alt="A flying bull-headed superhero."
title="I'm scarier than I look." >
```

If you specify the title attribute, it's always used for pop-up text. However, browsers differ in their behavior if you *don't* specify the title attribute. Internet Explorer uses the alt text instead. Firefox uses the correct approach, and doesn't show any pop-up text at all.

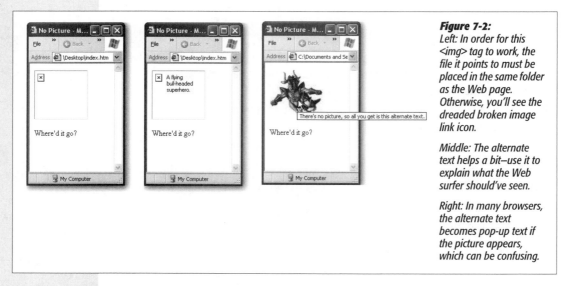

Figure 7-2:
*Left: In order for this
<img> tag to work, the
file it points to must be
placed in the same folder
as the Web page.
Otherwise, you'll see the
dreaded broken image
link icon.*

*Middle: The alternate
text helps a bit—use it to
explain what the Web
surfer should've seen.*

*Right: In many browsers,
the alternate text
becomes pop-up text if
the picture appears,
which can be confusing.*

Picture Size

When you start thinking about the size of your images, it's important to remember that the word *size* has two possible meanings: the dimensions of the picture (how big it appears in the browser, or the *picture dimensions*), and the actual size of the file (the number of bytes it takes to store it, or the *file size*). To Web page creators, both of these factors are very important.

The file size is important because it determines how long it takes to send the picture over the Internet to the browser. Large pictures can slow down a Web site significantly, especially if you're using multiple pictures in a page and the Web surfer is struggling with a slow Internet connection. If you're not careful, impatient surfers might just give up and surf somewhere else if the page is taking too long to appear. To understand file size and how you can control it, you need to understand the different file formats Web browsers use, a topic discussed in the next section.

The picture dimensions are important because they determine how much screen real estate an image occupies. The dimensions of Web graphics are always measured in pixels. Each pixel is one tiny dot on a screen (see the discussion on page

110). Fixed units like inches and centimeters aren't useful in the Web world, because you never know how large a monitor your visitor's using, and how many pixels it can cram in. Page 112 has a detailed discussion about screen size and how to design your pages to satisfy the largest number of potential viewers.

Interestingly, the <img> tag gives you the ability to resize a picture with its optional height and width attributes. For example, consider this tag:

```
<img src="photo01.jpg" width="100" height="150">
```

In this line of code, the picture is given a width of 100 pixels and a height of 150 pixels. If this doesn't match the real dimensions of the source picture, the picture is stretched and otherwise mangled to fit (see Figure 7-3).

Figure 7-3:
You should never use the height and width attributes to resize a picture, because the results are almost always unsatisfying. Enlarged pictures are jagged, shrunken pictures are blurry, and if you change the ratio of height to width (as with the top-right and bottom images shown here), the picture can get squashed out of its normal proportions.

Note: Approach the height and width attributes with extreme caution. Sometimes, novice Web authors use them to make *thumbnails*, which are small versions of large pictures. The problem is that if you use the height and width attributes to scale down a large picture, the browser still needs to download the original file, which is still just as big, byte-wise. On the other hand, if you create your thumbnails in a graphics program like Photoshop Elements, you can save them with smaller file sizes, ensuring that your pages download much speedier.

Many Web page designers leave out the height and width attributes when they're adding images. However, experienced Web mavens sometimes add height and width attributes using the *same* dimensions as the actual picture. As odd as this sounds, there are a couple of reasons to use this technique.

First, when you include these sizing attributes, the browser can quickly tell how large the picture is and it can start laying out the page. On the other hand, if you don't include the height and width attributes, the browser won't know the dimensions of the picture until it's fully downloaded, at which point it will rearrange the page. This rearrangement is potentially distracting if your Web visitor has a slow connection, and has already started reading the page.

The second reason is because these attributes control how big the picture box is if the image can't be downloaded. (See for instance Figure 7-2.) If you don't use these attributes, the picture box is reduced until it's just big enough to show the error icon and any alternate text. In a complex Web page, this might mess up the alignment of other parts of your page.

So should you use the height and width attributes? It's up to you, but they're probably more trouble than they're worth for the average Web site. If you use them, you'll need to make sure you update them if you change the size of your picture, which quickly gets tedious.

Note: Many HTML editors, like FrontPage, automatically add the height and width attributes when you insert a picture.

File Formats for Graphics

Browsers can't display every type of image. In fact, browsers are limited to a relatively few image formats, including:

- **GIF** (pronounced "jif") format is suitable for graphics with a very small number of colors (like simple logos or clip art). It gives terrible results when used to display photos.

- **JPEG** (pronounced "jay-peg") format is suitable for photos that can tolerate some loss of quality. (As you'll learn more about in a moment, JPEG format shrinks down, or compresses, an image's file size so that it will download more quickly.) JPEG doesn't work well if your picture contains text or line art.

- **PNG** (pronounced "ping") format is suitable for all kinds of images, but it isn't supported on old browsers, and doesn't always compress as well as JPEG.

All of these formats are known as bitmap or *raster* graphics, because they represent pictures as a grid of dots. *Vector* graphics, which represent pictures with mathematically outlined shapes, aren't supported in Web pages.

Raster graphics generally have much larger file sizes than vector graphics. For that reason, Web designers spend a lot of their time worrying about *compression*—or how they can take a picture and reduce the amount of disk space it needs. Web page graphics use two types of compression: *lossy*, which compresses the most effectively but reduces image quality; and *lossless*, which preserves the same image quality but doesn't compress as much. For the full details, see the sidebar "How Compression Works in JPEG, GIF, and PNG files." Table 7-1 gives you a quick overview of the different image formats.

Table 7-1. *Image File Formats for the Web*

Format	Type of Compression	Color Support	Best Suited For:
GIF	Lossless	8-bit color (256 colors)	Logos and graphical text
JPEG	Lossy	24-bit (16.7 million colors)	Photos
PNG-8	Lossless	8-bit color (256 colors)	Rarely used, since it's similar to GIF but with less browser support
PNG-24	Lossless	24-bit (16.7 million colors)	Images that would normally be GIF files, but need more colors

Note: Some browsers give you a few more options, but you're better off steering away from them so that you can ensure a wide range of browsers can display your pages. For example, Internet Explorer supports bitmaps (image files that end with the .bmp file name extension). Don't ever use them—not only will they confuse other browsers, they're also ridiculously large because they don't support compression.

You'll probably end up using different file formats throughout your site, depending on what kind of pictures you're using; each format has its own niche (see Figure 7-4).

In the following sections, you'll get some guidance that will help you decide when to use each format.

Compression

In Web graphics, space is a key concern. You may have tons of storage space on your Web server, but larger files take more time to send across the Internet, which means more frustrating, toe-tapping seconds for your Web surfers until your page appears. To make a graphics-heavy Web site run smoothly—and these days, what Web site *doesn't* have lots of graphics?—you need to make sure you pare down the size of your pictures.

Of course it's not quite that simple. JPEG gives the best compression, but it has to throw out some detail in the process (see the box "How Compression Works in JPEG, GIF, and PNG files"). As you compress a JPEG image, you introduce various problems, which are known as *compression artifacts*. The most common compression artifacts you'll notice are blocky regions, halos around edges, and a general blurriness. Some pictures are more prone to showing these flaws than others. (It depends, for example, on the amount of detail.)

Tip: Most graphics programs let you choose how much you compress a picture, and many even let you preview the result before you save anything.

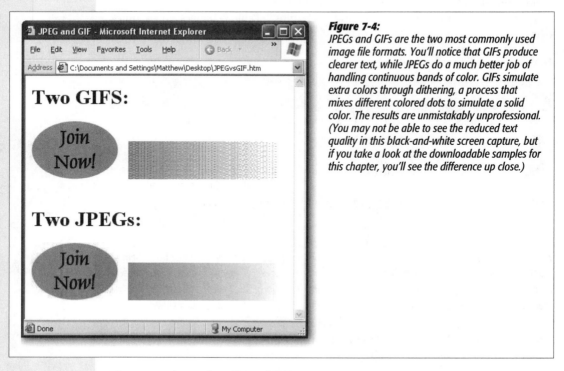

Figure 7-4:
JPEGs and GIFs are the two most commonly used image file formats. You'll notice that GIFs produce clearer text, while JPEGs do a much better job of handling continuous bands of color. GIFs simulate extra colors through dithering, a process that mixes different colored dots to simulate a solid color. The results are unmistakably unprofessional. (You may not be able to see the reduced text quality in this black-and-white screen capture, but if you take a look at the downloadable samples for this chapter, you'll see the difference up close.)

Figure 7-5 shows the effect of different compression settings on a small section of a picture of a church.

Choosing the right image format

It's important to learn which format to use for a given task. To help you decide, walk through the following series of questions.

Is your picture a hefty photo or does it contain fine gradations of color?
YES: JPEG is the best choice for cutting large, finely detailed pictures down to size. Depending on the graphics program you use, you may be able to choose how much compression you want to apply.

Does your picture have sharp edges, text, or does it contain clip art images? Does it use 256 colors or less?
YES: GIF is your man—it compresses pictures without creating blurred edges around text and shapes (the way JPEG files often do). However, keep a watch on your file size, because GIF can't compress quite as well as JPEG.

Does your picture have sharp edges and need more than 256 colors?

YES: PNG is the best answer here. It supports full color, gives you lossless compression, and you don't lose any detail. However, there are two caveats. PNG isn't supported on very old browsers.

100% Quality, 984 KB

75% Quality, 298 KB

50% Quality, 247 KB

15% Quality, 231 KB

Figure 7-5:
Compression can work—up to a point. In this example, cutting the quality factor from 100 percent to 75 percent shaves the file size of the picture to one-third without compromising the appearance. Reducing the quality further doesn't save much more disk space, and introduces a raft of compression artifacts. Note that the file sizes listed are for the whole picture, which is much bigger than the small portion shown here.

Also, keep an eye on the file size—even though PNG offers very good compression, not all graphics programs take advantage of it, in which case your PNG files won't be as small they should be. If PNG doesn't work for you (either because you need to support old browsers or you can't find a graphics program that uses it and makes small enough files), you can try JPEG. However, keep in mind that JPEG can easily introduce too much blurriness. You can also try GIF, but look out for mangled colors as a result of ugly dithering (Figure 7-4).

Does your picture include a transparent area?

YES: Use GIF. Although PNG supports transparency (and even goes further, with support for partially transparent areas), support for this feature is sketchy in many browsers. But think twice before you use transparency—the next section explains the problems you'll face.

Putting Pictures on Colored Backgrounds

Image files are always stored as rectangles. This is a problem, because not all pictures are rectangular. For example, a smiley face, of course, is a circular shape. If you create a graphic with a smiley face, the image file contains the smiley face surrounded by a white rectangle.

Graphics Programs

It's up to you to choose the format you use when you save your image files. In most good graphics programs (such as Macromedia Fireworks and Adobe Photoshop) you save your documents in a specialized file format that lets you perform advanced editing procedures. (In Photoshop, for example, this is the .psd format.) When you're ready to put your picture into a Web page, you then need to save a copy of the file in a *different* format that's specially designed for the Web, like JPEG or GIF. Usually, you can call up this feature by choosing File → Save As from the program's menu (although sometimes it's File → Export or File → Save For Web).

As a general rule of thumb, you always need at least two versions of every picture you create—a copy in the original format used by your graphics program, and a copy in the GIF, JPEG, or PNG format for your Web site. You need to keep the original file so that you can make changes more easily, and make sure the image quality for future versions of the picture are as high as possible.

Once you choose your Web format, your graphics program gives you a number of other options that let you customize details like the compression level. At higher compression levels, your image file is smaller but of lower quality. Some really simple image editors (such as the Paint program that

ships with Windows) don't let you tweak these settings, so you're stuck with whatever (usually unsatisfactory) settings are built into the program.

Graphics programs usually come in two basic flavors—*image editors* that let you apply funky effects to graphics and retouch pictures, and *drawing programs* that let you create your own illustrations by assembling shapes and text. Adobe Photoshop (and its lower-priced, less powerful sibling, Photoshop Elements), Corel Photo-Paint, and Corel Paint Shop Pro are well-known image editors. Adobe Illustrator, CorelDRAW, and Macromedia Freehand are popular drawing programs. Which type of tool you use depends on what you're trying to do. If you're splicing pictures of the office party to cut out an embarrassing moment, an image editor makes sense. If you're creating a logo for your newly launched cookie company, you need an illustration program.

If you don't have the luxury of getting a professional graphics program, you can surf to the shareware sites discussed in Chapter 4 (page 82). You can also check out *http://graphicssoft.about.com/od/pixelbased/a/bybphotoeditor.htm*, which provides a good overview of different photo editors for different tasks (and in different price ranges).

On a white background, this doesn't pose a problem. That's because the box that surrounds your smiley face blends in with the rest of the page. But if you've given your page a different background color using the *background-color* style property (page 151), you'll run into the graphical clunkiness shown in Figure 7-6.

Web designers came up with two solutions to this problem. One nifty idea was to use transparency, a feature supported by GIF graphics (and by PNG graphics, although not all browsers support it). The basic idea is that your graphic contains *transparent pixels*—pixels that don't have any color at all. When the browser comes across these, it doesn't paint anything. Instead, it lets the background of the page show through. To use transparency, you define a transparent color using your graphics program.

Although transparency seems like a handy way to make sure your image always has the correct background color, in practice, transparent regions rarely look good. The problem that you'll usually see is a jagged edge where the colored pixels of your picture end and the Web page background begins (see Figure 7-7).

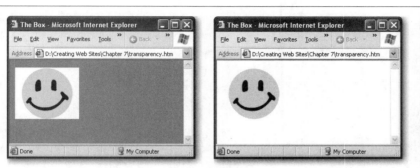

Figure 7-6:
Left: With a non-white background, the white box around your picture is glaringly obvious.

Right: But when you place the picture on a page with a white background, the smiley face blends right in.

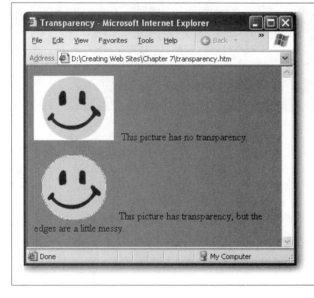

Figure 7-7:
The picture at the bottom of this page uses transparency, but the result—a jagged edge around the smiley face—is less than stellar. To take away this edge, graphics programs use a sophisticated technique called anti-aliasing, which blends the picture color with the background color. Web browsers can't perform this feat, so the edges they make aren't nearly as smooth.

The best solution is to use the correct background color when you create your Web graphic. In other words, when you're drawing your smiley graphic, give it the same background color as your Web page. Your graphics program can then perform the anti-aliasing to make the edges look nice. When you put the image on the page it will blend right in.

The only limitation with this approach is the lack of flexibility. If you change your Web page, you need to edit all your graphics. Sadly, this is the price of creating polished Web graphics.

How Compression Works in JPEG, GIF, and PNG files

All three of the common Web image formats use *compression* to shrink down picture information. However, the type of compression you get with each format differs significantly.

The GIF and PNG formats support *lossless compression*, which means you don't *lose* any information from your picture. Instead, the compression system saves your file in such a way that the receiving browser can perform a few tricks to reconstruct the file's original data. Lossless compression uses a variety of techniques to perform its space-shrinking magic—for example, it might find a repeating pattern in the file, and replace each occurrence of it with a short abbreviation.

The JPEG format uses *lossy compression*, which means that some information about your picture gets discarded, or *lost*. As a result, your picture's quality diminishes, and there's no way to get it back to its original tip-top shape. However, the JPEG format is crafty, and it tries to trick the eye by discarding information that doesn't harm the picture that much. For example, it might convert slightly different colors to the same color, or replace fine details with smoothed-out blobs, because the human eye isn't that sensitive to small changes in color and shape. Usually, the overall result is a picture that looks softer and (depending how much compression you use) more blurry. On the other hand, the size-shrinking results that you get with lossy compression are more dramatic than those offered by lossless compression, because lossy compression can shrink files much more dramatically.

Images and Styles

The <img> tag supports a few optional attributes that you can use to control alignment and borders. But in the modern world, these attributes are considered obsolete, and you won't use them in this book. Instead, you'll learn the best way to position images—with style sheets.

The following sections show all your image-alignment options, and help you practice some of the style sheet smarts you picked up last chapter.

Inline Images in Text

If you don't take any extra steps, every image you insert with an <img> tag is placed right into the flow of HTML text. The bottom edge is lined up with the baseline of the text that surrounds it (see Figure 7-8).

You can change the vertical alignment of text using the vertical-align property. Specify a value of top, middle, or bottom, depending on whether you want to line the picture up with the top, middle, or bottom of the line of text.

Here's an example with an inline style that uses the vertical-align property to line the picture up with the top of the line of text.

```
<img src="happy.gif" alt="Happy Face" style="vertical-align: top">
```

This technique is worthwhile if you're trying to line up a very small picture (like a fancy bullet). However, it doesn't work very well with large images. That's because no matter which vertical-align option you choose, only one line of text can appear alongside the picture (as you can see in Figure 7-8). If you want to create floating pictures with wrapped text, read on (page 194).

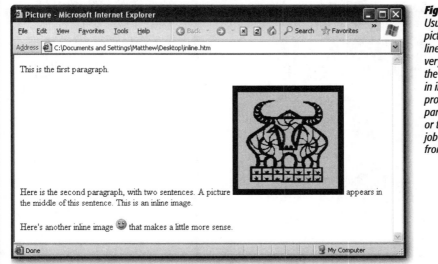

Figure 7-8:
Usually, you don't want a picture inside an ordinary line of text (unless it's a very small emoticon, like the kind of symbols used in instant message programs). You can use paragraphs, line breaks, or tables to do a better job of separating images from your text.

Borders

On page 169 in Chapter 6, you considered the style properties that let you add and modify borders around text boxes. It should come as no surprise that you can use these borders just as easily around images.

For example, here's a style that applies a thin, grooved border to all sides of an image:

```
img.GrooveBorder {
  border-style: groove;
  border-width: 3px;
}
```

As with all style sheet rules, you need to place the rule in an internal style sheet in the current Web page or in an external style sheet that your page uses (see p. 138 for a discussion of the difference).

Notice that this style is given a class name (GrooveBorder). That's because it shouldn't be automatically applied to every picture. Instead, you want to choose when to apply it by using the class attribute:

```
<img src="food.jpg" alt="A Meal" class="GrooveBorder">
```

Figure 7-9 shows the basic border styles. Remember, you can change the thickness of any border to get a very different look.

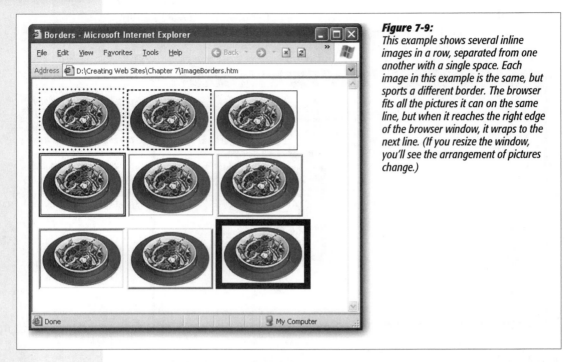

Wrapping Text Around an Image

Using inline images is the simplest way to arrange pictures. When you use inline images, the pictures and the text are usually in separate parts of your Web page. You use paragraphs (<p>), line breaks (<br>), horizontal rules (<hr>), and other divisions to separate your images from your text. For example, you might decide to put a picture in between two paragraphs, like this:

```
<p>This paragraph is before the picture.</p>
<p><img src="food.jpg" alt="A Meal"></p>
<p>This paragraph is after the picture.</p>
```

Inline images are locked into place. They never move anywhere you don't expect.

However, sometimes you want a different effect. Instead of separating images and text, you want to put them alongside each other. For example, maybe you want your text to wrap *around* one side of a picture.

Images that have text wrapped on one side or the other are called *floating* images, because they float next to an expanse of text (see Figure 7-10). You can create a floating image using a CSS property named *float*. The value can be either left or right, which lines the image up on either the left or the right edge of the text.

```
img.FloatLeft {
  float: left;
}
```

Typical File Sizes for Images

How much disk space does a typical picture occupy?

There's no single answer to this question, because it depends on several factors, including the dimensions of the picture, the file format you use, the amount of compression you apply, and how well the picture responds to compression techniques. However, here are a few basic examples that you can keep in mind.

The file size of a typical Web site logo is vanishingly small. Amazon's small logo (about 150 x 50 pixels) has a file size of a paltry 2 kilobytes (KB), which is less than most Web pages. Google's signature logo banner clocks in nearly as tiny, at 10 KB. Both are GIF files (page 186).

A picture can take up much more disk space. A small news picture in an article on the *New York Times* Web site rarely uses more than 20 KB. A typical eBayer includes a picture of her product that's 30 to 150 KB. At this size, the picture usually takes up a large portion of your browser window. However, that's nothing compared to the size the picture

would need if you weren't using compression. For example, a 1-megapixel camera can take a raw, uncompressed picture of about 3,000 KB. In a Web page, you might compress this to 300 KB or less by using a JPEG file format with a lower quality level (see page 191).

Of course, the important number is how long it takes a Web visitor to download a Web page that has a picture. Obviously, this depends on the speed of their Internet connection—a broadband connection won't blink while grabbing a huge graphic, while a surfer on a relatively slow 56 K dial-up modem can only get about 5 KB each second, meaning it takes about 20 seconds to see all of a 100 KB eBay picture. In Internet time, 20 seconds is a lifetime.

The best advice for keeping your pictures small is to crop them to the right dimensions, use the right image format, and try lowering the quality level of JPEGs to get better compression.

Notice that this image uses a class name. You probably don't want every image in your entire Web page to become a floating image, so it's always a good idea to use a class name. Here's an <img> that uses this class, followed by some text:

```
<p>
  <img src="food.jpg" alt="A Meal" class="FloatLeft">
  If you place a floating image at the beginning of a paragraph,
  it floats in the top-left corner, with the text wrapped along
  the right edge.
</p>
```

At the same time that you use the float attribute, it makes sense to adjust the margin settings to put a little breathing room between your image and the rest of the text:

```
img.FloatLeft {
  float: left;
```

```
    margin: 10px;
}
```

Figure 7-10 shows several floating images.

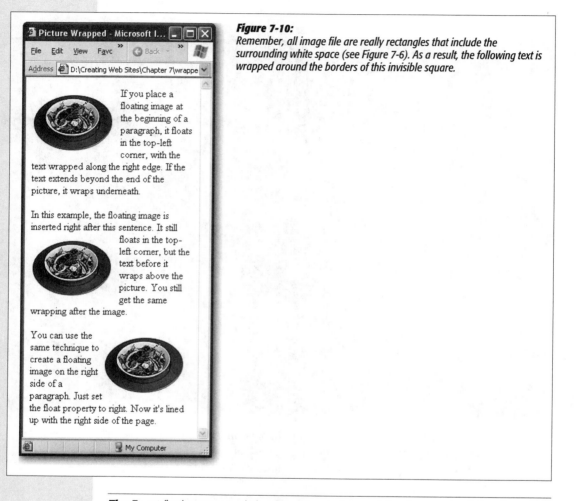

Figure 7-10:
Remember, all image file are really rectangles that include the surrounding white space (see Figure 7-6). As a result, the following text is wrapped around the borders of this invisible square.

Tip: To get floating text to work the way you want, always put the <img> tag just *before* the text that should wrap around the image.

Wrapping text can get a little tricky, because the results you get depend on the width of the browser window. A wide browser might fit the text in just a couple of lines, allowing the rest of the page to bump up next to your floating graphic, which isn't what you want (see Figure 7-11). To prevent this sort of problem, you can use tables (discussed in Chapter 9), or you can manually stop wrapping at any point using the *clear* property in a line break (<br>) tag:

```
<br style="clear: both;">
```

Place this line at the end of the wrapped paragraph, like so:

```
<p>
  <img src="food.jpg" alt="A Meal" class="FloatLeft">
  Here is a paragraph with a floating image.
  <br style="clear: both;">
</p>
<p>
  <img border="0" src="food.jpg" class="FloatLeft">
  This should be a separate paragraph with another
  floating picture.
</p>
```

The <br> tag ensures that the next paragraph starts after any floating pictures (see Figure 7-11).

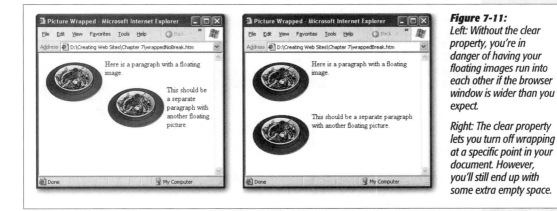

Figure 7-11:
Left: Without the clear property, you're in danger of having your floating images run into each other if the browser window is wider than you expect.

Right: The clear property lets you turn off wrapping at a specific point in your document. However, you'll still end up with some extra empty space.

Based on these examples, you might think that the *float* property sends a picture to the left or right side of the page. But this isn't exactly what happens. Remember, in CSS each HTML tag on the page is treated as a container. When you create a floating image, the image actually goes to the left or right side of the containing element. In the previous examples, this means the image goes to the left or right of the paragraph, because the paragraph is the containing tag.

In this example, the paragraph takes the full width of the page. However, this isn't always the case. If you use style rules to put the paragraph into a padded note box, you'll get a completely different effect.

To try this out, you need to wrap the image and the paragraph in a <div> tag, like this:

```
<div class="Box">
  <p>
    <img src="food.jpg" alt="A Meal" class="FloatLeft">
    <b>But Wait!</b> A tip box can interrupt the discussion
```

to let you know just how good mixed veggies can taste.
Of course, this tip box is really just an ordinary paragraph with
the right border and margin style properties.
</p>
</div>

You can then apply a fancy border to the <div> tag through a style rule:

```
div.Box {
    margin-top: 20px;
    margin-bottom: 10px;
    margin-left: 70px;
    margin-right: 70px;
    padding: 5px;
    border-style: dotted;
    border-width: 2px
}
```

Figure 7-12 shows the result.

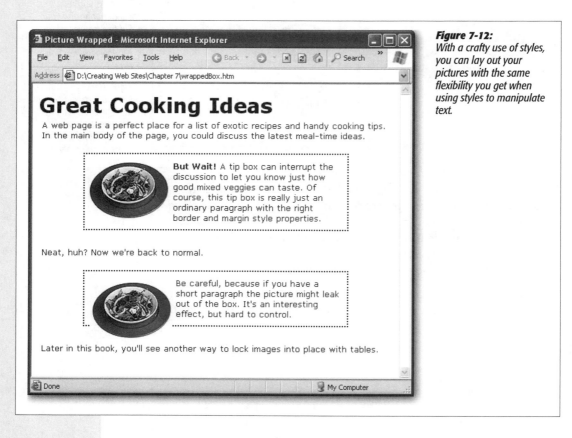

Adding Captions

Another nice touch is to give your pictures a caption above or below the image. You can easily do this with inline images (just put a line of text immediately above or after the picture, separated by a line break). However, it's not so easy when you have a floating image. In this case, you need to have your image *and* the caption text both float in the same way.

As it happens, the solution is quite easy. You simply need to take the FloatLeft style rule shown earlier (page 195), and change the name from img.FloatLeft to .FloatLeft, so that it can be used with any tag:

```
.FloatLeft {
  float: left;
  margin: 10px;
}
```

Next, you need to wrap the <img> tag and your text into a <span> tag. You can then make the entire <span> tag float, by using the FloatLeft style rule:

```
<span class="FloatLeft">
  <img src="planetree.jpg" alt="Plane Tree"><br>
  <i>The bark of a plane tree</i>
</span>
```

Figure 7-13 shows the result.

Note: The reason you use a <span> in this example instead of a <div> is because you can place a <span> *inside* other block elements, like paragraphs. The <div> element is designed to be placed on the outside (so it contains other block elements). In other words, by using a <span> tag, you can easily put your picture inside another paragraph.

Background Images

CSS makes it possible to set a background image that sits underneath the rest of the page content. This technique can be a little distracting, and so it's fallen out of favor with Web gurus in recent years. However, it's still worth considering if you want to add a really dramatic touch, and it's particularly handy for creating a "themed" Web site. For example, if you're creating a literary Web site, you could use a light parchment paper background. A Buffy fan site might put a darker cemetery image to good use.

Tip: Background images can make your Web site seem tacky. Be wary of using them for a résumé page or a professional business site. On the other hand, if you want to go a little kitschy, have fun!

Background images are almost always *tiled*, which means a smaller picture is copied over and over again to fill the browser window (see Figure 7-14). There's no way you could use a single image to fill the browser window, because you have no

---

way to know how wide and tall to make the picture. Even if you did, the picture you'd need to create would be ridiculously large, and downloading it would take an impractically long amount of time.

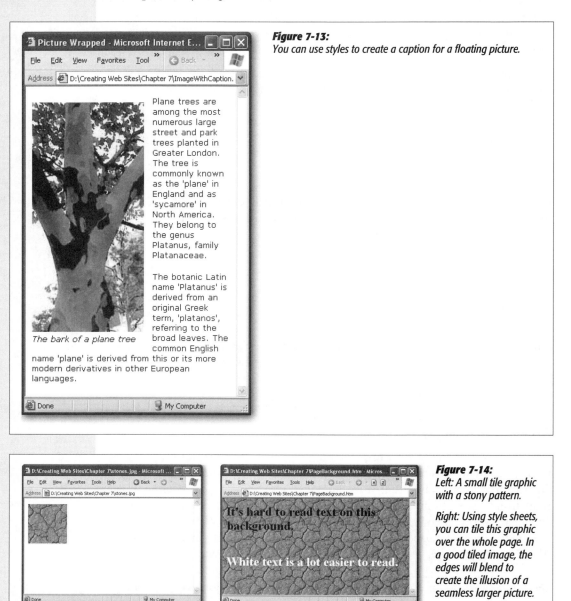

Figure 7-13:
You can use styles to create a caption for a floating picture.

Figure 7-14:
Left: A small tile graphic with a stony pattern.

Right: Using style sheets, you can tile this graphic over the whole page. In a good tiled image, the edges will blend to create the illusion of a seamless larger picture.

To take an image and use it to create a tiled background, you use the *background-image* style property. Your first step is to apply this style property to the <body>

element, so that the whole page is affected. Next, you need to provide the file name of the image using the form *url('filename')*, as shown here:

```
body {
   background-image: url('stones.jpg');
}
```

This takes the image *stones.jpg* and tiles it across the page to create your background.

Keep these points in mind when creating a tiled background:

- Use the JPEG format (page 186) when creating your background image file, since JPEGs can display the most colors of any of the Web-ready image formats.

- Make your background light, so the text remains legible. (If you really must go dark, you can use white, bold text to stand out. But don't do this unless you're creating a Web site for a trendy new band or opening a gothic clothing store.)

- Set the page's background color to match the image. For example, if you have a dark background picture with white writing, make the background color black. That way, if the image can't be downloaded, the text will still be visible.

- Use small tiles to reduce the amount of time your visitors need to wait before they can see the page.

- If your tiled image has an irregular pattern, make sure the edges line up. The left edge should continue the right edge, and the top edge should continue the bottom edge. Otherwise, when the browser tiles your image, you'll see lines where the tiles are stitched together.

Tip: The Web is full of common background images, like stars, blue skies and clouds, fabric and stone textures, fires, dizzying geometric patterns, borders, and much more. You can find these easily by searching on Google for "backgrounds," or head straight to top sites like *www.grsites.com/textures* (with over 5,000 backgrounds indexed by dominant color), *www.backgroundcity.com*, and *www. backgroundsarchive.com*.

Background "watermarks"

Most background images that you see on the Web have been created using tiling, but that's not your only option. Instead, you can take an image and place it at a specific position on your page. (Think, for example, "Top Secret and Confidential" splayed across your home page.) This is sometimes called a *watermark*. (The name stems from the process that's use to place a translucent logo on paper while the paper in still saturated with water.) To make a good watermark, you should use a background picture that's pale and unobtrusive.

To add a watermark to your page, you use the same background-image property you learned about above. However, you also need to add a few more style properties to the mix (see Table 7-2). First, you have to use the *background-repeat* property to turn off tiling. At the same time, it also makes sense to use the *background-position* property to align your picture to one of the sides of the page or in the center.

Table 7-2. *Background Image Properties*

Property	Description	Common Values	Oldest Supported Browsers	Can Be Inherited
background-image	The image file you want to show in the background.	A URL pointing to the image file, as in url('mypig.jpg').	IE 3, Netscape 4	No[a]
background-repeat	Whether or not the image should be tiled to fill the entire page. You can turn off tiling altogether, or turn it off in one dimension (so that images are tiled vertically but not horizontally, for example).	repeat repeat-x repeat-y no-repeat	IE 4, Netscape 4	No
background-position	Where the image should be placed. Use this only if you *aren't* tiling the image.	top left top center top right center left center center right bottom left bottom center bottom right	IE 4, Netscape 6	No
background-attachment	Whether the image should be fixed in place when the page is scrolled. Use this only if you *aren't* tiling the image.	scroll fixed	IE 4, Netscape 6	No

[a] Background pictures aren't inherited (page 148). However, if you don't explicitly assign a background color to a tag, it's given a transparent background, which means the background of the containing tag will still show through

Here's an example that places a picture in the center of the Web page:

```
body {
    background-image: url('smiley.jpg');
    background-repeat: no-repeat;
    background-position: center;
}
```

Note: The center of the document isn't necessarily the center of the window. If you have a long Web page and you position your image in the center, it won't appear until you scroll down.

You can also turn off scrolling to give the rather odd effect of an image that's fixed in place (see Figure 7-15). For example, use this style to create a background image that sits squarely in the center of the window:

```
body {
  background-image: url('smiley.gif');
  background-repeat: no-repeat;
  background-position: center;
  background-attachment: fixed;
}
```

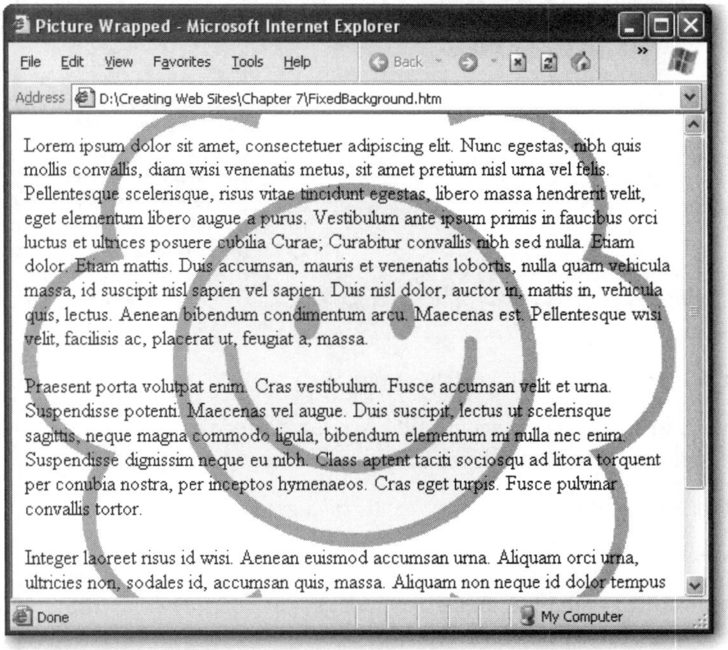

Figure 7-15:
This staring smiley face remains perpetually in the center of the window, even when you scroll up or down. It's a little creepy.

Techniques with Graphics

Now that you've mastered the <img> tag, it's time to learn a few tricks of the trade. In the following sections, you'll tour three common techniques used by Web gurus everywhere to create more polished pages.

Graphical Text

In Chapter 6, you learned that using exotic fonts on Web pages can be risky, since you don't know for sure which typefaces are installed on your Web surfer's computer. Although there's no way to get around this problem when you've got large blocks of text, enterprising Web artists commonly put the text for headings, buttons, and logos into picture files. That way, you get *complete* control of what your text looks like.

Here's a high-level look at what you need to do:

1. **Fire up your favorite image editor or drawing program.**

   Figure 7-16 shows an example with Adobe Illustrator.

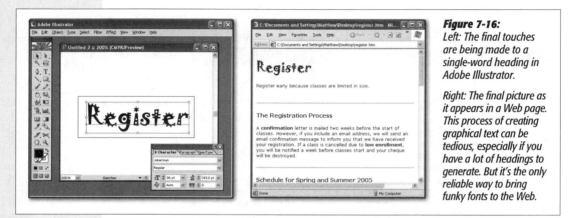

Figure 7-16:
Left: The final touches are being made to a single-word heading in Adobe Illustrator.

Right: The final picture as it appears in a Web page. This process of creating graphical text can be tedious, especially if you have a lot of headings to generate. But it's the only reliable way to bring funky fonts to the Web.

2. **Fill in a background color that matches your Web page.**

   In some programs, the easiest way to fill a section with color is to draw a shape (like a rectangle), and then give it the proper fill color.

3. **Choose your font, and type the text over the background color.**

4. **Cut your image down to size.**

   Ideally, you want to make the image as small as you possibly can without clipping off any of the text.

5. **Save your picture.**

   GIF is the best format choice, but you might need PNG if you have more than 256 colors. Don't use JPEG, or your text will have blurred edges.

Tip: Often, graphical pieces of text are turned into clickable buttons that can take you from page to another. You'll learn more about links in Chapter 8, and you'll find out how to make fancy graphical buttons in Chapter 15.

Backgrounds on Other Elements

You don't need to apply a background to a whole page. Instead, you can bind a background to a single paragraph or, more usefully, a <div> tag. Usually, you'll want to add a border around this tag to separate it from the rest of your Web page. You might also need to change the color of the foreground text so it's legible (for example, white shows up better than black on dark backgrounds).

Here's an example of a background image that can be used with any container element:

```
.pie {
   background-image: url('pie.jpg');
   margin-top: 20px;
   margin-bottom: 10px;
   margin-left: 70px;
   margin-right: 70px;
   padding: 10px;
   border-style: double;
   border-width: 3px;
   color: white;
   background-color: black;
   font-size: large;
   font-weight: bold;
   font-family: Verdana,sans-serif;
}
```

This style specifies a background image, sets the margins and borders, and chooses background and foreground colors to match.

Here's a <div> tag that uses this style:

```
<div class="pie">
   <p>Hungry for some pie?</p>
</div>
```

Figure 7-17 shows the result.

Graphical Bullets in a List

In Chapter 5, you looked at how you can use the <ul> tag to create a bulleted list. However, you were limited to a small set of predefined bullet styles. If you look around on the Web, you'll see more interesting examples that use tiny pictures to create custom bullets.

You could add custom bullets by hand using the <img> tag. However, there's an easier option. You can use the *list-style-image* style property to set a bullet image. Here's an example that uses a picture named *3Dball.gif*:

```
ul {
  list-style-image: url('3Dball.gif');
}
```

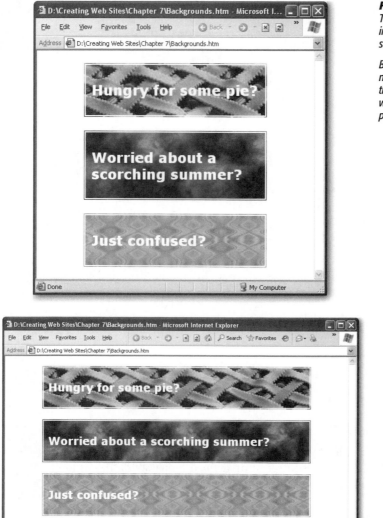

Figure 7-17:
Top: Using background images in small boxes is surprisingly slick.

Bottom: A particularly neat feature is the way the picture content grows when you resize the page, thanks to tiling.

Once you've created this style rule and placed it in your style sheet, it applies automatically to an ordinary bulleted list like this one:

```
<ul>
  <li>Are hard to miss</li>
  <li>Help compensate for feelings of inadequacy</li>
  <li>Look so darned cool</li>
  <li>Remind people of boring PowerPoint presentations</li>
</ul>
```

Figure 7-18 shows the result.

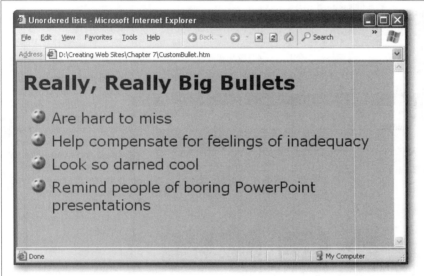

Figure 7-18:
Graphical bullets range from simple arrows and check boxes to extravagant three-dimensional soccer balls, like those shown here.

Finding Free Art

The Web is awash in graphics. In fact, finding a Web page that isn't chock full of images is about as unusual as spotting Bill Gates in a dollar store. But how does an ambitious developer generate all these pictures? Do you really need to spend hours in a drawing program fine-tuning every picture you need?

The answer depends on exactly what type of pictures you need. However, you'll be happy to hear that there are a variety of great resources on the Web where you can find ready-to-use pictures.

Finding Photos

It's not hard to find pictures on the Web. In fact, you can even use a handy Google tool to search for graphics on a specific subject (type *http://images.google.com* into your browser and search away). Unfortunately, *finding* an image usually isn't good enough. In order to use the image without worrying about a nefarious lawyer tracking you down, you also need the *rights* to use the picture. If you get lucky, you might be granted the permission you want after you send a quick email to the Web site owner. But on many sites, that means opening your wallet and shelling out real money.

Fortunately, there are free community sites made up of photo enthusiasts who post their pictures for the world to see. On some of these sites, you're able to search for and reuse anything you want, completely for free. One of the most remarkable is Stock.XCHNG (pronounced "stock exchange," after *stock photography*, the name for the vast catalogues of reusable pictures that graphic designers collect). To get to Stock.XCHNG, surf to *http://sxc.hu*. Figure 7-19 shows a Stock.XCHNG search in progress.

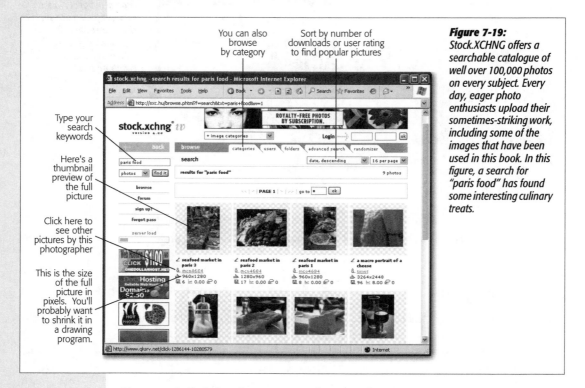

Figure 7-19:
Stock.XCHNG offers a searchable catalogue of well over 100,000 photos on every subject. Every day, eager photo enthusiasts upload their sometimes-striking work, including some of the images that have been used in this book. In this figure, a search for "paris food" has found some interesting culinary treats.

If you can't find the picture you want on Stock.XCHNG, you may never find it (at least not without going to a more specialized commercial service). But if you'd like to look at some other alternatives, check out the article on finding free photographs at *www.masternewmedia.org/news/2005/04/01/where_to_find_great_free.htm*.

Finding Clip Art

Stock.XCHNG is great when you need rich photographs, but it doesn't help when you want standard clip art. Clip art includes cartoon-like business graphics, common symbols like arrows, buttons, and starbursts, and more.

A lot of so-called free clip art sites are choked with ads and subscription demands. However, there are a few bright spots, including *www.grsites.com/webgraphics*, *www.clipartconnection.com*, and *www.myfreeclipart.com*. Some clip art sites restrict your ability to use their pictures on commercial Web sites, so be sure to read the fine print.

Tip: If you have a copy of Microsoft Office, you can also download clip art straight from the Office Online Web site. You'll need to open this clip art with a graphics program and save it as a Web image format (like JPEG or GIF), but it's a small price to pay for gaining access to a large, free clip art connection. Head to *http://office.microsoft.com/clipart* to start searching.

Linking Pages

So far in this book, you've concentrated on one Web page at time. While creating a single page is the crucial first step in building a Web site, sooner or later you'll want to wire several pages together so a Web trekker can easily jump from one to the next. After all, surfing is what the Web's all about.

It's astoundingly easy to create links—officially called *hyperlinks*—between pages. In fact, all you need to do is learn a single new tag: the *anchor* tag. Once you've mastered this bit of HTML lingo, you're ready to start organizing your Web site into separate folders and transforming your humble collection of Web pages into a full-fledged Web site.

Understanding the Anchor

In HTML, you use the anchor tag to create a link that, when clicked, transports the Web site reader to another page.

The anchor tag is a straightforward container tag. It looks like this:

```
<a>...</a>
```

Inside the anchor tag, you put the clickable content:

```
<a>Click Me</a>
```

The problem with the above link is that it doesn't *point* anywhere. To turn this into a fully functioning link, you need to supply the URL of the destination page using the *href* attribute (which stands for *hypertext reference*). For example, if you want a click to take the reader to a page named *LinkedPage.htm,* you'd create this link:

```
<a href="LinkedPage.htm">Click Me</a>
```

In order for this line to actually work, the *LinkedPage.htm* file must reside in the same folder as the Web page that contains the link. You'll learn how to become more organized and sort your pages into different subfolders on page 215.

Tip: To create a link in FrontPage, select the clickable text, and hit Ctrl+K. You can then browse to the correct page, and FrontPage will create the relative link. Dreamweaver and Nvu work the same way, when you press Ctrl+L.

The anchor tag is an inline tag (page 116) that fits inside any other block element. That means it's completely acceptable to make a link out of just a few words in an otherwise ordinary paragraph, like this:

```
<p>
   When you're alone and life is making you lonely<br>
   You can always go <a href="Downtown.htm">downtown</a>
</p>
```

Figure 8-1 shows this link example in action.

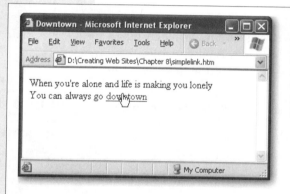

Figure 8-1:
If you don't take any other steps to customize the anchor tag, the text appears with the familiar underline and blue lettering in the browser. When you move the mouse over a hyperlink, the mouse pointer turns to a hand. You can't tell by looking at a link whether or not it works. If the link points to a non-existing page, you'll get an error only after you click it.

Internal and External Links

Links can shuffle you from one page to another in the same Web site, or they can transport you to a completely different Web site on a far-off Web server. Depending on which task you're performing, you use a different type of link.

Conceptually, there are two types of links:

- **Internal links** point to other pages or resources (for example, downloadable files) in your Web site.

- **External links** point to pages or resources in other Web sites.

For example, if you want visitors to surf from your bio page (*MyBio.htm*) to another page on your site with your address information (*ContactMe.htm*), you need to create an internal link. In all likelihood, you'll have stored both files in the same folder, and even if they aren't they're still part of the same Web site on the same Web server. On the other hand, if you want visitors to surf from your favorite books page (*FavBooks.htm*) to somewhere on Amazon (*www.amazon.com*), you need an external link. Clicking this type of link transports the reader out of your Web site and on to a new site, located elsewhere on the Web.

HOW'D THEY DO THAT?

Changing Link Color with Style Sheets

Virtually everyone born since the year 1900 has an instinctual understanding that blue underlined text is there to be clicked. But what if blue links are at odds with the overall look of your site? Thanks to style sheets, you don't need to play by the rules.

Based on what you learned about CSS in Chapter 6, you can quickly build a style sheet rule that changes the text color of all the link-producing anchor tags in your site. Here's an example:

```
a {
   color: fuchsia;
}
```

But watch out: making this change creates two problems. First, ordinary links look different after you've clicked them (they turn from blue to red). The style sheet rule in this example overrides that subtle modification, which many Web surfers depend on to know which links they've clicked in a site. Second, if you apply a rule to all anchor tags, it also affects any bookmarks (see page 224), which probably isn't the behavior you want.

A better way to create colorful links is to use another style sheet trick: *pseudo-selectors*. Pseudo-selectors are more specialized selectors (page 141) that rely on other details that the browser keeps track of behind the scenes. For example, an ordinary selector applies to a given tag, like <a>. A pseudo-selector can apply specifically to clicked or unclicked links. Pseudo-selectors are a mid-range CSS feature, which means they don't work on very old browsers like Internet Explorer 4 and Netscape 4.

There are four pseudo-selectors that help you format links. They are *:link* (for links that point to virgin ground), *:visited* (for links that have already been visited), *:active* (the color a link turns while you're clicking it, just before the new page appears), and *:hover* (the color a link turns when you move the mouse over the link). As you can see, pseudo-selectors always start with a colon (:).

Here's a style rule that uses pseudo-selectors to create a misleading page—one where visited links are blue and unvisited links are red:

```
a:link {
   color: red;
}
a:visited {
   color: blue;
}
```

If you want to apply these rules to some, but not all, links, you can use a class name with your pseudo-selector rule:

```
a.BackwardLink:link {
   color: red;
}
a.BackwardLink:visited {
   color: blue;
}
```

Now the anchor tag needs to specify the same class to get this style, as you can see in this line:

```
<a class="BackwardLink" href="...">...
</a>
```

When you create an internal link, you should always use a *relative URL*, which tells the browser the location of the target page *relative* to the current folder. In other words, it gives instructions on how to find the new folder by moving up or down from the current folder. (Moving *down* means moving from the current folder into a subfolder. Moving *up* is the reverse—you travel from a subfolder into the parent folder that contains it.)

All the examples you've seen so far use relative URLs. For example, imagine you surf to this page:

```
http://www.GothicGardenCenter.com/Sales/Products.htm
```

The *Products.htm* page includes a relative link that looks like this:

```
Would you like to learn more about our purple
<a href="Flowers.htm">hydrangeas</a>?
```

In this case, Flowers.htm is a relative URL. If you click this link, the browser automatically assumes that *Flowers.htm* is stored in the same location as *Products.htm*, and it fills in the rest of the URL. That means the browser actually requests this page:

```
http://www.GothicGardenCenter.com/Sales/Flowers.htm
```

HTML gives you another option, called an *absolute URL*, which defines the whole URL exactly, including the domain name, folder, and page. For example, you could convert the previous example into an absolute URL that looks like this:

```
Would you like to learn more about our purple <a href=
 "http://www.GothicGardenCenter.com/Sales/Flowers.htm">hydrangeas</a>?
```

So which approach should you use? Deciding's easy. There are exactly two rules you should keep in mind:

- **If you're creating an external link, you must use an absolute URL.**

  In this situation, a relative URL just won't work. For example, imagine you want to link to the page *home.html* on Amazon's Web site. If you create a relative link, the browser will assume that *home.html* refers to that file on *your* Web site. Clicking the link won't take your visitors where you want them to go (and may not take them anywhere at all, if you don't have a file with that name on your site).

- **If you're creating an internal link, you really, really should use a relative URL.**

  Technically, either type of link works in this situation. However, relative URLs have several advantages. First, they're shorter and make the HTML more readable and easier to maintain. More importantly, relative links are flexible. You can rearrange your Web site, put your files into a different folder, or even change the domain name of your Web site without disturbing your relative links.

One of the nicest parts about relative links is that you can test them on your own computer, and they'll work the exact same way as they do online. For example, imagine you've developed the *www.GothicGardenCenter.com* Web site on your own computer and have stored it inside the folder *C:\MyWebSite* (that'd be *Macintosh HD/MyWebSite*, in Macintosh-ese). If you click the relative link that leads from the *Products.htm* page to the *Flowers.htm* page, the browser looks for the target page in the *C:\MyWebSite* (*Macintosh HD/MyWebSite*) folder.

Once you've polished your work to perfection, say you upload the site to your Web server, which has the domain name *www.GothicGardenCenter.com*. Because you've used relative links, you don't need to change anything. Now, when you click on a link, the browser requests the corresponding page in *www.GothicGardenCenter. com*. If you decide to buy a new, shorter domain name like *www.GGC.com* and move your Web site there, the links keep on working.

FREQUENTLY ASKED QUESTION

Navigating and Frames

How do I make a link that opens in a new browser window?

When visitors click on external links, you might not want to let them get away that easily. A common trick that Web sites use is to open external Web sites in separate browser windows. This way, your Web site remains open in its original window, ensuring the reader won't forget about it.

To make this work, you need the help of another HTML feature—*frames*. Using frames, you can open a document in a specific section of the browser window or even in an entirely new window. Chapter 10 covers frames in detail. However, you don't need to understand frames just to open a link in a new window. All it requires is one extra attribute in your anchor tag, like this:

```
<a href="LinkedPage.htm" target="_blank">
Click Me</a>
```

The target attribute names the frame where the destination page should be displayed. The value *_blank* indicates that the page should be loaded into a new frame, in a new, empty browser window.

Some people love this feature, while others think it's an immensely annoying and disruptive act of Web site intervention. If you use it, apply it sparingly on the occasional link.

It's also worth noting that some vigilant *pop-up blockers* intercept this type of link and prevent the new window from appearing altogether. (Pop-up blockers are standalone programs or browser features designed to prevent annoying pop-up ads from appearing.) Internet Explorer 6 includes its own pop-up blocker, but its standard settings allow links that use target="_blank".

Relative Links and Folders

So far, all the relative link examples you've seen have assumed that both the *source page* (the one that contains the link) and the *target page* (the destination you arrive at when you click the link) are in the same folder. There's no reason to be quite this strict. In fact, your Web site will be a whole lot better organized if you store groups of related pages in *separate* folders.

For example, consider the Web site shown in Figure 8-2.

Note: The root folder is the starting point of your Web site—it contains all other files and folders. Most Web pages include a page with the name *index.htm* or *index.html* in the root folder. This is the *default page* (page 55). If a browser sends a request to your Web site domain without supplying a file name, the Web server sends back the default page. For example, requesting *www.TripToRemember.com* automatically returns the default page *www.TripToRemember.com/index.htm*.

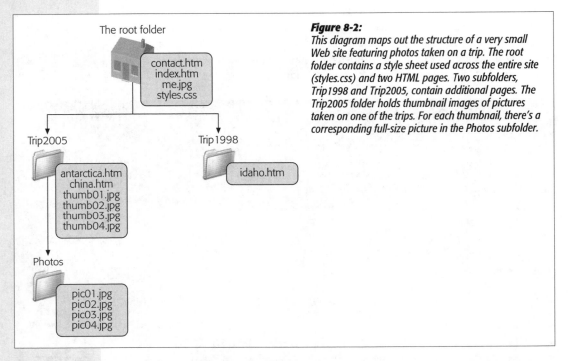

The root folder

contact.htm
index.htm
me.jpg
styles.css

Trip2005

antarctica.htm
china.htm
thumb01.jpg
thumb02.jpg
thumb03.jpg
thumb04.jpg

Trip1998

idaho.htm

Photos

pic01.jpg
pic02.jpg
pic03.jpg
pic04.jpg

Figure 8-2:
This diagram maps out the structure of a very small Web site featuring photos taken on a trip. The root folder contains a style sheet used across the entire site (styles.css) and two HTML pages. Two subfolders, Trip1998 and Trip2005, contain additional pages. The Trip2005 folder holds thumbnail images of pictures taken on one of the trips. For each thumbnail, there's a corresponding full-size picture in the Photos subfolder.

The Web site shown in Figure 8-2 uses a variety of different relative links. For example, imagine you need to create a link from the *index.htm* page to the *contact.htm* page. Both of these pages are in the same folder, so all you need is a relative link:

```
<a href="contact.htm">About Me</a>
```

You can also create more interesting links that move from one folder to another, which you'll learn how to do in the following sections.

Tip: If you'd like to try out this sample Web site, you'll find all the site's files on the "Missing CD" page at *www.missingmanuals.com.* Thanks to the magic of relative links, all the links will work fine no matter where you copy the files on your computer (PC or Mac), as long as you keep the same subfolders.

Moving down into a subfolder

Say you want to create a relative link that jumps from the *index.htm* page to the *antarctica.htm* page in the Trip2005 folder. Now you need to include the name of the subfolder in your relative link, like this (remember, this line of code should be on the *index.htm* page):

```
See pictures from <a href="Trip2005/antarctica.htm">Antarctica</a>
```

This link gives the browser two instructions—go into the subfolder Trip2005, and get the page *antarctica.htm.* In the link, the folder name ("Trip2005") and the file name ("antarctica.htm") are separated by a slash (/). Figure 8-3 shows both sides of this equation.

Figure 8-3:
Using a relative link, you can jump from the main index.htm page (top) to a page with picture thumbnails (bottom). Each picture is itself a link—click it to see a larger-sized version of the picture.

Interestingly, you can use relative paths in other HTML tags, like the <style> tag and the <img> tag. For example, imagine you want to show the picture *photo01.jpg* in the page *index.htm.* This picture is two subfolders away, but that doesn't stop you from linking to it:

```
<img src="Trip2005/Photos/photo01.jpg" alt="A polar bear">
```

Using these techniques, you can dig even deeper into subfolders of subfolders of subfolders. All you need to do is add the folder name and a slash character for each subfolder, in order.

But remember, links are always relative *to the current page.* If you want to display the same picture in the *antarctica.htm* page, that <img> tag above won't work, because the *antarctica.htm* page is in the Trip2005 folder (take a look back at Figure 8-2 if you need a visual reminder of the site structure). From the Trip2005 folder, you only need to go down one level, so you need this link:

```
<img src="Photos/photo01.jpg" alt="A polar bear">
```

By now, you've probably realized that the important detail is not how many folders you have in your site, but how you've organized them. Remember, a relative link always starts out from the *current* folder, and works it way up or down to the folder holding the target page.

Tip: One you start using subfolders, you shouldn't change the names of any of the folders or move them around. That said, many Web page editors (like FrontPage) are crafty enough to help you out if you do make these changes. When you rearrange pages or rename folders inside these programs, they can adjust your relative links automatically to take into account the new structure. It's yet another reason to think about getting a full-featured Web page editor.

Moving up into a parent folder

The next challenge you'll face is going *up* a folder level. To accomplish this task, you need to use the character sequence ../ (two periods and a slash). For example, if you want to add a link in the *antarctica.htm* page that returns the reader to the *index.htm* page, it would look like this:

```
Go <a href="../index.htm">back</a>
```

And as you've probably guessed by now, you can use this command twice in a row to jump up two levels. For example, if you have a page in the Photos folder, you would need this link to get back to the index page:

```
Go <a href="../../index.htm">back</a>
```

For a more interesting feat, you can combine both of these tricks to create a relative link that travels up one or more levels and then travels down a different path. For example, you'd need this sort of link if you wanted to jump from the *antarctica.htm* page in the Trip2005 folder to the *idaho.htm* page in the Trip1998 folder. Here's the link you need:

```
See what happened in <a href="../Trip1998/idaho.htm">Idaho</a>
```

This link moves up one level to the root folder, and then back down one level to the Trip1998 folder. You follow the same process when you're browsing files on your computer.

Moving into the root folder

The only problem with the relative links that you've seen so far is that they're difficult to maintain if you ever end up reorganizing your Web site. For example, imagine you have a Web page in the root directory of your Web site. Say you want to feature an image on that page that's stored in the *images* subfolder. You'd use this link:

```
<img src="images/flower.gif" alt="A flower">
```

But then, a little later on, you decide your Web page really belongs in *another* spot—a subfolder named *plant*—so you move it there. The problem is that the link now points to *plant/images/flower.gif*, which doesn't exist. As a result, your image link is broken.

There are a few possible workarounds. In programs like FrontPage, when you drag a file to a new location, the HTML editor updates all the relative links automatically, saving you the hassle. Another approach is to try to keep related files in the same folder, so that you always move them as a unit. However, there's a third approach, called *root-relative* links.

So far, the relative links you've seen have been *document-relative*, because they're based on the current location of the Web page document that contains the link. *Root-relative* links are based on the root folder in your Web site. They always start with the slash (/) character (which indicates the root folder).

Here's the <img> tag for *flower.gif* with a root-relative link:

```
<img src="/images/flower.gif" alt="A flower">
```

The remarkable thing about this link is that it works no matter where you put the Web page that contains it. For example, if you copy this page to the *plant* subfolder, the link still works, because the first slash refers to the root folder.

The only trick to using root-relative folders is that you need to keep the real root of your Web site in mind. When using a root-relative link, the browser follows a simple procedure to figure out where to go. First, it strips all the path and file name information out of the current page address, so that it's left with nothing but the domain name. It then adds the relative link on the end. So if you're on this page:

```
http://www.jumboplants.com/horticulture/plants/annuals.htm
```

The browser strips away the /horticulture/plants/annuals.htm portion, adds the relative link, and then looks for the picture here:

```
http://www.jumboplants.com/images/flower.gif
```

This makes perfect sense. But consider what happens if you don't have your own domain name. In this case, your pages are probably stuck in a subfolder on another Web server. Here's an example:

```
http://www.superISP.com/~user9212/horticulture/plants/annuals.htm
```

In this case, the domain name part of the URL is *http://www.superISP.com*, but for all practical purposes, the root of your Web site is your personal folder *~user9212*. That means you need to add this detail into all your root-relative links. To get the result you want with the *flower.gif* picture, you'd need to use this messier root-relative tag:

```
<img src="/~user9212/images/flower.gif" alt="A flower">
```

Now the browser strips out just the domain name part of the URL (*http://www.superISP.com*) and then adds the relative part of the path, starting with your personal folder.

The Rules for Relative URLs

The rules for correctly writing a URL in an anchor tag are fairly strict, and there are a few common mistakes that creep into the best Web pages. Here are some pointers to help you avoid these headaches:

- When creating an absolute URL, it must start with the protocol (usually http://). You don't need to follow this rule when typing a URL into a browser. For example, if you type *www.google.com*, most browsers are intelligent enough to assume the http:// part. However, in an HTML document it's mandatory.

- Don't mix up the backslash (\) and the ordinary forward slash (/). In the Windows world, the backslash is used in file paths (like *C:\Windows\win.ini*). In the Web world, the forward slash separates subfolders (as in *http://www.ebay.com/Help/index.html*). Once again, many browsers tolerate backslash confusion, but the same mistake in an anchor tag will break your links.

- Don't ever use file paths instead of a URL. It's possible to create a URL that points to a file on your computer using the *file* protocol (as in *file:///C:/Temp/myPage.htm*). However, this link won't work on anyone else's computer, because they won't have the same HTML file on their hard drive. Sometimes, design tools like FrontPage may insert one of these so-called local URLs (for example, it can occur if you drag and drop a picture file into your Web page). Be vigilant—check all your links to make sure this doesn't happen.

- Don't use spaces or special characters in your file or folder names, even if these special characters are allowed. For example, it's perfectly acceptable to put a space in a file name (like *My Photos.htm*), but in order to request this page, the browser needs to translate the space into a special character code (*My%20Photos.htm*). To prevent this confusion, just steer clear of anything that isn't a number, letter, dash (-), or underscore (_).

Linking to Other Types of Content

Most of the links you write will point to bona fide HTML Web pages. But that's not your only option. You can link directly to other types of files. The only catch is that it's up to the browser to decide what to do when someone clicks a link that points to a different type of file.

Here are some common examples:

- **You can link to a JPEG, GIF, or PNG image file (page 186).** When the visitor clicks this link, the browser displays the image in the browser window without any other content. Web sites often use this approach to let visitors take a look at large graphics. For example, the trip Web site presented in the previous section has a page chock full of small image thumbnails. Click on one of these, and you'll see the full-size image appear.

- **You can link to a specialized type of file, like a PDF file, a Microsoft Office document, or an audio file (like a WAV or an MP3).** When you use this technique, you're taking a bit of a risk. These links rely on the browser having a plug-in that recognizes the file type, or a suitable program installed on the computer. If the surfer's computer doesn't have the right software, the only thing they'll be able to do is download the file to their computer (see the next point), where it will sit like an inert binary blob. However, if they do have the right plug-in, a small miracle happens. The Office, PDF, or audio file opens up right inside the browser window, as though it were a Web page!

- **You can link to a file you want others to download.** If a link points to a file of a specialized type and the browser doesn't have a plug-in that wants to deal with that file type, the browser usually gives the Web surfer a choice. The visitor can ignore the content altogether, open it using another program on their computer, or save it on the computer. This is a handy way to distribute large files (like a ZIP file featuring your personal philosophy of planetary motion).

- **You can link to an email message.** Everybody's favorite form of note-sending these days is email. It's easy to build a link into a Web page that fires up your visitors' favorite email program and helps them send a note to you. Page 315 has all the details.

Image Links and Image Maps

It's worth pointing out that you can also turn images into links. The trick is to put an <img> tag inside an <a> tag, like this:

```
<a href="LinkedPage.htm"><img src="MyPic.gif"></a>
```

Pictures that are linked in this way get a thick blue border that indicates they're clickable. Usually, you'll turn this clunky looking border off using the style sheet border properties (page 170) or by adding a *border* attribute and setting it to 0

(which is the old-fashioned approach). Either way, when a visitor hovers his
mouse over a linked picture, the mouse pointer changes to a hand.

In some cases, you might want to create distinct clickable regions *inside* a picture.
For example, consider Figure 8-4.

Figure 8-4:
*Left: An ordinary picture,
courtesy of the <img>
tag.*

*Right: An irregularly
shaped region inside the
mouth becomes a hot
spot—a clickable region
that takes the surfer to
another page. In this
example, the hot spot is
visible because it's being
edited in FrontPage.
Ordinarily, hot spots are
invisible when you're
looking at the page in a
Web browser.*

To add a hotspot to a picture, you need to start by creating an *image map* using the
<map> tag. This part's easy—all you need to do is choose a unique name for your
image map so you can use it later on:

```
<map name="FaceMap">
</map>
```

Inside the <map> tag, between the start and end tags, you need to define each
hotspot. You can add as many hotspots as you want, although they shouldn't overlap. (If they do, the one that's defined first takes precedence.)

To define each hotspot, you add an <area> tag. The area tag identifies three
important details: the target page you'll get to if the link is clicked (the *href*
attribute), the shape of the hotspot (the *shape* attribute), and the exact dimensions
(the *cords* attribute). Here's an example:

```
<area href="MyPage.htm" shape="rect" coords="5,5,95,195">
```

This hotspot defines a rectangular region. When clicked, it takes the surfer to
MyPage.htm.

Three types of shapes are supported for the *shape* attribute, each of which corresponds to a different value for the *shape* attribute. You can use circles (*circle*), rectangles (*rect*), and multi-edged shapes (*polygon*). Once you've chosen your shape,
you need to supply the coordinates, which are a bit trickier to interpret. In order to

understand hotspot coordinates, you need to first understand how browsers measure pictures (see Figure 8-5).

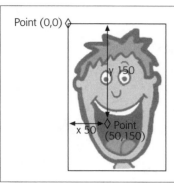

Figure 8-5:
Setting coordinates on an image map requires a quick trip back to Graph-Reading 101. Browsers designate the top-left corner in a picture as point (0, 0). As you move down the picture, the y-coordinate gets bigger. For example, the point (0, 100) is at the left edge of the picture, but 100 pixels from the top. As you move to the right, the x-coordinate gets bigger. That means the point (100, 0) is at the top of a picture, 100 pixels from the left edge.

You need to enter the coordinates as a list of numbers separated by commas. For a circle, list the coordinates in this order: center point (x-coordinate), center point (y-coordinate), radius. For any other shape, supply the corners in order as a series of x-y coordinates, like this: x1, y1, x2, y2, and so on. For a polygon, you supply every point. For a rectangle, you only need two points—the top-left corner, and the bottom-right corner.

That means the rectangle described earlier is defined by these two points: (5,5) at the top-left and (95, 195) at the bottom right. The more complex polygon that represents the mouth region in Figure 8-4 is defined like this:

```
<area href="MyPage.htm" shape="polygon"
  coords="38, 122, 76, 132, 116, 110, 102, 198, 65, 197">
```

In other words, this shape is created by drawing lines between these five points: (38, 122), (76, 132), (116,110), (102, 198), and (65, 197)

Tip: Getting coordinates correct is tricky. Many Web editors, like FrontPage and Dreamweaver, have built-in hotspot editors that let you create an image map by dragging shapes over your picture, which is a lot easier than trying to guess the correct values. To use this tool in Dreamweaver, select a picture, and look for the three hotspot icons (circle, square and polygon) in the Properties panel. In FrontPage, you use similar icons in the Picture toolbar. If the Picture toolbar isn't visible, right-click the picture and then select Show Pictures Toolbar.

Once you've perfected all your hotspots, there's one step left. You need to apply the hotspot to an image by adding the *usemap* attribute to your <img> tag. The *usemap* attribute matches the name of the map, but starts with the hash (#) character, which indicates that the image map is defined on the current page:

```
<img src="mouth.gif" usemap="#FaceMap">
```

Here's the complete HTML for the mouth hotspot example:

```
<html>
<head>
<title>Image Map</title>
<style>
  img {
    border-style: none;
  }
</style>
</head>

<body>
<p>Click inside his mouth...</p>
<p>
  <map name="FaceMap">
  <area href="http://edcp.org/factsheets/handfoot.html" shape="polygon"
   coords="38, 122, 76, 132, 116, 110, 102, 198, 65, 197">
  </map>
  <img src="mouth.gif" usemap="#FaceMap">
</p>
</body>

</html>
```

The hotspots you create are invisible (unless you've drawn lines on your picture to indicate where they are). However, when visitors hover over a hotspot the mouse pointer changes to a hand. Clicking on a hotspot has the same effect as clicking an ordinary <a> link—surfers get transported immediately to the new page.

Note: It's tempting to use image maps to start creating your own navigation systems. However, sophisticated Web sites go many steps further with menus and buttons that become highlighted when the mouse moves over them. To implement this nifty trick you need the JavaScript know-how you'll learn in Chapters 14 and 15.

Adding Bookmarks

Most links lead from one page to another. When you make the jump to a new page, the browser plunks you down at the very top of the page. However, it's also possible to create links that direct the Web surfer to a specific part of a Web page. This is particularly useful if you're creating long, scrolling pages and you want to direct your visitors' attention to a particular passage.

You can use this technique to create a link that leads to another position on the current page (see Figure 8-6), or a specific place in another Web page. Technically, this specific place where you want to send the reader is called a *fragment*.

Creating a link that points to a fragment is a two-step process. First, you need a way to identify that fragment. For example, imagine you want to send a visitor to the third level-three heading in a Web page named *sales.htm*. In order to make this work, you need to embed a marker just before that level-three heading. This marker is called a *bookmark*.

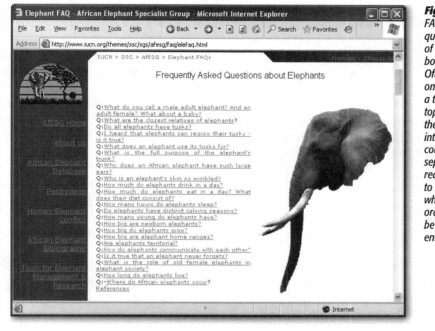

Figure 8-6:
FAQ (frequently asked questions) pages are one of the best examples of bookmarks at work. Often, an entire FAQ is only one long page, and a table of contents at the top lets you jump to just the topic you're interested in. A FAQ could be broken into separate pages, but then readers wouldn't be able to scan through the whole list of questions in order, and there wouldn't be any way to print the entire document at once.

To create a bookmark you use the <a> anchor tag, but with a twist. You don't supply the href attribute, because this anchor won't actually lead anywhere. All you supply is a *name* attribute that gives your bookmark a descriptive name. It's up to you whether you put any text inside the anchor—technically you don't need to, but most people find it easier to lock the bookmark into place around a specific word or title.

Here's an example:

```
...
<a name="Canaries"><h3>Pet Canaries</h3></a>
<p>Pet canary sales have plummeted in the developed world, due in large part
to currency fluctuations and other macroeconomic forces.</p>
...
```

In this example, the bookmark surrounds a heading and has the name Canaries.

Once you've created a bookmark, you can write a URL that points to that bookmark. The trick is that you need to add the bookmark information to the end of the URL. To do this, you add the number sign symbol (#), followed by the bookmark name.

For example, if you're sending the reader to a bookmark named Canaries in the *sales.htm* page, here's the link you'd use:

```
Learn about recent developments in <a href="sales.htm#Canaries">canary
sales</a>.
```

When you click this link, the browser heads to the *sales.htm* page and scrolls down the page until the Canaries bookmark is at the very top of the browser window.

Tip: If your bookmark is near the bottom of the page, the browser might not be able to scroll the bookmark all the way to the top of the window. Instead, the bookmarked section will appear somewhere in the middle of the browser window. This occurs because the browser hits the bottom of the page, and can't scroll down any further. If you think there's some potential for confusion (perhaps because you have several bookmarked sections close to each other on the same page), you can add a few line breaks at the end of your document, which will allow the browser to scroll down further.

Sometimes you might want to create a link that points to a bookmark in the *current* page. In this case, you don't need to specify the page name at all. Just start with the number sign, followed by the bookmark name:

```
Jump to the <a href="#Canaries">canary</a> section.
```

Using bookmarks effectively is an art. Resist the urge to overcrowd your pages with links that direct the reader between relatively small sections. Only use bookmarks to tame large pages that take several screenfuls of scrolling.

When Good Links Go Bad

Now that you've considered all the ways to build links, it's a good time to consider what can go wrong. Links on a site can break when you rename or move files or folders. Links to other Web sites are particularly fragile—they can break at any time, without warning. You won't know that anything's gone wrong until you click the link and get a "page not found" error message.

Broken links are so common that Web developers have coined a term to describe how Web sites gradually lose their linking abilities: *link rot*. Sadly, you can upload a perfectly working Web site today, and return a few months later to find that many of its external links have died off. They point to Web sites that no longer exist, have moved, or were rearranged.

Link rot is an insidious problem because it violates the confidence of your Web visitors. They see a page that promises to lead them to other interesting resources, but when they click one of the links to try and complete the deal, they're disappointed. Experienced Web surfers won't stay long at a Web site that's suffering from an advanced case of link rot—they'll assume that the site is updated infrequently and move on to a snazzier site somewhere else.

So how can you reduce the problem of broken links? First, you should rigorously test all your internal links—the ones that point to pages within your own site. Check for minor errors that can stop a link from working, and travel every path at least once. Leading HTML editors include built-in tools that can help automate this drudgery.

External links pose a different challenge. You can't create iron-clad external links, because link destinations are beyond your control and can change at any time. You could reduce the number of external links you include in your Web site to minimize the problem, but this isn't a very satisfying solution. Part of the beauty of the Web is the way a single click can take you from a comprehensive rock discography to a memorabilia site with hand-painted Elvis office supplies. As long as you want to connect your Web site to the rest of the world, you'll need to include external links. A better solution is to test your Web site regularly with a *link validator* that will walk through every page and check each link to make sure it still leads somewhere.

In the following sections, you'll take a quick look at Web site management and link validators.

Site Management

Nvu, Dreamweaver, FrontPage, and many other HTML editors include site management tools that let you see your entire Web site at a glance. In most cases, you need to specifically define a Web site in order to take advantage of these features (a process described on page 97). Once you've defined the Web site, you get a bird's eye view of everything it holds (see Figure 8-7).

In many ways, looking at the contents of your Web site folders isn't as interesting as studying the Web of links that binds your pages together. Many Web page editors give you the ability to get an at-a-glance look at where all your links lead (see Figure 8-8).

Link Checkers

A *link checker* is an automated tool that scans through one or more of your Web pages. It tests each link it finds by trying to retrieve the target page (the page your link is pointing to). Depending on the tool and the type of validation you're performing, link checkers might only scan internal links, or they might branch out to follow every link in every page until they've completely covered your Web site.

Sophisticated link checkers are built into programs like FrontPage and Dreamweaver, and they're great for digging through your Web site and finding problems. In Dreamweaver, use the command Site → Check Links Sitewide to perform a link check. In FrontPage, you can use a similar feature by choosing View → Reports → Problems → Hyperlinks.

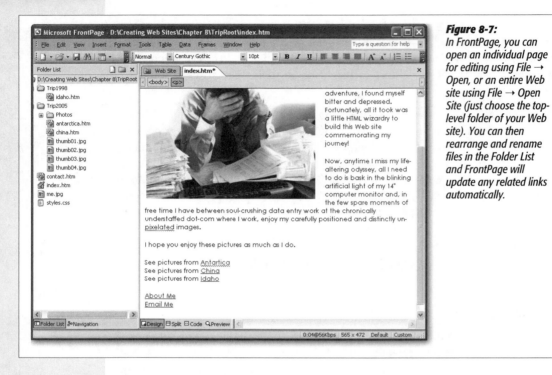

Figure 8-7:
In FrontPage, you can open an individual page for editing using File → Open, or an entire Web site using File → Open Site (just choose the top-level folder of your Web site). You can then rearrange and rename files in the Folder List and FrontPage will update any related links automatically.

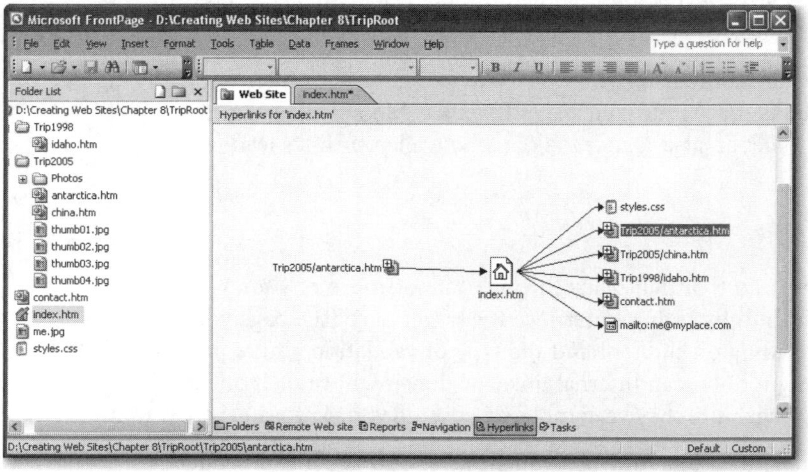

Figure 8-8:
In FrontPage, choose View → Hyperlinks, and you'll see this view, which shows you how the currently selected page fits into your Web site. In this example, the current page is index.htm. Arrows pointing away from index.htm represent links that lead to other pages. Arrows pointing to index.htm represent links in other pages that lead to index.htm. Click one of the plus (+) boxes next to another page, and you'll see all the links for that page, too.

The link checkers that are built into HTML editors work on the copy of your Web site that's stored on your computer. That's the best way to keep watch for errors as you're developing your Web site, but it's no help once your Web site's out in the wild. For example, it won't catch mistakes like linking to a local file on your hard drive or forgetting to upload a file you need to the Web server.

To get the final word on your Web site's links, you might want to try a free online link checker. The World Wide Web Consortium provides a solid choice at *http://validator.w3.org/checklink*. To start your free online link check, follow these steps:

1. **Surf to *http://validator.w3.org/checklink*.**

   This takes you to the W3C Link Checker utility.

2. **Enter the full URL for the page you want to check in the text box.**

   If your Web site has a default page like *index.htm*, you can type in just the domain name without explicitly supplying a file name.

3. **Choose the options you want to apply (Figure 8-9).**

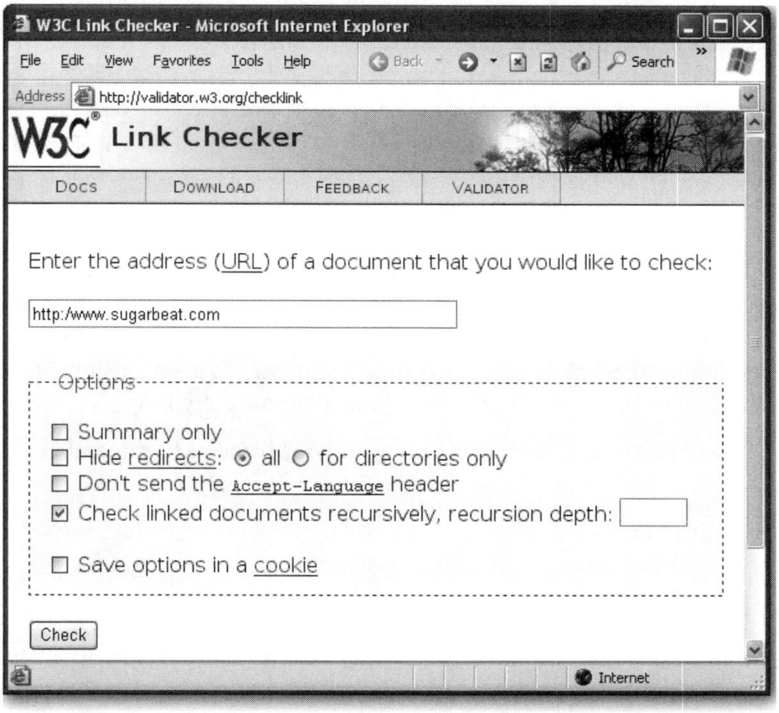

Figure 8-9:
Start by choosing the Web page you want to check, and whether or not you use recursion (which is used in this example). For more on how recursion works, see step 3, page 230. Then click Check to get started.

Select "Summary only" if you don't want to see the detailed list of steps that appears as the link checker examines each page. However, it's better to leave this option turned off, so you can get a better understanding of exactly what pages the link checker is examining.

Select "Hide redirects" if you want to ignore instructions that would redirect the link checker to another page (page 231). Usually, redirects indicate that your link still works, but should be updated to a new page.

The "Don't send the Accept-header" option tells the link checker not to tell the Web site about its language preferences. This setting only has an effect if you're creating a multilingual Web site, which is beyond the scope of this book.

The "Checked linked documents recursively" option allows you to search more than one page at a time using recursion. If you don't use this option, the link validator simply checks every link in the page you specify, and makes sure it points to a live Web page. If you use recursion, the link validator checks all the links in the current page, and then it *follows* each link. For example, if you have a link that points to a page named *info.htm,* the link checker first verifies that *info.htm* exists. Then it finds all the links in *info.htm,* and starts testing them. In fact, if *info.htm* links to another page (like *contact.htm*), the link checker branches out to that page and starts checking *its* links as well.

Note: The link checker is smart enough to avoid checking the same page twice. It also doesn't use recursion on external links. That means that if you start your link checker on the home page of your Web site, it will follow the links to get to every other page on your site, but it won't go any further. In other words, recursion is a great way to drill through all the links in your entire Web site in one go.

If you want to limit recursion (perhaps because you have a lot of pages and you don't need to check them all), you can supply a "recursion depth," which is the maximum number of levels you want to dig down. For example, if the recursion depth is 1, the link checker will only follow the first set of links. If you don't supply a recursion depth, the link checker checks everything.

4. **Select "Save options in a cookie" if you want your browser to remember these choices.**

   If you use this option, the next time you use the link checker, the browser will fill in the check boxes using your previous settings.

5. **Click Check to start checking links.**

6. **The link checker shows a report that lists each link it checks (Figure 8-10). This report is updated while the link checker works. If you're using recursion, you'll**

see the link checker branch out from one page to another. The report adds a separate section for each page.

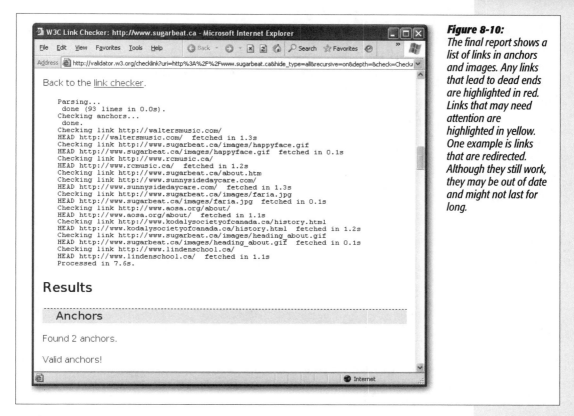

Figure 8-10:
The final report shows a list of links in anchors and images. Any links that lead to dead ends are highlighted in red. Links that may need attention are highlighted in yellow. One example is links that are redirected. Although they still work, they may be out of date and might not last for long.

Using Redirects

In order to be a good Web citizen, you also need to respect people that are linking to your Web site. That means once you create your Web site and it becomes popular, try to avoid tinkering with page and folder names. Making a minor change could disrupt someone else's link, making it impossible for an eager Web surfer to get to your site.

Some Web gurus handle this problem using *redirects*. When they rearrange their sites, they keep all the old files. However, they remove the content from the old files, and replace it with a *redirect*—a special instruction that tells the browser to automatically navigate to a new page. The advantage of using a redirect is that it prevents a broken link, but it doesn't lock you into the old structure of your Web site if you've decided it's time to make a change.

To create a redirect, you need to add a special <meta> tag to the <head> portion of your Web page. This tag indicates the new destination using an absolute URL, and lists the number of seconds to wait before performing the redirect. Here's an example:

```
<!doctype html public "-//w3c//dtd html 4.0 transitional//en">
<html>
<head>
  <meta http-equiv="REFRESH"
   content="10; URL=http://www.mysite.com/homepage.htm">
  <title>Redirect</title>
</head>
<body>

  <h1>The page you want has moved</h1>
  <p>
    Please update your bookmarks. The new home page is
    <a href=" http://www.mysite.com/homepage.htm">
    http://www.mysite.com/homepage.htm</a>.
  </p>
  <p>
    You should be redirected to the new site in 10 seconds. Click <a
    <a href=" http://www.mysite.com/homepage.htm">
    here</a> to visit the new page immediately.
  </p>
</body>
</html>
```

To adapt this page for your own purposes, just change the number of seconds (currently at 10) and the redirect URL. When the browser loads this page, it shows the temporary page for the indicated number of seconds, and then automatically requests the new page.

Redirect pages really serve two purposes. They keep your pages working when you change your Web site's structure, and they inform the Web visitor that the link is obsolete. That's where the time delay comes in—it provides a few seconds to notify the visitor that they're entering the Web site the wrong way. Many Web sites keep their redirect pages around for a relatively short amount of time (for example, a few months), after which they remove the page altogether.

Page Layout Tools: Tables and Styles

When HTML was first created, the focus was on delivering basic information: the score in yesterday's ball game, the price of coffee beans in Colombia, reasons why the Macarena rules. As strange as it seems, no one thought formatting and layout tools were really that important. Fortunately, a few pioneering Web designers recognized the problem and set out to rescue the Web from the engineers who invented it. These Web-heads invented a number of clever workarounds that gave the HTML universe a much-needed blast of pizzazz.

The best known of these tactics is the *invisible table*. Using an invisible table, you can align content, pictures, and headings along the lines of an invisible grid. It's impossible to overstate how important invisible tables were in the early days of the Web—they saved us almost single-handedly from a world of drab, plain text pages. But now that styles are on the scene, invisible tables are starting to outgrow their usefulness. Although invisible tables are still widely used, many Web developers find that they're just too awkward to manage.

Today, invisible-table–based layout is slowly but surely giving way to *style-based layout*. Style-based layout uses the positioning rules of CSS to place panels, columns, and pictures in specific spots on a Web page. When you use style-based layout, your HTML markup is easier to understand, and you'll have less trouble replicating your design across multiple pages. With a little planning, you can even create flexible pages that can be completely rearranged without touching a line of HTML—all you need to do is modify the linked style sheet. (See Chapter 6 for all the details on how to get started working with style sheets.) But style-based layout isn't perfect, and there are a few browser quirks and compatibility problems that everyone still has to contend with.

In this chapter, you'll learn how to use both table-based and style-based layout.

Note: Overall, style-based layout is the most elegant, and neatly structured, approach—it's the wave of the future. Table-based layout has remained around, thanks to the compatibility it offers with old browsers, and for a few special scenarios where style-based design is unnaturally difficult. But that doesn't mean you should think about ignoring tables altogether. You'll still use them for laying out dense grids of information.

HTML Tables

A table is a grid of cells that's built out of rows and columns. Originally, HTML tables were used (predictably) to show tables of information. But crafty Web developers quickly discovered that *invisible* tables offered a perfect way to get around the limits of plain vanilla HTML, allowing Web page creators to lay out content in a variety of new ways (see Figure 9-1).

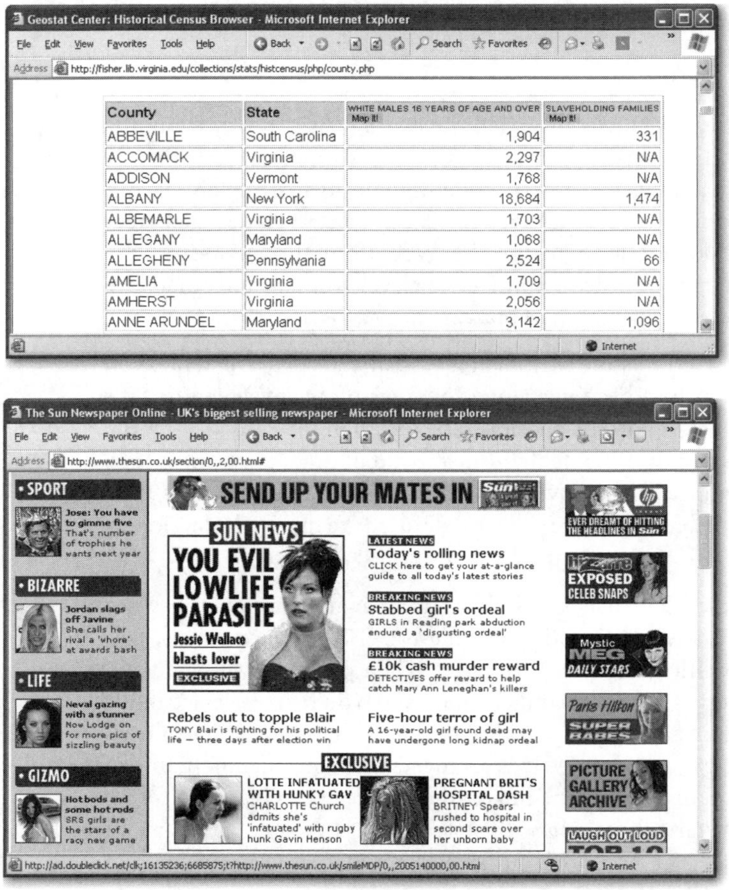

Figure 9-1:
Top: This detailed census information from 1790 makes perfect sense in an ordinary table.

Bottom: A combination of invisible tables (technically, tables with no borders) gives you all the underpinning you need for this headache-inspiring, multi-columned newspaper view.

In the following sections, you'll explore how to create a table using HTML.

The Anatomy of an HTML Table

All you need to whip up a table is a few new tags:

- **<table>** wraps the whole shebang. This is the starting point for every table.

- **<tr>** represents a single table row. A <table> contains a series of one or more <tr> tags.

- **<td>** represents a table cell (it stands for table data). Inside each <tr> tag, you add one <td> tag for each cell in the row. Inside the <td> tag, you place the text (or numbers, or <img> tags, or pretty much any HTML you like) that should appear in that cell. If you place text here, it gets displayed with the same font as ordinary body text.

- **<th>** is an optional tag used to define column headings. You can use a <th> tag instead of a <td> tag at any time, although it makes most sense in the first row of the table. The text inside the <th> tag is formatted in almost the same way as the text in a <td> tag, except it's bold and centered (unless you've applied different formatting rules with a style sheet).

Note: There are a few other table-specific tags that have fallen by the wayside. These tags, which either aren't needed or aren't supported in all browsers, include <thead>, <tbody>, <tfoot>, and <caption>.

Figure 9-2 shows a table at its simplest. Here's a portion of the HTML used to create the table in Figure 9-2:

```
<table>
  <tr>
    <th>Rank</th>
    <th>Name</th>
    <th>Population</th>
  </tr>
  <tr>
    <td>1</td>
    <td>Rome</td>
    <td>450,000</td>
  </tr>
  <tr>
    <td>2</td>
    <td>Luoyang (Honan), China</td>
    <td>420,000</td>
  </tr>
  <tr>
    <td>3</td>
    <td>Seleucia (on the Tigris), Iraq</td>
```

```
        <td>250,000</td>
    </tr>
    ...
</table>
```

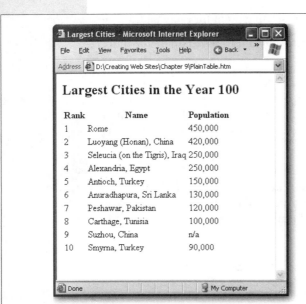

Figure 9-2:
Top: A basic table doesn't have any borders, but you'll still spot the signature sign that you're looking at a table: text lined up neatly in rows and columns.

Bottom: This behind-the-scenes look at the HTML powering the table above shows the <table>, <tr>, <th>, and <td> tags for the first three rows.

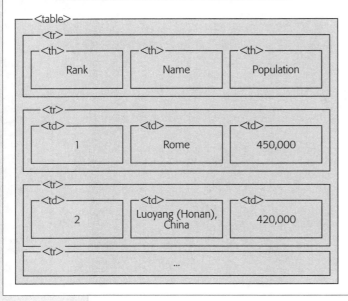

In this example, the tags are indented to help you see the structure of the table. Indenting your table tags like this is always a good idea, as it helps you spot mismatched tags. In this example, the only content in the <td> tags is ordinary text. But you can also add other HTML tags into a cell, including hyperlinks (the <a> tag) and images (the <img> tag).

Tip: You might be able to avoid writing tables by hand, as most Web design tools include their own table editors that let you point and click your way to success. These table-creation features are similar to those you'd find in a word processor.

Formatting Table Borders

Traditional tables have borders around each cell. You can turn on table borders using the *border* attribute. The *border* attribute specifies the width (in pixels) of the line that is added around each cell and around the entire table. Here's an example:

```
<table border="1">
  ...
</table>
```

Although you can choose the line thickness, you can't control the style of a table border. Most browsers use a solid black line with a raised edge to outline a table.

If this lack of control troubles you, you can always use style sheets. The basic trick is to create a borderless table and then apply a border to the <tr> and <table> tags. Style sheet border properties are described on page 170.

The following style sheet rules set a thin blue border around every cell, and create a thick blue border around the entire table:

```
table {
  border-width: 3px;
  border-style: solid;
  border-color: blue;
}
td, th {
  border-width: 1px;
  border-style: solid;
  border-color: blue;
}
```

Figure 9-3 shows the result.

Tip: Borders aren't the only style sheet feature you can apply to table cells. You can also change the font and text alignment, the padding and margins (page 165), and the colors. You can even set a background image for an individual cell or the whole table using the background-image property (page 199). And if you want to apply style rules to individual cells (rather than the whole table), you just need to use class names (page 173).

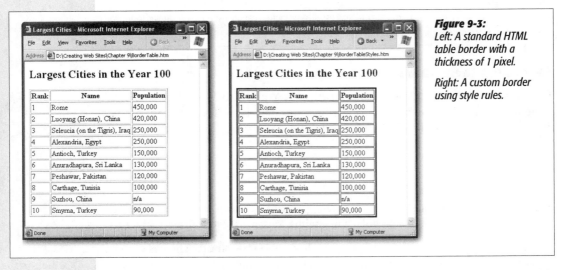

Figure 9-3:
Left: A standard HTML table border with a thickness of 1 pixel.

Right: A custom border using style rules.

There's one hiccup to watch out for when creating tables with borders. Empty table cells will appear to be "collapsed," which means they won't get any borders at all (see Figure 9-4).

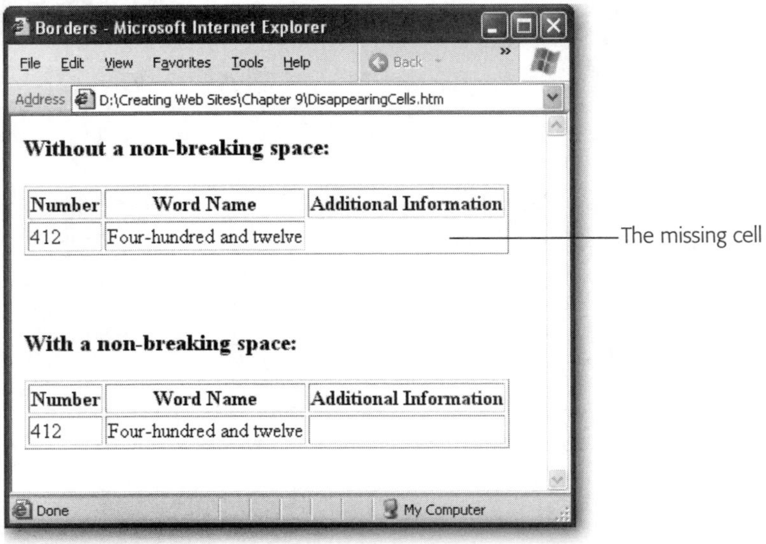

Figure 9-4:
If you don't include a non-breaking space, you'll lose the borders around your empty cells.

The missing cell

To prevent your cell from collapsing, add a single non-breaking space:

```
<td> </td>
```

This space won't be displayed in the browser, but it will ensure the borders stay put.

Cell Spans

HTML tables support *spanning*, a feature that allows a single cell to stretch out over several columns or rows. Spanned cells let you tweak your tables in all kinds of funky ways.

You can use a *column span* to stretch a cell out over two or more columns. To make this happen, just add the *colspan* attribute to the <td> tag you want to extend, and specify the total number of columns you want it to occupy. Here's an example that stretches a cell out over two columns, so that it actually occupies the space of two full cells:

```
<table border="1" cellpadding="2" width="100%" id="table1">
  <tr>
    <td>Column 1</td>
    <td>Column 2</td>
    <td>Column 3</td>
    <td>Column 4</td>
  </tr>
  <tr>
    <td> </td>
    <td colspan="2">Look out, this cell spans two columns!</td>
    <td> </td>
  </tr>
  ...
</table>
```

Figure 9-5 shows this trick in action.

In order to make sure your table doesn't get mangled when you're using column spanning, you need to keep track of the total number of columns you have to work with in each row. In the previous example, the first row starts off by defining the four basic columns:

```
<tr>
  <td>Column 1</td>
  <td>Column 2</td>
  <td>Column 3</td>
  <td>Column 4</td>
</tr>
```

In the next row, the second column extends over the third column, thanks to column spanning. As a result, the next <td> tag actually becomes the *fourth* column. That means you need only three <td> tags to fill up the full width of the table:

```
<tr>
  <!-- This fills column 1 -->
  <td> </td>

  <!-- This fills columns 2 and 3 -->
  <td colspan="2">Look out, this cell spans two columns!</td>

  <!-- This fills column 4 -->
  <td> </td>
</tr>
```

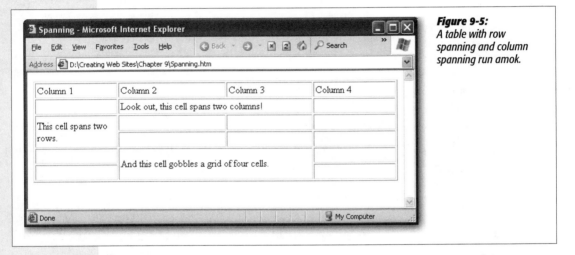

Figure 9-5:
A table with row spanning and column spanning run amok.

The same principle works with *row spanning* and the *rowspan* attribute. In the following example, the first cell in this row leaks through to the second row:

```
<tr>
  <td rowspan="2">This cell spans two rows.</td>
  <td> </td>
  <td> </td>
  <td> </td>
</tr>
```

In the next row, the first cell is already occupied by the cell from above. That means the first <td> tag you declare actually becomes the second column. All in all, this row needs only three <td> tags:

```
<tr>
  <td> </td>
  <td> </td>
  <td> </td>
</tr>
```

If you miscount and add too many cells to a row, you'll end up with an extra column at the end of your table.

Tip: Many HTML editors let you create spans by joining cells. In Nvu, just select a group of cells, right-click them, and select Join Selected Cells. In FrontPage and Dreamweaver it's the same process, but the menu command is named Merge Cells.

Sizing and Aligning Tables

If you don't explicitly set the size of a table, each column grows just wide enough to fit the longest line of text (or to accommodate any picture you add with an <img> tag). Likewise, the table grows big enough to fit all the columns. However, there's one exception—if these adaptations would cause the table to grow outside the bounds of the browser window, the table's width is limited to the browser window size. In that case, text gets wrapped inside each column.

Tip: Need more space inside your table? Style rules can make it easy. To add more space between the cell content and its borders, increase the padding property for the <td> and <tr> tags. To add more space between the cell borders and any adjacent cells, up the margin width for the <td> and <tr> tags. Page 167 has more on adjusting these dimensions.

In most cases, you'll want to explicitly set the width of your table and its columns. Once again, style sheets provide the best approach. All you need to use are the height and width properties, as explained in the next section.

Sizing the table

You have two choices when specifying table dimensions.

- **Relative sizing** sizes the table in sync with the dimensions of the browser window. You supply the percentage of the window that the table should fill.

- **Absolute sizing** uses pixel sizes to set an exact size for the table.

For example, the following style sheet rule ensures that this table always occupies the full width of the browser window:

```
table {
  width: 100%;
}
```

Thus, the table gets sized *in relation to* the size of the browser window. And this rule limits the table to half of the current window:

```
table {
    width: 50%;
}
```

Either way, the table resizes dynamically as you resize the browser window.

If you use exact pixel widths, you choose the exact size you want. For example, the following rule creates a table that's a generous 500 pixels wide.

```
table.Cities {
    width: 500px;
}
```

Because this is a very specific width, it will only be suitable for certain tables. To prevent the rule from being applied to every table, this example uses the class name Cities. Therefore you'll need to edit your HTML so that only specific tables adopt this class:

```
<table class="Cities">
    ...
</table>
```

You can also set the height of a table. Usually, you'll set the height using an absolute size, as shown here:

```
table.Cities {
    height: 500px;
}
```

Although you can set a table height as a percentage of the browser window, that creates a strange, rarely seen effect (a table that grows taller and shorter as you resize the page).

There's one important caveat to table sizing. Although you can enlarge a table as large as you want (even if it stretches off the borders of the page), you don't have the same power to shrink a table. If you specify a table size that's smaller than the minimum size needed to fit the table's data, the table appears at this minimum size (see Figure 9-6).

Sizing a column

Now that you know how to expand the size of a table, you're probably wondering where the extra space goes. Assuming the table has reached its standard size (just large enough to fit all the data), the extra space is distributed proportionately so that every column grows by the same amount.

Of course, this isn't necessarily what you want. You might be planning to create a wide descriptive column paired with a narrow column of densely-packed text. Or, you might just want to set columns to a specific size so that all your pages look the same, even if the content differs.

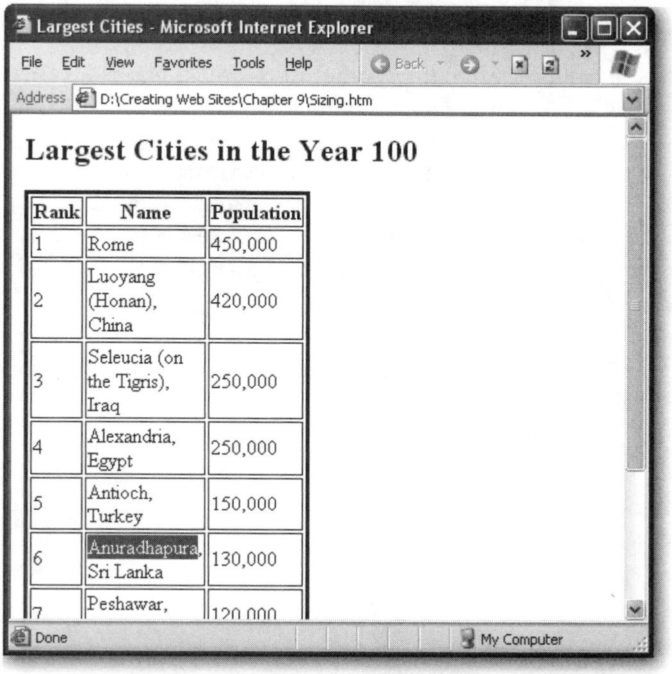

Figure 9-6:
In this example, the table was explicitly sized to a width of 1 pixel. However, the browser doesn't actually shrink it down that far, thus preventing individual words from being awkwardly chopped in two. In this table, the city name Anuradhapura is the longest un-splittable value, so it determines the width of the column. If you really want to ratchet the size down another notch, try shrinking the text by applying a smaller font size.

To set a column's size, you simply need to use the *width* property with the <td> and <th> tags. Once again, you can do this proportionately, using a percentage, or exactly, using a pixel width. However, percentages have a slightly different meaning when used with columns. When you use a percentage value for the table width, you're in effect sizing the entire table up against the width of the page. So, for example, 50 percent means 50 percent of the full width of the page. But when you use a percentage value to set a column width, you're defining the percentage of the *table* that the column should occupy. So a column with a 50 percent width takes up 50 percent of the table.

When you size columns, you need to create style rules that use class names (page 173). That's because each table column is potentially a different width—you can't just write a single style rule that applies to every column.

The following style rules set different widths for each of the three columns that you see in Figure 9-6.

```
th.Rank {
  width: 10%;
}
th.Name {
```

```
    width: 80%;
  }
  th.Population {
    width: 10%;
  }
```

In this example, the class names match the column titles, which makes it easier to keep track of which style rule applies to each column.

Note: When you're using percentage widths for columns, you don't need to specify values for all three columns. If you leave one out, the browser will size it to fill the rest of the space in the table. If you do decide to include widths for each column (as in the previous example), make sure they add up to 100 percent, to avoid confusion. Otherwise, the browser will need to override one of your settings, and you won't know how your table will actually appear.

In order for these rules to take effect, you need to apply them to the corresponding cells:

```
<table class="Cities">
  <tr>
    <th class="Rank">Rank</th>
    <th class="Name">Name</th>
    <th class="Population">Population</th>
  </tr>
  <tr>
    <td>1</td>
    <td>Rome</td>
    <td>450,000</td>
  </tr>
```

Notice that the widths are applied only to the first row (which contains the cell headers in this example). You could apply the rule to every single row, but there's really no point. When the browser builds a table, it scans the whole table structure to determine the required size, based on the cell content and any explicit width settings. If you apply a different width to more than one cell in the same column, the browser simply uses the largest value.

Tip: It's a good idea to size your table by applying style rules to the first row. This makes your HTML more readable, because it's immediately obvious what the dimensions of your table are.

Sizing a row

You can size a row just as easily as you size a column. The best approach is to use the *height* property on the <tr> attribute, as shown here:

```
t5.TallRow {
  height: 100px;
}
```

Once again, percentages and pixel values are both acceptable. When you resize a row, you affect every cell in every column. However, you're free to make each row in the table a different height, using the techniques just described.

Organizing a Page with Tables

So far, the tables you've seen have been fairly typical grids of information. But on many Web sites, tables play another role—they organize the page into separate regions.

One of the most common Web site designs is to divide the page into two or three columns. The column on the left typically has navigation buttons or links. The column in the middle takes the most space, and has the main content for the page. The column on the right, if present, has additional information, an advertisement, or another set of links. Figure 9-7 shows how it all breaks down.

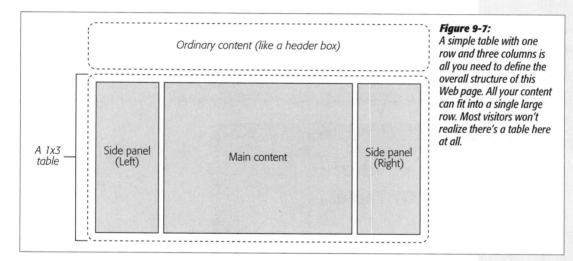

Figure 9-7:
A simple table with one row and three columns is all you need to define the overall structure of this Web page. All your content can fit into a single large row. Most visitors won't realize there's a table here at all.

In order to make this design work, you need to consider several details:

- **Vertical text alignment.** Ordinarily, row content is centered between the top and bottom edge of the row. This effect isn't what you want in an extremely large row. Instead, you want to make sure each cell is aligned with the top of the table, so the content in the side panels remains at the top of your page, and is immediately visible.

- **Borders.** If you decide to use borders, you'll want them only on *some* edges to emphasize the separation of content. You won't want them around every cell and the entire table. In many cases, you'll do away with borders altogether and just use different background colors or images to separate the sections of your page.

- **Sizing.** Typically, the sidebars will be fixed in size. The middle panel needs to command the most space.

Figure 9-8 gives you a taste of what a finished page that uses a table for layout might look like. You can see this example with the downloadable content for this chapter.

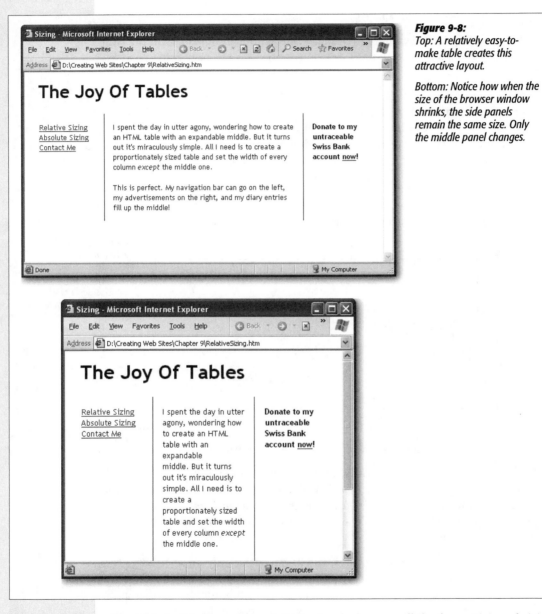

Figure 9-8:
Top: A relatively easy-to-make table creates this attractive layout.

Bottom: Notice how when the size of the browser window shrinks, the side panels remain the same size. Only the middle panel changes.

The table in this example is relatively simple, because all the formatting and sizing details are maintained separately, in the style rules. Therefore, all you need to do is create an ordinary table with one row and three columns. Each column is then mapped to a different style using a class name.

```
<table>
  <tr>
    <td class="Left">
      <a href="RelativeSizing.htm">Relative Sizing</a><br>
      <a href="AbsoluteSizing.htm">Absolute Sizing</a><br>
      <a href="mailto:no-one">Contact Me</a><br>
    </td>
    <td class="Middle">
      I spent the day in utter agony, wondering how
      to create an HTML table with an expandable middle...
    </td>
    <td class="Right">
      Donate to my untraceable Swiss Bank account
      <a href="http://www.paypal.org">now</a>!
    </td>
  </tr>
</table>
```

The style sheet rules start by choosing a font for the whole document:

```
body {
  font-family: Trebuchet MS, serif;
}
```

Next, the table is sized to fill the window:

```
table {
  width: 100%;
}
```

Every cell is given some standard settings for text alignment, font size, and padding (to give a little extra space between the column border and the text):

```
td {
  font-size: x-small;
  padding: 15px;
  vertical-align: top;
}
```

Finally, the column-specific rules set the widths and the borders. The side panels are given fixed, 100-pixel widths:

```
td.Left {
  width: 100px;
}
td.Right {
  width: 100px;
  font-weight: bold;
}
```

The middle panel isn't given an explicit width. Instead, it's sized to fit whatever space remains. It's also given left and right borders to separate the side panels:

```
td.Middle {
  border-left-width: 1px;
  border-right-width: 1px;
  border-top-width: 0px;
  border-bottom-width: 0px;
  border-style: solid;
  border-color: blue;
}
```

There's one last detail you might want to consider changing. This example uses proportional sizing for the table, which allows the middle panel to grow and shrink as the browser window is resized. Although this is the most flexible option, in dense, graphics-rich Web sites, absolute sizing is a must, because it gives you tighter control over how the page looks. Absolute sizing prevents the table from being resized and mangling your layout.

You can convert this example to use absolute sizing by changing the table style rule, as shown here:

```
table {
  width: 600px;
}
```

Now the table is 600 pixels wide. The left and right panels are still 100 pixels each, and the middle column gets whatever's left in the table after the left and right panels are sized. That means it's always exactly 400 pixels wide (based on a total width of 600 pixels, minus 100 pixels for each panel). Figure 9-9 shows the difference.

If you use relative sizing, you need to think quite carefully about the size of monitor your visitors are using to surf your site. Choose a column width that's narrow enough for the average visitor. (As discussed on page 112, a typical monitor resolution is 800 x 600 pixels, which gives a maximum width of 800 pixels if the browser window is maximized. Many Web designers use a width of 760 pixels, to make sure there's room left over for a vertical scroll bar, if needed.) If the content is too wide for the browser window, visitors will need to scroll from side to side to read each line.

Style-Based Layout

Although the table-based approach seems perfect at first, it has a few frustrating quirks. One of the most daunting problems is that once you've perfected your table-based layout, you need to painstakingly copy the exact table structure to every other page in your Web site. This is tedious, and tables are notorious for going haywire when a single tag goes missing. Even worse, what happens once you've copied your table-based layout into a hundred different pages, and then decide you want to improve it with a minor change?

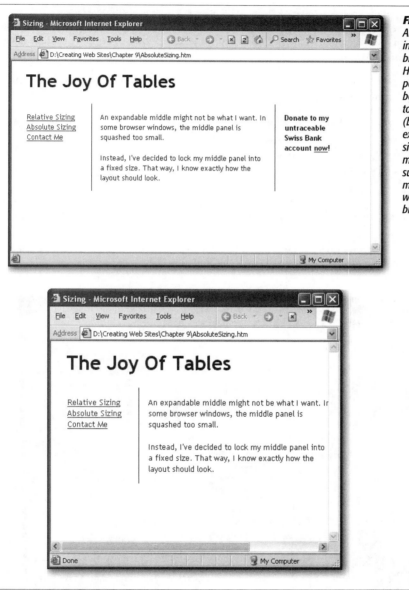

Figure 9-9:
Absolute sizing keeps the integrity of your layout as the browser window is resized. However, the tradeoff is the possibility that visitors might be forced to scroll from side to side to see everything (bottom), which is sure to exasperate them. Another side effect is that the page might appear barren for surfers with high-resolution monitors due to all the empty white space they'll see in the browser window.

In the early lawless days of the Web, HTML tables went unchallenged. But when styles appeared, leading Web designers began to explore new layout options. For most Web-heads, style-based layout takes a little bit longer to grasp, but causes fewer long-term headaches. Here are some of the benefits:

- The HTML for a page that uses style-based layout is cleaner and easier to read.

- Ideally, all the style information is stored in a separate style sheet so that it can be applied to multiple pages with little effort.

- When you modify the style sheet, you can reconfigure the layout of every linked page in one (immensely gratifying) fell swoop.

You've already taken your first tentative steps towards this nirvana by learning about style-based layout using boxed text and floating images (Chapter 7). But before you go any further, you need to consider a few more style sheet features that make it all possible.

Tip: Many of the layout features you'll read about below are more recent than the meat-and-potatoes properties for text formatting, colors, and borders. Some are a part of CSS2 (rather than the original CSS1 standard). As a result, it's even more important to test a page on as many different browsers as possible when you use style-based layout. As a rule of thumb, don't expect perfect layout if you're dealing with browsers that are older than Internet Explorer 5 and Netscape Navigator 6.

POWER USERS' CLINIC

Nested Tables

In sophisticated Web sites, the show doesn't end with a single table. Instead, tables are placed *inside* of other tables, which are then placed in yet more tables. For example, you might create a basic three-column setup using one table, and then divide the right column into a series of distinct ads using a second table. When a table is placed in another table, it's called a *nested table*.

Creating this design is easy (although it can be a little difficult to keep track of everything). The trick is to define a table inside one of the cells in an existing table. For example, if you have this table with three columns:

```
<table>
  <tr>
    <td class="Left">...</td>
    <td class="Middle">...</td>
    <td class="Right">...</td>
  </tr>
</table>
```

You can slide a table right into the <td> tags for the third column:

```
<table>
  <tr>
    <td class="Left">...</td>
    <td class="Middle">...</td>
    <td class="Right">
      <table>
        <tr>...</tr>
        <tr>...</tr>
      </table>
    </td>
  </tr>
</table>
```

Resizing all the parts of these two tables can get confusing. It's easiest to size the nested table using a relative size of 100 percent. This way, the nested table expands or shrinks to fit the column that contains it.

The <div> Tag

Before you can start placing elements in the right positions, you need a way to bundle up all the related content into a single neat package. In the HTML table examples, that package was the table cell. When you're using styles, that package is the <div> tag—the all-purpose container described on page 125.

For example, imagine you want to create a box with several links on the left side of your page. Trying to position each link separately is as much fun as peeling grapes. By using the <div> tag, you can group everything together:

```
<div class="Menu">
  <a href="...">Home Page</a>
  <a href="...">Buy Our Products</a>
  <a href="...">File a Lawsuit</a>
  ...
</div>
```

Whenever you create a <div> tag, choose a class name that describes the type of content (like LeftPanel, Menu, Header, AdBar, and so on). Later on, you can create a style rule that positions this <div> tag and sets its font, colors, and borders.

Remember, a <div> doesn't define any formatting. In fact, on its own, it doesn't do anything at all. The magic happens when you combine your <div> with a style sheet rule.

Even Better Selectors

In Chapter 6, you learned a variety of different ways to write *selectors*. A selector is the part of a style sheet rule that identifies what you want to format. The most common type of selectors are *type* selectors, which format every occurrence of a specific HTML tag, and *class* selectors, which format every tag that uses the same class name. However, there are a few ways you can get even craftier.

Contextual selectors

Contextual selectors are stricter than ordinary type selectors. Whereas a type selector matches a tag, a contextual selector matches a tag *inside another tag*. To understand the difference, take a look at this type selector:

```
b {
  color: red;
}
```

This selector formats all bold text in red. But what if you want to work only on bold text that appears inside a bulleted list? You can do this using the following contextual type selector, which matches the unordered list tag (<ul>) and then finds any bold tags inside it:

```
ul b {
  color: red;
}
```

To create a contextual type selector, you simply need to put a space between the two tags.

Contextual selectors are useful, but thinking through the different possibilities for combining tags can get a little dizzying. The real benefit occurs when you use a contextual selector to match a specific type of tag inside a specific type of class.

For example, imagine you want to change how all the links look inside the menu panel described above. The menu panel is represented by a <div> tag with the class name Menu. Here's the rule you need:

```
div.Menu a {
  color: red;
}
```

The first part of this selector gets all the <div> tags in your page. The second part limits the matches to <div> tags that have the Menu class—which is exactly one. The third and final part of the selector extracts the <a> tags inside the menu panel.

The end result is that this rule changes every anchor in the menu panel to have red lettering. However, the anchors in the rest of the Web page are left alone. This technique is frequently used in Web pages that use CSS-based layout, because contextual selectors make it easy for you to define formatting rules for different sections of a page.

id selectors

There's one other type of selector that you need to know about: the *id selector*. The id selector is actually a lot like the class selectors you've been using up until now. Like a class selector, the id selector lets you pick a descriptive name for your rule. But instead of a period (.), you separate the tag name from the id name with a hash character (#), as shown here:

```
div#Menu {
  border-width: 2px;
  border-style: solid;
}
```

This example defines a rule named Menu that can apply only to <div> tags.

Like a class rule, id rules aren't applied unless you specifically indicate that they should be used in your HTML. However, instead of using the *class* attribute to switch them on, you use the *id* attribute.

For example, here's a <div> tag that uses the Menu style:

```
<div id="Menu">...</div>
```

At this point, you're probably wondering what's the point of all this—after all, the id selector seems almost exactly the same as the class selector. The only difference you've seen so far is in the name of the attribute that links the tag to the style rule.

But there is one more restriction: You can have only *one* tag in a page with a given id. In other words, if you define an id selector for formatting a menu, you can use it in your Web page only once. This restriction doesn't apply to classes, which you can reuse inexhaustibly.

Web designers like the id selector for page elements that occur only once, because they're clearer. For example, a page has only one menu, or one navigation bar. By using the id attribute, you clearly communicate this fact. Of course, the reason you need to understand id attributes is because you'll frequently see them in the wild (for example, you'll find them in the *www.csszengarden.com* examples shown in Figure 9-12). Now that you know they're just a version of class attributes, you won't have any trouble understanding how they work.

Incidentally, you can use id selectors in all the same ways as other selectors. That means you can combine them with the comma (,) or you can create contextual selectors like the one shown here, which acts only on anchors inside a <div> menu:

```
div#Menu a {
   color: red;
}
```

Floating Boxes

Most of the example pages in previous chapters used *relative positioning*, which is the original HTML model. When you use relative positioning, elements are ordered based on where they appear in the document. For example, if you have one <div> followed by another <div>, the second <div> is placed below the first one.

To get richer layouts—for example, to create either of the pages you see in Figure 9-10, bottom—you need different ways to position content. One option is a *floating layout*, which you used to make pictures float off to the side in Chapter 7. A floating layout works just as readily with <div> tags, with one exception—you need to supply the correct width for the box.

Note: When you float an image, the floating box is automatically made as wide as the image in the box. When you float a text box, it's up to you to choose how wide you want it.

Here's an example that defines a box that floats on the right side of some text:

```
.Float {
   float: right;
   width: 150px;
   background-color: red;
   border-width: 2px;
   border-style: solid;
   border-color: black;
   padding: 10px;
   margin: 8px;
```

```
    font-weight: bold;
    color: white;
}
```

With floating content, text wraps around the edges (see Figure 9-10).

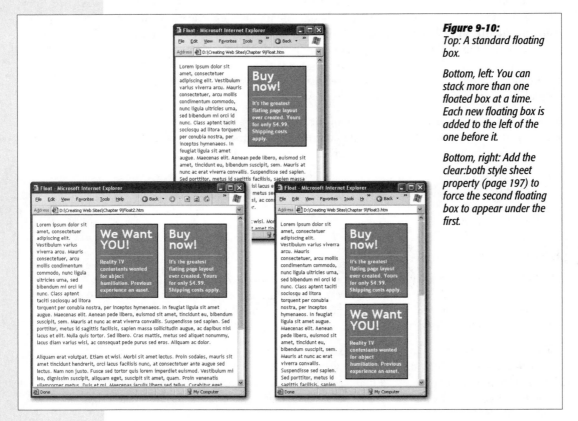

Figure 9-10:
Top: A standard floating box.

Bottom, left: You can stack more than one floated box at a time. Each new floating box is added to the left of the one before it.

Bottom, right: Add the clear:both style sheet property (page 197) to force the second floating box to appear under the first.

Absolute Positioning

Style sheets also let you place elements at fixed locations on a page, with no wrapping involved. This technique is handy for creating multi-columned pages (see Figure 9-11).

To use absolute positioning, you simply need to set the position property of your <div> tag to *absolute*. Then, you set the location of your <div> tag using a combination of the *top, left, right,* and *bottom* properties.

For example, the following style rule defines a panel that's 150 pixels wide and positioned along the left side of the page. The left edge of the box is 10 pixels from the edge of the browser window, and the top edge of the box is 70 pixels from the top of the browser window.

```
.LeftPanel {
    position: absolute;
```

```
  top: 70px;
  left: 10px;
  width: 150px;
}
```

It's just as easy to create a fixed panel on the right side. Just use the top and right position properties to space the box out from the right edge of the browser window:

```
.RightPanel {
  position: absolute;
  top: 70px;
  right: 10px;
  width: 150px;
}
```

The final step is to define a content section that sits between the two panels. You can't use absolute positioning for this part, because you don't know how large the browser window will be. Fortunately, you don't need to—all you need is to create enough spacing from either edge with the margin properties. Given that the panels are both 150 pixels wide, left and right margins of 151 pixels will do the trick:

```
.CenterPanel {
  margin-left: 151px;
  margin-right: 151px;
  padding-left: 12px;
  padding-right: 12px;
}
```

This panel also adds some padding to make sure the text isn't too crowded along the left and right edges.

Once you've defined the main regions of your page, you can insert content into them using <div> tags. But because the <div> tags are placed precisely on the page, it doesn't matter how you order the <div> tags in your Web page. For example, you might want to define the content for your left and right panels, and *then* your center panel. The point is, the order that you lay down your <div> tags doesn't matter. Here's an example:

```
<div class="LeftPanel">
  <h1>Links</h1>
  <a href="...">Page 1</a><br>
  <a href="...">Page 2</a><br>
  ...
</div>

<div class="RightPanel">
  <h1>Contact Us</h1>
  ...
</div>
```

```
<div class="CenterPanel">
   Styles are remarkably powerful. All you need to do is position
   a few &lt;div&gt; tags, and your content flows...
</div>
```

Figure 9-11 shows the results.

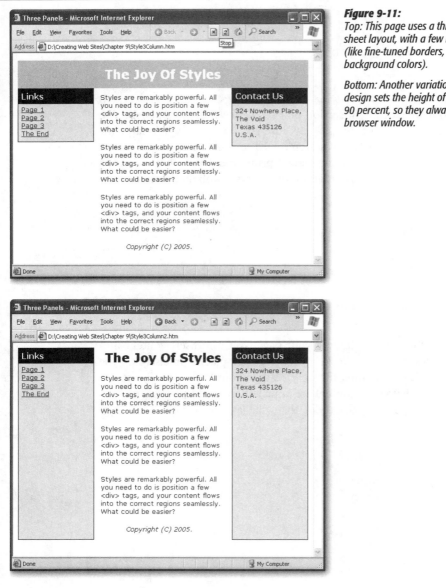

Figure 9-11:
Top: This page uses a three-panel style sheet layout, with a few more refinements (like fine-tuned borders, fonts, and background colors).

Bottom: Another variation of the same design sets the height of the side panels to 90 percent, so they always fill up the browser window.

The remarkable part about this example is that the HTML code is completely free of the messy formatting details. Instead, it's a small miracle of clarity, with content divided into several easy-to-understand sections. The same structure in a table would be cluttered with table tags, making it more difficult to interpret. And if you've saved your styles into an external style sheet (page 138), you can start building a second page that uses the same layout without spending any time puzzling out the correct formatting.

To use style-based layouts, begin by planning your page as a collection of separate regions. Next, put every region into a <div> tag with a different class, even if you don't intend to apply style sheet rules for the section yet. Finally, write the style sheet rules that position and format each element. This part is the most time-consuming, but don't worry—you can tweak your rules at any time without disturbing the HTML content. Figure 9-12 shows a Web site that takes this concept to the extreme.

Figure 9-12:
One page, dozens of different looks. The Web site www.csszengarden. com demonstrates the holy grail of style-based formatting: a page that can be thoroughly reformatted and rearranged just be switching the style sheet it uses. Best of all, you can download the HTML for this page and the sample style sheets to try it out for yourself.

Layering

It may have occurred to you that you need to position elements very carefully when using absolute positioning, to make sure you don't overlap one element over another. Interestingly, advanced Web pages sometimes overlap elements deliberately to create dramatic effects. For example, you might overlap two words to create a logo, or create a heading that partially overlaps a picture. These tricks use overlapping *layers*.

When using overlapping layers, the browser needs to know which element goes on top. This is accomplished through a simple number called the *z-index*. Elements with a high z-index are placed in front of elements with a lower z-index.

For example, here are two elements that are positioned absolutely so that they overlap:

```
.Back {
  z-index: 0;
  position: absolute;
  top: 10px;
  left: 10px;
  width: 150px;
  height: 100px;
  background-color: orange;
  border-style: dotted;
  border-width: 1px;
}
.Front {
  z-index: 1;
  position: absolute;
  top: 50px;
  left: 50px;
  width: 230px;
  height: 180px;
  font: xx-large;
  border-style: dotted;
  border-width: 1px;
}
```

The first class (Back) defines an orange background square. The second class (Front) defines a large font for text. The z-index is set so that the Front box (which has a z-index of 1) is superimposed over the Back box (which has a z-index of 0). A dotted border is added around both elements to make it easier to see how they overlap on the page.

Tip: The actual value of the z-index isn't important, only how it compares to other elements. For example, if you have two elements with the z-indexes of 48 and 100, you'll have the same effect as two elements with the z-indexes 0 and 1—the second element overlaps the first.

In your HTML, you need to create both boxes with <div> tags. It also makes sense to supply some text content for the Front box:

```
<div class="Back">
</div>
<div class="Front">
This text is on top.
</div>
```

In the browser, you'll a block of text that stretches over part of the orange box and out into empty space (see Figure 9-13, left).

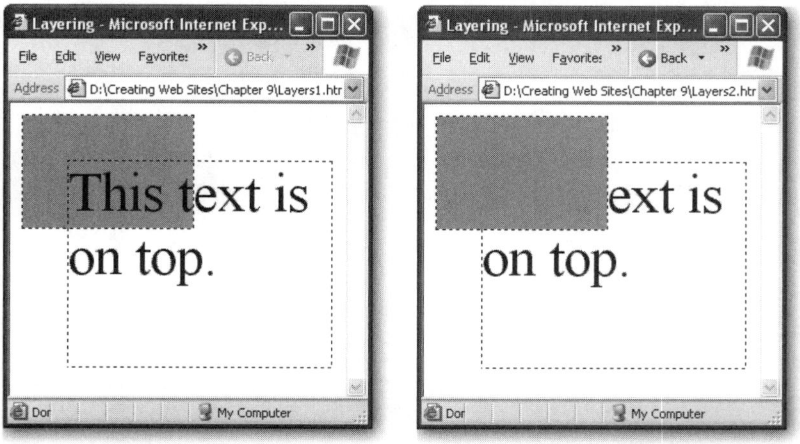

Figure 9-13:
Left: The colored box has the lower z-index.

Right: The colored box has the higher z-index, and obscures the text.

DESIGN TIME

Become a Style Sheet Guru

Style sheets are one of the hottest topics in Web development today. The Web is buzzing with discussion groups, articles, and tutorials that show how to create slick style-powered designs. If you want to become a style guru, there's still quite a bit to learn, including the ins and outs of browser quirks, workarounds for style sheet limitations, and innovative ways to combine graphics and text. Here are a few of the best resources:

- **Style sheet basics.** Is your style sheet expertise a little wobbly? Brush up with the tutorials at *www. w3schools.com/css*.

- **Style sheet examples (the barebones).** See some of the basic style sheet designs (like two- and three-column layouts) at the Layout Reservoir (*www. bluerobot.com/web/layouts*) and Glish (*http://glish. com/css*), along with handy links to other good online resources.

- **Style sheet examples (full-featured).** See dozens of different painstakingly perfected style sheets that can all be used to format the same HTML document. This small miracle of CSS design is at *www. csszengarden.com*. There's even a book tie-in named *The Zen of CSS Design* (Peachpit Press) that discusses some of the more exotic examples.

- **Advanced style sheet resources.** Planning to become a cutting-edge Web designer? Check out the legendary books by Eric Meyer (such as *Eric Meyer on CSS* (New Riders Press)) and surf by the Web site at *www.westciv.com/style_master/house*.

You can also reverse the z-index to change the example:

```
.Back {
  z-index: 1;
  ...
}
.Front {
  z-index: 0;
  ...
}
```

Frames

As you start to build bigger and more elaborate Web sites, you'll no doubt discover one of the royal pains that come with being a Web maven: getting a common element (like a navigation bar) to appear on every page in your site.

For example, you might decide to add a menu of links that let a visitor jump from one section of your Web site to another. You can place these links in a table or a <div> tag (two techniques demonstrated in Chapter 9). However, either way, there's a problem—in order to show this menu on every page, you'll need to do a fair bit of copying and pasting. If you're not careful, one page will end up with a slightly different version of the same menu. And when you decide to make a minor change to the menu, you'll be faced with the nightmare of updating dozens of pages.

One way to tackle this problem is with *frames*, a sometimes-controversial HTML feature that lets you show more than one Web page in the same browser window. In this chapter, you'll learn how to use frames to tame large Web sites.

The Problem with Repeating Content

By this point, you've amassed a solid toolkit of Web-page building tactics and tricks. You've learned to polish up your Web pages with modern fonts and colors, gussy them up with a trendy layout, and add images and links to the mix. However, as you apply these techniques to a complete Web site, you'll run into some new challenges.

One of the first consequences you'll face when you go from one Web page to a dozen is how to make them all consistent. If you carefully plan the structure of your Web site and you use external style sheets (Chapter 6), you'll be able to apply a common look and feel to as many pages as you want. However, style sheets won't help you if you need to have the same *content* in more than one page. That's a problem, because modern Web sites have specific elements that repeat on every page—typically a header and a set of navigation buttons (see Figure 10-1).

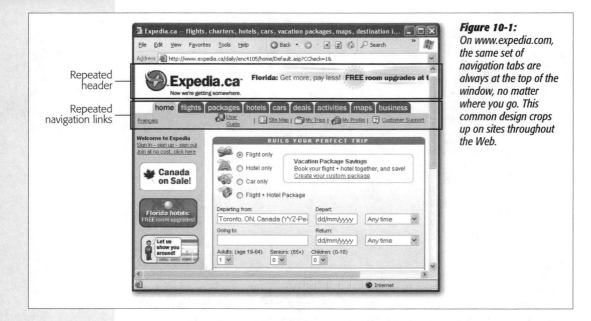

Repeated header

Repeated navigation links

Figure 10-1:
On www.expedia.com, the same set of navigation tabs are always at the top of the window, no matter where you go. This common design crops up on sites throughout the Web.

In a large Web site, pasting the same bit of HTML into every page just isn't an option—it's a management disaster.

The problem could easily be solved if HTML supported a way to dynamically insert the contents of one HTML file into another. For example, imagine you had an <include> tag you could use like this:

```
<html>
  <head>...</head>
  <body>
    <h1>Welcome to the First Page</h1>

    <!-- This tag doesn't really exist. -->
    <include src="menu.htm">

    <p>This is the welcome page. Just above this
    text is the handy menu for this site.</p>
  </body>
</html>
```

Presumably, when the browser found the <include> tag it would request the *menu. htm* document and inject its HTML into the current location of the page. That way, you could create one copy of the *menu.htm* file and reuse it in several pages. Sadly, this feature never materialized in ordinary HTML, and Web developers have been forced to rely on other compromise measures.

Note: Many Web *programming* platforms do have an include feature. Examples include ASP, PHP, and ASP.NET (and a host of other techno-cool acronyms). Almost all of the Web's most popular sites are actually so-called *Web applications* (powerful programs that generate HTML on the fly) so they don't face the hassle of maintaining the same content in dozens of different files. Expedia (Figure 10-1) is one example.

But don't rush off to pick up a degree in computer science just yet. Programming is a completely different cup of tea. Unless you have a lot of time to spare for removing cryptic bugs from computer code (a process known as debugging) and even more time to put them there in the first place (politely known as programming), you're better off using the techniques in this chapter instead.

Without a handy include feature, what's an enterprising Web designer to do? HTML doesn't include a feature for dynamically inserting a block of HTML into another file, but it does have a feature for splitting a Web browser window into several regions, or *frames*. Once you split the window in this way, you can show a different Web page in each frame. This feature is *almost* as good as the missing include feature (see the box below for some of the reasons why it's not quite the same).

FREQUENTLY ASKED QUESTION

The Frames Controversy

Are there reasons to avoid frames?

The Web developer community has been steadily moving away from frames for several years. Although they're still alive and well in small- and medium-sized Web sites, you're unlikely to see them turn up in a large-scale Web site such as eBay or Amazon.

Some of the reasons that frames have a bad reputation are historical—for example, ancient browsers didn't support them that well, and Web newbies used them in all the wrong ways. However, frames also have a few quirks of their own.

Here are the reasons that top-level Web professionals look like they've just bit into a lemon when you tell them you're thinking about using frames:

- **Search engine confusion.** When you use a frame, you display several pages at once. This has the potential to confuse search engines when their automatic indexing robots stumble across just one file in a set that's meant to be shown together. They might have difficulty interpreting what your page is about, because the important content is stored in a separate page. Or, they might index your content page by itself. In this case, when someone follows the search engine link they'll wind up seeing your page without

any of the other frames. These idiosyncrasies aren't the end of the world, but they aren't ideal.

- **Frame abuse.** Some Stone Age Web developers used frames to keep part of their Web site visible when the visitor clicked on an external link. The effect is like an ad bar that never goes away. This leech-like use of frames is universally despised and almost completely expunged from today's Internet. One of the few Web sites that still uses it is *www.about.com*.

- **Future compatibility and accessibility.** On page 47 you learned about XHTML, the eventual successor to HTML. Although the earlier transitional versions of XHTML support frames, the latest versions don't. While frames will probably never disappear from the Web completely, they are slowly being phased out because they're not easily viewable by people with disabilities (who often use screen-reading devices) or those who use cell phones to surf the Web.

- **Less-effective URLs.** When you surf to a frames page, the Web browser grabs the initial page for each frame. There's no way to supply visitors with a URL that lets them surf straight to the page they want—they'll need to click their way through. You'll learn more about this issue on page 277.

Throughout the rest of this chapter, you'll explore frames and learn how to use them to deal with repeating Web site content like headers and navigation bars.

Frame Basics

Frames work by splitting a browser window into two or more regions, and showing a different HTML page in each region. The first step to using frames is to create a *frameset* document, which holds the smaller Web pages and defines how the browser window should be split.

A frameset page isn't like an ordinary HTML page. It still starts with an <html> tag, and it includes a <head> section, where you can define the title for the page, but it doesn't continue with the familiar <body> tag, where you usually put the content of the page. Instead, it includes a <frameset> tag that divides the page into separate frames, and a <noframes> tag that supplies content that is shown if frames aren't viewable on the browser that's loading the pages. Here's a summary of the code you might see on a frameset page:

```
<html>
  <head>
    <title>A Sample Frames Page</title>
  </head>
  <frameset>...</frameset>
  <noframes>...</noframes>
</html>
```

The <noframes> portion is the easiest to fill in. Just enter the HTML content you want to show if the browser doesn't support frames. Many Web sites include little more than a couple of lines of text, like this:

```
<noframes>This Web site uses frames and your browser doesn't
support them.</noframes>
```

This approach, although common, isn't terribly helpful. Later in this chapter (page 276), you'll learn how to include some much more respectable content in the <noframes> section, without going to much extra work.

Some of the reasons that a browser might not support frames include:

- The browser is really old. This is incredibly rare today. Netscape's supported frames since version 2.

- It's a mobile browser, like those used on small devices like cell phones. Of course, if you want to support these devices, you need to design your site with their small screens and limited display powers in mind.

- The Web surfer is viewing-impaired and is using a *screen-reading* program (a program that "speaks" text on a Web page). To make the page accessible to screen readers, you should definitely use the <noframes> technique shown later on page 276.

Defining the Frameset

The information inside your <frameset> tags is the heart of your frameset page. It's where you decide how to split the browser window into rows or columns of specific sizes (with each row or column occupying its own frame). You define the width of each column using the *cols* attribute, or the height of each row using the *rows* attribute. For every column or row you want to add to your page, you need to add a measurement indicating its width or height, respectively. Here's an example that splits the page into two even columns:

```
<frameset cols="50%,50%">
    ...
</frameset>
```

Here's an example that creates three rows, with the middle section being the largest:

```
<frameset rows="25%,50%,25%">
    ...
</frameset>
```

Figure 10-2 shows what this example looks like in a browser.

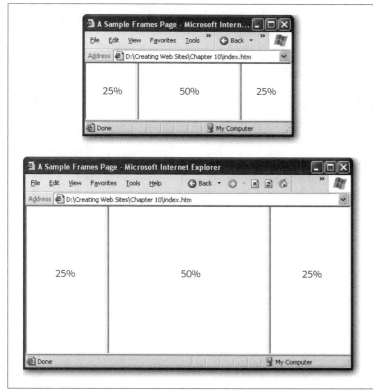

Figure 10-2:
These figures show the same frameset, with a 25/50/25 percent split. Because frame size was set using a percent value (rather than specifying an exact pixel size), all the frames get resized proportionately when the browser window is stretched.

In these examples, the size of each column or row is defined using a percentage value. For example, if you use 50 percent for a column, it will occupy half of the browser window.

Another option is to specify an exact pixel size. For example, here's a three-column example where the left and right columns are always 100 pixels each:

```
<frameset cols="100,*,100">
  ...
</frameset>
```

This example introduces another nifty trick—using the asterisk (*). You use this to tell the browser to make that frame occupy the remaining space. For example, if the browser window is 800 pixels wide, you'll have two 100-pixel columns on the flanks and a 600-pixel column in the leftover space. Figure 10-3 shows what this looks like.

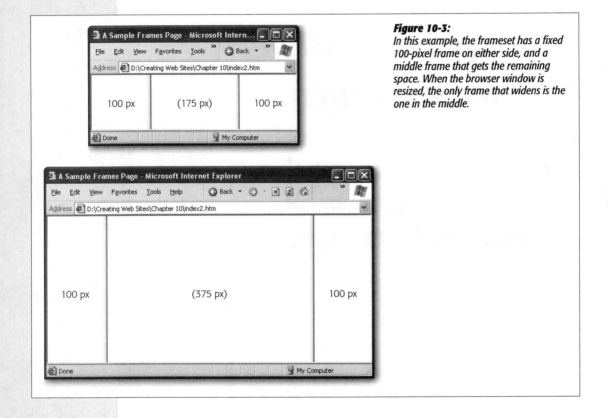

Figure 10-3:
In this example, the frameset has a fixed 100-pixel frame on either side, and a middle frame that gets the remaining space. When the browser window is resized, the only frame that widens is the one in the middle.

Note: If you specify fixed pixel sizes for every row or column, the browser gives them the requested size and then checks if there's more space left over in the browser window. If there is, the browser expands all frames proportionately. This probably isn't the effect you want, so it's a good idea to use the asterisk to give all the extra space to a specific frame.

As you've probably figured out by now, frames always occupy rectangular regions of a browser window. There's no way to create frames with fancy shapes. However, that doesn't mean you can't create the *illusion* of a shaped frame. All you need to do is create a regular rectangular frame and use the background-image property discussed in Chapter 7 (page 199) to add some sort of shaped or curved background picture behind your frame. Figure 10-4 shows an example.

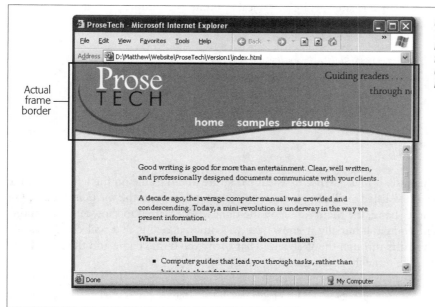

Figure 10-4:
You can create the illusion of a curved frame by adding the correct background image, as shown here.

Putting Documents in a Frameset

Splitting the window into frames is a good first step, but in order to see some actual content on your pages, you'll need to define the *frame source*. The frame source is the HTML document that contains the content you want to show in an individual frame.

To define the frame source, you need to add one <frame> tag for each column and row your frameset includes. You add these <frame> tags inside the <frameset> tags, keeping the same order that was used to list the columns (left to right) or rows (top to bottom).

Here's the basic skeleton for a page with two frames:

```
<frameset cols="30%,*">
  <frame>
  <frame>
</frameset>
```

To link your page to the frame you want to incorporate, you can set various attributes of the <frame> tag. The most important are *src* (which lists the Web page file name) and *name* (which gives the frame a descriptive title you can use to refer to the frame later). Here's a typical example of a complete frameset page:

```
<html>
  <head>
    <title>A Sample Frames Page</title>
  </head>
  <frameset cols="30%,*">
    <frame name="Menu" src="menu.htm">
    <frame name="Main" src="welcome.htm">
  </frameset>
</html>
```

In this case, it makes sense to assume that the Menu frame on the left (that is, the first frame listed) will always show the same menu from the *menu.htm* page. On the other hand, the Main frame on the right will be reused to show all kinds of different content—initially it shows the welcome page, but that will change as the reader surfs through the Web site. That's why the frame name and the HTML file name don't match in the second <frame> tag.

Tip: When you supply the source for a frame, you follow all the same rules you follow when supplying the source for an image or hyperlink. That means you include just the file name if the file is in the same folder as the current page, or you can use a relative or absolute path (see page 214).

To try this example out, save the frameset page using the file name *index.htm*.

Tip: Many Web servers treat *index.htm* as the entry point of your Web site. That means they send it to the browser automatically if they receive a request that doesn't specify a page. See page 55 in Chapter 3 for more.

Next, create the *menu.htm* and *welcome.htm* pages. All the *menu.htm* page needs is a simple list of links, as shown here:

```
<html>
  <head><title></title></head>
  <body>
    <a href="welcome.htm">Welcome</a><br>
    <a href="page1.htm">Page 1</a><br>
    <a href="page2.htm">Page 2</a><br>
    <a href="page3.htm">Page 3</a>
  </body>
</html>
```

When displaying frames, the browser uses the title that's defined in the frameset page. That means the title in the *menu.htm* and *welcome.htm* pages has no effect. However, it's a good idea to still include the <title> element, because it's a required part of HTML. Additionally, the title information sometimes appears in search engine listings.

Note: In the examples in this chapter, the <title> tag is left blank if it won't appear in a browser. That way, you can quickly sort out which titles are most important.

The *welcome.htm* page can show some straightforward content:

```
<html>
  <head><title></title></head>
  <body>
    <h1>Welcome</h1>
    <p>This simple welcome page shows how two frames can be joined in happy
    matrimony. On the left is a menu with a set of links.
    Over here on the right, there's a heading and an ordinary paragraph,
    which makes up a content page.</p>
  </body>
</html>
```

As always, you could use styles to make these two pieces look a lot more impressive (see Chapter 6 for more on styles). But these pages are enough to give you an idea of how all this frames business works. Assuming all the pages are in the same folder, you'll see a single integrated window when you request *index.htm* (see Figure 10-5).

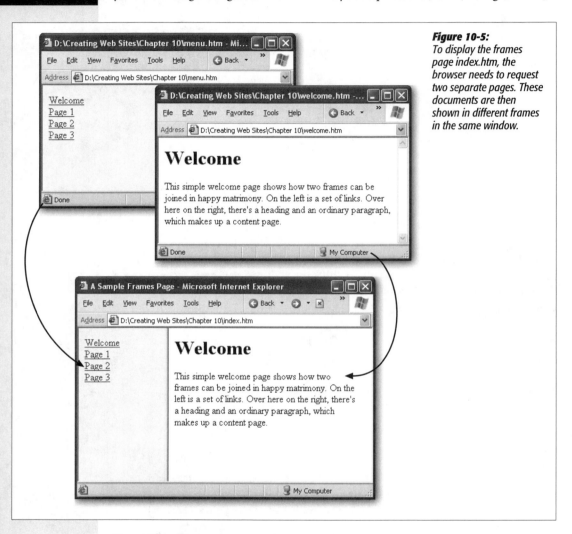

Figure 10-5:
To display the frames page index.htm, the browser needs to request two separate pages. These documents are then shown in different frames in the same window.

Targeting Frames

There's actually a small but important flaw in the frameset shown in the previous example. When you click one of the navigation links, the target page of the link opens in the frame where the link is placed (see Figure 10-6).

To correct this problem, you need to change your links so that they explicitly tell the browser to open the target page in the Main frame. To take care of this, you need to add the *target* attribute to the <a> tag. Use this attribute to supply the name of the frame where the page should be displayed.

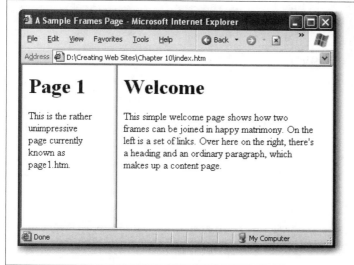

Figure 10-6:
Here's what happens when you click the Page 1 link on the left-hand frame shown in Figure 10-5. The target page (page1.htm) appears, but in the frame where the menu bar used to be. Now you're stuck, with no navigation controls to move around.

Here's how you should rewrite the *menu.htm* page to target your links:

```
<a href="welcome.htm" target="Main">Welcome</a><br>
<a href="page1.htm" target="Main">Page 1</a><br>
<a href="page2.htm" target="Main">Page 2</a><br>
<a href="page3.htm" target="Main">Page 3</a>
```

Figure 10-7 shows the corrected behavior.

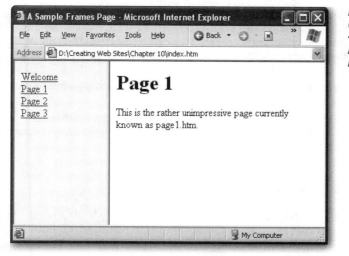

Figure 10-7:
Once you add the target attribute to the <a> tag, menu links open the target in the Main frame on the right, keeping the menu links visible at all times.

Rather than changing every link in your page, it would be nice if there were a way to set a single target frame that would apply to every link in the page. Fortunately, HTML makes this easy with the *<base>* tag. Using the <base> tag, you could rewrite the menu page like this:

```
<html>
  <head>
    <base target="Main">
    <title></title>
  </head>
  <body>
    <a href="welcome.htm">Welcome</a><br>
    <a href="page1.htm">Page 1</a><br>
    <a href="page2.htm">Page 2</a><br>
    <a href="page3.htm">Page 3</a>
  </body>
</html>
```

There are also four reserved target names that have special meanings. You can use these target names with individual links or with the <base> tag instead of naming an actual frame. For example, you can use these targets to open a pop-up window, as shown here:

```
<a href="contact.htm" target="_blank">Welcome</a><br>
```

Table 10-1 has the list of these target names.

Table 10-1. *Reserved Target Names*

Name	Description
_top	Opens the target in the "top" level of the window. That means every frame is cleared away to make room for the new document. It's equivalent to typing the URL of the target page into the browser's address box.
_parent	Opens the target in the frameset that contains the current frame. In the examples you've seen so far, there's only one frameset, so this is equivalent to the _top target. However, if you start deploying nested frames (page 278) the _parent target comes in handy.
_self	Opens the target in the current frame. This is the standard behavior, unless you've changed it using the <base> tag.
_blank	Opens the target in a brand new pop-up window. This technique should be used sparingly, because it can quickly litter the unsuspecting visitor's monitor with a confusing mess of extra windows.

Building Better Frames Pages

So far, you've learned enough about frames to create a basic Web site that sports a never-changing navigation bar (just like the one shown in Figure 10-7). In this section, you'll learn about a few refinements that help make sure your frames look respectable, as well as a way to create more complex site structures using nested frames.

Frame Borders and Resizing

When you create a basic frameset, the browser adds a thick gray bar between each frame. The Web surfer can drag this bar to resize your frames at will, potentially scrambling your content (see Figure 10-8).

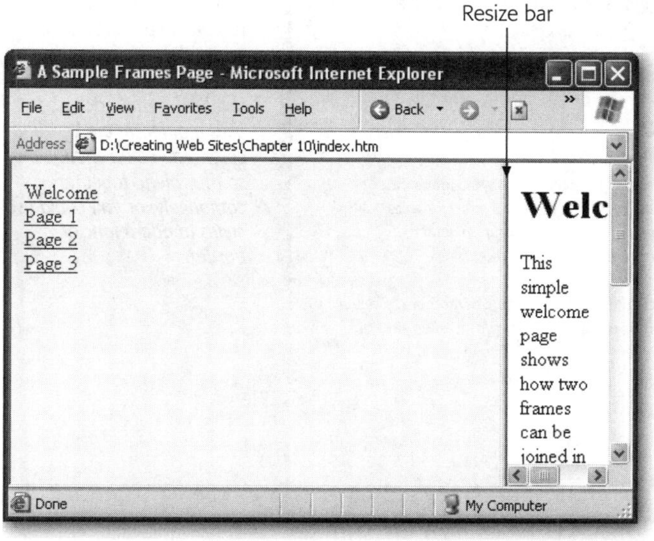

Resize bar

Figure 10-8:
Resizable frames just give your Web visitors too much control.

Although resizable frames are occasionally useful, very few Web sites use them. Instead, most Web sites add the *noresize* attribute to lock frames into place. That way, you decide what the page looks like—and stays like. You need to apply the *noresize* attribute to each <frame> tag, like so:

```
<frame noresize ... >
```

Many Web pages go even further, and hide the ugly gray bar altogether, by using the *border* attribute of the <frameset> tag. You also need to add a number to the border attribute that represents the width of the bar (in pixels). Set this number to 0 and the border disappears, so the page blends into one seamless whole:

```
<frameset border="0" ... >
```

Here's a cleaned-up version of the frameset demonstrated earlier:

```
<html>
  <head>
    <title>A Sample Frames Page</title>
  </head>
```

```
<frameset cols="30%,*" border="0">
  <frame name="Menu" src="menu.htm" noresize>
  <frame name="Main" src="welcome.htm" noresize>
</frameset>
</html>
```

Figure 10-9 shows the result.

Figure 10-9:
This frames page might as well be an ordinary Web page—the only indication that there are two pages involved is that each page uses a different background color. You could change this so they blend together completely, or you could use styles to add a fancier border.

Scrolling

Frames have one unmistakable feature—the scroll bar. When the content of one page grows larger than the size of its frame, scrollbars appear. But what makes this scrolling feature different than in an ordinary Web page is the fact that you can scroll each frame *independently*, as shown in Figure 10-10.

Note: The fact that you *don't* see independently scrolling page sections is one way you can tell that a Web site like Amazon *isn't* designed using frames. When you scroll a page on the Amazon Web site, everything—content, menu, and header sections—scrolls as part of the same page.

In order to prevent confusion, it's a good idea to keep as little content as possible in the non-content frames (like the menu panel) to prevent having more than one set of scrollbars, which can confuse the hardiest Web fan.

Alternatively, you can change the scrolling behavior of a frame using the *scrolling* attribute. The standard setting, *auto* (which you get if you don't list any attribute) shows scrollbars only when they're needed. Your other options are *no* (to never show scrollbars) or *yes* (to always show them).

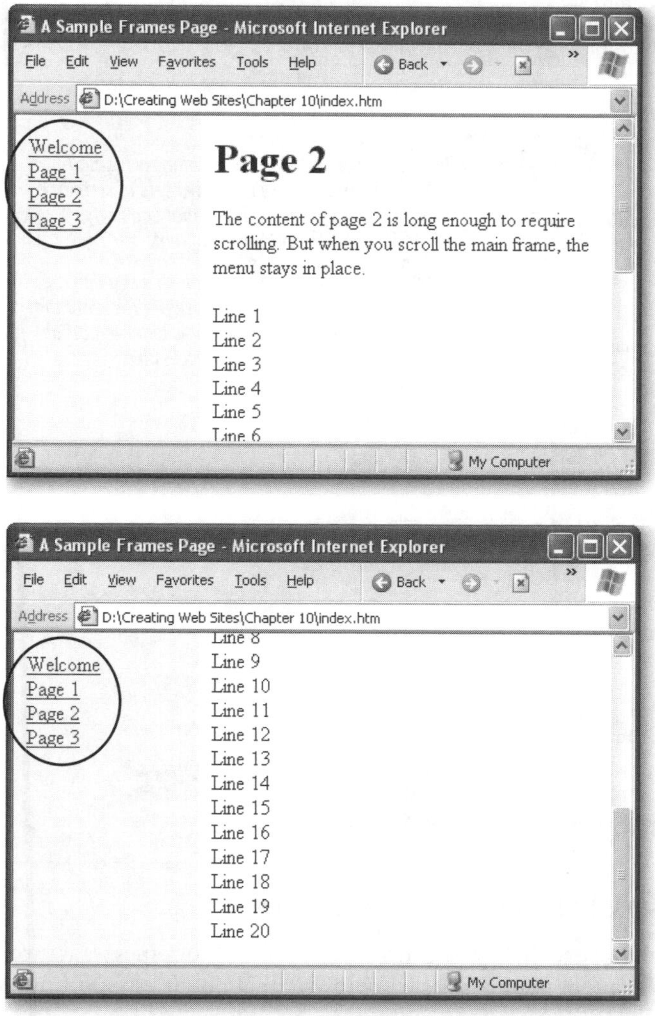

Figure 10-10:
Frames support independent scrolling. That means that when you scroll down to see a lengthy content page, other frames (like the navigation controls circled in this example) remain locked in place.

Here's an example that disables scrolling for the menu frame:

```
<frame name="Menu" src="menu.htm" noresize scrolling="no">
```

Figure 10-11 shows the difference.

Note: Resist the temptation to turn off scrolling, because it might be needed if the browser window is very small. Ideally, you should test your Web site at the minimum expected browser window size (see page 112 in Chapter 5 for a discussion about screen resolutions), and ensure that at this size, the only scrollbars that appear are in the main content page. The only time you may want to turn off scrolling is when you show a small frame for a navigation bar or a page banner.

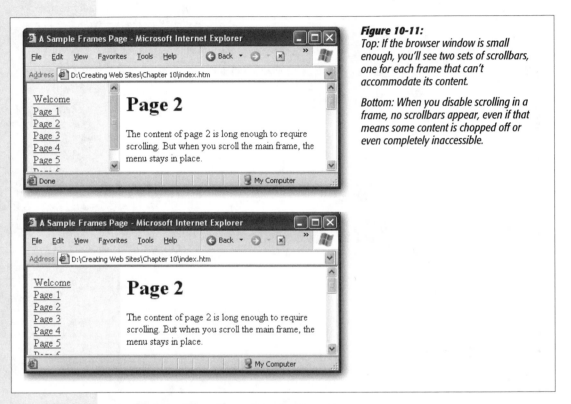

Figure 10-11:
Top: If the browser window is small enough, you'll see two sets of scrollbars, one for each frame that can't accommodate its content.

Bottom: When you disable scrolling in a frame, no scrollbars appear, even if that means some content is chopped off or even completely inaccessible.

Handling Browsers That Don't Support Frames

Earlier in this chapter (page 264) you learned about the <noframes> tag, which allows you to define content that appears in a browser that doesn't support frames. Although it's rare that you'll run into any trouble, it's still a good idea to plan an alternative option for surfers who can't view your frames. Fortunately, HTML gives you an option that doesn't require a lot of work.

For example, consider the two-frame example you've been reading about throughout this chapter. It uses frames to show a menu alongside a content page. At a bare minimum, browsers that don't support frames should still be able to read the content pages one at a time, in an ordinary browser window. The easiest way to accomplish serve up these individual pages is to copy the HTML from the *menu. htm* file into the <noframes> section, as shown here:

```
<html>
  <head>
    <title>A Sample Frames Page</title>
  </head>
  <frameset>...</frameset>
  <noframes>
    <body>
      <h1>Choose a Topic</h1>
      <a href="welcome.htm">Welcome</a><br>
      <a href="page1.htm">Page 1</a><br>
      <a href="page2.htm">Page 2</a><br>
      <a href="page3.htm">Page 3</a>
    <body>
  </noframes>
</html>
```

Notice that the <noframes> section picks up where the rest of the HTML document leaves off—with the <body> tag that defines the start of the HTML content.

Now, when the page is viewed on a browser that doesn't support frames, the visitor will see a heading and the list of pages from the menu. The visitor can click through to see each content page. The solution isn't perfect (for example, in order to move from the content page back to the menu, the visitor needs to click the browser's Back button), but it does provide a rudimentary view of your site's pages. You also need to remember to copy the menu HTML back into the <noframes> section of the *index.htm* document every time you change it.

Tip: It's also a good idea to add content to the <noframes> section so any search engine that stumbles across your page can find out more about it, increasing the likelihood your Web site will be cataloged and searchable. Chapter 11 discusses search engines and how they find your Web site in more detail.

Better URLs for Framesets

There's no law against requesting a frameset page. You can type its URL into your browser window or link to it in the same way you link to any page. However, frameset pages are a lot less flexible, because they combine several pages into one URL. To understand the problem that can create, it helps to consider an example.

When you head to a frameset page (say, *index.htm*), the browser requests the initial page for each frame. For example, the browser might request *navbar.htm* to get a menu and *start.htm* to show a start page. When you start clicking links in the navigation bar, the browser performs the nifty little trick you saw earlier—it keeps the same frame layout, but it loads in new Web pages. For example, if you click Contact Us, the link might swap the *start.htm* page with *contact.htm*.

But here's the problem: The URL in the browser window never changes. No matter what page you're looking at, the URL still reflects the name of the initial frameset page (*index.htm*). That means that there's no way to surf back to the arrangement of frames that has *contact.htm* loaded up. Instead, when you type *index.htm* into your browser you'll see the initial set of frames (which includes *start.htm*), and you'll need to click your way through to *contact.htm*.

Note: The limitation discussed in this section actually doesn't apply to the Favorites feature in Internet Explorer. That's because IE is crafty enough to store information about what page should be loaded into each frame, so it can restore the exact arrangement of frames. However, this limitation does apply to other browsers like Firefox. More significantly, it applies if you need to type the URL in by hand, send it in an email message, or provide a link from another Web site.

You might think you could solve this problem by requesting *contact.htm* directly. But that would get you just the *contact.htm* page, *not* the frameset. As a result, you wouldn't see the content in other frames, like the ever-so-important navigation bar.

One way around this problem is to create extra frames pages. For example, if you want a way to get back to the *contact.htm* page, you could create a frames page named *contact_frames.htm*. This frames page would use the exact same frameset as *index.htm*, with one minor difference. Instead of loading the *start.htm* page initially, it would load the *contact.htm* page. If you want to point someone to the Contact Us page, just use *contact_frames.htm*. Think of it as an open front door that gives surfers another way into your Web site.

The only problem with this approach is that you need to create a lot of extra frameset pages—as much as one for each ordinary content page. If you decide to change your layout later on, you're stuck with a lot of updating.

Note: A more advanced approach is to add JavaScript code to each page. The idea is that each content page should check if it's a frameset when it's shown in a browser. If it isn't, the content page should send the surfer back to the frames page, with specific instructions about what frames to show. If you want to experiment with this more complex approach, work through the JavaScript section in Chapter 14, and then read the solution at *http://javascript.about.com/library/blframe.htm*.

Nested Framesets

As you get more comfortable with frames, you may begin to plan more ambitious layouts. Sooner or later, you'll want to divide and subdivide the browser window with wild abandon. The good news is that this isn't that difficult to accomplish—you simply need to *nest* one set of frames inside another.

For example, imagine you want to divide a page into two rows, and place the header information into the top row. Then, you want to subdivide the remaining content into two columns, featuring the menu controls and content page. Figure 10-12 shows the result of this kind of slicing and dicing.

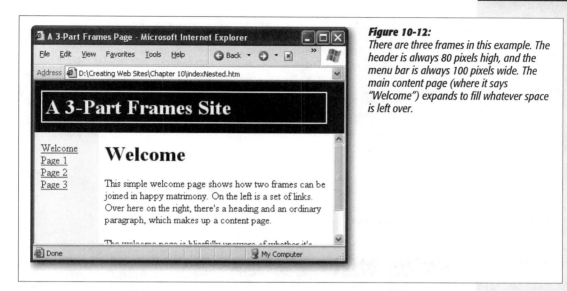

Figure 10-12:
There are three frames in this example. The header is always 80 pixels high, and the menu bar is always 100 pixels wide. The main content page (where it says "Welcome") expands to fill whatever space is left over.

In this case, you need two framesets. The outer frameset defines the two rows, and the inner frameset splits one of these rows into columns. Here's the complete code for the frames page:

```html
<html>
  <head>
    <title>A 3-Part Frames Page</title>
  </head>

  <frameset rows="80,*" border="0">
    <frame name="Header" src="header.htm">

    <frameset cols="100,*" border="0">
      <frame name="Menu" src="menu.htm" noresize>
      <frame name="Main" src="welcome.htm" noresize>
    </frameset>

  </frameset>
</html>
```

The only challenge in writing a nested frameset is determining the correct order to use for dividing your page. If you reverse the nesting in this example (so you split the window into columns first and *then* into rows), you'll end up with a different result.

```
<html>
  <head>
    <title>A 3-Part Frames Page</title>
  </head>

  <frameset cols="100,*" border="0">
    <frame name="Menu" src="menu.htm" noresize>

    <frameset rows="80,*" border="0">
      <frame name="Header" src="header.htm">
      <frame name="Main" src="welcome.htm" noresize>
    </frameset>

  </frameset>
</html>
```

Figure 10-13 shows this reorganized version.

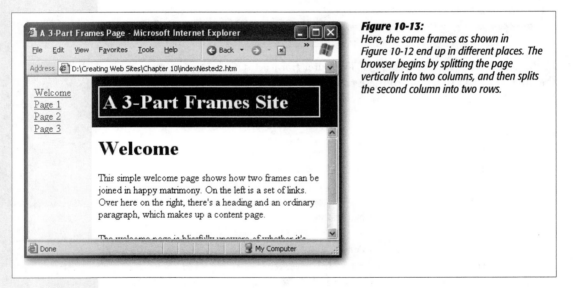

Figure 10-13:
*Here, the same frames as shown in
Figure 10-12 end up in different places. The
browser begins by splitting the page
vertically into two columns, and then splits
the second column into two rows.*

Another Way to Nest Frames

There is one limitation with defining all your frames in a single frames page. To understand the problem, it helps to consider a new example.

Figure 10-14 shows a page that's divided into a typical layout of three frames: a header at the top, a topic panel at the left, and a content region at the right. However, the way these frames are used is different from the previous examples. If you click one of the topic links on the left, you'll jump to a different portion of the current page. If you click one of the header links at the top, you'll surf to a whole new page with a different set of topics.

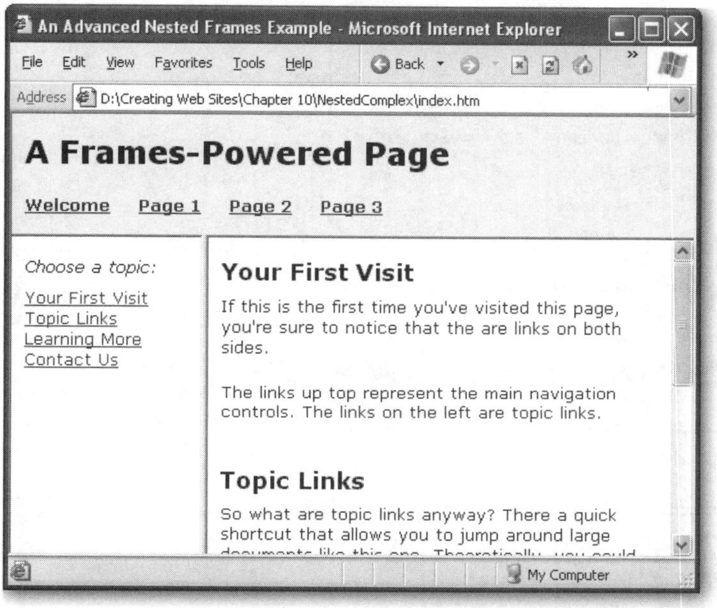

Figure 10-14:
In this page, the main navigation links are all a part of the header panel on the top. The panel on the left shows something new: topic links that allow the reader to quickly jump from one part of the current page to another (using the bookmark feature you learned about on page 224). While the header menu never changes, every page has its own set of topic links.

Tip: Topic links are a great way to break down large pages and make them easier to navigate on the Web. Add these links to your pages by using bookmarks (as described on page 224).

The problem that this example presents is that every time the reader clicks a new link in the header, you need to replace *both* of the frames underneath. That's because you need to load a new content page and a new list of topic links. Unfortunately, if you implement this design using a single frames page, that isn't possible. Every time you click a link in the header, you can change only a single frame.

The workaround to this problem is to create more than one frames page. The first frames page is *index.htm,* which defines the overall structure of the site. It simply splits the page into a header frame and another frame underneath, as shown here:

```
<html>
  <head>
    <title>An Advanced Nested Frames Example</title>
  </head>
  <frameset border="0" rows="94,*">
    <frame name="Header" scrolling="no" noresize src="header.htm">
    <frame name="Main" src="welcome_frame.htm">
  </frameset>
</html>
```

The trick here is that the frame underneath points to *another* frame document, which is named *welcome_frame.htm*. The *welcome_frame.htm* file then splits the page *again*, this time into two columns:

```
<html>
  <head><title></title></head>
  <frameset cols="150,*">
    <frame name="TopicLinks" src="welcome_topics.htm" scrolling="no">
    <frame name="Content" src="welcome.htm" >
  </frameset>
</html>
```

The frame on the left, TopicLinks, holds the topic links. The frame on the right, Content, holds the actual text (see Figure 10-15).

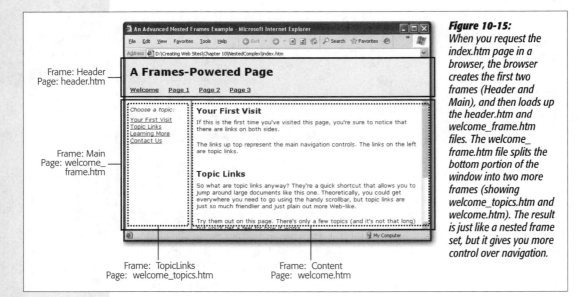

Frame: Header
Page: header.htm

Frame: Main
Page: welcome_
frame.htm

Frame: TopicLinks
Page: welcome_topics.htm

Frame: Content
Page: welcome.htm

Figure 10-15:
When you request the index.htm page in a browser, the browser creates the first two frames (Header and Main), and then loads up the header.htm and welcome_frame.htm files. The welcome_frame.htm file splits the bottom portion of the window into two more frames (showing welcome_topics.htm and welcome.htm). The result is just like a nested frame set, but it gives you more control over navigation.

In order for this model to work, you need to create a frame document for every content page. That's the messy bit. For example, when the Page 1 link is clicked, you would replace the bottom frame with the *page1_frame.htm* page. Here's the link you'd put in the *header.htm* document:

```
<a href="page1_frame.htm" target="Main">Page 1</a>
```

The *page1_frame.htm* document looks exactly the same as *welcome_frame.htm*, because it defines the same two column frames, in exactly the same positions. The only difference is that the source changes to point to a new topic page and a new content page, as shown here:

```
<html>
  <head><title></title></head>
  <frameset cols="150,*">
    <frame name="TopicLinks" src="page1_topics.htm" scrolling="no">
    <frame name="Content" src="page1.htm" >
  </frameset>
</html>
```

That's all you need to make this example work. As you can see, by creating more than one frames page, you buy yourself oodles more flexibility. However, this approach requires some extra effort. In order to complete this solution, you need a frames page, topic page, and content page for each link in the header. Sadly, there's no way to dodge this work.

Tip: Of course, high-powered HTML editors like FrontPage and Dreamweaver do provide tools that make it easier to work with frames. For example, you can edit all the pages that belong to a frameset in one window. The same support isn't available in Nvu.

Part Three: Connecting with Your Audience

3

Attracting Visitors

Over the past ten chapters, you've polished your Web designing mettle and learned how to build a variety of sleek pages. Now it's time to shift to an entirely different role, and become a Web site *promoter*.

The best Web site in the world won't do you much good if it's sitting out there all by its lonesome self. In order for your site to flourish, you need to find the best way to attract visitors—and keep them flocking back for more. In this chapter, you'll learn some valuable tricks for promoting your site. You'll also see how search engines work, how to make sure they regularly index your site, and how to work your way up the rankings. Before you know it you'll be more popular than chocolate ice cream.

Your Web Site Promotion Plan

Before you plunge into the world of Web site promotion, you need a plan. So grab a pencil and plenty of paper, and get read to jot down your ideas for global Web site domination (fiendish cackling is optional).

Although all Webmasters have their own tactics, it's generally agreed that the best way to market a Web site is to follow these steps:

1. **Build a truly great Web site.**

   If you start promoting your Web site before there's anything to see, you're wasting your effort (and probably burning a few bridges). Nothing says "never come back" like an empty Web site with an "under construction" message.

2. **See step 1.**

If in doubt, polish and perfect your Web site! Fancy graphics aren't the key concern here—the most important detail is whether or not you have some genuinely useful content. Ask yourself—if you were surfing the Web, would you stop to take a look at this site? Make sure you've taken the time to add the kinds of add-on features that will keep visitors coming back. One great option: a discussion forum (see the next chapter for more details on how to add one to your site).

3. **Share links with friends and like-minded sites.**

This step is all about building community. Contrary to what you might expect, this sort of small-scale, word-of-mouth promotion might bring more traffic to your Web site than high-powered search engines like Google.

4. **Perfect your Web site's meta tags.**

Meta tags are hidden tags that convey important information about your Web site's content, like a list of keywords and a site description. Search engines use them as one way to determine what your Web site's all about.

5. **Submit your Web site to Internet directories.**

Like search engines, directories help surfers find Web sites. The difference between directories and search engines is that directories are generally smaller catalogs put together by humans (rather than huge sprawling text indexes amassed by computers).

6. **Submit your Web site to Internet search engines.**

Now you're ready for the big time. Once you submit your Web site to Web heavyweights like Google, it officially enters the public eye. However, it still takes time to climb up the rankings and get spotted.

7. **Figure out what happened.**

In order to assess the successes and failures of your strategy, you need to know measure some vital statistics—how many people are surfing to your site, how long they're staying, and how many visitors are coming back for more. To take stock, you'll need to crack open tools like hit counters and server logs.

Throughout this chapter, you'll tackle these steps, get some new ideas, and build up a collection of promotion strategies.

Spreading the Word

Some of the most effective promotion you can do doesn't involve any high-tech HTML wonkery, but instead amounts to variations on the theme of good old fashioned advertising.

The first step is to find other Web sites like yours. If you're creating a topic-oriented site—your musings on, say, golf, fine jewelry, or jeweled golf clubs—these kinds of similar sites are friendlies that make up the larger online community to which you now belong. So why not introduce yourself? Strike up a *reciprocal link* relationship (see the next section).

On the other hand, if you're creating a business site, similar sites are, obviously, your competitors. As a result, you're unlikely to share links. However, it's a great idea to Google your competition. You'll probably find other sites—business directories, news sites, content sites, and so on—that link to these competitive sites. Once you've found these places, you can advertise your Web site in them as well.

Reciprocal Links

A reciprocal link is a link-trading agreement. The concept is simple. You find a Web site with similar content, and you strike a bargain: Link to my site, and I'll link to yours. Reciprocal links are an important thread in the underlying fabric of the Web. If you're not sure where to start searching for potential link buddies, pay a visit to Google and use the *link:* operator (as explained in Figure 11-1) to see who's linking to sites similar to yours.

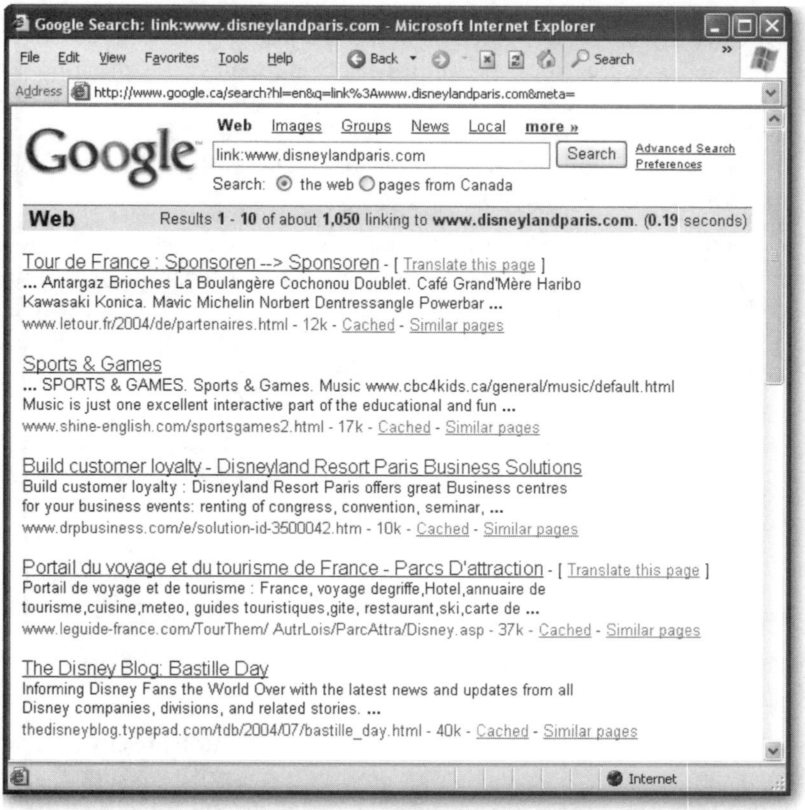

Figure 11-1:
Google has a little-known search keyword that lets you search for links (to your site or to anyone else's for that matter). It's the link: operator. If you type in link:www. disneylandparis.com, you'll find all the Web sites that link to the EuroDisney home page. You can use any URL you want (for example, try link:www.disneylandparis. com/uk/introduction.htm to find out who's linking to the English-language intro page). Just remember to always leave out the http:// part of the URL.

Reciprocal links only work if there's a logical connection between the two sites. For example, if you've created the Web site *www.ChocolateSculptures.com*, it probably makes sense to exchange links with *www.101ChocolateRecipes.com*. But *www.HomerSimpsonForPresident.com* is a far stretch, no matter how much traffic it gets.

Topic isn't the only consideration. You should also look for a site that feels professional. If a similarly themed site is choked with ads, barren of content, formatted with fuchsia text on a black background, and was last updated circa 1998, keep looking.

Once you've found a site you want to exchange links with, dig around on the site for the Webmaster's email address. Send an email message explaining that you love *www.101ChocolateRecipes.com*, and plan to link to it from your site, *www.ChocolateSculptures.com*. Then, gently suggest that you think your Web site would be of great interest to the readers of *www.101ChocolateRecipes.com*.

Tip: Reciprocal linking can require a little finesse. It's best to look for sites that complement yours, but don't necessarily compete with it. You'll also have more luck if you approach a Web peer (a site that's of similar quality or has a similar amount of traffic to yours).

Once you enter into a link agreement—even if it's just an informal exchange of emails—remember to keep your end of the deal. Don't remove the link from your Web site without letting the other Webmaster know about your change. It's also a good idea to keep checking on the other site to make sure your link remains prominent. If it disappears, don't fly into an Othellian rage—just send a polite email asking where it went or why it disappeared.

Reciprocal links are also a good way to start working your way up the search engine rankings (see page 304). That's because one of the criteria Google takes into account when determining how to order results in a Web search is how many sites link to your Web site. The more popular you are, the more likely you'll climb up the list.

Note: There are some companies that sell reciprocal link services. The basic idea is that they try to pair up different Web sites (for a fee) in a link-sharing agreement. Don't fall for it. Your traffic might increase, but the visitors you'll get won't really be interested in the content of your site, and they won't hang around for long.

Web Rings

A Web ring is similar to a reciprocal link, but instead of sharing a link between two partners, it binds a group of Web sites together.

For example, imagine you've created a brilliant new site featuring reality TV trivia. To get more exposure, you could join a Web ring dedicated to reality TV. You agree to put a block of HTML on your Web site that advertises the ring and lets surfers visit other sites in the ring. As payback, you become another stop on the ring (see Figure 11-2). Web rings are almost exclusively used with topic-based sites.

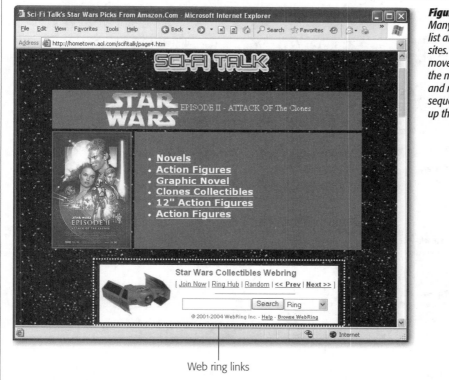

Figure 11-2:
Many Web rings don't list all their member sites. Instead, surfers can move from one site to the next using previous and next links. This sequence of sites makes up the "ring."

Web ring links

Sadly, the majority of Web rings consist of gaudy, amateurish Web disasters. Pair up with these nightmares, and your Web site will be deemed guilty by association. However, with a little research you may find a higher quality ring. To search for one, use Google (see Figure 11-3). If you want to establish and manage your own ring, check out *http://dir.webring.com/rw* or *www.bravenet.com*.

Note: The biggest disadvantage of Web rings is that they usually require you to add a fairly ugly set of links to your page. Before you sign up, carefully evaluate if the extra traffic is worth it, and travel to all the other sites to see if they're of similar quality. If you're linked in a ring with low-quality sites, it can hurt your reputation.

Shameless Self-Promotion

To get your Web site listed on many popular sites, you'll need to fork over some cold, hard cash. However, some of the best advertising doesn't cost anything. The trick is to look for sites where you can promote *and* contribute at the same time.

For example, if you've created the Web site *www.HotComputerTricks.com*, why not answer a few questions on a computing newsgroup or discussion board? It's considered tactless to openly promote your Web site, but there's nothing wrong with dispensing some handy advice and following it up with a signature that includes your Web site URL.

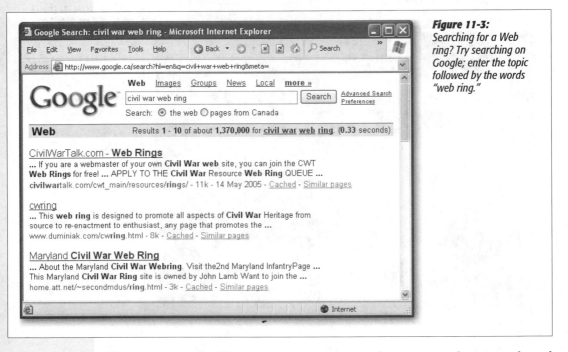

Figure 11-3:
Searching for a Web ring? Try searching on Google; enter the topic followed by the words "web ring."

Here's an example of how you can answer a poster's question and put a good word in for yourself at the same time:

> Jim,
>
> The problem is that most hard drives will fail when submerged in water. Hence, your fishing computer idea won't work.
>
> Sasha Mednick
>
> www.HotComputerTricks.com

An answer posting is much better than sending an email directly to the original poster, because on a popular site, hundreds of computer aficionados with the same question will read your posting. If even a few decide to check out your site, you've made great progress.

If you're very careful, you might even get away with something that's a little more explicit:

Jim,

The problem is that most hard drives will fail when submerged in water. Hence, your fishing computer idea won't work. However, you might want to check out my home-made hard-drive vacuum enclosure (www.HotComputerTricks.com), which I developed to solve the same problem.

Sasha Mednick

www.HotComputerTricks.com

Warning: This maneuver requires a very light touch. The rule of thumb is that your message should be well-intentioned. Only direct someone to your Web site if there really is something specific there that addresses their question.

Some sites allow you to post tips, reviews, or articles. In this case, you can use variations of the same technique. Remember, dispense some useful advice, and then follow up with a byline at the end of your message. For example, if you submit a free article that describes how to create your groundbreaking vacuum enclosure, end it with this:

Sasha Mednick is a computer genius who runs the first-rate computing Web site www.HotComputerTricks.com.

Promotion always works best if you believe in your product. So make sure there's some relevant high-quality content on your site before you boast about it. Don't ever send someone to your site based on some content you plan to add (someday).

Return Visitors

Attracting fresh faces is a critical part of Web site promotion, but novice Webmasters often forget something equally important—return visitors. In order for a Web site to become truly popular, it needs to be able to attract visitors who will return again and again. Many a Web site creator would do better to spend less time trying to attract new visitors and more time trying to keep the attention of the current flock.

If you're a marketer, you know that a customer that comes back to the same store three or four more times is a lot more likely to make a purchase than someone who's there on a first visit. These regulars are also more likely to get excited and recruit their friends to come and take a look. This infectious enthusiasm can lead more and more people to your Web site's virtual doorstep. The phenomenon is so common it has a name: the *traffic virus*.

Tip: Return visitors are the ultimate measuring stick for a Web site. If you can't interest someone enough to come back again, your Web site's just not fulfilling its destiny.

So how does your Web site become a favorite stopping point for Web surfers? The old Internet adage says it all—*content is king*. Your Web site needs to be chock full of fascinating must-read information. Just as important, this information needs to change regularly and noticeably. If you update information once a month, your Web site barely has a pulse. If you update information two or three times a week, you're ready to flourish.

Never underestimate the importance of regular updates. It takes weeks and months of up-to-date information to create a return visitor. However, one dry spell—say, three months without changing anything more than the color of your buttons—doesn't just stop attracting newcomers, it can actually kill off your current roster of return visitors. That's because savvy Web surfers immediately realize when a Web site's gone stale. They have much the same sensation you feel when you pull out a once-attractive pastry from the fridge and find it's as hard as an igneous rock. You know what happens next—it's time to toss the pastry away, clear out the Web site bookmarks, and move on.

Tip: Signs of a stale site include old-fashioned formatting, broken links, and references to old events (like a Spice Girls CD release party or a technical analysis of why the dot-com boom may not last as long as everyone thinks).

The other way to encourage return visitors is to build a *community*. Discussion forums, promotional events, and newsletters are like glue. They encourage visitors to feel like they're participating in your site, and sharing your Web space. If you get this right, hordes of visitors will move in and never want to leave. You'll learn specific techniques for community building in the next chapter.

GEM IN THE ROUGH

Favorite Icons

Your first challenge is to get a Web surfer to add your site to her browser bookmarks. However, that's not enough to guarantee a return visit. Your Web site also needs to be fascinating enough that it beckons from the bookmark menu, tempting the visitor to come back. If you're a typical surfer, you regularly visit only about five percent of the sites you've bookmarked.

One way to make your Web site stand out from the crowd is to change the icon that appears in the bookmark or favorites menu (technically called a *favicon*). This technique is browser-specific, but it works reliably in most versions of Internet Explorer, Firefox, and Safari. The illustration in this box shows the favicons for Google and Amazon.

To create a favicon, just add an icon file to the top-level folder of your Web site, and make sure it's named *favicon. ico*. The best approach is to use a dedicated icon editor (see the shareware sites listed on page 82) because that will

let you create an icon file that has both a 16-pixel x 16-pixel and larger 32 x 32 version of your icon in the same file. That's handy because some operating systems and browsers use the favicon when you drag a shortcut to the desktop. If you don't have an icon editor, just create a bitmap (a .bmp file) that's exactly 16 pixels wide and 16 pixels high.

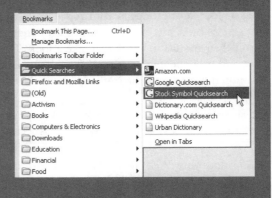

Adding Meta Tags

Meta tags give you a way to attach descriptive information to your Web pages, which is important because some Web search engines rely on these tags to help surfers find your work. Figure 11-4 explains how it all works.

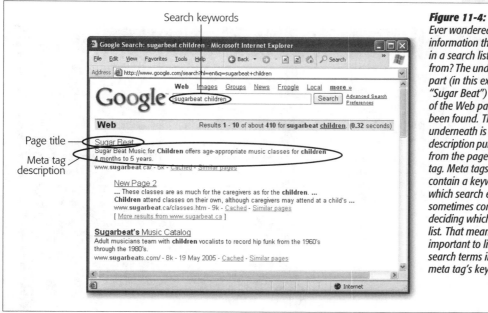

Figure 11-4:
Ever wondered where the information that you see in a search listing comes from? The underlined link part (in this example, "Sugar Beat") is the title of the Web page that's been found. The text underneath is a hidden description pulled directly from the page's meta tag. Meta tags can also contain a keyword list, which search engines sometimes consult when deciding which results to list. That means it's important to list likely search terms in your meta tag's keyword list.

Note: Fun fact for etymologists and geeks alike: the term meta tag means "tags about," as in "tags about your Web page."

All meta tags are placed in the <head> section of the page. Here's an example meta tag that assigns a description to a Web page:

```
<html>

<head>
  <meta name="description"
        content="Noodletastic offers custom noodle dishes made to order.">
  <title>Noodletastic</title>
</head>

<body>...</body>

</html>
```

All meta tags look more or less the same. The tag name is <meta>, the *name* attribute indicates the type of meta tag, and the *content* attribute supplies the relevant information.

Meta tags don't show up when your page appears in a browser. They're intended for the programs that read your Web page—like browsers and Web search engines (see the box below).

UP TO SPEED

How Web Search Engines Work

A Web search engine like Google is built out of three separate pieces. The first piece is an automated program that roams the Web, downloading everything it finds. This program (often known by more picturesque names like *spider*, *robot*, or *crawler*) will eventually stumble across your Web site and copy its contents.

The second piece is an indexer that chews through the Web page, and extracts a bunch of meaningful information, including the Web page title, the description, and the keywords. The indexer also records a great deal of more esoteric data. For example, a search engine like Google keeps track of what words crop up the most often on a page, what other sites link to your page, and so on. The indexer inserts all of this digested information into a giant catalog (technically, a *database*).

The final piece of the search engine is the part you're probably the most familiar with—the front-end, or search, page. You enter the keywords you're hunting for, and the search engine scans the catalog looking for suitable pages. Different engines have different ways of ranking pages, but the basic idea is that the search engine attempts to make sure the most relevant and popular pages turn up early in the search. In a search engine like Google, Web sites aren't ranked individually. That is, there's no such thing as the world's most popular Web page (in the eyes of Google). Instead, pages get ranked in terms of how they stack up against whatever search keywords have been entered. That means that a slightly different search (say, "green tea health" instead of just "green tea") could get you a completely different set of results.

In theory, there's no limit to the types of information you can place inside a meta tag. For example, FrontPage is notorious for inserting meta tags that identify that your pages were built with its software. (Don't worry; once you understand meta tags, you'll recognize this harmless fingerprint and you can easily remove it.) Another Web page might use a meta tag to record the name of the Web designers who created it, or the last date it was updated.

Although there's no limit to the information you can put in meta tags, in practice, there are two meta tags that are more important than all others, because they're the only ones heeded by search engines. These are the *description* and *keywords* meta tags. These details, in conjunction with the <title> tag, constitute the basic information the search engine needs to know about your page. That means you need to make sure you put these tags in every page you create.

The Description Meta Tag

The description of your page is the simplest part. You simply need a few sentences that distill the content of your site into a few plain phrases. Here's an example:

```
<meta name="description" content="Sugar Beat Music for Children offers age-
appropriate music classes for children 4 months to 5 years old.">
```

This tag is split over two lines in this book because there's not enough room for it on one line. But when you're composing a description in your HTML, file make sure you don't hit the Enter key. If you do, your description could get broken up over multiple lines when it appears on a search results page.

Although you can stuff a lot of information into your description, it's a good idea to limit it to a couple of focused sentences that total no more than around 50 words. Some search engines use the description text, while others rely more heavily on the text in the page. Even if your description is shown on a search result page, you'll see only the first part, followed by an ellipsis (…) where it gets cut off.

DESIGN TIME

The Importance of Titles and Image Text

A search engine draws information from many parts of your page, not just the meta tags. To make sure your pages are search-engine–ready, you should check that you're using the <title> tag in all your pages, and alternate text with all your images.

Alternate image text is the text that's shown if an image can't be retrieved. You specify this text using the alt attribute in the <img> tag (see page 183). Search engines also pay attention to the alternate text—for example, Google, uses it as the basis for its image-searching tool (*http://images. google.com*). If you don't have alt text, Google has to guess what the picture is about by looking at nearby text, which is less reliable.

The <title> tag also plays several important roles. You already know that it sets the text in the title bar of the browser window. The <title> tag also helps identify your Web page in a search (see Figure 11-4). Finally, the <title> tag contains the text that appears in the bookmarks menu if a surfer bookmarks your page. Keep that in mind, and refrain from adding long slogans. "Ketchup Crusaders—Because ketchup isn't just for making food tasty" is about the longest you can stretch a title, and even that's iffy. On the other hand, remember not to omit essential information. The title "Welcome" or "New Page 2" (a FrontPage favorite) isn't very helpful.

The Keyword Meta Tag

The keyword list should contain a list of about 25 words or phrases (or less) that represent your Web site. Each word in the list is separate by a comma. Here's an example:

```
<meta name="keywords" content="sugarbeat, sugar, beat, music, children,
musical, classes, movement, babies, infants, kids, child, creative">
```

The keyword list is a great place to add key terms (like "horseback riding"), alternate spellings ("horse back riding"), synonyms or related words ("equestrian"), and even common misspellings ("ecquestrian"). Keywords aren't case-sensitive.

Unfortunately, there's a huge caveat. Most search engines don't use the keyword list any longer. That's because it was notorious for abuses (many a Web page stuffed their keyword list full of hundreds of words, some only tangentially related to what was actually on the site). Search engines like Google take a more direct approach—they look at all the words in your Web page, and pay special attention to words that appear more often, appear in headings, and so on.

Note: To find out which Web search engines still support the keyword list, check out *http://searchenginewatch.com/webmasters/article.php/2167891*.

Even though search engine support is spotty, it's a good idea to keep using the keyword list. Just don't expect it to do that much for you.

FREQUENTLY ASKED QUESTION

Keyword Tricks

Can I make my Web site more popular by adding hidden keywords?

There are quite a few unwholesome tricks that crafty Web-weavers use to game the search engine system (or at least try). For example, they might add a huge number of non–meta-tagged keywords, but hide the text so it isn't visible on the page. (White text on a white background is one oddball option, but there are other style-sheet tricks.) Another trick is to create pages that aren't really a part of your Web site, but are stored on your Web server. You can fill these pages with repeating keyword text. To complete this trick, you can use a little JavaScript code to make sure real people who arrive at the page are directed to the entry point of your Web site, while search engines get to feast on the keywords. (JavaScript is discussed in Chapter 14.)

As seductive as some of these tricks may seem to lonely Web sites (and their owners), the best advice is to avoid them altogether. The first problem is that they pose a new

set of headaches and technical challenges, which can waste hours of your day. But more significantly, search engines learn about these tricks almost as fast as Web developers invent them. If a search engine catches you using these tricks, they may ban your completely, banishing your site to the dustbin of the Web.

If you're still tempted, keep this in mind: Many of these tricks just don't work. In the early days of the Web, primitive search engines gave a site more weight based on the number of times a keyword cropped up, but modern search engines like Google use much more sophisticated page-ranking systems. A huge whack of keywords might not move you up the search list one iota, and it'll make you as popular as Enron.

Directories and Search Engines

Now that you're well on your way to perfecting and popularizing your site, it's time to start looking at the second level of Internet promotion—search engines. Getting your Web site into the most important search engine catalogs is a key step in publicizing your Web site. Working your way up the rankings so Web searchers are likely to find you takes more work, and monopolizes the late-night hours of many a Webmaster.

Directories

Directories are searchable site listings, with a difference: They're created by humans. That means a small army of computer workers painstakingly puts together a collection of sites, neatly sorted into categories. The advantage of directories is that they're well-organized. A couple of clicks can get you a complete list of California regional newspapers. The unquestioned disadvantage is that they're dramatically smaller than *full-text search* catalogs. That means directories aren't very useful for those in search of a piece of elusive information that doesn't easily fall into a category, like the most commonly misspelled words. Over the years, as the Web's ballooned in size, directories have become increasingly specialized, and full-text searching tools have become the most common way to hunt for information.

So, given that directories are just the unattractive cousins of full-text search engines, why do you need to worry about them? Two reasons. First, many Web surfers still use directories, even if they don't use them as often as full-text search engines. Second, some search engines (including Google) pay attention to directory listings, and tend to rank sites higher if they turn up in certain directories. Getting into the right directories can help you start to move up the list in a full-text search. And just like college, getting into a directory requires that you submit an application, which you'll learn about next.

The Open Directory Project

The most important directory to submit your site to is the Open Directory Project (ODP) at *http://dmoz.org*. The ODP is a huge, long-standing Web site directory that's staffed entirely by thousands of volunteer editors, who review submissions in countless categories. The ODP isn't the most popular Web directory (that honor currently goes to the Yahoo directory), but it is used behind the scenes by other search engines, including Google, Yahoo, AOL, HotBot, and Lycos. In fact, Google's own directory service (*http://directory.google.com*) is based on the ODP.

Before submitting to the ODP, take the time to make sure you do it right. An incorrect submission could result in your Web site not getting listed at all. You can find a complete description of the rules at *http://dmoz.org/add.html*, but here are the key requirements:

- Don't submit your site more than once.

- Don't submit your site to more than one category.

- Don't submit more than one page or section of your site (unless you have a really good reason, like the separate sections are dramatically different).

- Don't submit sites that contain "illegal" content. (By the OPD definition, this is more accurately described as unsavory content, like pornography, libelous content, or material that advocates illegal activity—you know who you are.)

- Clean up any broken links, outdated information, or any other red flags that might suggest to an editor that your site isn't here for the long term.

• When you submit your site, describe it carefully and accurately. Don't promote it. In other words "Ketchup Masters is a manufacturer of gourmet ketchup" is acceptable. "Ketchup Masters is the best food-oriented site on the Web—the Louisville Times says you can't miss it!" is not.

• Don't submit a site that's not completed. Your "under construction" page won't get listed.

Next step is to spend some time at the *http://dmoz.org* site, until you've found the single best category for your site (see Figure 11-5).

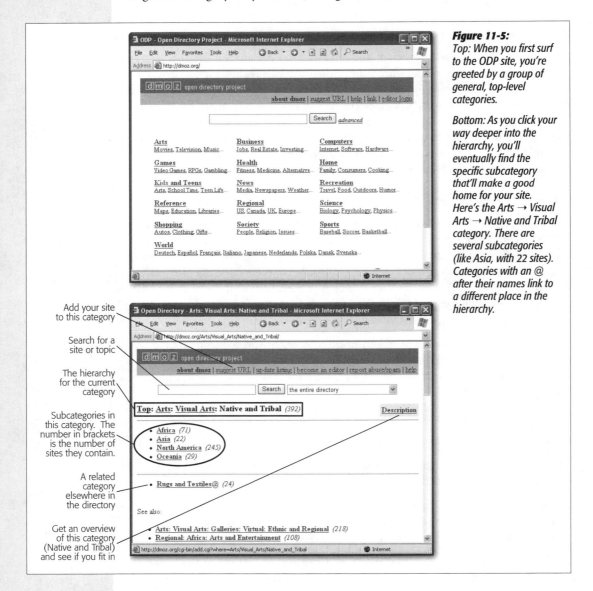

Figure 11-5:
Top: When you first surf to the ODP site, you're greeted by a group of general, top-level categories.

Bottom: As you click your way deeper into the hierarchy, you'll eventually find the specific subcategory that'll make a good home for your site. Here's the Arts → Visual Arts → Native and Tribal category. There are several subcategories (like Asia, with 22 sites). Categories with an @ after their names link to a different place in the hierarchy.

Once you've found the right section, click the "suggest URL" link at the top of the page and fill out the submission form (see Figure 11-6). The form includes your URL, the title of your site, a brief description, and your email address.

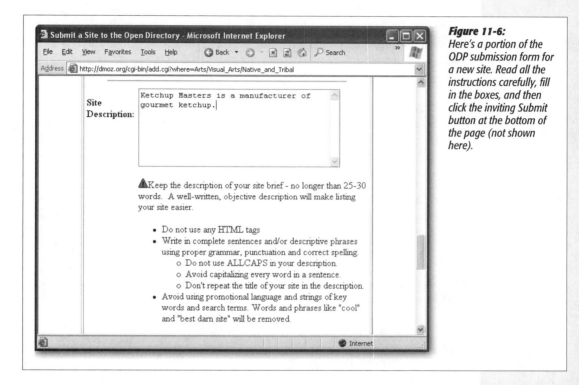

Figure 11-6:
Here's a portion of the ODP submission form for a new site. Read all the instructions carefully, fill in the boxes, and then click the inviting Submit button at the bottom of the page (not shown here).

Tip: If you have some free time on your hands, you can offer to help edit a site category—just click the "become an editor" link. And even if you don't have editorial aspirations, why not check out the editor guidelines at *http://dmoz.org/guidelines* to get a better idea of what's going on in the mind of an ODP editor, and how he'll evaluate your Web site submission?

Once you've submitted your site, there's nothing to do but wait (and submit your site to the other directories and search engines discussed in this chapter). If two or three weeks pass without your site appearing in the listing, and you haven't received an email describing any problems with your site, try submitting again. If that still doesn't work, it's time to contact the editor of the category where you submitted your site. Write a polite email asking why your site wasn't added to the listing, and include the date of your submission(s) and the name, URL, and description of your site. You can find the email address for the category editor at the very bottom of the category page (see Figure 11-7).

Other directories

ODP is a great starting point, but it isn't the only directory on the block. The other two heavyweights are Yahoo and Looksmart. Unfortunately, getting your site on these directories takes considerably more work. If you've created a commercial site, you'll almost certainly need to pay a fee. If you've created a non-commercial site, you can probably get in free, but it may take persistence, emails, multiple submissions, and a bit of luck.

Here are some links to get your started:

- For Yahoo (*www.yahoo.com*), the official submission guidelines are at *http://docs.yahoo.com/info/suggest*. However, you'll be much happier with the *unofficial* write-up at *www.apromotionguide.com/yahoo.html*, which discusses your free and for-fee options, and explains what the cryptic rejection emails Yahoo sends you really mean.

- For Looksmart (*www.looksmart.com*), it gets more confusing. You'll probably want to dodge the high fees and try to get in through the back door through a related Web site called Zeal (*www.zeal.com*). You can read the Zeal guidelines at *www.zeal.com/guidelines/user*, and get a walkthrough of the horribly convoluted process at *www.apromotionguide.com/looksmart.html*.

Once you're done with directories (or just ready to move on), it's time to take a look at full-text search engines.

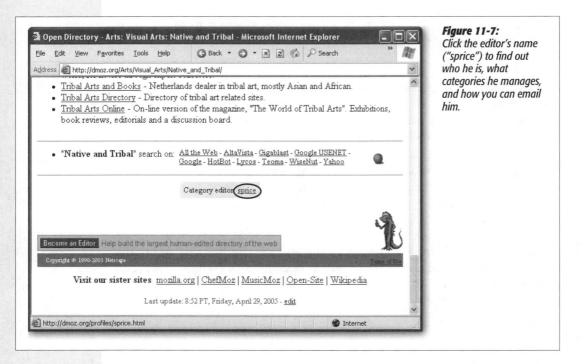

Figure 11-7:
Click the editor's name ("sprice") to find out who he is, what categories he manages, and how you can email him.

Search Engines

For most people, search engines are the one and only tool for finding information on the Web. In order for the average person to find your Web site, you need to make sure your site is in the most popular search engine catalogs, and turns up as a result for the right searches. This task is harder than it seems, because the Web is full of millions of sites jockeying for position. In order to get noticed, you need to spend time developing your site and enhancing its visibility. You also need to understand how search engines rank pages (see the box below for an example).

The undisputed king of Web search engines is Google (*www.google.com*). Not only is Google far and away the most popular search engine, it also powers other search engines (usually without being credited). Google performs an amazing amount of work—every day it chews through hundreds of millions of search requests.

Tip: For more information about search engines, including who's on top and who owns whom, check out *www.searchenginewatch.com*.

UP TO SPEED

How Google's PageRank Works

Google uses a rating system called *PageRank* to size up different Web pages and determine how they rank when someone conducts a search.

PageRank isn't used to *find* search results; instead, it's used to *order* them. When you perform a search with Google, it pulls out all the sites that match your search keywords. Then, it orders its results according to the PageRank of each page.

The basic idea behind the PageRank system is that the value of your Web site is determined by the community of other Web sites that link to it. There are a few golden rules:

- The more sites that link to you, the better.

- A link from a more popular site (a site with a higher PageRank) is more valuable than a link from a less popular site.

- The more links a site has, the less each link is worth. In other words, if someone links to your site and just a handful of other sites, that link is valuable. If someone links to your site and *hundreds* of other sites, the link's value is diluted.

Although Google regularly fine tunes its secret PageRank recipe, Web gurus spend hours trying to deconstruct it. For some fascinating reading, you can learn more about how PageRank works (loosely) at *www.akamarketing.com/google-ranking-tips.html* and *www.markhorrell.com/seo/pagerank.html*. The original formulation of PageRank is described in an academic paper by Google co-founders Sergey Brin and Larry Page at *http://www-db.stanford.edu/~backrub/google.html*.

For way more information about Google and its internal workings, be sure to check out *Google: The Missing Manual*.

It's not too difficult to get noticed by Google. By the time your site's about a month old, Google will probably have stumbled across it at least once, usually by following a link from another site or the ODP. A link to your site is the best way to introduce yourself to Google. As described in the box above, Google takes outside links into consideration when sizing up a site, so the more sites that link to you the more likely you are to turn up in someone's search results.

If you're impatient or you think Google's passing you by, you can introduce yourself directly using the submission form at *www.google.com/addurl.html* (see Figure 11-8). Most popular search engines include a submission form like this. Just make sure you keep track of where you've submitted, so you don't inadvertently submit to the same search engine more than once.

Figure 11-8:
You can safely skip filling in the comments section on this page but make sure to include the http:// prefix at the start of your Web page's URL.

Rising up in the rankings

You'll soon discover that it's not difficult to get into Google's catalog. However, you might find that it's exceedingly hard to get noticed. For example, suppose you've submitted the site *www.SamMenzesHomemadePasta.com*. To check if you're in Google, try an extremely specific search that targets just your site, like "Sam Menzes Homemade Pasta." This should definitely lead to your doorstep. Now, try searching for just "Homemade Pasta." Odds are, you won't turn up in the top 10, or even the top 100.

So how do you create a site that the casual searcher's likely to find? There's no easy answer. Just remember that the secret to getting a good search ranking is having a good PageRank, and getting a good PageRank is all about connections. In order to stand out, your Web site needs to share links with the other leading sites in your category area.

If you want to delve into the nitty-gritty of *search engine optimization* (known to Webmasters as SEO), consider becoming a regular reader of *www.webmasterworld. com* and *www.searchenginewatch.com*. You'll find articles and forums where Webmasters discuss the good, bad, and downright seedy tricks to try and get noticed.

Tip: It's possible to get too obsessed about search engine rankings. Here's a good rule of thumb–don't spend more time trying to improve your search engine ranking than you spend improving your Web site. In the long term, the only way to gain real popularity is to become one of the best sites on the block.

Google AdWords

As a Web surfer, you've no doubt seen several lifetimes' worth of flashing messages, gaudy banners, and invasive pop-ups, all trying to sell you some hideously awful products. It probably comes as no surprise to learn that these types of ads aren't the way to promote your site—they're more likely to alienate people than entice them.

However, there are respectable paid placements that can get your site in front of the right readers, at the right time, and with the right amount of tact. One of the best choices is AdWords (*https://adwords.google.com*), Google's insanely flexible advertising system.

The idea behind AdWords is that you create text ads that Google will show alongside its regular search results. The neat part is that the ads aren't shown indiscriminately. Instead, you choose the search keywords that you want your ad to be associated with (see Figure 11-9).

The neat (and slightly confusing) part about AdWords is that you *bid* for the keywords you want to use. For example, you might tell Google you're willing to pay 25 cents for the keyword "food." Google takes this into consideration with everyone else's bids, and shows the higher bidders more often. (Google will tell you the highest bid, in case you just want to beat that by a penny.) However, you don't get charged anything for appearing on Google's page. You owe money only when someone clicks on your ad to get to your site.

By this point, you might be getting a little nervous. Given the fact that Google handles hundreds of millions of searches a day, isn't it possible for a measly one-cent bid to quickly put you and your site into bankruptcy? Fortunately, Google's got the solution for this, too. You just tell Google how much you're willing to pay per day. Once you hit your limit, Google stops showing your ad.

Interestingly, the bid amount isn't the only factor that determines how often an ad appears. Popularity is also important. If Google shows your ad over and over again and it never gets a click, Google realizes that your ad just isn't working, and lets you know with an automatic email message. It may then start showing your ad significantly less, or refrain from showing it altogether until you can improve it.

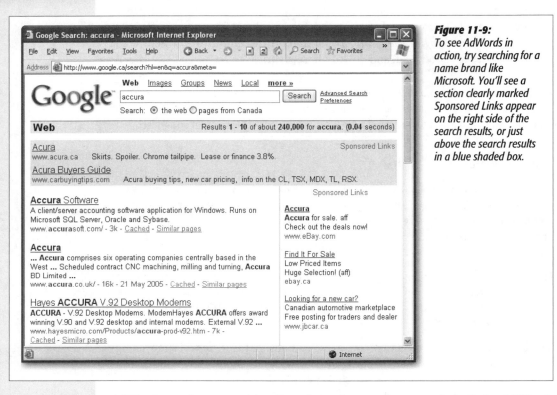

AdWords can be competitive. In order to have a chance against all the AdWords sharks, you need to know how much a click is worth to your site. For example, if you're selling monogrammed socks, you need to know what percentage of visitors actually buy something (the *conversion rate*) and how much they're likely to spend. A typical cost per click hovers around 35 cents, but there's a wide range. At last measure, the word *free* topped the charts at $1.33, while *capitalism* could be had for a song—a mere 10 cents. (And in recent history, law firms have bid "mesothelioma"—an asbestos-related cancer that could have a class action lawsuit in the making—up close to $100.) Before you sign up with AdWords, it's a good idea to conduct some serious research.

Note: You can learn more about AdWords from *Google: The Missing Manual*, which includes a whole chapter about it. You can also get an online introduction at *http://searchenginewatch.com/sereport/article.php/2164591*. Finally, for a change of pace, surf to *www.iterature.com/adwords* for a story about an artist's attempt to use AdWords to distribute AdWords, and why it failed.

Hiding from search engines

In rare situations, you might create a page that you *don't* want to turn up on a search engine. The most common reason is because you've posted some information that you want to share with only a few friends, like the latest Amazon e-coupons. If Google indexes your site, thousands of visitors could flood your way, sucking up your bandwidth for the rest of the month. Another reason may be that you're posting something semi-private that you don't want other people to stumble across, like a story about how you stole a dozen staplers from your boss. If you fall into the latter category, be very cautious. Keeping search engines away is the least of your problems—once a site's on the Web, it *will* be discovered. And once it's discovered, it won't ever go away (see the box below).

But there is at least one thing you can do to minimize your site's visibility or, possibly, keep it off search engines altogether. To understand how this procedure works, recall that search engines do their work in several stages (page 303). In the first stage, a robot program crawls across the Web downloading sites. You can tell this robot not to index your site, or a portion of it, in several ways. (Not all search engines respect these rules, but most—including Google—do.)

UP TO SPEED

Web Permanence

You've probably heard a lot of talk about the ever-changing nature of the Web. Maybe you're worried that the links you create today will lead to dead sites or missing pages tomorrow. Well, there's actually a much different issue taking shape–old site copies that just won't go away.

Once you put your work on the Web, you've lost control of it forever. The corollary to this sobering thought is: Always make sure you aren't posting something that's illegal, infringes on copyright, is personally embarrassing, or could get you fired. Because once you've put this material out on the Web, it may never go away.

For example, imagine you accidentally reveal your company's trade secret for carrot-flavored chewing gum. A few weeks later, an excited customer links to your site. You realize your mistake, and pull the pages off your Web server. But have you really contained the problem?

Assuming the Google robot has visited your site recently (which is more than likely), Google now has a copy of your old Web site. Even worse, people can get this *cached* (saved) copy from Google if they know about the *cache* keyword. For example, if the offending page's URL is *www.*

GumLover.com/newProduct.htm, a savvy Googler can get the old copy of the page using the search "cache:www. GumLover.com/newProduct.htm." (Less savvy surfers might still stumble onto the cached copy of a page by clicking the Cached link that appears after each search result in Google's listing.) Believe it or not, this trick's been used before to get accidentally leaked information, ranging from gossip to software license keys.

You can try to get your page out of Google's cache as quickly as possible using the remove URL feature at *http:// services.google.com/urlconsole/controller*. But even if this works, you're probably starting to see the problem–there's no way to know how many search engines have made copies of your work. Interested people who notice you've pulled down the information will hit these search engines and copy the details to their own sites, making it pretty near impossible to eliminate the lingering traces of your mistake. There are even catalogs dedicated to preserving old Web sites for posterity (see the Wayback Machine at *www. archive.org*).

To keep a robot away from a single page, add the *robots* meta tag to your page. Use
the content value noindex, as shown here:

```
<meta name="robots" content="noindex">
```

Remember, like all meta tags, you place this in the <head> section of your HTML
document.

Alternatively, you can use the content nofollow to tell the robot to index the current page, but not to follow any of its links:

```
<meta name="robots" content="nofollow">
```

If you have larger portions of your site that you want to block off, you're better off
to create a specialized file called *robots.txt,* and place it in the top-level folder of
your site. The robot will check this file before it goes any further. The content
inside the *robots.txt* file sets the rules.

If you want to stop a robot from indexing any part of your site, add this to the
robots.txt file:

```
User-Agent: *
Disallow: /
```

The User-agent part identifies the type of robot you're addressing. (An asterisk
represents all robots.) The Disallow part indicates what part of the Web site is off
limits. (A single forward slash represent the whole site.)

To rope off just the Photos subfolder in your site, use this:

```
User-Agent: *
Disallow: /Photos
```

To stop a robot from indexing certain types of content (like images), use this:

```
User-Agent: *
Disallow: /*.gif
Disallow: /*.jpeg
```

As this example shows, you can put as many Disallow rules as you want in the
robots.txt file, one after the other.

Remember, the *robots.txt* file is just a set of guidelines for search engine robots. It's
not a form of access control. In other words, it's similar to posting a "No Flyers"
sign on your mailbox—it works only as long as advertisers choose to heed it.

Tip: You can learn much more about robots, including how to tell when they visit your site, and how to
restrict the robots coming from specific search engines, at *www.robotstxt.org*.

Tracking Visitors

As a Web site owner, you'll try a lot of different tactics to promote your site. Naturally, some will work while others won't—and you'll need to keep the good strategies and prune those that fail. In order to do this successfully, you need a way to assess how your Web site is performing.

Almost every Web hosting company (except for those that don't charge a fee) give you some way to track the number of visitors to your site (see Figure 11-10). Ask your Web hosting company how to use these tools. Usually, you need to log on to a "control panel" or "my account" section of your Web host's site. You'll see a variety of options there—look for an icon labeled "site counters" or "Web traffic."

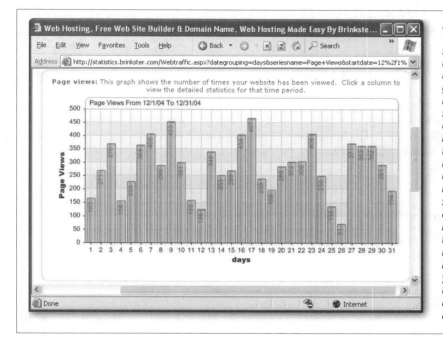

Figure 11-10:
This Brinkster page view summary shows the number of hits (page requests) received on a given day. The chart below this summary (not shown) shows the total amount of bytes of information downloaded from your site. It's important to realize that a hit is defined as a request for any page. If a single visitor travels around your Web site, requesting several pages, they'll generate several hits. In order to find out how many unique visitors you have, you need to use a separate log analysis program, described below.

Web Server Logs

With more high-end hosting services, you often have more options for viewing your site's traffic statistics. For example, you might be able to get a report by time of day, or get an indication of how many pages each visitor is reading. But to get really detailed information, you need to grab the raw *Web server logs*. Many commercial Web hosts provide the server logs, but you may need to ask their technical support department how you can download them.

The Web server logs are important because they have detailed, blow-by-blow information about every visitor. This information includes the time visitors came, their IP addresses (page 54), their browsers, what site referred them to you, whether they ran into an error, what pages they ignored, what pages they loved, and so on. The information in a Web server log is richer by several orders of magnitude than the simple Web traffic analysis offered by your Web host.

You won't be able to interpret a server log on your own, but you can feed it into a *log analysis* program for more detailed breakdowns. For example, you can use a log analyzer to pick out your most popular pages, the sites that are leading visitors to you, and what browsers and operating systems your fans use. This information can help you tailor your Web site *and* your promotional tactics.

Log analyzers are notoriously complex, but you can get a good overview of a few free choices from *www.thefreecountry.com/webmaster/loganalyzers.shtml*.

Hit Counters

The best choice is to work with a dedicated analysis program and review the raw server logs. However, this isn't an option for everyone. Low-priced Web hosts might not make the server logs available. In fact, free Web hosts probably won't even give you a single tool for traffic analysis.

In this case, you may want to use a free *hit counter* service from another company. A hit counter is a page element that counts up the number of times your page has been requested. The appearance of a hit counter varies—some hit counters show the number of hits directly on the page (usually with a small picture), while others are invisible and collect their data silently for later analysis.

Here's how a typical hit counter service works:

1. **You add a very small bit of HTML to your page.**

   For example, this HTML might include an <img> tag that shows the hit counter picture.

2. **When someone requests your page, they see an image that shows how many people have visited so far.**

   Here's the trick: When your page loads and requests the image from the hit counter Web site, the Web site makes a note of this request, and increases the counter by one. In other words, every time you display the hit counter, the hit counter site logs what happened.

3. **Later on, you can log on to the hit counter Web site to get more detailed information.**

   For example, you might be able to find the difference between *page hits* (the number of time a page on your site is requested) and *unique visitors* (the number of *different* people who visited that same page). If someone looks at the same page several times (or just hits the Refresh button), the number of page hits goes up, but the number of unique visitors doesn't change.

Hit counters don't all work in the same way, and be on the lookout for hit counting services that try to convince you to insert ads into your page. For a list of free hit counter services, see *www.thefreecountry.com/webmaster/loganalyzers.shtml*. Or, to try out a free hit counter that doesn't require an image (and is completely invisible to the Web site surfer), check out the popular StatCounter service at *www.statcounter.com*.

CHAPTER 12

Letting Visitors Talk to You (and Each Other)

The Web is the crowded home of several million people. When you put your Web site online, it doesn't just drop into a vacuum. Instead, it takes center stage in front of an audience that's always interested, often opinionated, and occasionally irritable.

In order for your site to really fit in with the rest of the Web, you need to participate with your visitors. The idea of dialogue—back-and-forth communication between peers—is hard-wired into the Internet's DNA. Heated discussion flows over all sorts of different channels, and includes insightful postings on discussion groups, scathing reviews on Amazon, shout-outs on Web site guestbooks, daily blog entries, email, instant messages, chat rooms, and much more. The online discussions never stop—they just billow across the globe like giant clouds of hot air.

In this chapter, you'll learn how to connect with your audience by using basic tools like your email inbox and how to incorporate the often rollicking world of Web-based groups and discussion forums into your site.

Transforming a Site into a Community

The Web sites you've created so far are lonely affairs. Visitors can come and look around, but there aren't any avenues for them to really participate. If this were a one-way medium like cable television or newspapers, this wouldn't be a problem. But the Internet is all about *community*, which means you need to let your visitors react, respond, and (occasionally) harass you.

How do you start transforming your Web site into a Web community? The first trick is to change your perspective, so that you plan your Web site as a meeting place instead of just a place to vent your (admittedly brilliant) thoughts. Here are a few tips to help you get in the right frame of mind:

- **Clearly define the purpose of your site.** For example, the description "www. BronteRevival.com is dedicated to bringing Charlotte Bronte fans together to discuss and promote her work" is more community-oriented than "www. BronteRevival.com contains information and criticism of Charlotte Bronte's work." The first description indicates what the site aims to accomplish, while the second reflects what it contains, thereby limiting its scope. Once you've defined a single-sentence description, you can use it in your description meta tag (page 296) or in a mission statement on your homepage.

UP TO SPEED

Talking the Talk

Community is so important to the Web that ubergeeks have their own catchy jargon to describe the process of people meeting up online. Here are some popular terms so you won't feel left out of the discussion:

- A **netizen** is an active, responsible citizen of the Internet—someone who takes Web community as seriously as life in the real world.

- **Flaming** is a blistering exchange of insults on a public forum. If you post your personal theory about how an alien race created the human species on a discussion group about evolution, you're sure to be flamed.

- **Trolling** is the act of enticing people to flame you, either to make them look ridiculous or just for sport. For example, if you ask for donations for your "Hillary for President" campaign on a Web site for young Republicans, you're trolling.

- **Blogging** is the practice of posting regular, dated entries on a special kind of Web site (which is called a *blog*—short for Web log). Blogs can contain anything from detailed technical articles to rambling, random thoughts. Often, bloggers let other people add comments to their blog entries, which allows blogs to become another forum for community interaction. You'll learn about blogs in Chapter 17.

- **Build gathering places.** No one wants to hang around a collection of links and static text. Jazz your site up with discussion forums or chat boards, where your visitors can kick up their heels. You'll learn how to get these bits in place later in this chapter.

- **Give your visitors different roles.** Successful community sites recognize different levels of contribution. At one extreme, the right people can grow into leadership roles and even coordinate events, newsletters, or portions of the site. At the other end are visitors who are happiest lurking in the background and watching what others do. There are different ways to recognize individual contribution—some sites use a personal feedback rating system that adds gold stars (or some other sort of icon) next to a person's name. Another approach is to give certain visitors more powers—like the ability to manage members in a Google group (page 326).

- **Advertise new content before and after you add it.** In order to get visitors coming back again and again, you need lots of new content. But new content on its own isn't enough—you need to build up visitors' expectation of new content so that they know to return, and you need to clearly highlight the new material so that they can find it once they do. To help this work smoothly, try adding links on your first page that lead to newly added content, along with a quick line or two about upcoming content you're planning to add (and when it'll be there).

- **Introduce regular events.** It's hard to force yourself to update your site regularly—and even when you do, visitors have no way to know when there's something that makes a return visit worthwhile. Why not help everyone keep track of what's going on by promoting regular events (like a news section that's updated weekly or a promotional drawing that happens on a set date)?

- **Create feedback loops.** It's a law of the Web—good sites keep getting better, while bad sites magnify their mistakes. To help your site get on the right track, make sure there's a way for visitors to tell you what they like. Then, spend the bulk of your time strengthening what works (and tossing out what doesn't).

To get some more ideas for community building, check out the book *Community Building on the Web* by Amy Jo Kim. You can read portions of it online at *www. naima.com/community*.

Now that you have your Web site good-citizenship philosophy straight, it's time to learn how to build the ingredients every Web community needs.

POWER USERS' CLINIC

Planning for the Future

The techniques you'll learn about in this chapter will help you start and manage a small Web community. However, keeping up with all the tools you'll need to use takes effort, and as your site starts to grow, you might not have the time to manage mailing lists by hand or keep track of your visitors.

All large communities on the Web are supported with some type of nifty software that can manage these tasks. Only a small fraction of Web site creators build their own software. Most buy an existing program.

You won't learn about full-fledged community software in this chapter (aside from some free solutions for setting up forums). However, you can take your search online to hunt down professional software. *Missing Manual* parent O'Reilly Media, for example, uses Lyris (*www.lyris.com*) to manage its internal discussion groups and newsletters.

Helping Visitors Email You

The first step in audience participation is letting your visitors email you. This is a very small-scale type of interaction, because it's exclusively between two people (you and one visitor) and the conversation is private. Later on in the chapter you'll see how to expand the discussion to include a whole gaggle of surfers.

Mail-To Links

Unlike the standard-issue hyperlinks you learned about back in Chapter 8, there's one special type of link that you haven't seen yet—the *mail-to* link. This link automatically starts an email message when clicked. It's still up to the Web surfer to send the message, but you can supply some boilerplate subject and body text.

Note: The mail-to link is a great way to get feedback from others, but in order for it to work there, must be an email program installed on the Web surfer's computer, and the email program must be properly configured.

To create a mail-to link, you supply a path that starts with the word *mailto*, followed by a colon (:) and the email address. Here's an example:

```
<a href="mailto:me@myplace.com">Email Me</a>
```

Most browsers also let you supply some text for the subject and body of the email message, which the Web visitor can then edit as she sees fit. To do this, you need to use a slightly wonky syntax that follows these rules:

• After the email address, put a question mark.

• To declare the subject, add "subject=" followed by the subject text.

• If you also want to define some body text, add the character sequence "&" after the subject text. Then, begin the body by writing "body=" followed by the body text.

• Replace every space in the subject and body text with the character sequence "%20". This gets quite tedious and makes the message hard for you to read as you're composing it, but it's required in order for this trick to work with all browsers.

Confused? The easiest way to grasp these rules is to take a look at a couple of examples. First, here's a mail-to link that includes the subject text "Automatic Email":

```
<a href="mailto:me@myplace.com?subject=Automatic%20Email">
Email Me</a>
```

And here's a link that includes both subject text and body text:

```
<a href=
"mailto:me@myplace.
com?subject=Automatic%20Email&amp;body=I%20love%20your%20site.">
Email Me</a>
```

When you click this link, you'll see an email pop up like the one shown in Figure 12-1.

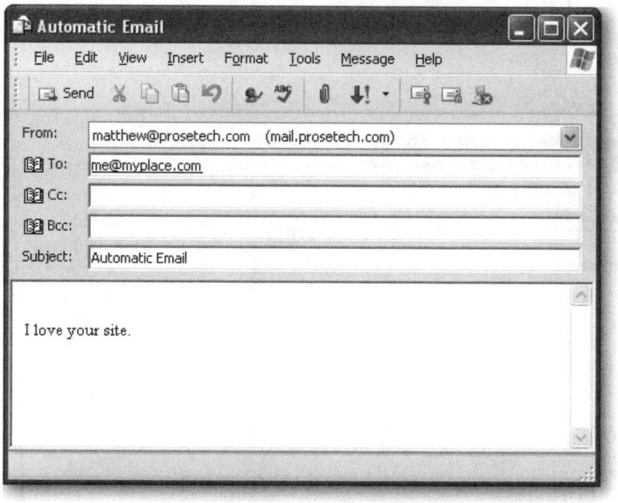

Figure 12-1:
When you click a mail-to link, an email message is created (as shown here). The recipient, subject, and body are filled in according to the link, although whoever's clicked the link has the ability to change these details (or just to close the window without clicking Send). The actual email window differs, depending on what email program is installed on the Web surfer's computer. This example shows the send mail window from Outlook Express.

HTML Forms

HTML forms is a corner of the HTML standard you haven't explored yet. It defines tags that you can use to create graphical widgets (like text boxes, buttons, checkboxes, and lists). Visitors can interact with these widgets, which are commonly called *controls*. Figure 12-2 shows an example of an HTML form in action

HTML forms are an indispensable technology for many Web sites, but you probably won't get much mileage out of them. The problem is that HTML forms are best suited for high-powered Web applications, not the static Web sites you're creating.

For example, consider the account creation form shown in Figure 12-2. Once you, the visitor, fill out all the details and click the Submit button at the bottom, the browser does something special—it collects the information you've entered and the selections you've made in every control, and patches it together into one long piece of text. Then, it sends a request back to the server with all this information. That's where the Web application comes in. It examines the submitted data, chews through it, and then carries out some sort of action. This action might involve sending back another page with different HTML (for example, if the application detects an error), or storing the information in a database on the Web server.

Forms are the basic building block of highly dynamic Web sites. If you're not a Web programmer, you probably won't use forms all that often. However, you can still use forms as a basic way to collect information. To do this, you configure your forms to send an email message at the moment that they're submitted. In other words, when someone clicks the Submit button on the form, the collected data isn't sent to a program—instead, it's mailed to you as an email message. You'll need to sift through the emails yourself (which can be a major chore if you're receiving hundreds of messages a day). However, you've opened up a valuable channel for feedback.

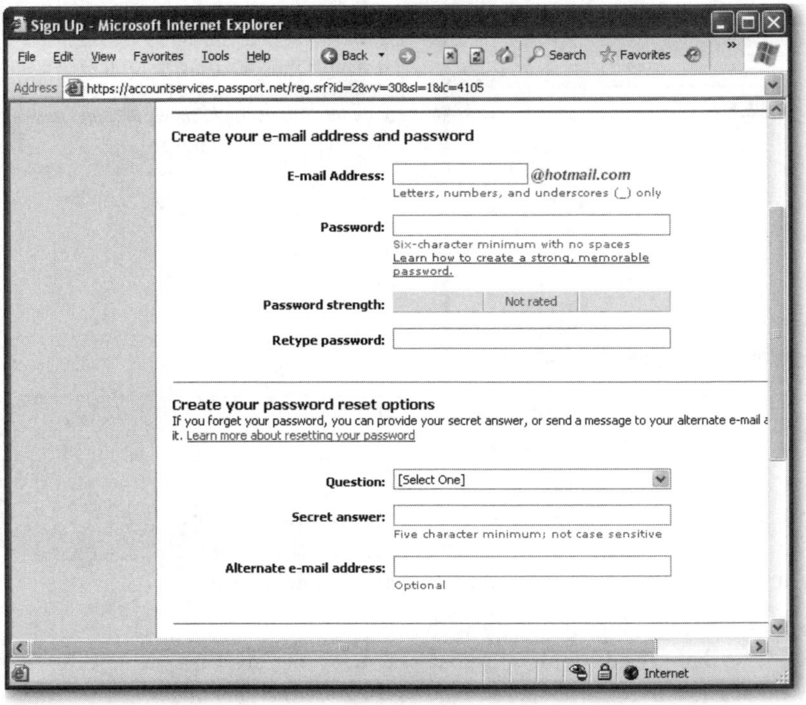

Figure 12-2:
Before Microsoft will grant you an email account, you need to submit some seriously detailed information. The textboxes, lists, and buttons you use are all part of an HTML form.

Form basics

Every HTML form starts out with a <form> tag. The <form> tag is a container tag (page 30), and everything inside is automatically deemed to be part of your form.

```
<form>
  ...
</form>
```

Form tags are also block elements (page 116), which means when you start a form, the browser adds a little bit of spacing and starts you off on a new line.

What goes inside your form tag? Ordinary HTML content (like text) can go inside a form tag, or it can go outside—it really doesn't matter. However, controls (those graphical widgets like buttons, text boxes, and lists) should always go *inside* a form tag. Otherwise, you won't have any way to capture the information that visitors enter into these controls.

POWER USERS' CLINIC

Becoming a Programmer

Want to unleash forms throughout your site and become a hard-core programmer? It's not easy going, but it can open up a lot of options for a stylin' site. The first task is to choose the programming framework you want to use. Here are some options:

- **JavaScript** is a simplified way to program for the Web. It won't power a professional Web site, because it runs only inside the browser (not on the Web server). However, it's a good way to start out with a kind of programmer's training wheels. You'll get a basic introduction to JavaScript in Chapter 14.

- **CGI** (Common Gateway Interface) is the favorite of Internet traditionalists. It's a thorny but widely adopted standard that has been around since the dawn of the Internet. CGI isn't for the faint of heart, because it requires jargon-filled languages like C and Perl. If you aren't familiar with these languages, you might still be able to download a CGI script file from the Web and get it working for you. Surf over to *www.cgi101.com/book* to dip a toe into CGI.

- **ASP** (Active Server Pages) and **ASP.NET** (a newer version) are Microsoft technologies that are a good fit for people familiar with friendly programming languages like Visual Basic. You can learn some ASP basics at *www.w3schools.com/asp*, or tackle the more complex but much more capable ASP.NET at *www.w3schools.com/aspnet*.

To create controls, you use yet another set of HTML tags. Here's the weird part—most form controls use the *exact same* tag. That tag is named <input>, and it represents information that you want to get *from* the visitor. You choose the type of input control by using the *type* attribute. For example, to create a checkbox, you use the *checkbox* type:

```
<input type="checkbox">
```

To create a text box, you use the text type:

```
<input type="text">
```

To create a complete form, you just mix and match <input> tags with ordinary HTML:

```
<html>
<head>
  <title>A Form-idable Test</title>
</head>

<body>
  <form>
    First Name: <input type="text"><br>
    Last Name: <input type="text"><br>
    Email Address: <input type="text"><br>
```

```
        <br>
        <input type="checkbox">Add me to your mailing list
    </form>
    </body>
    </html>
```

Figure 12-3 shows the page this creates.

Figure 12-3:
This very basic HTML form brings together four controls: three text boxes and one checkbox. Everything else is just ordinary HTML content. To make everything look nicer (and align it more neatly), you can use all the tricks you've learned about in previous chapters, including tables and styles. But one thing's still missing: a way for your visitor to actually send you the form's info. You'll learn how to fix that shortcoming below.

Every <input> tag also supports the *value* attribute, which is usually used to set the initial state (setting) of the control. For example, if you want to put some text inside a textbox when the page first appears, you could use this tag:

```
<input type="text" value="<Enter the first name here>">
```

Checkboxes are a little different. You can start them off so that they're turned on by adding the *checked* attribute, as shown here:

```
<input type="checkbox" checked>
```

Not all controls use the <input> tag. In fact, there are two notable exceptions. The <textarea> tag is used to grab large amounts of text that span more than one line (don't ask why a new tag was used for this purpose—it's largely for historical reasons). The <option> tag is used to create a list (inside of which the surfer can select an item). Table 12-1 lists all of the most common controls.

Table 12-1. *HTML Form Controls*

Control	HTML Tag	Description
Single-line Textbox	`<input type="text">` `<input type="password">`	Shows a textbox where the visitor can type in any text. If you use the password type, the text isn't displayed in the browser. Instead, surfers see an asterisk (*) appear in the place of each letter, hiding it from prying eyes.

Table 12-1. *HTML Form Controls (continued)*

Control	HTML Tag	Description
Multi-line Textbox	`<textarea></textarea>`	Shows a large textbox that can fit multiple lines of text.
Checkbox	`<input type="checkbox">`	Shows a checkbox that can be turned on or off.
Option Button	`<input type="radio">`	Shows a radio button (a circle that can be turned on or off). Usually, you'll have a group of radio buttons next to each other, in which case the visitor can select only one.
Button	`<input type="submit">` `<input type="reset">`	Shows the standard clickable button. A *submit* button always gathers up the form data and sends it to its destination. A *reset* button simply clears the visitor's selections and text in all the input controls of the form.
List	`<select>...</select>`	Shows a list where your visitor can select one or more items. Each item in the list is represented by an <option> tag.

Right now, the only problem with the form in Figure 12-3 is that it doesn't actually do anything. You need a way for the visitor to send the form to you. In order to make this happen, you need to take two steps. First, you need to add a *submit* button. Use the *value* attribute to set the text that appears inside this button.

```
<input type="submit" value="OK">
```

Next, you need to modify the <form> tag so that it uses a *mailto* link to identify the email address where the form data should be sent:

```
<form action="mailto:myaccount@HelloThere.com"
 method="post" enctype="text/plain">
```

Note: As with the mailto links shown in the previous section, this technique only works if Web surfers have an email program installed and correctly configured on their computers.

Finally, you need a way to uniquely identify each control. Otherwise, you won't be able to separate the first name from the last name from the rest of the form information. The solution is to give each control a name with the *name* attribute.

Here's the revised form:

```
<form action="mailto:myaccount@HelloThere.com"
 method="post" enctype="text/plain" >
  First Name: <input type="text" name="FirstName"><br>
  Last Name: <input type="text" name="LastName"><br>
  Email Address: <input type="text" name="Email"><br>
  <br>
  <input type="checkbox" checked name="MailCheck">
  Add me to your mailing list<br><br>
```

```
<input type="submit" value="OK">
</form>
```

Now, say a visitor fills out the form with the information shown in Figure 12-4.

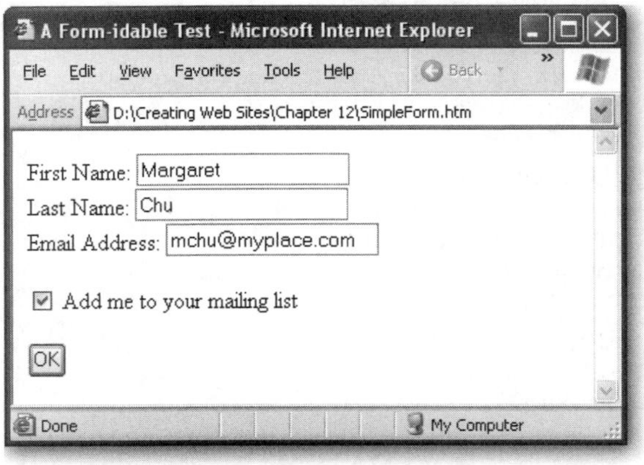

Figure 12-4:
A form with some visitor-supplied information.

When the visitor clicks OK, the information is added to an email message, and sent to your email address. Here is the content of the email that you'll receive:

FirstName=Margaret

LastName=Chu

Email=mchu@myplace.com

MailCheck=on

All this email contains is a list of *name-value pairs*. The name (on the left side of the equal sign) identifies the control. The value (on the right side) indicates the value that the visitor supplied. As you can see, it could take a lot of work to read all these emails and add them to an email list in your email program if you have a popular Web site. A nicer, but far more complex, approach is to have some sort of program that can understand this type of message, and carry out the correct actions automatically.

Tip: Your browser may show a warning when you click the submit button, advising you that you are about to send an email. Similarly, spyware catchers and virus programs might block this behavior. If you're concerned about these potential roadblocks, you can add a note to your page informing visitors that when they click the submit button they may see a message, which they'll need to review before they can send an email.

Creating a feedback page with a form

The next example you'll see uses a form to create a *feedback page* (see Figure 12-5). Visitors use this page to supply their deepest thoughts, and whisk them off to you with a single click of a button.

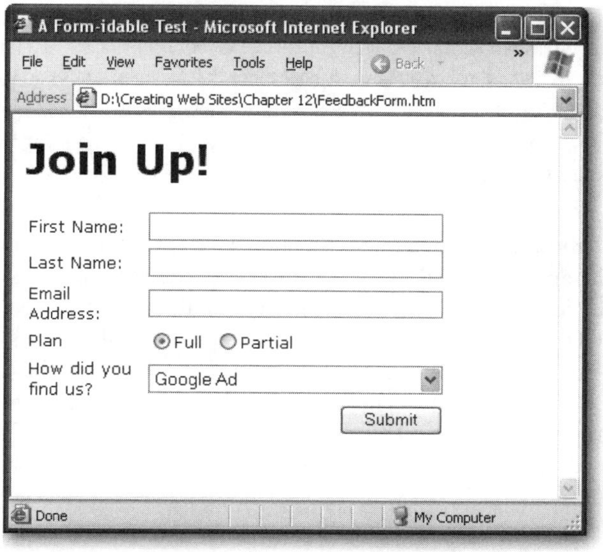

Figure 12-5:
This form aligns its controls neatly, and features a radio button selection and a drop-down menu.

This form is a fair bit more interesting than the previous one. First of all, it includes two instances of a new form tag—the radio button—which is created with the *radio* type of <input> tag. Here's the HTML that makes it all happen:

```
<input type="radio" name="Plan" value="Full" checked>Full
<input type="radio" name="Plan" value="Part">Partial
```

The trick is to make sure you give every radio button in the group the same name. That way, the browser knows they belong together, and when you click one option, the others are unselected. You also need to give every radio button a unique value. That's how you tell, when you receive the form results, which option was selected. For example, if the surfer clicks Full and submits the form, this is the corresponding line you'll see in the emailed data:

```
Plan=Full
```

The drop-down menu uses the <select> tag to define the list (and choose a name), and the <option> tags to define each item in the list (and choose a unique value for each one). Here's the HTML:

```
<select name="PromoSource">
  <option value="Ad">Google Ad</option>
  <option value="Search">Google Search</option>
```

```
      <option value="Psychic">Uncanny Psychic Intuition</option>
      <option value="Luck">Bad Luck</option>
   </select>
```

Now, if someone selects the first option, the email message will contain this line:

```
PromoSource=Ad
```

Tip: You can switch your menu from its drop-down appearance to a large list box using the *size* attribute. For example, if you write <select size="3"> you'll create a scrollable list box that fits three items into view at once. If you want to allow multiple selections, add the attribute *multiple*. Now, a visitor can select several items at once by holding down the Ctrl key (or @cmd, if she's using a Mac). For more low-level HTML form details, check out *www.w3schools.com/html/html_forms.asp*.

The last interesting detail about the form shown in Figure 12-5 is that it uses tables and styles to neaten up its appearance. Various style rules set the fonts and sizing of the different controls. (See the downloadable content for this chapter—available from the "Missing CD" page at *www.missingmanuals.com*—to take a look at the details.) Additionally, each item is placed inside a separate table row so they all line up neatly. The table has two columns. The leftmost column holds the caption text, and the rightmost column has the control.

Here's the first part of the table structure:

```
<table>
  <tr>
    <td>First Name:</td>
    <td><input type="text" name="FirstName"></td>
  </tr>
  <tr>
    <td>Last Name:</td>
    <td><input type="text" name="LastName"></td>
  </tr>
  <tr>
    <td>Email Address:</td>
    <td><input class="TextControl" type="text" name="Email"></td>
  </tr>
  ...
</table>
```

This technique is a handy way to rein in sprawling forms.

Adding Forums and Groups to Your Site

In the early days of the Internet, Web sites weren't at the heart of the action. Instead, the most interesting and lively interactions took place on a mammoth collection of online bulletin boards called *Usenet*. Sadly, Usenet fell into decline as the

Web grew, suffering as well from an onslaught of spam, and losing its luster as slick graphical sites become the norm. More recently, the collection of Usenet groups was bought by Google, and is experiencing a small renaissance as a part of Google Groups (see *http://groups.google.com*).

Although Usenet isn't ever going to recapture the limelight, different types of discussion forums are still ragingly popular. But instead of subject-based, administrator-moderated groups that are controlled by a single organization, forums are cropping up as a bonus feature on all sorts of different Web sites. Here are some examples:

- Technology vendors large and small use them to provide community support and spread information. For example, Microsoft veterans and newbies exchange Office tips on the boards at *www.microsoft.com/office/community/en-us*.

- Topic sites use them to host rollicking discussions. For example, you can tear reality TV to shreds on the popular *http://p085.ezboard.com/bsurvivorsucks* or register your Office frustration at *www.officefrustration.com*.

- Individuals use them to provide technical support and get feedback. For example, popular computer book author Jesse Liberty helps readers with questions about his technical books at *http://forums.delphiforums.com/LibertyBooks*.

One of the best parts about forums is they drive themselves. Once you get the right ingredients in place, a forum can succeed without you needing to intervene. Think of it as a dinner party that you're hosting, and all you need to do is get the conversation started before making a polite retreat. And if you use forums to answer technical questions, you can reduce your workload immensely. For example, on many forums the emphasis is on different customers or experts helping each other. That means easy questions are answered for you, and you might only need to step in to clear up a long-running debate.

Although discussion forums are wildly popular, they come in many different flavors. All the examples in the previous list run on different software. Some of it's free, other options cost money, and still other options are developed by hand by Web site programmers and aren't for sale to the public.

To create your own groups, you have a few choices. You could purchase an expensive product, install it on your own in-house Web server, and have complete control over everything: what your discussion pages look like, who gets to post messages (or not), and so on. This approach makes sense for a gargantuan company like American Express, but it doesn't fit the bill for the small- to medium-sized site. Instead, what you'll probably want to do is use an online service provided by another company. In this scenario, you provide a link on your site that leads to the other company's Web server, where the discussion forum is hosted. The only catch? Usually, most companies that provide a discussion forum sell advertising space. That means that as you read messages in the group, you're likely to see some ads on the sidelines.

In the remainder of this chapter, you'll learn how to create a forum with one of the most capable discussion forum tools—Google Groups.

About Google Groups

Google Groups is a thriving community of discussion forums. Although it hasn't been around as long as some other forum hosts, it includes a collection of useful features that rivals any of its competitors. And, of course, it's all free.

Here are some important details about Google Groups:

- When you create a group, you're given a unique, easy-to-remember URL. That's the group address, and it never changes.

- Group members can search through group postings with some of the best search tools on the planet. For bragging rights, nothing rivals the catalog of searchable Usenet content that Google has acquired, which ranges back to 1981.

- The group creator (you) controls who can and who can't post.

- Google manages the registration process itself. That means you don't need to manually add and remove group members.

- Each group member can choose whether they like to read group messages online, or receive them in regular emails that Google will send automatically.

- Google's page layout is a frazzled Web surfer's dream. It's easy to search posts, see all the replies to a post at a glance, bookmark the posts you want to follow, and more.

- Although Google will display ads in the corners of your group windows, it does its best to choose relevant ad content. For example, if the most common topic in a group is favorite DVDs, you're likely to start seeing ads that promise cutting edge DVD players, mail-order movie clubs, and DVD e-commerce shops.

You can learn more about Google Groups by surfing to *http://groups.google.com/intl/en/googlegroups/about.html*.

Note: Google is continuously improving its offerings. At the time of this writing, some parts of the Google Groups features are considered to be "in beta." Technically, that means they may get tweaked a bit, and may have a few unexpected hiccups along the way.

Creating a Group

To create a new group, follow these steps:

1. **Head on over to *http://groups.google.com*. Look for a link inviting new members to join, and click it.**

    You'll need to register (with a valid email address and password) before you can create a group. Once you've completed the process and activated your account, you're ready to return to the group setup page.

2. Click the "Create new groups" link to get started.

3. When asked, log in with your user name and password. The "Create a group" page appears, as shown in Figure 12-6).

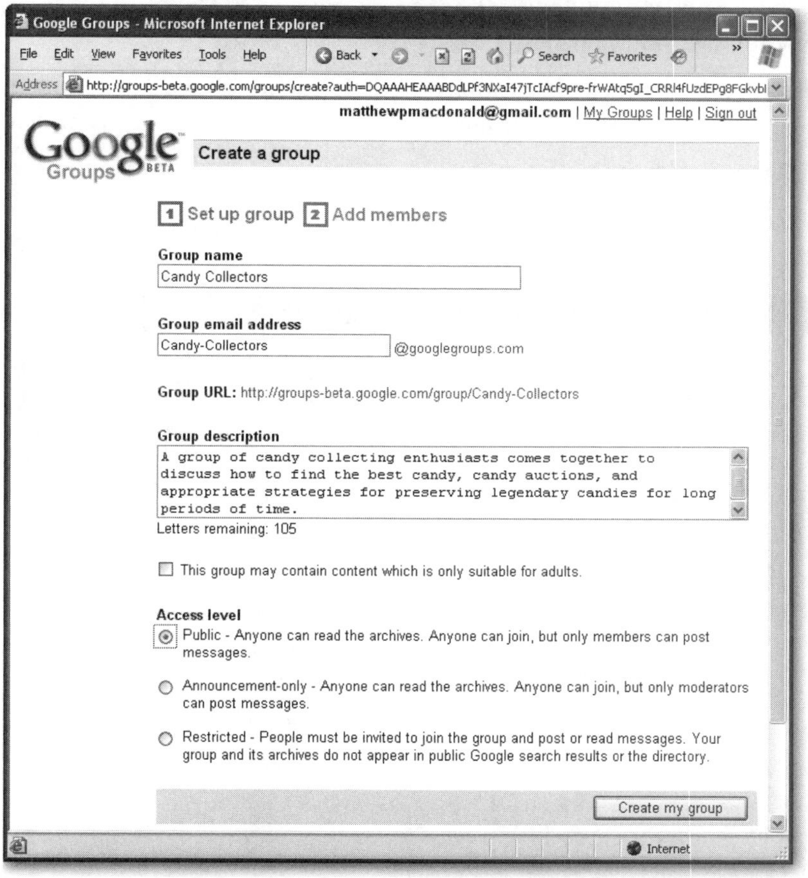

Figure 12-6:
Creating a Google group takes two steps. In the first step, you define all the basic information about your group, including its name and email address.

4. Fill in all the information for your group.

The *group name* identifies your group, like *Candy Collectors*.

The *group email address* is a version of the name that will work as an email address or URL. Spaces aren't allowed, but *Candy-Collectors* and *CandyCollectors* work. The email address also becomes part of the group URL, so make sure it's memorable.

The *group description* explains what the group's all about, using two or three sentences.

The *access level* indicates who's allowed to post. If you want to create a completely open group that accepts all comers, choose *Public*, which makes sense for most Web groups. Anyone who stumbles across the group can join at will, without your intervention. If you want to use the group solely as a place to post your own musings, choose *Announcements-only*. However, you're probably better off to put these announcements right on your Web site instead of in a group. Finally, if you want to have micromanaged control over who's allowed in and who's kept out, choose *Restricted*. That way, the only people allowed to join are those you specifically invite.

Finally, you'll see a checkbox to allow adult content. If you don't allow this, naughty posts may be blocked automatically, saving you some embarrassment.

5. **Click the "Create my group" button.**

   The second step appears (see Figure 12-7).

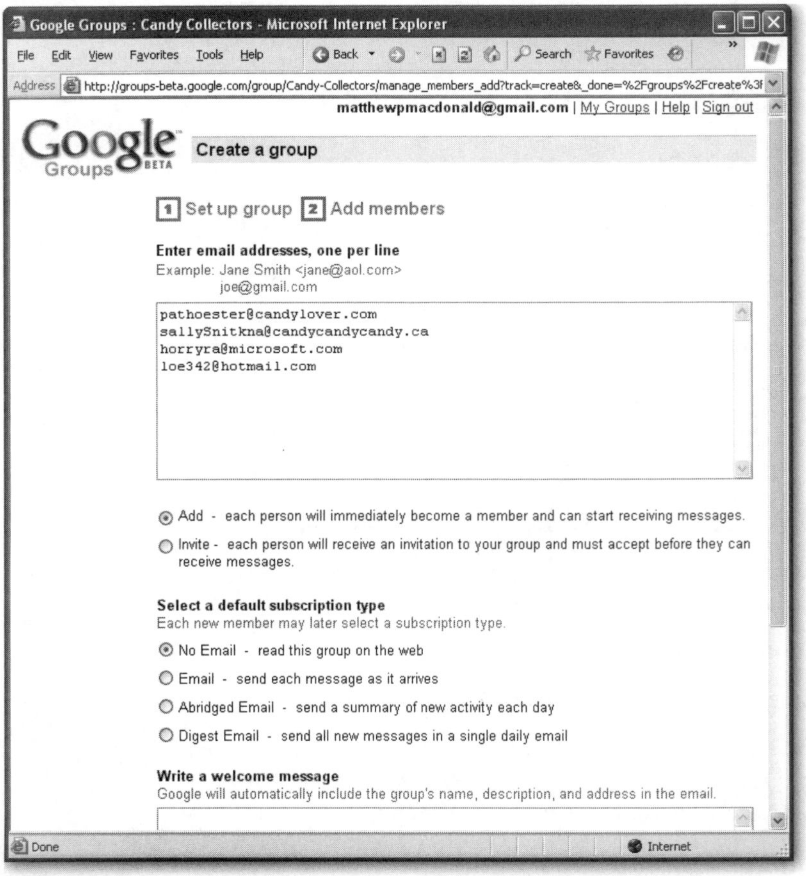

Figure 12-7:
In the second step, you choose your initial group members. Remember, if you're creating a public group, new people can join at any time through Google.

6. **Fill in the initial set of group members.**

   Supply a list of email addresses, with one address per line. Google will email these people to tell them they've been allowed into the group.

If you choose Add, each of these members is automatically a group member. If you choose Invite, they'll need to visit the site to opt in and become a member. Either way, if the recipient doesn't have a Google account, they'll need to create one before they can do anything.

The subscriber type allows you to choose how these people will use the group. They can choose to read the group posts on the group Web site, or to have every message delivered to them by email (a bad idea unless it's a quiet discussion group). There are also two more specialized options. If you choose Abridged Email, the subscriber receives one email message per day (as long as there's been at least one new post), and this email message contains a list of message titles, with a link to the full text next to each. This option is a handy way to stay on top of group activity, and keep an eye out for interesting posts. The other option is Digest Email, which sends all the new content once per day in a single gargantuan email. This option won't clutter your email inbox as much as receiving each message separately, but in an active group, it's impractical to browse through such a long email.

No matter what subscriber type you choose, each group member can change this to match their personal preference later on.

Finally, supply some text for a welcome message. Once you create the group, every member receives a welcome message letting them know the group's been set up (see Figure 12-8).

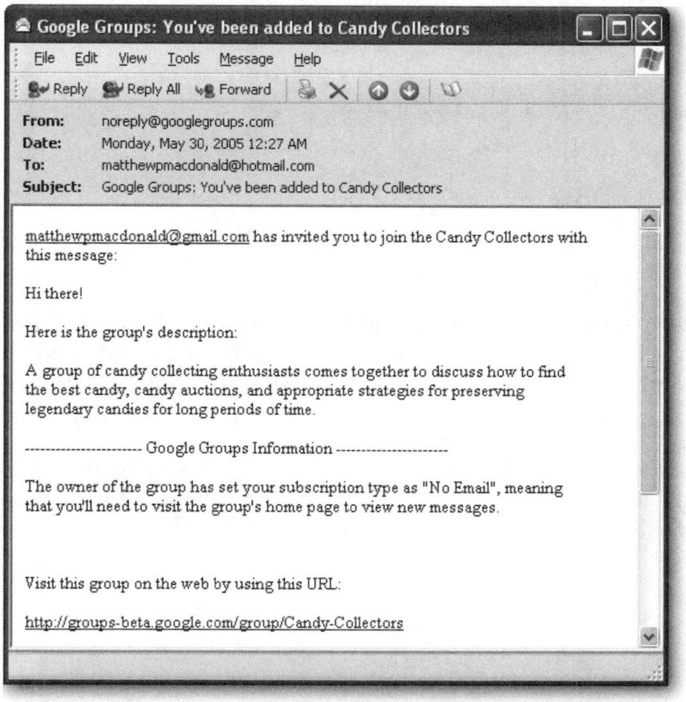

Figure 12-8:
Welcome aboard. You're a new member of a Google group.

Tip: Don't worry if you don't have email addresses handy. You don't need to invite anyone now. You can return to this page to invite more people later on, after you've created the group.

7. **Click Done.**

Google creates the group, and shows you a summary (Figure 12-9). Sometime shortly thereafter, it sends welcome messages to the initial set of group members.

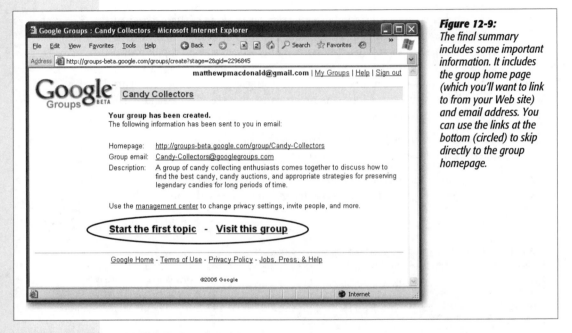

Figure 12-9:
The final summary includes some important information. It includes the group home page (which you'll want to link to from your Web site) and email address. You can use the links at the bottom (circled) to skip directly to the group homepage.

Participating in a Group

When you first head over to your group, you'll find that it's barren. To get the discussion started, why not post the first topic?

Google gives you two different ways to post a topic. You can add a topic right from the Web page by clicking the "Start a new topic" link. Or, if you're really in a hurry, you can simply send an email message to the group email address. The email message is then automatically converted into a group topic (Figure 12-10).

Of course, discussions are all about back-and-forth exchanges. Once a message has been posted, you can read it and click the Reply link to post a reply. Posts and replies are *threaded*, which means they're grouped together so that you can easily see what message goes with what topic, no matter when the posts were made (see Figure 12-11).

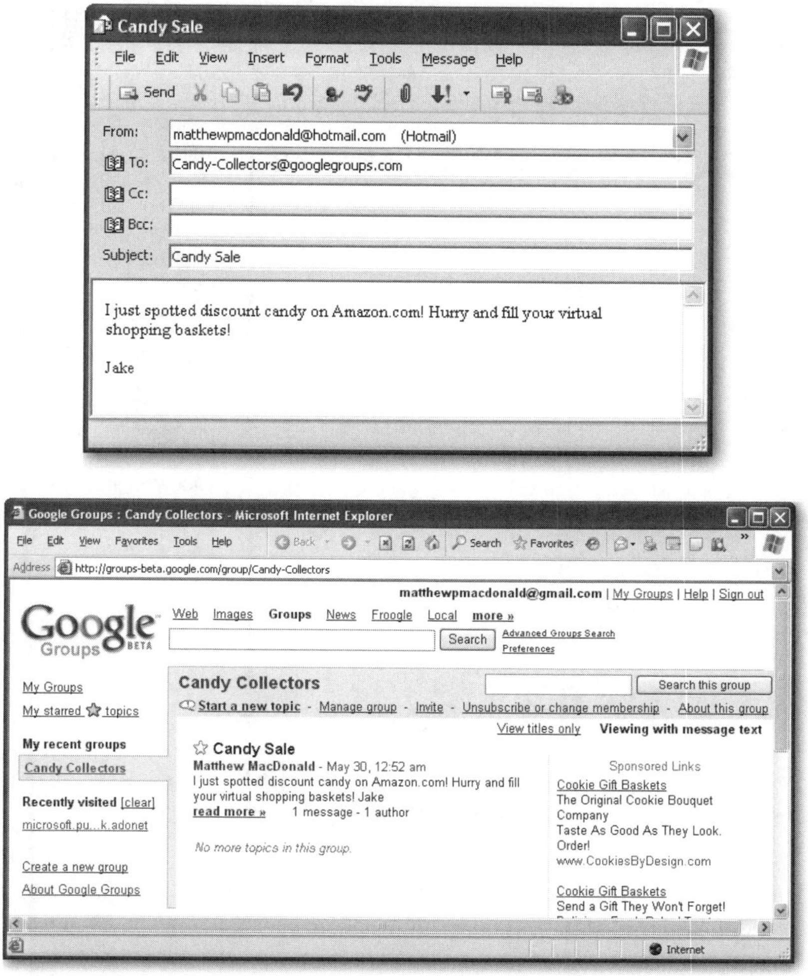

Figure 12-10:
Top: This email is about to be sent to a Google group.

Bottom: Once the email's received, it becomes an ordinary posting. Interestingly, even with a single topic Google's already picked out some ads it thinks are related (shown on the right). As people use your group, Google will refine the types of ads it uses, based on which ones are the most popular (and get the most clicks from group members).

You now have a fully functioning group. From this point on, the challenge isn't in using the group, but attracting enough interesting people that it becomes a lively community.

Managing Your Group

When an ordinary group member visits a group, he'll have the option of posting new messages, replying to existing messages, or changing his delivery settings by clicking the "Unsubscribe or change membership" link. Use this last option to have group messages automatically emailed to you or to see a summary of group activity (page 330).

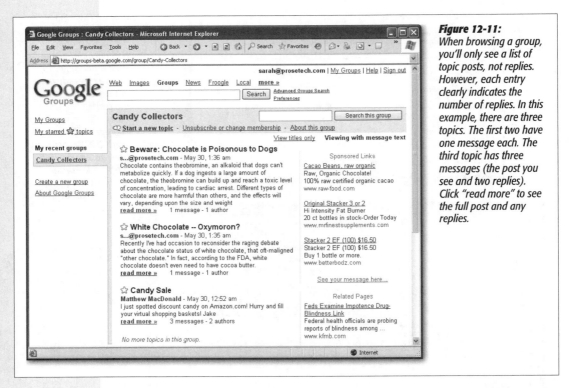

Figure 12-11:
When browsing a group, you'll only see a list of topic posts, not replies. However, each entry clearly indicates the number of replies. In this example, there are three topics. The first two have one message each. The third topic has three messages (the post you see and two replies). Click "read more" to see the full post and any replies.

On the other hand, when the group creator visits the group, some additional links appear in the display. Along with the customary links for posting and changing the membership settings, you'll also see an Invite link, which allows you to send welcome messages to a new batch of groupies. You'll also see the "Manage group" link, which allows you to take control of a lot more (see Figure 12-12).

On the whole, the group membership page is well-organized and quite clear. You'll have no trouble using the various options. Here are some of the highlights:

- **The Access settings.** These settings allow you to define who's allowed to read messages (anybody, or only group members), who's allowed to invite new members (just you, or any group member), and who's allowed to join. The last option is the most interesting. You can allow everyone, restrict the group to just people you invite, or force people to apply for group membership. If you use the last choice, anyone can apply to join through Google, but you'll have the chance to review the application and give the final acceptance or refusal. You can even tell Google to give hopeful applicants a specific question. You can then review their answer to determine whether they are group-worthy.

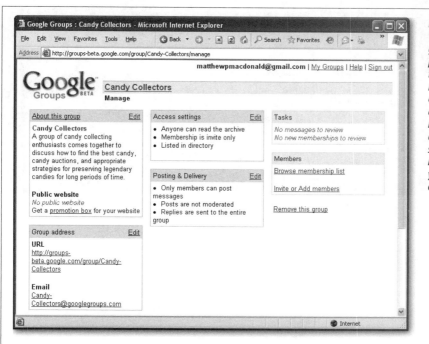

Figure 12-12:
When you click "Manage group," you'll see this page, which allows you to change the group name and description, change the level of access, and invite new members or remove existing ones. The settings offered here are more detailed than those you saw when you created the group.

- **Posting & Delivery settings.** These settings let you define who's allowed to post to your group. You can choose any group member, just you, or anyone. Additionally, you can choose to use *moderated messages*. With moderated messages, every new message is sent to you for review. Messages won't appear on the group until you give them a thumbs-up (and if you don't, they'll never reach the group). Only use moderated messages if you have a lot of spare time.

- **Browse membership list.** Use this link to delve into the details about group members. You can review the full list of group members, see who hasn't responded to a group invitation, ban troublemaking posters, and give other members managerial powers.

FREQUENTLY ASKED QUESTION

Group Restrictions

Should I restrict people from joining my group or posting messages?

It's tempting to force group members to apply to your group, but resist the ego trip. On the Web, people are impatient and easily distracted. If you place barriers in the way of potential group members, they may just walk away.

On the other hand, there are some cases where restricted group membership makes a lot of sense. Two examples are if you want to discuss semi-secret information like company strategies, or if you're afraid your topic might attract the wrong kind of crowd. For example, if you set up a group called Software-Piracy to discuss the social implications of software piracy, you might find yourself deluged with requests for the latest versions of cutting-edge software. As

a general rule of thumb, restrictions make sense only if they're being used to maintain group quality control.

The same holds true for message moderation. Most healthy online communities are self-regulating. If a member inadvertently offends the general community, others will correct him or her; if it's deliberate, most will eventually ignore the provocation. You might need to step in occasionally to ban a member, but screening every message is overkill. It also adds a huge amount of extra work for you, and severely cramps the dynamic of your group, because most messages won't appear until several hours after they've been written (at least). For fans of the Web who expect instant gratification, this isn't good news.

CHAPTER 13

Making Money with Your Site

If it's not for sale on the Web, it's probably not for sale at all. It's no secret that the Internet is a global bazaar with more merchandise than a decade's worth of garage sales. Surfers generate huge amounts of traffic hunting for Amazon coupons, discussing hot deals, and scouring eBay for bargains. So how can you get your share of Web capital?

One obvious option is to sell a real, tangible product. The Internet abounds with specialty shops hawking art, jewelry, and handmade goods. But even if you have a product ready to sell, you still need a few specialized tools to transform your corner of the Web into a bustling e-commerce storefront. For example, you'll probably want a virtual *shopping cart*, which lets visitors collect the items they want to buy as they surf. And when they finally head for the checkout, you'll need a secure way to accept their cash—usually by way of a credit card transaction. In this chapter, you'll learn how to get both these features using PayPal's merchant tools.

But even if you aren't looking for a place to unload your hand-crafted fishbone pencils, your Web site can still help fatten your wallet. In fact, just about any Web site can become profitable, either by selling ad space or recommending other companies' products. In this chapter, you'll consider how you can use two of the Web's most popular *affiliate programs*—Google AdWords and Amazon Associates—to collect some spare cash.

Note: Not a U.S. citizen? Don't worry—all the money-making ideas in this chapter rely on companies that provide services worldwide. Google, Amazon, and PayPal will let you rake in the cash no matter what country you live in.

Money Making the Web Way

The Web offers many paths to fiduciary gain. Here are some of the most popular ways Web sites make money:

- **Donations.** It sounds crazy, but some Web sites badger their visitors for spare change. Donations might work if your Web site provides some truly valuable and unique content (see Figure 13-1). Otherwise, don't bother. Don't be seduced into logic like "If 1000 visitors come and every visitor pays just 10 cents…." They won't. (If you still want to add a Donate button to your Web pages, you can use a payment service like PayPal, which is discussed later in this chapter.)

Figure 13-1:
www.treadmilldoctor.com—a popular site with information about a dizzying array of exercise treadmills—goes so far as to ask visitors for money (see the donation box, circled). It's a rare success story. Because TreadmillDoctor.com spends so much time compiling detailed research, and since they've decided not to accept sponsored links (which would compromise their objectivity), many visitors are willing to pay up every once in a while.

- **Advertisements.** The most popular way to make money on the Web is by selling small spaces of Web-page real estate. Unfortunately, this is also a great way to exasperate your visitors, especially if the ads are distracting, unrelated to your site, or simply take up too much space. Not long ago, ads were the worst thing you could do to your pages. Fortunately, in the 21st century, monitors are bigger, and companies like Google provide targeted, unobtrusive ads that fit right in with the rest of your site.

- **Affiliate Programs.** Rather than plastering ads across your site, why not put in a good word for a company you really believe in? Many affiliate programs let you get a commission for referring customers to other sites. For example, if you review gourmet cookbooks, why not include links to the books on Amazon's Web site? If an interested reader buys a book, Amazon's associate program will fork over a few dollars.

- **Sell Stuff.** If you have your own products to sell, the Web is the perfect medium, since the costs required to set up shop online are so much less than in the real world. You can build a slick store, with product pictures and a shopping cart, with surprisingly little work.

- **Pay-For-Content.** If you have really great content, you can ask for cash *before* letting your visitors read it. Warning: This is even harder to pull off than asking for donations, because visitors need to take a huge leap of faith. It's a technique that's used by established media companies (like the *Wall Street Journal*) and hucksters promising secret ways to conquer the real estate market or get free camcorders.

Note: Pay-for-content is the only money making scheme that you won't learn to pull off in this chapter. That's because in order for it to work, you need a way to *authenticate* visitors—in other words, you need to be able to identify visitors in order to tell if they've paid or not. This needs some heavy-duty programming (or a pay service from another company).

Google AdSense

Even if you don't have any products to sell, you still have one valuable asset: the attention of your visitors. The good news is there are a huge number of companies ready to pay for it.

Some of these companies pay you a minuscule fee every time someone requests a page that has an ad, while others pay only when an ad is clicked, or when an ad is clicked and the visitor goes on to actually buy something on the sponsor's site. Fortunately, you don't need to waste hours checking out all these options, because Google offers an advertising program that handily beats just about every other system out there.

The program's called Google AdSense, and it requires you to show small, text-only advertisements on your Web site. You sign up, set some space aside on one or more Web pages, and paste in some HTML that Google supplies (see Figure 13-2). Google takes care of the rest, filling in the space with a group of ads every time someone requests the page.

Showing Google AdSense ads doesn't get you anything, but whenever a visitor clicks on one of the ad links, you earn a few cents. When your total reaches $100, Google mails you a check.

Note: There's no way to know for sure how much money an individual click is worth with AdSense. That's because Google advertisers compete by bidding for different keywords (see page 305 in Chapter 11) and keyword prices can fluctuate over time. Google *does* let you know how much your clicks were worth (in total) when it pays you. A typical click can net you about 20 cents.

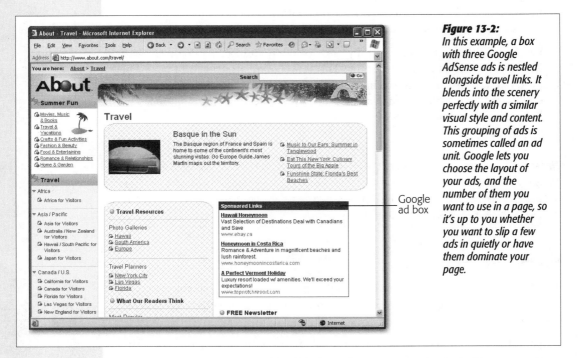

Figure 13-2:
In this example, a box with three Google AdSense ads is nestled alongside travel links. It blends into the scenery perfectly with a similar visual style and content. This grouping of ads is sometimes called an ad unit. Google lets you choose the layout of your ads, and the number of them you want to use in a page, so it's up to you whether you want to slip a few ads in quietly or have them dominate your page.

Before you become an AdSense devotee, you need to know what makes AdSense different from other ad programs. Here are some of its top advantages:

- **AdSense ads are relevant.** Google automatically scans your site, and matches ads based on keywords. That means that if you've got a Web site devoted to Sponge-Bob SquarePants, Google will provide ads hawking SpongeBob DVDs, inflatable dolls, and birthday gear. Using keyword-based ads is far, far better than aggravating your visitors with offers for completely unrelated products like high-tech spy cameras. It also dramatically increases the chance that a visitor will click an ad and generate a click-through fee. And if you're worried about a competitor's site turning up in an advertisement, you can tell Google to filter it out.

- **AdSense ads can blend in with the scenery.** Google gives you a wide range of ad layout and color options. This ensures that you can generate ads that match the slick color scheme of the rest of your Web site.

- **Google gives fair payment terms.** As you learned in Chapter 11, Google charges advertisers different amounts of money for different keywords. Most advertising providers would just swallow the extra money, and pay their members the same amount for any click-through. Not Google. It pays you according to the current value of the keyword, which guarantees that you're always getting a competitive rate.

- **There are no start-up charges.** The AdSense program is completely free to join.

Tip: Don't try to cheat AdSense. Devious Web developers have tried to game the system by clicking on their own ads over and over again, or even firing up automating programs that do it for them. The problem is that Google uses various techniques to spot suspicious usage patterns. If it sees a ridiculous number of clicks over a short period of time all originating from the same computer, it's likely to spot the deception and ban your site outright.

Signing Up for AdSense

You can learn much more about the specifics of Google's ad program by surfing to *www.google.com/adsense*. There's also a great, not-too-detailed walkthrough of the AdSense service at *www.google.com/services/adsense_tour*.

When you're ready to get started, follow these steps to sign up:

1. **On the AdSense homepage, click the Click Here to Apply button.**

   Google asks you if you already have an AdWords account (which you can use to pay for advertisements that appear on Google's Web site, as described on page 305). If you do, you can use that to login and skip the account creation steps.

Note: Even if you have a Gmail account, you still need to register for AdSense. Gmail login information and the AdSense information are separate, because Google needs a few more details before it can conduct business with you.

---

2. **To create a new account, you need to supply your email address and a password, and click Continue.**

   Google starts the process of getting the account information it needs. First, you'll need to identify whether you're applying as an individual or as a registered business. Registered businesses that are based in the U.S. need an EIN (Employer Identification Number). U.S. citizens who are applying as individuals need to give an SSN (Social Security Number). Citizens of other countries need to apply for a U.S. TIN (Taxpayer Identification Number)—see *www.google.com/adsense/taxinfo* for the lowdown.

3. **Next, you'll need to supply the typical identification information, like your name and address.**

The interesting part comes when it's time to choose the type of AdSense feature you want. You'll find these options in the Products section at the bottom of the page (see Figure 13-3).

Figure 13-3:
Google gives you the option of ordinary AdSense (called "AdSense for content"), which you've learned about so far, and a search-based feature called "AdSense for search." With "AdSense for search," you can provide a Google search box on your page that visitors can use to search the Web. When ads crop up in the search results, they're treated like ads on your Web site (see page 351 for more). You may as well choose both AdSense programs, since you can decide later which to use.

4. **Once you're finished, click Submit.**

   The next page shows a summary of all the information you supplied.

5. **Click Continue to finish the process.**

   Now you need to wait for Google to contact you by email to confirm your account. There are two steps in this process.

   First, Google sends you an email confirmation message almost immediately. This message contains a link that you need to click to confirm your email address. However, this still doesn't finish the job.

   Instead, someone at Google needs to take a quick look at your Web site to confirm it really exists and isn't promoting illegal activity (for example, offering pirated copies of Windows XP). Once this process is finished (usually two days later), you'll get a second email confirming your account has been activated.

Creating an Ad

Now that you have an AdSense account, you're ready to generate some ads and put them in your Web site. Just go to *www.google.com/adsense*, and log in with your email and Google password. You'll see the Google AdSense page (see Figure 13-4).

Note: Before you can generate the right ad unit, you need to have a basic idea of where you plan to put your ads. Consider whether you want a vertical or horizontal strip of ads, and try to assess how wide or long that bar should be. You can skip ahead to Figure 13-6 to see a preview of some of your layout options.

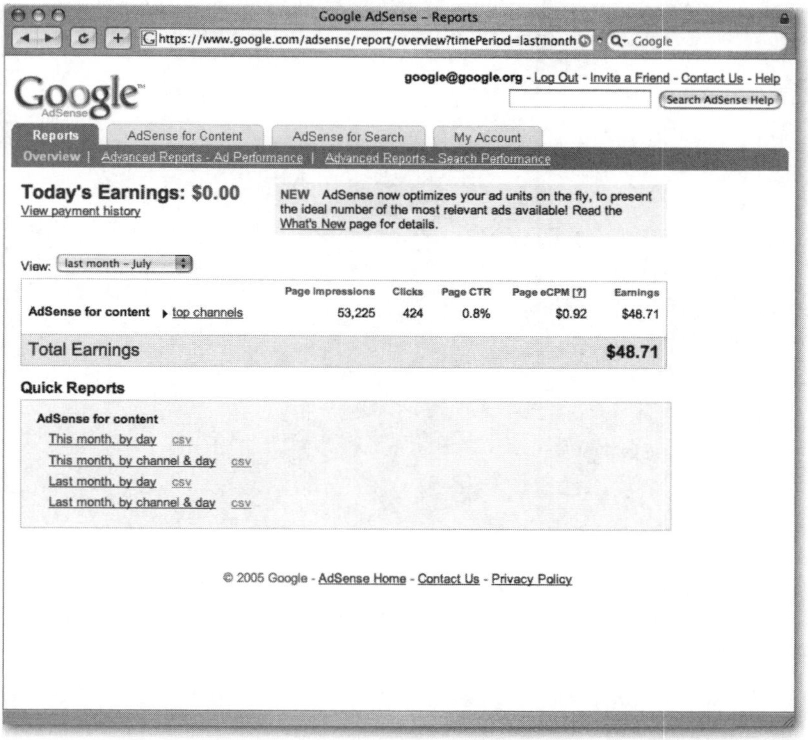

Figure 13-4:
The AdSense page is divided into several tabs. Initially, you begin at the Reports tab, where you can survey a day-by-day breakdown of the money you've made.

The AdSense page has four central sections, which are represented by tabs at the top of the page. These sections include:

- **Reports.** This tab helps you assess the performance of your AdSense ads. You'll see a summary of the money you've made today and over the last week. To get more detailed information, you can click a report link (like "This month, by day," which gets the earnings for this month, totaled by day). Google won't tell you what each individual click was worth, or which particular ad caught the reader's eye. You can also view a payment history that records each check that Google's mailed out to you (click the "View payment history" link).

- **AdSense for Content.** This is your starting point for generating AdSense ads— it's where you specify the type of ad you want, and get the HTML code you need to insert into your Web pages. You also have access to some advanced features here, such as filtering out ads from specific Web sites.

- **AdSense for Search.** Using this tab, you can generate the HTML for a Google search box that you can place on your Web pages. When a visitor performs a search through this Google box, they may see some relevant ads, and if they click one, you'll get the usual commission.

UP TO SPEED

AdSense Rules

Google enforces a handful of rules that your Web site must follow in order to be a part of AdSense. Many of these are common sense, but it's still worth taking a quick look at them.

- You can't put the ads that Google supplies you with in email messages or pop-up windows—the temptation for spammers to abuse the system is just too great.

- You can't put ads on pages that don't feature any "real" content. This includes error, login, registration, welcome, and under-construction pages. You definitely can't create pages that include nothing but ads.

- You can't try to obscure parts of the ad (for example, by placing other elements overtop with a style sheet). The entire content of an ad must be visible.

- You can't click your own ads. You also can't use programs that do this for you. Finally, you can't entice your visitors to click your links using threats or incentives.

- Your Web site can't include excessive profanity, copyrighted material, pornography, content about hacking hi-tech security systems, advocacy for illegal drugs, hate speech, or anything related to gambling.

For the full AdSense policy, surf to *www.google.com/adsense/policies*.

- **My Account.** This tab lets you update most of the information you supplied when you registered. This includes details like your mailing address and tax information.

Now that you're acquainted with AdSense, you're ready to dive in and build your first ad unit. Here's how:

1. **On the AdSense page, click the "AdSense for Content" tab.**

   The "AdSense for Content" tab has several clickable subcategories, including "Ad layout code," which is selected when you arrive on the "AdSense for Content" page. Using this "Ad layout code" sub-tab, you can generate the HTML code for a Google ad unit.

2. **Choose the type of ad you want to create—either an ad unit or a link unit.**

   An *ad unit* is a group of one or more ads, complete with descriptive text or (optionally) images. When a visitor clicks an ad, the visitor winds up at the advertiser's Web site (and you get paid). If you're used to seeing AdSense ads on Web pages, ad units are what you've probably seen most of in the past.

   A *link unit* is a slim box of links with no descriptive text. The title of the box is "Ads by Google" and the links are one- or two-word entries, like "Digital Cameras" or "Consumer Electronics." If a visitor clicks on one of these links, Google serves up a new page that's filled with ads for that topic. If the visitor then clicks one of these ads, you get paid.

Google AdSense

Note: Google is constantly tweaking and refining the types of ads it offers. Don't be surprised if you find even more types of ad formats available when you check out the AdSense program.

3. **Choose the exact type of ad (from the list box next to ad unit or link unit).**

If you're creating a link unit, you're limited to choosing how many links appear in the box.

If you're creating an ad unit, you can choose whether you want to use text or image ads. Generally, image ads stand out more than text ads. However, you need to balance two conflicting goals—the desire to make money by attracting clicks with eye-catching ads, and the desire to minimize the distraction on your Web page by choosing ad types that are less obtrusive.

Figure 13-5 shows one possible ad type and page layout selection.

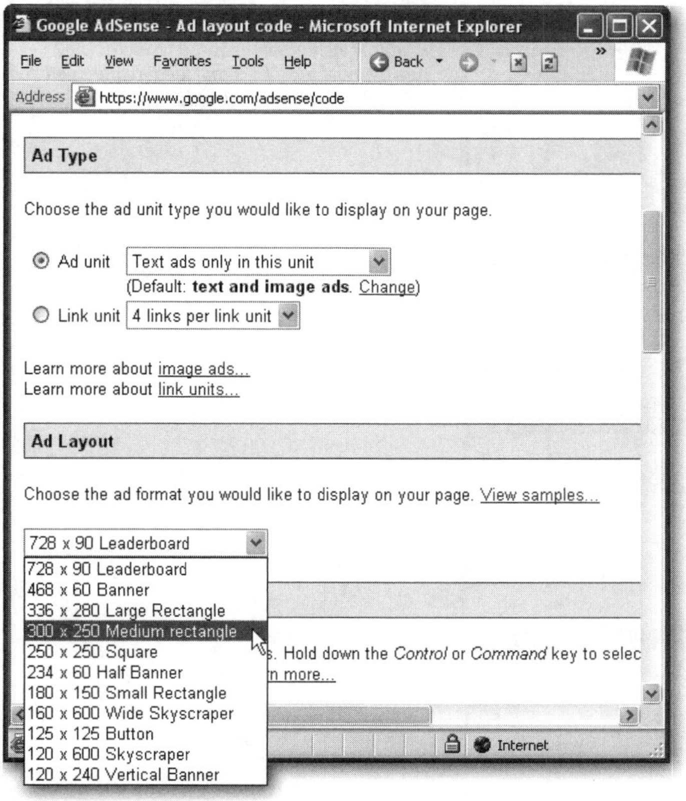

Figure 13-5:
This example uses text-only ad units. The ad layout is a 300 x 250 pixel rectangle, which holds four ads, one on top of the other. Of course, the only way you'll know how many ads fit into this layout is by checking out Google's sample-ad page (see Figure 13-6).

4. Choose the ad layout.

The ad layout determines the size of an ad. If you've chosen a text-only ad, Google uses a box with several ads inside it. The ad layout option also determines how many ads you'll see at once (from one to five).It's usually impossible to picture what the different ad layouts really look like. To orient yourself, click the View Samples link, which opens a new window with an example of every ad layout option (see Figure 13-6). Using this page, you can find the format that best suits your Web site.

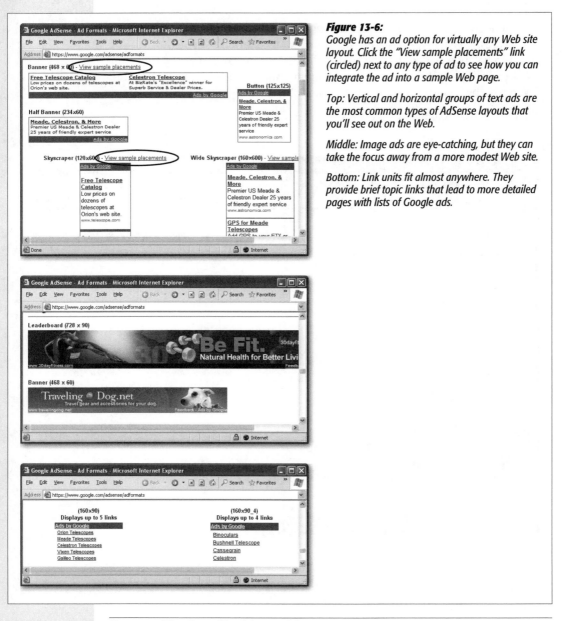

Figure 13-6:
Google has an ad option for virtually any Web site layout. Click the "View sample placements" link (circled) next to any type of ad to see how you can integrate the ad into a sample Web page.

Top: Vertical and horizontal groups of text ads are the most common types of AdSense layouts that you'll see out on the Web.

Middle: Image ads are eye-catching, but they can take the focus away from a more modest Web site.

Bottom: Link units fit almost anywhere. They provide brief topic links that lead to more detailed pages with lists of Google ads.

5. **Choose a color palette. (This step is optional.)**

The *color palette* sets the colors that are used for the ad text, background, and border. Google has preset palettes, with names that rival designer paint lines ("Mother Earth" and "Fresh Mint" are two examples). As you choose the palette you want to use, Google demonstrates the result with a small preview ad on the right.

If you want complete control over your colors and want to make sure they match the ones you're using in your Web site, you need to create a custom color palette. Click the "Manage color palettes" link (see Figure 13-7).

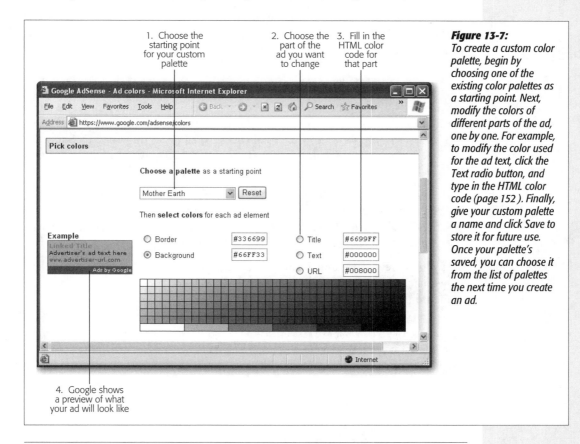

Figure 13-7:
To create a custom color palette, begin by choosing one of the existing color palettes as a starting point. Next, modify the colors of different parts of the ad, one by one. For example, to modify the color used for the ad text, click the Text radio button, and type in the HTML color code (page 152). Finally, give your custom palette a name and click Save to store it for future use. Once your palette's saved, you can choose it from the list of palettes the next time you create an ad.

Note: Usually, you'll choose ad backgrounds and text colors that match the colors you're already using in your Web pages. For some advice about how to choose HTML colors, see page 153.

6. **Choose an alternate ad. (This step is optional.)**

When you first place the ad unit on a page, Google doesn't yet know what ads are a good match for your content. Instead it uses some generic ads, like news headlines or messages from nonprofit organizations. Google's text-sniffing software pays a visit to your page shortly after, and the real ads materialize within a couple of days.

If you don't want to put up with the generic ads for any period of time, you can choose alternate content. You have two options—you can choose an alternate color, in which case Google will insert a block of color and not give you any ad content. The idea is that you'll use a color that matches the background of your page, so it disappears entirely. Your second option is to specify a URL for a page you want to use. Until the real ads are ready, that's the content that appears in your page.

Note: Alternate ads probably aren't worth the trouble. It's better to use the generic ads, because the ad layout is the same, which makes it easy to place the ad in the right place and get an idea of what it looks like alongside the rest of your site's content.

7. **Choose a channel. (This step is optional.)**

   Ordinarily, if you generate a half-dozen ads, and scatter them on different pages throughout your site, you don't know which ones are making you money. Google's report only shows you the total clicks for all pages on your site. Some site owners need more detailed information about which ads are working. Enter Google's *channels* feature.

   If you want to track the performance of different ads or different pages, you need to create distinct channels. The idea is that you place each ad in a separate, virtual "channel." Google then lets you create reports that compare each channel, so you can tell which one is performing best.

   If you've created a channel, you can select it from the list. To create a new channel, click the "Manage channels" link, which takes you to the page shown in Figure 13-8.

Tip: Channels are a great way to try out different ad strategies, and see which ad formats and ad placements have the most success garnering clicks from your visitors.

8. **If the page where you're going to place the ad uses frames, turn on the "Ad will be placed on a framed page" checkbox.**

   If your Web page uses frames, Google needs to know about it, so it can scan the content of the correct frame. When using frames, you need to put your ad in the content part, not in other frames (like titles or navigation bars). If you put an ad in a page without any content, Google won't be able to figure out what kind of ads are relevant to your Web site. For more on frames, see Chapter 10.

9. **The text box at the bottom of the page now has your complete, customized ad unit code (see Figure 13-9).**

Click in the text box to select it, and then copy its contents by pressing Ctrl+C (⌘-C). You're now ready to paste it, by clicking Ctrl+V (⌘-V) into one or more Web pages, as described in the next section.

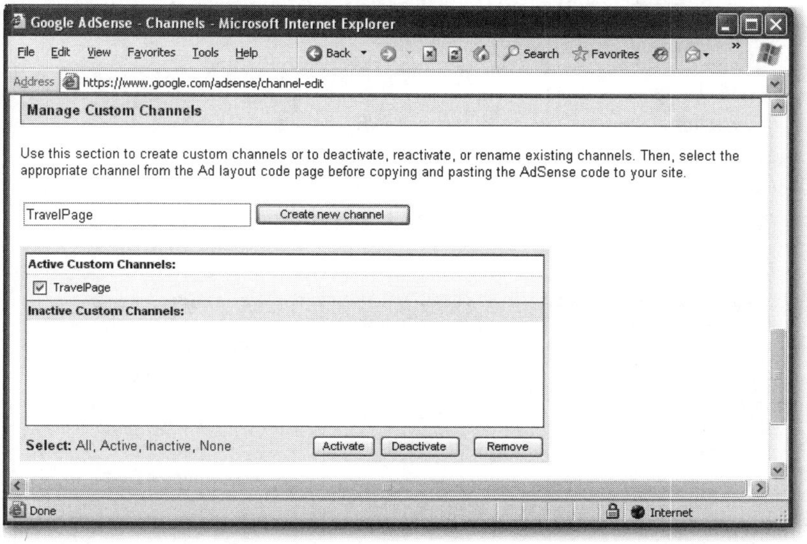

Figure 13-8:
Creating a custom channel is easy—just type in a name, click "Create new channel," select your channel, and then click Activate. You can add multiple ads to the same channel to track them as a group, or you can create a separate channel for each ad you use.

Placing Ads in Your Web Pages

Once you've generated the ad script, you're ready to pop it into any Web page. Horizontal strips are easiest to position. You simply need to paste the entire script right where you want it to appear.

Here's an example that places the ads at the bottom of a page:

```
<html>
<head>...</head>
<body>
  <h1>A Trip to Remember</h1>
  <p><img border="0" src="me.jpg" class="floatLeft">
   After returning from my three-month travel adventure...</p>
  <p>I hope you enjoy these pictures as much as I do.</p>
  <p>See pictures from...</p>

  <script type="text/javascript"><!--
   google_ad_client = "pub-5867479552359052";
   google_ad_width = 728;
   google_ad_height = 90;
   google_ad_format = "728x90_as";
   google_ad_type = "text";
```

```
      google_ad_channel ="";
      google_color_border = "006600";
      google_color_bg = "FDF5E6";
      google_color_link = "000000";
      google_color_url = "0033FF";
      google_color_text = "000000";
    //--></script>
    <script type="text/javascript"
      src="http://pagead2.googlesyndication.com/pagead/show_ads.js">
    </script>
  </body>
</html>
```

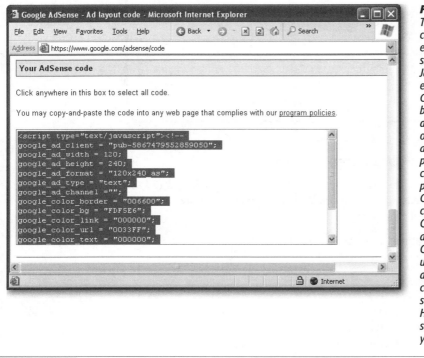

Figure 13-9:
The ad unit doesn't consist of HTML elements—instead, it's a snippet of code written in JavaScript (which you'll explore in Chapter 14). Google uses a script because it needs to be able to generate blocks of ads dynamically, according to the preferences you've chosen. Whenever your page gets requested, the Google ad script runs, communicates with the Google Web servers, and asks for a set of ads. The Google Web server looks up some relevant ads, applies your layout and color options, and then sends the final block of HTML back to the script so it can be inserted into your page.

Figure 13-10 shows the result.

Positioning vertical ad strips requires a little more work, but it's easy once you learn the trick. The challenge is that you want the rest of your page content to flow beside the vertical ad. As you learned in Chapter 9, there are two techniques that can help you accomplish this feat. You can use invisible tables and lock the ad unit into a specific cell, or you can use style sheet rules to float the ads on the side of the page. .

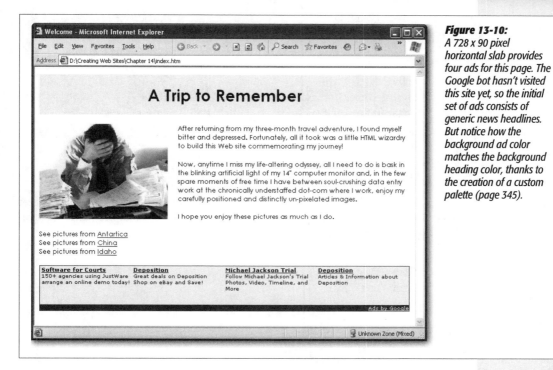

To use the style sheet approach, begin by wrapping your script in a <div> tag. Here's an example featuring the same content you saw in Figure 13-10; the <div> tag lines are highlighted:

```
<html>
<head>...</head>
<body>
  <div class="floatRight">
    <h1>A Trip to Remember</h1>
    <script type="text/javascript"><!--
    google_ad_client = "pub-5867479552359052";
    google_ad_width = 120;
    google_ad_height = 240;
    google_ad_format = "728x90_as";
    google_ad_type = "text";
    google_ad_channel ="";
    google_color_border = "006600";
    google_color_bg = "FDF5E6";
```

```
    google_color_link = "000000";
    google_color_url = "0033FF";
    google_color_text = "000000";
  //--></script>
  <script type="text/javascript"
   src="http://pagead2.googlesyndication.com/pagead/show_ads.js">
   </script>
  </div>
  <p><img border="0" src="me.jpg" class="floatLeft">
   After returning from my three-month travel adventure...</p>
  <p>I hope you enjoy these pictures as much as I do.</p>
  <p>See pictures from...</p>
</body>
</html>
```

Notice that the <div> tag (which has no formatting of its own), uses the style sheet class *floatRight*. In your style sheet, you use this rule to make the <div> section float with the *float* attribute (see page 195). Here's what you need:

```
.floatRight {
  float: right;
  margin-left: 20px;
}
```

Figure 13-11 shows the result.

Google-Powered Searches

Google has one more way for you to please your visitors (and earn some cash in the process). You can add a Google search box to a Web page, letting visitors launch their Google queries right from your site. Even better, you get the earnings for any ads they click in the search results—a feature Google calls (rather unimaginatively) "AdSense for search."

Once you have an AdSense account, it's easy to get the Google search box so you can add it to your site:

1. **Log in to your AdSense account, and click the "AdSense for Search" tab.**

   The "AdSense for Search" page is a lot like the "AdSense for Content" page. It asks you a series of questions, and gives you a block of HTML you can copy into your Web page at the end.

2. **Select the language and country of your Web site.**

   The standard options are English and United States. As you probably know, Google has country-specific pages that can tweak search results, providing them in different languages or giving priority to local sites.

3. Choose Google Search (if you want visitors to be able to explore the whole Web, including your site) or Google SiteSearch (if you want them to be confined to just searching the pages on your site).

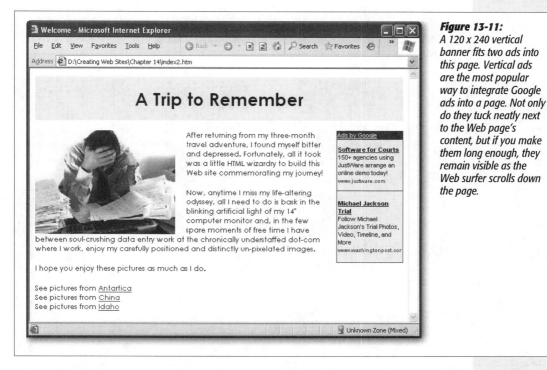

Figure 13-11:
A 120 x 240 vertical banner fits two ads into this page. Vertical ads are the most popular way to integrate Google ads into a page. Not only do they tuck neatly next to the Web page's content, but if you make them long enough, they remain visible as the Web surfer scrolls down the page.

Google Search is the original Google search engine we all know and love.

Google SiteSearch is an innovative idea—it's a search box just for searching *your site*. For example, if you have dozens of pages of travel stories, a visitor could home in on the page they want by typing "funny story about rubber chicken in Peru" into a SiteSearch box. However, there's one catch. SiteSearch still uses Google's standard, centralized catalog of Web pages; it just limits the search to the pages from your site. But if Google doesn't have the page in its catalog (either because you just created it or because Google doesn't know your site exists), SiteSearch won't find it.

If you want to provide both options (Google Search and Google Site Search), just follow these instructions twice to create two different text boxes. But be careful you don't wind up confusing your visitors.

Tip: If you decide to use SiteSearch, use the search engine tips in Chapter 11 to make sure Google knows you're alive.

4. **If you want to filter out profanity and sexual content from search results, choose the SafeSearch option.**

   SafeSearch is useful in two situations. First, it's de rigueur for sites that provide children's content. Second, it's handy if your Web site deals in a topic that shares some keywords with adult-only sites. For example, if you're creating a breast cancer awareness page, you don't want searches for "breast exam" to dig up the wrong goods.

How AdSense Creates Targeted Ads

Every time you serve up a Web page that contains Google ads, the AdSense script sends a message to the Google Web server asking for ads. This message includes your ad preference information and your unique client ID. (Your client ID is something like *pub-5867479552359052*; you can see it in the script code.)

The first time Google receives this request, it realizes that it hasn't examined your page yet, and it doesn't know what types of ads are best suited for it. Instead, Google sends you a block of generic ads (or sends back your alternate content, if you choose that feature as described on page 344). Google also adds your page to a list of pages it needs to visit. Sometime in the next couple of days, the AdSense robot heads over to your site and analyzes its content. From that point forward, you'll see ads that are based on the content of your page.

If 48 hours pass and you still aren't getting targeted ads, there could be a problem. One of the most common mistakes is putting ads on pages that don't have much text, in which case Google can't figure out what your site is really all about. (Remember, Google only considers a single page—the one with the ad unit—not any other pages in your site.) Another potential problem occurs if you put your ad in an inaccessible page. For example, the Google bot can't get to any page that's not on the Internet—pages on your personal computer or a local network just can't cut it. Likewise with pages that are password-protected. Some Web sites block off robots using exclusion rules (page 307 in Chapter 11). These also stop the AdSense bot cold.

---

5. **Tailor the appearance of the Google search box.**

   You can tweak the background color, width, and placement of the logo and search button (see Figure 13-12).

6. **Choose any optional features you want.**

   Select "Open search results in a new browser window" if you want a new page to pop up with the results of the visitor's search. Pop-up windows are usually annoying to Web surfers, but are handy if you want to make sure your Web site sticks around on the visitor's desktop.

   Choose a style palette for the search results page. This way, the search results can blend in with the color scheme used in the rest of your Web site. Style palettes are almost the same as the color palettes discussed with ad creation (page 344), except they also let you add a custom logo.

Choose a channel if you want to track the ad dollars you make from this search box. See page 346 for more information about channels.

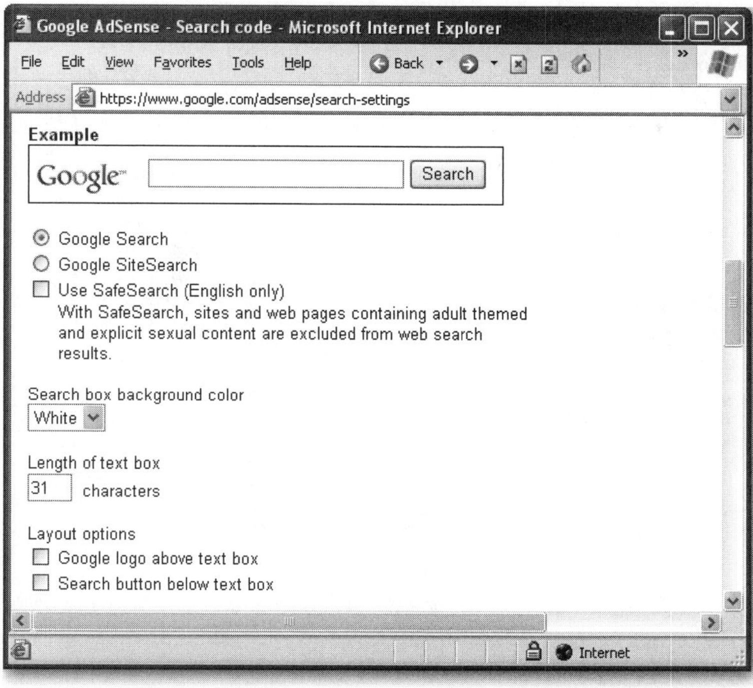

Figure 13-12:
There's not a lot to change here, but Google gives you a little flexibility to alter how the search box appears.

7. **The text box at the bottom of the page now has your complete, customized search engine box (see Figure 13-13).**

   You can copy this HTML with a quick Ctrl+C (⌘-C) and paste it, via Ctrl+V (⌘-V) into any Web page.

Note: For even more details and tips about the Google AdSense program, check out *Google: The Missing Manual.*

Amazon Associates

As popular as ads are, they have one serious drawback—they clutter up your Web site. Once you've perfected a design beauty with carefully chosen pictures and style sheets, you might not want to insert someone else's ad. And although Google ads aren't as visually distracting as other types of ads (like animated banners and pop-up windows), they still chew up valuable screen space. If you can't bear to disturb your Web page masterpieces, you might be interested in subtler affiliate programs.

The Amazon Associates program is the Web's longest running affiliate program. If you have a personal site with a "favorite books" page, or you just refer to the odd book here and there, you might be able to make some extra money by signing up.

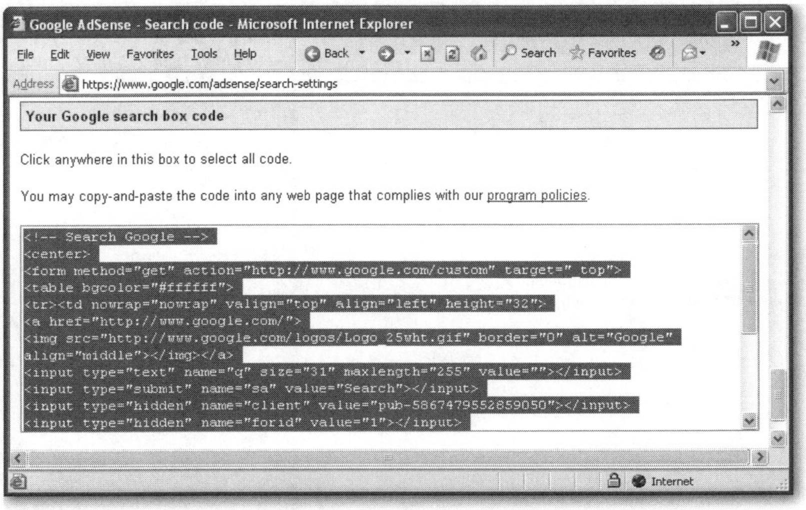

Figure 13-13:
Unlike with Google ads, the search box doesn't require a script. Instead, it includes the actual HTML tags, including an invisible table, logo, and input controls. As tempting as it might seem, Google forbids you from editing the HTML to create a really customized Google search box.

The basic idea behind the Amazon Associates program is that you provide links to book pages and other product pages on the Amazon Web site. For example, if you write a blurb about a great recipe you tried, you could add a link that, when clicked, takes the reader to the Amazon page that sells the cookbook you're quoting from. The link itself is a nice feature for your Web site, since it provides your visitor with more information. But the best part is what happens if a visitor decides to buy a copy. You'll wind up making a healthy commission of 4 percent to 7.5 percent of the book's Amazon sale price.

Tip: Amazon commissions aren't just for books. You can provide links to pretty much everything that's for sale on Amazon (excluding items sold by other retailers, like Target and Office Depot). But there are limits to how much you can make on non-book items. For example, with personal computers, you're capped at a maximum $25 commission. These rules change from time to time, so make sure you scour the Amazon Associates Web site carefully to get the lowdown.

The specific payments terms are a little convoluted, and they're discussed in detail at *www.amazon.com/gp/browse.html/?node=3435371*. Here are a few rules of thumb:

• You make the most money if you lead Amazon fans directly to a specific book, and they buy that book.

- If you lead a surfer to the main Amazon page, or you lead them to a specific book but they go on to buy something different, you still make a commission, but it'll be smaller.

- If your Web site is responsible for generating a huge number of sales, you earn even more (up to a total 10 percent commission). Amazon calculates your bonus based on the total number of sales in the quarter. To be eligible for the bonus percentage points, you need to help sell at least 21 products.

It may take a graduate degree in number theory to really sort out the final commissions you'll get from an Amazon sale. Fortunately, it doesn't matter that much—most associates are happy to add a few links to specific books they like, and then see how much money it nets.

Note: Without a doubt, the best feature of Amazon Associates is that it doesn't tamper with your Web site. You're in complete control of where you place the link and what it looks like.

Signing Up as an Associate

Signing up for an Amazon Associates program is even easier than joining AdSense. Just follow these steps:

1. **Surf to *www.amazon.com/gp/browse.html/?node=3435371* and find the "Click here for easy registration" link.**

   If that link is too much to remember, just surf to Amazon's main site and search the help information for "associates."

2. **Log in with your Amazon email and password.**

   In order to join the associates program, you need to already be an Amazon customer. If you aren't, create a customer account before you go any further. (Don't worry, it's easy. Just head to the main *www.amazon.com* site and look for a sign-up link.)

3. **Enter your payment information and click Continue.**

   You need to supply your name, address, and preferred form of payment (check, Amazon certificates, or direct deposit to a U.S. bank). Check payments don't go out until you make at least $100, while other payment types kick in once you reach $10.

4. **Enter your Web site information and click Continue.**

   You need to supply a Web site name, URL, and a brief description (see Figure 13-14).

5. **Review the summary and click Continue to submit your application.**

   The final page lets you confirm all the information you've entered so far.

Shortly after you've submitted your application, you'll get a confirmation message that approves you on a trial basis. This email also supplies you with your unique associate ID. This is important, because it's the single piece of information you need to put in all your Amazon links to start earning commissions. You can now start using the associate tools at *http://associates.amazon.com* (see the next section).

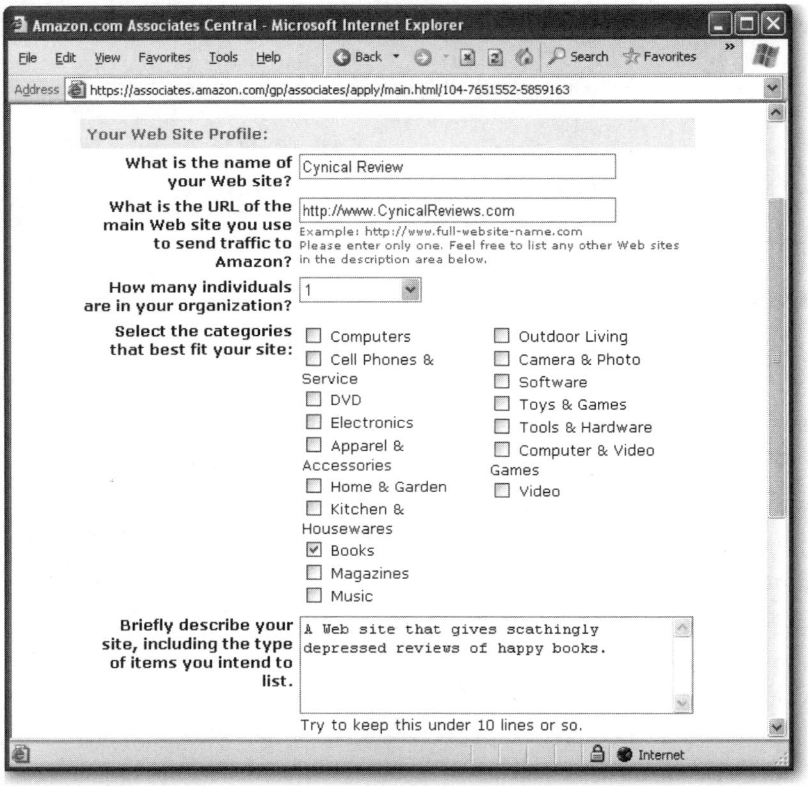

Figure 13-14:
To become an Amazon associate, you need to supply some basic information about your site. Don't skip over this step, because someone from Amazon will take a quick look at your site before it approves you for the program.

A couple of days later, when someone at Amazon has verified your site exists and isn't running afoul of the law, you'll get a second email confirming that you're in for good.

Generating Associate Links

Once you have your associate ID (which is found in the first confirmation email Amazon sends you), you're ready to start creating *associate links,* the hyperlinks that will bring your site visitors over to Amazon. The trick is formatting the URL in the right way.

Associate links always have the associate ID at the very end. For example, the first email Amazon sends shows an example of how you can link to the Amazon home-page. It looks like this:

```
http://www.amazon.com/exec/obidos/redirect-home/prosetech-20
```

In this example, the associate ID is *prosetech-20*. (Replace it with your own ID to create a link for your Web site.) If someone follows this link and buys something, you'll earn the minimum 4 percent commission.

Here's how you could use this link in an anchor (page 211 in Chapter 8):

```
Visit <a href="http://www.amazon.com/exec/obidos/redirect-home/prosetech-20">
Amazon</a> and help me save up to buy a Ferrari.
```

Note: Amazon encourages you to advertise the fact that you're an Amazon associate. If you'd like to boast, Amazon provides a collection of ready-made Amazon logos and banners at *http://associates. amazon.com/gp/associates/network/build-links/banner/main.html*. You can add these to your site, and even put them in anchor tags to transform them into associate links. (Before you can view the banner page, you'll need to be signed up as Amazon associate, as described on page 355.)

Product links

You'll get better commissions with more useful links that lead directly to a specific product. Amazon supports several associate link formats, and here's one of the simplest:

```
http://www.amazon.com/exec/obidos/ASIN/0141181265/prosetech-20
```

In this link, there are two details you need to customize, the ASIN (Amazon Standard Item Number) and the associate ID. In this link, the ASIN is 0141181265 (which leads to the book *Finnegans Wake*) and the associate ID is *prosetech-20*. Figure 13-15 shows you where to find an ASIN.

Here's an example of a complete link:

```
The development of the modern personal computer was first presaged in Joyce's
<a href="http://www.amazon.com/exec/obidos/ASIN/0141181265/prosetech-20">
Finnegans Wake</a>.
```

That's all you need.

Advanced links

Amazon offers a set of specialized tools designed to help you generate links. Using these tools, you can create a wide range of snazzier links. Your options include:

• Links with thumbnail pictures.

- Links to product categories (like equestrian magazines or bestselling kitchen gadgets).

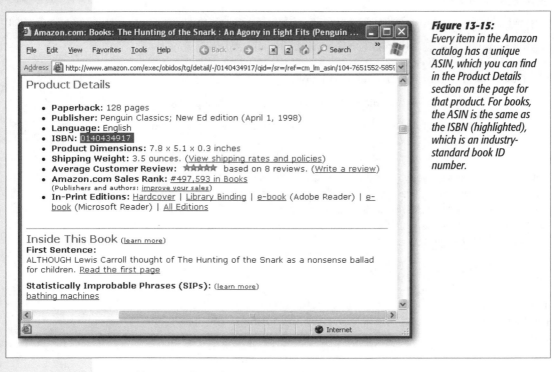

Figure 13-15:
Every item in the Amazon catalog has a unique ASIN, which you can find in the Product Details section on the page for that product. For books, the ASIN is the same as the ISBN (highlighted), which is an industry-standard book ID number.

- Ad banners that advertise a specific Amazon department.

- Amazon search boxes that let visitors perform their own queries.

Even if you don't want these fancier links (and if your life isn't dedicated to selling books, you probably don't), there's still good reason to build links with the tools Amazon provides. That's because these links have built-in tracking, which lets you determine how many people saw your Amazon link.

Note: Amazon tracking is very clever. Essentially, Amazon embeds a tiny one-pixel image alongside each link. If someone requests a page that contains one of these links, his browser automatically fetches the invisible picture from Amazon. When Amazon gets the request for the invisible picture, it knows someone is looking at the link, and so it records a single *impression* in its tracking database.

Here's how you can use Amazon's link building tools:

1. **Surf to** *http://associates.amazon.com* **and log in.**

   This takes you to the Associates Central home page, which has a number of useful resources for associates (Figure 13-16).

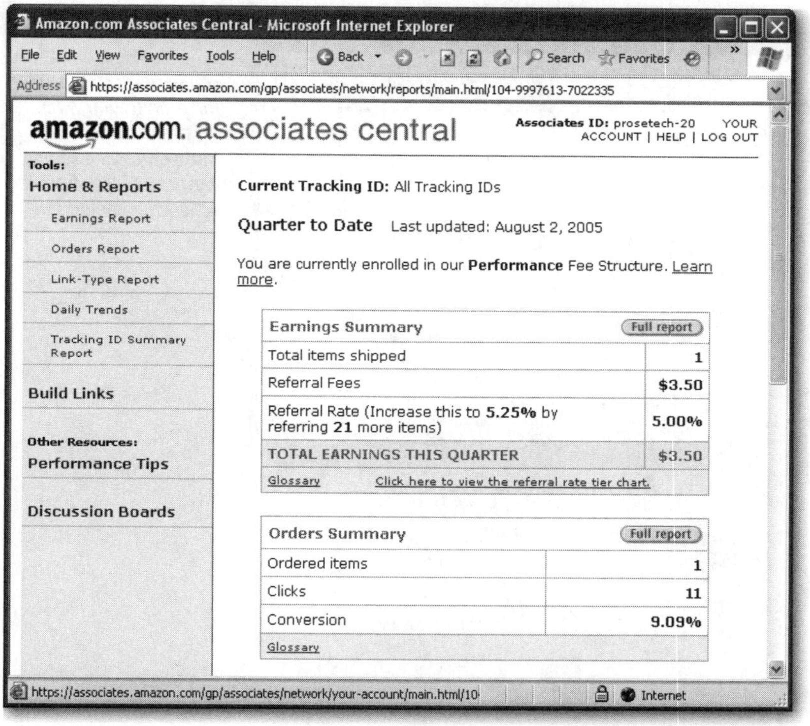

Figure 13-16:
The Associates Central home page gives you a variety of reports for checking your progress to date, as well as tools for building links. You can also get invaluable advice from other associates by visiting the discussion forums.

2. **Click Build Links → Product Links.**

   Product links point to individual items on Amazon's site. They're the most lucrative type of link (and generally the most useful for your site's visitors). But if you're planning to go Amazon-crazy, feel free to explore all the other types of links.

3. **Type in the ASIN for your product and click Go.**

   If you don't know the ASIN, select the best category and type in the product name. When you click Go, Amazon performs the search and shows a list of all the results that match (see Figure 13-17).

4. **Click the Get HTML button next to the product you want to link to.**

You'll see a text box with the HTML code required to create an ad linking to the book or whatever product you're linking to. You can copy this code directly into your page. However, if you want an ordinary text link, you need to do a little more work.

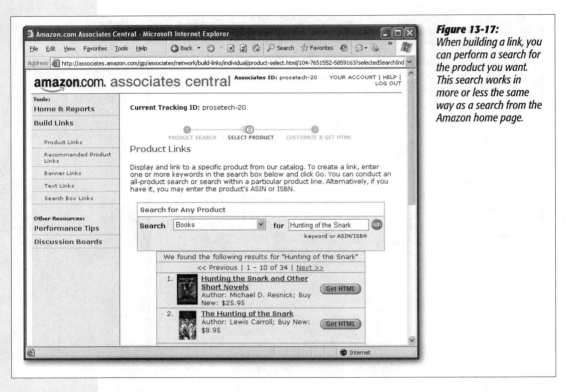

Figure 13-17:
When building a link, you can perform a search for the product you want. This search works in more or less the same way as a search from the Amazon home page.

5. **Click the Show button next to the Customize Link heading. Then, choose the link options you want.**

The page you're looking at shows a set of options for configuring the link to be as fancy or simple as you want (see Figure 13-18). To create a text link, click Basic Display, and choose Text Only in the Image box.

You can also choose where the link goes by choosing from the Link Destination drop-down menu (see Figure 13-18, bottom). Your two options are Detail Page (the full product description, with reviews) and Offer Listing Page (which shows third-party sellers that have new or used copies for sale).

6. **Click Update HTML.**

Now you can copy the HTML from the text box and paste it in any Web page on your site.

When you create a text link, Amazon generates an anchor tag that looks fairly complex. (As described earlier, the anchor tag contains an <img> tag for an invisible picture that lets Amazon track how many times the link is shown.) However, like all anchor tags, it's relatively easy to put this tag where you want it. Just pop it into an existing paragraph, like this:

```
<p>Lewis Carroll's work as a mathematician may have driven him insane,
as his famous book
<a href="http://www.amazon.com/exec/obidos/...">The Hunting of the Snark</a>
<img src="http://www.assoc-amazon.com/..." width="1" height="1" border="0"/>
attests.</p>
```

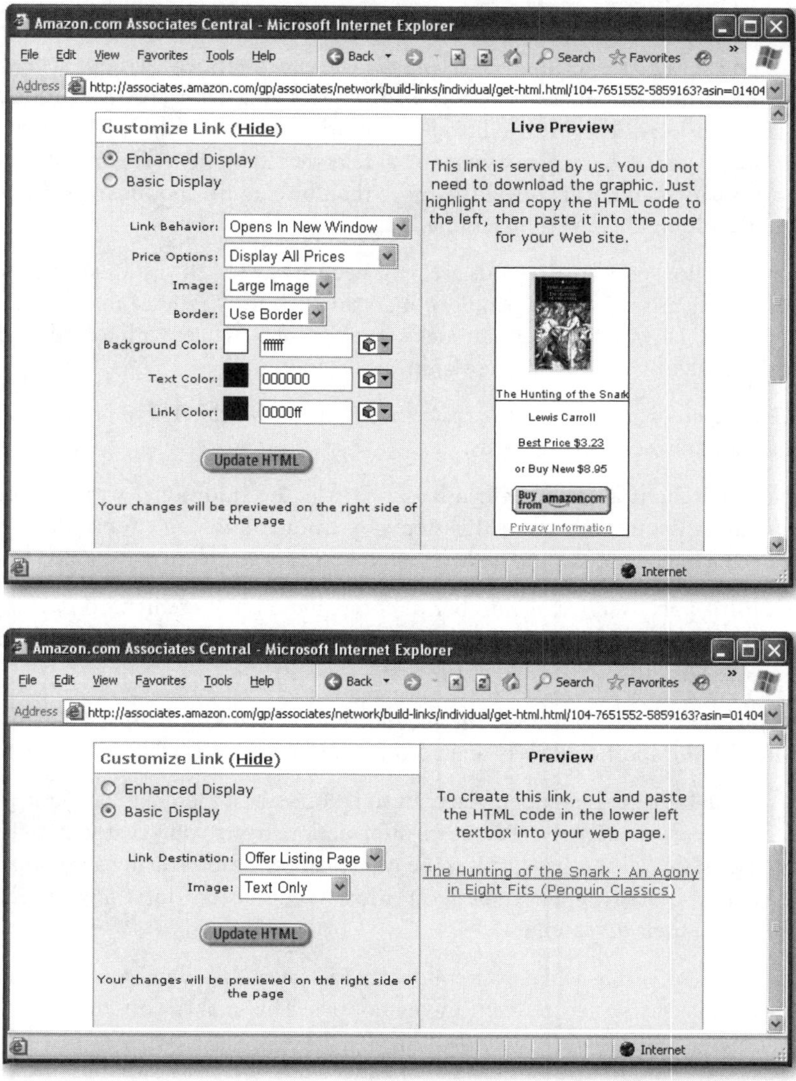

Figure 13-18:
As you choose your link options, Amazon shows you a preview of what the link will look like. You can choose a graphical image (top) or a plainer, easier-to-integrate text link (bottom).

Tip: Inside the anchor tag, Amazon puts the full title of the book. This title might be a little longer than you intend, because it might include information about the edition or a byline. If so, just cut it down to the title you want to use.

PayPal Merchant Tools

Unless your Web site is wildly popular, ads and other affiliate programs will only net you spare change. If you have all-consuming dreams of Web riches, you need to actually sell something.

You don't need to go far to run into self-made Internet commerce kingpins. A surprisingly large number of people have made their living with creative products. Examples include t-shirts with political catchphrases, empty bottles of wine with Titanic labels, and collectable toys from a relative's basement. Your path to a thriving e-business might involve little more than buying tin spoons from Honest Ed's and decorating them with macramé.

But no matter how good your goods are, you need a way to sell vast quantities easily and conveniently. Very few people will go through the hassle of mailing you a personal check. However, if they can make an impulse purchase with a credit card, your odds of making a sale improve significantly.

But accepting credit cards isn't the easiest thing in the world. There are two ways an e-business can accept credit cards:

• **Open a merchant account with a bank.** This is the traditional way to accept credit cards. Requirements for this step vary from country to country, but you may need a business plan and an accountant, and some up-front capital.

• **Use a third-party service.** A number of companies accept credit card payments on your behalf in exchange for a flat fee or a percentage of the sale. In this chapter, you'll learn how to use one of the best—PayPal.

Unless you have a large business, the second option is always better. The reason has to do with the additional risks that accompany Web-based sales.

First of all, the Internet is an open place. Even if you have a merchant account, you need a *secure* way to accept credit card information from your customers. That means the credit card number needs to be *encrypted* (scrambled using a secret key) so that Internet eavesdroppers can't get it. Most Web masters don't have a secure server sitting in their basement.

Another problem is that when you conduct a sale over the Web, you don't have any way to collect a signature from the e-shopper. This makes you vulnerable to *chargebacks* (see the following sidebar).

Note: PayPal is a staggeringly large Internet company that offers payment solution in 45 countries, and has 71 million account members worldwide. PayPal was established in 1998 and purchased by eBay in 2002. .

FREQUENTLY ASKED QUESTION

Understanding Chargebacks

What's a chargeback?

A chargeback occurs when a buyer asks their credit card company to remove a charge from their account. The buyer may claim that the seller didn't live up to their end of the agreement, or claim that they never made the purchase in the first place. A chargeback can occur weeks or months after the item is purchased.

From the buyer's point of view, a chargeback is relatively easy. The buyer simply phones the credit card company and reverses the transaction. The money you made is deducted from your account, even though you've already shipped the product. If you want to dispute the buyer's complaint, you're in the unenviable position of trying to convince a monolithic credit card company to take your side. Many small businesses don't dispute chargebacks at all, because the process is too difficult, expensive, and unsuccessful.

However, when you use a third-party service, the odds tilt in your favor. If the buyer asks for a chargeback, the chargeback is made against the third-party company that accepted the payment (like PayPal), not you. And even though PayPal isn't as large as the average multinational bank, it's still a major customer of most credit card companies, which means it has significant clout to argue against a chargeback.

The end result is that buyers are less likely to charge back items to PayPal. And even if they do, PayPal gives you the chance to dispute the chargeback. PayPal even lets you contact the buyer to see if there's a simple misunderstanding (for example, to check whether you sent the item to the wrong address). And if you're really paranoid, you can use PayPal's Seller Protection Policy, which insures you for up to $5,000 of loss, if you take a few additional steps (like giving PayPal your bank information and retaining proof of delivery). For more information about how PayPal handles chargebacks, check out *www.paypal.com/cgi-bin/webscr?cmd=xpt/seller/ChargebackRisk-outside*. To learn about PayPal's seller protection, refer to *www.paypal.com/cgi-bin/webscr?cmd=p/gen/protections-outside*.

Singing Up with PayPal

Once you sign up with PayPal, you'll have the ability to accept payments from customers across the globe. Here's how you do it:

1. **Head to the PayPal Web site (*www.paypal.com*). Click the Sign Up Now button on the home page.**

   This sends you to the Sign Up Web page

2. **Choose the type of account you want to create: Personal, Premier, or Business.**

   A *personal account* is ideal if you want to use PayPal to buy items on eBay. With a personal account, you can buy items using your credit card or an account funded from a bank account. You can also accept payments from other people, without having to pay any fees. However, there's a significant catch—credit card payments aren't supported, which means your customers need to get money into their account first (either from a transaction with another PayPal account holder or from a linked bank account) before they can do business with you.

A *premier account* is the best way to run a small business. You get the ability to send money (great if you crave a rare Beanie Baby on eBay) and accept any type of payment that PayPal supports, including credit cards and bank account debit. You'll also get to use PayPal's e-commerce tools. However, You'll be charged a fee on every payment you receive, which varies by volume but ranges from 1.9 percent to 2.9 percent of the total value (with a base fee of 30 cents). That means on a $25 sale, you pay PayPal about $1.

A *business account* is almost identical to a premier account, except it supports multiple logins. The business account is the best choice if you have a large business with employees who need to use PayPal to help manage your site.

3. **Choose your country and click Continue.**

   The next page collects the typical account details.

4. **Enter your name, postal address, and email address. Next, supply a password.**

   Make it good—you don't want a malicious hacker guessing your password and using your PayPal account to go on an electronic buying binge.

Tip: As a general rule of thumb, guard your PayPal account information the same way you guard your bank PIN. If you're really paranoid, don't use your PayPal account to buy items on other Web sites, and don't supply your credit card information.

---

5. **Finally, review the PayPal user agreement and privacy policy and indicate your agreement. Click Sign Up to complete the process.**

   PayPal sends you an email confirmation message immediately. Once you click the link in this message, your account is active and you can start creating PayPal buttons and shopping carts to collect payments.

Accepting Payments

PayPal makes it ridiculously easy to make e-commerce Web pages. In this section you'll see how to add a Buy Now button to any Web page on your site.

1. **Head to *www.paypal.com*, and sign in.**

   Once you've signed in, you have access to several tabs crammed with goodies (see Figure 13-20).

   Use the My Account tab to update your account information, see what transactions you've made, and request withdrawals.

   Use the Send Money tab to email someone some cash (which you'll need to supply from a real-world bank account or a credit card), and the Request Money tab to send an email asking for the same.

Use the Merchant Tools tab to build buttons that you can add to your Web pages to sell items.

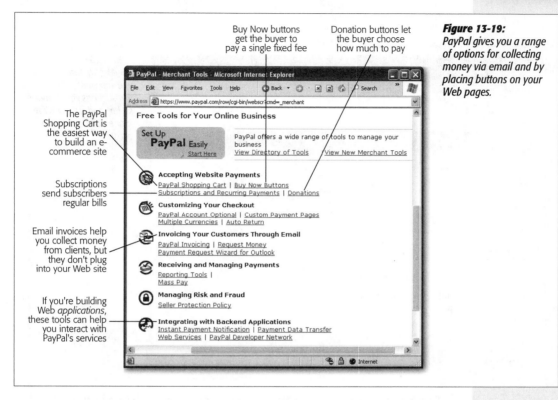

Buy Now buttons get the buyer to pay a single fixed fee

Donation buttons let the buyer choose how much to pay

Figure 13-19:
PayPal gives you a range of options for collecting money via email and by placing buttons on your Web pages.

The PayPal Shopping Cart is the easiest way to build an e-commerce site

Subscriptions send subscribers regular bills

Email invoices help you collect money from clients, but they don't plug into your Web site

If you're building Web *applications*, these tools can help you interact with PayPal's services

Use the Auction Tools tab to use PayPal to sell items on eBay. (eBay is still one of the most popular places to set up an e-business.)

2. **Click the Merchant Tools tab.**

Scroll down the page, and you'll see a variety of tools for collecting money, as explained in Figure 13-19.

3. **Click the link Buy Now Buttons.**

PayPal shows a page where you can configure your button's appearance and set the price of your product (Figure 13-21).

4. **Give your item a name and (optionally) a product code that you use to keep track of it. Then supply the price, currency, and a default country.**

Don't worry about locking out international visitors when you set your currency. Credit card companies are happy to charge Canadian customers in U.S. dollars, U.S. customers in euros, and European customers in rupees. Just choose the currency that your buyers expect to see.

The country setting isn't terribly important. If you think most of your customers are from the U.S., then choose United States. However, enterprising surfers from Luxembourg can still change this setting when they fill out their payment forms.

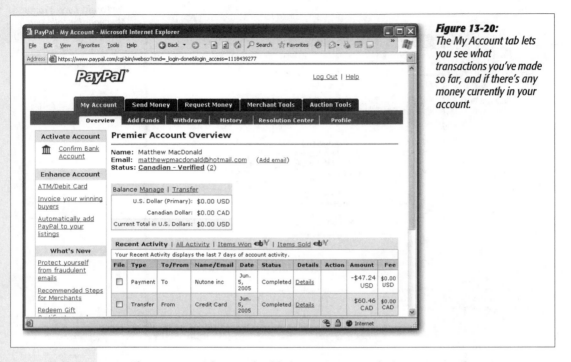

Figure 13-20:
The My Account tab lets you see what transactions you've made so far, and if there's any money currently in your account.

5. **Choose to use the standard button picture or design a custom button.**

   The standard Buy Now button is nice, but a little plain. If you've created a nicer button (see Chapter 15 for tips) and uploaded it to your site, just supply the URL for that button image here. Either way, you can always change the HTML that PayPal generates later on if you want to use a different button picture.

6. **Choose whether you want to use encryption for your price information.**

   This bit's slightly confusing. PayPal *always* uses bulletproof encryption when it gets payment details (like a credit card number) from a customer. Anything less would be scandalously irresponsible. However, this option lets you choose whether or not to encrypt the price information that you've entered, so it can't be changed.

   If you choose not to encrypt the price information, a nefarious user could create a copy of your Web page, change the price from $500 to $0.50, and then make a payment. This deception isn't the end of the world—unless you're selling hundreds of different products, you're likely to notice the incorrect payment and refuse to ship the item.

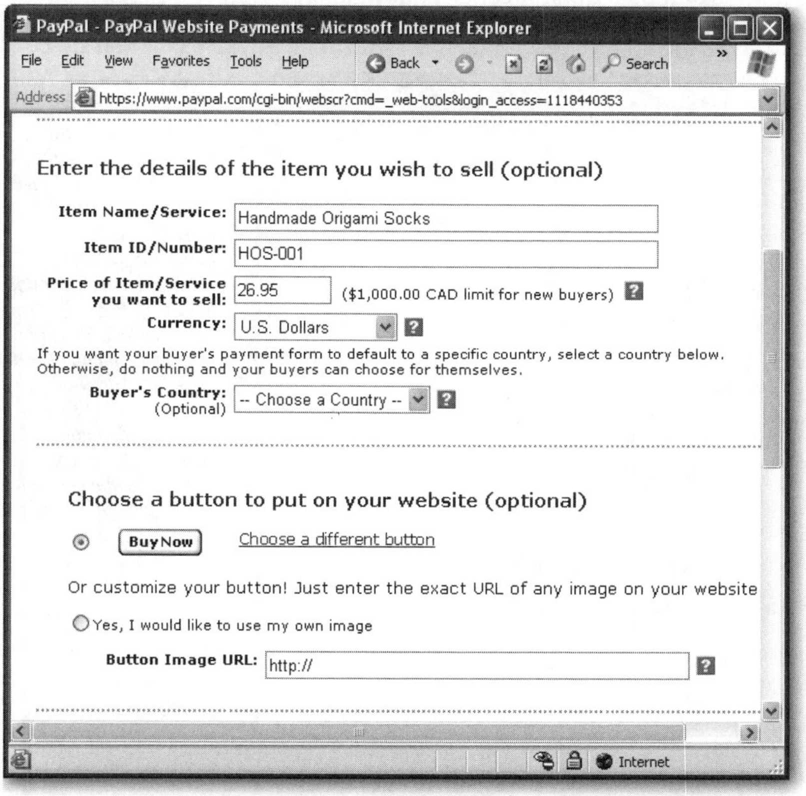

Figure 13-21:
The basics of a Buy Now button.

If you use encryption, buyers can't attempt this kind of fraud. However, it also prevents you from using *option fields*, a PayPal feature that lets customers choose various options about the product they're buying.

7. **Click the Add More Options button.**

The Add More Options page gives you a heap of extra possibilities. You can add a flat surcharge for shipping and a percentage for taxes. You can also let customers fill in comments with their payments, and supply a URL on your Web site where purchasers should be redirected after they complete a payment or cancel it. But two of the niftiest features are option fields (described in Figure 13-22), and the ability to customize your "buyer's experience."

Essentially, the buyer experience section lets you tell PayPal where to send shoppers when they complete a transaction or cancel it. Rather than using the generic PayPal pages, you can send your shoppers to a specific URL on your Web site with a detailed description about your shipping policies and provide them with additional support contact information.

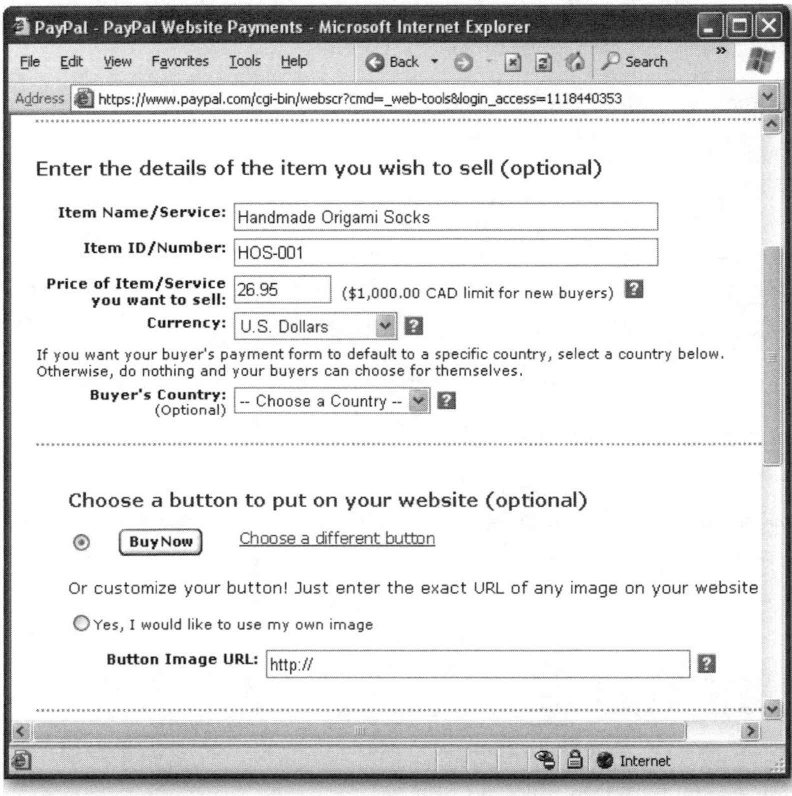

Figure 13-22:
With an option field, you can collect additional information about the type of product the buyer wants. This is useful if you offer the same item in multiple colors or sizes. To create an option field, you choose the type of control you'll use (a drop-down menu or text box). For a drop-down menu, you then supply the allowed options from which the buyer can choose. PayPal lets you create two option fields.

Note: Option fields are only available if you've chosen not to use encryption (see the description for step 7).

8. **Click Create Button Now.**

   You'll see a text box with the HTML for your customized Buy Now button. All you need to do now is copy it out of the text box and paste it into a Web page.

When you create a Buy Now button, PayPal puts everything inside a <form> tag (explained on page 318 in Chapter 12). If you haven't used encryption, you might be able to figure out what's going on inside your form.

Here's the example that was generated over the last few steps for a pair of hand-made origami socks:

```
<form action="https://www.paypal.com/cgi-bin/webscr" method="post">
  <input type="hidden" name="cmd" value="_xclick">
  <input type="hidden" name="business" value="matthewpmacdonald@hotmail.com">
  <input type="hidden" name="item_name" value="Handmade Origami Socks">
  <input type="hidden" name="item_number" value="HOS-001">
  <input type="hidden" name="amount" value="26.95">
  <input type="hidden" name="no_note" value="1">
  <input type="hidden" name="currency_code" value="USD">
  <table><tr><td>
  <input type="hidden" name="on0" value="Color">Color</td><td>
  <select name="os0">
    <option value="Yellow">Yellow
    <option value="Green">Green
    <option value="Tomato">Tomato
    <option value="Chartreuse">Chartreuse
  </select>
  </td></tr></table>
  <input type="image" src="https://www.paypal.com/en_US/i/btn/x-click-but23.gif"
    border="0" name="submit" alt="Make payments with PayPal">
</form>
```

Remember, when you submit a form, all the information in any <input> fields gets sent along with it. PayPal puts the product name, number, and price in the input fields, along with your business name. If you don't use encryption, this is the part that a troublemaker could tamper with and attempt to pay you less than you or your product are worth.

If you've added any option fields, you'll see <select> and <option> tags that define the list boxes you need (page 323 in Chapter 12). Finally, the form ends with a submit button that sends the form to PayPal. You can change the src attribute of this button to point to a different image file.

Tip: As long as you don't tamper with the <input> fields, and you keep everything inside the <form> tags, you can tweak the HTML PayPal has created for you. For example, you can add other tags in the form, or apply style sheet formatting. Or, you might want to remove the invisible table (represented by the <table>, <tr>, and <td> tags) that's used to organize your button and your option fields to get a different layout.

What happens when the shopper submits this form? The action attribute in the very first line of the above code tells the story. It has the URL *https://www.paypal.com/cgi-bin/webscr*. This URL tells you the information is sent to PayPal over a secure channel (that's why it starts with "https" instead of "http").

Lastly, it's just as important to realize what PayPal *hasn't* generated—namely, it doesn't provide any information about the item you're selling. You'll need to put the item name, picture, description, and price into your Web page (probably before the Buy Now button). Here's an example:

```
<html>
<head>...</head>

<body>
  <h1>Handmade Origami Socks</h1>
  <p><img border="0" src="origami.jpg" class="float">
  You've waited and they're finally here. Order your own
  pair of origami socks for only $26.95 and get them in time
  for the holidays. What better way to show your loved ones how
  poor your gift giving judgement really is?</p>
  <form action="https://www.paypal.com/cgi-bin/webscr" method="post">
    ...
  </form>
</body>
</html>
```

Figure 13-23 shows the result. In this example, the standard PayPal ordering page is shown, but you can customize this page with your own logo. You'll learn how in the next section.

Building a Shopping Cart

The Buy Now button gives you a great way to make a quick sale. But if your dreams are about a Web e-commerce empire, you'll need to create a store where visitors can collect several items, and pay for them all at once. This setup requires a shopping cart, and it's a staple on e-commerce Web sites. With PayPal, you don't need to program your own shopping cart—instead, you can use a pre-built shopping cart service that integrates smoothly into your Web site.

Creating a shopping cart is remarkably similar to creating a Buy Now button (so if you haven't tried that, you might want to play around with it before you go any further). The basic idea is that you create a separate Add To Cart button for each item you're selling on your site. When you create this Add To Cart button, you get many of the same options you saw when you created the Buy Now button—for example, you set the price, product code, shipping charges, and so on. The difference is that when a visitor clicks the Add To Cart button, they aren't sent straight to a checkout page. Instead, a shopping cart page pops up in a new window. Visitors can keep shopping, and then complete the purchase when they've collected everything they want.

To demonstrate how this works, the following example takes the page shown in Figure 13-24 as a starting point. This example also demonstrates a great use of style-based layout. Check out the downloadable samples—available from the "Missing CD" page at *www.missingmanuals.com*—to try it out for yourself.

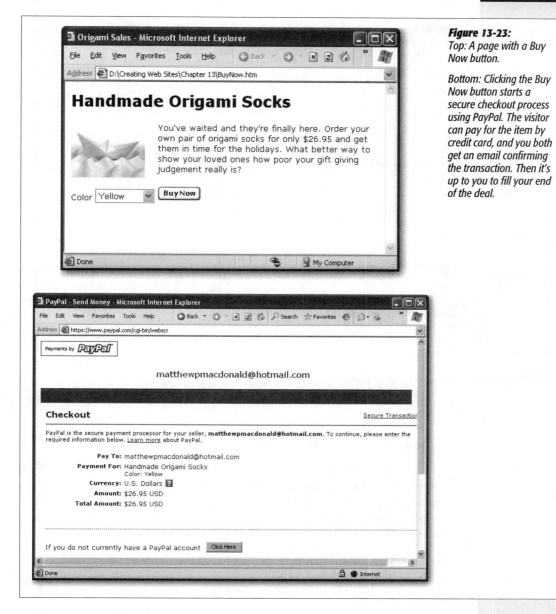

Figure 13-23:
Top: A page with a Buy Now button.

Bottom: Clicking the Buy Now button starts a secure checkout process using PayPal. The visitor can pay for the item by credit card, and you both get an email confirming the transaction. Then it's up to you to fill your end of the deal.

Creating a custom page style

Before you create your shopping cart, there's an extra step you can take to really personalize the payment pages. If you're happy with the PayPal standards, feel free to skip straight to the next section. But if you'd rather have your company logo appear in the shopping cart pages, keep reading.

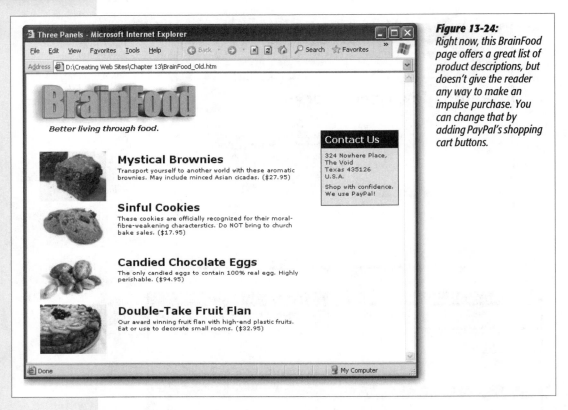

Figure 13-24:
Right now, this BrainFood page offers a great list of product descriptions, but doesn't give the reader any way to make an impulse purchase. You can change that by adding PayPal's shopping cart buttons.

1. **If you're not already there, head to *www.paypal.com*, and sign in.**

2. **Select the My Account tab, and then the Profile sub-tab.**

   You see a page with a slew of information about your preferences, grouped into three main categories: Account Information (who you are and where you live), Financial Information (your bank, credit card, and payment history information), and Selling Information (extra options you can use with the merchant tools). In this case, you're interested in the Selling Information section.

3. **Scroll down to find the Custom Payment Page link, and click it.**

   This takes you to the Custom Payment Page Styles page, where you can set up page styles or edit existing ones.

4. **Click Add to create a new page style.**

   You start off with only a single page style—the PayPal standard, which sports a basic PayPal logo.

5. **Supply the information for your page style.**

Page Style Name is a descriptive title to help you remember which style is which.

Header Image URL is a URL that points to a picture on your Web site. This picture is the logo you want to show at the top left of the PayPal shopping cart page. The image you use can be a maximum size of 750 pixels wide by 90 pixels high.

Note: Because PayPal's shopping cart page is a secure page, when you use a custom logo, the shopper may get a message informing them that there are some insecure items on the page (namely, your picture). If you want to avoid this message, talk to your Web hosting company about putting your picture on a secure (https) server.

Header Background Color, Header Border Color, and Background Color let you set the page colors with six-digit HTML color codes (see page 125 in Chapter 6). This part is optional—leave it out if you're happy with the standard white.

6. **Click Save to store the page style.**

   You can also click Preview to take a sneak peek at what the PayPal payment page will look like.

Generating the shopping cart buttons

Now you're ready to build the buttons that add your items to an e-shopper's cart. Here's how to do it:

1. **If you're not already there, head to *www.paypal.com*, and sign in.**

2. **Click Merchant Tools and then click the PayPal Shopping Cart link.**

   PayPal shows a page where you can configure the Add To Cart button for a single item.

3. **Give your item a name and (optionally) a product code that you use to keep track of it. Then supply the price, currency, and default country.**

   These settings are exactly the same as for a Buy Now button (see Figure 13-25). Choose to use the standard button picture (by clicking the Add To Cart radio button) or create a custom button (by clicking "Choose a different button") .

4. **Click the Add More Options button.**

   Now you can set all the options you learned about above, including shipping and sales tax (page 367). You also get two new shopping-cart–only features.

   Your shopping cart solution wouldn't be complete without a button that lets the shipper see what's in the cart (and then head to the virtual checkout counter). PayPal let's you use the standard View Cart button, or supply a URL that points to a button picture of your own design.

In the Customize Your Payment Pages section, you can also choose a custom page style. This lets you change the look of the PayPal shopping cart page. If you followed the instructions on page 370 to create a custom page style, select it now.

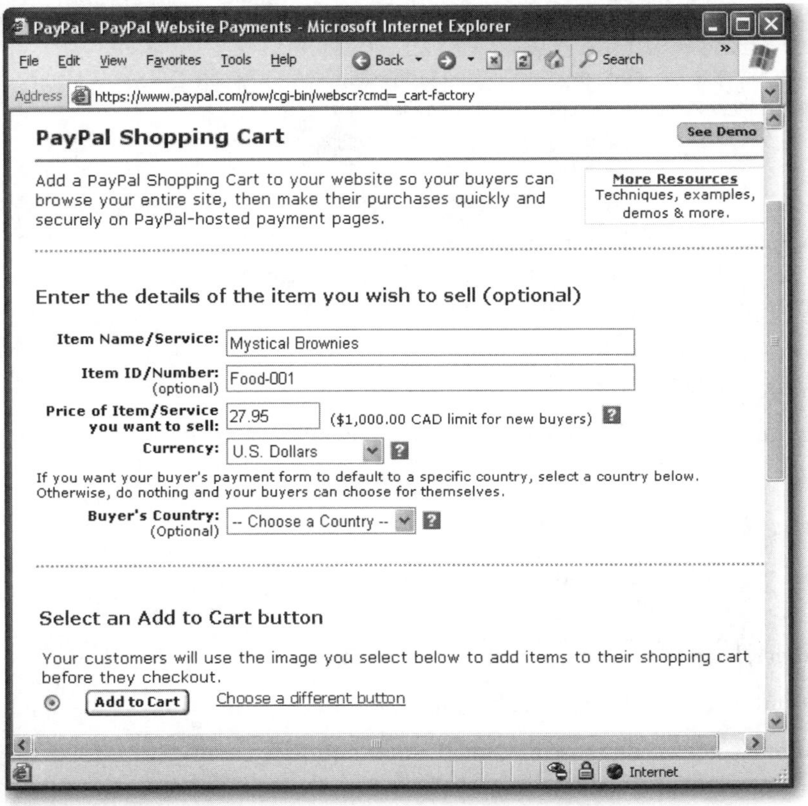

Figure 13-25:
*Here's the information
you need to supply to
create an Add To Cart
button that selects the
Mystical Brownies.*

5. **Click Create Button Now.**

   You'll see a text box with the HTML for your customized Add To Cart and View Cart buttons. But remember, the Add To Cart code you generated is good for one button only. If you have more than one item (as in the BrainFood example), you need to generate multiple buttons. Click Create Another Button and head back to step 3.

Tip: If you aren't using encryption, there's a shortcut that lets you create additional buttons. Just copy the block of HTML from your first button and find the input tags inside. Look for the product name, product code, and price, and edit these details by hand. This is also a great way to make a price change without regenerating the whole button.

Once you've created your buttons, you simply need to add them all to your page. Figure 13-26 shows the final result.

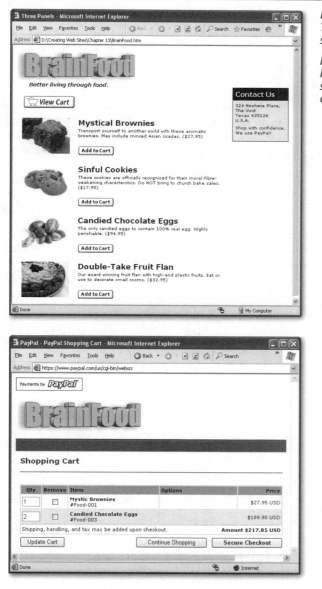

Figure 13-26:

Top: Here's the revised BrainFood page, with shopping cart buttons.

Bottom: After clicking a few Add To Cart buttons, here's the shopping cart page your visitors will see (in a separate window). All they need to do is click Secure Checkout to make the purchase.

Withdrawing Your Money

Every payment you get through PayPal is safely stashed in your PayPal account (which is kind of like a virtual bank account). You can see the balance at any time after you log in and click the My Account tab.

If you've earned a small amount of money, you may be happy just using it to buy other stuff on Web sites like eBay and *www.buy.com*. But if you're raking in significant dough, you'll want to withdraw some of that money into the real world. PayPal gives you a few options.

- **You can transfer money to a bank account.** In order to do this, you'll need to provide PayPal with your bank account information. Depending on the country where you live, PayPal waives its fee as long as your withdrawal meets a certain minimum (like $150). However, your bank may apply a standard electronic transaction fee.

- **You can request a check.** PayPal will mail you the amount to your postal address. Once again, you may need to meet a certain minimum to get your money without a fee.

To get started with either of these approaches, log in, select My Account → Withdraw, and follow the instructions there.

Part Four: Web Site Frills

JavaScript and DHTML: Adding Interactivity

JavaScript is a simplified programming language designed for beefing up HTML pages with interactive features. JavaScript aims to give you just enough programming muscle to add some fancy effects, but not enough to cause any serious damage if your code goes wonky. JavaScript is perfect for creating pop-up windows, marquee-style scrolling text, and buttons that light up when a visitor moves his or her mouse pointer over them. On the other hand, JavaScript can't help you build a hot e-commerce storefront (for that, you need the PayPal tools described in Chapter 13).

The goal of this chapter isn't to teach you all the details of JavaScript. Instead, by the time this chapter's through, you should know enough to find a great script online, understand it well enough to make basic changes, and paste it into your pages to get the results you want. Since the Web's got dozens of JavaScript sites, offering thousands of ready-made scripts for free, these basic skills can come in very handy.

Understanding JavaScript

The JavaScript language has a long history—it first hit the scene with the Netscape Navigator 2 browser in 1995, and Internet Explorer jumped on the bandwagon by adding JavaScript compatibility to IE version 3. Today, all modern browsers support JavaScript, and it's become wildly popular as a result. However, some justifiably paranoid surfers turn off the JavaScript switch in their browser settings (since malicious developers have, on occasion, used JavaScript-fueled agents to attack computers with pop-up ads and other types of browser annoyances). That means the best rule of thumb is to use JavaScript to improve your page, but make sure your page still works (even if it doesn't look quite as nice) when JavaScript has been disabled.

Note: JavaScript is thoroughly different from the Java language (although the code sometimes looks similar, because they share some syntax rules). Java was developed by Sun Microsystems, and is a full-fledged programming language, every bit as powerful—and complicated—as C++, C#, and Visual Basic.

So what can JavaScript do?

- JavaScript can dynamically insert some HTML into a Web page, or modify an existing HTML tag. For example, you can show a personalized message, or make a title grow and shrink perpetually (an example of which is shown on page 399).

- JavaScript can gather information about the current date, the surfer's browser, and the choices he's made when presented with a form element like a drop-down menu or a radio button. You can display any of this information or use it to make decisions about what page to show next. For example, you could stop surfers from going any further until they type in an email address.

- JavaScript can react to events that happen in the browser. For example, you can write code that runs when something specific happens (like when a page has finished loading or when a surfer clicks a picture).

It's just as important to understand what JavaScript *can't* do. JavaScript code is *sandboxed,* which means the browser locks your page into a carefully controlled place in memory (known as the sandbox) so it can't access anything on the Web surfer's computer. This design, which is necessary to ensure good security, effectively prevents JavaScript from sending orders to the printer, reading or writing (creating or editing) files, running other programs, reformatting your hard drive, and so on. Just about the only thing JavaScript is allowed to do is read and modify the HTML of the current Web page.

Server-Side and Client-Side Programming

In order to understand how JavaScript fits into the Web universe, it's important to understand that there are two types of programming on the Web.

When you surf to a search engine like Google or an e-commerce Web site like Amazon, you're actually connecting to a high-powered piece of software that runs on a Web server. This program is what's known as a *server-side application.* When you're using one of these Web sites, you send the program some information (like the keywords you want to search for, or the book you want to buy) and the application consults a massive database and spits out some HTML that creates the page you see in your browser.

Server-side applications rule the Web world, because there's virtually nothing they can't do. However, they're insanely difficult to program. Not only do developers need to worry about generating the HTML for the browser, they also need to run all kinds of complex routines and consult giant databases—and they need to do it all in a way that performs just as well when millions of people are clamoring for attention as it does when there's only one person surfing the site. This is hard work, and it's best handled by the poor souls we call programmers.

Client-side applications, on the other hand, use a completely different model. They embed a small, lightweight program inside an ordinary HTML page. When a browser downloads this page, the browser itself can then run the program (assuming it hasn't been disabled by security settings or compatibility issues). Client-side applications are much less powerful—for example, they have no reliable way to access the huge databases stored on Web servers, and for safety reasons they're prevented from directly changing most things on your home computer. However, they're much simpler to create. If you've ever played a game of Java checkers in your browser (see Figure 14-1), you've used a client-side program.

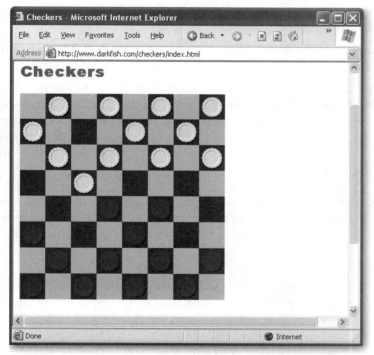

Figure 14-1:
This game of Java checkers looks like an ordinary Web page, but something very different is taking place behind the scenes. In fact, the checkerboard is actually a complete Java program that's embedded inside the Web page.

Scripting Languages

Even client-side applications can be a challenge for ordinary non-technogeeks. For example, to build the checkers game shown in Figure 14-1, you need to know your way around the highly sophisticated Java programming language. However, a whole class of client-side applications exist that aren't nearly as ambitious. They're called *scripts*, and their purpose in life is to give the browser a list of instructions (like "scroll that heading from left to right" or "pop up an ad for fudge-flavored toothpicks in a new window").

Scripts are written in a simplified *scripting language*, and even if you don't know all the ins and outs of a language, you can often copy and paste a cool script from another Web site to get instant gratification. Two examples of scripting languages are JavaScript and VBScript (a scripting language that uses syntax that resembles Visual Basic).

This chapter focuses exclusively on scripts created with JavaScript, the only scripting language that's reliably supported on most browsers.

JavaScript 101

Now that you've learned a bit about JavaScript and why it exists, it's time to dive right in and start creating your first real script.

The <script> Tag

Every script starts with a <script> block that you slot somewhere into an HTML document. Really, you have only two options:

- **The <body> section.** Put scripts in the <body> section that you want to run right away, when the browser's in the process of reading (and displaying) your page. The browser launches your script as soon as the browser reaches the script in the HTML document. This means if you put your script at the beginning of the <body> section, the script gets fired up before the rest of the HTML is displayed in the browser.

Tip: Usually, JavaScript fans put their scripts at the *end* of the <body> section. That way, you avoid errors that might occur if you use a script that relies on another part of the page, and the browser hasn't read that other section yet. Because browsers read an entire page quite quickly, these scripts execute almost immediately.

- **The <head> section.** If you place an ordinary script in the <head> section, it runs immediately, before the browser has processed any part of the HTML for the page. However, it's more common to use the <head> sections for scripts that contain *functions* (see page 388). Functions don't run immediately— instead, they're summoned when some kind of action happens on the page (for example, when the Web surfer moves her mouse).

Note: You can place as many <script> blocks in a Web page as you want.

A typical script block consists of a series of programming instructions. To get a handle on how these instructions work, consider the following example, which causes the browser to display a JavaScript alert box.

```
<html>

<head>
  <title>JavaScript Test</title>
</head>

<body>
  <h1>You Will Be Wowed</h1>
  <p>This page uses JavaScript.</p>
  <script type="text/javascript">
    alert("Welcome, JavaScript coder.")
  </script>
</body>

</html>
```

This script pops up a window with a message, as shown in Figure 14-2. When you click OK, the message disappears, and it's back to life as usual for your Web page.

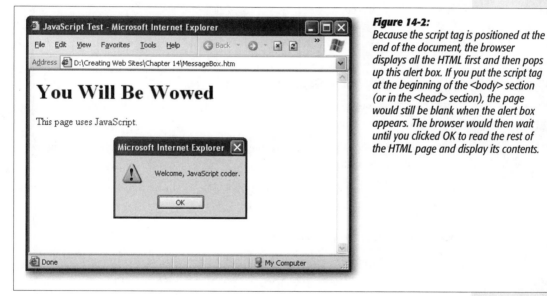

Figure 14-2:
Because the script tag is positioned at the end of the document, the browser displays all the HTML first and then pops up this alert box. If you put the script tag at the beginning of the <body> section (or in the <head> section), the page would still be blank when the alert box appears. The browser would then wait until you clicked OK to read the rest of the HTML page and display its contents.

You're probably wondering exactly how this script works its magic. When the browser processes the script, it runs all the code, going one line at a time. In this case, there's only one line:

```
alert("Welcome, JavaScript coder.")
```

This line uses the built-in JavaScript function named *alert*. A *function* is a programming routine consisting of one or more lines of code that performs a certain task. JavaScript offers many built-in functions, and you can build your own.

The alert( ) function requires one piece of information, or an *argument*, in programmer-speak. In this case, that piece of information is the text you want to show in the alert box. If you were supplying an ordinary number, you could type it in as is—that is, you'd just write in the number. However, text poses a bit more of a problem, because there's no way for the browser to tell where the text starts and stops. To handle this problem in JavaScript, you must put your text inside single apostrophe quotes (') or double quotation marks ("), as in this example.

Note: In programmer-speak, a distinct piece of text that's used in a program is called a *string*; "a," "The friendly fox," and "Rumpelstiltskin" all qualify as strings.

That's it. All this simple script does is call the alert( ) function. (Spend enough time around programmers and JavaScript fans, and you'll soon learn that "call" is the preferred way to describe the action of summoning a function into action.) The alert( ) function does the rest, popping up the correct-sized window and waiting for the surfer to click OK.

Note: In order to write this script, you need to know that there's an alert( ) function ready for you to use—a fact you can find out on one of the many JavaScript tutorial sites.

Based on what you now know, you should be able to change this script in the following ways:

- Display a different message (by changing the argument).
- Display more than one message box, one after the other (by adding more lines in your <script> block).
- Display the message box before the Web page is shown (by changing the position of the <script> block).

It's not much to keep you occupied, but it does demonstrate how easy it is to get started using and changing a simple script.

Scripts and really, really old browsers

Sometimes, scripts are written with the comment markers shown here:

```
<script type="text/javascript">
<!--
  alert("Welcome, JavaScript coder.")
//-->
</script>
```

Placing the comment markers like this hides the script from Paleolithic browsers like Netscape 2, which don't understand scripts and are dimwitted enough to display the actual script text in the browser window. The chances of running into one of these beasties today is quite rare, so many JavaScript coders don't even bother with this extra step.

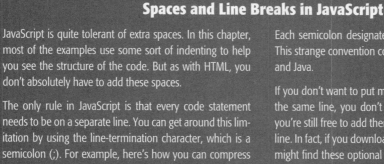

Spaces and Line Breaks in JavaScript

JavaScript is quite tolerant of extra spaces. In this chapter, most of the examples use some sort of indenting to help you see the structure of the code. But as with HTML, you don't absolutely have to add these spaces.

The only rule in JavaScript is that every code statement needs to be on a separate line. You can get around this limitation by using the line-termination character, which is a semicolon (;). For example, here's how you can compress three code statements onto one line:

```
alert("Hi"); alert("There");
alert("Dude");
```

Each semicolon designates the end of a code statement. This strange convention comes from the Bizarro world of C and Java.

If you don't want to put more than one code statement on the same line, you don't need the semicolons. However, you're still free to add them if you want, at the end of each line. In fact, if you download a script from the Web, you just might find these optional semicolons, which is often a tip-off that a C or Java programmer wrote the script.

Even if you aren't expecting really old browsers to come by your Web site, you might want to use the <noscript> tag. This tag defines some alternate content that's used by browsers that understand the meaning of the <script> tag, but have JavaScript switched off. It's also used for browsers that don't support the script language you're using. For example, most non-IE browsers don't support VBScript, a scripting language based on Visual Basic.

You place the <noscript> tag immediately after the <script> tag. Here's an example that shows a paragraph of text in the page when JavaScript support is lacking:

```
<script type="text/javascript">
  alert("Welcome, JavaScript coder.")
</script>
<noscript>
  <p>Welcome, non-JavaScript-enabled browser.</p>
</noscript>
```

Variables

Every programming language includes the concept of *variables*, which are temporary storage containers where you can keep track of important information. Variables can store numbers, objects, or pieces of text. As you'll see throughout this chapter, variables play a key role in many JavaScripts, and they're a powerful tool in any programmer's arsenal.

Declaring variables

To create a variable in JavaScript, you use the *var* keyword, followed by the name of the variable. You can choose any name that makes sense to you, as long as you're consistent (and avoid spaces or special characters). Here's an example that creates a variable named *myMessage*:

```
var myMessage
```

To put information into a variable, you use the equal sign (=), which copies the data on the right side of the equal sign into the variable on its left. Here's an example that puts some text into myMessage.

```
myMessage = "Everybody loves variables"
```

Remember, you need to use quotation marks whenever you've got a text string. In contrast, if you want to copy a *number* into a variable, you don't need quotation marks:

```
myNumber = 27.3
```

Note: JavaScript variables are case-sensitive, which means a variable named myMessage isn't the same as MyMessage. If you try to use them interchangeably, you'll wind up with a scripting error (if your browser is nice) or a bizarre mistake in the page (which is usually what happens).

Often, you'll want to create a variable and fill it with some useful content in the same step. JavaScript lets you do perform this maneuver by placing the equal sign immediately after the variable name when you declare it:

```
var myMessage = "Everybody loves variables"
```

To make matters a little confusing, JavaScript lets you use variables that you haven't declared. Doing so is considered extremely bad form and is likely to cause all sorts of problems. However, it's worth knowing that these undeclared variables are permissible, because they're the source of many an unexpected error.

Modifying variables

One of the most useful things you can do with numeric variables is perform *operations* to change your data. For example, you can use arithmetic operators to perform mathematical calculations:

```
var myNumber = (10 + 5) * 2 / 5
```

These calculations follow the standard order of operations (parentheses, then addition and subtraction, then multiplication and division). The result of this calculation is 6.

You can also use operations to join together multiple pieces of text into one long string. In this case, it's the plus (+) operator that you use:

```
var firstName = "Sarah"
var lastName = "Smithers"
var fullName = firstName + " " + lastName
```

Now the fullName variable holds the text "Sarah Smithers".

An example with variables

Although you'd need to read a thick volume to learn everything there is to know about variables, you can pick up a lot from a simple example. The following script inserts the current date into the Web page. Each line of script code is numbered to make it easy to reference.

```
<html>
<head>
  <title>JavaScript Test</title>
</head>

<body>
  <h1>What Day Is It?</h1>
  <p>This page uses JavaScript.</p>
  <p>
  <script type="text/javascript">

1        var currentDate = new Date( )
2        var message = "The current date is: "
3        message = message + currentDate.toDateString( )
4        document.write(message)

  </script>
  </p>
</body>
</html>
```

Here's what's happening, line by line:

1. This line creates a new variable named *currentDate*. It fills the currentDate variable with a new Date object. You'll know an object is being created when you see the keyword *new*. (You'll learn more about objects on page 396; for now, it's enough to know that objects come with built-in functions that work more or less the same way as the functions you learned about earlier.)

2. This line creates a new variable named *message,* and fills it with a generic welcome message.

3. This line adds some new text to the end of the message. The new text comes from the currentDate object. The tricky part is understanding that the currentDate object comes with a built-in toDateString( ) function that converts the date information into a piece of text suitable for displaying in the browser (see

Figure 14-3). Once again, this is the kind of detail you can only pick up by studying a good JavaScript reference.

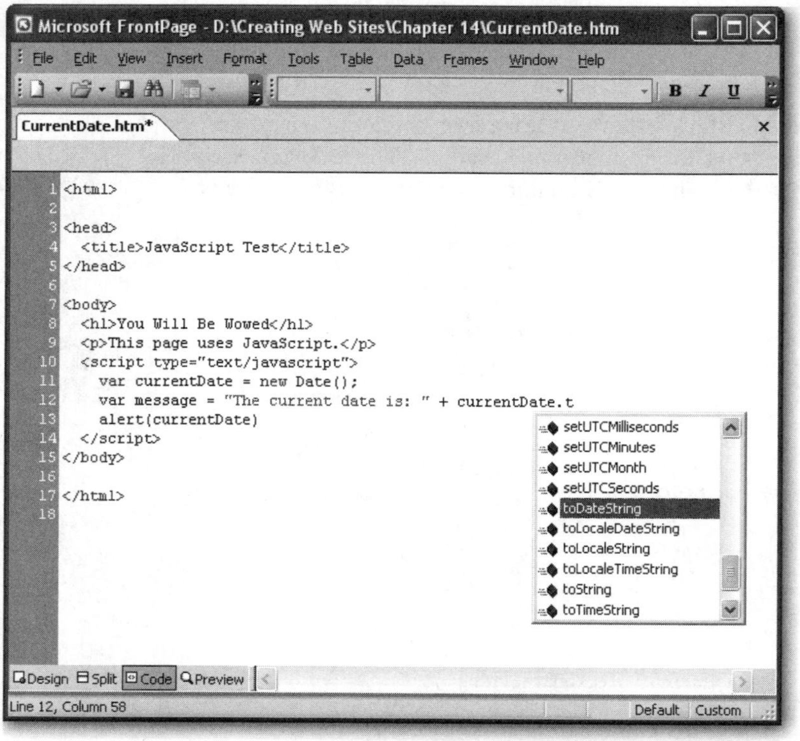

Figure 14-3:
Some HTML editors will help you out when you write JavaScript code. For example, FrontPage shows a drop-down menu that shows you all the functions an object provides. Although this probably isn't enough for you to figure out how to use the Date object for the first time, it's a great way to refresh your memory later on.

4. This line uses the *document* object, which has a function named *write( )*. The write( ) function copies a piece of text into the page at the current location. The final result is a page that shows your welcome message (see Figure 14-4).

Scripts can get much more complex than this. For example, they can use loops to repeat a single action several times, or use conditional logic to make decisions. You'll see examples of some of these techniques in this chapter, but you won't get a blow-by-blow exploration of the JavaScript language—in fact, that would require a small book of its own. If you want to learn more, check out the box "Becoming a JavaScript Guru."

Functions

So far, you've seen simple scripts that use only a few lines of code. More realistic JavaScript scripts can take dozens of lines, and if you're not careful, they can grow into a grotesque tangle that leaves the rest of your page difficult to edit. To control the chaos, smart JavaScripters almost always use *custom functions*.

A function is a series of code instructions that you group together and give a name. In a way, functions are sort of like miniature programs, because they can perform a series of operations. The neat thing about functions is that you only need to create them once, and then you can reuse them anywhere.

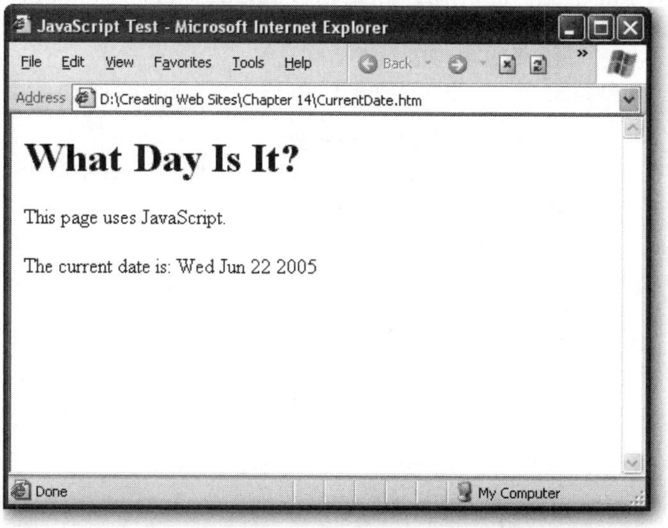

Figure 14-4:
The document.write( ) command inserts your text directly into the page, wherever the script block is positioned. In this case, it shows the current date.

Declaring a function

To create a JavaScript function, start by deciding what your function is going to do (like show an alert message) and then choose a suitable name (like *ShowAlertBox*). As with most things in the programming world, the function name can't have any spaces or special characters.

Armed with this information, you're ready to put a <script> block in the <head> section of your page. But this <script> block looks a little different from the examples you've seen so far. Here's a complete function that shows an alert box with a predefined message:

```
<script type="text/javascript">
  function ShowAlertBox( ) {
    alert("I'm a function.")
  }
</script>
```

To understand what's going on here, it helps to break this example down and consider it piece by piece.

Every function declaration starts with the word *function*, which tells JavaScript what you're up to.

```
function
```

Next is the name of your function and then two parentheses. The parentheses can be used to get extra information to feed into your function, as you'll see on page 391.

```
function ShowAlertBox( )
```

At this point, you've finished *declaring* the function. All that remains is to put the code you want *inside* that function. To do this, you need the funny curly braces shown above. The { brace indicates the start of your function code and the } brace indicates the end. In between, you can put as many code statements as you want.

One tricky part of function writing is the fact that JavaScript is notoriously loose about line breaks. That means you can create an equivalent JavaScript function that moves the curly brace down a line, and looks like this:

```
<script type="text/javascript">
  function ShowAlertBox( )
  {
    alert("I'm a function.")
  }
</script>
```

But don't worry—both functions work exactly the same.

Tip: You can put as many functions as you want in a single <script> block. Just add them one after the other.

Calling a function

Creating a function is only half the battle. On their own, functions don't do anything. It's up to you to call the function somewhere else in your page to actually run the code. To call a function, you use the function name, followed by parentheses:

```
ShowAlertBox( )
```

Note: Don't leave out the parentheses after the function name. Otherwise, the browser will assume you're trying to use a variable rather than call a function.

You can call ShowAlertBox( ) anywhere you'd write ordinary JavaScript code. For example, here's a script that shows the alert message three times in a row to really hassle your visitors:

```
<script type="text/javascript">
  ShowAlert( )
  ShowAlert( )
  ShowAlert( )
</script>
```

This is the same technique that, earlier, you saw used to call the alert( ) function. The difference is that alert() is built into JavaScript, while ShowAlertBox( ) is something you created yourself. Also, the alert( ) function requires one argument, while ShowAlertBox( ) doesn't use any.

Functions that receive information

The ShowAlertBox( ) function is beautifully simple. You simply call it, and it displays an alert box with the built-in message. Most functions don't work this easily. That's because in many cases you need to send specific information to a function, or take the results of a function and use them in another operation.

For example, imagine you want to show a welcome message with some standard information (like the current date). However, say you want to have the flexibility to change part of this message by supplying your own witty words each time you call the function. In this case, you need a way to call a function *and* supply a text string with your message.

To solve this problem, you can create a ShowAlertBox( ) function that accepts a single argument. This argument represents the customized piece of information you want to incorporate into your greeting. You choose a name for it, and place it in between the parentheses after the function name, like so:

```
function ShowAlertBox(customMessage) {
   ...
}
```

There's no limit to how many pieces of information a function can accept. You just need to separate each argument with a comma. Here's an example with three arguments:

```
function ShowAlertBox(messageLine1, messageLine2, messageLine3) {
   ...
}
```

The following example shows the finished ShowAlertBox( ) function. It accepts a single argument named customMessage, and uses it to customize the text that's shown in the alert box:

```
<script type="text/javascript">
1        function ShowAlertBox(customMessage)
2        {
3          // Get the date.
4          var currentDate = new Date( )
5
6          // Build the full message.
7          var fullMessage = "** IMPORTANT BULLETIN **\n\n"
8          fullMessage += customMessage + "\n\n"
9          fullMessage += "Generated at: " + currentDate.toTimeString( ) + "\n"
10         fullMessage += "This message courtesy of MagicMedia Inc."
11
12         // Show the message.
13         alert(fullMessage)
14       }
</script>
```

Here are some helpful notes to help you wade through the code:

• Any line that starts with // is a comment (see lines 3 and 6). Good programmers include lots of comments to help others understand how a function works. The browser ignores them.

• To put line breaks into an alert box, you need to use the code \n in your strings (lines 7, 8, and 9). Each \n is equivalent to one line break. (This rule is for message boxes only. When writing HTML, you need to add the <br> tag to create a line break.)

• To build the text for the fullMessage variable (lines 7 to 10), the code uses a shortcut with the += operator. This operator automatically takes whatever's on the right side of the equal sign and pastes it onto the end of the variable that's on the left side. In other words, this...

```
8      fullMessage += customMessage + "\n\n"
```

...is equivalent to this longer line:

```
8      fullMessage = fullMessage + customMessage + "\n\n"
```

Using this function is easy. You just need to remember that when you call the function, you must supply the same number of arguments as you defined for the function, separating each one with a comma. In the case of ShowAlertBox( ), you only need to supply a single value for the customMessage variable. Here's an example:

```
<script type="text/javascript">
  ShowAlertBox("This Web page includes JavaScript functions.")
</script>
```

Figure 14-5 shows the result of this script.

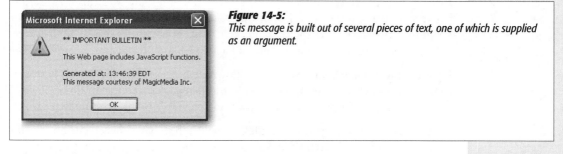

Figure 14-5:
This message is built out of several pieces of text, one of which is supplied as an argument.

Functions that return information

Arguments let you send information *to* a function. You can also create functions that send some information back to the script code that called them. The trick to doing this is the *return* command, which you should place right at the end of your function. The return command ends the function immediately, and spits out whatever information you want your function to generate.

Of course, a sophisticated function can accept *and* return information. For example, here's a function that multiplies two numbers (supplied as arguments) and returns the result to anyone who's interested:

```
<script type="text/javascript">
  function MultiplyNumbers(numberA, numberB)
  {
    return numberA * numberB
  }
</script>
```

Here's how you can use the function elsewhere in your Web page:

```
<p>The product of 3202 and 23405 is
<script type="text/javascript">
  var product = MultiplyNumbers(3202, 23405)
  document.write(product)
</script>
</p>
```

This displays the following text in a paragraph on your page:

```
The product of 3202 and 23405 is 74942810
```

To use a typical script from the Web, you'll need to copy one or more functions into your page. These functions are likely to look a lot more complex than what you've seen so far. However, now that you understand the basic structure of a function, you'll be able to wade through the code to get a basic understanding of what's taking place (or at least pinpoint where the action is going down).

External Script Files

Reusing scripts inside a Web page is neat, but did you know you can share scripts between individual pages and even different Web sites? The trick is to put your script into an external file and then link to it. This procedure is similar to the external style sheet linking you learned about back in Chapter 6.

For example, imagine you perfect the ShowAlertBox( ) routine so that it performs a complex task exactly the way you want, but it requires a couple of dozen lines of code to do so. To simplify your life, you could create a new file to store that script.

Script files are always plain text files. Usually, they have the extension .js (for JavaScript). Inside the script file, you put all your code, but you don't include the <script> tags. For example, you could create a JavaScript file named *ShowAlert.js* and add this code to it:

```
function ShowAlertBox( )
{
  alert("This function is in an external file.")
}
```

Now save the file, and place it in the same folder as your Web page. In your Web page, you define a script block, but you don't supply any code. Instead, you add the src attribute and indicate the script file you're linking to:

```
<script type="text/javascript" src="ShowAlert.js">
</script>
```

When the browser comes across this script block, it requests the *ShowAlert.js* file and treats it as though the code were inserted right in the page. Here's a complete HTML test page that uses the *ShowAlert.js* file. The ShowAlertBox( ) function is called by a script in the body of the of the page:

```
<html>

<head>
  <title>Show Alert</title>
  <!-- Make all the functions in the ShowAlert.js file
   available in this page. Notice there's no actual content here. -->
  <script type="text/javascript" src="ShowAlert.js">
  </script>
</head>

<body>
  <!-- Test out one of the functions. -->
  <script type="text/javascript">
```

```
        ShowAlertBox( )
      </script>
    </body>

    </html>
```

There's no difference in the ways that embedded and external scripts work. However, placing your scripts in separate files helps keep your Web site organized and makes it easy to reuse scripts across several pages. In fact, you can even link to JavaScript functions on another Web site—the only difference is the src attribute in the <script> block needs to point to a full URL (like *http://SuperScriptSite.com/ShowAlert.js*) instead of just a file name.

Note: Using separate script files doesn't improve your security one iota. Because anyone can request your script file, a savvy Web surfer can figure out what scripts your page uses and take a look at them. So never include any code or secret details that you don't want the world to know about in a script.

Dynamic HTML

JavaScript underwent a minor revolution in the late 1990s, adding support for a set of features called *Dynamic HTML* (DHTML). Dynamic HTML isn't a new technology—instead, it's a fusion of three distinct ingredients:

- Scripting languages like JavaScript, which let you write code.

- The CSS (Cascading Style Sheet) standard, which lets you control how an HTML element appears and how it is positioned.

- The HTML *document object model* (or DOM), which lets you treat an HTML page as a collection of *objects*.

The last point is the most important detail. DHTML extends scripting languages like JavaScript so they can interact with the page as a collection of *objects*. This is a radical shift in Web programming. Each HTML element you add, including images, links, and even the lowly paragraph, is treated like a separate programming ingredient that your JavaScript can play with. And when you mix in style sheet attributes, your code can change what each element looks like or even where it gets placed on the page.

Note: Most DHTML operations require Internet Explorer 4 or later, Netscape 7 or later, Opera 7 or later, or Firefox. Although these options represent the browsers that are most commonly in use today, you should test your pages with older browsers if you need to support them, too. Also, be wary of proprietary features (like the innerHTML property that only Internet Explorer supports).

HTML Objects

Clearly, DHTML requires a whole new way of thinking about Web page design. Your scripts no longer look at your Web page as a static block of HTML. Instead, they see a combination of *objects*.

UP TO SPEED

Understanding Objects

In many programming languages, including JavaScript, everything revolves around objects. What exactly is an object?

In the programming world, an object is nothing more than a convenient way to group some related features or information. For example, say you wanted to change the picture that's shown in an <img> tag in a Web page (useful, if you wanted to write a script that flashed a series of images). The easiest way to interact with an <img> tag in JavaScript is to use the corresponding *image* object. In effect, the image object is a container holding all sorts of potentially useful information about what's happening inside an <img> tag (including its dimensions, its position, the name of the image file associated with it, and so on). The image object also gives you a way to manipulate the <img> tag—that is, to change some or all of these details.

For example, you can use an image object to get information about the image, like this:

```
document.write("The tooltip says" +
image.title)
```

Or, you can even change one of these details. For example, you can modify the actual image that an <img> tag is showing by using this code:

```
image.src = "newpic.jpg"
```

You'll know an object's at work by the presence of a dot (.) in your code line. The dot separates the name of the variable (the first part) from one of the built-in functions it provides (called *methods*), or one of the related variables (called *properties*). The properties and methods are always placed after the period.

In the previous examples, src and title are two of the image object's properties. In other words, the code *image.src = "newpic.jpg"* is the equivalent of saying "Hey, Mr. Object-named-Image: I have a new picture for you. Change your src to point to *newpic.jpg*."

Programmers embraced objects long ago, because they're a great way to organize code conceptually (not to mention a great way to share and reuse it). You might not realize it at first, but working with the image object is actually easier than memorizing a few dozen different commands that manipulate an image.

Before you can manipulate an object in your Web page, you need a way to uniquely identify it. The best choice is the *id* attribute. Add this attribute to the tag for the element you want to manipulate, and choose a unique name, as shown here:

```
<h1 id="PageTitle">Welcome to My Page</h1>
```

Once you give your element a unique ID, it's easy to dig up (and use) the matching object in your code. JavaScript has a trick for just this purpose—it's the document.getElementById( ) method. Basically, *document* is an object that represents your whole HTML document. It's always available and you can start using it any time you want. The document object, like any object worth its name, provides some handy properties and methods. The getElementById( ) method is one of the coolest—it's able to scan the whole page looking for a specific HTML tag.

When you call the document.getElementById( ) method, you supply the ID of the HTML element you're looking for. Here's an example that digs up the object for an HTML tag with the ID *PageTitle*:

```
var titleObject = document.getElementById("PageTitle")
```

This gets the object for the <h1> element (shown earlier), and stores it in a variable named titleObject. That way, you can perform a series of operations with the heading without having to look it up more than once.

What exactly can you do with an HTML object? To a certain extent, it depends on the type of element. For example, if you have a hyperlink, you can change the URL. If you have an image, you can change the source. And there are some actions you can take with most HTML elements, like changing the style information, or modifying the text that appears between the beginning and ending tags. As you'll see, these tricks are useful when you're making a page more dynamic—for example, you want your page to change when your visitors do something. That way, they feel like they're using an intelligent, responsive program, instead a plain, inert Web page.

For example, here's how you could modify the text inside the just-mentioned <h1> element:

```
titleObject.innerText = "This Page Is Dynamic"
```

If you run this code in a script, the header's text changes immediately when the script runs.

The trick that makes this script work is the innerText *property*. Like all properties, innerText is just one aspect of an HTML object that you can alter. In order to write code statements like this, you need to know what properties there are for you to play with. Obviously, some properties are for specific tags only—like the src attribute of an image. However, modern browsers boast a huge catalog of DOM properties that you can use for just about any tag. Table 14-1 lists some of the most useful.

Tip: To get the properties that a specific HTML tag supports, check out the reference at *www.w3schools.com/htmldom/dom_reference.asp*.

Currently, this example works in two steps (getting the object, and then manipulating it). Although this two-step maneuver is probably the clearest approach, it's possible to combine these two steps into one line, which scripts often do. Here's an example:

```
document.getElementById("PageTitle").innerText = "This Page Is Dynamic"
```

The advantage of getting an object first is that you can change several properties one after the other, without needing to look up the HTML object using getElementById( ) each time.

Table 14-1. Common HTML Object Properties

Property	Description
className	Lets you retrieve or set the class attribute (see page 174). In other words, this property determines what style (if any) this element uses. Of course, this style needs to be present in an embedded or linked style sheet, or you'll just end up with the plain-Jane default formatting.
innerText	Lets you read or change the text inside this element. innerText is insanely useful, but has two quirks.
	First, any tags you include are automatically converted to plain text using the HTML character entities (see page 46). In other words, if you set this property with the text <b>Hi</b>, it's converted to <b>Hi</b> which is displayed as the text <b>Hi</b>. If you want to actually make the text bold, you'll need to use the style property instead (which is also described in this table).
	Second, if you use a tag that has other tags inside it, the innerText refers to the text between the opening tag and the first nested tag. So if you have a paragraph with bolded text, as in "<p>This <b>word</b> is bold</p>," the innerText is just the first part: "This." Using innerText can be quite confusing, so it's recommended that you don't use it on tags that contain other tags. If you want to modify a specific piece of a paragraph, wrap that piece in a <span> tag.
parentElement	Provides the HTML object for the tag that contains this tag. For example, if the current element is a <b> tag in a paragraph, this gets the object for the <p> tag. Once you have this object, you can modify the paragraph. Using this technique (and other similar techniques in DHTML), you can jump from one tag to another.
style	Bundles together all the CSS attributes that determine the appearance of the HTML element. Technically, the style property returns a full-fledged style object, and you need to add another dot (.) and the name of the style attribute you want to change, as in myObject.style.fontSize. You can use the style object to set colors, borders, fonts, and even positioning.
tagName	Provides the name of the HTML tag for this object, without the angle brackets. For example, if the current object represents an <img> tag, this returns the text "img".
value	In an <input> tag (page 323), the value attribute has a special meaning. For example, in a checkbox, it indicates whether or not the checkbox is turned on; in a text box, it indicates the text inside the box; and so on. Other tags don't use the value attribute.

Using HTML objects in a script

The easiest way to come to grips with how HTML objects work is to look at an example. The Web pages shown in Figure 14-6 includes a paragraph that continuously grows and then shrinks, as your code periodically tweaks the font size.

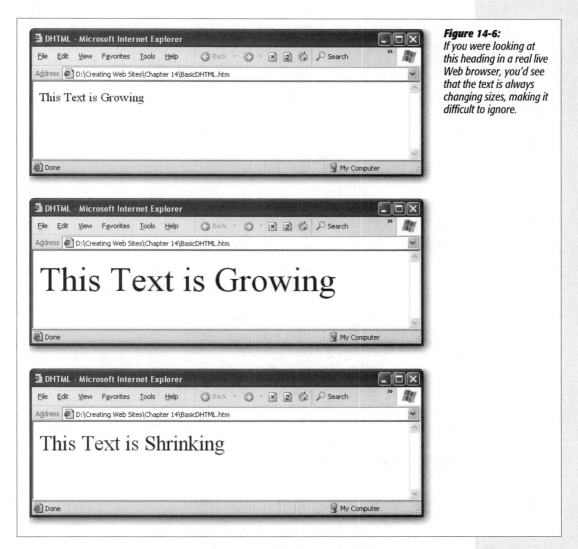

Figure 14-6:
If you were looking at this heading in a real live Web browser, you'd see that the text is always changing sizes, making it difficult to ignore.

The way this example works is quite interesting. First of all, in the <head> section of the underlying HTML, two variables are defined. The *size* variable keeps track of the current size of the text (which starts at 10 pixels). The *growIncrement* variable determines how much the text size changes each time the code runs (initially, it grows by two pixels at a time).

```
<html>

<head>
  <title>DHTML</title>
  <script type="text/javascript">
    // The current font size.
    var size = 10

    // The amount the font size is changing.
    var growIncrement = 2
```

Next, the script defines a function named ChangeFont( ). This function retrieves the HTML object for the <p> tag that should have the growing and shrinking text. Once again, the getElementById( ) function does the job.

```
function ChangeFont( ) {
    // Find object that represents the paragraph
whose text size you want to change.
    var paragraph = document.getElementById("animatedParagraph")
```

Now, using the size and growIncrement variables, it's easy to perform a calculation to determine the new size for the paragraph.

```
size = size + growIncrement
```

And it's just as easy to set the new size using the paragraph.style.fontSize property:

```
paragraph.style.fontSize = size
```

If this code runs perpetually, you'll eventually end up with text that grows so ridiculously huge you can't see any of it on the page. To prevent this from happening, the code has a safety valve.

When the text size hits 100, it's time to stop growing and start shrinking. At that point, the growIncrement variable is switched to subtract two pixels, and the paragraph text is also changed to let you know what's taking place. The next time this code runs, it will shrink the text instead of growing it. To make this happen, the code uses conditional logic courtesy of the *if* statement. Here's what it looks like:

```
// Decide whether to reverse direction from
// growing to shrinking (or vice versa).
if (size > 100) {
    paragraph.innerText = "This Text is Shrinking"
    growIncrement = -2
}
```

Of course, you don't want the shrinking to go on forever either. So it makes sense to add one last check that tests if the text has shrunk to 10 pixels or less, in which case it's time to go back to enlarging the text.

```
        if (size < 10) {
          paragraph.innerText = "This Text is Growing"
          growIncrement = 2
        }
```

Now here comes the really crafty bit. JavaScript includes a setTimeout( ) function, which lets you give an instruction to the browser that says "call this function, but wait a bit before you do." The setTimeout( ) function is very handy when creating interactive pages. In this example, the setTimeout( ) function instructs the browser to call the ChangeFont( ) method again in 100 milliseconds (0.10 seconds).

```
        setTimeout("ChangeFont( )", 100)
      }
    </script>
  </head>
```

Because the ChangeFont() always uses setTimeout( ) to call itself again, the shrinking and resizing never stops. However, you could alter this behavior. For example, you could add conditional logic so that the setTimeout( ) method is called only a certain number of times.

The last detail is the <body> section, which contains the actual paragraph that's being resized and a script that calls ChangeFont( ) for the first time, starting the whole process.

```
  <body>
    <p id="animatedParagraph">This Text is Growing</p>
    <script type="text/javascript">
      ChangeFont( )
    </script>
  </body>

  </html>
```

Although the resizing paragraph trick is absurdly impractical, the same technique is the basis of many much more impressive scripts (to download the whole script and play around with it yourself, download the script from the "Missing CD" page at *www.missingmanuals.com*). For example, you can easily find scripts that animate text in various ways, making it fly in from the side of the page (see *www.codejunction.com/detailed/sequential-fly-in-text-effect.html*); showing words appear one letter at a time, typewriter-style (*www.javascript-page.com/tickert.html*); or making a sparkle float over a title (*www.flooble.com/scripts/animate.php*). Each of these examples uses the same basic approach but adds significantly more code, and gives you a much slicker solution.

Events

The most exciting JavaScript-powered pages are *dynamic*, which means they perform various actions while your visitors interact with the page (moving their mice, typing in text, clicking things, and so on). A dynamic page is far more exciting than an ordinary HTML page, which appears in the browser in one shot and sits there, immobile.

To make dynamic pages, you need to program your pages to react to JavaScript *events*. Events are notifications that an HTML element sends out when specific things happen.

For example, JavaScript gives every <a> tag an event named onMouseOver. As the name suggests, this event takes place (or *fires*, to use programmer-speak) when the mouse pointer moves over an HTML element like a paragraph, link, image, table cell, or text box. At that point, the event is triggered and your code flies into action.

Note: The capitalization of JavaScript events is a little controversial. As you learned in Chapter 2, HTML isn't case-sensitive, and it doesn't care what mix of uppercase and lowercase letters you use. Long-time scripters have a tradition of capitalizing the first letter of each word in the event (except the first word "on"), as in onMouseClick. Although this is the most common approach, if you want to upgrade to XHTML (page 47) in the future, you may as well get used to less-readable, all-lowercase names, like onmouse-click. That's what XHTML requires.

Here's an example that displays an alert message when a surfer moves his mouse pointer over a link:

```
<html>
<head>
  <title>JavaScript Test</title>
</head>

<body>
  <h1>You Will Be Wowed (Again)</h1>
  <p>When you hover over <a href="SomePage.htm"
  onMouseOver="alert('Colorless green ideas sleep furiously.')">
this link</a>
   you'll see a secret message.
  </p>
</body>
</html>
```

When you use an event, you don't absolutely need a script block (although it's a good idea to use one anyway, as described in the next section). Instead, you just put your code in between quotation marks next to the event attribute:

```
<a onMouseOver="[Code goes here]">...</a>
```

There's one detail to keep in mind. In this example, the text argument ('Colorless green...') uses single quotes instead of double quotes. That's because the event attribute uses double quotes, and using them for two different purposes at the same time will horribly confuse the browser.

Figure 14-7 shows the result of running this script and moving the mouse pointer over the link.

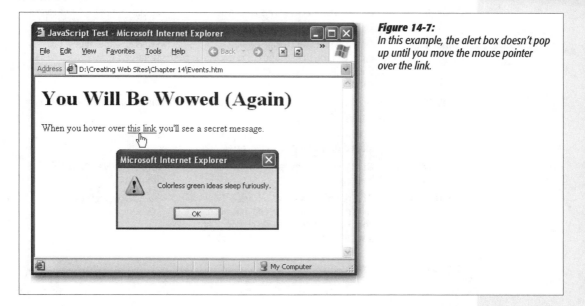

Figure 14-7:
In this example, the alert box doesn't pop up until you move the mouse pointer over the link.

In order to use events effectively, you need to know what events there are, and what HTML tags support them. Although the events you can use depend on the HTML tag they're applied to, Table 14-2 provides a list of commonly used events (and you can find a more complete reference at *www.w3schools.com/htmldom/dom_reference.asp*). In the following sections, you'll see two common scenarios that use some of these events.

Table 14-2. *Common HTML Object Properties*

Event	Description	Applies To
onClick	Occurs when you click an element.	Almost all
onMouseOver	Occurs when you move the mouse pointer over an element.	Almost all
onMouseOut	Occurs when you move the mouse pointer away from an element.	Almost all
onKeyDown	Occurs when you press a key.	<select>, <input>, <textarea>, <a>, <button>
onKeyUp	Occurs when you release a pressed key.	<select>, <input>, <textarea>, <a>, <button>
onFocus	Occurs when a control receives focus (the cursor appears there so you can type something). Controls include text boxes, checkboxes, and so on—see page 319 in Chapter 12 for a refresher.	<select>, <input>, <textarea>, <a>, <button>

Table 14-2. *Common HTML Object Properties (continued)*

Event	Description	Applies To
onBlur	Occurs when focus leaves a control.	`<select>`, `<input>`, `<textarea>`, `<a>`, `<button>`
onChange	Occurs when you change a value in an input control. In a text box, this event doesn't fire until you move to another control.	`<select>`, `<input type="text">`, `<textarea>`
onSelect	Occurs when you select a portion of text in an input control.	`<input type="text">`, `<textarea>`
onError	Occurs when an image can't be downloaded (usually due to an incorrect URL).	`<img>`
onLoad	Occurs when a new page finishes downloading.	`<img>`, `<body>`, `<frame>`, `<frameset>`
onUnload	Occurs when a page is unloaded. (This typically occurs after a new URL has been entered or a link has been clicked. It fires just *before* the new page downloads.)	`<body>`, `<frameset>`

Image Rollovers

The most popular way to use mouse events is to create *image rollovers*. With an image rollover, you start by creating an `<img>` tag that shows a specific picture. Then, when the mouse pointer moves over the `<img>` tag, a new picture appears, thanks to the onMouseOver event. Creating an image rollover is a fairly easy task. All you need to do is get the HTML object for the `<img>` tag and modify the src property.

In this situation, you can't get everything done with a single line of code. You could pile your entire script into the event attribute (using semicolons to separate each line), but it would be dreadfully confusing. A better choice is to put your code in a function. You can then call the function using the event attribute.

For example, here's the function you need to swap an image. This function is written in a very generic way using parameters, which lets you reuse the function over and over, as you'll see in a moment. Every time you call the function, you specifically indicate which image you want to change (by name) and what new image file you want to use. That way, you can call the same function for any image rollover, anywhere on your page.

```
<script type="text/javascript">
  function ChangeImage(imageName, newImageFile) {
    // Find the object that represents the <img> tag.
    var image = document.getElementById(imageName)

    // Change the picture.
```

```
        image.src = newImageFile
    }
  </script>
```

When creating an image rollover, you need to use two events. Use the onMouseOver event to switch to the rollover picture. Additionally, use the onMouseOut event (which occurs when the mouse pointer moves *off* the HTML element) to switch back to the original picture.

```
<img id="SwappableImage" src="pic1.gif"
  onMouseOver="ChangeImage('SwappableImage', 'LostInterestMessage.gif')"
  onMouseOut="ChangeImage('SwappableImage', 'ClickMe.gif')" >
```

Figure 14-8 shows the result.

Figure 14-8:
A rollover image in action.

If you want to add more rollover images, just add a new <img> tag with a different name. The following tag uses the same initial image, but shows a different rollover image each time the mouse pointer moves on and off the image:

```
<img id="SwappableImage2" src="pic1.gif"
  onMouseOver="ChangeImage('SwappableImage2', 'MouseOverPicture.gif')"
  onMouseOut="ChangeImage('SwappableImage2', 'InitialPicture.gif')" >
```

If you want to get really fancy, you can even use the onClick event (which occurs when the element is clicked) to throw yet another picture into the mix.

Note: You'll get your hands dirty with more image rollovers when you create fancy buttons in Chapter 15.

Collapsible Text

Another nifty way to use events is to create *collapsible pages*. The basic idea behind a collapsible page is this: If you've got a lot of information to show your viewers, but don't want them to digest it all at once, you can hide (or collapse) chunks of text behind headlines that they can then click to read the details (see Figure 14-9).

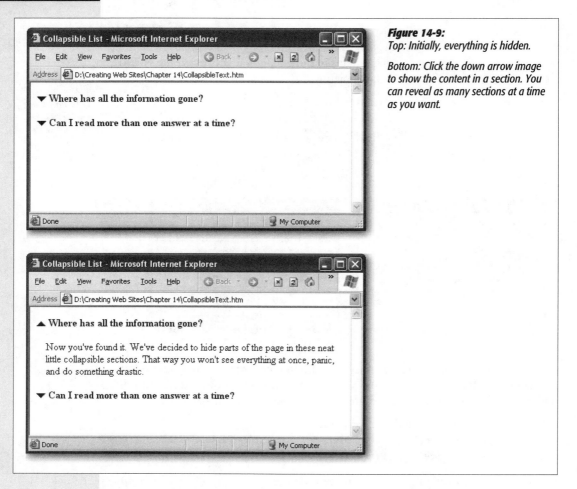

Figure 14-9:
Top: Initially, everything is hidden.

Bottom: Click the down arrow image to show the content in a section. You can reveal as many sections at a time as you want.

DHTML gives you many ways to trick the browser into hiding text to create a collapsible page, but one of the best techniques is shown in the next example. One of the advantages of this example is that it works well with old browsers (those before Internet Explorer 5). Old browsers will simply display all the content, including the information that should be hidden. The page won't be as impressive, but at least nothing will go missing.

The technique revolves around the CSS *display* property. When the property is set to *block*, an item appears in the HTML page in the normal way. But when set to *none*, the element completely disappears, along with everything inside it.

The first ingredient in making a collapsible page is to create the function that performs the hiding and the showing. The function requires two parameters: the name of the open/close image, and the name of the element you want to hide or show. The function actually does double duty. It checks the current state of the section, and then changes it. That means a hidden section is automatically shown and a displayed section is hidden, thanks to conditional logic. At the same time, the open/close image is changed to display a different type of arrow.

Note: This practice, where you always reverse the current state of an item, is called *toggling* by jargon-happy programmers.

```
<script type="text/javascript">
  function ToggleVisibility(image, element){
    // Find the image.
    var image = document.getElementById(image)

    // Find the element to hide/unhide.
    var element = document.getElementById(element)

    // Check the element's current state.
    if (element.style.display == "none"){
      // If hidden, unhide it.
      element.style.display = "block"
      image.src = "open.png"
    }
    else
    {
      // If not hidden, hide it.
      element.style.display = "none"
      image.src = "closed.png";
    }
  }
</script>
```

The code starts out by looking up the two objects you need, and storing them in the variables *image* and *element*. Then it gets to work. It looks at the current state of the paragraph, and makes a decision (using an *if* statement) about whether it needs to show the paragraph or hide it. Only one part of this conditional code runs. For example, if the image is currently hidden (the display style is *none*), the function runs just these two lines and then skips to the bottom of the function and ends:

```
element.style.display = "block"
image.src = "open.png"
```

On the other hand, it the image isn't hidden, this code gets a chance to prove itself instead:

```
element.style.display = "none"
image.src = "closed.png";
```

To use this function, you need to add the <img> that performs the toggling into your Web page. You also need to add the HTML section that contains the hidden content. You can show or hide virtually any tag, but a good all-purpose choice is to use a <div> tag. That way, you can stuff whatever you want to hide inside the <div> tag.

Here's an example:

```
<p>
  <img id="Question1Image" src="closed.png"
  onClick="ToggleVisibility('Question1Image','HiddenAnswer1')">
  <b>Where has all the information gone?</b>
</p>

<div id="HiddenAnswer1" style="display:none">
  <p>Now you've found it. We've decided to hide parts of the
  page in these neat little collapsible sections. That way you won't
  see everything at once, panic, and do something drastic.</p>
</div>
```

The first part (between the <p> tags) defines the question heading, which is always visible. It contains the image and the question (in bold). The second part (in the <div> tag) is the answer, which can be alternately shown or hidden.

Notice that the <div> tag uses a style rule (display:none) to explicitly hide the section. If you want a section to start off being visible, just remove the style attribute, so the <div> tag is declared like this:

```
<div id="HiddenAnswer1">
```

Best of all, because you've put all the complicated stuff into a function, you can reuse your function quite easily to make more collapsible sections. These sections have the same structure, but have different contents:

```
<p>
  <img id="Question2Image" src="closed.png"
  onClick="ToggleVisibility('Question2Image','HiddenAnswer2')">
  <b>Can I read more than one answer at a time?</b>
</p>

<div id="HiddenAnswer2" style="display:none">
  <p>You can expand as many or as few sections as you want.
  Once you've expanded a section, just click again to collapse it back up
  out of sight. The only rule is that when you leave this page and come back
  later, everthing will be hidden all over again. That's just the way
  JavaScript and DHTML work.</p>
</div>
```

Notice that each <img> and <div> tag needs a unique id, or your function won't know which picture to change and which section to hide. This is all you need to run the example shown in Figure 14-9.

Optionally, you can change this page around to give it a different feel but keep the same collapsing behavior. For example, you can make the page easier to use by letting the surfer expand and collapse sections by clicking the heading text (instead of just the image). The easiest way to do this is to pop the image and the bold heading into a <div> tag, and then handle the onClick event of that <div> tag. Here's the change you need:

```
<div onClick="ToggleVisibility('Question1Image','HiddenAnswer1')">
  <p>
  <img id="Question1Image" src="closed.png">
  <b><u>Where has all the information gone?</u></b>
  </p>
</div>
```

You could even underline the heading text so it looks like a link, which lets the viewer know something will happen if it's clicked. Use style sheet formatting or the <u> tag to get your underlining.

Note: You'll see more collapsible text effects when you tackle collapsible menus in Chapter 15.

An Interactive Form

Some of the most powerful examples of JavaScript appear when you combine Java-Script with HTML forms. As you learned in Chapter 12 (page 318), HTML forms allow you to create graphical widgets like text boxes, checkboxes, buttons, and more. Without using a client-side programming language like JavaScript or a more powerful server-side programming language, forms are quite limited. However, if you start using JavaScript and add in a dash of programming savvy, you can create pages that have their own intelligence.

For example, consider the page shown in Figure 14-10. It provides several text boxes where viewers can type in numbers, and then it performs a calculation when they click a button.

Building this example is surprisingly easy. The trickiest part is creating the function that powers the underlying calculations. This function needs several pieces of information, corresponding to the values in the three text boxes (feet, inches, and pounds). The function also needs the name of the element where it should display the results. Here's what the function looks like to start with:

```
<script type="text/javascript">
  function CalculateBMI(feet, inches, pounds, resultElementName) {
```

Tip: You could create a CalculateBMI( ) function that doesn't take any arguments. Instead, the function could just search for all the controls on the page by name. However, using arguments is always a good idea, because it makes your code more flexible. Now you can use the CalculateBMI( ) function on all kinds of different pages, with or without a form.

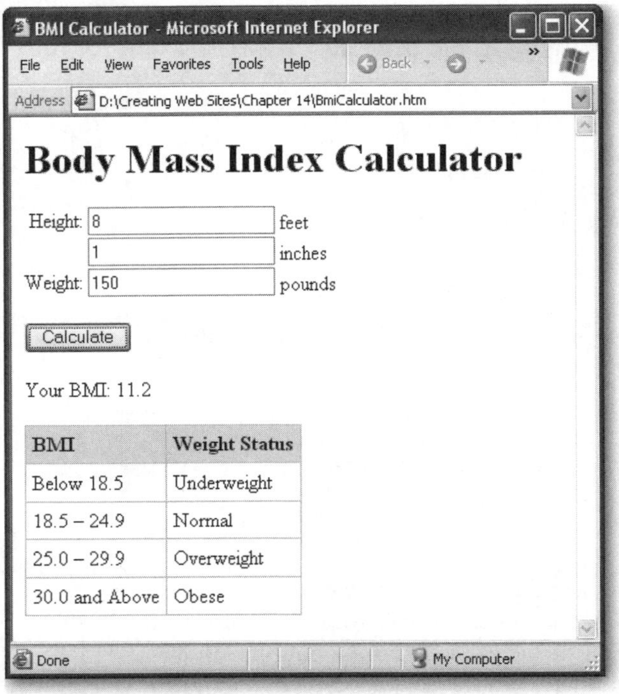

Figure 14-10:
BMI, or body-mass index, is a popular way to calculate a person's overall health by taking their height and weight into consideration. It produces a single number that you can compare against a few standard values. The BMI calculation is thought to be accurate for most people, but there are, of course, always exceptions.

The function code that follows isn't much different from what you've seen before. One trick is that it begins by using a Number( ) function that's hardwired into JavaScript. This function converts the text that's been typed in to numbers that can be used in calculations. If you don't take this step, you might still get the right answer (sometimes), because JavaScript can automatically convert textual strings into numbers as needed. However, there's a catch—if you try to *add* two numbers together and JavaScript thinks they're strings, it will just join the two strings together into one piece of text (so 1+1 would get you 11). This mistake can really scramble your calculations, so it's best to always use the Number( ) function, like so:

```
inches = Number(inches)
pounds = Number(pounds)
feet = Number(feet)
```

The actual calculation isn't too interesting. It's taken straight from the definition of BMI (which you can find on the Internet).

```
var totalInches = (feet * 12) + inches
```

Finally, the result is displayed on the page:

```
    var resultElement = document.getElementById(resultElementName)
    resultElement.innerText =
    Math.round(pounds * 703 * 10 / totalInches / totalInches) / 10
  }
</script>
```

Creating the form that uses this function is the easy part. All you need to do is create the text boxes with <input> tags, and give them names that are easy to remember. In this example, the form uses a table to make sure the text boxes line up neatly next to each other.

```
<form>
  <table>
    <tr>
      <td>Height: </td>
      <td><input type="text" name="feet"> feet</td>
    </tr>
    <tr>
      <td> </td>
      <td><input type="text" name="inches"> inches</td>
    </tr>
    <tr>
      <td>Weight: </td>
      <td><input type="text" name="pounds"> pounds</td>
    </tr>
  </table>
```

Finally, at the bottom of the form, you create a button that calls the CalculateBMI( ) function with the form values. To have the button make this call, you need to program your page to react to the onClick event. To look up a value in a form, you don't need the getElementById( ) function. Instead, you can access them by name through the *this.form* object, which represents the current form:

```
<p>
  <input type="BUTTON" name="calc" value="Calculate"
  onClick="CalculateBMI(this.form.feet.value, this.form.inches.value,
this.form.pounds.value, 'result')">
  </p>
</form>
```

The final ingredient is the tag that displays the result. In this case, you want it to appear inside another paragraph, the <span> tag makes more sense than the <div> tag. (See page 125 in Chapter 6 to review the difference.)

```
<p>
  Your BMI: <span id="result"></span>
</p>
```

You can use all sorts of other form-related scripts. For example, you can check the information people enter for errors before allowing them to continue from one page to another. To learn more about these tricks, you'll need to take your search to the Web, as described in the next section.

Script Categories

To get a handle on what types of scripts are available, look through the different Dynamic Drive categories. Here's a sampling of what you'll find:

The Calendars category has scripts that produce nifty HTML that looks like a calendar—great for displaying important dates or letting surfers plan in advance.

The Date & Time category has live clocks and countdowns to a specific date.

The Document Effects category has page transitions and background effects (like fireworks or floating stars).

The Dynamic Content category has menus that slide out, sticky notes, and scrollable panels.

The Form Effects category has scripts for managing forms (see page 412). You can use them to make sure forms are submitted only once, check for invalid entries, and more.

The Games category has complete miniature games, like tic-tac-toe and Tetris. These games stretch the capabilities of JavaScript and DHTML as far as they can go.

The Image Effects category has slideshow and image gallery scripts, along with dynamic images that change pictures when you move the mouse.

The Links & Tooltips category has fancy links that flash, button tricks, and pop-up text boxes that capture your visitors' attention.

The Menus & Navigation category has handy collapsible menus and navigational bars that let visitors move through your site, like the ones you'll see in Chapter 15.

The Mouse and Cursor category has scripts to change the mouse pointer and add those annoying mouse trails (pictures that follow the mouse pointer wherever it goes).

The Scrollers category has marquee-style scrolling text, like you might see in a news ticker.

The Text Animations category has scripts that bring text to life, making it shake, fly, glow, or take on even more bizarre characteristics.

The User/System Preference category has scripts that dig up information about the browser that's currently displaying your page.

The Window and Frames category has scripts for a dozen different types of pop-up windows.

Scripts on the Web

JavaScript is a truly powerful tool. If you're a diehard alpha nerd who likes to program your TiVo to talk to your BlackBerry, you'll enjoy long nights of JavaScript coding. However, if you don't like to lie awake wondering what *var howMany = (trueTop > 1 ? "s" : "")*; really means, you'll probably be happier if you let someone else do the heavy lifting.

If you fall into the non-programmer camp, this chapter has some very good news. The Web is flooded with free JavaScript. In fact, it's easier to find free scripts than clip art, style sheets, or MIDI music. Most of the time, these scripts include step-by-step instructions that explain where to put the functions, what tags to use in your page, and how to hook your tags up to functions using events.

Although the list of JavaScript sites is too long to print, here are some good starting points:

- *http://webdeveloper.earthweb.com/webjs*

  Offers a huge collection of JavaScript standards.

- *http://javascript.internet.com*

  Provides a solid catalog of 2,000 bread-and-butter scripts.

- *www.javascript-2.com*

  Tips the scales with a staggering 9,000 scripts.

- *www.dynamicdrive.com*

  Provides a smaller set of scripts that emphasize modern DHTML-based programming techniques. Includes exotic scripts like glowing green letters that tumble down the page, Matrix-style. Offers many scripts that are IE-only, but clearly indicates browser support for each script.

- *www.javascripter.net/faq*

  Unlike the other sites, this one doesn't offer a catalog of complete downloadable scripts. Instead, it's organized as a set of frequently asked JavaScript questions, with the relevant code for each answer.

- *http://webmonkey.wired.com/webmonkey/programming/javascript*

  Unlike the other sites, this one offers a smaller set of detailed JavaScript tutorials instead of a huge variety of standalone scripts. Useful if you want to learn more about some of the core JavaScript techniques.

Using this list, you can dig up everything from little frills to complete, functioning Tetris clones. But keep in mind that a script is only as good as the coder who created it. Even on sites with good quality control, you could stumble across a script that doesn't work on all browsers or slows your page down to a sluggish crawl. As a rule of thumb, always try out each script thoroughly before you start using it on your site.

Tip: The hallmark of a good script site is that it's easy to navigate. You'll know you've found a bad script site if it's so swamped in ads and pop-ups that you can't find out where the scripts are.

Finding a Cool Script

Ready to hunt for scripts online? The next series of steps takes you through the process from beginning to end.

1. **Fire up your browser and choose your site.**

   In this example, you'll use *www.dynamicdrive.com*.

2. **Choose the category that you want from the site's home page (Figure 14-11).**

   In this case, you'll use the Documents Effects category. For a sample of what else you can find, see the box "Script Categories."

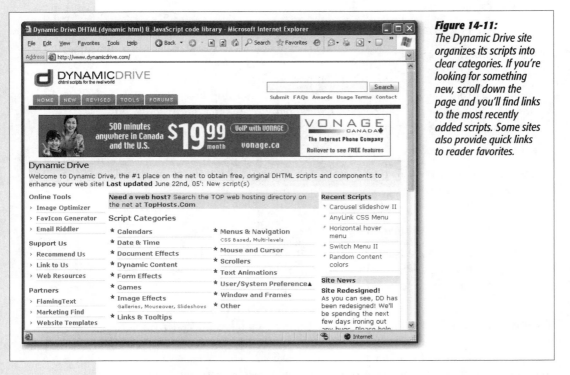

Figure 14-11:
The Dynamic Drive site organizes its scripts into clear categories. If you're looking for something new, scroll down the page and you'll find links to the most recently added scripts. Some sites also provide quick links to reader favorites.

3. **Scroll through the list of scripts in your category (Figure 14-12), and click one.**

   In this case, you'll use the Top-Down Stripy Curtain Script.

4. **The next page shows an example of the script (Figure 14-13).**

   Once the next page loads, you'll find a script description, the author's name, and a link to try the script out (if it wasn't already used on the page). Under-

neath all this information are the step-by-step instructions you need to use the
script.

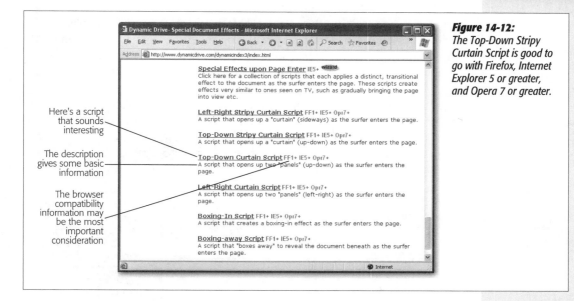

Figure 14-12:
*The Top-Down Stripy
Curtain Script is good to
go with Firefox, Internet
Explorer 5 or greater,
and Opera 7 or greater.*

Here's a script that sounds interesting

The description gives some basic information

The browser compatibility information may be the most important consideration

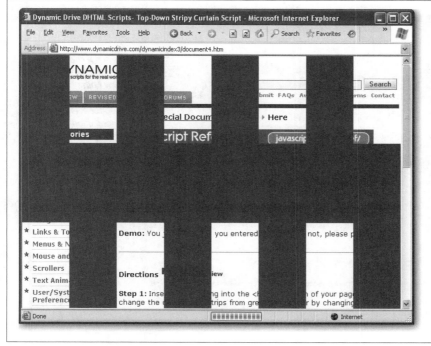

Figure 14-13:
*Here's the Top-Down
Stripy Curtain Script in
action. It fills in the page
by drawing alternating
black strips, some from
top to bottom and others
from bottom to top. It all
happens in a flash.*

5. **Follow the instructions to copy and paste the different parts of the script into your page (Figure 14-14).**

Often, you'll get a set of functions (which you need to place in the <head> portion of your page) and then some HTML tags (which you need to place in the <body> section). In some cases, you'll be able to customize your scripts—for example, you might modify numbers and other values to tweak your script code, or you'll change the HTML tags to provide different content

---

Note: Many scripts include a set of comments with author information. If they do, the rule usually is that you need to keep these comments in your script file, so other developers who check your site out will know where the code originally came from. This practice is just part of giving credit where credit's due. Ordinary Web visitors won't even think to look at the script code, so they won't have any idea whether or not you wrote the script from scratch.

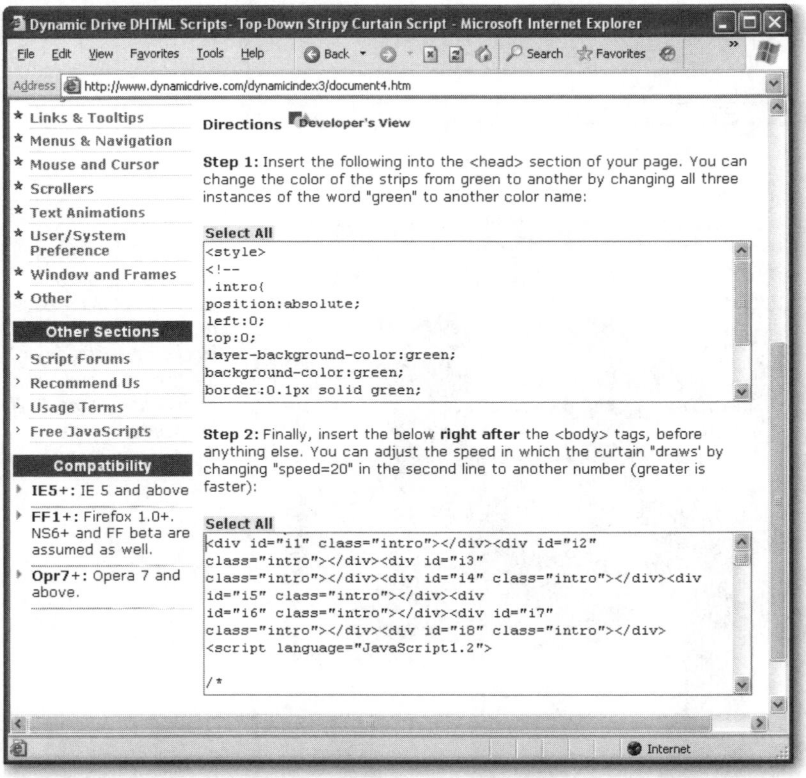

Figure 14-14:
The Top-Down Stripy Curtain Script has two components. The first part is a style definition that defines the solid background curtain that's wiped away with the page content. The second part creates the background curtain (as a <div> tag) and includes the script code that performs the transition. Copy both of these to any page, and you're set. (And for even better organization, consider placing the code in a separate JavaScript file, as described on page 394.)

CHAPTER 15

Fancy Buttons and Menus

Chapter 14 gave you a crash course in JavaScript, the secret ingredient you need to add slick features and frills to ordinary Web pages. Although JavaScript is quirky, arcane, and sometimes frustrating, learning the basics pays off. In this chapter, you'll see how you can use the JavaScript you learned in Chapter 14 to create fancy buttons and menus that will liven up any Web site.

Although buttons and menus that pulse, swirl, and unfurl may seem like small potatoes, they're actually a hallmark of contemporary Web design. In fact, a stylized button or well-designed collapsible menu is sometimes all the polish you need to make your site stand out.

Fortunately, you don't need to be a JavaScript guru to add these sophisticated buttons and menus to your site. As you'll see in this chapter, there are plenty of great tools (both in Web editing programs like FrontPage and Dreamweaver and in free online scripts) that can help you get the results you want without forcing you to endure an all-night JavaScript coding binge.

Creating Fancy Buttons

In Chapter 8, you learned how to use links to let visitors travel from one page in your Web site to another. Although ordinary links work perfectly well, they just aren't showy enough for creative Web masters. Instead, modern Web sites usually let surfers move around by clicking graphical buttons, as shown in Figure 15-1.

A graphical button is really just an image (represented by the familiar <img> tag) that's been turned into a link. There are two ways you can perform this transformation. You can put the image inside an anchor tag, as described in Chapter 8. Here's what that looks like:

```
<a href="targetPage.html"><img src="myPicture.jpeg"></a>
```

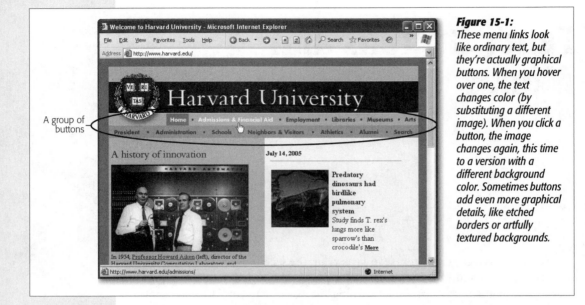

A group of buttons

Figure 15-1:
These menu links look like ordinary text, but they're actually graphical buttons. When you hover over one, the text changes color (by substituting a different image). When you click a button, the image changes again, this time to a version with a different background color. Sometimes buttons add even more graphical details, like etched borders or artfully textured backgrounds.

This adds an ugly blue border around your image to indicate it's a link. To get rid of the blue border, you can use the CSS *border-style* attribute (page 170 in Chapter 6) and set it to *none*.

Alternatively, you can use the <img> tag in conjunction with the onClick event attribute (page 403). This is a good approach if you want to run some JavaScript code instead of just redirecting the visitor with a URL. For example, you used this technique in Chapter 14 (page 409) to create the BMI calculator, which performs a calculation and displays it in the current page when you click a button.

Here's an example of this technique:

```
<img onClick="DoSomething()" src="myPicture.jpeg">
```

In this case there's no ugly blue border, and you don't need the border-style attribute.

Neither of these techniques is new. However, things get a little more interesting if you decide to make *dynamic* buttons. Dynamic buttons (also known as *rollover buttons*) change subtly but noticeably when a visitor to your site hovers the mouse pointer over them. This change lets the visitor know that she's poised over a real, live button, and all she needs to do is click the button to complete the deal.

When you're ready to create a dynamic button, you're going to use the image rollover technique described on page 404. Here's a quick overview of how the maneuver works. Your button reacts to JavaScript events like onMouseOver and onMouseOut to swap the button picture with another picture that's similar, yet slightly different. Then, when the visitor clicks the button, off she goes to whatever link's associated with the button.

Really slick dynamic buttons have *three* pictures—one for the initial state, one for when the mouse pointer hovers over the button, and one for when the button is clicked (just before the new page appears).

GEM IN THE ROUGH

Free Button Makers

Creating a cool rollover button is an age-old problem, with plenty of solutions.

On the Web, you'll find a wide range of online button-making tools. These tools usually start with a page where you specify the button details (like the text, color, background, and so on). Once you're finished, you simply click a button and a program running on the Web server creates the button image (or images) and displays them in a new page. All you need to do is download the images and start using them in your own pages.

Some examples of online button-making tools include *www.buttongenerator.com* (which is demonstrated in this chapter), *http://cooltext.com/ButtonBrowse.aspx*, and *www.grsites.com/button*. Not all of these button makers can create mouse-over images. However, you can usually run the button generator multiple times and choose a slightly different color scheme to create the highlighted button image. For a change of pace, try *www.flashbuttons. com*, which lets you create animated buttons that are actually miniature Flash animations (as described later on page

461 in Chapter 16). Although these types of buttons are impressive, few Web sites use them because they aren't usable on browsers that don't have Flash installed.

The most powerful button-making tools aren't Web-based. Instead, they're separate programs that you can download and install on your computer. These programs often give a richer range of choices, more configurable options, and features that let you create a pile of buttons at once. Unlike online button-makers, if you go this route you'll need to shop around a bit before you find a program that runs on your operating system (for example, Windows or Mac) and has the right price (free or close to it).

Your best place to find free button-making software is one of the shareware sites discussed on page 82. Windows fans might be interested in trying out the free *http://free-buttons.org*. And if you have FrontPage, skip ahead to page 432 to find out about its integrated button generator.

Creating a dynamic button presents you with two challenges:

• **Creating the button pictures.** Not only should these buttons look eye-catchingly cool, the different versions you use (the normal version and the mouse-over version) need to line up exactly. If the selected version of your button has text that's a slightly different size or in a slightly different place, it makes for a jarring effect when the browser swaps the images.

• **Loading the images.** Every dynamic button on your site can use up to three images. For best performance, the browser needs to download all these images when it first requests the page. That way, when someone moves the mouse pointer over a button there isn't a noticeable delay while the appropriate mouse-over image is downloaded.

In the next two sections, you'll learn how to create button images and make them dynamic with a dash of JavaScript.

Generating Button Pictures

If you're graphically inclined, you can create the pictures for a rollover button by hand, using just about any graphics program (Adobe Photoshop and Macromedia Fireworks are two popular choices). However, getting buttons to look good isn't always easy. It's also hard to mass-produce buttons, because you need to make sure every button has a consistent size, background, color palette, and text placement.

Fortunately, if you need a bunch of buttons in a hurry, or your artistic abilities are feebler than those of Koko the painting Gorilla, there's an easier option. You can use a specialized *button creation* program. These programs have no purpose in life other than to help you create attractive buttons with the text, colors, and backgrounds you choose.

The Web's teeming with a wide range of button creation tools (see the box "Free Button Makers"). The following example shows how you can use one of these (the site *www.buttongenerator.com*) to get what you need.

1. **Surf to *www.buttongenerator.com*.**

   This is the ButtonGenerator home page. Scroll down the page until you see the section with the title "Select the button you wish to edit."

2. **In the Show list, choose Only Free Buttons. Figure 15-2 shows the list you'll see.**

   ButtonGenerator has a large catalog of button styles, and it offers a rotating selection of these for free. For a small yearly fee, you can join as a member and get access to more powerful features and the full catalog of buttons.

   If you stick with the free option but find something you like in the full catalog, look for the "Will be FREE in" message underneath the button, which indicates when this style will be offered for free (typically less than a week).

3. **Once you find a button you like, click to select it.**

   Now you'll see a page that lets you customize your button.

4. **In the "Choose a mode" list, select Advanced Form.**

The Advanced Form lets you create an ordinary button image *and* the rollover image at the same time. It also lets you create several buttons at once. (The plain vanilla Easy Form lacks both these valuable features.)

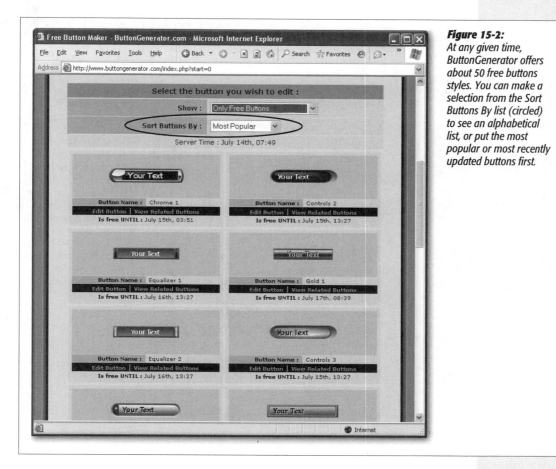

Figure 15-2:
At any given time, ButtonGenerator offers about 50 free buttons styles. You can make a selection from the Sort Buttons By list (circled) to see an alphabetical list, or put the most popular or most recently updated buttons first.

5. **Choose a different picture or a different background for the mouse-over version of your button (see Figure 15-3).**

To create a good dynamic button, you need to differentiate your ordinary button image (called the *initial state* button) from the image that appears when the mouse pointer hovers over the button (called the *mouse-over state* button). The difference should be noticeable, yet subtle.

6. **In the Background Transparency section, choose Light Background or Dark Background, depending on where you want to place your buttons.**

Button images often need to use some transparency because they aren't exact rectangles. The Light Background option creates an image that tends to look better when the page has a light background showing through (like white, gray, or yellow). The Dark Background is a better choice if you're creating Web pages with a black background.

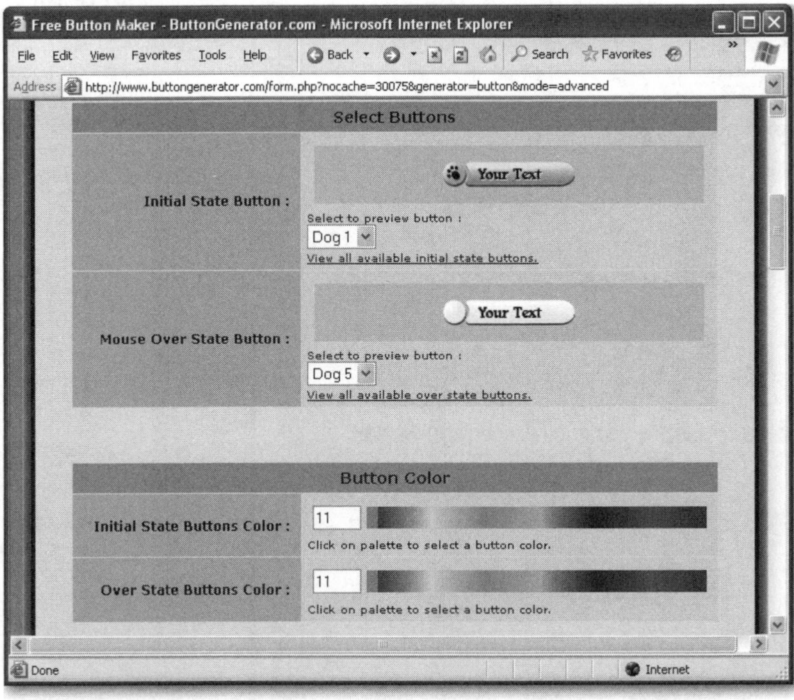

Figure 15-3:
The best way to distinguish an ordinary button from a selected button is by choosing a different state image, as in this example. The ordinary button uses the Dog 1 state, while the selected button uses Dog 5, which is lighter and doesn't have the paw print icon. If your button doesn't provide multiple state choices, you'll need to choose a different background color to make the distinction instead.

7. **In the Text Labels section, enter the text you want to appear on the button (see Figure 15-4).**

If you enter multiple lines of text, each line of text creates a separate button. This is a great trick for generating a pile of buttons in one go.

8. **In the Text Font section, choose a font for the button text, the font size, and whether or not you want to use anti-aliasing.**

When choosing a font, you're limited to a relatively small number of choices. These are the fonts that the ButtonGenerator site uses to create the buttons—it doesn't matter what fonts your site visitors have installed on their computers, since these buttons are going to be transformed into graphics.

Anti-aliasing is a feature that smoothes the edges of a font by blending them in with the background. Usually, this makes the button look more professional.

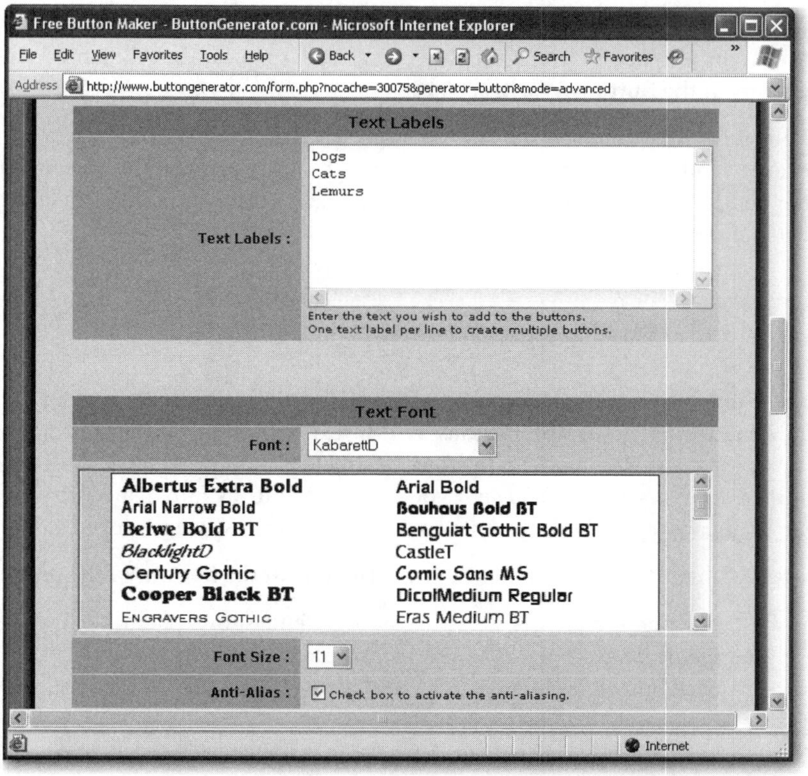

Figure 15-4:
In this example, three buttons are being created at once (with the text "Dogs," "Cats," and "Lemurs," respectively). The options underneath let you choose the best font.

9. In the Text Alignment section, choose left, right, or center alignment, depending on whether the text should be flush with the left edge, lined up on the right, or centered in the middle.

   You can also use the X and Y text boxes to offset the text slightly in either direction. Use these settings only if you find out that your button text isn't aligned perfectly after you generate it. For example, if you create a button with lowercase text, you might find that the text is positioned too low on the button. You can correct this by using a negative number for the Y value.

10. Optionally, tweak the colors for various parts of the button in the Text Color and Mouse Over Buttons Text Color sections.

   The Text Color section corresponds to the initial button image. The Mouse Over Buttons Text Color section corresponds to the image that's shown when the mouse pointer hovers over the button. If you like the current colors, you don't need to change any of these details.

11. **Optionally, choose an image from the list in the Icon Insertion section.**

    If you want, you can embed a small image *inside* your button, like an arrow or flag. However, you're limited to the options that the ButtonGenerator gives you. Usually, you don't need a button icon—it's overkill.

12. **If you want all your buttons to be the same size, turn on the All Same Width checkbox in the Buttons Width section.**

    If you use this option, the ButtonGenerator calculates the width it needs to fit the largest button (the one with the longest text), and makes all the buttons that same width. If you don't choose this option, each button is sized to fit its text exactly.

Tip: If you plan to stack more than one button in a column (for example, to create a navigation bar), make sure you use the All Same Width option. Otherwise, your buttons won't line up.

There's one other option. If you have a specific width in mind, you can enter that value (in pixels) in the Buttons Width text box. Now all the buttons will have the size you specify. The Buttons Width text box overrides the All Same Width setting. It's a good choice if you're fitting buttons into a specific part of your Web page layout and you know exactly how much space you need to fill.

13. **Click the Click Here to Generate Your Button link at the bottom of the page.**

    The ButtonGenerator creates all your buttons, and shows them all in a new page (see Figure 15-5). Now it's time to download the pictures (or click your browser's Back button and try again).

Tip: Once you create your button images, they can't be edited in the ButtonGenerator. For that reason, it's a good idea to keep track of the settings you used (like colors, font, text size, and button width). That way, you can generate replacement buttons later on if you need to change the wording, or if you need to create additional buttons that match those you already have.

---

14. **You need to download the pictures one at a time. To save a picture on a Windows PC, right-click the button and choose Save As (the actual wording depends on your browser). If you've got a Mac, Control-click the button to access your Save As options.**

    The Save Picture dialog box appears.

Note: All unregistered button fanatics are kindly asked to include a link to the ButtonGenerator site somewhere on their Web page. (It's completely kosher to bury this detail on an About Us or Credits page.) The HTML you need for this link is also provided on the ButtonGenerator page, below your button pictures.

---

15. In the Save Picture dialog box, browse to your Web site folder, type in a button name, and click Save. Return to step 14 to save the next picture, and continue until you've saved every image.

It's important to use a good naming convention for your button pictures, so you don't get lost in a tangle of picture files. One approach is to give each button a descriptive name, followed by an underscore, and then the button state. For example, the two pictures for the Dogs button could be named *DogsButton_Normal.png* and *DogsButton_MouseOver.png*.

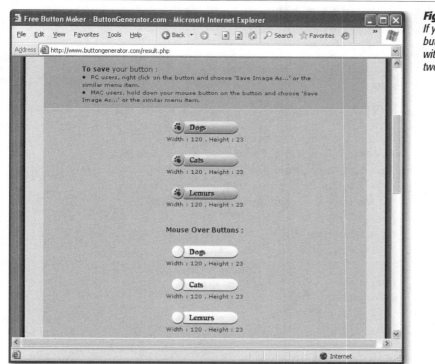

Figure 15-5:
If you create three buttons, you'll end up with six pictures in total, two for each button.

Building a Rollover Button

Now that you have the button images you need, you're ready to incorporate them in a Web page. You can use the exact same ChangeImage( ) function you used in Chapter 14 (page 404).

Note: If you're using Dreamweaver, you don't need to write the JavaScript on your own. Instead, skip ahead to page 432 (or keep reading if you're curious to learn how rollover buttons really work).

The following example shows a complete Web page that includes the ChangeImage( ) script and a single <img> tag, which represents one button. This button is placed inside an anchor tag so it can be clicked to move to another page; and the blue border gets removed thanks to a style sheet rule.

Here's the full HTML, including several comments to help guide you along the way:

```html
<html>

<head>
  <title>Fancy Buttons</title>
  <style>
    /* Hide the blue link border on all images. */
    img {
      border-style: none;
    }
  </style>

  <script type="text/javascript">
    // This is the script for swapping button pictures.
    function ChangeImage(imageID, newImageFile) {
      // Find the object that represents the <img> tag.
      var image = document.getElementById(imageID)

      // Change the picture.
      image.src = newImageFile
    }
  </script>
</head>

<body>
  <p>
    <!-- Create the link with the dynamic button inside. -->
    <a href="Dogs.html">
      <img id="Dogs" src="DogsButton_Normal.png"
      onMouseOver="ChangeImage('Dogs', 'DogsButton_MouseOver.png')"
      onMouseOut="ChangeImage('Dogs', 'DogsButton_Normal.png')">
    </a>
  </p>
```

```
</body>

</html>
```

Figure 15-6 shows the result.

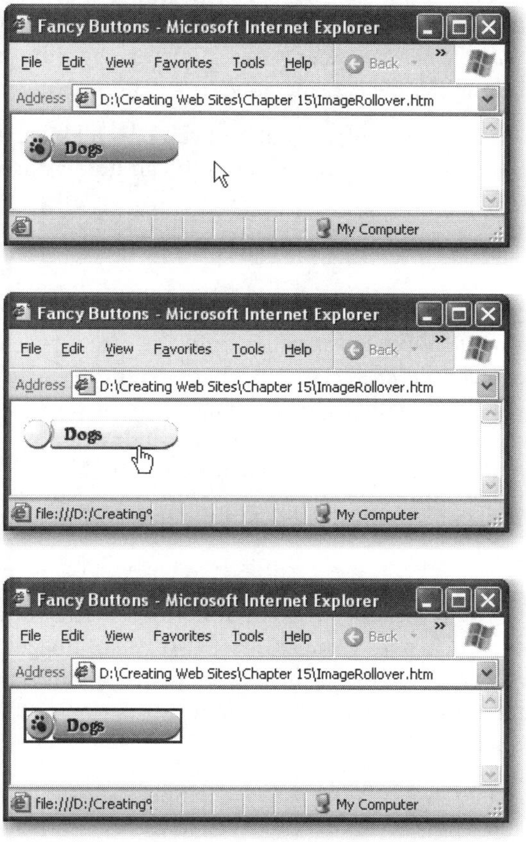

Figure 15-6:
Top: The rollover button in its initial state.

Middle: The rollover button while the mouse pointer hovers overtop.

Bottom: The rollover button without the style rule that hides the border. Without this ever-important style rule, a blue rectangle appears as a clumsy indication that the button's a link.

Using image lists

Although this page gets the job done, it's a little more complicated than it needs to be. The problem is that the declaration for the <img> tag is quite long. Worse, if you make a slight mistake when you type in the image ID or picture URLs, the code won't work. In a page with dozens of buttons, keeping all this straight can become quite a headache, especially if your pictures are stored in a subfolder (in which case the URLs can become very long). And if you add the image preloading technique discussed a bit later (on page 431), you're in even more danger of derailing your code with a minor mistake in the picture URL.

To help minimize the chance of error, pages that use rollover buttons commonly add another JavaScript technique. They declare all the picture URLs in a single list, and they place this list in a script block at the start of the page. Each picture is associated with a number, like 1 for the first button, 2 for the second, and so on. From that point onward, the rest of your page can refer to each picture by number, which shortens your HTML and simplifies life considerably.

To create the picture list, you use a JavaScript ingredient that you haven't seen yet: the *array*. An array is an object that represents a list of items. It can hold as many objects as you want.

Here's an example that creates an array:

```
var myArray = new Array( )
```

Initially, this array is empty. To actually put information into the array, you use square brackets to indicate the *index number*. This is where arrays get a little wonky, because they use *zero-based numbering*. This is a fancy way of saying the first item is given the index number 0, the second item has the index number 1, and so on. Strange as it seems, programmers always start counting at 0.

Here's an example that puts a text string into the first slot in the array:

```
myArray[0] = "This is the first item"
```

In the dynamic button example, you're dealing with three buttons. Each button has an initial image and a mouse-over image. To track these two sets of images, it makes sense to create two arrays, one for normal images (which you can name imgN) and one for selected buttons (imgS). Here's the complete code you need to create the array and store all the picture URLs:

```
<script type="text/javascript">
  // The image lists.
  var imgN = new Array( )
  imgN[0] = "DogsButton_Normal.png"
  imgN[1] = "CatsButton_Normal.png"
  imgN[2] = "LemursButton_Normal.png"

  var imgS = new Array( )
  imgS[0] = "DogsButton_MouseOver.png"
  imgS[1] = "CatsButton_MouseOver.png"
  imgS[2] = "LemursButton_MouseOver.png"
  ...
```

Now you can rewrite the button so that it pulls the names of the images from the array, rather than using the file names directly:

```
<a href="Dogs.html">
  <img id="Dogs" src="DogsButton_Normal.png"
  onMouseOver="ChangeImage('Dogs', imgS[0])"
  onMouseOut="ChangeImage('Dogs', imgN[0])">
</a>
```

There's another change you can make to streamline your code and make the ChangeImage( ) function easier to use. Right now, the current version of the ChangeImage( ) function uses two arguments—the ID of the image tag and the new image file name. Check it out:

```
function ChangeImage(imageID, newImageFile) {
```

You can simplify life by modifying the ChangeImage( ) function so that it accepts an object that represents the <img> tag, instead of the *name* of the <img> tag. Here's the modified version:

```
// This is the script for swapping button pictures.
function ChangeImage(image, newImageFile) {
  image.src = newImageFile
}
</script>
```

As you can see, this means there's no longer a need to go hunting for the image object with the document.getElementById( ) method. However, this change also allows for a handy shortcut. When you call ChangeImage( ), you can pass the current tag using a special keyword named *this*. The *this* keyword always refers to the object for the current tag—in this case, the object that represents the <img> tag. Here's how it works:

```
<a href="Dogs.html">
  <img src="DogsButton_Normal.png"
  onMouseOver="ChangeImage(this, imgS[0])"
  onMouseOut="ChangeImage(this, imgN[0])">
</a>
```

Take a moment to compare this to the more painful version on page 426. Now you no longer need to give the <img> tag a unique ID to keep track of it. You also don't need to type in the picture URLs every time you call ChangeImage( ). Instead, imgS[0] refers to the first selected button image, and imgN[0] refers to the first normal button image.

Note: Keen eyes may notice that the image URL still appears in the src attribute. You might wonder if there's a way to set this detail through JavaScript code using the imgN array. Although it's possible, it's not a good idea. That's because the current approach works even when the browser doesn't support JavaScript. (In that situation, the fancy rollover effect doesn't work, but the ordinary button image is still shown.) If you relied entirely on JavaScript, the buttons wouldn't appear at all on feebler browsers.

To complete this example, you need an <img> tag for each button. In the following code, all the buttons are grouped into a <div> tag so the buttons can be placed together along the side of the page.

```
<div class="Menu">
  <p>
    <a href="Dogs.html">
      <img src="DogsButton_Normal.png"
       onMouseOver="ChangeImage(this, imgS[0])"
       onMouseOut="ChangeImage(this, imgN[0])">
    </a>
  </p>
  <p>
    <a href="Cats.html">
      <img src="CatsButton_Normal.png"
       onMouseOver="ChangeImage(this, imgS[1])"
       onMouseOut="ChangeImage(this, imgN[1])">
    </a>
  </p>
  <p>
    <a href="Lemurs.html">
      <img src="LemursButton_Normal.png"
       onMouseOver="ChangeImage(this, imgS[2])"
       onMouseOut="ChangeImage(this, imgN[2])">
    </a>
  </p>
</div>
```

Here's the style rule that formats this <div> tag, lining it up neatly on the left side of the page:

```
div.Menu {
  float: left;
  margin-right: 20px;
  margin-top: 20px;
  height: 1000px;
}
```

For a quick refresher on style sheet-based layout, pop back to page 248.

Figure 15-7 shows the final result.

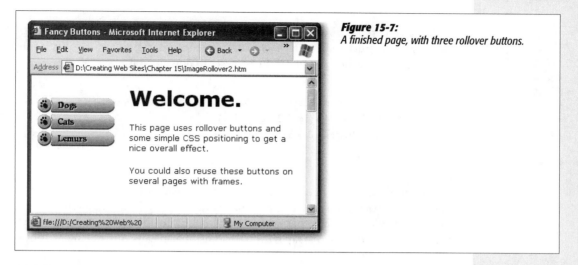

Figure 15-7:
A finished page, with three rollover buttons.

Preloading images

With the current example, it's only a little bit more work to use *image preloading*. This technique ensures that the mouse-over pictures are downloaded the first time the page is requested (instead of when the surfer moves her mouse pointer over a button). Although you won't notice the difference when you run a Web page from your computer's hard drive, preloading images makes the buttons more responsive when visitors interact with a page over the Internet, particularly if they've got a slow connection.

The technique for preloading images requires a bit of a quirky workaround. Basically, you need to trick the browser into thinking that you're using the rollover pictures right away. This convinces the browser to download the images without delay.

Then, later on, when the mouse pointer moves over a button and the ChangeImage( ) method runs, the browser gets ready to download the mouse-over picture. However, being a relatively clever program, the browser immediately realizes that it *already has* the picture stored away in its *cache* (a temporary location in memory or on disk for storing recently visited pages and other recently downloaded files). As a result, no download is needed—the browser just uses the image it already has.

To use image preloading, you need to add a function that downloads the rollover pictures. The first step is to create a dummy image object in memory. You won't actually use this image to do anything, but the browser doesn't know that.

```
function PreloadImages( ) {
  // Create a "dummy" image.
  var preloadedImage = new Image( )
  ...
```

Next, the code reads through the entire imgS list of rollover pictures, using a programming construct called a *for loop*. Each time it finds an image, it stuffs it into the image object, which convinces the browser to download it.

```
  ...
  // Load all the pictures into this image, one after another.
  for (var j = 0; j < imgS.length; j++) {
    preloadedImage.src = imgS[j]
  }
}
```

A for loop repeats code a certain number of times using a built-in counter. In this case, the counter is a variable named *j* that starts at 0, and keeps increasing until it matches imgS.length—in other words, until it gets to the last item in the imgS array. Assuming the imgS array has three items, that means this statement is executed three times:

```
  preloadedImage.src = imgS[j]
```

The first time is when j is 0, and the code loads up the first image in the list. The second time j is 2, and it digs up the second image. You can guess what happens the third time.

Strangely enough, that's all you need to do. Even though you're not using the images, the browser still obligingly fetches them from your Web server and stores them in its cache when you refer to them in this way.

The only remaining step is to make sure you call the PreloadImages( ) function when the page is loaded. You accomplish this by adding the onLoad event attribute to the <body> tag, as shown here:

```
  <body onLoad="PreloadImages( )">
```

That's it. Your rollover buttons are now Web-ready!

Creating Rollover Buttons in Dreamweaver and FrontPage

If you're using an HTML editor like Dreamweaver or FrontPage, you don't need to write your own JavaScript code. Both programs provide a built-in way to quickly create rollover buttons.

In Dreamweaver, all you need to do is select Insert → Image Objects → Rollover Image. You see an Insert Rollover Image dialog box, which you can use to set all the important details (Figure 15-8). Click OK, and Dreamweaver creates the <a> and <img> tags and adds the JavaScript code for swapping images.

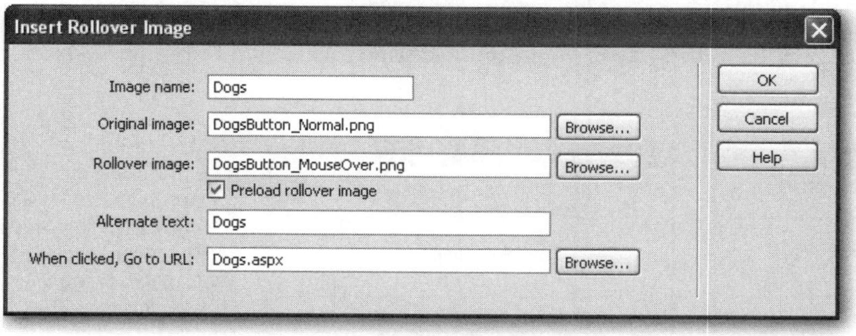

Figure 15-8:
To create a rollover button in Dreamweaver, just supply a unique button name, the normal state and mouse-over images, any alternate text that should appear if the image can't be shown, and the target URL. You can also click the "Preload rollover images" button to generate JavaScript code that downloads all the rollover buttons when the page loads.

The only way to improve on this feature is with a tool that not only inserts a rollover button, but can also create the button images you need, based on the text and style options you choose. FrontPage provides the goods with a feature it calls *interactive buttons*.

To create an interactive button in FrontPage 2003, start by selecting Insert → Web Component from the FrontPage menu. The Insert Web Component dialog box appears. In the "Component type" box, choose Dynamic Effects, and in the "Choose an effect" box, select Interactive Button. Then click Finish. You're presented with an impressively featured button generator (see Figure 15-9).

When you save your Web page, FrontPage 2003 prompts you to choose file names for all the button pictures you've created using the Interactive Buttons dialog box.

The best part about the FrontPage button generator is that it's fairly easy to modify your button settings and regenerate the button pictures later on. Just double-click the interactive button in the editor, modify the settings in the Interactive Buttons dialog box, and click OK to generate the new images.

Tip: The FrontPage button generator is new in FrontPage 2003. However, if you have an earlier version of the program, you can download a similar tool named 3D Button Visual Editor from Microsoft at *www.microsoft.com/downloads/details.aspx?familyid=23e6b5ad-c173-4aa4-8348-f400d670e0ac*. (If you don't want to type in this horrendous URL, use the link from the "Missing CD" page at *www.missingmanuals.com*.)

Creating Fancy Menus

Rollover buttons are wildly popular on the Web, and it's easy to see why. There's something irresistible about a button that lights up when you're over it. However, you can have too much of a good thing, and stuffing too many rollover buttons into a page is a surefire way to create an overdone turkey of a Web site.

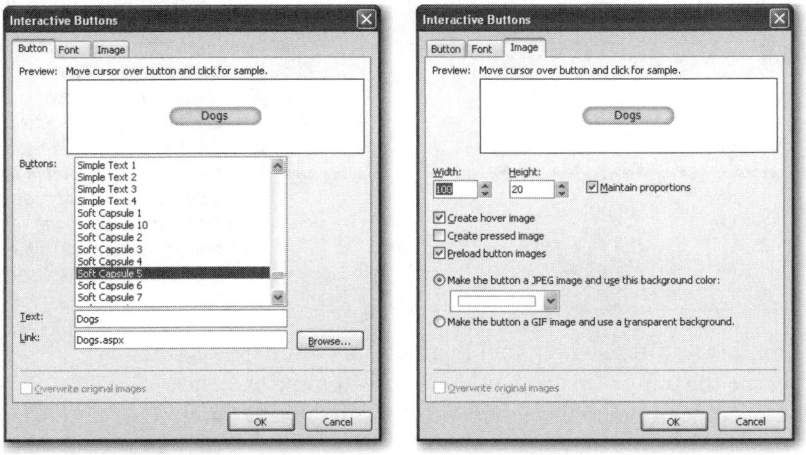

Figure 15-9:
Left: The FrontPage button generator lets you choose from a long list of button styles, ranging from metallic rectangles to soft glow tabs. You supply the text and target link.

Right: Use the Image tab to set the button size and background color. Turn on the "Create hover image" checkbox to generate a mouse-over image along with the initial button image, and turn on "Create pressed image" if you want a third image, one that appears when the button is clicked (just before the browser navigates to the new page).

More recently, the Web's seen a small renaissance of simplicity, and a trend away from rollover buttons. This change is caused in part by the increasing complexity of the Web—quite simply, a handful of rollover buttons is no longer enough to guide a reader around a typical Web site. Instead, Web sites use more detailed multilevel menus that can swallow up dozens of links.

Note: Fancy buttons and fancy menus play a similar role in taking surfers from one page to another. If you have a relatively small site, you may choose to use buttons exclusively. If you have a large Web site, you're more likely to use a combination of menus and buttons.

A typical menu starts with a collection of anchor tags, organized into logical groups, that are placed together on a page. For example, a company Web site might have a group of product pages, a group of pages with contact and location information, and another group of tech support pages. By arranging links into separate groups, it's much easier for visitors to find what they're looking for.

So far, this menu design doesn't require anything special. Using the linking skills you picked up in Chapter 8, and the layout smarts you gained in Chapter 9, you can easily create a side panel with a grouped list of anchors. But really neat menus add another trick—they're *collapsible*. That means you don't need to see the whole menu at once. Initially, you see only the group headings. When you click a group, a list of related links pops open just underneath.

There are a variety of ways to create collapsible menus. Some are fairly easy, while others are dizzyingly complicated. In the following sections, you'll learn how to build a simple collapsible menu of your own, and use a more complicated menu system, courtesy of a free JavaScript site.

Do-It-Yourself Collapsible Menus

You can create a respectable menu of your own using the collapsible DHTML tricks described in Chapter 14 (page 405). The basic idea is to use JavaScript to hide and show specific HTML elements by changing the CSS *display* property (page 406).

For example, imagine you want to create the cool two-level tabbed menu shown in Figure 15-10. This page splits its links into three separate groups, each of which is represented by a tab. Only one tab shows its sublinks at a time.

This design might seem a little intimidating, but it only consists of two separate parts: the tabs at the top of the page, and the link boxes that appear dynamically underneath them. In order to make these regions easy to deal with, it makes sense to wrap them in <div> and <span> tags, as you've seen throughout this book.

Note: In the rest of this section, you'll get a chance to look at the solution piece by piece. To see the complete page, check out the downloadable content for this chapter, available from the "Missing CD" page at *www.missingmanuals.com*.

Because the three tabs appear next to each other on the same line, the <span> tag is the easiest choice. (Remember, the <div> tag adds a line break and some space between each element. The <span> tag is an inline element, which means you can fit it inside an existing paragraph and place more than one <span> side by side.)

Here's the HTML you'll start with:

```
<span class="Tab">About Me</span>
<span class="Tab">My Store</span>
<span class="Tab">Really Cool Stuff</span>
```

These <span> tags have the descriptive class name Tab. That associates them with the following style sheet rule, which gives the tabs the correct font and borders:

```
.Tab {
  font-weight: bold;
  padding: 5px;
```

```
    border-style: solid;
    border-width: 1px;
}
body {
    font-family: Veranda, sans-serif;
}
```

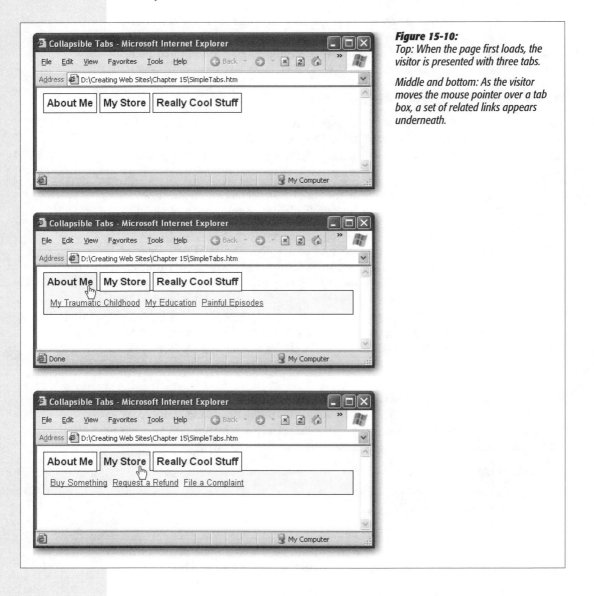

Figure 15-10:
Top: When the page first loads, the visitor is presented with three tabs.

Middle and bottom: As the visitor moves the mouse pointer over a tab box, a set of related links appears underneath.

After you declare the <span> tags, it makes sense to add the link groups. Each link group can be represented by a <span> or <div> tag, but a <div> tag makes most sense because the links are placed separately on the page (meaning they aren't inserted into another paragraph). Each <div> tag needs to have a unique ID, because you'll need to use that in your code to show the group of links you want.

Here's the <div> tags for the three link groups:

```
<div id="AboutMe" class="Links">
  <a href="...">My Traumatic Childhood</a> 
  <a href="...">My Education</a> 
  <a href="...">Painful Episodes</a>
</div>
<div id="MyStore" class="Links">
  <a href="...">Buy Something</a> 
  <a href="...">Request a Refund</a> 
  <a href="...">File a Complaint</a>
</div>
<div id="ReallyCoolStuff" class="Links">
  Just kidding.
</div>
```

Even though these <div> tags are stacked one on top of the other, they won't ever appear at the same time. When the page first appears, they're all hidden, thanks to the style rule for the Links class:

```
.Links {
  display: none;
  border-width: 1px;
  border-style: solid;
  padding: 10px;
  background-color: lightyellow;
  font-size: x-small;
}
```

These style sheet rules, <span> tags, and <div> tags create the basic framework for your page. The final step is to create a script that can show one of the hidden <div> tags, depending on which tab your visitor selects.

The code you need is quite similar to what you used with the ToggleVisibility( ) function demonstrated in Chapter 14 (page 407). The difference is that in this case, you're not interested in hiding and showing individual sections. Instead, you want to show a single section (depending on the selected tab) and hide everything else. In this page, that task is handled by a custom function named MakeVisible( ).

Here's a simplified version of the MakeVisible( ) function. As you can see, it takes an element name, finds the element, and changes the style settings to make it appear on the page.

```
function MakeVisible(element){
  // Find the element and unhide it.
  var element = document.getElementById(element)
  element.style.display = "block"
}
```

Now you can hook up this function to all of the tab buttons. You have a choice here—you could react to clicks using the onClick attribute, or to a mouse pointer hovering using the onMouseOver attribute. This example uses the latter approach.

```
<span class="Tab" onMouseOver="MakeVisible('AboutMe')">About Me</span>
<span class="Tab" onMouseOver="MakeVisible('MyStore')">My Store</span>
<span class="Tab" onMouseOver="MakeVisible('ReallyCoolStuff')">Really Cool
  Stuff</span>
```

The page still isn't quite right. Although the MakeVisible( ) function shows the correct tab, it doesn't hide anything. That means that if you pass the mouse pointer over all three tabs, you'll see all three groups of links at the same time, one above the other.

To correct this problem and hide the other tabs, you need to get a little craftier. The problem is that MakeVisible( ) knows what tab it's supposed to show, but it doesn't know anything about the other tabs. To find these tabs, your code needs to search through the rest of the page. In this example, the basic approach is to look for any <div> tag that has the class name Links, and hide it. You can perform this step at the beginning of the MakeVisible( ) function, so that everything is hidden. Then, you need the code you saw before to show just the link box you want.

Here's the corrected MakeVisible( ) function:

```
function MakeVisible(tab, element) {
  // Get an array with div tags.
  var links = document.getElementsByTagName("div")

  // Search the array for link boxes, and hide them.
  for (var j = 0; j < tabs.length; j++) {
    if (links[j].className == 'Links') links[j].style.display = "none"
  }

  // Find the element and unhide it.
  var element = document.getElementById(element)
  element.style.display = "block"
}
```

This code is a little tricky. As with the rollover example earlier in this chapter (page 428), it uses an array and a for loop. In this case, the array has a list of all the <div> objects on your page. As the code moves through this list, it checks the class name of each <div> tag. If the class name indicates that you've found a link box, the code makes it disappear from the page by changing the display style.

The code in the downloadable example gets slightly fancier—it also fiddles with the tab to change the background border color and hide the border for the selected tab. However, the basic approach is still the same.

Note: If the stranger aspects of JavaScript still look like Danish, don't worry. If you're inclined, you can learn about JavaScript programming features like arrays, loops, and if statements from a dedicated book or Web site (see page 390 in Chapter 14 for some good resources). Or, you can keep your sanity and rely on the examples provided with this book and find great free scripts online.

Third-Party Menus

If you've had enough fun writing your own JavaScript code, you'll be happy to hear that the Web is chock-full of free menu scripts that you can use completely for free. Many of these have more dazzle than the tabbed menu shown in the previous example. Some of the extra features you might find include:

- Multilevel menus that let your visitors drill down into specific subcategories.

- Pop-up menus that appear "above" your Web page when you click them.

- Ridiculously showy effects, like shaded highlighting and transparent backgrounds.

To find a good menu, you can use any of the JavaScript sample sites described in Chapter 14 (see page 413). You'll find that there's quite a bit more diversity in menus than in rollover buttons. Every menu looks and behaves a little differently. Some pop up, others slide out, and others try to emulate the look and feel of popular programs like Microsoft Outlook.

To get a glimpse of what's out there, head over to the examples at Dynamic Drive, which has a set of nifty menus at *www.dynamicdrive.com/dynamicindex1* and a particularly interesting specimen (called, rather unimaginatively, Top Navigational Bar II) at *www.dynamicdrive.com/dynamicindex1/topnavbar.htm*. Figure 15-11 shows this menu with the same menu structure that was used in the tabbed menu example from earlier in this chapter.

Tip: Before you choose a navigation bar for your own Web site, you'll want to test drive quite a few. This section walks you through the process, but you'll want to compare the result with other navigation bars before you commit.

In the following sections, you'll download the script code you need for Top Navigation Bar II, and use it to create your menu.

Note: Top Navigational Bar II works in Internet Explorer and Opera, but not Firefox. To get better support, you should definitely check out Top Navigational Bar III (*www.dynamicdrive.com/dynamicindex1/topmen3*), which provides a similar effect but works in just about every modern browser. (The Web page for the script provides a table with detailed browser compatibility information.)

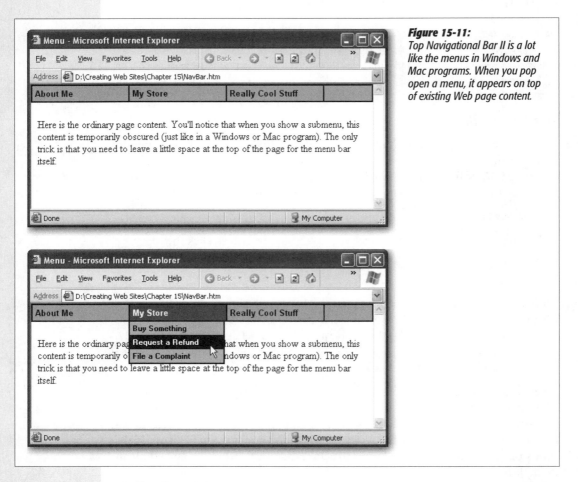

Figure 15-11:
Top Navigational Bar II is a lot like the menus in Windows and Mac programs. When you pop open a menu, it appears on top of existing Web page content.

Getting the script

To download Top Navigational Bar II, follow these steps:

1. **Surf to** *www.dynamicdrive.com/dynamicindex1/topnavbar.htm*.

   You'll see a page that demonstrates the navigation bar, and provides step-by-step instructions for using it.

2. **In the Step 1 section, copy all the code, and paste it into the <head> section of any Web page.**

You can create a new Web page for this purpose, or use a Web page you've already created.

3. **As instructed in the Step 2 section, change the <body> tag in your Web page to <body onload="init( )">.**

   This tells your code to call the init( ) method to set up the menu when the page loads.

4. **In Step 3, click to download and open the ZIP file named *exfiles.zip*. Unzip these files (using any unzip tool you have) into the same folder where you've stored your Web page.**

   The *exfiles.zip* file contains three text files that are full of JavaScript code that supports the navigation bar. Fortunately, you never need to look at (or understand) any of this code, unless you're irrationally curious.

5. **Try the page out in your Web browser.**

   You'll see a sample menu with a series of headings and subheadings. To change this menu into the menu you really want, you need to edit the JavaScript code that you pasted into your Web page (not the ones in the separate script files). As you'll see in the next section, it's pretty easy.

Creating the menu

Every JavaScript menu has a slightly different procedure for creating it. Some menus make you define the menu in a separate text file. Other menus, like Top Navigational Bar II, force you to modify the actual JavaScript code to define the links you want.

In the previous section, you pasted the script code into a Web page, and wound up with the sample menu. To customize this menu, you need to open up the Web page, and scroll to the very top of the script.

You'll see this code, which creates the special menu objects:

```
<script language="JavaScript">
var myNavBar1 = new NavBar(0);
var dhtmlMenu;
```

Note: The code in this example looks a little different because every statement ends with a semicolon (;). This is a C programming convention that's supported (but optional) in JavaScript. Programming types like it because it clearly indicates where each line ends. We use it in this section because that's the way the Top Navigational Bar II is written.

From this point on, the rest of the code builds up the particular menu structure for your page. The code performs this task one submenu at a time. You can delete the code that's there (to remove the existing menus) or just modify it to create the menu items you really want.

To create a submenu, you begin by creating a new NavBarMenu object, and supplying two numbers. The first number is the width (in pixels) of the top-level menu heading. The second number is the width of the menu that pops up underneath the top-level heading. Here's an example that makes both 150 pixels wide, which is a good size to start with. The longer your text, the wider the space you'll need on your Web page.

```
dhtmlMenu = new NavBarMenu(150, 150);
```

Now, you need to add the top-level heading for this menu item. You do this by calling dhtmlMenu.addItem( ), and passing in a new NavBarMenuItem object, like this:

```
dhtmlMenu.addItem(new NavBarMenuItem("About Me", ""));
```

When you create a NavBarMenuItem you supply two details: the menu text ("About Me"), and the link. In the case of a top-level menu item, you don't need the link. Technically, you *can* make the top-level menu heading clickable, but that behavior confuses just about everyone.

Note: Remember, you don't need to understand how this code works (or why the syntax is the way it is) in order to use it. You simply need to copy the sample code exactly, and replace the menu captions and page links with yours. (You should also test your page with a range of different browsers and on different operating systems.)

You now know just about everything you need to create fancy menus for your site's navigation menu. You simply need to repeat the previous step to create each menu item. Here's how you would add three more menu items, representing the three items in the About Me menu:

```
dhtmlMenu.addItem(new NavBarMenuItem("My Childhood", "Child.html"));
dhtmlMenu.addItem(new NavBarMenuItem("My Education", " Education.html "));
dhtmlMenu.addItem(new NavBarMenuItem("Painful Episodes", "Pain.html "));
```

The only rule you need to keep in mind is that you create the menu items in the same order you want them to appear on the page. The first menu item is always the heading that you'll see at the top.

Finally, when you've completed a submenu, end with this statement, which adds the submenu to the navigation bar:

```
myNavBar1.addMenu(dhtmlMenu);
```

Now you just repeat the whole process to add the next submenu. Here's the complete code that creates the My Store submenu:

```
dhtmlMenu = new NavBarMenu(150, 150);
dhtmlMenu.addItem(new NavBarMenuItem("My Store", ""));
```

```
dhtmlMenu.addItem(new NavBarMenuItem("Buy Something", "..."));
dhtmlMenu.addItem(new NavBarMenuItem("Request a Refund", "..."));
dhtmlMenu.addItem(new NavBarMenuItem("File a Complaint", "..."));
myNavBar1.addMenu(dhtmlMenu);
```

You can continue this process of defining submenus indefinitely, until you get all the menus you want.

CHAPTER 16

Audio and Video

There comes a point when every new Web designer wants more than mere text and pictures. Even spruced-up fonts and elegant page layouts don't satisfy the design envy that many newcomers feel when they spot a site loaded with sounds and motion. It's understandable: You want to use *multimedia* to trick out your pages with audio and video. In this chapter, you'll learn how to do exactly that, and create Web pages with background music, animations, and even full-frame movies.

But before you go any further, take a moment to consider the pitfalls you'll face. If you think of the most common examples of multimedia on the Web, you're likely to come up with a long list of Web annoyances. These abuses include flashing banner ads, irritating background music, exasperating pop-ups, time-wasting intro pages, and bandwidth-sucking commercials. Occasionally, you'll find a worthwhile movie promo or interactive game, but they're far outnumbered by budget Web pages blurting out irritating jingles.

So before you jump on the multimedia bandwagon, it's important to think about exactly what you want to accomplish. Are you planning to showcase your musical compositions or provide downloadable recordings of Junior's first moments? If so, multimedia probably makes sense. But if you're just looking for a way to dazzle surfers with an animated logo sequence, think twice. It's probably not worth the considerable effort to design something that will only aggravate most of your visitors.

Understanding Multimedia

Multimedia is a catch-all term that includes a variety of different technologies and file types, all of which have dramatically different computer requirements and pose different Web design challenges. Before you can jazz up your site with audio or video, you need to understand a few basics.

Linking and Embedding

One of the key choices you'll make when outfitting your Web pages with multimedia is whether to link or embed the files you're adding.

Linking to your multimedia content is the simplest but least glamorous approach. The basic idea is that you create a link that *points* to the audio or video file that you've stored alongside all the other HTML and image files on your site. There's really nothing to creating linked multimedia. All you need is the lowly anchor tag (see Chapter 8) to create the link. The *href* attribute of the link points to your file, as in this example:

```
Would you like to hear <a href="IndustrialNoiseBand.mp3">Industrial Noise</a>?
```

Figure 16-1 shows what happens when you click one of these babies.

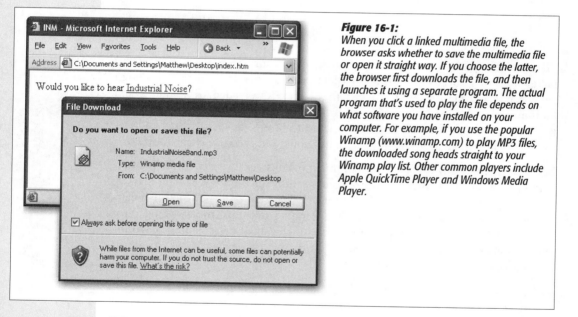

Figure 16-1:
When you click a linked multimedia file, the browser asks whether to save the multimedia file or open it straight way. If you choose the latter, the browser first downloads the file, and then launches it using a separate program. The actual program that's used to play the file depends on what software you have installed on your computer. For example, if you use the popular Winamp (www.winamp.com) to play MP3 files, the downloaded song heads straight to your Winamp play list. Other common players include Apple QuickTime Player and Windows Media Player.

Note: It makes absolutely no difference what kind of software is running on your Web server when you add linked audio to your site. The audio is always downloaded to the Web surfer's computer and played there.

Embedding multimedia is a more advanced approach that aims to integrate ordinary HTML content with background music or a video window. Embedding multimedia can be a challenge. Depending on what kind of file you're embedding, your visitor's browser might not support it. Another problem is that you might need to have special software on your Web server. Usually, the role of this software is to take a large multimedia file (like a five-minute movie clip), and send it out to browsers piece by piece. This process, known as *streaming*, allows the Web surfer's computer to start playing the multimedia file before it's completely downloaded.

Note: The distinction between linking and embedding multimedia is the same as the difference between linking to a picture (with the <a> tag), and embedding it right in your page (with the <img> tag). The only difference is that images are a basic, well-supported part of the HTML standard, so embedding never causes much concern. However, embedding audio and video takes you into less-charted waters.

Types of Multimedia Files

The decision to link or embed will be decided, at least partly, by the type of multimedia content you want to show. Because HTML doesn't have any multimedia standard of its own, other companies have innovated to fill the gaps. Today, there's a slightly bewildering field of choices.

Here are the types of multimedia you'll see in this chapter:

- **Synthesized music (MIDI).** MIDI files are very small, low-quality music files. Although the audio quality depends on the sound hardware in your site visitor's computer, the results most commonly resemble a cheesy Casio keyboard. But because they're lightweight and supported on almost all browsers, MIDI files are the most common type of Web page background music. (MIDI stands for Musical Instrument Digital Interface.)

- **Digital audio (WAV and MP3).** These file types store recorded audio, which makes for far better quality. However, WAV files are enormous, which makes them unsuitable for all but the most bloated Web sites. MP3 files are 10 times slimmer, but browsers often don't support them directly, which means you can't always embed MP3 files.

- **Digital video (MPEG, AVI, MOV, and WMV).** These file types are the heavy hitters of multimedia. They allow you to show full video that ranges in quality from a jerky thumbnail-sized window to DVD-quality playback. Digital video is a challenge for any Web page creator, because it's ridiculously large. In order to have even a chance of making it work, you need to compress, shrink, and reduce the size and quality of your video clips with video editing software.

- **Animated GIFs.** Animated GIFs are small animations that actually consist of a sequence of static images shown one after the other (like a flipbook). If you see a Web site with a dancing carton character, spinning text, or pulsing globe (don't ask), you're probably looking at an animated GIF. Most Web-heads don't consider these to be real multimedia, because they're so simple. However, GIF files are small, pretty easy to create, and they're widely supported.

- **Flash.** Flash is an animation standard that's designed especially for the Web. Flash movies are *vector-based*, which means they're built out of animated shapes rather than a series of video frames. That makes them much smaller than digital video, and perfect for creating animated logos, commercials, and dazzling intro screens (see Figure 16-2). Flash animations can also be interactive, which means a Flash guru can use Flash to build slick menus and games. However, in order to create a Flash animation, you need to buy specialized software from Macromedia, which runs into the hundreds of dollars. And even if you shell out the cash, you'll find that creating the professional Flash animations you want requires the skill of a talented Flash artiste. Finally, Flash movies won't even appear at all in a Web surfer's browser unless it has the Flash plug-in installed (which most do). (A plug-in is a small program that extends the browser with extra features, like the ability to handle otherwise foreign types of files.)

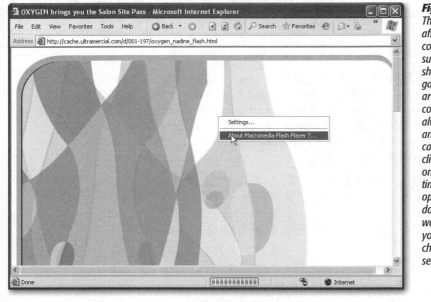

Figure 16-2:
The news and current affairs site www.salon.com makes non-subscribers sit through a short commercial before gaining access to any articles. Though the commercial varies, it's always a Flash animation—a fact you can confirm by right-clicking (Control-clicking, on a Mac) on it at any time. Instead of seeing options that let you download it (as you would with a picture), you'll see a command for changing playback settings.

It's difficult to digest all the information in this list at once. If you're still mulling over you're different choices, take a look at the scenarios in Table 16-1 to help you sort out the roles of the different multimedia types.

Table 16-1. Multimedia Scenarios

If You Want To:	Then Use:	Embedded or Linked
Play a synthesized version of your favorite pop tune in the background	MIDI files	Embedded

Table 16-1. Multimedia Scenarios (continued)

If You Want To:	Then Use:	Embedded or Linked
Play a short loop of digital audio continuously in the background	Flash (You can use the MP3 format instead, but not all browsers will support it, and the looping is less precise.)	Embedded
Let visitors download your band's newest indie recordings	MP3 files (Record your music using WAV files and then covert them into MP3 format to save space.)	Linked
Show a stock animation effect, like clapping hands, a flashing star, or a dancing bean	Animated GIFs	Embedded
Let visitors see your favorite home movie	MPEG, AVI, or MOV files (But make sure you use video editing software to dramatically reduce the file size.)	Either one (although linking is easiest).
JavaScript or Flash (JavaScript only works with Internet Explorer; Flash works with all browsers, but takes more work)	Flash (This can also be done through JavaScript, but browser support is more limited.)	Embedded
Show an animated intro screen or commercial	Flash (Animated GIFs are used sometimes, but they look chintzy.)	Embedded
Show a humorous animated story that you've created	Flash	Embedded

Tip: If you plan to create a Web site with a significant amount of digital audio and video, you'll need to reconsider your space and bandwidth requirements (see page 66). Unlike ordinary HTML and Web graphics, multimedia files can grow quite large.

Background Music

Most people like to browse the Web in peaceful silence. That means no trance-hypno-ambient background tracks, no strange disco beats, and no sudden cymbal crashes. This aversion to noise may be due to the fact that something like 98 percent of all Web surfing takes place on company time.

But if you like to startle and annoy people, or if you're absolutely convinced that your Web audience really *does* want some funky beats, keep reading to bring on the background music.

The <embed> Tag

Although the HTML standard doesn't include official support for background music, almost all browsers support the <embed> tag, which was first pioneered by Netscape browsers in the early days of the Web. You can put the <embed> tag anywhere on your page. Here's a basic example of a Web page that includes background music:

```html
<html>
<head>
  <title>Background Music</title>
</head>

<body>
<h1>Automatic, Unsolicited Music</h1>
<p>The music now blaring from your speakers is
Scarlatti's first sonata (K. 500).
I hope you didn't tell your colleagues you were working!</p>
<embed src="soundfile.mid">
</body>

</html>
```

When using the <embed> tag, you have a slew of different options that allow you to control whether or not the playback controls are shown, and whether the music starts automatically. If you use the <embed> tag without specifying any of these details (as in the previous example), your visitors will see a page like the one shown in Figure 16-3.

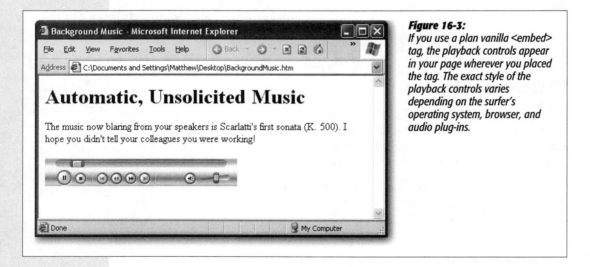

Figure 16-3:
If you use a plan vanilla <embed> tag, the playback controls appear in your page wherever you placed the tag. The exact style of the playback controls varies depending on the surfer's operating system, browser, and audio plug-ins.

Music playback isn't always this seamless. Because every browser performs this task a little differently, you can run into problems like the ones shown in Figure 16-4. The best advice is to test your Web page on as many browsers as possible.

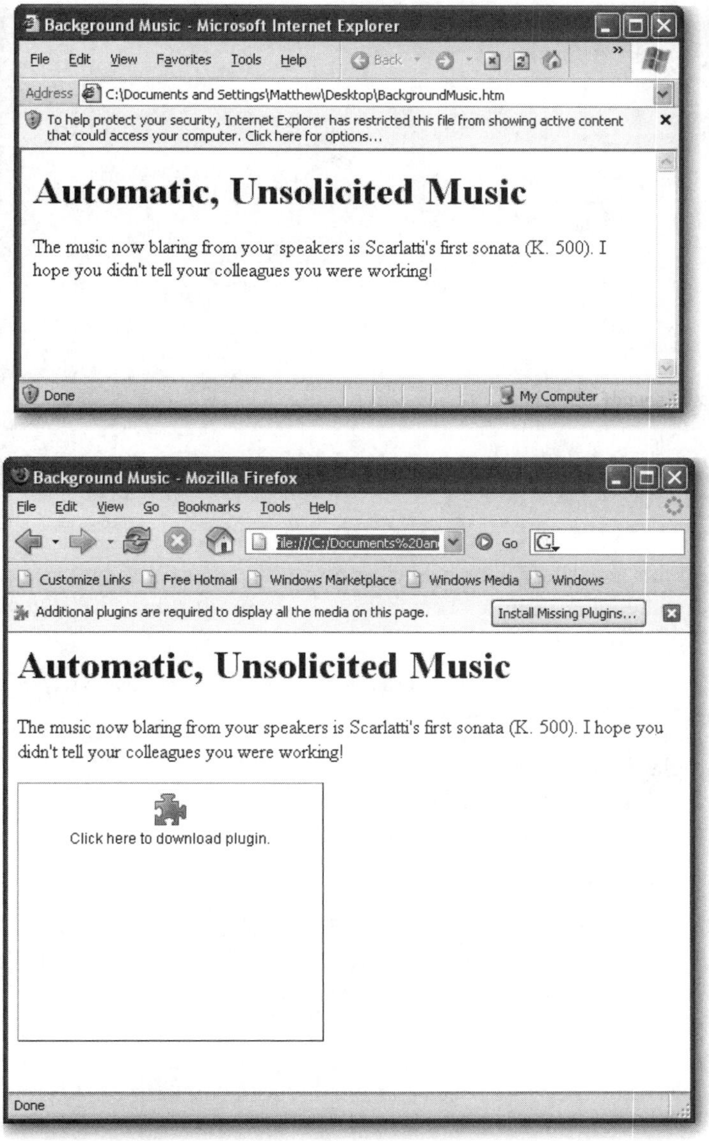

Figure 16-4:
Top: Paranoid surfers sometimes step up their security settings, which can lock out your music.

Bottom: Depending on what a Web surfer has installed and uninstalled, the browser might not find the components it needs to play your background music.

Ordinarily, the <embed> tag starts the music playing as soon as the music file is downloaded. Visitors can kill the sound with a quick click of the stop button, but if they're not expecting to hear a burst of music, it's still enough to frazzle some nerves.

A more polite option is to show the playback controls but not start the music until the visitor clicks the play button. This design is easy—just use the *autoplay* attribute:

```
<p>If you'd like some soft music to browse by, click the play button.</p>
<embed src="soundfile.mid" autoplay="false">
```

Turning off autoplay is considered very good Web etiquette. A much poorer idea is the *hidden* attribute, which lets you hide the playback controls altogether. All too often, you'll find Web pages that use <embed> tags like this:

```
<embed src="soundfile.mid" hidden="true">
```

In this example, the sound file plays automatically. Because the playback controls are hidden, the only way to stop it is to lunge for the volume control. Web sites that put their visitors through this ordeal rarely see a return visit.

Note: Unfortunately, autoplay and hidden playback controls are all too common. Some Web designers become intoxicated with their newfound multimedia abilities, and decide it's not enough to let visitors listen to music—they need to force them to do it. Resist the urge.

Quite a few more frills are available for the <embed> tag. Table 16-2 has the full list.

Table 16-2. *Attributes for the <embed> tag*

Attribute	Description
src	The URL that points to the audio file.
autoplay	A true or false value that indicates whether the audio should start playing immediately (true) or wait for the Web surfer to click the play button (false).
hidden	A true or false value that indicates whether the playback controls are visible.
loop	A true or false value that indicates whether the audio should be played once (from start to finish), or repeated endlessly. When looping audio, you'll notice a distinct pause before the audio restarts.
volume	A percentage between one percent and 100 percent (100 percent is the loudest you can get). 50 percent tends to produce the standard volume on a Windows computer; on Macs, the equivalent effect comes with a value of 75 percent. Set it to 100 percent, and you can be sure you won't get any repeat visitors. When you use the volume attribute, just supply a number (leave out the % sign).
border, width, and height	These attributes let you set the dimensions of the playback controls and the border around them, in pixels. You can achieve greater customization by applying a style sheet rule (see Chapter 6).

Other Audio Formats

As you learned earlier on, MIDI files are remarkably small because they don't store recorded sound. Instead, they contain a series of musical notes that are played using the built-in instruments on your computer's soundcard. As a result, they don't usually sound that great, and they don't sound the same on everyone's computer. MIDI files are fun, but they often make a site seem amateurish.

What if you want something a little more upmarket? You could use a WAV file, which is an uncompressed digital audio file format first introduced by Microsoft but now supported everywhere. Most computers have software for recording WAV files—for example, on Windows computers you can usually find a program called Sound Recorder lurking in the Programs → Accessories → Entertainment section of the Start menu. Mac fans may want to use the free program Audacity (*http://audacity.sourceforge.net*), which is also available in a Windows version.

You can use a WAV file with the <embed> tag in exactly the same way as a MIDI file:

```
<embed src="soundfile.wav" autoplay="false">
```

The problem with WAV files is that they're really, *really* big. In fact, they're enormous. Think of the file size of an MP3 file, and multiply it by ten. As a result, it rarely makes sense to use WAV files in a Web page. On a typical mid-speed connection, your visitor would have a long wait before the complete music file trickled down and playback started.

Note: A typical MIDI file is even smaller than a typical image. A 100 kilobyte (KB) MIDI file could handle the first movement of a detailed symphony.

Another option is to use MP3 files. This approach works great in newer browsers, but older browsers may ignore your command or launch another program.

```
<embed src="soundfile.mpg" autoplay="false">
```

If you're interested in trying this option, keep your file small and try it out on the browsers your visitors use. A 10-second MP3 file takes a modest 170 KB. As a rule of thumb, most Web authors suggest you keep your audio clips limited to 30 seconds if you use autoplay.

Sadly, the <embed> tag won't help you create those nifty looping soundtracks. Even though you can use the loop attribute, the results aren't good, because the <embed> tag doesn't loop cleanly. Instead, it pauses each time it reaches the end of your audio file. If you want a slick looping soundtrack, you'll need to use Flash, as described on page 464.

Tip: There's lots of great shareware available for recording WAV audio files and converting WAV audio files into the more compact MP3 format. Two bargain basement choices that are free to try are GoldWave (*www.goldwave.com*) and FlexiMusic (*www.fleximusic.com*). If all you want to do is convert existing WAV files to MP3 format, you can use Apple's iTunes software, available for both Windows and the Mac (*www.apple.com/itunes*). You can get the job done by right-clicking (Control-clicking) any song name and choosing, from the pop-up menu, "Convert Selection to MP3."

Sound Effects

Ever wanted to create one of those Web pages where every mouse movement unleashes a sound? For example, maybe you want a whoosh when your visitors move over a button or an audible click when they click a link.

Sadly, there's no perfect solution that will work with every browser. But there are two compromises:

- Use Flash, which lets you construct an entire page with sound effects for the most minute of actions. The problem here is that the browser needs to have the Flash plug-in installed.

- Use the <bgsound> tag (short for background sound) along with the JavaScript technique you'll learn about next. The key limitation with this technique is that it only works with Internet Explorer 5 and later—most other browsers and older versions of IE ignore your background sound effects altogether.

Several versions of this script are available online. The one you'll see in the next example (and available via the "Missing CD" page at *www.missingmanuals.com*) is one of the simplest. If you dig around on the Internet, you can find similar versions that preload their audio files, which delivers better performance. Without preloaded sounds, your visitors may experience a slight delay the first time they play an audio file because the file needs to be downloaded.

To use JavaScript-powered sounds, start by adding a <bgsound> tag in the <head> section of your Web page. The <bgsound> tag is an IE-specific version of the <embed> tag. The trick is, you won't supply any source file for this tag. Instead, you'll set the source to start playing only when something actually happens on the page:

```
<bgsound src="" id="SoundEffect" autostart="true" loop="1">
```

Notice that the <bgsound> tag is named SoundEffect. (The *id* attribute uniquely identifies a tag in your document—for a refresher, see page 252.) The last two attributes in the <bgsound> tag instruct it to play audio files immediately (*autostart="true"*) and play them exactly once (*loop="1"*).

The next step is to add the script with the PlaySound( ) function to the <head> portion of your page. The PlaySound( ) function has one role—it finds the <bgsound> tag and points it to the music file you want to play:

```
<script type="text/javascript">
function PlaySound(soundfile) {
  if (document.all && document.getElementById)
  {
    document.getElementById("SoundEffect").src=soundfile
  }
}
</script>
```

In other words, it's up to you call the PlaySound( ) function and supply a sound file name. The PlaySound( ) function then adjusts the <bgsound> tag by setting its *src* attribute, and the background sound plays immediately.

Remember, functions just hang around idly until you call them. Your Web page won't make a beep until a JavaScript event occurs and triggers the PlaySound( ) function. Here's how you can use the PlaySound( ) function to play a sound named *soundeffect.wav* when a visitor moves her mouse pointer over a link:

```
<a href="http://www.somesite.com"
onMouseOver="PlaySound('ding.wav')">Click Me</a>
```

The only problem here is that if you want to add sound effects like this to several links, you need to hook up every single link *separately,* even if they all use the same audio file. But don't despair. There's a solution courtesy of *www.dynamicdrive. com.* A second JavaScript function, named BindSound( ), lets you add a sound effect to all the tags of a certain type in a certain container.

For example, if you want to add a sound effect to a group of links, pop them into a <div> tag, like this:

```
<div>
  <a href="http://www.somewhere.com">Click Me</a>
```

```
<a href="http://www.somewhere.com">Click Me</a>
...
</div>
```

Now, instead of adding the onMouseOver attribute to every <a> tag, you can attach it to the <div> container using the BindSound( ) function. The BindSound( ) function takes three arguments—the type of tag that you want to hook up, the sound effect file name, and the container that contains the tags you want to hook up. Here's an example:

```
<div onMouseOver="BindSound('a', ding.wav', this)">
  <a href="http://www.somewhere.com">Click Me</a>
  <a href="http://www.somewhere.com">Click Me</a>
  ...
</div>
```

Notice that for the first argument, it's important to leave out the angle brackets (for example, use "a" to hook up every <a> anchor tag). For the third argument, you can always use the keyword *this*, which refers to the current tag (in this case, the <div> container). The end result of this example is that every anchor in the <div> section is linked to the *ding.wav* audio file.

You can use this trick to put sounds on your entire page—just add the onMouseOver attribute to the <body> tag that contains the whole Web page.

You can get the full code with the BindSound( ) function from the "Missing CD" page for this chapter at *www.missingmanuals.com*.

Tip: Looking for some free sound effects to use with this script? Try out *www.grsites.com/sounds* and *www.freeaudioclips.com*.

Video Clips

Video clips haven't quite taken off, but with the recent wave of digital cameras that shoot movies, video cell phones, and other video gadgets, interest is growing. Family members, tourists, and adventurers all regularly keep in touch by posting video clips, and the blogging community (see Chapter 17) is getting excited, too. Bloggers are in the midst of coining a new word for Web sites that feature regular video postings. (Current candidates include "videoblogs," "vidblogs," "vogs," and "vlogs;" check out *http://videoblogging-universe.com* for some neat samples.)

Surprisingly, you can pop a video into your Web page using the exact same techniques you used with digital audio. That means you can link to a video so that it opens up in another browser window:

```
Click to download or open my home movie
<a href="ouch.mpg">Ouch, That Hurts</a>.
```

Or, you can use the <embed> tag to place a video window right inside your Web page.

```
<embed src="ouch.mpg" autoplay="false">
```

If you use the <embed> tag, make sure you turn *off* the autoplay behavior. Otherwise, surfers with feeble dial-up connections will see their Web pages slow to a crawl while your video downloads.

The video window shows up wherever you place the <embed> tag (see Figure 16-5).

Figure 16-5:
You can add a video window to your Web pages almost as easily as adding basic audio playback controls. If you don't specify a fixed size, the video window automatically adjusts to the dimensions of your video.

If this seems too easy to be true, that's because it is. There are two stumbling blocks that you'll encounter when using video in a Web page. The first challenge is getting the video in the first place. Not just any video will work—you need a highly compressed format that won't choke your visitors' browsers.

The second problem is the fact that it takes a while to download a video file. When you use the <embed> tag, your video won't start playing until it's completely downloaded. Internet techies found a way around this unbearable wait, by inventing *streaming video* (see page 460). Their solution works great, but it requires special software on the Web server, which most budget Web hosting companies won't provide.

Note: Modern media players can perform streaming on the Web browser's computer with certain file types. For example, both QuickTime Player (with .MOV files) and Windows Media Player (with .ASF files) can start playing audio before it's completely downloaded. This technique is called a *progressive download*, and it doesn't require special Web server software.

Creating Your Own Movies

Putting personal video on a Web site is a task meant for ambitious multimedia mavens. The key stumbling block is the sheer size of your files when you start dealing with digital video.

For example, consider a popular MiniDV camcorder, which stores an hour of video on a single tape. You can download that video to your computer—but only if you have a spare 13 gigabytes handy! The ugly truth is that every second of raw, high-quality video chews through a sizeable 3.5 megabytes of space. Not only is that enough to take a bite out of any Web master's Web space and bandwidth allocation, it's too big for even the speediest surfers to download.

What can you do to make a respectable Web video? You can always use someone else's Web-ready video (or just pay a video editing company lots of money to trim yours down to Web proportions). Assuming that's not what you want, you have two choices.

- **Record at a lower quality.** In some cases, you may have the option to record your video using lower quality settings. Some video cameras allow you to record lower-quality video just for the purpose of putting it on a Web site. Usually, this video gets stored on a memory card instead of a tape. Cell phones, tiny computer spy cams, and digital cameras all create low-quality movies, letting you dodge the conversion headaches and enable you to send your video straight to your Web site. In fact, some video fans find the best solution is to have two types of recording devices—one for ordinary home movies and one for lower-quality Web movies.

- **Lower the quality afterwards.** More commonly, you'll need to start with your high-quality video and go through a long process of *re-encoding* to convert it to a size that's more suitable for the Web. In order to do this, you'll need a video editing program. Video cameras generally include some sort of tool to help you out, although you may want to pony up for more powerful software. Two popular choices are iMovie (for the Mac) and Windows Movie Maker (which is included with Windows XP).

Note: For full details on how to operate Windows Movie Maker, check out *Windows XP Home Edition: The Missing Manual.* If you're using iMovie, take a look at *iMovie HD & iDVD: The Missing Manual.* You'll also find some great articles on Web video preparation at *www.internetvideomag.com.*

Here are the basic steps you need to follow to get your video ready for the Web:

1. **First, film your movie.**

   Video gurus are careful to film their video in a way that makes it easier to compress and introduces less distortion. For example, if you keep camera movements smooth and gradual, and don't film complex patterns, your compressed video will be smaller and look better.

2. **Fire up the video capture program that was included with your video camera. Use this program to download your movie to your computer's hard drive.**

   Typically, this step involves connecting your camera to your computer using a *FireWire* cable. (USB cables need not apply—they're just not fast enough to keep up with huge chunks of raw video data.)

3. **Now you need to use a video editing program to snip out the part you're interested in posting to your site.**

   Depending on the program you're using, you might use this moment to add music or special effects.

4. **Next, you need to re-encode just that piece of video in a highly compressed format. If all the format information in your program sounds like gobbledygook, look for an option that clearly says "Web video" when you save your clip.**

   Technically, you're making three choices in this step—the video format (the algorithm used to encode the video), the dimensions of the playback window (Web pages usually fall somewhere between 176 x 144 to 320 x 240 pixels), and the quality (as with JPEGs, the greater the compression, the more detail you lose in the picture).

Tip: There are a wide range of competing Web video formats, but the most common is MPEG-4. Just to make life more interesting, MPEG-4 has all kinds of quality settings, so you can use it to create DVD-quality movies or Web-friendly video clips. If in doubt, double check the final file size of the movie. If you can get 60 seconds of video into a file that's one megabyte on your hard drive, you're doing well.

Re-encoding video is a time-consuming operation—even the speediest computer may take five times as long as the length of the original clip to re-encode the video. The good news is that at the end of the process, you'll have a more manageable Web-ready video file—say, two megabytes for a full 90-second clip.

Tip: Need more space for your video files? Even Web-sized videos can consume more Web server space and bandwidth than you have. Consider using a free video hosting service, which lets you put your videos on another server. The disadvantage is that if that Web server is slow or buggy, your videos won't work as well. There's a good list of options at *www.internetvideomag.com/ProductReviews/Services/ FreeVideoHosting102.htm.*

Streaming Media

Streaming video is designed to take the pain out of video playback on the Web. The key idea is that instead of sending a video file in one large piece, the Web server sends small chunks to the browser as they're needed. Modern computers, which are quite adept at doing two things at once, simultaneously play the current chunk while requesting the next one. The only drawback is that streaming video can sometimes bog down a bit (especially if the viewer's got a pokey Internet connection); in that case, the video will pause briefly until the next chunk downloads.

On the whole, streaming video is much more satisfying than downloading the whole enchilada first. Some Web mavens also like streaming video because it makes it more difficult (although not impossible) for the viewer to save a copy of the video on their own computer.

In order to use streaming video, the browser and the Web server need to enter into a more detailed conversation than usual. Rather than the standard "Give me this file" instruction, a browser needs to ask, "Can you give me a piece of that data?" and, when appropriate, "I'm ready for some more." This requires special software on the Web server. You can ask your Web hosting company if they provide this feature. If they don't (or you're unwilling to pay the extra price), you do have another option. Recently, free streaming servers have started to crop up on the Web. They let you store your video on their Web servers. And because they have the streaming software, you can stream the video through your Web pages. Right now these services are still pretty unreliable, but check out *www.pixparty.com* if you're interested in giving it a whirl.

Animations

Web animations are a simpler, more flexible alternative to video. They let you show a series of changing pictures, floating text, and cartoon-like characters. In the hands of a talented Web artiste, animations can become complete, miniature movies.

Animations are much more common on the Web than video for two reasons. First, they're dramatically smaller, and therefore much more practical. Second, a Web designer can build an animation with nothing more than a mouse and some specialized software. No camera or lengthy conversion process is required.

In this section, you'll take a quick look at two types of animation—animated GIFs and Flash.

Animated GIFs

Animation is one of the features built into the GIF standard (page 186). Animated GIFs are really a poor man's form of animation. They don't let you design complex animations like Flash, they aren't interactive, and they certainly don't let you show real video like the MPEG format. An animated GIF is really just a series of separate GIFs that are shown one after the other, with a specified delay in between each frame. Animated GIFs are short and usually loop, which means they restart their animation when they reach the last frame. Figure 16-6 shows how an animated GIF works.

Figure 16-6:
This simple animated GIF consists of three static images, which are shown one after the other (with a brief delay after each frame) to create the illusion of a cartoon character banging a drum. It's taken from the online Microsoft Office clip art collection.

Note: Just as with any other GIF, animated GIFs are limited to a paltry 256 colors. There's no such thing as animated JPEGs.

You can build animated GIFs using a shareware tool (search on *www.zdnet.com* to find candidates), or a professional tool like Macromedia Fireworks. However, animated GIFs aren't generating much interest these days, and all the cool people have moved on to Flash.

If you're looking for some free animated GIFs, you'll find ancient sites strewn across the Web. Check out *www.gifanimations.com*, *www.webdeveloper.com/ animations*, and *www.animatedgif.net* to get started. Microsoft Office also has animated GIFs in its copious clip art library.

Flash Animations

A Flash animation can be anything from a simple animated-GIF replacement to an alternate way to build an entire Web site. That's because Flash animations have several unique characteristics.

The good

First, Flash animations are stored as a series of instructions. So instead of, say, saving three dozen pictures of a circle in slightly different positions to simulate a ball in flight (like you would with an animated GIF), you simply instruct Flash to "move this shape from here to there, at this speed." That makes complex animations much easier to create and edit.

Flash animations also can include video and compressed audio. That makes them perfect for creating talking characters or background music.

Finally, Flash uses programming code. That means you can program in all kinds of devious logic, like making shapes move and sounds play when the Web surfer moves the mouse or clicks a portion of the animation. This ability brings all the tricks of client-side programming (Chapter 14) together with all the tools of graphic design to make really slick animations. Best of all, your Web server doesn't need any special software because the Flash browser plug-in does it all.

Note: To get a sense of what's possible with Flash, check out the gorgeous graphics in the free Flash games at *www.ferryhalim.com/orisinal*, or take on the detailed negotiation simulations at *www.zapdramatic.com*, which pit you against a host of unsavory characters.

The bad

The disadvantage to Flash is that it really isn't HTML. In fact, Flash animations are really miniature programs that Web visitors download to their computers, and then run using a browser plug-in. (You can download the plug-in at *www.macromedia.com/go/getflashplayer*.)

For example, imagine you want to create a part of your Web site with Flash. To do this, you create a Flash file (a .swf file) using the Flash editing software. Then, you insert that file into your Web pages using an <embed> or <object> tag. When the browser reads the page, it downloads your Flash file, and uses a browser plug-in in to display the animation.

One significant side effect to using Flash: The content you put inside your Flash animations can't be read by a search engine. The quirks don't end there. Flash animations also require that pesky browser plug-in. By now, most avid Web surfers have it (and it is supported on virtually all browsers and computer platforms). However, if someone's stubbornly decided not to download the Flash player, they won't see any Flash content—or even a substitute.

Note: Sometimes, developers use Flash to create animated buttons. Dreamweaver even has a built-in feature for just this purpose. But it's a dangerous game to play, because surfers without the Flash plug-in will be locked out of your buttons (and by extension, the rest of your Web site) altogether.

Finally, with great power comes great responsibility—or at least, enough complexity to send you running for the hills. To really use the animation and programming muscle in Flash, you'll need to plunk down about $400 for this premier Web design tool, and get ready to learn a whole lot more. Everything you've learned so far (HTML, styles, and so on), won't help you much in the world of Flash. Even once you have the right software, you'll find it takes more than a modicum of artistic skill to create a professional Flash animation.

As a result, the rest of this chapter concentrates on guiding you to some free Flash animations. If you'd like to learn more and develop your inner animator, check out the Web tutorials at *www.flashkit.com/tutorials* and *www.w3schools.com/flash*, or pick up a dedicated book on the subject.

Free Flash animations

The best things in Flash aren't free, but you can dig up some interesting Flash files by searching on Google. Figure 16-7 shows a free Flash animation generator, good for creating introduction page greetings; you'll find the tool at *www.freeflashintros.com*.

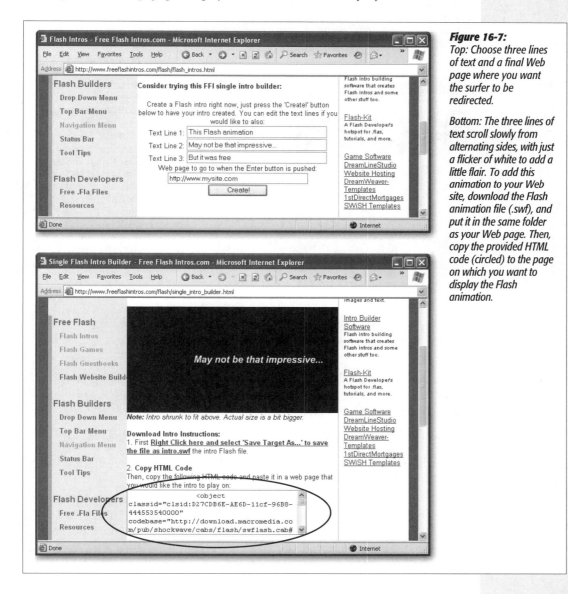

Figure 16-7:
Top: Choose three lines of text and a final Web page where you want the surfer to be redirected.

Bottom: The three lines of text scroll slowly from alternating sides, with just a flicker of white to add a little flair. To add this animation to your Web site, download the Flash animation file (.swf), and put it in the same folder as your Web page. Then, copy the provided HTML code (circled) to the page on which you want to display the Flash animation.

If you absolutely must have background music, Flash is probably the best way to go. The trick is to use an invisible (audio-only) Flash animation. Flash compresses audio even more snugly than the MP3 format, and it lets you seamlessly loop audio (for non-stop playing). Many Web sites sell audio loops; you can download from a large catalog of free choices at *www.flashkit.com/loops* (see Figure 16-8). Altogether, this site features nearly 10,000 loops that range from ambient to urban.

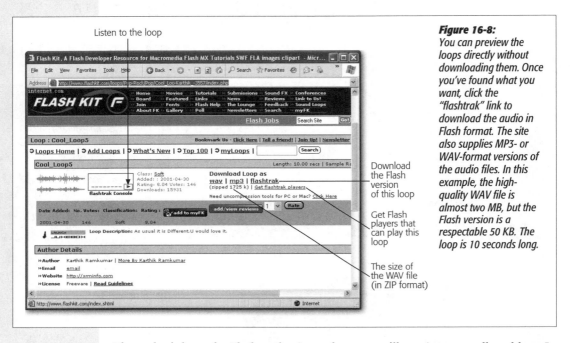

Figure 16-8:
You can preview the loops directly without downloading them. Once you've found what you want, click the "flashtrak" link to download the audio in Flash format. The site also supplies MP3- or WAV-format versions of the audio files. In this example, the high-quality WAV file is almost two MB, but the Flash version is a respectable 50 KB. The loop is 10 seconds long.

If you don't have the Flash authoring software, you'll run into a small problem. In order to get your Web page ready to play a background audio track using Flash, you actually need two things:

- The file that contains the actual audio for the loop. This is a .swf file.

- A flashtrak player. This is a program (designed in Flash and a .swf itself), that plays the audio file.

So far, you have the audio file, but not the player. But thanks to the Flash Kit site, it's not hard to find one. Just look for the "Get flashtrak players" link. You'll find a range of jukebox-style controls, each of which is actually a Flash program. Most of these show snazzy effects while the music's playing (like pulsing lines or expanding circles).

Note: When you download the flashtrak player, you may end up with more files than you actually need. For example, you don't need any files that end with ".fla" (these are Flash files that you edit in the Flash software). You can delete these files. Also, when you download a player, you'll probably find yourself with a pile of extra song files. Delete the ones you don't want, or your player will cycle through them all.

Once you've downloaded the two pieces you need, you're ready to play your audio loop in a Web page. A simple <embed> tag that points to the player file will take care of things:

```
<embed src="StarPlayerMultiTrackWithAutoStart.swf">
```

Figure 16-9 shows what you'll see when you run the page that contains this tag.

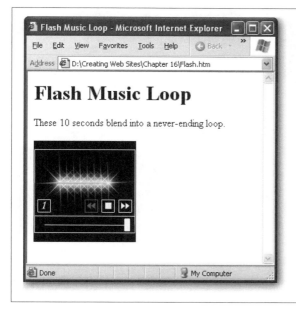

Figure 16-9:
Here's the Flash-based audio controls in action, complete with playback buttons and soothing graphics. The best way to try out this example is to download the sample content for this chapter, available from the "Missing CD" page at www.missingmanuals.com.

Some HTML editors also include features that allow you to quickly insert Flash animations. For example, FrontPage provides an Insert → Picture → "Movie in Flash Format" command that inserts the <embed> tag you need. If you look at the HTML FrontPage generates, you'll find it's actually a fair bit more complicated than the example shown above. (For example, FrontPage also inserts an <object> tag, which is recommended for wide-ranging browser compatibility, but rarely needed.)

Part Five: Blogs

5

Chapter 17: Blogs

Blogs

Throughout this book, you've learned how to craft a personalized Web site using the basic ingredients: HTML, style sheets, and JavaScript. Armed with this know-how, you can build a fairly impressive site.

However, *maintaining* a Web site requires a significant investment of your time. You need to regularly review what you have, add fresh material, keep site navigation menus up to date, check old links, and periodically update your pages to incorporate the latest Web design trends. For some people, this constant grooming is fun—after all, you get to tweak and fiddle with the most minute details until you get everything exactly the way you want it. But not everyone's that ambitious. Some people prefer to spend less time managing their Web site, and more time just creating content.

In this chapter, you'll learn about *blogs*, a self-publishing format that can help you avoid the headaches of Web site management. Blogs are a fresh, straightforward, and slightly chaotic way to communicate on the Web. To maintain a blog, you publish short entries whenever the impulse hits. Your blog posts are collected, organized (chronologically), and presented in HTML pages by high-powered blogging software. That means if you don't want to fuss with the fine details of Web site management, you don't need to. All you need to worry about is sending in the postings—and with some blogging software, that's as easy as firing off an email.

In this chapter, you'll see how to create your own blog with Blogger, one of the leading free services.

Understanding Blogs

The word "blog" is a nerdy abbreviation of *Web log*, which makes sense because blogs are made up of regular, dated blurbs—sort of like a cross between a diary entry and a newsgroup postings. "Blog" is also a verb, as in "I just ate at a terrible restaurant; when I get home I'm going to blog about it." Figure 17-1 dissects the anatomy of a basic blog.

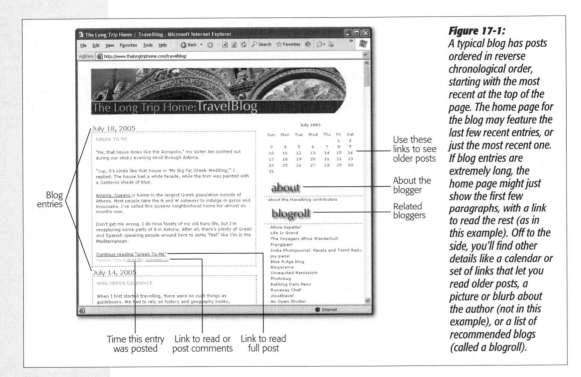

Figure 17-1:
A typical blog has posts ordered in reverse chronological order, starting with the most recent at the top of the page. The home page for the blog may feature the last few recent entries, or just the most recent one. If blog entries are extremely long, the home page might just show the first few paragraphs, with a link to read the rest (as in this example). Off to the side, you'll find other details like a calendar or set of links that let you read older posts, a picture or blurb about the author (not in this example), or a list of recommended blogs (called a blogroll).

Although blogs simplify Web posting, it's unfair to say that blogs are just a simplified way to work the Web. Rather, blogs are better understood as a wholly different form of online communication. And although there's no definitive test to decide what is and what isn't a real blog, there are several characteristics that most blogs share:

- **Blogs are personal.** There are topic-based blogs, work-based blogs, and many more blogs filled with random, offbeat musings. However, blogs always emphasize the author's point of view. There's rarely any attempt to be objective—instead, blogs contain unapologetically idiosyncratic *opinions*. Blogs are always written in the first person.

- **Blogs are organized chronologically.** When you design a Web site, you spend a great deal of time deciding how to best organize the material. Ideally, you need a menu or set of links that can guide the visitor through an assortment of different topics. Blogs take a radically different approach. They don't have any organization other than a loose, chronological ordering of postings. Anything else would just slow down restless bloggers.

- **Blogs are updated regularly.** Blogs emphasize fast, free communication rather than painstakingly crafted Web design. Bloggers are known to add content obsessively (sometimes as often as hourly). Because blog entries are dated, it's glaringly obvious if you aren't keeping your blog up to date. If you can't commit to blogging regularly, don't start a blog—just set up a simple Web page instead.

- **Blogs are flexible.** There's a bit of blog wisdom that says no thought's too small for a blog. And it's true—whether you want to write a detailed discussion about the viability of peanut-butter Oreos or a three-sentence summary of an uneventful day, a blog post works equally well.

- **Blogs create a broader conversation.** Blogs form communities more readily than Web sites. Not only are blogs more conversational in nature, they also support comments and links that can tie different blogs together into a conversation. If an interesting item is posted in one blog, a legion of fellow bloggers often add links to it within hours. Scandalous blog gossip is known to rocket right around the globe in a startlingly short period of time.

Note: When a large amount of activity, information, and opinion erupts around a particular subject or controversy in the *blogosphere*, it's sometimes called a *blogstorm,* or blog swarm. You can find more blogtastic jargon at *http://en.wikipedia.org/wiki/Weblog*.

The actual content of a blog isn't fixed—it can range widely, from political commentary to personal travelogues. There are hundreds of thousands of blogs online today. In fact, the Blogger service alone hosts several million blogs, of which several thousand are considered active blogs.

The best way to get a feeling for blogdom is to check out some popular examples. To see an example of widely read political commentary, surf over to arch-conservative Andrew Sullivan's blog at *www.andrewsullivan.com*. Or check out the insights of Salam Pax, the Baghdad blogger (now a *Guardian* columnist), who captivated the media world with a frank, gripping account of life in war-torn Baghdad at *http://dear_raed.blogspot.com*. For somewhat lighter fare, visit the curiously popular *www.wilwheaton.net*, a blog by Wil Wheaton, the actor who played the nerdy upstart Wesley Crusher of *Star Trek* fame. For expertise and observations from security guru Bruce Schneier, surf to *www.schneier.com/blog*. The list goes on—from journalists to hobbyists to sports heroes and porn stars, it seems almost everyone's willing to psychoanalyze their life or chat about water-cooler topics with an audience of millions via a blog.

Tip: Blogs are a specialized niche that can't compete with a lot of the other types of sites you've seen. For example, you can't effectively sell a line of clothes for dogs on a blog. However, many people start blogs *in addition* to ordinary Web sites. This is a great combination. Visitors love blogs because they crave a glimpse behind the scenes. They're also sure to visit again and again if they can count on a regularly updated blog to offer a steady stream of news, gossip, and insights.

Syndication

One of neatest features about blogs is *syndication*. Syndication is a feature that allows avid blog readers to monitor their favorite blogs using a specialized program (called a *feed reader*, or *news aggregator*). You fire up your feed reader, and enter links to all your favorite blogs. The feed reader periodically checks these blogs for new postings, and lets you know when they show up. Quite simply, a feed reader lets you stay up to date with all your friends in the blogiverse, without forcing you to surf back to every blog 94 times a day to check if anything's new. Feed readers are the only practical option if you need to follow lots of blogs regularly.

Note: Feed readers are a little like email programs, which, of course, let you regularly check to see if you have new messages from any of your friends. This is a lot more efficient than contacting them each individually and asking if they have anything new to say. Similarly, you can use a feed reader program whenever you want to check up on blog activity. If there's nothing new, you find out in an instant.

Although most blogs work with feed readers, some don't. In order to work with a feed reader, a blog needs to provide a *feed* (Figure 17-2). A feed contains recent blog postings in a computer-friendly format. Feed readers know to interpret feeds to get important information like the title, description, and date. Feed readers also use feeds to determine whether or not there are any new postings. Technically, feeds are in an XML-based format, because XML is a data standard that can be interpreted on any computer platform.

If you want to try using a feed reader, you've got lots of choices:

- Online feed readers require a subscription, but you don't need to install anything. You read the feed right inside a Web browser window. Popular examples include *www.bloglines.com*, *www.newsisfree.com*, and *www.newsgator.com*.

- Desktop feed readers run on your computer; you'll need to find a version that runs on your operating system. You can track down many desktop feed readers on popular shareware sites like *www.zdnet.com*. If you're using a Windows computer, you can purchase the excellent FeedDemon (see Figure 17-3) for a nominal fee. Mac fans might like the highly-touted NetNewsWire (which sells for around $25 at *http://ranchero.com/netnewswire*).

- Browsers are increasingly adding features like feed reading. If you're using Firefox, you can use a feature called *live bookmarks* (see Figure 17-4) or you can download a more powerful feed reader plugin. The next version of Internet Explorer promises new feed-reading features, and the latest version of Apple's Safari browser has a feed reader built in.

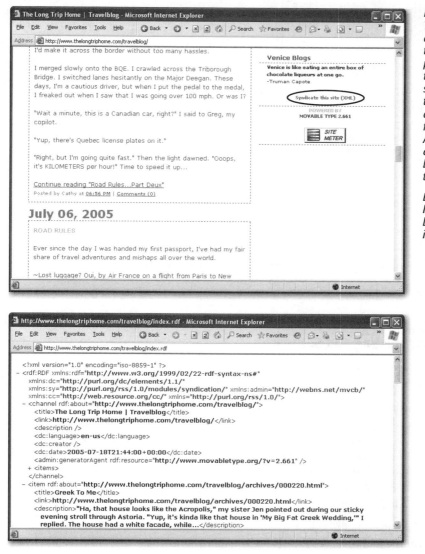

Figure 17-2:
Top: Most blogs will have a link somewhere on their home pages that provides a feed. Look for the word feed or syndication. Sometimes, the link includes the actual name of the feed format, like RDF, RSS, or Atom (all of which are designed with XML), so be on the lookout for these words too.

Bottom: The feed won't look like much to you, but your feed reader can interpret it.

Tip: For an article that describes different feed readers, see *http://weblogs.about.com/od/aggregators.*

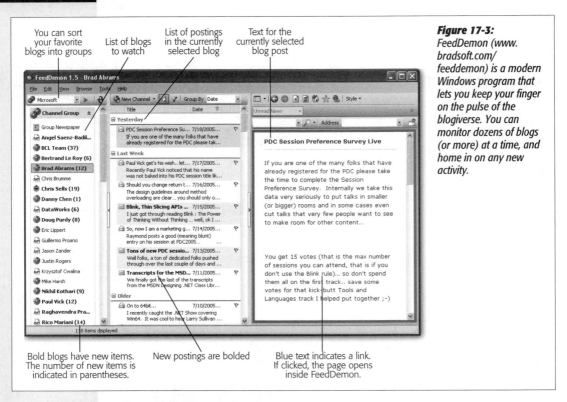

You can sort your favorite blogs into groups

List of blogs to watch

List of postings in the currently selected blog

Text for the currently selected blog post

Figure 17-3:
FeedDemon (www. bradsoft.com/ feeddemon) is a modern Windows program that lets you keep your finger on the pulse of the blogiverse. You can monitor dozens of blogs (or more) at a time, and home in on any new activity.

Bold blogs have new items. The number of new items is indicated in parentheses.

New postings are bolded

Blue text indicates a link. If clicked, the page opens inside FeedDemon.

Blog Hosting and Software

Before you can set up a blog, you need to understand the different kind of blog-making options out there. There are really three types of blogs:

- **Hosted blogs.** With a hosted blog, you simply sign up with a blog provider and start blogging. Adding a blog entry is as simple as just filling out a form in your Web browser. You never need to hassle with a separate program or figure out how to upload content files, because the blog provider stores all the HTML files for your blog on its Web servers. You don't even need to have a Web site. Hosted blogs are the best bet for new bloggers. They're completely painless and remarkably flexible.

  Examples of hosted blog companies include MSN Spaces (*http://spaces.msn. com*), Radio UserLand (*http://radio.userland.com*), TypePad (*www.typepad. com*), Live Journal (*www.livejournal.com*), and Xanga (*www.xanga.com*).

- **Self-hosted blogs.** If you're a hardcore high-tech geek and you have a Web server in the basement, you might be interested in hosting a blog entirely on your own. In order to do this, you need to find some blog hosting software that works on your Web server platform, install it on your Web server, and configure everything correctly. This approach gives you unlimited flexibility (and it may get you better performance). However, it probably isn't for you unless you enjoy do-it-yourself challenges like making your laptop talk to your coffee maker.

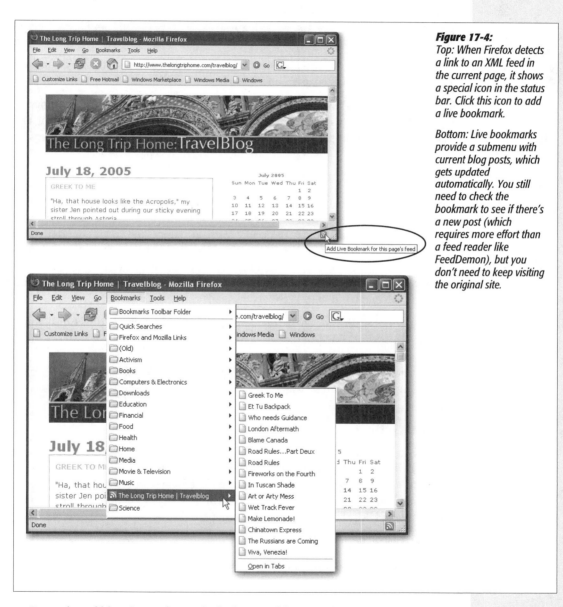

Figure 17-4:
Top: When Firefox detects a link to an XML feed in the current page, it shows a special icon in the status bar. Click this icon to add a live bookmark.

Bottom: Live bookmarks provide a submenu with current blog posts, which gets updated automatically. You still need to check the bookmark to see if there's a new post (which requires more effort than a feed reader like FeedDemon), but you don't need to keep visiting the original site.

Examples of blogging software include Movable Type (*www.movabletype.org*), Blosxsom (*www.blosxom.com*), and WordPress (*http://wordpress.org*).

- **Remote weblog systems.** This category is really a hybrid between hosted blogs and do-it-yourself blog hosting software. The basic idea is that you use a blogging system that's hosted by a blog provider, and you have the *option* to choose where you want to store the final blog files. You can choose to host them with the blog provider (in which case, this option is the same as an ordinary hosted blog), or you can ask the blogging system to transmit any updates to your own Web server. This model gives you the ease of hosted blogs along with some extra features (like the ability to place your blog on a part of your Web site).

  Examples in this category include Blogger (*www.blogger.com*), the blog software demonstrated in this chapter, and WebCrimson (*www.webcrimson.com*).

In this chapter, you'll spend your time using one blogging tool, called Blogger. Blogger is simple to use yet powerful, which makes it the best candidate for all-around blogging champ.

Getting Started with Blogger

Blogger is the most commonly used blogging tool. It provides the easiest way to start a blog, and is chock-full of nifty blog management tools. Once upon a time, Blogger was offered in both a basic free version (supported by ads) and a more full-featured premium version, which required a small yearly contribution. In early 2003, that all changed when Google bought Blogger. Now, all of Blogger's features are part of the free package and blogs are much more reliable, thanks to Google's stacks of cash and rock-solid Web servers.

Creating a blog with Blogger is ridiculously easy. In the following sections, you'll learn how to create a blog, add posts, and take charge of a few neat features.

Tip: You can also check out the official catalog of Blogger help at *http://help.blogger.com* and the discussion board *www.bloggerforum.com*, where bloggers share tips, ask questions, and vent their frustrations.

Creating a Blog

Before you create your blog, it's a good idea to assess your goals, and decide exactly what type of content you plan to showcase in your blog. Will it contain random thoughts, a chronicle of daily life, or more targeted, topic-specific posts? Once you know how you want to position your blog, you'll be able to choose a snappy name and a suitable URL. Then, start with these steps:

1. **Surf to** *www.blogger.com.*

   This is the home page for the Blogger service.

2. Click the "Create a Blog" button.

Creating a blog is a three-step process. The first step is creating an account (see Figure 17-5).

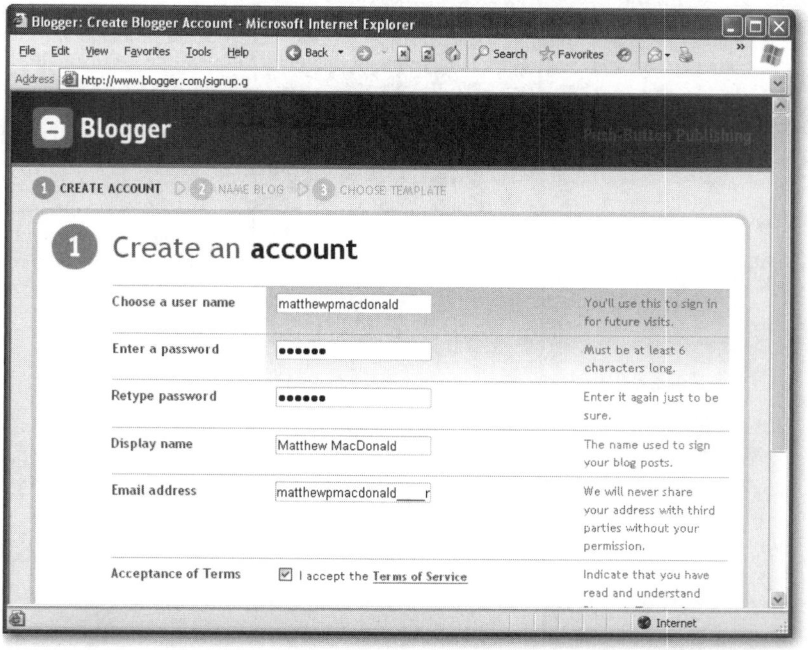

Figure 17-5:
In the first step, you create your account.

3. **Type in your account information, which consists of a user name, a password, and an email address. You also need to turn on the checkbox at the bottom of the page to officially accept the Blogger rules.**

If you're still trying to think of a good user name, try the first part of your email address. For example, if your email address is lemur_tamer01@hotmail.com, lemur_tamer01 probably makes a good user name. If your user name is already taken, you'll be asked to enter a new one. Don't worry about anonymity—you can choose a different display name for your blog, and other people never need to know your user name.

Tip: You only need to create an account once. However, you can create multiple blogs for the same account.

4. Click Continue to move to the next step.

The second step is where you actually create the blog (see Figure 17-6).

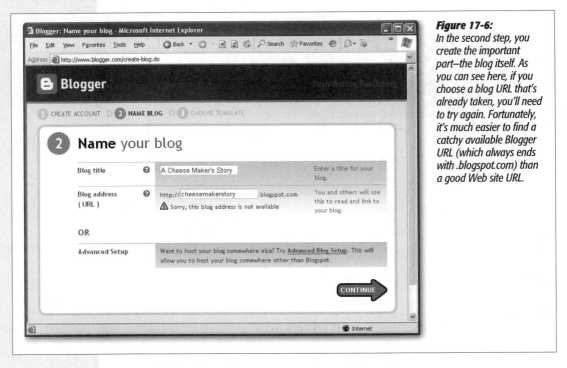

Figure 17-6:
In the second step, you create the important part—the blog itself. As you can see here, if you choose a blog URL that's already taken, you'll need to try again. Fortunately, it's much easier to find a catchy available Blogger URL (which always ends with .blogspot.com) than a good Web site URL.

5. Supply the title and URL you want your blog to have.

A blog title is just like a Web page title—it's the descriptive bit of text that appears in the browser title bar.

The URL is the really important part, because you don't want to change this later on (or you risk losing your readers). It's the address that eager Web surfers will use to find your blog. Blogger is surprisingly generous with URLs—unlike free Web hosting providers, Blogger lets you have just about any URL, so long as it ends with *.blogspot.com*. Although other bloggers will already have taken some of the most obvious names, it's still reasonably easy to create short-and-sweet blog names like *http://secretideas.blogspot.com* or *http://richwildman. blogspot.com*.

If you really *must* have your own completely customized domain name, you have two choices. You can use the domain-forwarding technique described in Chapter 3 (page 60) to forward visitors from your domain to the URL for your blog. Or, you can use a more seamless approach, and tell Blogger you'll host your blog on another Web server (page 496).

Note: Just under the section where you choose your URL is an option that lets you use advanced setup to host your blog on another Web server. You don't need to set this up right away. Instead, you can choose ordinary hosting to start with, and change your hosting settings later on to move your blog to another Web server (as described on page 496).

6. **Click Continue to move to the next step.**

   In the third step, you choose a template for your blog (see Figure 17-7).

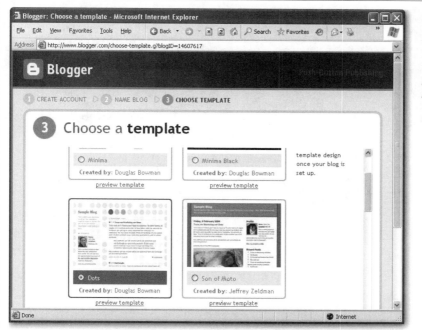

Figure 17-7:
Blogger templates just may qualify for coolest feature of the year. You choose one of the slick presets, and your blog postings are formatted with the template's color, graphics, and layout.

7. **Scroll down through a list of templates, and select the one you want to use.**

   Click the "preview template" link to get a sneak preview of what it looks like. Don't worry too much about your decision—you can choose a different template at any time later on.

8. **Click Continue to finalize your blog.**

   You see a page with a "Creating your blog" message for a few seconds, followed by a confirmation message.

9. **Click Start Posting to carry on to create your first blog post.**

   You can return to manage your blog at any time by surfing to *www.blogger.com*. Or, continue with the next step to create your first blog entry.

10. **Enter the title for your entry, and then type the content of your post into the large text box, which acts like a miniature word processor (see Figure 17-8).**

Don't worry about all the fancy frills in the editing window just yet—you'll learn all about that in the next section.

Note: A blog entry can be as long or short as you want. Some people blog lengthy stories, while others blog one- or two-sentence posts that simply provide a link to an interesting news item (or, more commonly, a post from another blogger).

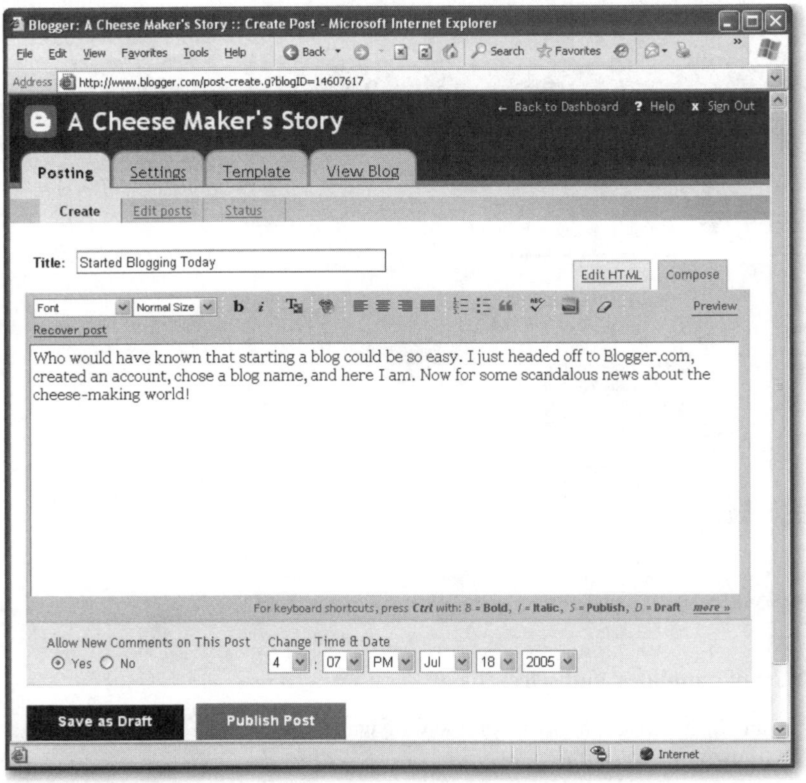

Figure 17-8:
Blogger uses a tabbed page layout that's organized around four tasks—posting, changing settings, choosing a template, and viewing your blog. When you create a post, you'll use the Posting tab, which provides three links—one for creating a new post, one for editing an existing post, and one for checking the status of your last blog posting.

11. **Choose whether you want to allow or prevent comments at the bottom of the page. Also, verify that the indicated date is correct (and if it isn't, change it).**

You'll learn more about comments later.

The date is probably incorrect, because you haven't yet set the time zone for your blog. You'll learn how to update this later on page 485, but for now, change the date by hand so that readers know when you created the entry. (The date appears at the bottom of each blog post.)

12. **Click Publish Post to create the blog entry.**

> You see a status page informing you that your blog entry is being published. A few seconds later, you'll get a confirmation informing you that your new entry is online.

> If you want to take some time to think over your blog post, click Save Draft instead. That way, the text you've entered so far will be waiting for you the next time you return to your blog.

Now's a great time to check out what your post looks like. You can click the View Blog tab to show your blog in a new window, or just type your blog URL into a browser window by hand. Figure 17-9 shows what you'll see.

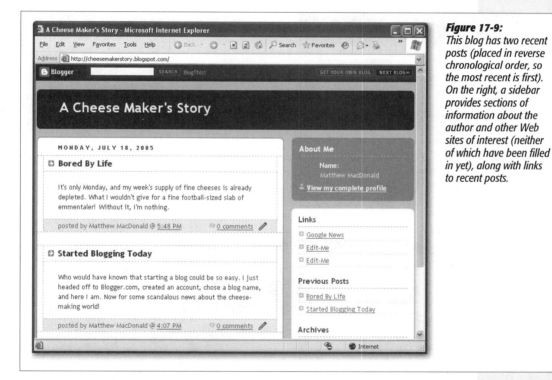

Figure 17-9:
This blog has two recent posts (placed in reverse chronological order, so the most recent is first). On the right, a sidebar provides sections of information about the author and other Web sites of interest (neither of which have been filled in yet), along with links to recent posts.

Managing a Blog

Once you've created your blog, you can do exactly two things when any kind of blog-related urge strikes:

- Surf to your blog, using whatever URL you picked when you created it. Here you can read all of the blog entries you've posted, and any feedback left by others.

- Surf to *www.blogger.com* and sign in. Here you can add posts and manage your blog.

To try this second option out, head to *www.blogger.com* and sign in. You'll see a page called the Dashboard (see Figure 17-10).

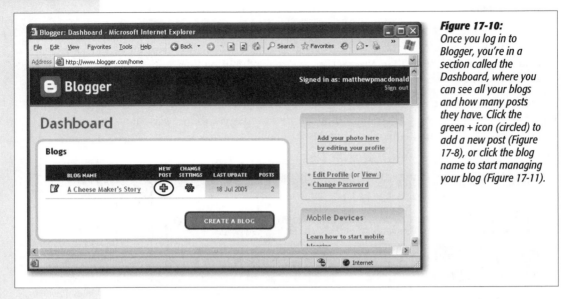

Figure 17-10:
Once you log in to Blogger, you're in a section called the Dashboard, where you can see all your blogs and how many posts they have. Click the green + icon (circled) to add a new post (Figure 17-8), or click the blog name to start managing your blog (Figure 17-11).

Once you click a blog name, you end up back on Blogger's multi-tabbed page with the Posting tab selected (see Figure 17-11). However, this time, Blogger sends you to the "Edit posts" page, which lets you review the posts you've made and edit them.

The four tabs

The Posting tab has three options

Figure 17-11:
The "Edit posts" page lets you review what you've written, search for specific content (type something in the Search box and click Go), or even edit an old post (click the Edit button next to the entry you want to change). If you have second thoughts about something you've posted, click Delete to remove it.

To do more with Blogger, you need to find your way around its multi-tabbed page layout. There are four tabs:

- **Posting.** Use this tab to create a new post, edit an existing post, or review the status of your last post and republish your blog (so that recent changes appear).

- **Settings.** This tab groups a dizzying number of options into several subgroups. Here you set everything from basic information about you and your blog to comment and hosting options.

- **Template.** This tab lets you choose a new template for your blog. If you aren't happy with the current look and feel, this gives your blog an effortless make-over.

- **View Blog.** This tab opens a separate browser window for your blog site. After you make changes to your blog, you'll use this command to take a look at the results.

WORD TO THE WISE

The Hazards of Blogging

There's something about the first-person nature of a blog that sometimes lures people into revealing much more information than they should. Thanks to reckless moments of blogging, lovers have discovered their cheating spouses, grandmothers have read memorable accounts of their daughter's sexual conquests, and well-meaning employees have lost their jobs.

The dangers of impulse blogging are particularly great in the working world. In most countries, companies have the ability to fire employees who make damaging claims about a business (even if they're true). Even famously open-minded Google ditched Mark Jen (*http://blog.plaxoed. com*) after he blogged a few choice words about a Google sales conference that he claimed resembled a drunken frat party. The notable part of his story is that he didn't set out to undermine Google or make his blog widely available. In fact, only his close friends and family even knew he had a blog. Unfortunately, a few Google-watching sites picked up on the blog post and posted the link around the Internet. There are many more stories like these, where employees lose their jobs after revealing trade secrets, admitting to inappropriate on-the-job conduct (for example, posting ris-qué at-work photos or bragging about time-wasting games of computer solitaire), or just complaining about the boss.

To protect yourself from the hazards of blogging, remember these rules:

- "Anonymous" never is.

- If you plan to hide your identity, adopt a pseud-onym, or conceal personal details, remember the first rule.

- Funny is in the mind of the beholder. Your humor-ous work stories will be seen in a different light when read by high-powered executives without your finely developed sense of irony.

- Think before you write. There's a fine line between company secrets and information in the public domain.

- There's no going back. Although tools like Blogger let you edit or remove old posts, they can stick around in search-engine caches indefinitely.

Tweaking a few common settings

To get started and add a few more details to your blog, follow the steps below that lead you through several fine details that can improve any blog. You'll add a description, choose how many posts you want to see on your front page, and set a time zone to make sure your posts get the right date stamp.

1. **Click the Settings tab.**

   The Settings tab provides eight separate options. Initially, the Basic page of settings is shown.

2. **Add a description for your blog.**

   The description appears just under the blog title. Typically, it should only be a sentence or two that hints at the flavor of your blog. For example, two good descriptions are "The sober confessions of an unlicensed meat handler," and "An on-again, off-again look at my life and adventures."

3. **Scroll down and click Save Settings.**

   When you save your settings, you'll see a message appear at the top of the page, informing you that you need to republish the site before any changes appear. Don't do that yet—there are still a few more changes to make.

4. **Click the link for the Archiving subgroup.**

   Archiving is the process Blogger uses to group together old posts and shuffle them out of sight. Every archive gets a link on your page. For example, if you have Blogger set to create monthly archives, your blog will have links like "January 2006, February 2006, and so on. If your visitors click an archive link, they'll see the posts from that period.

5. **Set the archive frequency, and choose whether or not you want each post to have its own page.**

   The archive frequency can be monthly, weekly, or daily. Most casual bloggers find that monthly is the best choice. If you blog every day, it might be better to split posts into weekly groups, but you'll end up cluttering your index page with a lot of extra links (one for every week you've blogged).

   The post page option determines whether or not each post has its own dedicated page. Usually, you want posts to have their own dedicated pages. That way, a reader can blog in response to your posting, and provide the exact link to your post. The post page option is also required if you want to support blog comments.

Note: Even though each blog posting has its own page, Blogger still shows multiple entries at once on the home page and archive pages.

---

6. **Click Save Settings.**

Once again, it's not quite time to republish yet.

7. **Click the link for the Formatting subgroup.**

The Formatting group lets you choose how many postings are shown on your blog home page, and how dates are formatted (see Figure 17-12).

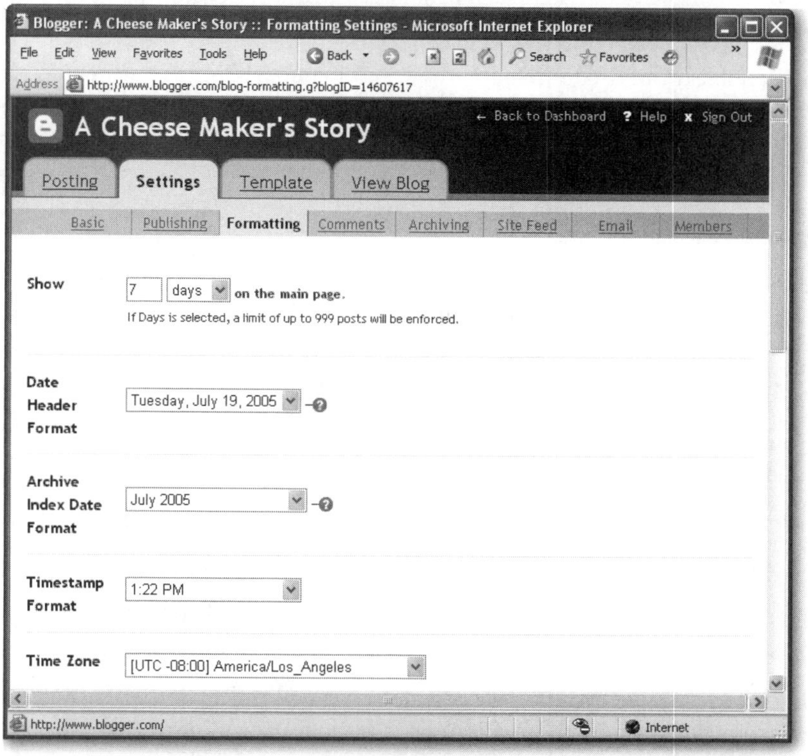

Figure 17-12:
This example shows how you can configure your blog to show a week's worth of posts.

8. **Choose the number of posts you want to appear on your first page.**

You can set a number of days or a number of posts. For example, you could ask Blogger to show the last 14 days of posts, or just the three most recent posts. Ideally, you don't want to crowd your front page with too many entries. If you post daily, stick to showing a small number of posts or just topics from the current week.

9. **Set the date format you want to use, and specify your time zone.**

The date is displayed for every blog post, usually at the beginning or end of the post (depending on the template). By setting the correct time zone, you won't need to manually set the correct date every time you create a new post.

10. **Click Save Settings.**

Now you're ready to republish.

11. **Click Republish.**

When you republish a blog, Blogger recreates all the HTML files for your blog, based on the new settings. Blogger keeps the same content (which is safely tucked away in a database on the Blogger server), but it changes details like the formatting depending on your settings. For a large blog, this process may take a little time. Once it finishes, you can click View Blog to see the results of your work.

The Republish Index command is similar to Republish, but it regenerates only the blog home page, not the archive pages and post pages. Typically, you'll only use the Republish Index command if you want to preview the effect of your changes before you go ahead and apply them to the whole blog.

Configuring your user profile

Interested in customizing the information that appears at the side of your blog posts on your blog home page? This information is drawn from your user profile, and it's easy to customize. Just follow these steps:

1. **Head to the Dashboard area on Blogger's main page.**

If you're in the tabbed view, click the Back To Dashboard link at the top of the window. Otherwise, surf to *www.blogger.com* and sign in.

2. **Click the Edit Profile link (which appears to the right of your blog list).**

Your profile page appears.

3. **Edit your profile information (see Figure 17-13). Pay special attention to the Display Name, Photo URL, City, State, Country, and About Me sections.**

The profile page lets you supply a wide range of information about yourself. Only some of those details will appear on your blog home page. The most important include your name (Display Name), an optional link to your photo (Photo URL), your location (City, State, and Country), and the descriptive text in About Me box.

4. **Once you've entered all the profile information you want to supply, click Save Profile.**

Now that your profile is saved, its time to head back to Blogger's main page.

5. **Click the Back to Dashboard link.**

Even though you've updated your profile information, the changes won't appear until you republish your blog. That's the next step you need to perform.

6. **Select your blog in the list. Then, click the Posting tab and then the Status subgroup.**

   This brings you back to the multi-tabbed page you use for managing blogs. The Status subgroup is where you need to go to republish your blog.

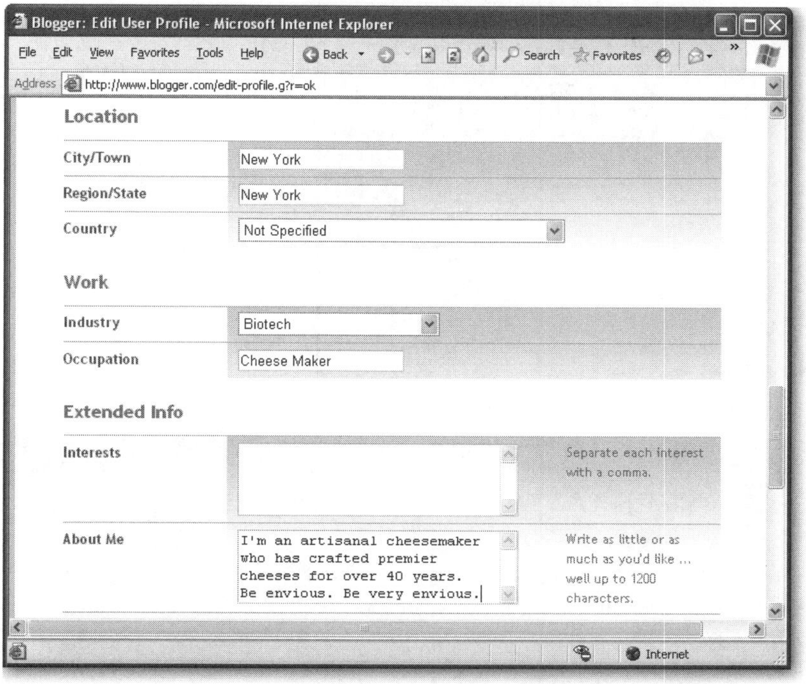

Figure 17-13:
The About Me section is one of the most important parts of your profile, because it's displayed prominently on your blog home page. Other sections, like Interests and Occupation, aren't (although readers can find them by clicking the "View my complete profile" link on your blog home page).

7. **Click Republish Entire Blog.**

   If you want to see the effect of your changes, click the View Profile button. Figure 17-14 shows the result.

Templates

Templates are keenly important in Blogger. They don't just determine what your blog looks like (irreverent, serious, technical, breezy, and so on), they also set the overall layout, and allow you to add specific ingredients, like a set of links that point to your favorite fellow bloggers, or a sidebar of targeted Google ads (page 337). You can also remove parts of the template you don't like.

When you first create a blog, you'll want to choose a template that suits your content, and has more or less the right layout and formatting. After you've found the right template, you'll probably want to edit it to add more features. Once you crack open the HTML inside a template, you're free to use the skills you've learned throughout this book to change virtually anything.

Figure 17-14:
Here's a fine-tuned blog home page that shows a custom description and About Me text.

Team Blogs

Having trouble keeping your blog up to date? If you want to be part of the blogosphere but just can't manage to update more than once a month, consider sharing the effort with some friends. Look for a natural reason to band together—for example, colleagues often create blogs to discuss specific work projects, and families create them to keep in touch.

Creating a team blog in Blogger is easy. All you need to do is take your ordinary blog, choose the Settings tab, and click Members. Then, click Add Members to add fellow bloggers.

You supply the email address and an optional welcome message. Blogger sends an email to inform each blogger that they're now a part of your blog.

All bloggers have the ability to post entries. Additionally, you can give some bloggers administrator status, which means they can add more bloggers (and delete existing ones).

Applying a new template

Finding the right template is often a trial-and-error process. Fortunately, it's easy.

1. **Click the Template tab.**

   The Template tab gives you two choices. You can edit the HTML for the current template by hand (click "Edit current") or choose a new preset design (click "Pick new"). The second option is the best starting point.

2. **Click "Pick new."**

Find the template you want to try and click Use This Template. If you're not sure yet which one you want, try clicking the template picture to see a larger preview of what it looks like.

When you select a template, you may see a warning message informing you that any customization you've made to the current template will be lost. Since you haven't invested any effort in changing the template yet, you can safely ignore this message.

Once you select a template, you're sent back to the "Edit current" section, where you can make any changes to the template you chose.

3. **Click Republish or Republish Index to update your blog.**

If you want to test out your template and you have a large blog, click Republish Index to republish just the home page. If you don't mind waiting, or you're sure you've got the right template, click Republish instead.

4. **Click View Blog to take a look at your changes (see Figure 17-15 for an example).**

If you don't like what you see, you can head back to step 2 and keep going to pick a new template.

Customizing a template

To get complete control over your blog's home page, you can edit its template by hand.

The blog template is really just an HTML document that defines your blog pages. At first glance, this seems a little unusual—after all, a modest blog has dozens of pages, and you only have one template! The trick is that the template defines special replaceable regions. When Blogger builds your home page or creates a new post, it starts with the template, and then fills in the appropriate details wherever it finds a matching code.

For example, if Blogger finds this code:

```
<head>
  <title><$BlogPageTitle$></title>
  ...
```

It replaces the highlighted code with the title of your blog. The final HTML file for your home page will actually contain this text:

```
<head>
  <title>A Cheese Maker's Story</title>
  ...
```

You can recognize Blogger codes by the fact that they're always bracketed by the character combinations <$ and $>. In addition, you'll also find some tags that are used exclusively by Blogger and have no meaning in HTML. For example, here's part of the definition for a blog entry in a template. It adds the date using a level-two heading (formatted according the date-header style sheet class).

```
<BlogDateHeader>
  <h2 class="date-header"><$BlogDateHeaderDate$></h2>
</BlogDateHeader>
...
```

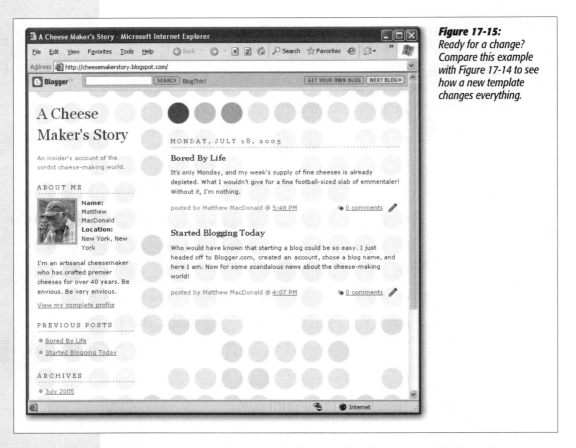

Figure 17-15:
Ready for a change? Compare this example with Figure 17-14 to see how a new template changes everything.

Note the presence of the wacky <BlogDateHeader> tag, which doesn't mean anything to a browser. When Blogger creates a page, it uses these tags to identify the structure of the page and determine where to insert content. In then strips them out before creating the final HTML.

Tip: To get detailed reference information on Blogger template tags, check out Blogger's online help on the subject at *http://help.blogger.com/bin/topic.py?topic=39.*

The upshot of all this is that you can edit how your blog looks using all the HTML and CSS skills you've acquired throughout this book. Although a typical template is quite long, the overall organizational rules are fairly straightforward.

- It splits the page into separate regions using <div> tags, just as you did in Chapter 9 (page 251).

- It places the sidebars using the floating behavior in CSS, which you saw in Chapter 9 (page 253).

- It uses an embedded style sheet (page 138 in Chapter 6) to define all the styles for different regions of the page.

- It includes HTML comments to point out important regions (for example, places where you might want to add content).

Editing a template is quite a bit easier than creating one. Now that you know how templates work, here are some of the tasks you might want to perform:

- Modify the style settings to change the formatting of a portion of the page.

- Move content around the page, by cutting it from one <div> tag and popping it into another.

- Add new content on the page, such as a set of links or a block of Google ads (see page 337 in Chapter 13).

The following series of steps explains how to edit the current template to add a new section with your favorite links. Although some templates already have a links section, not all do (and even if they do, you'll need to edit the template to change the title and any other formatting details you want to fiddle with).

Here's how it works:

1. **Click the Template tab.**

   You'll start with the "Edit current page" link selected, which is what you want.

2. **Choose a color for the Blogger NavBar.**

   The NavBar is the thin strip that appears at the top of your blog. It has quick links that let visitors travel from one blog to another, sign up for their own blog, or (most usefully) search your blog for specific keywords. This search feature uses the Google SiteSearch feature described in Chapter 13 (page 351), which means it homes in exclusively on the content in your blog.

   You can't get rid of the NavBar. However, it's a good idea to choose a color that matches your template, so it blends in with the scenery.

Note: If you really, really must remove the NavBar (and Blogger frowns on this), see *www.diaphaneity.com/layouts/2004/08/how-to-disable-navbar.html* for a workaround.

---

3. Edit the template in the large text box in the middle of the page (see Figure 17-16).

This is where the real work takes place.

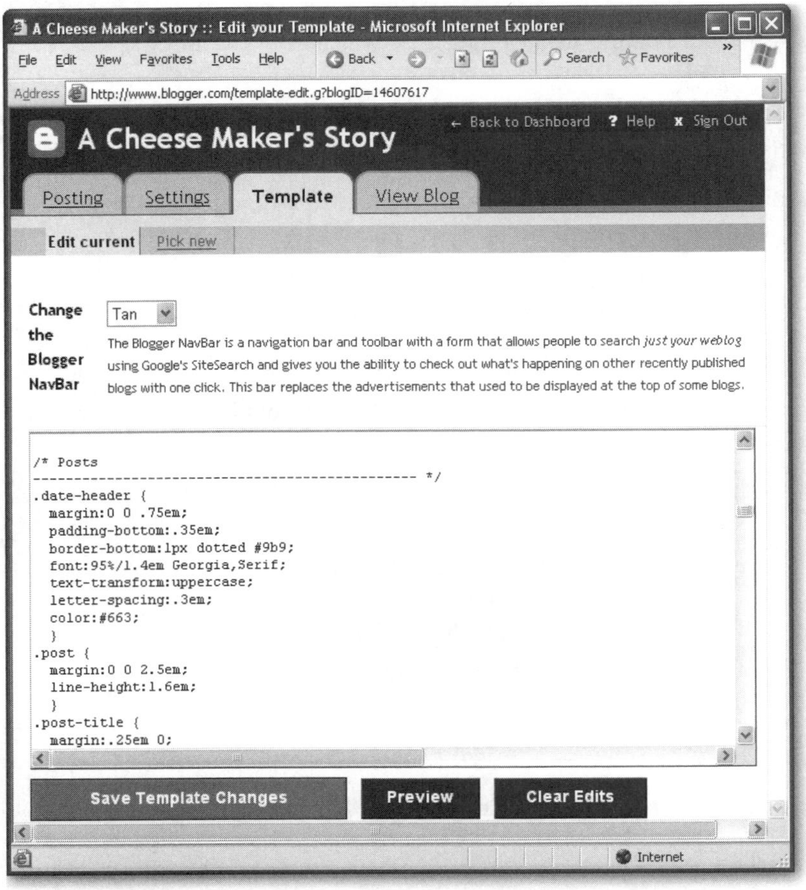

Figure 17-16:
The first part of the template is filled with style sheet rules that format your blog.

If you want to modify style properties, it's easy—just find the appropriate style rule, and use the style sheet settings you've used throughout this book. For example, change the *post-title* style sheet rule to set the formatting for the title of each blog entry. All the style rules are at the top of the template.

If you want to add new content, you need to find the right section in which to add it. The template is divided into a few key regions using <div> tags. You can identify each section based on the id attribute in the <div> tag:

- **content** contains the whole page.

- **sidebar2** defines the side panel with the About Me section and archive links.

- **main2** defines the center column that contains the blog posts.

- **footer** defines an optional footer at the bottom of the page.

***

Note: You'll notice that some <div> tags are defined twice, the second time with the number 2 at the end. For example, there's a sidebar <div> that contains the sidebar2 <div> where the real content is. This curious detail is actually a workaround for a bizarre Internet Explorer bug. You're best off not to think about it too long.

***

The sidebar2 panel is the best place to add your own content, like a set of links or ads. That's the task you'll complete in the following steps.

1. **Start by looking for this line in the template:**

   ```
   <div id="sidebar"><div id="sidebar2">
   ```

   Right after this line, the About Me information is defined. Scroll past this information. You should see a comment indicating the end of the profile section:

   ```
   <!-- End #profile -->
   ```

   And then you'll see the spot where the list of previous posts appears.

   ```
   <h2 class="sidebar-title">Previous Posts</h2>
   ```

***

Note: Some templates already include a group of links or a similar section. In this case, it makes more sense to edit this section rather than create a new one.

***

2. **Just before this <h2> heading, add your own set of links.**

   Here's an example of the links you might create:

   ```
   <h2 class="sidebar-title">My Favorite Links</h2>
   <a href="http://www.cheese.com">All About Cheese</a><br>
   <a href="http://ask.yahoo.com/ask/20020610.html">Why Swiss Cheese Has Holes
   </a><br>
   <a href="http://www.gourmetsleuth.com/fondue.htm">Cheese Fondue</a><br>
   ```

   Notice you don't need to worry about spacing or formatting, because the style sheet rules take care of that automatically. Just make sure you use the sidebar-title style for your heading.

3. **Click Save Template Changes to store your new template, and use Republish or Republish Index to update your blog accordingly.**

   Figure 17-17 shows the result.

Tip: Once you've perfected the template, it's a good idea to back it up before you make any more changes. Otherwise, you could muck it up and have no way to get back to the right version. To make a backup, just copy the full template text from the text box, and paste it into a text editor. Save it somewhere where you won't forget it on your computer, with a name like *BloggerBackupTemplate.htm*.

Figure 17-17:
Thanks to style sheet rules, the new section blends effortlessly into the rest of the template.

Tip: One great reason to use the technique you've just seen is to add Google AdSense ads to help your blog earn you some cash. Just use the same technique to place the AdSense code into a sidebar. For a walkthrough and some information about the best ad types to use, see *http://help.blogger.com/bin/answer.py?answer=974*.

Creating Formatted Posts

So far, you've only seen how to post text-only content in a blog. But Blogger actually lets you run rampant with HTML and perform all sorts of fancy design maneuvers, from highlighting text to inserting graphics. You just need to know your way around the editor.

To try out some of these changes, start a new post by clicking the Posting tab and choosing Create. Type something in the Compose box in the middle of the page. Next, select some text, and try out some of the buttons in the toolbar to format it (see Figure 17-18).

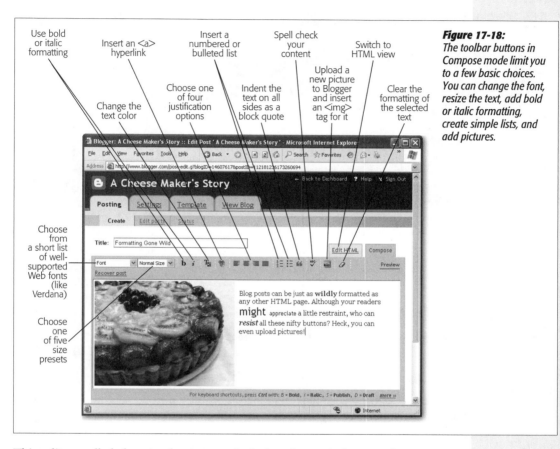

This editor, called the *visual composer*, is designed to mimic a word processor. However, if you're itching for some HTML action, click the Edit HTML link at the top right of the edit window. Now you can add tags and other HTML goodies directly (see Figure 17-19).

Figure 17-20 shows the splashy result.

Tip: Blogger recently released a tool that lets you post blogs from right inside Microsoft Word. Surf to *http://buzz.blogger.com/bloggerforword.html* to check out this effortless alternative.

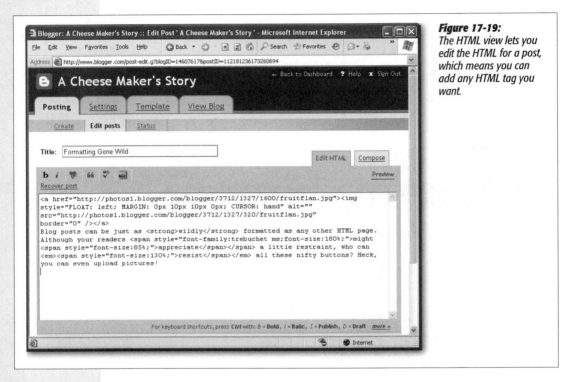

Figure 17-19:
The HTML view lets you edit the HTML for a post, which means you can add any HTML tag you want.

Hosting Your Blog on Your Web Site

In the past, cutting-edge bloggers took off on their own because hosted providers just weren't stable enough. All too often, blog messages would disappear or blog tools would become temporarily unresponsive. Fortunately, Blogger has evolved into a remarkably reliable blog host. However, there are still some reasons that you might want to host your blog on your own Web site. One of the most obvious reasons is because you already have a URL, and you want your blog to use that URL. For example, if you have the site *www.CheeseMaker.com*, you could put your blog at *www.CheeseMaker.com/blog*. The best part is that you can still use Blogger to create the appropriate HTML pages for your blog, but now you get to tell Blogger to upload them directly to your Web site.

To set this up, you need to have a few pieces of information at your fingertips. Namely, you need to know the FTP address for your Web host, and the user name and password you use to log in to their FTP server. You need to provide all this information to Blogger. That way, every time you add a post, Blogger can connect to the FTP site and transmit the newly generated files to your site.

Here's how you set this up:

1. **After you've logged into Blogger, click the Settings tab and choose Publishing.**

   The first line on this page indicates where your blog is hosted. You'll see the line "You're publishing on blogspot.com" unless you've already followed these steps to switch your blog over to another Web site.

Figure 17-20:
A blog post with wacky formatting and a picture. The picture is hosted on Blogger's Web server, just like the HTML for your blog pages.

2. **Next to the "Switch to" heading, click either FTP or SFTP, depending on the type of publishing system you use with your Web hosting provider.**

   FTP is most common. SFTP is a secure version that uses encryption to hide your password when it makes the connection.

3. **Enter all the information about your FTP server.**

   FTP Server is the URL for your server (like *ftp.website.com*).

   Blog URL is the Web address where you can see this part of your site (like *http://www.website.com/blog*).

   FTP Path is the subfolder of your Web site where you want to store your blog. Usually, you won't put the blog right in the root (main) folder, because that's where your Web site goes. Instead, you can use a path like *blog/* to tell blogger to go into the blog subfolder. Make sure you include the trailing forward slash character.

Blog Filename is the filename that you want Blogger to use when it creates your blog home page. For example, you might use *index.html*. If this page already exists at the same location, it will be overwritten when Blogger transfers your blog.

FTP Username and FTP Password compose the user information you supply to connect to the FTP server. You can leave these values blank, in which case you need to supply them every time you publish your blog.

4. **Click Save Settings to abandon your blogspot.com-based blog and switch over to your own server.**

   From this point on, any time you publish your blog, Blogger will attempt to connect to your FTP server and transfer all the files.

5. **It's a good idea to test this out right away by clicking Republish.**

GEM IN THE ROUGH

Emailing a Blog Entry

To take advantage of all of Blogger's features, it makes sense to use the editor on the Blogger Web site. However, if you find yourself on the go with only limited time to spare, you might appreciate Blogger's ability to accept emails and turn them into posts automatically. It really comes in handy if you want to email in a post from a mobile phone that's got email capability, or if you've got a sporadic Internet connection. If that's the case, you can prepare a post in your email program, and then connect to the Internet just long enough to send in the posting.

To use Blogger's email posting features, you first need to enable them. Click the Settings tab and choose "email." Then, in the Mail-To-Blogger section, enter a secret word to use in your email address and turn on the Publish checkbox.

The secret word prevents other people from sneaking their posts onto your blog, because they won't know the exact address. For example, if your user name is lisajones and your secret word is antelope12, you need to send a message to *lisajones.antelope12@blogger.com*.

When you send an email, the subject line immediately becomes the title of your blog entry, and the message text becomes the body of the post. Blogger inserts the date automatically, based on your time zone (see page 485).

BlogThis

A huge number of blog postings simply call attention to online interesting news stories, scandalous gossip, or funny pictures. If you're an infrequent blogger, you can beef up your blog by adding this type of short entry. And thanks to a remarkable tool called *BlogThis*, adding these links is now easier than ever.

There are two ways to use BlogThis. If you're using Internet Explorer and the handy Google Toolbar (see *http://toolbar.google.com*), there's a BlogThis button waiting for you to use. If you aren't currently using the Google Toolbar and you don't want to start, you have another option—you can add a special BlogThis link to your list of bookmarked sites. To do that, head to *http://help.blogger.com/bin/*

answer.py?answer=152&topic=17. You'll see some explanatory information and a link with the text "BlogThis." Add this link to your favorites menu.

Note: BlogThis works through a funky assortment of JavaScript code. This code runs when you click the BlogThis button (on the Google Toolbar) or the BlogThis favorite link.

Once you're set up to use BlogThis with one of these two approaches, the fun really starts. Surf around, and when you find a page that interests you, click the BlogThis button (on the Google Toolbar) or the BlogThis favorite link.

When you do, a new pop-up window appears (see Figure 17-21), with a text box that's similar to the one you use when creating a new entry.

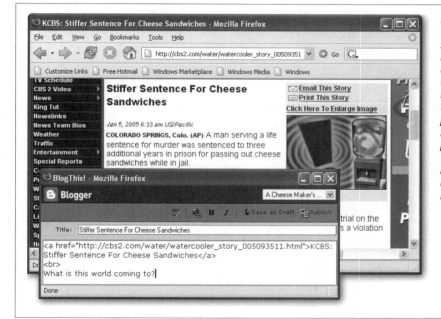

Figure 17-21:
When you've found something unique online, let the world know by adding it to your blog with BlogThis. When you use BlogThis, the text box (with the content for your post) is automatically filled in with a link to the page you're looking at. You simply need to type in a few words underneath, and click Publish to post it.

Figure 17-22 shows the posted blog entry.

Promoting Your Blog

Blogs need to be promoted just like any other Web site. Although you can use everything you learned in Chapter 11, there are some techniques that are unique to the blogosphere.

Here are some important tips to help get you started:

- **Add a blogroll to your site.** A blogroll is really just a set of links that lead to bloggers you like (similar to the set of links you learned how to add to the template on page 493). However, the blogroll also makes a statement. It says "these are the people I like" or "this is the crowd I want to be associated with." In other words, a blogroll is social networking at its best.

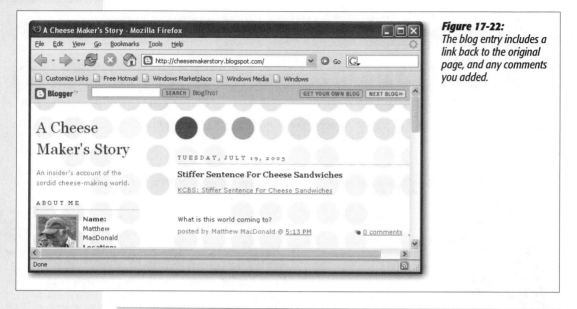

Figure 17-22:
The blog entry includes a link back to the original page, and any comments you added.

Tip: If you don't want to keep updating your template to change your blogroll, consider a service that can help you manage a blogroll and insert it into your blog for you, like *www.blogrolling.com*.

- **Tell the world when your blog is updated.** Blogger includes a setting to tell *Weblogs.com* every time your blog is updated. *Weblogs.com* is a blog update notification service that many people (and many other services) use. That way, your blog will crop up in "recently updated" lists across the Web. To find this setting, on Blogger.com choose the Settings tab and the Publishing section. The setting is named Ping Weblogs.com. Set it to Yes.

- **Participate with others.** Bloggers are an open-minded bunch. If you leave an insightful comment in response to someone else's blog entry, odds are good at least some readers will head over to your blog to see what else you have to say. If you let them comment on your posts, they're even more likely to come back for more.

- **Use the Email This Post feature.** You need to capitalize on the enthusiasm of your visitors. If you blog about a truly fascinating piece of gossip or news, readers might just decide to tell all their friends—if you make it easy enough. To help them give into the impulse, you can add a quick link that lets the reader email the story link to friends. To add this feature, choose the Settings tab and click the Basic section. Set "Show Email Post links" to true and republish.

- **Make sure you're in Blogger's listings.** You're probably already there, but it's good to double-check. Choose the Settings tab and click the Basic section, and make sure the "Add your blog to our listings" setting is set to Yes. If not, you're hiding from the world.

- **Provide a feed.** Feeds, discussed on page 472, work with feed readers. True blog aficionados love them, because they can track dozens or even hundreds of blogs all the time. Odds are, your site is already enabled for feeds. To check, choose the Settings tab and click the Site Feed section. Make sure Publish Site Feed is set to Yes. On this page, you'll also see the feed URL for your blog (for example, *http://cheesemakerstory.blogspot.com/atom.xml*), which is the URL you need to supply to a feed reader so it can start watching your blog.

Part Six: Appendixes

6

HTML Quick Reference

HTML (HyperText Markup Language) is the language of the Web. It's the standard used to create all Web pages, whether you're promoting a local bake sale or running a Fortune 500 company. Chapter 2 introduced HTML in detail, and since that point, you've steadily added to your arsenal of HTML techniques.

This appendix provides a quick HTML reference, organized alphabetically. Each entry features a brief description of what the tag does, and many provide cross-references to more detailed examples in other chapters. You'll also get a quick refresher of HTML character entities (codes that you use when you want to display special characters on a Web page).

Note: This appendix tackles HTML. HTML is slowly but surely giving ground to XHTML, which borrows the same basic set of tags, but has stricter rules about using them. To learn more about XHTML, see page 47.

HTML Tags

As you already know, the essential idea behind the HTML standard is *tags*—specialized codes in angle brackets that tell the browser how to format text, when to insert images, and how to link different documents together. Throughout this book, you've examined just about every important HTML tag that's in use today. Now you're ready for a quick reference that can refresh your memory and help you find the information you need elsewhere in this book.

Note: You won't see every HTML tag in this chapter. Some are old, obscure, and rarely used, while others are redundant or have been superseded by the CSS (Cascading Style Sheet) standard. For the full HTML standard, check out *www.w3.org/MarkUp*, or try *www.htmlhelp.com/reference/html40* for a reference that's easier to digest.

<a> (Anchor Tag)

The anchor tag has two roles. The most common use of the <a> tag is to create a link that, when clicked, takes a visitor from one page to another. To insert this type of link, you supply the destination URL using the *href* attribute, and put the clickable link text between the opening and closing tags.

```
<a href="LinkedPage.htm">Click Me</a>
```

The href can be *relative* (which means it points to a page in your own Web site) or *absolute* (which means it includes a full URL starting with "http://"). For a review of the differences and when to use each type, see page 214 (Chapter 8).

Creating clickable image links is just as easy as creating clickable text links. The trick is to put an <img> tag inside an <a> tag, like this:

```
<a href="LinkedPage.htm"><img src="MyPic.gif"></a>
```

Finally, you can create a link that doesn't transfer the visitor to a new page, but instead pops up an email message with the address information filled in. You do this by creating a mail-to link, as shown here:

```
<a href="mailto:me@myplace.com">Email Me</a>
```

For more information about the ins and outs of the mail-to link, see page 316 (Chapter 12).

Anchors can also take a *target* attribute, which instructs the browser to open the destination page in a specific frame, or in a new browser window (as shown here).

```
<a href="LinkedPage.htm" target="_blank">Click Me</a>
```

You can learn about this technique on page 270 (Chapter 10).

The anchor tag also lets you create a *bookmark* in a specific spot on a page. Once you've created a bookmark, you can create a link that heads straight to your bookmark.

To create a bookmark, you use the <a> anchor tag, but with a difference. You don't supply the href attribute, because the anchor doesn't lead anywhere. You also don't put any text inside the anchor, because it's not clickable. Instead, all you supply is a *name* attribute that gives your bookmark a descriptive name. Here's an example:

```
<a name="Canaries">Pet Canaries</a>
```

Once you've created a bookmark, you can write a URL that points to that bookmark. The trick is that you need to add the bookmark information to the end of the URL. To do this, you add the number sign symbol (#) followed by the bookmark name, as shown here:

```
Learn about recent developments in <a href="sales.htm#Canaries">canary
sales</a>.
```

You can learn more about bookmarks and ordinary links in Chapter 8.

<acronym>

The acronym tag lets you give the full version of an abbreviation. For example, wouldn't your visitors like to know that the hipster slang AFAIK stands for "as far as I know"? You can provide this information like this:

```
<acronym title="As Far As I Know">AFAIK</acronym>
```

On your Web page, the information in the *title* attribute doesn't appear right away. But it's available for automated programs that scan Web pages, and more interestingly, many Web browsers (including Internet Explorer) show the full title text in a pop-up text box if you hover over the acronym.

If you use the <acronym> tag, consider applying some style sheet formatting to make sure your acronym appears differently from the rest of the body text (perhaps with a different background color). That way, the visitor will know there's some extra information waiting to be uncovered with a mouseover.

<address>

An occasionally used tag that identifies contact information (like a Web or postal address). Here's an example:

```
<address>If you have any questions about the content of this site,
 phone our offices at 555-5555.
</address>
```

Most browsers format addresses in italics, just as though you used the <i> tag. The only value in using the <address> tag is the fact that it lets automated programs that scan Web pages extract some useful address information.

<area> (Image Map)

Defines a clickable region (known as a *hotspot*) inside an image map (generated with the <map> tag; see page 516). When defining an area, you need to supply the target URL (using the *href* attribute), the type of shape (using the *shape* attribute), and the coordinates (using the *coords* attribute). The shape can be a circle, square, or polygon.

For a circle, the coordinates are in this order: center point (x-coordinate), center point (y-coordinate), radius. For any other shape, you supply the corners in order as a series of x-y coordinates, like this: x1, y1, x2, y2, and so on. Here's an example that creates a square-shaped hotspot:

```
<area href="page1.htm" shape="square" coords="5,5,95,195">
```

The square is invisible. If you click anywhere inside this square, you'll be transported to *page1.htm.* For more information, see the <map> tag on page 516. For a full-fledged image map example, see page 221 in Chapter 8.

<b> (Bold Text)

Displays text in bold. HTML gurus suggest using <strong> instead of <b>, because it more clearly indicates the relative importance of your text, rather than giving a strictly typographic instruction about how to format it. However, the <b> tag is much more common.

```
Here is some <b>bold</b> text.
```

You can get much more control over every aspect of formatting using style sheet rules.

<base> (Base URL)

Defines a document's *base URL,* which is a Web address that's used to interpret all relative paths. You must place the <base> tag in the <head> section of a page, and you can use two attributes—*href* (which supplies the base URL) and *target* (which supplies a target frame for links).

For example, if you have a link that points to a file named *MySuperSunday.htm* and the base URL is *http://www.SundaysForever.com/Current,* the browser interprets the link as *http://www.SundaysForever.com/Current/MySuperSunday.htm.* The base URL is rarely used in this way, because it almost always makes more sense for the base URL to be drawn from the current page. In other words, if you're looking at *http://www.SundaysForever.com/Current/Intro.htm,* the browser already knows that the base URL is *http://www.SundaysForever.com/Current.* For more information about the difference between absolute and relative links, see page 214 (Chapter 8).

There is one useful purpose for the base URL tag—you can use it to set the target frame that will be used for all the links on the page (unless otherwise indicated). Here's an example:

```
<base target="Main">
```

You can learn much more about frames in Chapter 10.

<big> (Large Text)

Steps the text size up a notch to create larger text. The <big> tag is out of vogue, and you're better off using style sheets to control the formatting of your text.

<blockquote> (Block Quotation)

Used to identify a long quotation (which stands on its own, separate from other paragraphs) as a *block element*. As with all other block elements, the browser adds a line break and some space before the beginning and after the end of a <block-quote>:

```
<blockquote>It was the best of times, it was the worst of times.</blockquote>
```

Usually, the <blockquote> element is rendered as italic text and indented on the left and right side. However, it makes more sense to use the <blockquote> element to denote the meaning of your text (for example, that it's a passage quoted from a book), in conjunction with style sheet rules that apply the specific formatting you want.

If you want a shorter quotation that you can place inside another block element (like a paragraph), use the <q> element instead.

<body> (Document Body)

The body tag is a basic part of the structure of any HTML document. It occurs immediately after the <head> section ends, and it contains the complete content of your Web page, including all its text, images, tables, and links.

 (Line Break)

The break tag is an inline element that splits two lines using a single hard return. No extra spacing is added in between the two lines. For example, you can use <br> to split address information in a paragraph:

```
<p>Johny The Fever<br>
200 Easy Street<br>
Akimbo, Madagascar</p>
```

<button> (Button)

Lets you create a clickable button in a form, with any content inside (for example, you can place a phrase or an image between the start tag and the end tag). As with any other form control, you need to supply a unique name and a value that will be submitted when the surfer clicks the button. You place the button text between the opening and closing tags:

```
<button name="submit" value="order">Place Order</button>
```

The <button> tag is more powerful than the <input> tag for creating buttons, because it puts whatever content you want on the face of a button, including images.

```
<button name="submit" value="order"><img src="Order.gif" alt="Place Order">
</button>
```

\<caption> (Table Caption)

Defines a text title for a table. If used, this must be the first element in a \<table> tag:

```
<table>
  <caption>Least Popular Vacation Destinations</caption>
  ...
</table>
```

No automatic formatting is applied to the caption—it's just placed at the top of the table as ordinary text (and wrapped to fit the width of the table). However, you can apply whatever formatting you want through style sheet rules.

\<cite> (Citation)

Used to identify a *citation,* which is a reference to a book, print article, or other published resource.

```
<p>Charles Dickens wrote <cite>A Tale of Two Cities</cite>.</p>
```

Usually, the \<cite> element is rendered as italic text. However, it makes more sense to use the \<cite> element to denote the meaning of your text, in conjunction with style sheet rules that apply the specific formatting you want.

\<dd> (Dictionary Description)

Used to identify the description in a dictionary list. For more information, see the very simple example under the \<dl> tag description, below, or refer to page 129 (Chapter 5).

\<del> (Deleted Text)

A rarely used tag that identifies text that was present but has now been removed. Browsers that support this tag display crossed-out text to represent deleted material. Another tag sometimes used to indicate a revision trail is \<ins>.

\<dfn> (Defined Term)

A rarely used tag that indicates the defining instance of a term. For example, the first time you learn about a new term in this book, like *froopy,* it's italicized. That's because it's considered the defining instance, and a definition usually follows. Browsers render the \<dfn> tag in italics.

\<div> (Generic Block Container)

The division tag is used to group together one or more block elements. For example, you could group together several paragraphs, a paragraph and heading, and so on. Here's an example:

```
<div>
  <p>...</p>
```

```
<p>...</p>
</div>
```

On its own, the <div> tag doesn't do anything. However, it's a powerful way to apply style sheet formatting. In the example above, any formatting you apply to the <div> tag is automatically applied to the two nested paragraphs.

To learn more about how to use the <div> tag to apply style rules, see page 177 in Chapter 6. You should also refer to the <span> tag (page 125), which applies formatting inside a block element.

<dl> (Dictionary List)

Defines a definition list (also known as a dictionary list), which is a series of terms, each one followed by a definition in an indented block of text that appears immediately below it. In theory, you could put any type of content in a dictionary list, but it's recommended that you follow its intended use and include a list of points and explanations. Here's an example:

```
<dl>
<dt>tasseomancy</dt>
<dd>Divination by reading tea leaves.</dd>
<dt>tyromancy</dt>
<dd>Divination by studying how cheese curds form during cheese making.</dd>
</dl>
```

<dt> (Dictionary Term)

Used to identify the term in a dictionary list. For more information, see the very simple example under the <dl> tag description, above, or refer to page 129 (Chapter 5).

<em> (Emphasis)

Has the same effect as the <i> tag, but is preferred by some HTML experts because it indicates the relative importance of your text, not just the way it should be formatted. After all, you might use style sheet rules to change the formatting of this tag so that it's emphasized in some other way, and doesn't necessarily use italic formatting.

<form> (Interactive Form)

The form tag creates an interactive form, where you can place graphical widgets like text boxes, checkboxes, selectable lists, and so on (represented by the <input>, <textarea>, <button>, and <select> tags). By placing these widgets in a <form> tag, you can create pages that are able to collect the information the surfer enters with these controls, and submit this information to a Web application. Web applications are outside the scope of this book, but you can learn how to create a basic form that emails you the relevant information in Chapter 12.

<frame> (Frame)

Defines a *frame*—a rectangular subset of the browser window—inside a <frameset>. Each frame can show a different Web page. When defining a frame, you can supply a frame name with the *name* attribute (which you use to identify the frame in your links) and the page that should be shown in the frame with the *src* attribute.

```
<frame name="Menu" src="menu.htm">
```

You can also create a fixed, non-resizable frame by adding the *noresize* attribute to the frame tag, and you can prevent scrolling the frame by adding *scrolling="no"*.

For much more information about frames and how to use them, refer to Chapter 10.

<frameset> (Frameset)

Defines a frameset page—a page that contains one or more frames. Each frame is a rectangular region in the browser window that can show a different Web page. The <frameset> tag also sets the size of each frame (using absolute pixel sizes or percentages of the current browser window). If you're splitting the page horizontally, you use the *rows* attribute. If you're splitting the page vertically, you use the *cols* attribute.

Here's an example with two frames split vertically. The first frame is 100 pixels, and the second frame occupies the remaining space.

```
<frameset cols="100,*">
  <frame name="Menu" src="menu.htm">
  <frame name="Main" src="welcome.htm">
</frameset>
```

You can also control the size of the border that's shown between frames by adding the *border* attribute and setting it to a pixel size (use 0 for no border at all).

```
<frameset cols="100,*" border="0">
  ...
</frameset>
```

For much more information about frames and how to use them, refer to Chapter 10.

<h1>, <h2>, <h3>, <h4>, <h5>, <h6> (Headings)

Headings are section titles. They display in bold lettering, at various sizes. The size of the heading depends on the heading level. There are six heading levels, starting at <h1> (the biggest), and moving down to <h6> (the smallest). Both <h5> and <6> are actually smaller than regularly sized text. Here's an <h1> tag in action:

```
<h1>Important Information</h1>
```

When you use headings, always make sure your page follows a logical structure that starts with <h1> and gradually works its way down to lower heading levels. Don't start with <h3> just because the formatting looks nicer. Instead, use style sheets to change the formatting of each heading to suit you, and use the heading levels to delineate the structure of your document.

<head> (Document Head)

Defines the header portion of an HTML document. The <head> tag is placed immediately before the <body> tag. While the <body> tag contains the Web page content, the <head> tag includes other information like the Web page title (the <title> tag), descriptive metadata (one or more <meta> tags), and styles (the <style> or <link> tags).

<hr> (Horizontal Rule)

Defines a horizontal rule (a solid line) that's drawn to separate block elements:

```
<p>...</p>
<hr>
<p>...</p>
```

Although the <hr> tag still works perfectly well, HTML gurus prefer using border settings in a style sheet rule to get much more control over the line style and color. Here's an example that defines a style sheet rule for a solid blue line:

```
.border { border-top: solid medium navy }
```

And here's how you could apply it:

```
<p>...</p>
<div class="border"></div>
<p>...</p>
```

For more information about the style sheet border settings, refer to page 170 in Chapter 6.

<html> (Document)

The <html> tag is the first tag in any HTML document. It wraps the rest of the document. If you're creating an ordinary Web page, the <html> tag contains two other essential ingredients—the <head> tag that defines the title, metadata, and linked style sheets, and the <body> tag that contains the actual content. If you're creating a frames page, the <html> tag contains a <head> tag, a <frameset>, and a <noframes> region.

<i> (Italic Text)

Displays some text in italics. HTML gurus suggest using <em> (emphasis) instead of <i>, because it more clearly indicates the relative importance of your text, rather than giving a strictly typographic instruction about how to format it. However, the `<i>` tag is much more common.

```
Here is some <i>italicized</i> text.
```

You can get much more control over every aspect of formatting using style sheet rules.

`<iframe>` (Inline Frame)

Creates an *inline frame*—an embedded, scrollable window that shows another Web page inside the current one. You supply the attributes *src* (the page to show in the frame), *name* (the unique name of the frame), *width*, and *height* (the dimensions of the frame in pixels). You can also turn off the border by setting the *frameborder* attribute to 0, or disable scrolling by adding the *scrolling="no"* attribute. Here's one use of the `<iframe>` tag:

```
<iframe src="MyPage.html" width="100" height="250"></iframe>
```

Inside the `<iframe>` tag, you can put some content that will be displayed on browsers that don't support the `<iframe>` tag.

```
<iframe src="MyPage.html" width="100" height="250">
  <p>To see more details, check out <a href="MyPage.html">this page</a>.</p>
</iframe>
```

`<img>` (Image)

The `<img>` tag points to a picture file you want to show in a page. The *src* attribute identifies the picture (using a relative or absolute link—see page 214 in Chapter 8). The *alt* attribute supplies some text that's used if the picture can't be shown.

```
<img src="OrderButton.gir"
alt="Place Order">
```

Internet Explorer uses the alternate text for a picture pop-up text box, while some more standards-aware browsers (namely Firefox) don't. In either case, you can supply a pop-up text box in just about any browser using the *title* attribute. This is the best way to add a pop-up text box to an image.

The `<img>` tag also supports *height* and *width* attributes that you can use to explicitly size a picture:

```
<img src="photo01.jpg" width="100" height="150">
```

In this example, the picture is given a width of 100 pixels and a height of 150 pixels. If these dimensions don't match the actual size of the source picture, the picture is stretched and otherwise mangled to fit.

Never use the width and height attributes to resize an image; instead, make those kinds of edits in a proper image-editing program. You can use the width and height attributes to tell the browser how big your picture is, so it can lay out the page before it's downloaded the whole image (see page 184 in Chapter 7 for more details).

To learn more about supported image types, how to organize pictures on a page, and where to find the best material, refer to Chapter 7. To learn how to create images that serve as fancy clickable buttons, check out Chapter 15.

Finally, you can create clickable regions on an image by defining an image map, and then linking that image map to your image with the *usemap* attribute of the <img> tag. For more information, see the <map> section (page 516).

<input> (Input Control)

The input tag is the most common ingredient in a HTML form (represented by the <form> tag). The input tag can represent different onscreen widgets (called *controls*) that collect information from the Web surfer.

The type of control is determined by the *type* attribute (see page 320 in Chapter 12 for a detailed list). Table A-1 lists the most common types. Additionally, every control should have a unique *name* associated with it.

Table A-1. *HTML Form Controls*

Control	HTML Tag	Description
Single-Line Text Box	<input type="text">	Shows a text box where the visitor can type in any text.
Password Text Box	<input type="password">	Shows a text box where the visitor can type in any text. However, the text isn't displayed in the browser. Instead, you'll see an asterisk (*) appear in the place of every letter, hiding it from prying eyes.
Checkbox	<input type="checkbox">	Shows a checkbox that can be turned on or off.
Option Button	<input type="radio">	Shows a radio button (a circle that can be turned on or off). Usually, you'll have a group of radio buttons next to each other, in which case the visitor can select exactly one.
Button	<input type="submit">	Shows a standard push button that submits the form, with all its data.
Button	<input type="reset">	Shows a standard push button that simply clears the user selections and entered text in all the input controls of the form.

Here's an <input> tag that creates a text box. When the page is submitted, whatever the surfer typed in will be sent along, with the descriptive identifier "Last-Name".

```
<input type="text" name="LastName">
```

For more information about forms and how you can use them to collect data, refer to page 317 in Chapter 12.

<ins> (Inserted Text)

A rarely used tag that identifies newly inserted text. It lets you create an HTML Web page with limited change tracking. (Of course, you don't really want too much change tracking information in a page, because you want to keep your page sizes as small as possible so they can sail across the Internet without a care.)

The <ins> tag can be used around block elements, or inside a block element. Another change revision tag is <del>.

<li> (List Item)

Represents a single item in an ordered (numbered) list or unordered (bulleted) list. For more information, see the <ol> tag for ordered lists and the <ul> tag for unordered lists.

<link> (Document Relationship)

The <link> tag describes a relationship between the current document and another document. For example, you might use it to point to another document that's the previous version of the current document. More commonly, it's used to point to an *external style sheet* that provides the styles for the current page. The <link> tag is always placed in the <head> section of the page. Here's one possible use:

```
<link rel="stylesheet" href="NyStyles.css" type="text/css">
```

By using external style sheets, you can define your styles in one file, and use them in multiple pages. Chapter 6 has much more about style sheets and how to use them.

<map> (Image Map)

Defines an *image map*—a picture with one or more clickable regions. When creating an image map, you assign a unique name that identifies it using the *name* attribute. You then add one <area> tag inside the <map> tag for each clickable region, specifying the coordinates and destination URL (see the <area> tag on page 507 for more on how the coords attribute works). Here's an example of an image map with three clickable regions:

```
<map name="ThreeSquares">
  <area href="page1.htm" shape="square" coords="5,5,95,195">
  <area href="page2.htm" shape="square" coords="105,5,195,195">
  <area href="page3.htm" shape="square" coords="205,5,295,195">
</map>
```

Finally, to use your image map, you need to apply it to an image with the *usemap* attribute. The usemap attribute matches the name of the map, but starts with the hash (#) character, which indicates that the image map is defined on the current page:

```
<img src="image.gif" usemap="#ThreeSquares">
```

The clickable regions are invisible (unless they're indicated within your picture). However, when you hover over a hotspot, the mouse pointer changes to a hand. Clicking on a hotspot has the same effect as clicking an ordinary <a> link—you're transported immediately to the new URL. For a full-fledged image map example, see page 221 in Chapter 8.

<meta> (Metadata)

Meta tags give you a way to attach descriptive information to your Web pages. This information is never shown to the Web surfer, but it is available to automated programs like Web search engines as they scan your site. You add metadata by placing <meta> tags in the <head> section of your page.

Every <meta> tag is made up of a *name* attribute (which identifies the type of information you're adding) and a *content* attribute (which supplies the actual information). Although there is an unlimited number of potential <meta> tags, the two most common are description and keywords, because they're used by some search engines:

```
<meta name="description" content="Sugar Beat Music for Children offers age-
appropriate music classes for children 4 months to 5 years old">
```

Page 295 in Chapter 11 describes meta tags in more detail, and explains how search engines use them.

<noframes> (Frames Alternate Content)

Defines the content that should be shown instead of a frames page if the browser doesn't support frames. The <noframes> tag must immediately follow the <frameset> tag on a frames page.

It's incredibly rare to stumble across a browser that's too old to support frames. (Netscape's supported frames since version 2.) Today, the only browsers you're likely to find that don't support frames are mobile browsers for small devices like cell phones, and screen reading programs (typically used by viewing-impaired visitors).

For much more information about frames and how to use them, refer to Chapter 10.

<noscript> (Alternate Script Content)

Defines the content that should be shown if a script can't run. The <noscript> tag must immediately follow the <script> tag. The most common reason a script can't run isn't due to lack of browser support—instead, it's usually because the Web surfer has specifically disabled this feature of the browser.

For more information about scripts, refer to Chapter 14.

<object> (Embedded Object)

Used to embed specialized objects in your page, like audio, video, and even *applets* (miniature programs that can run inside a Web page). For example, you might use an <object> tag to place a Flash movie inside a Web page, as described in Chapter 16.

<ol> (Ordered List)

An unordered list starts with the <ol> tag, and contains multiple list items, each of which is represented by the <li> tag. In an ordered list, each item is numbered consecutively, although the numbering can use numbers, letters, or roman numerals.

Here's a simple ordered list that numbers items from 1 to 3:

```
<ol>
  <li>Buy bread</li>
  <li>Soak stamps off letters</li>
  <li>Defraud government with offshore investment scheme</li>
</ol>
```

To start at a number other than 1, use the *start* attribute and supply the starting number. To change the list formatting, use the *type* attribute with one of these values: 1 (numbers), a (lowercase letters), A (uppercase letters), i (lowercase roman numerals), I (uppercase roman numerals).

Ordered lists are demonstrated in Chapter 5 (page 127).

<option> (Menu Option)

Defines an item in a selectable list control, inside a <select> tag. For example, if you want to create a drop-down menu for color picking that has the entries Blue, Red, and Green, you need one <select> tag with three <option> tags inside.

When you define the <option> tag, you can use attributes like *selected* (the choice is initially selected) and *disabled* (the choice is disabled, and can't be selected by the surfer). You can also use the *value* attribute to associate a uniquely identifying piece of information for this option, which is sent with the form data when the form is submitted.

For a basic example, see the description of the <select> tag on page 323.

<p> (Paragraph)

The paragraph tag contains a paragraph of text:

```
<p>It was the best of times, it was the worst of times ...</p>
```

Paragraphs are *block elements*, which means the browser automatically adds a line break and a little extra space between two paragraphs, or between a paragraph and another block element, like a list or a heading.

Empty paragraphs are ignored by the browser. If you want to create a blank paragraph that takes up the normal amount of space, use a non-breaking space like this:

```
<p> </p>
```

<param> (Object Parameter)

Defines extra information that's used with the <object> tag to send information to the applet or plugin.

<pre> (Preformatted Text)

Preformatted text breaks the normal rules. Inside a <pre> tag, the browser pays close attention to every space and line break you use, and it duplicates that exactly in the Web page. Additionally, the Web browser puts it all into a monospaced font (typically Courier), which means the results are usually ugly. The <pre> tag is an easy and quick way to get text to appear exactly where you want, which is useful if you're using it to show visual poetry or a snippet of programming code. However, you shouldn't use it to align large sections of ordinary text—use tables and CSS positioning rules (see Chapter 9) for those tasks.

```
<pre>
Tumbling-hair
                picker of buttercups
                                    violets
dandelions
And the big bullying daisies
                        through the field wonderful
with eyes a little sorry
Another comes
            also picking flowers
</pre>
```

<q> (Short Quotation)

Used to define a short quotation inside another block element, like a paragraph.

```
<p>As Charles Dickens once wrote, <q>It was the best of times, it was the
worst of times</q>.</p>
```

Usually, the <q> element is rendered as italic text. However, it makes more sense to use the <q> element to denote the meaning of your text, in conjunction with style sheet rules that apply the specific formatting you want.

If you want a longer quotation that stands on its own as a *block element*, use the <blockquote> element instead.

<script> (Client-Side Script)

Includes a client-side script inside your Web page. A script is a set of instructions written in a simplified programming language like JavaScript. These instructions are often used to create more interactive Web pages by adding effects like buttons that change color when you hover the mouse pointer over them. To learn some of the basics of JavaScript and see scripts in action, check out Chapter 14.

<select> (Selectable List)

Defines a list control inside a form. The Web surfer can select a single item in the list (or multiple items, if you add the *multiple* attribute). You use the *name* attribute to uniquely identify this control, as in the following example:

```
<select name="PromoSource">
  <option value="Ad">Google Ad</option>
  <option value="Search">Google Search</option>
  <option value="Psychic">Uncanny Psychic Intuition</option>
  <option value="Luck">Bad Luck</option>
</select>
```

Ordinarily, selection lists are shown as drop-down menus. However, you can create a scrollable list box using the *size* attribute. Just specify the number of rows you want to show at once:

```
<select name="PromoSource" size="3">
  ...
</select>
```

For a full form example, refer to page 323 in Chapter 12.

<small> (Small Text)

Steps the text size down one notch to create smaller text. The <small> tag is out of vogue, and you're better off using style sheets to control the formatting of your text.

<span> (Generic Inline Container)

The <span> tag is used to identify some text you want to format inside a block element. For example, you could format a single word in a paragraph, a whole sentence, and so on. Here's an example:

```
<p>In this paragraph, some of the text is wrapped in a span tag.
That <span>gives you the ability</span> to format it in some fancy
way later on.</p>
```

On its own the <span> tag doesn't do anything. However, it's a powerful way to apply style sheet formatting in a generic way.

You should also refer to the <div> tag (page 510), which can apply formatting to several block elements at once.

<strong> (Strong Emphasis)

Has the same effect as the <b> tag, but is preferred by some HTML experts because it indicates the relative importance of your text, not just the way it should be formatted. After all, you might use style sheet rules to change the formatting of this tag so it's emphasized in some other way, and doesn't necessarily use bold formatting.

<style> (Internal Style Sheet)

The <style> tag is used to supply CSS (Cascading Style Sheet) rules that format a Web page. It's always placed inside the <head> section of a Web page.

The <style> tag lets you define a style right inside a Web page. This is known as an *internal style sheet*. Here's an example that gives <h1> headings colored text.

```
<style type="text/css">
  h1 { color: fuchsia }
</style>
```

More commonly, you'll use the <link> tag instead of the <style> tag, so that you can link to a separate file that defines your styles. That way, you can apply the same styles to multiple pages without cluttering up your HTML. Chapter 6 has much more about style sheets and how to use them.

<sub> (Subscript)

Formats text so that it appears smaller and lower (the middle of the text is lined up with the bottom of the current line). It's best not to rely on this trick for formatting (use style sheets instead), but it is a handy way to deal with scientific terms like H20. Here's how you'd use it:

```
Water is H<sub>2</sub>0
```

<sup> (Superscript)

Formats text so that it appears smaller and higher (the middle of the text is lined up with the top of the current line). It's best not to rely on this trick for formatting (use style sheets instead), but it is a handy way to deal with exponents like 3^3. Here's the <sup> tag in action:

```
3<sup>3</sup> is 27
```

\<table> (Table)

The outermost tag that defines a table. Inside the \<table> tag, you define rows with the \<tr> tag, and inside each row, you place columns of data in cells with the \<td> tag. Here's a very basic table:

```
<table>
  <tr>
    <td>Row 1, Column 1</td>
    <td> Row 1, Column 2</td>
  </tr>
  <tr>
    <td>Row 2, Column 1</td>
    <td>Row 2, Column 2</td>
  </tr>
</table>
```

It looks like this:

Row 1, Column 1	Row 1, Column 2
Row 2, Column 1	Row 2, Column 2

For much more information about creating exotic tables and sizing them perfectly, refer to Chapter 9.

\<td> (Table Data Cell)

Represents an individual cell with text inside a table row (a \<tr> tag). Each time you add a \<td> tag, you create a column. However, it's perfectly valid to have different numbers of columns in subsequent rows (although it might look a little wacky). For a very basic table example, see the \<table> tag definition, above, and for a detailed table exposé, check out Chapter 9.

\<textarea> (Multiline Text Input)

Shows a large text box that can fit multiple lines of text, inside of a \<form>. As with all input controls, you need to identify the control by giving it a unique name. Additionally, you can set the size of the text box using the *rows* and *cols* attributes.

If you want some text to appear initially in the \<textarea> element, place it in between the beginning and ending tags, like so:

```
<textarea name="Comments">Enter your comments here.</textarea>
```

\<th> (Table Header Cell)

Represents an individual cell with heading text. The \<th> tag is used in the same way as the \<td> tag—the difference is that it's usually reserved for the first row (with the heading text), and has a basic bold formatting (which you can tailor using style sheets).

<title> (Document Title)

The <title> tag sets the title for the Web page, which is displayed in the browser title bar and used as the bookmark text if a surfer adds your site to his or her bookmark list. The <title> tag must be placed in the <head> section.

```
<title>Truly Honest Car Mechanics</title>
```

<tr> (Table Row)

Represents an individual row inside a table (a <table> tag). To add cells of information, you need to add the <td> tag inside the <tr> tag. For a very basic table example, see the <table> tag definition, above, and for a detailed table exposé, check out Chapter 9.

<tt> (Teletype Text)

Text in a teletype tag displays using a fixed-width (monospaced) font, like Courier. Programmers sometimes use it for snippets of code in a paragraph:

```
<p>To solve your problem, use the <tt>Fizzle()</tt> function.</p>
```

Teletype text is designed to be used inside a block element like a paragraph (because it's an *inline element*). For a similar effect in a *block element*, check out the <pre> tag.

<u> (Underlined Text)

Displays some underlined text. Be careful about using this tag, because it's all too easy for Web surfers to mistake underlined text for links.

```
Here is some <u>underlined</u> text.
```

<ul> (Unordered List)

An unordered list starts with the <ul> tag, and contains multiple list items, each of which is represented by the <li> tag. The browser indents each item in the list, and draws a bullet next to it.

Here's a simple unordered list:

```
<ul>
  <li>Buy bread</li>
  <li>Soak stamps off letters</li>
  <li>Defraud government with offshore investment scheme</li>
</ul>
```

Page 128 shows how you can change the bullet style in an unordered list with the type attribute. You can even use an image for a bullet, as demonstrated on page 205 (Chapter 7).

HTML Character Entities

HTML character entities are codes you can enter in a page that are then translated into other characters by the browser before they're displayed. All HTML character entities start with the ampersand (&) and end with the semicolon (;).

There are two reasons you might want to use HTML character entities. First of all, you might want to use a character that is considered to have a special meaning in the HTML standard. For example, if you type < in an HTML document, the browser assumes you're starting a tag, which makes it difficult to write a pithy bit of logic like "2 < 3." To get around this, you can replace the < symbol with a character entity that *represents* the less-than symbol. The browser will then insert what you want when it displays the page.

The other reason you might use HTML character entities is because you want to use a special character that's not easy to type, like an accented letter or a currency symbol. In fact, it's quite possibly not on your keyboard at all.

Table A-2 has the most commonly used HTML entities. For the complete list, which includes many more international language characters, see *http://webmonkey.wired.com/webmonkey/reference/special_characters*.

Table A-2. *HTML Character Entities*

Character	Name of Character	What to Type
<	Less than	&lt;
>	Greater than	&gt;
&	Ampersand	&amp;
"	Quotation mark	&quot;
©	Copyright	&copy;
®	Registered trademark	&reg;
¢	Cent sign	&cent;
£	Pound sterling	&pound;
¥	Yen sign	&yen;
€	Euro sign	€ (but € is better supported)
°	Degree sign	&deg;
±	Plus or minus	&plusmn;
÷	Division sign	&divide;
×	Multiply sign	&times;
µ	Micro sign	&micro;
¼	Fraction one-fourth	&frac14;
½	Fraction one-half	&frac12;
¾	Fraction three-fourths	&frac34;
¶	Paragraph sign	&para;

Table A-2. *HTML Character Entities (continued)*

Character	Name of Character	What to Type
§	Section sign	§
«	Left angle quote, guillemotleft	«
»	Right angle quote, guillemotright	»
¡	Inverted exclamation	¡
¿	Inverted question mark	¿
æ	Small ae diphthong (ligature)	æ
ç	Small c, cedilla	ç
è	Small e, grave accent	è
é	Small e, acute accent	é
ê	Small e, circumflex accent	ê
ë	Small e, dieresis or umlaut mark	ë
ö	Small o, dieresis or umlaut mark	ö
É	Capital E, acute accent	É

HTML Color Names

Only 16 color names are officially recognized by the HTML standard. These are listed in Table A-3.

Table A-3. *HTML Color Names*

Aqua	Navy
Black	Olive
Blue	Purple
Fuchsia	Red
Gray	Silver
Green	Teal
Lime	White
Maroon	Yellow

Although many browsers recognize more names, the safest option to get better colors is to use a color *code* (page 152).

Useful Web Sites

Throughout this book, you've learned about a number of great Web sites where you can download handy software or get valuable information. Odds are, you'll want to revisit some of these sites to keep honing your Web skills (or just get free stuff). To save you the effort of leafing through hundreds of pages, this appendix repeats all these links, grouped by chapter.

Tip: To avoid carpal tunnel syndrome, you don't need to painstakingly type these URLs into your browser. Instead, use the online version of this appendix that's located on the "Missing CD" page at *www. missingmanuals.com*. That way, once you've found the link you want, you're just a click away. Also, it's worth checking this page for late-breaking changes (like URLs that have moved to another location).

Chapter Links

The following tables list the links found in each chapter. Links are presented in the same order that they occur in the text. You'll find all kinds of links here. Some point to useful tutorial sites and articles, others to Web curiosities, and still more point to handy free tools or downloadable pictures and media. Particularly important or noteworthy links are printed in bold.

Chapter 1. Preparing for the Web

Description	URL
The history of the Internet	www.isoc.org/internet/history
	www.walthowe.com/navnet/history.html
Internet Explorer (browser)	www.microsoft.com/windows/ie
Firefox (browser)	www.mozilla.org/products/firefox
Netscape (browser)	http://channels.netscape.com/ns/browsers/download.jsp
Opera (browser)	www.opera.com
Safari (browser)	www.apple.com/safari
Summary of Mac browsers	http://darrel.knutson.com/mac/www/browsers.html
Spybot Search & Destroy (spyware removal tool)	www.safer-networking.org
Microsoft AntiSpyware (spyware removal tool)	www.microsoft.com/athome/security/spyware
Lavasoft Ad-Aware (spyware removal tool)	www.lavasoftusa.com/software/adaware
Online community of diary writers	www.opendiary.com
One of many free blogging services (see the Chapter 17 link list for more)	http://spaces.msn.com
Personal blogs of Microsoft employees	www.microsoft.com/communities/blogs
A fee-based service for testing a Web page with different browsers	www.netmechanic.com
What not to do in a Web page	www.angelfire.com/super/badwebs
The ultimate examples of bad Web design	www.webpagesthatsuck.com
	www.worstoftheweb.com

Chapter 2. Creating Your First Web Page

Description	URL
Java checkers	http://thinks.com/java/checkers/checkers.htm
ActiveX virus scanner	http://housecall.trendmicro.com
Flash games	www.ferryhalim.com/orisinal
XHTML tutorial	www.w3schools.com/xhtml
XHTML validator	www.htmlhelp.com/cgi-bin/validate.cgi

Chapter 3. Putting Your Page on the Web

Description	URL
Domain Direct (Web host)	*www.domaindirect.com*
Brinkster (Web host)	*www.brinkster.com*
Insider Hosting (Web host)	*www.insiderhosting.com*
Pair Networks (Web host)	*www.pair.com*
Sonic.net (Web host)	*www.sonic.net*
Yahoo GeoCities (free Web host)	*http://geocities.yahoo.com*
Angelfire (free Web host)	*http://angelfire.lycos.com*
Tripod (free Web host)	*www.tripod.lycos.com*
AOL Hometown (free Web host)	*http://hometown.aol.com*

Chapter 4. Power Tools

Description	URL
ZDNet (shareware)	*http://downloads-zdnet.com*
Download.com (shareware)	*www.download.com*
Tucows (shareware)	*www.tucows.com*
Nvu (HTML editor)	*www.nvu.com*
HTML-Kit (HTML editor)	*www.html-kit.com*
	www.chami.com/html-kit/plugins/info/hkh_w3c_offline
CoffeeCup (HTML editor)	*www.coffeecup.com*
FrontPage (trial software)	*www.microsoft.com/office/frontpage/prodinfo/trial.mspx*
Dreamweaver (trial software)	*www.macromedia.com/go/trydreamweaver*

Chapter 5. HTML Text Tags

Description	URL
Learn about the semantic Web	*http://logicerror.com/semanticWeb*
Special characters in HTML	*http://webmonkey.wired.com/webmonkey/reference/special_characters*

Chapter 6. Style Sheets

Description	URL
Browser usage statistics	*www.w3schools.com/browsers/browsers_stats.asp*
CSS compatibility tables for different browsers	*www.corecss.com/properties/full-chart.php*
	www.quirksmode.org
Web-safe colors	*www.w3schools.com/css/css_colors.asp*
Online color pickers	*www.webtemplates.com/colors*
	http://mediagods.com/tools/rgb2hex.htm
	www.colorschemer.com/online.html
Information about font support on different operating systems	*http://web.mit.edu/jmorzins/www/fonts.html*
	www.upsdell.com/BrowserNews/res_fontsamp.htm
Detailed information about CSS typography	*http://usabletype.com/ess*

Chapter 7. Adding Graphics

Description	URL
Overview of photo-editing software	*http://graphicssoft.about.com/od/pixelbased/a/bybphotoeditor.htm*
Free backgrounds	*www.grsites.com/textures*
	www.backgroundcity.com
	www.backgroundsarchive.com
Google image search (pictures aren't necessarily free to use)	*http://images.google.com*
Stock.XCHNG (free pictures)	*http://sxc.hu*
Overview of places to find free pictures	*www.masternewmedia.org/news/2005/04/01/where_to_find_great_free.htm*
Free clip art	*www.grsites.com/webgraphics*
	www.clipartconnection.com
	www.myfreeclipart.com
Microsoft Office clip art	*http://office.microsoft.com/clipart*

Chapter 8. Linking Pages

Description	URL
Link checker	*http://validator.w3.org/checklink*

Chapter 9. Page Layout Tools: Tables and Styles

Description	URL
A huge catalog of style sheet layout examples	*www.csszengarden.com*
CSS tutorial	*www.w3schools.com/css*
Style sheet templates	*www.bluerobot.com/web/layouts*
	http://glish.com/css
CSS resources	*www.westciv.com/style_master/house*

Chapter 10. Frames

Description	URL
How to force frames with JavaScript	*http://javascript.about.com/library/blframe.htm*

Chapter 11. Attracting Visitors

Description	URL
Web ring services	*http://dir.webring.com/rw*
	www.bravenet.com
The Open Directory Project	*http://dmoz.org*
	http://dmoz.org/add.html (submission rules)
	http://dmoz.org/guidelines (editor guidelines)
Google Directory	*http://directory.google.com*
Yahoo (submission guidelines)	*http://docs.yahoo.com/info/suggest*
	www.apromotionguide.com/yahoo.html (unofficial)
Looksmart/Zeal (submission guidelines)	*www.zeal.com/guidelines/user*
	www.apromotionguide.com/looksmart.html
How Google works	*www.akamarketing.com/google-ranking-tips.html*
	www.markhorrell.com/seo/pagerank.html
	www-db.stanford.edu/~backrub/google.html
Google (submission)	*www.google.com/addurl.html* (submit a site)
	http://services.google.com/urlconsole/controller (remove a site)
Search Engine Watch (industry news)	*www.searchenginewatch.com*
Webmaster World (industry news)	*www.webmasterworld.com*
Google AdWords	*http://adwords.google.com*
AdWords information	*http://searchenginewatch.com/sereport/article.php/2164591*
	www.iterature.com/adwords

Description	URL
Wayback Machine (archived Web pages)	www.archive.org
List of Web robots	www.robotstxt.org
Overview of free log analysis software	www.thefreecountry.com/webmaster/loganalyzers.shtml
Overview of free hit counters	www.thefreecountry.com/webmaster/loganalyzers.shtml
StatCounter (free hit counter)	www.statcounter.com

Chapter 12. Letting Your Visitors Talk to You (and Each Other)

Description	URL
Community building on the Web (book excerpts)	www.naima.com/community
Lyris (professional software for groups and newsletters)	www.lyris.com
CGI introduction	www.cgi101.com/book
ASP and ASP.NET introductions	www.w3schools.com/asp
	www.w3schools.com/aspnet
HTML forms tutorial	www.w3schools.com/html/html_forms.asp
Google Groups	http://groups.google.com
	http://groups.google.com/intl/en/googlegroups/about.html
Examples of discussion groups on the Web	www.microsoft.com/office/community/en-us
	http://p085.ezboard.com/bsurvivorsucks
	www.officefrustration.com
	http://forums.delphiforums.com/LibertyBooks

Chapter 13. Making Money with Your Site

Description	URL
Google AdSense	www.google.com/adsense (sign up)
	www.google.com/services/adsense_tour
	www.google.com/adsense/taxinfo
	www.google.com/adsense/policies
Amazon Associates	www.amazon.com/gp/browse.html/?node=3435371 (sign up)
	http://associates.amazon.com (log in)
	www.amazon.com/gp/browse.html/?node=3435371 (payment rules)
	http://associates.amazon.com/gp/associates/network/build-links/banner/main.html (banners)

Description	URL
PayPal	*www.paypal.com*
	www.paypal.com/cgi-bin/webscr?cmd=xpt/seller/ChargebackRisk-outside (about chargebacks)
	www.paypal.com/cgi-bin/webscr?cmd=p/gen/protections-outside (seller protection)

Chapter 14. JavaScript and DHTML: Adding Interactivity

Description	URL
JavaScript tutorials	*www.w3schools.com/js*
	www.echoecho.com/javascript.htm
	www.htmlgoodies.com/primers/jsp
	http://webmonkey.wired.com/webmonkey/programming/javascript
Text effect examples	*www.codejunction.com/detailed/sequential-fly-in-text-effect.html*
	www.javascript-page.com/tickert.html
	www.flooble.com/scripts/animate.php
JavaScript events	*www.w3schools.com/htmldom/dom_reference.asp*
EarthWeb (JavaScript samples)	*http://webdeveloper.earthweb.com/webjs*
The JavaScript Source (JavaScript samples)	*http://javascript.internet.com*
JavaScript 2 (JavaScript samples)	*www.javascript-2.com*
Dynamic Drive (JavaScript samples)	*www.dynamicdrive.com*
JavaScript FAQ	*www.javascripter.net/faq*

Chapter 15. Fancy Buttons and Menus

Description	URL
Button image generator	*www.buttongenerator.com*
Other button image generators	*http://cooltext.com/ButtonBrowse.aspx*
	www.grsites.com/button
Flash button generator	*www.flashbuttons.com*
Button making software (Windows)	*http://free-buttons.org*
FrontPage 3D Button Visual Editor add-in	*www.microsoft.com/downloads/details.aspx?familyid=23e6b5ad-c173-4aa4-8348-f400d670e0ac*
Navigation bars	*www.dynamicdrive.com/dynamicindex1*
	www.dynamicdrive.com/dynamicindex1/topnavbar.htm
	www.dynamicdrive.com/dynamicindex1/topmen3

Chapter 16. Audio and Video

Description	URL
Winamp (MP3 player)	www.winamp.com
Classical MIDI Archives	www.classicalarchives.com
Audacity (sound editor)	http://audacity.sourceforge.net
WAV/MP3 editors	www.goldwave.com
	www.fleximusic.com
iTunes	www.apple.com/itunes
Sound effects	www.grsites.com/sounds
	www.freeaudioclips.com
Video Blogs	http://videoblogging-universe.com
Internet Video Magazine	www.internetvideomag.com
Overview of cheap places to store video files	www.internetvideomag.com/ProductReviews/Services/FreeVideoHosting102.htm
Pixparty (free video hosting)	www.pixparty.com
GIF animations	www.gifanimations.com
	www.webdeveloper.com/animations
	www.animatedgif.net
Flash player	www.macromedia.com/go/getflashplayer
Impressive Flash examples	www.ferryhalim.com/orisinal
	www.zapdramatic.com
Flash tutorials	www.flashkit.com/tutorials
	www.w3schools.com/flash
Flash introduction generator	www.freeflashintros.com
Flash background music loops	www.flashkit.com/loops

Chapter 17. Blogs

Description	URL
Definition of "blog"	http://en.wikipedia.org/wiki/Weblog
Popular blog examples	www.andrewsullivan.com
	http://dear_raed.blogspot.com
	www.wilwheaton.net
	www.schneier.com/blog
	http://blog.plaxoed.com
Online feed readers	• www.bloglines.com
	• www.newsisfree.com
	www.newsgator.com
Windows feed reader	• www.bradsoft.com/feeddemon

Description	URL
Mac feed reader	• *http://ranchero.com/netnewswire*
Overview of feed readers	• *http://weblogs.about.com/od/aggregators*
MSN Spaces (hosted blogs)	*http://spaces.msn.com*
Radio UserLand (hosted blogs)	*http://radio.userland.com*
TypePad (hosted blogs)	*www.typepad.com*
Live Journal (hosted blogs)	*www.livejournal.com*
Xanga (hosted blogs)	*www.xanga.com*
Movable Type (blogging software)	*www.movabletype.org*
Bloxsom (blogging software)	*www.blosxom.com*
WordPress (blogging software)	*http://wordpress.org*
WebCrimson (hosted blogs, with the option to self-host)	*www.webcrimson.com*
Blogger (hosted blogs, with the option to self-host)	*www.blogger.com*
	http://help.blogger.com (information)
	http://help.blogger.com/bin/topic.py?topic=39 (template tag reference)
	http://help.blogger.com/bin/answer.py?answer=974 (putting Google ads in a blog)
	http://help.blogger.com/bin/answer.py?answer=152&topic=17 (create a BlogThis bookmark)
	*http://buzz.blogger.com/bloggerforward.htm*l (post a blog entry using Word)
Blogger discussion forum	*www.bloggerforum.com*
Removing the Blogger NavBar (unofficial workaround)	*www.diaphaneity.com/layouts/2004/08/how-to-disable-navbar.html*
Google Toolbar (for BlogThis)	*http://toolbar.google.com*
Blogrolling service	*www.blogrolling.com*

Index

S

T

<table> tag, 522
tables
borders, 237
cell spans, 239
contextual selectors, 251
design and, 245
<div> tag, 251
HTML, 235
id selectors, 252
invisible, 233
nested, 250
sizing, 241
columns, 242
rows, 244
text alignment, 245
tags, HTML (see HTML tags)
targeted ads, Google AdSense, 352
targets, framesets, 270
<td> tag, 522
teletype text, 133
templates, Blogger, 487
applying, 488
customizing, 489–493
terminology in communities, 314
text
alignment, 165–167
tables, 245
bold, 132
emphasized, 132
flow, 36
formatting, 132
graphical, 157, 203
inline images, 192
italic, 132
layout, 110
overview, 109
preformatted, 122
quotes, 123
spacing, 167
special characters, 134
strikethrough, 132
strong, 132
structure in tags, 37
subscript, 132
superscript, 132
table alignment, 245
teletype, 133
underline, 132
usage tips, 126
wrapping around images, 194

text editors
HTML documents and, 24
overview, 80
(see also HTML editors)
text tags, 115
formatting and, 131–135
headings, 120
horizontal lines, 121
line breaks, 118
ordered lists, 127
preformatted text, 122
text-align property, 166
<textarea> tag, 522
text-based HTML editors, 81
TextEdit, 24
<th> tag, 522
third-party menus, 439–443
threads, group discussions, 330
tiling background images, 199
titles, searches, 297
topical Web sites, 16
<tr> tag, 523
tracking visitors, 309
trolling, 314
<tt> tag, 523
type selectors, 142
types of Web sites, 14
typographic HTML tags, 112

U

<u> tag, 523
<ul> tag, 523
underline text, 132
unordered lists, 126, 128
uploads
browser-based, 74–76
Web hosting and, 66
Web sites
Dreamweaver, 105
FrontPage, 100
URLs (Uniform Resource Locator), 51
absolute, 214
bookmarks, 53
browsers and, 54
domains, 52
filename, 53
framesets and, 277
paths, 52
protocols, 52
query string, 53
relative, 213
rules, 220
Usenet, 324

Colophon

Mary Anne Weeks Mayo was the production editor for *Creating Web Sites: The Missing Manual*. Marlowe Shaeffer and Claire Cloutier provided quality control. Johnna VanHoose Dinse indexed the book.

Marcia Friedman designed the cover of this book, based on a series design by David Freedman. Marcia Friedman produced the cover layout with Adobe InDesign CS using Adobe's Minion and Gill Sans fonts.

David Futato designed the interior layout, based on a series design by Phil Simpson. This book was converted by Keith Fahlgren to FrameMaker 5.5.6 with a format conversion tool created by Erik Ray, Jason McIntosh, Neil Walls, and Mike Sierra that uses Perl and XML technologies. The text font is Adobe Minion; the heading font is Adobe Formata Condensed; and the code font is LucasFont's TheSans Mono Condensed. The illustrations that appear in the book were produced by Robert Romano, Jessamyn Read, and Lesley Borash using Macromedia FreeHand MX and Adobe Photoshop CS.

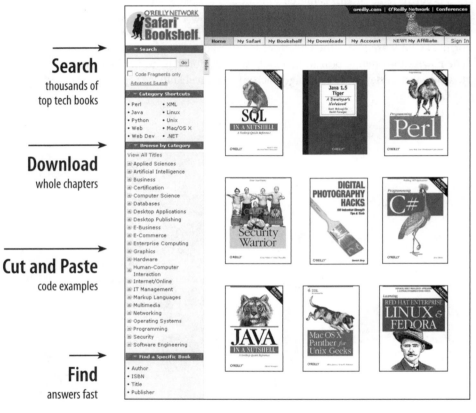